I0762964

The Complete Notebooks

Albert

The Complete Notebooks

Translated and Annotated
by Ryan Bloom

Camus

The University of Chicago Press
Chicago and London

The University of Chicago Press, Chicago 60637
The University of Chicago Press, Ltd., London

Published 2025
Printed in the United States of America

34 33 32 31 30 29 28 27 26 2 3 4 5

ISBN-13: 978-0-226-69481-8 (cloth)
ISBN-13: 978-0-226-74924-2 (ebook)
DOI: https://doi.org/10.7208/chicago/9780226749242.001.0001

Originally published in French as
Carnets I (1935–1942) © Éditions Gallimard, Paris, 1962
Carnets II (1942–1951) © Éditions Gallimard, Paris, 1964
Carnets III (1951–1959) © Éditions Gallimard, Paris, 1989

www.centrenationaldulivre.fr

Library of Congress Control Number: 2025015445.

♾This paper meets the requirements of ANSI/NISO Z39.48-1992 (Permanence of Paper).

Authorized Representative for EU General Product Safety Regulation (GPSR) queries: **Easy Access System Europe**—Mustamäe tee 50, 10621 Tallinn, Estonia, gpsr.requests@easproject.com
Any other queries: https://press.uchicago.edu/press/contact.html

Contents

Translator's Introduction

Like many writers, Albert Camus didn't keep his work all in one place. In 1935, when he began the first of the main notebooks included in this volume, he was already writing in another notebook, a black moleskine that he'd started using the year before and that he'd continue to use for about another year after. On the whole, Camus seems to have used the black moleskine as a more formal workspace, with the majority of its extant pages dedicated to the essays that would go on to become his first collection, *L'envers et l'endroit*,[1] whereas the first of the main notebooks in this volume is a less formal collection of observations and reflections, of drafts and quotes and plans for work to come. Nevertheless, the two *cahiers* do overlap in a variety of ways, with the black moleskine also containing plans and drafts for work beyond *L'envers et l'endroit*—most notably, a first attempt at a novel—and it's quite possible that the twenty-two pages that begin the first notebook in this volume were in fact torn from the black moleskine as well. Still, if the whole of the black moleskine isn't included here because it was seen as a structured drafting space for formal writings, the same logic can't be given for leaving out the notes that Camus had begun to keep in an earlier journal in April 1933, notes that in all respects resemble the entries that are included in the established notebooks, and which leave us with the question: What exactly *do* we have here?

What we know for sure is this: Sometime between 1937 and 1954, Albert Camus had typed copies made of his handwritten notebooks. Raymond Gay-Crosier, editor of the most recent French edition of the *cahiers*, indicates that "the first typed version of Notebook I, made well before the others, bears the date September 15, 1937."[2] Hiroyuki Takatsuka, who has gone so far as to analyze the type of ink and paper used to make the typescripts, argues, how-

1. In traditional usage, the phrase *l'envers et l'endroit* refers to the two sides of an embroidery: the clean, neat, finished side that the viewer is supposed to see, and the messier side with loose ends that the viewer is not supposed to see. In casual usage, the phrase means something like "front and back." With the essays that make up Camus's collection as context, a translation such as "the seen and unseen" would seem to capture the spirit of the French phrase, whereas the current English title, *The Wrong Side and the Right Side*, seems to imply a value judgment that is expressly at odds with the essays themselves, as well as Camus's larger body of work (see Notebook I, note 26, for example). For this reason, the title is given in French throughout.

2. Gay-Crosier, in Albert Camus, *Œuvres complètes*, vol. 2, ed. Jacqueline Lévi-Valensi (Bibliothèque de la Pléiade, 2008), 1382. Hereafter, all quotes from Camus's work are drawn from Albert Camus, *Œuvres complètes*, vols. 1–2, ed. Jacqueline Lévi-Valensi (Bibliothèque de la Pléiade, 2006), and vols. 3–4, ed. Raymond Gay-Crosier (Bibliothèque de la Pléiade, 2008).

ever, that September 15, 1937, is simply the date at which the first notebook ends, not the date at which it was typed.[3] Aside from this, both agree that notebooks II–VII were typed at a much later date, with Gay-Crosier giving the timeframe as around 1952–1953 and Takatsuka giving the date as around 1953–1954. In anonymous editorial notes prepared for the first French publication of Camus's travel journals, the editor, likely Roger Quilliot, states that he received typescripts of the then-complete set of notebooks from Camus in 1954.[4] The final two notebooks, VIII and IX, which run from August 1954 to December 1959, had not been typed at the time of Camus's sudden death in a car accident on January 4, 1960.

But why does it matter when the notebooks were typed? Camus's handwriting, though it changed somewhat over the course of his life, is incredibly difficult to read, and so as each of the seven notebooks were typed—likely, though not definitely, by Camus's secretary Suzanne Agnely—Camus reviewed them, filling in blanks where the typist couldn't make out a word or phrase, adding in bits of information, rearranging certain entries, and, in general, "correcting" the text. Ultimately, it seems Camus fully reviewed notebooks I–III, while only partially correcting IV–VII. Camus's notes were then integrated into a new typescript, and it's from these "corrected" typescripts, further edited by Camus's wife, Francine, and friend Roger Quilliot, that notebooks I–VII were originally published.

When we read intimate works, such as a writer's notebooks or letters, we tend to assume that we're encountering them in the raw, as they were originally written. But if Camus corrected these pages before they were published, then how different is what we have here from the original? To get a sense of that, Hiroyuki Takatsuka compared entries from the handwritten notebooks with the initial typescript and then with the final, published text. He gives the following example, from early in notebook I, in which the blanks represent words the typist couldn't make out (words Camus would add to the typescript with no change from the handwritten manuscript), bold letters indicate additions made by Camus (which don't appear in the manuscript), and strikethroughs indicate words crossed out by Camus, with his adjustment given in brackets:

---

3. Hiroyuki Takatsuka, "Les retouches et l'avant-textualité des *Carnets* d'Albert Camus: Entre la relecture des Cahiers I à VII et la rédaction du Premier Homme," *Etudes de langue et littérature françaises* 102 (2013): 153–69.

4. Fonds Albert Camus, Bibliothèque Méjanes, Aix-en-Provence, CMS2.Af4-05.05: Notes à propos des *Journaux de voyage*.

> **Grenier** à propos du communisme : « Toute la question est celle-ci : pour un idéal de justice, faut-il __________ à des sottises ? » On peut répondre oui : c'est beau. Non : c'est honnête.
>
> Toutes proportions gardées : ~~ce~~ [le] problème du _________isme. Le croyant s'embarrasse-t-il ___ __________ des évangiles et des ______ de l'Église ? Croire est-ce admettre l'Arche de Noé—est-ce défendre l'Inquisition ou le tribunal qui condamna Galilée ?
>
> Mais, d'autre part, comment concilier communisme et dégoût ? Si je tente les ______ _______, dans la mesure où elles atteignent l'absurde et l'inutile—je ~~viens au~~ [nie le] communisme. Et ce souci religieux . . .

As is visually apparent, Camus was mostly filling in blanks, words the typist couldn't read, and making minor adjustments, such as changing "this" to "the" or adding a full name where the original had only a single initial—but he also makes a more serious, significant change. In the original, handwritten notebook, the penultimate clause reads: "I come to Communism." In the typed, corrected version, it reads: "I reject Communism." While the above entry leaves some room for interpretation, if we place it alongside Camus's contemporaneous, August 21, 1935, letter to Jean Grenier, we get a clearer picture of Camus's thinking at the time: "You're right to advise me to join the Communist Party. I'm going to do so when I get back from the Balearics. I admit that everything is pointing me in that direction and that I was prepared to give them a try. The issues I have with Communism, well, it seems better to live with them."[5]

If the typescripts were in fact corrected around 1954, that means the above change was made almost twenty years after Camus wrote the initial entry, long after he had been expelled from the Algerian Communist Party for refusing to support their turn against Muslim nationalists and the working class—a move he saw as "playing into the hands of the colonialists"[6]— after he had already completed most of his major works, after he'd already published *The Rebel,* the book that led to the famous quarrel with Jean-Paul Sartre, which was, in many ways, a quarrel about the French Communist Party and its intellectual supporters, whom Camus had come to see as apologists for premeditated, organized, rationalized murder. So then, in correcting the initial typescript, an older Camus, one whose political beliefs had changed, over-

5. Jean Grenier and Albert Camus, *Correspondance 1932–1960* (Gallimard, 1981), 22.
6. Herbert Lottman, *Albert Camus: A Biography* (Gingko Press, 1997), 167.

ruled a younger Camus, intervening in these pages and rewriting his own history. This seemingly small tweak, a mere two words, has a rather large effect, giving Camus the appearance of having never believed in, of having never accepted, Communism, when, in fact, he once did.

But such changes don't end at political beliefs. In addition to his habit of tucking entries written on outside, looseleaf sheets of paper into the original notebooks, Camus also rearranged the chronological placement of certain entries, moving, for example, four passages that appear in the latter part of 1937 in one of the handwritten notebooks to the beginning of 1936 in the typescript while also, at the same time, rearranging the content of some of those entries, such that an entry that begins with a bit of dialogue about being a writer in the original notebook ends up beginning with a dialogue about being sentenced to death in the corrected typescript. All four of these entries concern his novel *The Happy Death,* and in moving and rearranging them Camus gives readers the impression that he had a clearer, more fully developed idea of the book earlier than he did.

To a similar end, in an entry from 1947, Camus indicates that after he has finished *The Plague, The Rebel,* and *The Just,* he plans to write *The Judgment* (an early working title for *The Fall,* which would be published in 1956) and *The First Man*—but these latter two titles don't actually appear in the original manuscript. In reality, they were added to the typed version at a later date, and Camus would continue to add the title *The First Man* to the typescript in several other places where it doesn't appear in the handwritten notebook. Whether these changes were simple matters of housekeeping for Camus or deliberate attempts to alter his biography, for readers interested in the writer's political and artistic development, they are details to bear in mind.

Aside from what has been completely lost, such as the pages that Camus appears to have ripped from the first notebook and destroyed, as well as the handful of pages still withheld, there are also a number of notes that do appear in both the handwritten notebook and the initial typescript but not in the final publication. In notebook VII, for example, the following entry, clearly the origin of Camus's celebrated short story "The Guest," appears in both the manuscript and the typescript, with the latter version initially corrected by Camus in black pen before he eventually crossed it out completely:

> Lebediev, a peasant, a Doukhobor, has to take charge of a prisoner for a leg. He refuses. The starosta says: "I'm no informant. I'll bring the prisoner over and

you can do as you like." Treats the prisoner like pilgrim, warmth, food, bed. The next morning 50 kopecks. Then leads him to a crossroads: one path goes to the prison, the other to freedom. He lets him choose. The prisoner takes the first path.[7]

On the other side of things, there are also instances of entire entries, and even sets of entries, being added to the typescript that do not exist in the original notebook. Not far from where Camus removed the above entry, for example, he also added five consecutive entries laying out the short stories that he would go on to include in *Exile and the Kingdom*, giving the impression, again, that he had a more developed idea of the collection at an earlier date than he may have. At various other points, Camus inserts outside sheets of paper into the notebooks, and though it is often clear that these sheets are not contemporaneous, the entries written on them would be printed in the final publication where Camus inserted them, without mention of their later addition.

All in all, what we have, then, is an officially sanctioned version of notebooks I–VII, as conceived by Camus at the time they were typed and corrected, as well as the edited version of the final two notebooks, VIII and IX. Whether Camus would have continued to edit the notebooks, whether, in time, he would have decided to add other materials, such as the notes from 1933 or the unpublished notebook he'd left in Oran as he moved around during the war years—a notebook that he didn't have access to when the other typescripts were made, and one that provides a more personal glimpse of what would become *The Myth of Sisyphus*, *The Happy Death*, and *The Stranger*—we simply cannot know.[8]

In the biography *Albert Camus: A Life*, Olivier Todd writes that the author "really wasn't one for first drafts," explaining that he "liked rewriting as much as the initial writing itself."[9] A quick glance at Camus's handwritten pages, whether for novels, newspaper articles, or essays and plays, illustrates the

7. Hiroyuki Takatsuka, "Albert Camus sur le chemin de Tolstoï: La genèse de « L'Hôte » dans le Cahier VII des *Carnets*," *Albert Camus au fil des rencontres. Littérature, théâtre, politique*, ed. Philippe Vanney, vol. 24, *Albert Camus* (2019): 171–83.

8. See appendix I, "The First Notebook: 1933," and appendix II, "The Oran Notebook: May 1938–August 1942."

9. Oliver Todd, *Albert Camus: Une vie* (Folio, 1999), 215–16.

point well, showing a fast, tight script that dashes from one side of the page to the other, sometimes slanting upward, sometimes down, individual words and letters, as well as entire paragraphs, crossed out and replaced by notes squeezed between lines or written along margins, top, bottom, and side, arrows and carets, circled words and all manner of additions and deletions, of corrections, often running throughout.

With Camus's notebooks, things are a little different, though no less complicated.

Given that notebooks VIII and IX were not typed during Camus's lifetime, the first challenge in transcribing them was simply trying to decipher his handwriting, a feat that could not always be accomplished without him around to fill in the blanks and correct possible misreadings. As a result, there remain in this published edition, as in the French edition, a variety of words, clauses, and occasionally even whole sentences that either could not be deciphered or that could only be deciphered with a bit of guesswork involved. In reviewing certain manuscript pages and cross-referencing them with other works, a handful of these passages have been cleared up for this English-language edition, though a good number of uncertainties remain. All such instances have been noted in the text.

If in revising and correcting the first seven of these notebooks, Camus occasionally intervened in their content, he seemingly made little attempt to change their character: When entries in the handwritten original appear clipped, elliptical, abstract, or even inscrutable, as they sometimes do, when a sentence lacks articles or trails off mid-thought, Camus usually leaves it that way in the typescript. As such, whenever possible, these characteristic features have been maintained in translation, though given differences in French and English syntax, doing so has not always been feasible. A similar effort has been made, especially in notebooks I, VII, and IX—the least uniform of the notebooks—to note the look and feel of the handwritten originals, though Camus so frequently skips lines and entire pages, crosses things out, indents paragraphs or doesn't, adds a divider between entries or doesn't, jots in the margins, abbreviates names and places, draws arrows, changes ink or pencil, eschews basic punctuation such as periods and the closing of quotes, that a consistent attempt to note or reproduce such surface features would likely result in an unreadable text. Still, the reader should bear in mind that such extemporaneous features and abridgments are a part of the original, so that even when Camus quotes from other sources in which, for example, punctuation is clearly present, he often does not carry it over to the notebook.[10] Even a cursory glance at the crossed-out entry about the Doukhobor Lebediev, given earlier, and the source material from which Camus drew it, *Tolstoï et les Doukhobors,* a collection of Tolstoy's writings translated into French in 1902 by J. W. Bienstock, plainly shows the often-abbreviated nature of the notebooks:

> **BIENSTOCK / TOLSTOY**
> Fiodor Lebediev traita le prisonnier comme un voyageur ; il le fit chauffer, lui donna à boire et à manger, et le garda la nuit pour dormir. Le matin, voyant que le prisonnier était un hommes très pauvre, il lui donna rouble 50 copées et lui proposa de le conduire hors du village.
>
> Fiodor Lebediev treated the prisoner like a pilgrim; he let him warm up, gave him something to eat and drink, and gave him a place to sleep for the night. In the morning, seeing that the prisoner was a very poor man, he gave him 50 kopecks and offered to show him the way from the village.
>
> **CAMUS**
> Traite le prisonnier comme voyageur, chauffé, nourri, couché. Le lendemain matin 50 kopeks.
>
> Treats the prisoner like pilgrim, warmth, food, bed. The next morning 50 kopecks.

Where Bienstock includes a proper name, "Fiodor Lebediev," Camus includes neither a proper name nor a personal pronoun; where Bienstock includes an article, "a pilgrim," Camus drops the article, leaving only "pilgrim"; where Bienstock fully describes "he let him warm up, gave him something to eat and drink, and gave him a place to sleep for the night," Camus writes only "warmth, food, bed"; and where Bienstock provides reasoning and explanation, writing, "In the morning, seeing the prisoner was a very

10. For this reason, all quotes given by Camus have been translated directly from his notebooks, as he rendered them. No attempt has been made to "fix" or "correct" Camus's particular manner of quoting, though when large differences between source and citation exist, they have been pointed out in a footnote. For works not originally written in French, Camus usually bases his rendering on the contemporary French translation; in a couple of instances, with texts originally written in English or Spanish, he quotes directly from the source language. All references to specific page numbers within the notebook entries themselves are, unless otherwise noted, to the then available French edition.

poor man, he gave him 50 kopecks and offered to show him the way from the village," Camus gives none, "The next morning 50 kopecks."

When source material such as this can be traced, the context it provides is invaluable in guiding the translation, both at the sentence level, with punctuation and grammar, as well as overall comprehension; the same is true when an entry from the notebooks was later incorporated into one of Camus's formal pieces of writing. Without having *Tolstoï et les Doukhobors* or "The Guest" available for reference, we could only guess at the meaning of "The next morning 50 kopecks." Perhaps, we might think, Camus had meant the line to indicate a twist: the next morning, after being treated well by his host, the prisoner *stole* 50 kopecks and tried to flee. Such a reading would inevitably color our understanding, and, depending on further context provided by the rest of entry, or the lack thereof, it's possible the remaining translation could also be affected.

Bearing this in mind, when neither outside sources nor Camus's own writings seem to shed light on an enigmatic entry, or when an entry is written in such a way as to leave room for possible confusion, the translation given leans slightly in the direction of readability, filling in the occasional dropped article, adding the occasional comma, and, in rare cases, providing a touch of clarification. That said, and by way of example, Camus is often careful to avoid the first-person "I" in these pages, even when it's clear he's relating a personal experience or opinion, and though this is somewhat easier to do in French than in English, an attempt has been made to maintain these sorts of deliberate decisions, even when the resulting English can sometimes be a little awkward, slightly unnatural, or, on occasion, burnt on the tongue. The guiding principle throughout is the recognition that, even if Camus did edit some of these notebooks, they ultimately remain informal writings—notes and jottings and drafts—and they should, no matter the language, read as such.

Still, no matter how carefully a translation attempts to reproduce a given text, it will always and inevitably be the interpretation of a given translator. Take the French word *révolte,* for example. More often than not, the word is translated here as "rebellion," rather than as the more transparent, similar sounding "revolt," because in most of the entries recorded here, Camus seems to be referring to the idea of an ongoing struggle, rather than to a concentrated burst of activity intended to overthrow a specific source of power. So, even though *révolte* looks and sounds more like "revolt" than it does "rebellion," and even though both words, *révolte* and *rébellion,* exist in French, nevertheless, what Camus often seems to be referring to in these particular entries is not "revolt," as described above, but "rebellion." What is clear, then, is that this is a translation choice made based on one person's understanding, and that other readers or translators may, with good reason, disagree about how Camus is using the word in any given entry, just as other readers or translators may disagree with the given English definitions themselves.

Perhaps the greatest loss in translating *révolte* as "rebellion" is the loss of the word's root connection to *révolution,* a connection Camus intentionally utilizes, both in these pages and in his book *The Rebel.* At the same time, translating *révolte* as "rebellion" in these pages, where the entries often provide little context to go by, helps to clarify the connection between certain notes and the book for which Camus was keeping them. And while some have argued that *L'homme révolté*'s English title is, in itself, a mistranslation, and that it should actually be rendered as *Man in Revolt,* it should be noted that Camus himself gave the book its English title and that his editor, Blanche Knopf, felt his English was strong enough that he could do some of his own English translations. For what it's worth, the French word *rébellion* does appear three times in a row right at the beginning of *L'homme révolté,* after which it appears nowhere else in the book, nor does it appear even a single time in these pages. So many questions and explanations for a single word only begin to hint at the beautifully complex, brutally ambiguous way in which translation so often works.

A Note About Notes

While the footnotes in this volume are drawn from a lifetime of research, reading, and rereading of Camus's work, many have also been adapted directly from Raymond Gay-Crosier's notes in the Pléiade edition of the *Carnets,* as well as from notes kept by early Camus scholars Philip Thody in *Carnets: 1935–1942* (Hamish Hamilton, 1963), Justin O'Brien in *Notebooks: 1942–1951* (Knopf, 1965), and Roger Quilliot in *Journaux de voyage* (Gallimard, 1978), all of whom examined, worked with, and commented on the notebooks in the years immediately following Camus's death. All English translations from the French, however—whether of Camus's own work or the works of others—remain my own.

Notebook I

MAY 1935–SEPTEMBER 1937

A brownish-orange composition notebook, 22 × 17 cm, with the word "Jupiter" preprinted on the cover. Camus drew a slash through "Jupiter" and wrote "May 1935" above it in large blue crayon and "September 37" below, initially in fine ballpoint, which was then overwritten with crayon. At the top of the cover, in the right corner, he wrote "Cahier no. 1" in smaller lettering, with the date "May 1935" below it, and then, in much larger, looser lettering, starting at top-left, he rewrote "Cahier no I."

The twenty-two pages that begin the notebook, hand numbered as such by Camus, are not actually part of the notebook itself; rather they were torn from another notebook—quite possibly the black moleskine—and placed at the start of this one (the twenty-two-page notebook signature, into which Camus inserted one additional outside page, still holds together, showing that Camus took a whole section from the other notebook and not diverse pages here and there; that said, the pages numbered 53–56 and 59–68 also appear to have come from this same outside notebook). The remains of the Jupiter notebook itself consist of fifty-seven squared pages, with at least three pages, if not more, clearly torn out.

Over the course of this first notebook, and throughout the notebooks as a whole, Camus's already difficult handwriting becomes smaller, tighter, and even harder to read. Initially, there is a good bit of variation from one entry to the next, with some being recorded in black ink, some in light pencil, and some in large, looping blue letters. Camus has a tendency here, as in certain other notebooks, to skip the verso page, sometimes returning to write on it at a later date.

As these official journals begin, Camus is twenty-one years old.

May '35.

My point is:

That a person can—without romanticism—feel nostalgic for lost poverty. A certain number of years lived in destitution is enough to develop a sensibility. In this particular case, the curious feeling the son carries for his mother constitutes *his entire sensibility*.[1] That this sensibility is expressed in such a wide variety of areas can be sufficiently explained by the latent, material nature of his childhood memories (a glue that sticks to the soul).

For those who realize this, the result is gratitude and thus a guilty conscience. The result of that, and, if they've changed social class, of comparison, is the feeling of lost riches. To rich people, the sky is but a natural gift, another given. For poor people, it retains its character of infinite grace.[2]

A guilty conscience needs to confess. A body of work is a confession; I must bear witness. I have only one thing to say, having given it serious thought. It's in this life of poverty, among these vain or humble people, that I've come closest to touching what seems to me the true meaning of life. Works of art will never be enough. For me, art isn't everything. Let it at least be a way.

What's also important is that terrible shame, those bits of cowardice, that unconscious esteem we grant the other world (the one of money). I believe the world of the poor is one of the few, if not the only, that is closed in on itself, that is an island in society. A person can play Robinson Crusoe there at little cost. But for those immersed in it, they have to say "out there" when talking about the doctor's place, which is just around the corner.[3]

All of this should be expressed through the mother and son.

---

1. In the original, handwritten notebook, *toute sa sensibilité* is underlined. Following standard practice, all passages underlined in the original manuscript will appear here in italics (*his entire sensibility*).

2. In the essay "Between Yes and No," Camus revises and clarifies the idea as follows: "At a certain level of wealth, the sky itself and the star-filled night seem natural assets, but at the bottom of the ladder, the sky regains its full significance: a priceless grace."

Camus, who was deeply steeped in the Bible and ancient Greek literature, sometimes echoes the language found there, as in the case at hand, which finds reference in Matthew 6, the central section of the Sermon on the Mount.

3. The paragraph to which this note is attached would, aside from the first sentence, be incorporated into *Louis Raingeard*, Camus's first attempt at a novel, which he wrote partly in these pages, partly in the black moleskine, and partly in other places. The novel would be abandoned after approximately twenty pages.

Olivier Todd notes in his biography that in Belcourt, the poor neighborhood where Camus grew up, if you were headed downtown, you would say that you were going "to Algiers," even though Belcourt was in Algiers.

This is generalization.
To be concrete and specific is much more complicated:
1) A setting. The neighborhood and its inhabitants.
2) The mother and her actions.
3) The son's relationship to the mother . . .
Which solution: The mother?
Last chapter: symbolic value achieved through the son's nostalgia???[4]

Grenier:[5] we always underestimate ourselves, though in poverty, sickness, and solitude we become aware of our eternity. "We have to be put to the test."

That's it exactly, no more, no less.

Vanity of the word experience. Experience is not formed through experiments. We don't bring it about. We undergo it. It's more like patience than experience. We wait patiently—rather, we endure.

---

4. The list at the end of the entry bears similarities to a plan for *Louis Raingeard* that Camus recorded elsewhere. It reads:

I. The P[oor] N[eighborhood]
Chap. I. The crisis point
Chap. II. The slow breakdown that brought this woman face to face with her son
  Grandmother's death
  Son's illness
  Separation from brother
Chap. III. Son's parallel experience, defeated by two things:
  Left by the woman across the way
  Elderly uncle's death
  Alone at both ends of the city—Seeing each other from time to time
  2 infinities
II. The M[other] and the S[on]
  First point of understanding
  Enduring appeal
III. The Last Stand
  Return to the essay: 8 days
  Symbol
  The old woman
  The old man
  Departure

5. Jean Grenier (1898–1971) was Camus's high-school philosophy teacher in Algiers. His book *Islands*, published just two years before Camus began these notebooks, was a great influence on Camus, who would go on to dedicate two of his own books—*L'envers et l'endroit* and *The Rebel*—to Grenier. The two friends would continue to correspond and visit each other throughout Camus's life.

In practice: after having an experience, you haven't acquired knowledge, you've become skilled—but at what???

———

2 friends: both very sick. But for one of them, it's nerves, recuperation is always possible. For the other: advanced tuberculosis. No hope.[6]

One afternoon, the tubercular woman is at her friend's bedside. The friend says:

"You see, until now, even in my very worst moments, there was always a reason to keep going. A sort of relentless hope for life. But now it seems there's nothing left to hope for. I'm so worn out it feels like I'll never get up again."

Then, with a wild flash of joy in her eyes, the friend takes the tubercular woman's hand and says: "Oh, but we'll make that great journey together."

The same two—the tubercular one dying, the other practically cured. She'd taken a trip to France and tried a new treatment, which put her on the road to recovery.

And the dying woman blames her for doing it. Apparently, she blames her friend for abandoning her. In truth, she can't bear to see her friend get better. She'd had this crazy hope that she wouldn't die alone—that she'd bring her dearest friend with her. She is going to die alone. And knowing it fuels her friendship with a terrible hatred.[7]

———

Stormy August sky. Scorching winds. Black clouds. But off to the east there's a band of delicate, see-through blue. Impossible to look at it. Its presence is unsettling to eyes and soul. Because beauty is unbearable. It drives us to despair, that eternal minute we'd like to extend over the whole of time.

———

He's at ease with sincerity. Very rare.

———

Playacting is also an important subject.[8] What saves us from our greatest sorrow is the feeling of being alone and abandoned, yet not so alone that

---

6. Though Camus had been showing symptoms for some time—coughing, vomiting blood, and fainting—it wasn't until 1931, at age seventeen, that he was officially diagnosed with tuberculosis. In those days, approximately 150 of every 100,000 French inhabitants died from the disease.

7. In the handwritten notebook, an additional sentence follows this one.

8. While the French word *comédie* often refers to the genre "comedy," it also carries the sense of someone putting on a show for other people, in the sense of "playacting," an idea that Camus returns to throughout these pages. See p. 21n24. The word *comédien* refers to a film or stage "actor."

Some of the ideas in this entry were first described in Camus's December 1934 essay "Voices from the Poor Neighborhood" and then taken up again in his later essay "Between Yes and No,"

"others" forget to "consider" us in our unhappiness. That's why we sometimes feel happiest when our feeling of abandonment fills and lifts us into an endless sadness. That's also why happiness is often no more than a feeling of pity for our own unhappiness.

Striking among the poor—God placed complacency[9] next to hopelessness, like a cure next to a sickness·

———

When I was young, I asked people for more than they could give: everlasting friendship, a permanent emotion.

Now I know to ask less of them than they can give: companionship, plain and simple. And then their emotions, their friendship, their noble gestures, in my eyes, they maintain the full value as the miracles they are. Entirely the result of grace.

———

. . . [10] They'd already had too much to drink and wanted to eat, but it was Christmas Eve and the place was full. Turned away, they insisted. They were shown the door. So then, they kicked the proprietor's wife, who was pregnant, and the proprietor, a frail young man with blond hair, grabbed a gun and fired. The bullet lodged in the man's right temple. His head swung sideways and came to rest on the wound. Drunk on alcohol and fright, his friend began to dance around the body.

---

where he writes: "We feel our distress and like ourselves the better for it. Yes, perhaps that's what happiness is, the feeling of pity for our own unhappiness."

9. The French word *complaisance* could equally be translated as "self-pity," "indulgence," or "resignation," though given the rest of the sentence, Camus may have had the term *attestation de complaisance* in mind, which refers to a "placebo prescription."

When the extant pages of *The First Man* were recovered from Camus's valise after his death, a copy of this entry and the one that follows were found on a sheet of paper inserted at the back of the manuscript. There, Camus had added a footnote after "our own unhappiness," which reads: "the grandmother's death." After the next entry, he added an arrow pointing to a marginal comment: "Marie Viton: airplane." Marie Viton was a friend from Algiers who flew planes and offered to take Camus up for his first flight.

10. The entry that follows is one of the few in the first notebook that was not written out by hand as part of the original manuscript; it was typed on a separate sheet of onionskin paper, folded in half, and inserted into the notebook at a later date. As Hiroyuki Takatsuka has pointed out in his article "Le meurtre de Noël," published in *Etudes camusiennes*, it is likely that this typed page was originally the second, now "missing," page of a typescript titled "The Neighborhood." The extant first page of that typescript ends mid-sentence with the words "The body wasn't," and the page inserted in the notebooks here picks up mid-sentence with "from this poor neighborhood," words Camus would later cross out in black ink, adding in their place "1935" followed by four dots.

It was a simple affair that would end with an article in the morning paper.[11] But at that moment, in that remote corner of the neighborhood, the occasional spot of light falling on the freshly soaked pavement, the long, wet sounds of cars sliding past, and the coming and going of loud, well-lit trams lent an eerie quality to that otherworldly scene: a cloying, lingering image of the neighborhood when the end of the day peoples its streets with shadows, when, rather, a single anonymous shadow, accompanied by muffled footsteps, by a hushed pattering of voices, sometimes suddenly appears, bathed in bloody glory, in the red glow of a pharmacy globe.

———

January '36.[12]

A garden on the other side of the window, and all I see are walls. And those few leaves caught in a stream of light. And higher up, more leaves. And higher up, the sun. Of all the jubilation to be felt out there, all the joy spread out over the world, all I see are the shadows of leaves playing against white curtains. And five rays of sunlight patiently spilling the honey-blond scent of dried grasses into the room. A breeze, and the shadows come to life on the curtains. Let a cloud pass over the sun, covering and uncovering it, leaving the blazing yellow of this vase of mimosa to emerge from the shadow. That's all it takes: that single nascent glimmer and I'm flooded with a faint and overwhelming joy.[13]

A prisoner of the cave, here I stand alone before the world's shadow. A January afternoon. Yet the cold remains hidden inside the air and a film of sunlight so thin it would crack beneath the tap of a fingernail coats everything,

---

11. On December 25, 1929, both *L'écho d'Alger* and *La dépêche algérienne*, the main newspapers in Algeria at the time, reported a story matching the details given in this entry. *L'écho d'Alger* identifies the restaurant as Père Babigne, located at 93 Rue de Lyon, which is also the address at which Camus's family then lived, their apartment being above the restaurant. Pieces of this entry would be used in both Camus's first novel, *The Happy Death*, as well as his last, *The First Man*.

12. At the top of this entry, Camus wrote and circled the word *Bon*, yet he also drew a pencil line through the first two pages, perhaps because the entry, with very few changes, would go on to form the heart of "L'envers et l'endroit," the title essay from his first collection.

A typed version of the entry, titled "I Watch Myself Being Born," hand dated January 20, 1936, was given by Camus to "Mireille and Lucien Bénisti, with the warmest of friendship."

13. Of note, given Camus's connection to his mother, who was partially deaf, is the use of the word *étourdissante*, here translated as "overwhelming," but also carrying the meaning "deafening." Variations of this word, as well as similar words, appear throughout the notebooks.

The references to the allegory of the cave in Plato's *Republic* would all be removed from the published essay.

graces everything with an eternal smile. Who am I and what can I do—aside from stepping into this play of leaves and light? To be that ray of sunlight in which my cigarette burns, that sweet, discreet passion breathing in the air. If I go in search of myself, I do so deep inside that light. And if I attempt to understand and savor the delicate flavor that reveals the world's secret, I find myself deep inside the universe. My self—that heightened sentiment that delivers me from the stage set. In only a moment, other things, other people will drag me back. So then, let me cut this moment from the fabric of time, in the way that others leave a flower between a book's pages, enclosing there a walk during which love brushed up against them. I, too, take walks, but it's a god who caresses me. Life is short and it's a sin to waste your time.[14] I waste my time all day long while others tell me how very much I'm doing. Today is a stopover, and my heart is going off to find itself.

If anxiety still grips me, it's on account of feeling this intangible instant slipping between my fingers like pearls of mercury. So then, let those who want to stand apart from the world do so. I no longer complain, as I can now see myself being born. I'm happy in this world, for my kingdom is of this world. A passing cloud and a fading moment. The self inside me dies. The book opens to a beloved page. How drab it is today, in the presence of the book that is the world. Is it true that I've suffered? Is it not true that I am suffering, and that this suffering intoxicates me, because it's this sun and those shadows, this warmth and that coldness felt far off in the distance, hidden deep inside the air? Am I really going to let myself wonder whether something is dying, whether men are suffering, when everything is written here in this window through which the heavens pour out their plenty? I can say, and I will say without hesitation, that what matters is to be human, to be simple. No, what matters is to be true, and then everything follows suit, humanity and simplicity. And when am I truer and clearer than when I am the world?[15]

A moment of precious silence. The people have fallen silent. But the world's song rises up, and I, chained deep inside the cave, I am filled before having desired. This here is the eternity I'd been hoping for. Now I can speak. I don't know that I could wish for anything more than the continuing pres-

---

14. In his copy of the published book, Louis Germain, Camus's schoolteacher, wrote next to this sentence: "This idea seems to have dominated Albert Camus's *entire life*."

15. The French *simple* is used here in the sense of living a simple life or, figuratively, being down-to-earth.

The middle of this paragraph, from "A passing cloud" to " this suffering intoxicates me, because it's," was cut from the final, published essay.

ence of my self within myself. It's no longer happiness I wish for now, only mindfulness. You think you're cut off from the world, but all it takes is an olive tree rising in the golden dust, all it takes are a few beaches sparkling beneath the morning sun, to feel the resistance inside you melt. And so it is for me. I'm conscious of the possibilities for which I'm responsible.[16] Every minute of life carries within it its value as a miracle and its face of eternal youth.

———

We think only in images. If you want to be a philosopher, write novels.[17]

———

Acquisition and realization.

At heart: the heroic values

———

In the Balearics: Last summer.[18]

Fear is what makes travel valuable. At any given moment, so far away from our homeland, from our language (a French newspaper becomes priceless, as do those late evening hours in cafes, looking to rub elbows with other people), a shapeless fear can seize us, and an instinctive desire to hide behind the shel-

---

16. In the handwritten notebook, the final two sentences are joined by: "—and I understand that".

17. In the October 20, 1938, edition of *Alger républicain*, Camus reviewed Jean-Paul Sartre's novel *Nausea*, opening the essay: "A novel is never anything but a philosophy put into images, and in a good novel, the philosophy is entirely conveyed through the images. If the philosophy overwhelms the characters and actions, that's all it takes for it to seem like a label slapped atop the work, for the plot to lose its authenticity and the novel its life. . . . This secret fusion of experience and thought, of life and reflection on its meaning, is what makes a great novelist. . . . The novel in question today upsets this balance and the theories damage the life. . . . What's striking about *Nausea* is how the novelist's emotional gifts, and the clearest, cruelest sort of intellectual gameplay, are simultaneously lavished and wasted."

A similar idea is expressed in *The Myth of Sisyphus*, where Camus writes: "The great novelists are philosophical novelists, which is to say the opposite of thesis writers. . . . It's precisely that they chose to write in images rather than in reasoning that reveals a certain manner of thinking shared among them, persuaded as they are of the uselessness of any explanatory principle and convinced of the instructive message of visible appearances."

18. In the summer of 1935, Camus traveled with his first wife, Simone Hié, to the Balearic Islands, where she was being treated for substance abuse. This entry would serve as the basis for the fourth paragraph of Camus's essay "Love of Life."

ter of old habits. This is the clearest benefit of travel. In such moments, we are feverish yet porous. The slightest impact shakes us to the core of our being. Let a cascade of light cross our path, and in it we see eternity. That's why we shouldn't say we travel for pleasure. There is no pleasure in traveling. I see it more as an ascetic experience. It's for culture that we travel, if by culture we mean the expression of our most intimate feeling, which is the feeling of eternity. Pleasure separates us from ourselves, as Pascal's diversion distances us from God. Travel, which is like a greater, more profound knowledge, brings us back to ourselves.

———

Balearics.
The bay.
San Francisco—Cloister.
Bellver.
Wealthy neighborhood (shade and old women).
Poor neighborhood (the window).
Cathedral (bad taste and a masterpiece).
Café chantant.[19]
Miramar Coast.
Valldemossa and the terraces.
Soller and the afternoon.
San Antonio (convent). Felantix.
Pollença: town. Convent. Pension.
Ibiza: bay.
La Peña: fortifications.
San Eulalia: The beach. The celebration.
The cafes around the harbor.
The stone walls and windmills in the countryside.

———

19. During the belle époque period in France, "singing cafés" were a sort of outdoor cabaret.

February 13, '36.

I ask more from people than they can give me. Vanity to pretend otherwise. But what a mistake, what hopelessness. And maybe I myself . . . [20]

Seek connections. All connections. If I want to write about people, how can I separate myself from the landscape? If I'm attracted to the sky or the light, will I forget the eyes or the voice of those I love? In each instance, I'm given the elements of a friendship, the fragments of an emotion, never the emotion itself, never the friendship itself.

You go to see an older friend to tell him everything. Or at least that something that's suffocating you. But he's in a rush. You talk about everything and nothing. The hour grows late. And now here I am, lonelier and emptier than before. This unsteady wisdom I'm trying to construct, how easily a distracted word from a fleeing friend can come and topple it! "Non ridere, non lugere . . ."[21] and doubts about myself and others.

March.

A day streaked with clouds and sun. Cold spangled with yellow. I should keep a daily weather journal. That beautiful, transparent sun yesterday, the bay trembling with light—like a wet lip.[22] And I spent the whole day working.

A title: The World's Hope.

---

20. On January 25, 1936, the Théâtre du Travail, assembled and directed by Camus, gave its first performance, an adaptation of André Malraux's *Le temps du mépris*. This entry is in reference to difficulties Camus was having at the time with some of the actors.

21. The quote comes from Spinoza's *Tractatus Theologico-Politicus*: "*Non ridere, non lugere, neque detestari, sed intelligere*" (Not to laugh, not to lament, not to detest, but to understand).

Parts of this entry would be used in Camus's essay "Between Yes and No."

22. Parts of this entry originally appeared in an essay titled "Courage," which Camus started in 1933 but never finished. He would later integrate the unfinished fragment into his essay "Irony," collected in *L'envers et l'endroit*, where he writes: "In the blue sky, you could sense the cold all spangled with yellow. The cemetery overlooked the city and you could see the beautiful, transparent sun as it fell over a bay trembling with light, like a wet lip."

In 1934, Camus had begun working for the university weather service. He would go on to be hired by the Institut de météorologie d'Alger in 1937.

Grenier, with regard to Communism: "The whole question is this: must we subscribe to stupidities to achieve an ideal form of justice?" You can say yes: it's a good thing to do. No: which is honest.[23]

All things considered: the same problem with Christianity. Do believers embarrass themselves in accepting the Gospel's contradictions and the Church's excesses? Does believing mean accepting Noah's Ark—defending the Inquisition or the tribunal that condemned Galileo?

But, what's more, how are we to reconcile Communism and disgust? If I push ideas to their extreme forms, to the point that they reach the absurd and useless—I reject Communism. And this religious concern . . .

———

Death gives the game[24] and heroism their true meaning.

———

Yesterday. The sun on the quays, the Arab acrobats, and the harbor shimmering with light.[25] It seems the country is pulling out all the stops, blossoming for my last winter here. This singular winter, blazing with cold and sun. Blue cold.

Lucid intoxication and smiling destitution—hopelessness in the virile acceptance seen on Greek stelae. What need do I have to write or create, to love or to suffer? Whatever in my life is lost isn't really what's most important. Everything becomes pointless.

---

23. On August 21, 1935, Camus wrote to Grenier: "You're right to advise me to join the Communist Party. I'm going to do so when I get back from the Balearics. I admit that everything is pointing me in that direction and that I was prepared to give them a try. The issues I have with Communism, well, it seems better to live with them." As the letter continues, we see early formulations of positions that would animate Camus's later political writing: "I'll always refuse to put a volume of *Capital* between life and man. All doctrines can and must evolve. . . . It seems to me that it's often life itself, rather than ideas, that leads to Communism." See the introduction to this volume for more.

24. Throughout the notebooks, as well as in his formally published works, Camus plays with the words *jeu*, *jouer*, and *joueur*, as well as the word *comédie*. In many cases, these passages seem to be getting at the idea of "playing the game" or "play acting," in the sense that Shakespeare has Jacques lament in *As You Like It* that "All the world's a stage / And all the men and women merely players." Perhaps more familiar to Camus at this point in his life would have been the Roman poet Juvenal's statement that "All of Greece is a stage, and every Greek's an actor."

In *The Myth of Sisyphus*, Camus writes: "So then, what is that unquantifiable feeling that deprives the mind of the sleep it needs to live? A world we can explain, even with the wrong reasons, is a familiar world. But on the contrary, in a universe suddenly devoid of illusions and illumination, man feels himself a stranger. There's no recourse for such an exile, given it's devoid of the memory of a lost homeland or the hope for a promised land. This divorce between man and his life, the actor and the stage setting, is precisely the feeling of absurdity."

25. This description would be incorporated into *The Happy Death*, part 1, chap. 2.

Neither hopelessness nor joy seem justified before this sky, beneath the sultry light pouring down from it.

March 16.

Long walk. Hills with the sea behind them. The sun delicate. White sweet-briars on all the bushes. Fat syrupy flowers with purple petals. Return to the sweetness of women's friendships. Young women with serious, smiling faces. Smiles, jokes, and intentions. We play the game, and, without believing in outer appearances, we all smile at them and pretend to give in to them. No false notes. I hold fast to the world with my every gesture, to people with all my gratitude.[26] From the hilltops, you can watch as the sun condenses the moisture left behind by the last rains, rebirthing it as fog. Even as I came down through the woods, sinking deeper into those balls of cotton, I could feel the sun above, a miraculous day haloing the trees. Trust and friendship, sun and white houses, subtleties barely recognized, O, my unspoiled happiness is already drifting away, and amid night's melancholy it will deliver me nothing more than a young woman's smile or the knowing look of a friendship that requires no words.

If time slips away so quickly, it's because we leave no landmarks.[27] Like the moon from zenith to horizon. That's why the years of our youth are so long, because they're so full, and the years of old age so short, because they're

---

26. This idea would appear in the penultimate paragraph of "L'envers et l'endroit," where Camus writes: "I hold fast to the world with my every gesture, to people with all my pity and gratitude. I don't want to choose between the seen and unseen world [*cet endroit et cet envers du monde*]. I don't like that we choose."

27. Camus would touch on this idea in his essay "La mort dans l'âme" (see p. 33n58), where he writes, "I decided to organize my days, to dot them with reference points," but it wasn't until the end of his life, over twenty years later, that the idea would begin to be fleshed out in his unfinished novel *The First Man*, where he writes: "Already poor people have a less nourished memory than the rich, because the memory of the poor has fewer physical landmarks, given that they rarely leave the place they live, and fewer landmarks in time, too, given a life that's uniform and gray. Of course, there's the heart's memory, which some say is the surest, but the heart's worn thin by hardship and work, and it quickly forgets beneath the weight of fatigue. The search for lost time is only for the rich. For the poor, it simply marks the faint traces of the road to death."

The rest of the entry informs a section of *The Happy Death*, in part 2, chap. 4, most explicitly when Camus writes: "Sometimes he'd take out a watch and stare at the hand passing from one number to the next, and he'd marvel at how five minutes could seem so interminable. That watch was probably what opened him to the painful, torturous path that leads to the supreme art of doing nothing."

already established. Note, for example, that it's nearly impossible to spend five minutes watching a hand turn round a clockface, so long and exasperating is the experience.

———

March.

Gray sky. But the light seeps through. A few raindrops a moment ago. The bay growing dimmer. The lights coming to life. Happiness and those who are happy. They have only what they deserve.[28]

———

March.

My joy has no end.

———

Dolorem exprimit quia movit amorem.[29]

———

March.

Clinic above Algiers. A rather strong breeze climbs the hill, rustling the grass and sunlight. But all this gentle, golden movement stops some distance from the peak, at the foot of the black cypresses that work their way up the ridge in tight rows. A glorious light flows from the sky. Down below, the sea is without a ripple, revealing its blue-toothed smile. Standing in the wind beneath a sun that warms only one side of my face, I watch as this singular hour flows by, unable to utter a word. But then a mental patient shows up with his nurse. He steps forward, a box held under his arm, his face serious.

"Hello, Mademoiselle" (to the young woman who's with me). "If you'll allow me to introduce myself, Monsieur, I'm Monsieur Ambrosino."

"Monsieur Camus."

"Oh! I knew a Camou. Had a truck company in Mostaganem. A relative, no doubt."

28. With this entry, the twenty-two-page notebook signature Camus inserted ends, and the notebook proper begins (see the note at the start of notebook I). It is clear that at least three pages of the Jupiter notebook, if not more, have been torn out from the beginning, as the very edges of the torn pages, with bits of writing on them, are still intact.

29. Another of Spinoza's aphorisms, slightly distorted as recorded here, where it roughly translates as: "Pain gains from love changed." This entry may be in reference to the breakdown of Camus's first marriage to Simone Hié. The couple would separate in September, with Camus going to live with his brother, Lucien.

"No."

"Well, doesn't matter anyway. May I sit with you a minute? I'm allowed out for a half-hour every day, though I have to bow down before the nurse to get him to take me. You're related to Mademoiselle?"

"Yes, Monsieur."

"Ah, well then, I should tell you that we're going to be engaged come Easter. My wife said it was okay. Here, Mademoiselle, please accept these meager flowers. And this letter, it's for you. Come sit next to me. I only have a half-hour."

"We have to go, Monsieur Ambrosino."

"Oh, really? But then when will I see you again?"

"Tomorrow."

"Ah, well, it's just that I only have a half an hour and I came to play a little music."

We set out. Red geraniums glow radiantly along the path. From his box, the mental patient pulls a reed that's been split lengthwise and patched with rubber tape. He draws a strange, plaintive, warm sound from it: "Il pleut sur la route . . ."[30] The music follows us down past the geraniums and large, daisy-filled flowerbeds, down to the sea and its imperturbable smile.

I opened the letter. It contained cut-out advertisements that had been carefully organized with numbers written in pencil.

M.[31]—He placed the weapon on the table every evening. The workday done, he'd put away his papers, draw the revolver close, and press it to his forehead, rolling it over his temples, using the cold iron to sooth his feverish cheeks. Then, he'd sit there like that for a long while, letting his fingers wander the length of the trigger and play with the safety, until the world around him fell silent and, already sleepy, his whole being snuggled up to that single sensation of cold-and-salty iron, to that thing from which death could come.

---

30. At the time of the encounter, Tino Rossi's song "Il pleut sur la route" would have been a new release. Tino Rossi was a favorite of Camus's mother, and his name appears in a couple of other places in Camus's writing.

For more on the advertisements that appear in the entry's final sentence, see p. 128n48.

31. This entry and the one that follows are notes for Camus's first novel, *The Happy Death*, with the initial *M* referring to the protagonist, Patrice Mersault. The passage recorded here appears in part 1, chap. 4.

Ray Davison notes in *Camus: The Challenge of Dostoyevsky* that this sketch bears similarities to a scene in Dostoyevsky's short story "The Dream of a Ridiculous Man."

The moment you decide not to kill yourself, you have to stop talking about life. And when he woke, his mouth was full of an already-bitter saliva, and he licked the barrel of the weapon, sticking his tongue inside of it, and then, groaning[32] with a fathomless happiness, repeated in amazement: "My joy is priceless."

M.—Part 2

Successive catastrophes—His courage—Life is woven from these misfortunes. He settles into that painful web, building his days around his evening returns, his solitude, his distrust, his disgust. People think he's stoic, resilient. Things appear to be going well from the look of it. One day, an insignificant incident: one of his friends speaks to him while only half paying attention.[33] He goes home. He kills himself.

———

March 31.

It seems as if I'm slowly emerging.

The pleasant, reserved friendship of women.[34]

———

Social issue settled. Balance restored. I'll take stock in 2 weeks. —My book, keep it at the front of my mind. My work, organize it without delay. Get started Sunday.

---

32. The French word used here, *râlant,* forms the base of the phrase, *râle d'agonie* (death rattle), a connection lost in translation.

33. Camus often took incidents from his life—in this case, the encounter with Jean Grenier noted a few pages back—and integrated them into his formal writing. The version expressed here would appear in "Between Yes and No," where Camus writes: "A man suffers and endures one misfortune after another. He deals with them, settling into his fate. People think well of him. And then, one evening, nothing: he meets a friend he likes a lot. The friend speaks to him only half paying attention. Back home, the man kills himself. So then, we speak of personal sorrows and secret dramas. Not so. Though if we absolutely must have a reason, then he killed himself because a friend spoke to him while only half paying attention."

Similarly, in *The Myth of Sisyphus,* Camus writes: "There are a lot of reasons for a suicide, and, generally speaking, the most obvious aren't usually the most important. People rarely commit suicide upon reflection (although it's not out of the question). What sets the crisis off is almost always unverifiable. The papers talk of 'personal sorrows' or 'incurable diseases,' and such explanations make sense. But we'd also need to know if on the given day a friend seemed uninterested while talking to the hopeless man. There's the culprit. Because that alone may be enough to trigger all the lingering resentment and weariness hanging about."

34. The reference is to Camus's friends, the couple Jeanne-Paule Sicard and Marguerite Dobrenn, with whom Camus rented a house on the heights of Algiers, at the corner of Rue Sidi-Brahim and Rue des Amandiers. Another friend, Christiane Galindo, would soon join them. The three

Build back up after this long period of hectic, hopeless life. Finally, the sun and my panting body. Keep the quiet—keep the faith.

April.

First hot days. Stifling. All the animals are laid out on their sides. As the day wanes, the air above the city takes on a strange quality. Sounds lift into it and are lost like balloons. People and trees remain perfectly still. On the terraces, Moorish people chat while awaiting the evening. Coffee is roasted, its scent also lifting upward. The hour is soft and desperate. Nothing to hold close. Nothing to bring you to your knees, wild with gratitude.

The heat on the quays—Enormous, crushing, it takes your breath away. Your throat is scraped clean by the overwhelming stench of tar. Annihilation and the taste of death. This here is the true climate of tragedy, not the night, as in preconceived notions.[35]

The senses and the world—Desires twirl together. And in this body that I'm holding against mine, I'm also holding that strange joy that flows from sky to sea.

Sun and death.[36] The longshoreman with the broken leg. Blooddrops dripping one by one onto the quay's burning stones. Sizzling. In the café, he tells me his life story. The others have all gone, leaving their six glasses behind. A little house in the banlieues. Lives alone, only goes home to cook dinner in the evenings. Has a dog, two cats, a male and female, six kittens. The female can't feed them. Her kittens die one by one. Every evening, a stiff dead body and excrement. Two smells accompany it: a mixture of urine and death. The last evening (he stretches his arms out on the table, gently spreading them apart, slowly pushing the glasses to the edge). The last cat dies. The mother had already eaten half of it. So then, a demi-cat, really. The excrement still lin-

---

friends called their home "The House Before the World," a name that would appear in several of Camus's formal writings.

In the copy of *L'envers et l'endroit* that he inscribed to Marguerite, Camus wrote: "For certain pleasant, reserved forms . . . of women's friendship."

35. Parts of this entry would appear in *The Happy Death*, part 1, chap. 2.

36. Several pieces of the entry appear in *The Happy Death*, while the portion about the cats appears in the essay "Between Yes and No."

gering. The wind howling through the house. A piano, far off in the distance. He sits amid these ruins, this misery, and then, all at once, the whole meaning of the world rises into his throat. (He continues to spread his arms, and the glasses fall one by one.) Stays there for several hours, his whole body racked with an enormous, wordless anger, his hands in the urine and thoughts on the dinner he has yet to make.

The glasses are all broken. He smiles. "It's fine," he says to the man in charge. "We'll pay for everything."

The longshoreman's broken leg. In a corner, a young man silently laughs.

"It's nothing. What hurt me most were abstract ideas."

Running after the truck, speed, dust, racket. Wild rhythm of winches and machines, masts dancing on the horizon, hulls rolling. On the truck: bouncing over the quay's uneven cobblestones. And in the chalky, white dust, amid the sun and the blood, against the immense, unbelievable backdrop of the port, two young men rush off at full speed, laughing like crazy, giddy and dizzy.[37]

MAY: Don't stand apart from the world. You can't go wrong in life if you live it in the light. All my effort, in all situations, in misfortune, in disillusion, goes to reestablishing connections. And even having this sadness inside me, still, what a desire to love, what intoxication at the mere sight of a hill against the evening sky.

Connect with truth. First and foremost, nature, and then art by those who've understood. And my art, if I'm capable of it. If not, the light and water and intoxication are still right there in front of me, as well as the wet lips of desire.

Smiling hopelessness. No exit, but endlessly exerting a domination we know to be in vain. The essential thing: not to lose yourself, and not to lose that part of yourself that lies dormant in the world.

MAY: All connections = Cult of the Self?[38] No.

37. This entry would appear in *The Happy Death*, part 1, chap. 2, as well as in *The Stranger*, part 1, chap. 3.

38. The reference may be to Maurice Barrès's *Le culte de moi* (*The Cult of the Self*), a trilogy of books published between 1888 and 1891. Camus would go on to write an article about Barrès in the April 5, 1940, issue of *La lumière*.

The cult of the self presupposes an amateur dilettantism or optimism. Both utter nonsense. Not to choose your life but to stretch it.[39]

Keep in mind: for Kierkegaard, the origin of our sickness is comparison.

Fully commit yourself. After that, accept yes and no with equal strength.

MAY. Those evenings in Algiers when the women are so beautiful.

MAY: At the edge—and beyond it: the game. I deny, am cowardly and weak, but I act as if I were assured, as if I were strong and brave. A matter of will = push absurdity as far as it will go = I am capable of . . .

That's why I take the game to be tragic in terms of the effort given to it but comic in its result (or rather, indifferent).

As such, don't waste your time. Seek extreme experience in solitude. Purify the game by conquering your self—knowing such conquest to be absurd.

Reconcile the Hindu sage and the Western hero.

"It's abstract ideas that have hurt me most."

This extreme experience must always stop before an outstretched hand. To be taken up again afterward. Outstretched hands are rare.[40]

God—Mediterranean: constructions—nothing natural.

Nature = equivalence.

Against relapse and weakness: effort—Beware the demon:
culture—the body
will—the work (phil.)

But the counterpart: the intercessors—every day
my work (the emotions)
extreme experiences.

Philosophical Work: absurdity.

Literary Work: strength, love and death under the banner of conquest.

---

39. Camus would get at a similar idea in *The Myth of Sisyphus*, as well as in a contemporaneous, previously unpublished notebook, where he writes: "Losing myself in that fathomless certainty, feeling that I was now enough of a stranger to my own life to stretch it out and explore it without the myopic eyes of a lover, in all of this I felt the birth of a certain kind of freedom, one that was finite, but one that took the place of those illusions of freedom that all succumb to death."

40. In the handwritten notebook, the margin of this note, and the six that follow it, is filled with illegible writing, as well as a series of arrows and brackets. Throughout the first notebook, there are many instances of such lines and arrows and circled words.

In the 2 cases, blend the 2 genres while respecting their particular tones. Write a book one day that will give this meaning.[41]

With regard to this tension: composure—Reject comparison.

———

An essay about death and Philosophy—Malraux.[42] India.

An essay about chemistry.[43]

———

MAY: That life is the strongest—truth, but also the principle of all cowardice. Clearly, we have to think the opposite.

———

And here they start to bray: I am an immoralist.

Translation: I need to give myself a moral code. So then, admit it, you fool. So do I.

———

Sounding another tune: you have to be simple, truthful, no literary leanings—to accept and give of yourself.[44] But that's all we ever do.

If you're quite convinced of your hopelessness, you have to act as if you have hope—or kill yourself. Suffering gives no rights.[45]

———

An intellectual? Yes. And don't ever deny it. An intellectual = a person who splits themself in two.[46] I like that. I'm happy to be both halves. "Can

---

41. In the handwritten notebook, these last four lines were added on the recto page, beneath the "Intellectual" entry, under which Camus drew two thick lines.

42. André Malraux (1901–1976), French novelist and, later in life, minister of cultural affairs. At the time this entry was recorded, Camus had just written an adaptation of Malraux's *Le temps du mépris*, which was performed by the Théâtre du Travail on January 25, 1936.

43. In the handwritten notebook, this is followed by "(cf. my readings)."

44. This idea of "giving of yourself" would appear not long after in a previously unpublished notebook (see appendix II). Camus would take up the idea again in *The Myth of Sisyphus*, the roots of which can be seen in the above entry, as well as the unpublished notebook.

On the typescript, the tone of this entry is a little different. There's a paragraph break here, followed by a crossed-out word: "Okay." Among other changes on the typescript, the final sentence, which is also crossed out, reads: "As if suffering gave them rights!"

45. In the preceding pages, as well as the pages that follow, the French word *désespoir*, often translated as "despair," is given as "hopelessness," emphasizing the shared root *espoir* (hope), which Camus often utilizes.

46. There is an oft-quoted, aphoristic translation of this passage ("An intellectual is someone whose mind watches itself. I like this, because I am happy to be both halves, the watcher and the watched.") that takes advantage of the French *se dédouble*, which more literally means "to double up" or "to split in two," and which Camus uses here in the sense of looking at a debate from both sides. But such a translation erases the elliptical nature of the entry, removing, even at a visual level, the "=" in favor of the smoother "is."

they be united?" A practical question. You have to get started trying. "I detest intelligence" really means "I can't deal with my own doubts."

I prefer to keep my eyes open.

———

November.

See Greece.[47] Mind and feeling, appetite for *expressions* as proof of decadence. Greek sculpture declines when smiles and gazes appear. Italian painting, too, with the 16th century and the "colorists."

Paradox of the Greek artist, great despite himself. The Doric Apollos are admirable because they have no expressions. Expressions were added on with paint (regrettable)—but the paint has gone, and the masterpiece remains.

———

Nationalities appear as signs of disintegration. Hardly had the religious unity of the Holy Roman Empire broken when: nationalities. In the East, the whole remains.

Internationalism attempts to return to the West its true meaning and calling. But the founding principle is no longer Christian, it's Greek. Contemporary humanism: it assures the gap that existed between East and West persists (case with Malraux). But it restores strength.

———

Protestantism. Nuance. In theory, an admirable attitude: Luther, Kierkegaard. In practice???

———

JANUARY. Caligula or the meaning of death. Four acts.[48]

I. (a) His accession. Joy. Virtuous speeches (Cf. Suetonius)
(b) Mirror
II. (a) His sisters and Drusilla
(b) Disgust with the grand
(c) Drusilla's death. Caligula's flight.
III.[49]

---

47. Camus had been planning to travel to Greece in 1939 but had to cancel the trip due to the war. It would be sixteen years before he was finally able to visit the country.

48. The first full version of *Caligula* was completed in 1938. Camus would continue to revise the play throughout the rest of his life.

49. Camus left the rest of this page blank, drew a line down it, then wrote the rest of the entry on the following page.

End: Caligula appears, opening the curtain:

"No, Caligula's not dead. He's there, and there. He's inside each one of you. If you were given the power, if you had the heart, if you loved life, you'd see it run wild, that monster or angel you carry inside you. Our day is dying for having believed in values, for believing things could be beautiful and could stop being absurd. Farewell, I'm headed back to history, where those who are afraid to love too intensely have kept me locked away for so long."

January.

Essay: The House Before the World.

—Around the neighborhood, people called it The House of the 3 Students.

—When you leave, it's to lock yourself away.

—The house before the world isn't a house where you have fun but a house where you're happy.[50]

"It's not just young ladies here," M. says, as X. stands there cursing.

M. and love:

"You've reached that age when people are happy to recognize themselves in someone else's child."

"He has to figure out Einstein's theory of relativity before he can make love."

"God forbid," M. says.

To climb it each time is to conquer it each time, so steep is the path that leads the way.

February.

Civilization doesn't reside in a greater or lesser degree of refinement but in the shared consciousness of an entire people. And such a consciousness is never refined. It may even be rudimentary. To make civilization out to be the work of an elite is to identify it with culture, which is something altogether

50. Two additional lines of dialogue, which Camus crossed out on the typescript, follow this one in the handwritten notebook.

different. There is a Mediterranean culture, but there's also a Mediterranean civilization. On the other hand, don't confuse civilization with the people.[51]

———

Touring theater.[52] In the morning there is a tender fragility to that Oran region that we know to be so terribly brutal in the full light of day: shimmering wadis lined with oleanders, the practically classic tones surrounding the rising sun, purple mountains fringed with pink.[53] All foretell a radiant day. But with a modesty and delicacy you can already feel coming to an end.

———

April '37.

Curious: inability to be alone, inability not to be. You accept both. Both have benefits.

———

The most dangerous temptation: to feel like nothing.[54]

———

Kasbah: A time always comes when you break with yourself. A small coal fire crackling amid a dark and viscous alley.

———

Madness—Beautiful setting for a splendid morning—Sun. Sky and bones. Music. A finger on the windowpane.[55]

———

51. In an entry that appears not long after this one, Camus quotes directly from Oswald Spengler's *The Decline of the West*, which it seems he was already in the process of reading when this entry was recorded. The majority of the quotations that follow come from the book's introduction. Here, as in the wide range of quotes that appear throughout the journals, Camus's citations tend to be somewhat inaccurate, regardless if he's quoting from a text translated into French, as with the Spengler, or quoting from a text originally written in French.

52. The word "theater" was added to the manuscript in thick red pencil.

53. In November 1936, Camus began touring as an actor with the troupe Radio-Alger, appearing as Olivier-le-Daim in a production of Théodore de Banville's *Gringoire*.

54. This idea also appears in Camus's essay "The Minotaur, or The Stop in Oran," which was written in 1939 but which, for reasons of censorship, wasn't published until 1946, at which point it appeared in a small literary magazine, *L'Arche*. In the essay, Camus writes: "'To be nothing!' For thousands of years, this great cry has raised millions of men to rebel against desire and grief. Its echoes have traveled across centuries and oceans to die here on the world's oldest sea, and they still bounce, barely audible, off Oran's compact cliffs. Everyone in this country listens to their advice, without comprehending it. Naturally, it's more or less in vain. Nothingness is no more attainable than the absolute."

55. This entry was written in the same thick red pencil as the word "theater" in the earlier entry.

The Need to be Right is the sign of a vulgar mind.

Narrative[56]—a man who doesn't care to justify himself. He prefers to let people make of him what they will. He dies, the only one aware of his true nature—Vanity of such consolation.

APRIL. Women—who prefer their ideas to their feelings.

—For the essay about the ruins:[57]

The desiccating wind—The old man as naked as an olive tree in the Sahel.

1) Essay about the ruins: the wind in the ruins or death in the sun.
2) Take up "with deep regret"[58] again—Presentiment.
3) The house before the world.
4) Novel—Work on it.
5) Essay about Malraux.
6) Thesis.

In a foreign country, the sun gilding the houses on a hill. A more powerful impression than the same sight in one's own country. It's not the same sun. I know very well it's not the same sun.

---

56. In French literature, there are three traditional categories of short story: *conte*, *nouvelle*, and *récit*. Here, Camus uses the term *récit*, which Geoffrey Hartman has identified as "a confessional narrative, a kind of dramatic monologue in prose," and for which Daniel Just gives Camus's *The Fall* as a prime example (see Hartman, "Maurice Blanchot: Philosopher-Novelist," and Just, "The Politics of the Novel"). André Gide, whose *L'immoraliste* (*The Immoralist*) is also considered a classic example of the *récit*, described the form as being told only from a single perspective, in contrast with the *roman* (novel), which has the ability to present a more complex, layered view of the world. Though he may have been willing to give a definition, Gide, as well as many other French writers, made a point of rejecting such traditional categorization.

57. The essay referenced here is "The Winds at Djemila," which was collected in Camus's second book of essays, *Noces*. Snippets of the essay originally appeared in a small Algerian journal, *Mithra*, in January–February 1939.

58. The essay Camus refers to here, "La mort dans l'âme," appears in his first collection, *L'envers et l'endroit*. The English rendering of the title, "Death in the Soul," a literal translation, loses the idiomatic sense of doing something with great reluctance or with a heavy heart. In concert with the last lines of the essay ("On the outskirts of Algiers, there's a small cemetery with black iron gates. If you go to the very back, you'll discover a valley set against a bay. You can dream for quite a while standing there before that offering sighing with the sea. But when you retrace your steps, you'll find 'Eternal Regrets' on the slab of an abandoned grave."), an English rendering that conveys the idiomatic sense of the phrase might be "With Deep Regret."

In the evening, the gentleness of the world above the bay—There are days the world lies, days it tells the truth. This evening, it's telling the truth—and with what sad, insistent beauty.

———

May.

Error of the complete psychological profile. People trying to find themselves, analyzing themselves. To know yourself, assert yourself. Psychology is action—not reflection on yourself. You create your self throughout your life. To know yourself completely is to die.[59]

———

1) The glamorous poetry that precedes love.

2) A man who fails at everything, even his own death.

3) In youth, we're more attached to a landscape than to another person. That's because the former allows itself to be interpreted.

———

MAY. Draft Preface for *L'envers et l'endroit*. For many people, these essays, as they're presented here, will seem to lack formal structure. This isn't the result of some convenient contempt for form—only of insufficient maturity. For those willing to take these pages for what they really are—essays, attempts—all that can be asked is that the reader follow their progression. In doing so, perhaps the reader will feel, from the first to the last, the faint steps that bring them together, that, I'd like to say, legitimize them, that is if such justification didn't seem pointless to me and if I didn't know that we always prefer the idea we have of a man to the man himself.[60]

———

To write is to be disinterested. A certain renunciation in art. Rewrite. The effort always brings some benefit, whatever it may be. A matter of laziness for those who don't succeed.

———

59. The idea of complete knowledge, whether scientific or otherwise, as a destructive force would recur throughout Camus's work, perhaps most humorously in his short story "Orgueil" ("Pride"), which appeared in French for the first time in 2008 and in an English translation in *Tin House* 72 (Summer 2017).

60. *L'envers et l'endroit*, published in Algiers in 1937 by Éditions Charlot, originally appeared without a preface, though Camus had been thinking about writing one at least since 1933, when he jotted several preparatory paragraphs in the notebook he bought at the Ferraris Bookshop (see appendix I). It wasn't until Gallimard reprinted the collection in 1958 that a preface would be added.

Luther: "It is a thousand times more important to firmly believe in absolution than to be worthy of it. This faith makes you worthy and constitutes true satisfaction."

(Sermon on *Justification* preached in Leipzig in 1519.)[61]

JUNE—Every day, the man who's been sentenced to death is visited by a priest. Because his neck will be severed, his knees bend, his lips attempt to form a name, and he drops to the ground, hiding from himself with a "My God, my God!"

And each time, resistance in the man, who doesn't want such an easy way out, who wants to ruminate on his fear. He dies without a word, his eyes filled with tears.

A philosophy is worth what the philosopher is worth. The greater the person, the truer the philosophy.[62]

Civilization versus culture

Imperialism is civilization in its purest form. Cf. Cecil Rhodes. "Expansion is everything"—civilizations are islets—Civilization as the fated culmination of culture (Cf. Spengler).

Culture: the cry of men faced with their fate.

Civilization, its decadence: man's desire when faced with wealth. Blindness.

A political theory about the Mediterranean.

"I speak of what I know."

---

1) Economic sense (Marxism).[63]

---

61. The translation given is from the French, as recorded by Camus. John W. Doberstein's standard English translation of the passage, which occurs at the end of the sermon, may have left Camus a little less enthused: "A thousandfold more depends on your firmly believing the judgment of the priest than your being worthy and doing sufficient works. Indeed, the selfsame faith makes you worthy and helps you to make a proper satisfaction."

62. From Spengler's *Decline of the West*.

63. In the handwritten notebook, the word "studies" is jotted next to this entry.

The French words *spirituel* and *évidence* can also mean "intellectual" and "foregone conclusion." The above entry could equally be read as: "Forgone economic conclusions" and "Foregone spiritual/intellectual conclusions."

2) Spiritual " "(Holy Roman Empire).

A suffering world's tragic battle. The futility of worrying about immortality. What interests us is our fate, yes—but not "after," "*before*."

The consoling power of hell.

1) For one thing, endless suffering holds no meaning for us—We imagine reprieves.

2) We can't comprehend the word eternity. It's inestimable for us. Except insofar as we speak of an "eternal moment."

3) Hell is life in this body—which is much better than annihilation.[64]

Logical rule: the unique has universal value.

Illogical " ":the tragic is contradictory.

Practical " ":a man who is intelligent in one field may be an imbecile in others.

To be deep through insincerity.[65]

The little darling, as seen by Marcel. "Her husband couldn't pull it off. One day, she says to me, 'It's never like that with my husband.'"

<u>The Battle of Charleroi,</u>[66]
as seen by Marcel.

"The rest of us, the Zouaves, they put us out there like that, as a skirmish-line. The major, he says, "Charge," and then we're going down into, it was like a ravine with trees. We were told to charge. There was no one else in front of us. So, we marched, we marched out in front like that, and then all of a sudden we're being machine-gunned, we're being hit, all of us, falling one atop the other. So many were wounded and dead and the bottom of the ravine was

---

64. Echoes of these reflections, some perhaps influenced by Camus's reading of Schopenhauer, can be found in the final, title section of *The Myth of Sisyphus*.

65. In the handwritten notebook, this is the only entry on the page.

66. The battle was fought between France and Germany on August 21, 1914, amid the larger Battle of the Frontiers.

Camus wrote Marcel's reflections on a looseleaf sheet of paper that he later glued in the notebook. The passage, with only slight alterations, would first appear in *The Happy Death*, spoken by the character Emmanuel, and then, twenty years later, would appear once more in *The First Man*.

so filled with blood that you could have crossed it with a pastera.[67] It was so awful. Some were crying out 'Maman.'"

———

"Oh, Marcel, look at all those medals, where did you earn all those medals?"

"Where did I earn all of these? In the war, I'd imagine."

"How'd you get them in the war?"

"What, you want me to show you the official documents with all the details? Should I read them to you, too? How about that? Is that what we should do?"

The "official documents" are brought out.

The "official documents" concern the entire regiment of which Marcel was one part.

———

Marcel. People like us, we're not rich, but we eat well. You see my grandson, well, he eats more than his father does. His father takes down a pound of bread, but him, he takes down a kilo. And bring on the sobrassada. And bring on the escabeche. Sometimes, as soon as he finishes, he says, "Mmm, mmm," and then eats some more.[68]

———

July

Countryside around La Madeleine.[69] Beauty that makes you long for poverty. I'm so far removed from my fever—so incapable of any pride but love. Keep a good distance. I have to say what fills my heart, have to say it right away.

———

"No relationship." *True novel.* He who defends a faith his whole life. His mother dies. He lets everything go. The true nature of his faith hasn't really changed. No relationship, that's just the way it is.

———

67. The word *pastera* doesn't come from French and could, depending on the source language, have several different meanings, though in the given context it most likely refers to a small rowboat.

68. This entry would later appear in Camus's essay "Irony," where he'd change the more particular "sobrassada" and "escabeche" to the more universal "sausage" and "camembert." The entry also aligns with later descriptions of Uncle Étienne/Ernest in *The First Man*.

69. La Madeleine was a neighborhood on the outskirts of Algiers, near El Biar.

Seaplane: a glory of sparkling metal above the bay, in the blue sky.

The pine trees, yellow with pollen and green with leaves.

Like Gide, Christianity asks man to restrain his desire. But Gide sees this as an additional pleasure, whereas Christianity finds it mortifying. In this sense, it's more "natural" than Gide—who is an intellectual—but less natural than the people, who satisfy their thirst at fountains, knowing satiety is the end of desire (an "Apology for Satiety").[70]

Prague. Running from yourself.
"I'd like a room."
"Certainly. For one night?"
"No. I don't know."
"We have rooms for 18, 25, and 30 crowns."
(no response)
"Which room would you like, Monsieur?"
"It doesn't matter which one" (gazing outside).
"Porter, take these bags to room No. 12."
(waking up)
"How much is that room?"
"30 crowns."
"That's too much. I'd like one of the rooms for 18 crowns."
"Porter, room No. 34."[71]

---

1) In the train carrying him to ". . . ," "X." looked at his hands.
2) The guy is still there. But coincidence.

Lyon.[72]
Vorarlberg-Halle.

---

70. These thoughts on Gide and Christianity would later appear as a footnote in "Summer in Algiers."

71. In his essay "Death in the Soul," Camus writes that he unwittingly ended up in the more expensive room and had to save money by eating poor-quality, nauseating food. The entry also appears in *The Happy Death*.

72. On the typescript, there's a scratched-out sentence preceding "Lyon." The word "July" can still be read, but the rest of the sentence is illegible.

Camus, his then wife Simone Hié, and their friend Yves Bourgeois had set out on a kayaking expedition that Camus had to abandon due to his health. Simone and Yves continued on without

Kufstein—The chapel and fields around the inn, beneath the rain. A solitude firmly anchored.

Salzburg—Jedermann.[73] Saint Peter's Cemetery. Mirabell Garden and its precious success. Rain and phlox—Lakes and mountains—walk on the plateau.

Linz—The Danube and the working-class districts. The doctor.

Budweis—The suburb. Small Gothic convent. Solitude.

Prague—*The first four days*. Baroque convent. Jewish cemetery. Baroque churches. Arrive at the restaurant. Hungry. No money. The dead man. Cucumbers in vinegar. The one-armed man with his accordion under his rear.

Dresden—Paintings.

Bautzen—Gothic cemetery. Geraniums and sunflowers in the brick archways.

Breslau—Drizzle. Churches and factory chimneys. A tragic air particular to this place.

Plains of Silesia: merciless and barren (dunes). Flights of birds in the humid morning, above the sticky earth.

Olmütz—Tender and slow plains of Moravia. Sour plum trees, distant, touching.

Brno—Poor neighborhoods.

Vienna—Civilization—Luxury piled up and hoarded, protected by the gardens. Private distress hidden in folds of silk.

———

Italy.

Churches—A particular feeling they have: Cf. Andrea del Sarto.

Painting: a grave, rigid world. Trust, etc.

Take note: Italian painting and its decadence.

———

The intellectual faced with becoming a member (fragment).[74]

———

him. Some of the notes and descriptions from the trip that Camus records here would later be incorporated into his essay "Death in the Soul."

73. Camus saw Max Reinhardt's production of Hugo von Hofmannsthal's play *Jedermann* (*Everyman*).

74. The French *adhésion* is used here in the sense of being faced with "joining" or "supporting" a particular group or political party, a topic Camus would often return to throughout his career. For more of Camus's early thoughts on the topic, see his November 11, 1938, article in *Alger républicain*.

July.

For women, what's unbearable is the loveless affection a man can show them.

For the man, it's bittersweet.

———

Couples: the man tries to look good in front of a third party. Immediately, the woman: "But you're also . . ." and tries to diminish him, to make him share in her mediocrity.

———

On the train: a mother to her child:

"Don't suck your fingers. Dirty."

or: "If you keep it up, you're gonna get it."

Id. Couples: the woman stands up on the packed train.

"Give it here," she says.

The husband searches his pocket and hands her the paper she needs.

———

July '37.

For the Novel about the Player.[75]

Cf. Les Pléiades: overflowing cadence. Play the game. Soul of luxury. The adventurer.

———

July '37—*Player*.

Revolution, fame, love, and death. What do they mean to me compared with that something inside me, so grave and true?

"What's that?"

"The heavy trail of tears," he said, "that underlies the entirety of my taste for death."

———

July '37.

The adventurer. Has the distinct feeling there's nothing left to be done in art. Nothing great or new is possible—at least not in Western culture. The

75. Camus may have initially been thinking of writing *Caligula* as a novel, given an early version of the play, dated 1939, bears the subtitle "or the Player."

only thing left is action. But anyone with a noble soul would only take part in such action out of desperation.

———

July.

When asceticism is voluntary, you can fast for 6 weeks (water is enough). When it's forced (famine), no more than 10 days.

Reservoir of real energy.

———

Breathing practices of Tibetan yogis. What we need to do is bring our positivist methodology[76] to experiences of this magnitude. To have "revelations" in which we don't believe. *What I like*: applying this lucidity to ecstasy.

———

Women in the street. The hot beast of desire that's carried coiled in the loins and that stirs with a fierce sweetness.

———

AUGUST—On the way to Paris: this fever beating in my temples, the strange and sudden letting go of the world and of people. Struggling against my body. On my bench, in the wind, emptied and hollowed out from the inside,[77] I kept thinking about K. Mansfield,[78] of that long, tender, and painful story of her struggle with illness. What awaits me in the Alps, along with the solitude and the idea that I'll be there to get better, is the *awareness* of my illness.

———

Carrying through to the very end isn't only a matter of enduring but also of letting go. I need to have a sense of myself, insofar as doing so means having a sense of what's bigger than myself. Sometimes I have to write things that

76. Positivist philosophy, which will appear again later in the notebooks, here carries the sense of "the scientific method."

77. The phrase "hollowed out from the inside" appears again later in the notebooks and also appears, in slightly altered form ("emptied from the inside" and "empty on the inside"), in *The Misunderstanding*.

78. Katherine Mansfield (1888–1923) was diagnosed with tuberculosis in December 1917 and died only a few years later, in January 1923, at the age of thirty-four, while seeking treatment in France. Her journal was published in English in 1927 and translated into French in 1932. It was later discovered that the journal, published by her husband, was heavily edited, and it wasn't until 2002 that the full, unedited edition was published.

are partly beyond me, but which, for that very reason, prove there are things in me that are greater than me.

———

August

Paris. The feeling and tenderness. The cats, the children, the people's retreat. The gray colors, the sky, a great parade of stone and water.

———

Arles.[79]

———

August '37–

He went deeper into the mountains every day, coming back mute, his hair full of grass, covered in a day's worth of scratches. And it was the same seductionless conquest every time. Little by little, he weakened that hostile country's resistance. He managed to make himself like those round, white clouds behind that single fir standing out on the ridge, to make himself like those fields of pinkish fireweed, of rowan trees and bellflowers. He melded with that aromatic, rocky world. Having reached that far-off summit, standing before that immense landscape so suddenly discovered, it wasn't the soothing calm of love that was born in him, but a sort of inner pact agreed upon with that foreign[80] nature, a truce established between two hard and fierce faces, the intimacy of two adversaries and not the ease of two friends.

———

Comfort of Savoy.

———

August '37.

A man who went looking for life where it's usually found (marriage, a steady job, etc.) suddenly realizes, while reading a fashion catalog, how much

79. In the handwritten notebook, this is the last word to appear on the page. The entry that follows this one was added to the manuscript at a later date.

80. In the entry below, also dated August '37, Camus lays out the basis for what would become *L'Étranger*, his first published novel. In the US, the book appeared with the title *The Stranger*, while in the UK it was titled *The Outsider*. While, for the sake of consistency and connection, the French word *étranger* is usually translated in these pages as "stranger," in the phrase that occurs here, *nature étrangère*, the translation "strange nature" would be idiosyncratic, if not outright misleading. In the given context, it's not that nature is strange, as in odd, but that it's unknown, as in the French *pays étranger* (foreign country).

of a stranger he's been to his own life (life as it's understood in fashion catalogs).

Part I—His life until then.

Part II—The game.

Part III—Letting go of compromise and truth in nature.

———

August '37.

Last chapter? Paris Marseille. Going down to the Mediterranean.

And he went into the water and washed from his skin the grimy, black images the world had left there. Suddenly, the scent of his skin came alive as his muscles flexed. Never before, perhaps, had he felt so in tune with the world, his trajectory so attuned to the sun's. At that hour, when the night was overflowing with stars, his movements were traced against the sky's vast and silent face. By moving his arm, he sketches the space separating this shining heavenly body here from the one seemingly blinking on and off over there, dragging a spray of stars in his wake, a train of clouds. It's like this that the sky's water is stirred by his arms, and the city, draped around him, is like a coat of glittering shells.

———

Two characters. One commits suicide?

———

August '37.

The player.

"That's going to be difficult, very difficult. But that's not a reason."

"Of course," Catherine said, lifting her eyes to the sun.[81]

———

The Player.

Mme X, aside from being a perfect old crone, was a very talented musician.

For novel.

Part I: Traveling theater. Cinema. Story of great Love (Collège Sainte-Chantal).[82]

———

81. In the handwritten notebook, Camus appears to have written "Paris" next to this entry.

82. In the handwritten notebook, there is one more line, "Yes, Madame," next to which, in the margin, Camus wrote "Algiers." The rest of the page is left blank, and then, near the bottom, he has written "Algiers" in the margin a second time.

August '37.

Draft outline. Combine roleplaying and life.

Part I.

A—Running from yourself.

B—M. and poverty. (All in the present tense.) The chapters in series A describe the player. Those in series B, life until the mother's death (Death of Marguerite—Different professions: brokerage, auto parts, prefecture, etc.)

Last chapter: going toward the sun and death (suicide—natural death).[83]

Part II.

Inverse.

A. in the present tense: Rediscovery of joy. House Before the World. Liaison with Catherine.

B. in the past tense. Playing the game. Sexual jealousy. Running away.[84]

Part III.

All in the present tense. Love and sun. No, the boy says.[85]

———

August '37.

Every time I hear a political speech or read something written by one of our leaders, I have the horrifying feeling I'm not hearing anything human. And this has been going on for years now. It's always the same words telling the same lies. And the fact that the people just go with it, that their wrath hasn't broken these puppets into pieces, in this I see proof that the people grant no importance to their government and that they play, yes, really, that they play with a whole part of their life and their so-called vital interests.

———

A2 or A5 of I.

What dismays me is the importance we attach to the movements of the soul. Are you melancholy? Then life with another person becomes impossible. For if you have a noble heart, you can't bear the many questions you

---

83. The first section of *The Happy Death* is titled "Natural Death."

84. The handwritten notebook reads: "Liaison that leads to sexual jealousy," and then, after "Running away," there is an arrow pointing toward the word "Algiers."

85. The handwritten notebook has an additional sentence here, which wasn't carried over to the typescript: "Woman who commits suicide." After that, the rest of the page is left blank. The two entries that follow this one each appear on their own notebook page.

are asked. Whereas such things may just be about as important as having an appetite or wanting to . . .

———

August '37.

Outline. 3 parts.

Part I: A in the present tense
B in the past tense.

Ch. A1—M. Mersault's day as seen from the outside.

Ch. B1—Paris's poor neighborhood. Horse butcher. Patrice and his family. The mute. The grandmother.

Ch. A2—Conversation and paradoxes. Grenier. Cinema.

Ch. B2—Patrice's illness. The doctor. "This sharp pain . . ."

Ch. A3—A month of traveling theater.

Ch. B3—Professions (brokerage, auto parts, prefecture).

Ch. A4—The story of true love: "You never felt like that again?" "Yes, Madame, with you." Revolver theme.

Ch. B4—Mother's death.

Ch. A5—Meeting with Raymonde.

———

or alternatively:

I A—Sexual jealousy.
B—Poor neighborhood—mother.
II A—House Before the World—stars.
B—Life overflowing.
III Running away—Catherine, whom he doesn't love.

———

Cut and condense. Story of sexual jealousy that leads to a feeling of being out of place. Coming back to life.

"The lesson he'd gone so far to find, yes, it was still just as valuable, but only for having been brought back to the land of light."

———

Arrival in Prague—until departure—illness.

Explanation—Lucile—Flight.

———

Part II[86]

A. in the present tense

B. in the past tense

Ch. A1—The House Before the World. Introduction.
Ch. B1—He remembers. Liaison with Lucienne.
Ch. A2—The House Before the World. His youth.
Ch. B2—Lucienne recounts her infidelities.
Ch. A3—House Before the World. Invitation.
Ch. B4—Sexual jealousy. Salzburg. Prague.
Ch. A4—House Before the World. The sun.
Ch. B5—Flight (letter). Algiers. Catches cold, gets sick.
Ch. A5—Night under the stars. Catherine.

———

Patrice tells the story of being sentenced to death: "I see him, that man. He's inside me. Every word he says pierces my heart. He lives and breathes with me. He's scared with me.

"and that other man who wants to break him, I can see him living, too. He's inside me. I send the priest to him every day to weaken him."

"I know now I'm going to write. There comes a time when the tree, after having suffered so much, must bear its fruit. Every winter ends in spring. I have to bear witness. Afterward, the cycle will begin again.

"I'll speak of nothing but my love of life. But I'll talk about it in my own way . . .

"Others write from temptations deferred. Each of their life's disappointments is made into a work of art, a lie woven from the lies of their life. But for me, my writings will come from my happiness. Even when those writings are cruel. I have to write as I have to swim—because my body demands it."

———

86. While reviewing the typescript, Camus moved the four following entries from their original location in the notebooks to an earlier point in the text, which is where they would appear in the first French publication. Raymond Gay-Crosier, editor of the Pléiade edition of the *Carnets*, noticed the chronological discrepancy and shifted the four entries later in the text, where he believed they were originally located. Not fully agreeing with this placement, Hiroyuki Takatsuka went back and examined the ink and paper used in the notebook to determine a more precise placement. For the present edition, the entries have been set in the location identified by Takatsuka as the original position of the entries. See the introduction for further details.

Part III (all in the present)

Chap. I.—"Catherine," Patrice says, "I know now I'm going to write. The story of a man sentenced to death. I've returned to my real purpose, which is to write."

Chap. II.—Coming down from the House Before the World to the port, etc. Taste of sun and death. Love of life.

———

6 stories:

Story of the brilliant game. Luxury.
Story of the poor neighborhood. Mother's death.
Story of the House Before the World.
Story of sexual jealousy.
Story of the person sentenced to death.
Story of descending toward the sun.

———

August.

Lack of Spanish philosophers.

———

Novel: the man who understands that to live you have to be rich, who devotes himself entirely to making money, who succeeds, lives and dies *happy*.[87]

———

SEPTEMBER. This August has been like a hinge—a deep breath before pouring it all out in a wild outpouring of effort.[88] Provence and something closing up inside me. Provence like a woman leaning backward.

You have to live and create. Live to the point of tears—as before this house with round tiles and blue shutters on this hillside dotted with cypress trees.[89]

———

87. A succinct overview of *The Happy Death* and the first time Camus refers to the project as a novel.

88. In French, *une charnière* can be used literally as "a hinge" and figuratively as "a turning point." The above translation attempts to maintain the link between *délier* and *délirant*, although a more natural rendering might read: "a deep breath before releasing it all in a frenzied effort."

89. In *The Happy Death*, Camus writes: "At that moment, Mersault, still seated, felt how close happiness is to tears, held entirely in that silent exhilaration where a life's mix of hope and hopelessness is forged."

Montherlant: I'm the one to whom something happens.

In Marseille, happiness and sadness—As far as I can go. Lively city that I love. But, at the same time, this bitter taste of solitude.[90]

Sept. 8.

Marseille, hotel room. Wallpaper with a gray background and large yellow flowers. Geographies of muck. Greasy, muddy corners behind a huge radiator. Slatted bed, broken switch. . . . The sort of freedom that comes from the dubious and disreputable.

M. Sept. 8.

The sun's long, glittering descent. Monaco and Genoa, full of flowers, oleanders. The Ligurian coast's blue evenings. My exhaustion and this desire to cry. This solitude and this thirst for love. Finally, Pisa, vivid and austere, its green and yellow palaces, its domes and, along the rigid Arno, its grace. All its nobility lies in this refusal to open up. A modest and sensible city. In night's deserted streets, so close to myself that—that walking them alone, my desire to cry is finally fulfilled. This open thing inside me is beginning to heal.[91]

On the walls in Pisa: *Alberto fa l'amore con la mia sorella.*[92]

Thursday, 9.

Pisa and its people lying in front of the Duomo. The Campo Santo, its straight lines, cypresses in all four corners. You can understand the quarrels of the 15th and 16th centuries. Every city matters here, each with its own face and profound truth.

My solitary steps along the Arno tap out the rhythm of the only life there is. The same one that writhed inside me on the train down to Florence. The

---

90. This description would be incorporated into *The Happy Death*.

91. The series of notes on Tuscany that begin with this entry and run through the end of the first notebook would go on to form the basis of the essay "The Desert."

The last word of this entry, *se cicatriser*, implies that the healing happens through the formation of scar tissue.

92. The graffito, which translates as "Alberto makes love to my sister," appears in "The Desert."

women's serious faces suddenly carried away with laughter. This one woman in particular, her long nose and proud mouth, laughing. In Pisa, a long hour spent lazing in the grass by the Piazza del Duomo. I drank from the fountains and the water was a little warm, but so smooth. On the way down to Florence, I lingered over the faces, I drank up the smiles. Am I happy or unhappy? The question is of little importance. I live with such intensity.

Things, people, are awaiting me, and probably I am awaiting them, too, desiring them with all the strength and sadness I have. But here I earn my keep through silence and secrecy.

The miracle of not having to talk about yourself.

———

Gozzoli and the Old Testament (dressed up).[93]

———

The Giottos in Santa Croce.[94] Saint Francis's inner smile, a lover of nature and life. He justifies those who have a taste for happiness. A soft, fine light over Florence. The waiting rain swelling the sky. Giottino's Entombment of Christ: the grief in Mary's clenched teeth.

———

Florence. In every church corner, displays of flowers, lush and shining, pearled with water, naive.

———

Mostra Giottesca.

It takes time to recognize that the faces you encounter every day in the street are the Florentine faces painted by the primitivists. It's because we've lost the habit of seeing the essence of a face. We no longer look at our contemporaries, no longer take anything from them but what serves our positioning (in every sense). The primitivists don't distort, they "realize."

In the Cloister of the Dead, in the Santissima Annunziata, a gray sky laden with clouds, the architecture austere, but nothing in the place speaks of death. There are tombstones and ex-votos, this one here a loving father and faithful husband, that one over there both the best of spouses and an astute merchant,

93. Benozzo Gozzoli (1421–1497), Italian Renaissance painter, who, from 1469 to 1485, painted twenty-four Old Testament murals in the Campo Santo.

94. The Basilica di Santa Croce (Basilica of the Holy Cross) in Florence is the final resting place of Michelangelo, Galileo, Rossini, Machiavelli, and several other well-known Italians. It features art by major figures such as Donatello and Vasari, as well as Giotto and others who are less well-known today. In summer 1937, Florence held a sexcentenary celebration honoring Giotto's work.

See Camus's 1933 essay "Art in Communion" for more on Giottino.

here a young woman, the model of all virtues, spoke French and English "si come il nativo." (They all created these moral obligations for themselves, and today children play leapfrog on the slabs intended to perpetuate their virtue.) Over there, a little girl was the hope of all her family, "Ma la gioia è pellegrina sulla terra." But none of this convinces me. Almost all of them, according to their inscriptions, resigned themselves, no doubt because they accepted their other obligations. I will not resign myself. With all my silence, I'll protest until the end. There's no need to say "you had to." What's right is my rebellion, and that joy like a pilgrim come to earth, that's what I have to follow, step by step.

Clouds are gathering over the cloister and night is gradually casting its shadow over the slabs on which the morals of the dead are inscribed. If I had to write a book of morals here, it would have a hundred pages, 99 of which would be blank. On the last one, I'd write: "I know of only one obligation and that is to love." For the rest, I say *no*. I say *no* with all my might. The slabs are telling me that it's all useless and that life is like "col sol levante, col sol cadente." But I don't see what uselessness takes away from my rebellion, I feel quite clearly what it adds.

I was thinking about all of this, sitting on the ground, leaning against a column, while children were laughing and playing. A priest smiled at me. Women looked at me with curiosity. In the church, the organ quietly played and the warm color of its pattern occasionally broke through the children's squealing. Death! If I go on like this, I'll really end up dying happy. I'll have eaten up all my hope.

———

SEPTEMBER—If you say: "I don't understand Christianity, I want to live without consolation," then you're narrow-minded and biased. But if, living without consolation, you say: "I understand the Christian position and I admire it," then you're a dilettante with no depth. I'm beginning to get over worrying about what people think.

———

Cloister of San Marco. The sun amid the flowers.

———

Sienese and Florentine primitivists. That they persistently make monuments smaller than people doesn't come from ignorance of perspective, but from an enduring respect for the people and saints they depict. Take inspiration from this for theatrical set design.

———

On this Sunday morning in Florence, late-blooming roses in the Cloister of Santa Maria Novella, and women with their breasts free, with eyes and lips that leave your heart beating, your mouth dry, and a warmth in your loins.[95]

Fiesole.[96] We lead a difficult life. We're not always able to adjust our actions to our vison of things. (And the color of my destiny, just when I think I catch sight of it, flees from before my eyes.) We labor and struggle to win back our solitude. But then one day the earth puts on that primitive, naive smile, and it's as if all the struggle and vitality inside us were instantly erased. Millions of eyes have contemplated this landscape, but for me it's like the world's first smile. It drives me wild[97] in the deepest sense of the expression. It assures me that everything outside my love is pointless and that even my love, if not innocent and without object, holds no value for me. It refuses me a personality and returns my suffering unheard. The world is beautiful, and that says it all. The great truth it patiently teaches is that the mind is nothing, that even the heart is nothing, and that a stone warmed by the sun, or a cypress brightened by the freshly cleared sky, mark out the only world where "being right" means anything: nature without man. This world annihilates me. It carries me to the end. It rejects me without anger. And I, consenting, vanquished, move toward a wisdom in which everything's already been conquered—if only these tears weren't filling my eyes, if only these great sobs of poetry swelling my heart wouldn't lead me to forget the world's truth.

Sept. 13

The scent of the bay trees you encounter on every street corner in Fiesole.

---

95. Camus removed the final clause, "a warmth in your loins," when he incorporated this entry into "The Desert." Parts of the next entry also appear in that same essay.

96. The word "Fiesole" was added to the typescript. In the manuscript, Camus crossed out four lines preceding the current start of the entry.

97. In French, the start of this sentence, *Il me met hors de moi*—which translates literally as "It puts me outside myself" but carries the sense of "until I can't take anymore" or, more colloquially, "it pushes my buttons"—and the start of the next sentence, *Il m'assure que hors de mon,* mirror each other in a way that is lost in the given translation, which attempts to preserve both the colloquial sense of ecstasy and the philosophical sense of a return to nature.

Sept. 15

In the Cloister of San Francesco in Fiesole, a small courtyard lined with arcades, full of red flowers, sunshine and yellow-and-black bees. In one corner, a green watering can. Everywhere, flies buzzing. Baked by the heat, the small garden slowly smolders. I'm sitting on the ground and I'm thinking about those Franciscans whose cells I saw earlier, whose inspiration I see now, and I truly feel that, if they're right, they're right with me. Behind the wall I'm leaning against, I know there's a hill hurtling down toward the city, down toward the offering that is the whole of Florence and its cypresses. But the world's splendor seems to justify these men. I pride myself in believing that it justifies me, too, and all those like me—those who know that the most extreme poverty always brings the world's luxury and richness together. If they choose to strip themselves down, it's for a greater life (and not for another life). That's the only meaning I'm willing to hear in the word "bareness." To be "bare naked"[98] always retains a sense of physical freedom, of that rapport between hand and flower, that loving harmony between the earth and the man delivered from mankind. How certainly I'd convert to all this if it wasn't already my religion.

Today, I feel free with respect to my past and what I've lost. I want nothing more than this tight, enclosed space—this lucid, patient fervor. Like warm bread kneaded and labored over, all I want is to take my life between my hands, as these men here have found a way to contain their life between flowers and columns. In doing so, life would become like one of those long nights on a train, nights during which you can talk to yourself, you can prepare yourself to live, your self laid out before yourself, living with that admirable patience to once again take up ideas, to stop them mid-flight, and to then move forward again. To lick your life like a string of rock candy, to shape it, sharpen it, to love it at last, in that same way you search for a word, an image, the definitive sentence, this one or that one that'll wrap things up, that'll bring things to a stop, the one with which you'll set out, which will form, from then on, all the colors through which your eyes view the world. Surely, I can stop there, can finally come to the end of a frantic, frenetic year of life.

---

98. In French, the comparison is between *dénuement* and *être nu*—both of which contain the root *nu*, meaning naked, but with *dénuement* carrying the primary sense of "deprivation," "destitution," and "poverty," and *être nu* carrying the primary sense, as Camus points out, of physical nakedness.

This feeling of myself being present to myself, my effort will now be to see it through to the end, to maintain it before the many facets of my life—even at the price of a solitude I now know is so difficult to bear. Don't give in: that says it all. Don't acquiesce, don't betray. All my savagery will help me with this, and where it leads me, my love will again join me, and with it, the furious passion for life that gives my days meaning.

Every time that you (that I) give in to your vanities, every time that you think and live in order to "appear," you betray. On every occasion, it's always the great mistake of wanting to appear that's diminished me before the truth.[99] You don't have to reveal yourself to others, only to those you love, because then it's no longer revealing yourself to appear but only to give. There's so much more strength in a person who appears only when necessary. To carry through to the end is to know how to keep your secret. I've suffered from being alone, but for having kept my secret, I've overcome the suffering of being alone. Today, I know no greater glory than to live alone and unknown. To write is my deepest joy! Give in to the world and enjoyment—but only in "bareness." I wouldn't be worthy of loving the "bare naked" beaches if I didn't know how to remain bare and naked before myself. For the first time, the meaning of the word happiness doesn't seem ambiguous to me. It's almost the opposite of what people normally mean when they say, "I am happy."

A certain amount of hopelessness ends up begetting joy. Those same men who live surrounded by red flowers in San Francesco keep the skulls of the dead in their cells as a means of nourishing their meditations; they have Florence at their window and death on their table. For my part, if I feel I'm at a turning point in my life, it's not because of what I've gained, but because of what I've lost. I feel a deep and powerful strength. It's on account of this that I must live as I'd like to live. If I feel so removed from everything today, it's because I only have the strength to love and admire. Life's face of tears and sunshine, life in salt and hot stones, life as I love it and wish it to be, it seems that in cherishing it, all my hopeless strength and love will come together. Today isn't a resting place between yes and no. It is yes and it is no. No, and rebel before all that isn't tears and sunshine. Yes to my life, whose future promise I feel for the first time. A burning, disorderly year is coming to an end, and Italy with it; the future's uncertain, but the freedom from my

99. The juxtaposition being between appearance and authenticity. Or, put another way: "that's diminished me in light of what's real."

past, from myself, is absolute. There lies my poverty and my singular wealth. It's as if I'm starting the game all over, neither happier nor unhappier, rather aware of my strengths, looking down on my vanities, and with this lucid fever pressing me toward my destiny.

Sept. 15, '37.[100]

100. Camus would leave Italy the next day, stopping in Arles before arriving back in Algiers September 19.

Notebook II

SEPTEMBER 1937–APRIL 1939

A water-stained, gray-green composition notebook, 22 × 17 cm, containing sixty-four pages, all written on except for page 18. At the top of the cover of this notebook, Camus wrote "Cahier no II." Below that are three large blocks of text that have been effaced with a pencil, below which a line is drawn, then a slash with "September 37" on the top and "April 39" on the bottom. In the top-right corner someone has written and circled "32." Possibly due to the water damage on the front cover, Camus rewrote "Cahier no. II" and the dates on the back cover. Unlike the first notebook, this one is a unified whole, its signatures all held together.

September 22.

The Happy Death.[1]

"You see, Claire, it's rather difficult to explain. There's only one question: do you know what you're worth? But to answer that, you have to set Socrates aside. To know yourself, you have to act, which isn't to say you can define yourself. The cult of I! Don't make me laugh. Which I and which personality? When I look at my life and its secret color, the I inside of me is like a trembling of tears. I am as much those lips I've kissed as those nights spent in the 'house before the world,' that poor child as that mad will to live and achieve that sometimes carries me away. A lot of people who know me don't always know it's me. And I feel in every way like that inhuman image of the world that is my own life."

"Yes," Claire said. "You're playing on two levels at once."

"Probably. When I was twenty years old, like everyone else I read that life could be an act, etc. But that's not what I'm talking about. Several lives, several levels, absolutely. But when the actor's on stage, the convention's accepted. No, Claire, we can clearly see this is serious—there's something telling us it is."

"Why?" Claire said.

"Because, if the actor played without knowing he was playing a part, then his tears would be tears and his life would be life. Every time I stop to consider the pain and joy coursing through me, I can clearly see, and with such a fit of rage, that the part I'm playing is the most serious and exciting of all.

"And I, I want to be that perfect actor. I couldn't care less about my personality. I don't feel the need to cultivate it. I want to be what my life makes of me and not make of my life an experiment. I am the experiment and it's life that shapes and directs me. If I had enough strength and patience, I know how much perfect impersonality I'd achieve, how far my strength could carry me toward active nothingness. What's always stopped me is my personal vanity. These days, I understand that to act, to love, and to suffer is in fact to live, but it's to live only insofar as you're clear-eyed and accepting of your fate as the unique reflection of a rainbow of joys and passions.

The route, etc.

But for that, you need time, and now I have time."

Claire, quiet for some time, looked Patrice in the face and said, slowly:

"Many sorrows await those who love you."

---

1. The title, *The Happy Death*, was added on the typescript; it does not appear in the handwritten notebook.

Patrice stood up, something desperate in his eyes, and said, vehemently: "Their loving me obligates me to nothing."

"That's true," Claire said. "I'm just telling you what I see. (You'll be alone, one day.)"[2]

———

September 23. *K. in P.F. (Philosophical Fragments).*

"The language is right to insist on the suffering of the soul in the word passion; whereas the use of the word passion makes us think more of a convulsive impetuosity that amazes us, and in this way we forget that suffering is at its root (pride—challenge)."[3]

id. The perfect actor (of life) is the one who "has acted"—and knows it—a passive passion.

———

"He woke sweating, disheveled, and wandered around the apartment for a few minutes. Then he lit a cigarette and sat down, head empty, gazing at the creases in his wrinkled pants. His mouth was filled with all the bitterness of sleep and cigarettes. His shapeless, listless day lapped around him like sludge."[4]

———

Rama Krishna, with regard to bargaining:

"The truly wise man holds nothing in contempt."

Don't confuse idiocy and sanctity.

———

September 23.

Solitude, luxury of the rich.

———

2. Parts of this dialogue appear in *The Happy Death* as a conversation between Zagreus and Mersault. Claire is not in the scene.

3. Kierkegaard's *Philosophical Fragments* appeared in French in 1937 under the title *Riens philosophiques*. The quote here is translated from the French, as Camus recorded it. The standard English translation, by Edna and Howard Hong, reads: "Our language correctly terms an uncontrolled emotional state [*Affekt*] a *suffering* of the mind [*Sindslidelse*], although when using the word 'affect' we usually think of the convulsive boldness that astounds us, and because of that we forget that it is a suffering. For example, arrogance, defiance, etc."

In Kierkegaard's text, the cited passage appears as a footnote to the remark: "At its deepest level, all offense is a suffering."

4. An entry used in *The Happy Death*.

September 26.

1) Precede the novel with diary fragments (end).[5]

2) Carry lucidity to the point of ecstasy.

Concrete description: Disappearance of friends.
Tramways (end of the line?)
Ideas—leitmotif.

He sunk from silence to silence, huddled inside himself . . .

. . . Reaching the point where lucidity can turn on itself. Immense effort: comes back to the world—drops of sweat—thinks of a woman's open legs—Goes to the balcony and pours his whole being into the world of flesh and light. "It's sanitary."

Then takes a shower and does chest exercises.

(Tractatus Theologico-Politicus)[6]

In Georges Sorel.[7] Dedicated to "the humanism of the left" that wants us to see Helvétius, Diderot, and Holbach as the summit of French literature.

The idea of progress that infests workers' movements is a bourgeois idea leftover from the 18th century. "All our efforts must go toward preventing bourgeois ideas from poisoning the rising class: that's why we'll never be able to do enough to break all ties between the people and the literature of the 18th century" (*Illusions of Progress*, p. 285 and 286).

———

5. *The Happy Death*, in its existing state, begins with a flash-forward rather than diary fragments. Camus would again play with the idea of using diary entries when he began outlining *The Plague*.

6. This was written at the very top of the page, enclosed in a box. Given the quotation in the previous notebook, coupled with the mention here, it's likely Camus was reading Spinoza's *Tractatus Theologico-Politicus*.

7. Georges Sorel (1847–1922) was a French intellectual and political theorist who emphasized the importance myth has on collective action (especially with regard to the general strike). His views were, at times, embraced across the political spectrum by Marxists and Fascists alike, though most of his mature political thought resembled syndicalism. Camus returns to Sorel throughout the notebooks, as well as in *The Rebel*, where he writes: "Sorel was perfectly correct in saying that the philosophy of progress was precisely the type of philosophy suited to a society eager to enjoy the material prosperity that comes with technological progress. When a person is assured that the natural order of things is such that tomorrow will be better than today, then that person can have their fun in peace. Progress, paradoxically, can serve to justify conservatism. A deal made based on future trust entitles the master to a clear conscience. To the slave, to those whose present life is miserable and who take no consolation in the heavens, we say that at least the future belongs to them. The future is the only type of property masters willingly concede to slaves."

September 30.

I always end up exhausting a person's possibilities. It's only a matter of time. A moment always comes when I feel the disconnect. What's interesting is that it always happens when the person, faced with something, gives me the feeling they are "incurious" about it.

Dialogue.

"And what do you do for a living?"

"I count, Monsieur."

"What?"

"I count. I say: one, the sea, two, the sky (oh, how beautiful it is!), three, the women, four, the flowers (oh, how happy I am!)."

"That ends up getting a bit silly, then."

"My God, your opinions must be shaped by your morning paper. Me? My opinions are shaped by the world. You think as the *Écho de Paris* does and I think as the world does. When it's filled with light, when the sun's beating down, I feel like hugging and loving, like flowing into bodies as into streams of light, like taking a bath in flesh and sun. When the world's gray, I'm melancholy and full of affection. I feel like a better person, capable of loving enough to get married. Either way, it doesn't matter."

After he leaves:

1) He's a fool.

2) Pretentious.

3) A cynic.

"Not at all," the teacher says. "He's a spoiled child, that's all. Go on, it's obvious. The son of a family that hasn't known life."

(because it's becoming clearer and clearer that, if you're able to find life beautiful and easy, you must have never known it.)

September 30.

It's so as to shine quicker that we refuse to rewrite. Despicable. Start over.

October 2.

"He walked on and on through the muddy streets, beneath a fine mist of rain. He could see no more than a few steps ahead of him. But he was the only one walking in that small town so far from everything. From everything and from himself. No, it was no longer possible. Crying in front of a dog, in front of everyone. He wanted to be happy. He had the right to be happy. He didn't deserve this."

October 4.[8]

"Until a few days, I believed that a person had to do something with their life and, more specifically, that if you were poor, you had to earn a living, have a steady job, settle down. I have to believe that this idea, which I still don't dare call a prejudice, was rooted somewhere deep inside me, seeing as it stuck around despite my ironies and categorical comments on the subject. And then, when I was appointed to Bel-Abbès, faced with what seemed a definitive settling down, all of it suddenly came rushing back. I refused the position, probably considering my security as nothing compared to my chances at a real life. I recoiled from such a dull, numbing existence. If I'd made it through the first few days, I'd have certainly surrendered. And that was the danger. I was afraid, afraid of the solitude and the finality of it all. To have rejected that life, to have closed myself off from what they call "a future," to continue on in uncertainty and poverty, even now I can't say whether it was strength or weakness. But at least I know that, if there's a conflict, it's for something worth the trouble. Unless, on a closer look . . . No. What made me run probably had less to do with the feeling of settling than with the feeling of settling into something ugly.

Now, am I capable of what others call "seriousness"? Am I lazy? I don't think so; I've proven that to myself. But does a person have the right to refuse their sentence on the grounds that they don't like it? I think idleness only cracks those who lack character. If I lacked it, there'd be only one solution."

October 10.

To have or not to have value. To create or not to create. In the first case, everything is justified. Everything, without exception. In the second case, it's

8. Camus had been offered a job teaching in Sidi-bel-Abbès, which was more than a ten-hour train ride from Algiers, a distance that led him to decline the offer.

complete Absurdity. The only thing left would be to choose the most aesthetically pleasing suicide: marriage + 40 hours or a revolver.[9]

———

On the way to La Madeleine—again that immense desire to be stripped bare before nature as beautiful as this.

———

October 15.

Giraudoux (for once)[10] "A being's innocence is the absolute adaptation to the world in which it lives."

Ex: the wolf's innocence—

the innocent is the one who doesn't explain.

———

October 17.[11]

On the paths above Blida, the night is like sweet milk, full of grace and meditation. Mornings on the mountain, with its shaggy head of hair tousled by autumn crocuses—the icy springs—the shadow and sun—my body consents then refuses. The concentrated effort the walk requires, the air in my lungs like a red-hot iron or a sharpened razor—everything applied to pushing myself and triumphing over the slope—a sort of self-knowledge through the body. The body, the true path of culture, shows us our limits.

———

Villages grouped around natural landmarks, each living its own life. Men draped in long, white fabrics, their simple, precise gestures silhouetted against an ever-blue sky. The narrow paths lined with Barbary fig, olive trees, carob trees, and jujube trees. Men leading donkeys laden with olives cross your path. Faces brown, eyes light. Between man and tree, gesture and mountain, a sort of consent is born that's both moving and joyous. Greece? No, Kabylia.

---

9. In an October 10 letter to Jacques Heurgon, a Latin professor at the University of Algiers during Camus's time there, Camus writes: "It seems I've finally made a sort of wager, one that forces me to create something that matters. Otherwise, it would be complete absurdity." To Liliane Choucroun, he writes: "If I'm unable to express what I carry inside me, it'll be complete absurdity, with all its attendant consequences for what's deepest in me." Throughout his writings, Camus sometimes capitalizes the word "absurd" and sometimes doesn't.

10. Camus's parenthetical "for once" is in reference to his dislike of Giraudoux, which would find fuller expression in his essay, "Jean Giraudoux or The Theatrical Lap of Luxury," which was published May 10, 1940, in *La lumière*.

11. This entry and the one that follows appear in *The Happy Death*.

It's as if the whole of Hellas was all at once, across the distance of centuries, transported to this spot between the sea and the mountains and reborn in its ancient splendor, its laziness and respect for Fate barely acknowledged by its neighbors to the East.

October 18.

In September, the carob trees spread the scent of love all over Algeria, and it's as if, after having given itself to the sun, the whole earth relaxed, its belly all wet with almond-scented seed.

On the path to Sidi-Brahim, after the rain, the scent of love descends from the carob trees, heavy and oppressive, weighed down by its watery burden. Then the sun sucks up all the water, and, colors again dazzling, the scent of love lifts, lightens, is barely noticed by the nostrils. It's like a mistress you go out into the street with after a long, sultry afternoon, one who gazes at you, shoulder to shoulder, amid the lights and crowds.[12]

Huxley. "After all, it is better to be a good bourgeois like the others than a bad bohemian, a false aristocrat, or a second-rate intellectual . . ."[13]

October 20.

The demand for happiness and the patient search for it. We don't have to exile melancholy, but we do have to destroy our taste for the difficult and fatal. Be happy with our friends, in harmony with the world, and earn our happiness by following a path that nevertheless leads to death.

"You'll tremble when faced with death."

---

12. The two parts of this entry appear in reverse order in *The Happy Death*, part 2, at the end of chap. 4.

13. After having sent a copy of *The Happy Death* to Jean Grenier, and having received a less-than-positive response, Camus replied: "After your letter, I was a bit disoriented. Things are better now. Only, before I get back to work, there's one thing I'd like to know from you because you're the only one who can tell it to me straight: Do you really think I should keep writing? Asking myself that question fills me with anxiety. Certainly, you know it's not a matter of making a career of it or profiting from it. I don't have many pure things in my life. Writing is one of them. But, at the same time, I've lived enough to know that it's better to be a good bourgeois than a bad intellectual or a mediocre writer. It's more dignified and, in any case, I'd like to know."

"Yes, but I won't have missed out on a single part of my mission, which is to live." Don't give in to convention and office hours. Don't give up. Never give up—always demand more. Be lucid even during those hours at the office. Aspire to the nakedness to which the world relegates us as soon as we are alone with it. But above all, to be, don't try to appear.

October 21.

A person needs significantly more energy to travel in poverty than to play the hunted traveler.[14] Taking fourth-class passage on a boat, arriving tired and hollowed out from the inside, traveling long distances third class, often having no more than a meal a day, counting your pennies while fearing every minute that some unforeseen accident might cut short a trip that's already so difficult in its own right, all of this requires a courage and will that makes it impossible to take those sermons on "uprooting" seriously. Traveling is neither merry nor easy. When you're poor and penniless, you need to have a taste for the difficult and a love of the unknown to bring dreams of travel to life. But if you really think about it, this serves as a warning against dilettantism, and I don't mean to say that having to travel cut-rate, being forced to stay in the same city for six days straight, is what's lacking in Gide and Montherlant, but I know very well that I can't, at a fundamental level, see things as Montherlant or Gide—on account of traveling cut-rate.

October 25.

Gossip—it's unbearable and degrading.

November 5.

El-Kettar cemetery. An overcast sky and rough sea facing hills filled with white gravestones. The earth and trees soaking wet. Pigeons between the white headstones. A single geranium, both red and pink, and a great sadness, lost and mute, that familiarizes us with the pure and beautiful face of death.

---

14. The phrase "hunted traveler" is in reference to a set of Henry de Montherlant's books collectively titled *Les voyageurs traqués* (*The Hunted Travelers*). Montherlant traveled extensively.

November 6.

Chemin de La Madeleine. Trees, earth, and sky. O, from my movements to that first star awaiting us on our return, what a distance between them, and what a secret understanding they share.

November 7.

Character. A.M. Invalid—two legs amputated—paralyzed on one side.

"They help me do my business. They wash me. They dry me. I'm practically deaf. Still, I'd never do anything to cut short a life I believe in so strongly. I'd put up with even worse. To be blind and deprived of all my senses—to be mute and unable to communicate—so long as I can feel within me that dark and fiery flame that is me, that is me living—I'll still be thankful to life for allowing me to go on burning."[15]

November 8.

At the local cinema, they sell mint pastilles with the words "Will you marry me one day?" written on them, and, "Do you love me?" Also, the responses: "Tonight," "A lot," etc. You pass one to the person sitting next to you and they respond in the same manner. Lives are committed through an exchange of mint pastilles.[16]

November 13.

Cviklinsky.[17] "I've always acted out of spite. Things are better now. Acting in a way that allows for happiness? If I must settle down, why not do it here in a country I like? But sentimental anticipation is always misguided—always. So then, we have to live however it's easiest for us to live. Don't force yourself, even if it's shocking. It's a little cynical, but it's also how the most beautiful girl in the world sees things."[18]

---

15. This bit of dialogue is spoken by Zagreus in *The Happy Death*, part 1.

16. This entry would go on to be used in the essay "Summer in Algiers."

17. Doctor Stanislas "Stacha" Cviklinsky (also Cviklinski) was a friend of Camus's in Algeria. In 1936, Stacha's wife, Morella, acted in *Le temps du mépris*, a play put on by Camus's Théâtre du Travail.

An edited version of the dialogue recorded here is spoken by Bernard, the doctor, in *The Happy Death*. The second paragraph is, in part, Mersault's reply.

18. The reference is probably to the French saying, "The prettiest girl in the world can only give what she has," a saying that many French writers, from Chamfort to Dumas, have utilized in their work.

A slightly more interpretive translation might read: "So then, we have to live however is most natural. Don't force yourself to do otherwise, even if the way you live shocks people."

Yes, but I'm not sure all sentimental anticipation is misguided. It's simply unreasonable. In any case, the only experience that interests me is the kind where everything happens exactly as we'd expected it to happen. *Doing a thing to be happy, and being happy as a result.* What attracts me is this link between the world and me, this double reflection that forces my heart to intervene and direct my happiness to the precise point, the limit, where the world can then complete or destroy it.

Aedificabo et destruam, Montherlant says. I prefer: Aedificabo et destruat.[19] The change in power isn't from me to me, but from the world to me and from me to the world. A question of humility.

November 16.

He says: "You have to have a love—a great love in your life, because it gives us an alibi for our overwhelming sense of hopelessness."[20]

November 17.

"Will to Happiness."

Part 3. Achievement of happiness.

Several years. Time passes in seasons and nothing else.

Part 1 (end). The invalid says to Mersault: "Money. It's through a sort of spiritual snobbery that people want to try to believe they can be happy without money."

M., returning home, examines the events of his life in light of these facts. Response: yes.

For a "highborn" man, to be happy is to take part in the same fate as everyone else, not with the will to renunciation, but with the will to happiness. To be happy, you need time, a lot of time. Happiness, too, is a long patience.

---

19. The Latin phrase *Aedificabo et destruam*, which is in the indicative, first-person singular, future tense, is usually translated as "I will build and I will destroy." Camus's adjustment puts the phrase in third-person singular subjunctive, which he likely intends to read: "I will build and it may destroy." In *Justice in the Revolution and the Church*, Pierre-Joseph Proudhon writes: "So then, I had a right, in 1845, to use those two words from Deuteronomy as an epigraph to *Economic Contradictions*: Destruam et aedificabo. It was a matter of taking negation as far as it could go through an in-depth critique of the social economy. Today, without any more pride than before, I could again use the motto by transposing the terms: *Aedificabo et destruam*. Exhibition of revolutionary ideas will indeed be the final blow to the Ancien Régime." Proudhon uses the phrase as a way of discussing the achievement of freedom through destruction of the State.

20. In *The Happy Death*, part 2, chap. 4, Mersault says to Lucienne: "All the same, that's why it's good to have had a great love, an unhappy passion in your life. At least it gives us an alibi for our overwhelming sense of hopelessness."

And time—it's the need for money that robs us of it. Time can be bought. Everything can be bought. To be rich is to have time to be happy, when you're worthy of being so.[21]

November 22.

It's normal to give up a little of your life so as not to lose the whole thing. Six or eight hours a day so as not to starve to death. Besides, there's profit in everything for those who wish to profit.

December.

A rain thick as oil on the windowpanes, the hollow sound of the horses' hooves, and the dull, persistent downpour, all took on a face from the past, a face whose heavy melancholy penetrated Mersault's heart like the water dampening his shoes and the cold chilling his knees, poorly protected by the thin fabric. All through the sky, black clouds continuously gathered, quickly dissipated, and were quickly replaced. The vaporized water that fell, neither mist nor rain, washed M.'s face like a light hand, laying bare the dark circles around his eyes. The pleats in his pants had disappeared and with them that warmth and confidence a normal man carries through a world that's made for him.

(In Salzburg.)[22]

Irony with Marthe—leaves her.

A guy who showed so much promise and who now works in an office. He doesn't do anything outside of work, goes home, goes to bed and smokes while waiting for dinnertime to come, goes back to bed and sleeps until the next day. On Sundays, he gets up very late, stands by the window, watches the rain or the sun, the passersby or the silence. So it goes the whole year. He's waiting. He's waiting to die. What good is promise, given that in any case . . .

Politics and the fate of the people is shaped by men without ideals or greatness. Those who have greatness in them don't go into politics. So it is with everything. But now we have to create a new man inside ourself. Now

21. A version of this entry is spoken by Zagreus in *The Happy Death*.

22. This description, apparently a memory of Camus's time in Salzburg, would be incorporated into *The Happy Death*.

men of action must also be men of ideals and poets industrialists. Now we have to live our dreams—to act on them. In the past, we gave up on them or got lost in them. Now we can't get lost in them or give up on them.

———

We don't have the time to be ourselves. We only have time to be happy.[23]

———

Oswald Spengler (*The Decline of the West*): I. Form and reality:

"I call understanding the world being at its level."

"He who defines doesn't know fate."

"There exists in life, aside from causal necessity—which I'll call the logic of space—also the organic necessity of fate—the logic of time . . ."

History lacks meaning for the Greeks. "History, from antiquity through the Persian Wars, is the product of an essentially mythical way of thinking."[24]

The Egyptian column started out as a column made of stone, the Doric as a column made of wood. In this, the Attic soul expressed its deep hostility to the idea of duration. "The Egyptian culture, the embodiment of concern." The Greeks, a happy people, have no history.

Myth and its antipsychological meaning. In contrast, at the beginning of the West's spiritual history, a fragment of intimate self-analysis exists, and it's the West's Vita Nuova. (Cf. mythical fragments about Hercules, the same from Homer through to Seneca's tragedies. A millennium. Which is to say: Antiquity = present.)

---

23. This line is given to Zagreus in *The Happy Death*, part 1, chap. 4.

After this entry, Camus skipped the verso page, then recorded three entries on the recto. On the typescript, he enclosed these three entries in a box and wrote: "* = see meteorological note."

24. In *The Rebel*, Camus writes: "As opposed to the Ancient world, the unity of the Christian world and Marxist world is striking. The two doctrines share a vision of the world that separates them from the Greek outlook. Jaspers defines it very well: 'To consider the history of mankind as strictly unique is a Christian thought.' The Christians were the first to consider human life and the sequence of events as a history that unfolds from a beginning to an end, in the course of which mankind either earns its salvation or deserves its punishment. The philosophy of history is born from a Christian image that a Greek mind would find surprising. The Greek notion of becoming shares nothing in common with our ideal of historical evolution. The difference between the two is the difference between a circle and a straight line. The Greeks saw the world as cyclical. Aristotle, to give a specific example, didn't see himself as being post-Trojan War. In order to spread throughout the Mediterranean world, Christianity had to become Hellenized, and in doing so its doctrines became more flexible."

Ex: "It was the Germans who invented mechanical clocks, the terrifying symbols of time passing, their sonorous strokes resounding day and night from the innumerable towers hanging over Western Europe, perhaps the most enormous possible expression of a historical sense of the universe."

"People of Western-European culture, endowed with historical sense, are an exception, not the rule."

Stupidity of the framework: Antiquity—Middle Ages—Modern Times.

"What can the idea of a superman mean to the Islamic world?"

"Civilization is the fate of a culture. In this way, the Roman succeeds the Hellenic. Greek *soul* and Roman *intelligence*. The transition from culture to civilization was accomplished in antiquity in the 4th century, in the West in the 19th century.

Our music and literature is for city-dwellers.

So then, we make the history of philosophy the only serious theme of all philosophy.

The whole question:

the antithesis of history and nature

↓ ↓

Mathematics History

and paintings (*review and revise*)[25]

December.

What moved him was the way she had of hanging onto his clothes, of squeezing his arm as she followed beside him, that surrender, that trust that stirred the manly part of him. Her silence, too, which entirely immersed her in whatever she was doing, completing her resemblance to a cat, together with the gravity she put into her kisses . . .

In the night, he felt a pair of icy, prominent cheekbones beneath his fingers, hot lips surrounding a warmth into which his finger sank. It produced a great cry inside him, fiery and selfless. Facing a night so filled with stars that

---

25. The quotations and references in this entry come from *The Decline of the West*'s preface and introduction. Camus's interest in Spengler's distinction between culture and civilization would seem to prefigure *The Rebel*'s analysis of the conflict between history and nature. The word *tableaux* could mean "paintings," as given above, or "tables," as in math tables.

it burst at the seams, the city below like an upside-down sky swollen with human lights, beneath the warm and fathomless breath that climbed from the harbor toward his face came the thirst for the source of that warmth, the unbridled desire to grasp all that inhuman and sleeping world's meaning on those lips that were so alive, like a silence enclosed in her mouth. He leaned over, and it was as if he were putting his lips on a bird. Marthe moaned. He nibbled her lips and, for a few minutes, mouth to mouth, inhaled the warmth that transported him, as if he were holding the world in his arms. She, on the other hand, clung to him as if drowning, surging up in flashes from the great depths of that hole into which she'd been thrown, pushing away those lips then pulling them close again, falling back into those icy, black waters that burned her like one of the chosen people.[26]

———

December.

A man who has a feel for playing the game is always happy in the company of women. Women are a good audience.[27]

———

It's always at the beginning that tiresome things grow tiring. Afterward comes death. "I could never lead that sort of life"; but it's leading it that enables you to accept it.

———

Novel. P. 1. Card games (brisque). Conversations.

"The rest of us, the Zouaves . . ."

"With my husband . . ."

A guy who's hammered: "You disgust me. You disgust me. I'm gonna tell you why. It's 'cause you're small-minded, and I don't like small-minded people. *You don't know how to live*."

---

26. In *The Happy Death*, part 2, chap. 3, these two paragraphs describe Lucienne, not Marthe. Some of the characters in *The Happy Death* have clear real-life counterparts: Marthe / Simone Hié; Rose / Marguerite Dobrenn; Claire / Jeanne-Paule Sicard; Catherine / Christiane Galindo. At the beginning of the year, when Christiane Galindo moved into the House Before the World, she and Camus began an open relationship. At the end of the year, Camus began two more relationships, one with Blanche Balain, whose poems he would urge Charlot to publish, and one with Lucette Maeurer, a pharmacy student with whom he enjoyed discussing politics and novels. The character of Lucienne seems to draw from both women.

27. This idea, reminiscent of Stendhal, will appear again later in the notebooks, as Camus begins to plan out his "Don Juan-Faust" project.

(Parc Saint-Raphaël.)

Novel. Titles: A Pure Heart
The Happy of the Earth
The Golden Ray.

"Do you know many 'magnetic'[28] men who'd refuse a pretty woman offering herself to him? And even if there are some, it's because they're not the hot-blooded sort."

"What you call hot-blooded is the total absence of serious feelings."

"Precisely. (At least in the way you mean 'serious.')"

Novel. P. 1.

Zagreus's residence in the countryside, in the banlieues. Murder. The room is too stuffy. Mersault, who can feel his ears getting red, is suffocating. When he leaves, he catches a cold (and from it the illness that will kill him).

Ch. IV: conversation with Z. begun with a certain "detachment."

"Yes," Z. says, "but you can't do that while working."

"No, because I'm in a state of rebellion and that, that's no good."

". . . Basically," M. says, "I'm a dangerous fanatic."[29]

Novel. P. IV. A passive woman.

"The mistake," M. says, "is in believing you have to choose, that you have to do what you want, that there are conditions for happiness. Happiness is or it isn't. It's the will to happiness that matters, a sort of enormous, ever-present awareness. The rest, women, works of art, worldly success, are nothing but pretexts. A canvas awaiting our embroidery."[30]

Novel. P. III.

---

28. As a noun, the French word *aimant* (magnet) can also, as in English, be used in the sense of *aimant à filles* (chick magnet). As an adjective, as in the case above, it often means "loving" or "affectionate."

In the handwritten notebook, Camus crossed out seven lines of dialogue preceding this one.

29. This is the first time the name Zagreus appears in the notebooks. It seems likely Camus intended the name as a reference to the Greek god dismembered by the Titans (sometimes referred to as Dionysus Zagreus). Camus's later notes about the Bacchantes confirm, at the very least, that he was familiar with the story.

30. In *The Happy Death*, part 2, chap. 4, Mersault speaks these lines to Catherine.

Not long after, Mersault announced his departure. He was going to travel first and then settle down somewhere around Algiers. A month later, he was back, certain that the trip represented a life now closed off to him. Travel seemed to him what it truly is: a happiness for the anxious.[31] That's not what M. wanted out of his search for conscious bliss. Anyway, he felt sick and knew what he wanted. For the second time, he prepared to leave the House Before the Sea.

———

February '38.

Here, men are sensitive to fate. That's what sets them apart.

———

The suffering that comes from not sharing everything and the misfortune that comes from sharing everything.

———

February '38.

The revolutionary mindset resides entirely in the human protest against the human condition.[32] In this sense, it is, in its various forms, the only eternal theme of art and religion. A revolution is always carried out against the Gods—beginning with Prometheus's. It's a stand man takes against his fate, an action for which tyrants and bourgeois puppets are but a pretext.

This mindset can no doubt be grasped in its historical action—but then it takes all Malraux's emotion not to give in to the will to prove something. It's

31. The entry, to this point, appears at the beginning of *The Happy Death*, part 2, chap. 4.

32. This entry introduces a philosophical complication that will run throughout the notebooks. In English, "mind" and "spirit" are two distinct words, whereas in French, as in German and other languages, the same word can be used for both "mind" and "spirit" (though it should be noted that "spiritual," which Camus also uses in these pages, is a separate word in French). Complicating things further, Camus often uses *esprit* in reference to Hegelian thought, where the German equivalent, *Geist*, is of central importance. Standard practice has been to translate Hegel's *Geist* into English as "spirit," though strong arguments have been made for using "mind" instead. To give just one example, in *Hegel: A Very Short Introduction*, Peter Singer argues that "to use 'spirit' is to prejudge, for the English-speaking reader, the whole question of what *Geist* really means for Hegel. In English, apart from special usages like 'spirit of the age' and 'team spirit,' the word 'spirit' has an inescapably religious or mystical flavor." Though Camus, like Hegel, seems sometimes to use the word in the sense of "spirit" and other times in the sense of "mind," "mind" is the English translation given throughout these pages, to make it clear that the same concept is being discussed.

easier to find it in its essence and its fate. In this respect, a work of art retracing the conquest of happiness would be a revolutionary work.[33]

Find the limitless in limitations.[34]

April '38.

How sordid and miserable is the condition of a workingman and a civilization founded on workingmen.

But it's a matter of holding on and not letting go. The natural reaction is always to spend all our energy outside of work, to create surface-level circles of approval around ourselves, an audience, a pretext for cowardice and role-playing (most households are created for this). Another inevitable reaction is pontification. Really, the two reactions can go together if we then, in addition, let ourselves go physically, neglect our body, and relax our will.

It's a matter of keeping quiet—of removing the audience and knowing how to be your own judge. Of balancing a conscious cultivation of the body and a conscious awareness of being alive. Of abandoning all pretension and focusing on the double-sided work of liberation—liberation from money and from your own vanities and cowardice. Live by your own rules. In a given lifetime, two years is not too long to reflect on a single point. You have to liquidate all prior states and put all your strength toward, first, not unlearning anything, then toward patiently learning.

---

33. This entry, in which we see early signs of *The Rebel*, shows the influence Malraux's ideas about art and revolution had on Camus. Some of the language Camus uses here comes straight from Malraux's preface to *Le temps du mépris* (translated as *Days of Wrath*), which Camus had adapted for the Théâtre du Travail in 1936. In the preface, Malraux writes: "One may wish the word Art to mean an attempt to give men a consciousness of their own hidden greatness. It isn't emotion that destroys a work of art but the desire to prove something; the value of such a work depends neither on its emotion nor its detachment, but on the melding of its content with the method of its expression."

After this entry, the rest of the notebook page was left blank. The entry that follows appears to have been added to the manuscript at a later date.

34. A part of the polemic *The Rebel* set off in France had to do with the question of what exactly Camus meant by the words *mesure* and *démesure*. Some argued Camus was supporting a sort of quietism, which, intentionally or not, reinforced the status quo, while others pointed to the word's roots in ancient Greek. The very short entry above—in French, *Trouver une démesure dans la mesure*—foregrounds the issue, especially as it relates to translation. In *The Rebel*, Camus links his conception of *mesure* with the myth of Nemesis. In English-language sources, Nemesis is often referred to as the goddess of "proportion" or "balance." In some depictions, she holds scales; in others, a variety of measuring devices. Nemesis was also known as the deliverer of divine retribution. In the most famous case, she led Narcissus to his death as punishment for his pride and vanity.

At this price, there's a one-in-ten chance of escaping the most sordid and miserable of conditions: that of the man who works.[35]

April.

Mail out 2 Essays. *Caligula*. Of no importance. Not mature enough. Publish in Algiers.

Go over: Philosophy and Culture. Drop everything else: Thesis
either Biology + agrégation[36]
or Indochina.
Make notes *every day* in this notebook; have *a work* written in two years.

April '38.

Melville chases after adventure and ends up in an office. He dies poor and unknown. By way of solitude and isolation (they're not the same thing) we can't help but eventually wear away even wickedness and slander. But we must always guard against the wickedness and slander inside us.

May.

Nietzsche. Condemnation of the Reformation that saves Christianity from the principles of life and love that Cesare Borgia was infusing into it. The Borgia Pope finally justified Christianity.[37]

---

35. There is a linguistically small but connotatively significant difference in the opening "workingman" and the closing "man who works," the first referring to an individual human being, the second referring to a condition of being. From the beginning of his life to the end, in novels, plays, and interviews, Camus continually expressed disgust at the idea of pointless work (or what anthropologist David Graeber has more bluntly termed "bullshit jobs"). The autobiographical origins of this feeling can be seen in *The First Man*, in which Camus's avatar, Jacques Cormery, is forced by his grandmother to take a job doing meaningless office work rather than something he sees as tangibly productive, such as working in a cooperage as his uncle does. In a broader, more political sense, the idea is most notably expressed in the play *State of Emergency*.

36. In France, the agrégation is a competitive examination for teaching positions in public education.

37. Likely in reference to Nietzsche's *The Anti-Christ*, section 61.

What attracts me to an idea is its piquancy and originality—the new and superficial. May as well admit it.

———

C., who plays at seduction, who gives too much to everybody and never takes to anyone. Who needs to acquire, to win love and friendship, and who is incapable of both. A lovely character for a novel and lamentable picture of a friend.

———

Scene: the husband, the wife, and the gallery.[38]

The man has his merits and likes to shine. The woman is mostly silent, but with a few, dry sentences, demolishes all her darling husband's impressions. That's how she's always showing her superiority. The man controls himself but suffers from the humiliation, and that's how hatred is born.

Ex. With a smile: "Don't make more of a fool of yourself than you are, my friend."

The gallery squirms and gives an uncomfortable smile. He reddens, goes over to her, smiles and kisses her hand: "You're right, my darling."

Face is saved and hatred fattens.

———

I still remember the feeling of hopelessness that gripped me when my mother told me that "now that I was old enough I'd get practical gifts for New Year's." To this day, I can't help but secretly wince when I get such gifts. And I probably knew even then that it was love speaking, but why is love sometimes expressed in such derisory language?

———

We think differently about the same topic in the morning and in the evening. But where does the truth lay: in nighttime thoughts or in the afternoon mind? 2 responses, 2 tribes of people.

———

May.

The old woman in the nursing home. She dies. Her friend, a friend she's had for three years, cries "because now she has nothing left." The concierge at the small morgue is Parisian and lives there with his wife. "Who would've thought that at 74 years old he'd end up in a nursing home in Marengo?" Her

38. Camus uses the word "gallery" here in its theatrical and figurative sense, as in "playing to the gallery."

son has a steady job. They came from Paris. The daughter-in-law didn't want them. Scenes. The old man ended up "raising his hand to him." His son put them in the nursing home. The dead woman's gravedigger friend. Sometimes they went to the village in the evening. The little old man who insisted on following the convoy to the church and the cemetery (2 km.). Being infirm, he can't keep up with the procession and walks twenty meters behind it. He's familiar with the countryside, though, and he takes shortcuts that allow him to catch up with the procession two or three times before falling behind again.

The Moorish nurse nailing the casket closed has an abscess on her nose and always wears a bandage.

The dead woman's friends: little old mythomaniacs. Everything was wonderful in the past. One speaking to the other: "Your daughter hasn't written to you?"

"No."

"She might remember she has a mother."

The other died—as a sign and warning for everyone else.[39]

June.

For *Happy Death*: a series of breakup letters. Familiar refrain: it's because I love you too much.

The last letter: a masterpiece of lucidity. But even there, the amount of playacting is priceless.

End. Mersault is drinking.

"Ah," Céleste said, wiping the bar. "You're getting old, Mersault."[40]

Mersault stopped short and set his glass down. He looked at himself in the mirror behind the bar. It was true.

Summer in Algiers.

39. This is one of the first entries definitively concerning *The Stranger* rather than *The Happy Death*. As evidenced by the entry that follows, Camus will continue to develop both novels simultaneously.

40. Céleste appears in both *The Happy Death* and *The Stranger*. In *The Happy Death*, it's Mersault who thinks Céleste has gotten old, while Céleste tells Mersault, "You haven't changed."

For whom is that spray of black birds in the green sky? The blind, deaf summer that seeps in and gives a purer meaning to the swifts' calls and the newsboys' cries.

JUNE. For the summer:
1) Finish Florence and Algiers.
2) Caligula.
3) Summer Impromptu.
4) Essay on theater.
5) Essay on 40 hours.
6) Rewrite Novel.
7) The Absurd.[41]

For Summer Impromptu:
"Audience member."
"Huh?"
"Audience member."
"Huh?"
"You're rare, audience member."
"What do you mean, rare?" (He looks around him.)
"Rare, that's what I mean! Not many of you. Only a few."
"We do what we can."
"Of course. As it is, you'll do just fine."

Novel.

"I have to admit I have some serious flaws," Bernard said. "For example, I'm a liar."

"?"

"Oh, I know. There are some faults a person never admits to having. And others it costs nothing to acknowledge. With a tone of false humility,

---

41. On this work plan, (1) refers to the essays "The Desert" and "Summer in Algiers," both of which would be published in *Noces*; (5) refers to the forty-hour workweek that had recently been put in place by the Popular Front, and about which Camus wrote an essay that he sent to Jean Giono at *Cahiers de Contadour*; in the notebook pages that follow, we can see the essay, which Giono didn't publish, being developed; (6) refers to *The Happy Death*; (7) likely refers to *The Myth of Sisyphus*, which Camus was beginning to work on in another notebook around this time. The essay about the theater would remain an unpolished rough draft, and the "Summer Impromptu," according to Philip Thody, was written for the Théâtre de l'Équipe, though the editors of Camus's *Complete Works* remain uncertain about the reference.

of course! 'Okay, it's true, I have a temper, I like food a little too much.' In a way, it flatters them. Being a liar, though, being conceited, envious, those are faults they don't admit. Other people are those things. And anyway, by admitting you have a temper, you avoid having to talk about all the rest. When a person accuses themselves all on their own, you don't go looking for other faults, do you?

"Me? I'm worthless. I've accepted myself. As a result, everything is quite simple."[42]

Caligula: "What you'll never understand is that I'm a simple man."

Essay about 40 hours.

In my family: work 10 hours. Sleep. Sunday—Monday.

Unemployment: the man cries. Man's great misery is that he must cry about and wish for what humiliates him (competition).

"There's a lot of talk these days about the dignity of work, about the necessity of it. M. Gignoux,[43] in particular, has some very strong opinions on the matter . . .

It's a con. There's dignity in work only when it's work freely undertaken. Only idleness is a moral value because it can be used to judge people. It's fatal only to the mediocre. That's its lesson and its greatness. Work, on the contrary, crushes everyone equally. It can't be used as a basis for judgment. It puts a metaphysics of humiliation into action. Our society of self-righteous[44] conformists have now made it a form of slavery, and the best don't survive it . . .

I propose we turn the classic model upside down and we make work a fruit of idleness. There's a dignity of work in the small barrels made on Sundays. There, work meets play and play yields to technique, becoming a work of art and the whole of creation . . . I know some rant and rave, "Hey, what're you looking at me for, my workers earn 40 francs a day . . ."

---

42. In this entry, we can see early hints of the mindset that Camus would impart to Clamence in *The Fall*.

43. Claude-Joseph Gignoux (1890–1968) was a conservative French politician and economist.

44. The French term *bien-pensant* (right-thinking) loses a little of its bite in English. The term might also be translated as "narrow-minded" or "reactionary."

At the end of the month, the mother says with an encouraging smile: "We'll have milk with our coffee this evening. Things do change every once in a while . . ."

But at least they'll be able to make love there . . .

———

The only brotherhood now possible, the only one we're offered and allowed, is the sordid, slimy brotherhood formed in the face of military death.

———

June.

At the cinema with her husband, the little woman from Oran cries her eyes out watching the hero's woes. Her husband begs her to stop. While still crying: "Really," she says. "Just let me enjoy it."

———

The Happy Death:

Zagreus is sitting in front of him on the train. Only instead of the black scarf he usually wore, he'd put on a very light summer tie. (After the murder, he goes back to his apartment. Doesn't change anything. Just puts up a new mirror).

———

The temptation common to all forms of intelligence: cynicism.

———

Misery and greatness of this world: it offers no truths but love.

Absurdity reigns, love redeems.

———

There's legitimate psychology in serial novels.[45] But it's a beneficent psychology. It doesn't pay attention to small details. It gives people credit. That's where it goes wrong.

———

The old woman's New Year's wishes: we don't ask for much, a little work and good health.

———

45. Serial novels (*roman-feuilleton*) developed as an offshoot of the supplemental, nonpolitical newspaper pages (*feuilleton*) introduced by the *Journal des débats* in 1800. In France, Alexandre Dumas's *The Three Musketeers* and Eugène Sue's *The Mysteries of Paris* were two early, instant successes that led to the expansion of the genre. The term *roman-feuilleton* is sometimes used today as shorthand for "soap opera" or "pulp fiction."

That singular vanity of the man who lets himself believe, who wants to believe, that it's truth he's longing for when really he's asking the world for love.

It's a hard thing to understand that a person can be superior to many without being a superior person. And that true superiority . . . [46]

August.

A room overlooking a courtyard—opens into a second room that receives the daylight from the first and that, in turn, opens into a third room without windows. In this room, three mattresses. Three people sleep there. But as the widest part of the room is not as wide as the mattresses, they've propped the tops of the mattresses against the wall and the men sleep in an arc.

The blind man and a friend of his who is also blind go out at night between 1:00 and 4:00 A.M., because they're sure not to run into anyone in the streets. If they run into a lamppost, they can have a good laugh about it. They do laugh. Whereas during the day, other people's pity prevents them from laughing.

"Write," the blind man says. "But no one would be interested. What interests people in a book is a pathetic existence. And our lives are never pathetic."

In writing, always err on the side of giving too little (rather than too much). No chit-chat, in any case.

The "real" experience of solitude is one of the least literary possible—a thousand miles from the literary idea of solitude.

Cf. what's degrading in all sufferings. Don't give in to the void. Try to overcome and to "fill." Time—don't let it get away.

The only possible freedom is freedom from death. The truly free individual is the one who, accepting death as it is, also accepts the consequences—which is to say the overturning of all life's traditional values. Ivan Karamazov's "everything is permitted" is the only expression of a coherent freedom. But we have to reach for the substance behind the slogan.[47]

---

46. The rest of the notebook page after this entry was left blank.

47. Camus expands on Karamazov's "everything is permitted" in the "Kirilov" section of *The Myth of Sisyphus*.

———

August 21, 1938.

"Only he who has known the 'present' truly knows what Hell is." (Wassermann.)[48]

———

Laws of Manu:

"A woman's mouth, a girl's breast, a child's prayer, sacrificial smoke, these are always pure."[49]

———

On conscious death, cf. Nietzsche. *Twilight of the Idols*, p. 203.[50]

N: "It's to the most spiritual souls, assuming they are the most courageous, that the most sorrowful tragedies are given to live, but it's for just this reason that they honor life, because it puts them up against its greatest adversity." (*Twilight of the Idols*.)

———

N: "What, then, do we desire on seeing beauty? To be beautiful. We imagine it must bring much happiness, but that's a mistake." (*Human, All Too Human*.)[51]

———

—The air is alive with cruel and dreadful birds.

———

To increase the happiness of a human life is to extend the tragedy for which it bears witness. The truly tragic work of art (if it bears witness) must

---

48. Jakob Wassermann (1873–1934) was a Jewish-German novelist whose 1928 book, *Der Fall Maurizius* (*The Maurizius Case*), Camus read in its French translation, *L'affaire Maurizius*. Here, Camus misquotes the French text, though he does so without changing the substance of the citation. The date of this entry is written in much larger numbers and letters than usual.

49. *Lois de Manu* is the French title of the ancient Hindu legal text *Manusmriti*. Differing versions of the text exist. In many, the quote Camus cites here retains only the first clause, "a woman's mouth." That said, it seems likely Camus took the quote from Nietzsche's *The Anti-Christ*, section 56, where Nietzsche discusses the *Laws of Manu* and cites the passage Camus has recorded here.

50. The reference is to "Raids of an Untimely Man," section 36, Morality for Doctors (the quote itself is from section 17). The page number given here matches Henri Albert's then-standard French translation. Camus would go on to title part 2 of *The Happy Death* "Conscious Death."

51. See section 149 of *Human, All Too Human*, "The Slow Arrow of Beauty."

be that of a happy man—because such a work of art will be completely blown away by death.[52]

———

The meteorological method. Temperature varies from one minute to the next. The experience is too fluid to be fixed in mathematical concepts. Here, observation represents an arbitrary sample of reality. It's only the concept of averages that allows us to provide an image of this reality.

———

Etruscan Bibliography. A. Grenier: Recherches Étrusques in the Revue des Études Anciennes, IX, 1935—219 sq.
B. Nogara: Les Étrusques et Leur Civilisation—Paris, 1936.
Fr. De Ruyt: Charon, Démon Étrusque de la Mort. (Reference?)

———

Belcourt. A young woman. Her husband is taking a nap and isn't to be disturbed by the children. Two rooms. She lays a blanket on the floor in the dining room and quietly entertains the children so that the man can sleep. She keeps the door to the landing open, because it's hot. Every so often she falls asleep, and you can see her as you pass by, slumped to the side, the children sitting silently around her, watching her body's gentle movements.

———

Belcourt. Shown the door.[53]

Doesn't dare tell her. Talks.

"Well, we'll have coffee in the evening. Things do change every once in a while."

He looks at her. He's often read stories about poverty in which the woman is "valiant." She hasn't smiled. She's gone back to the kitchen. Valiant? No, resigned.

———

52. In "Summer in Algiers," Camus writes: "In that Algerian summer, I was learning that there's only one thing more tragic than suffering, and that's the life of a happy man. Though it could also be the path to a greater life, as it causes you not to cheat."

See, also, the discussion between Mersault and Catherine in *The Happy Death*, part 2, chap. 4.

53. In French, *être mis à la porte* carries the sense of "to be fired" but can also mean, for example, "to be evicted."

A version of the quote that follows appears a little earlier in the notebooks in relation to the essay Camus was working on about the forty-hour workweek.

The former boxer who lost his son. "What're we doing here on Earth? We fritter around, we fritter around."

Belcourt. R.'s story.[54] "I knew this lady . . . let's say she was my mistress . . . I realized she'd been cheating on me." Story about the lottery tickets. (Did you buy one for me?) Story about the outfit and the sister. Story about the bracelets and the "evidence."

Calculation, 1300 francs. She doesn't have enough. "Why don't you work part-time? You'd make it a lot easier on me for all these little things. I bought you that outfit, I give you 20 francs a day, I pay your rent, and you, you drink coffee with your friends all afternoon. You give them coffee and sugar. Me? I give you money. I've done right by you and you do me wrong."

He asks for advice. He still has "feelings for his lay."[55] He wants a letter with "all the blows," with the "things that'll make her regret it."

Ex. "You just want to have fun getting off, that's all." Then: "I thought that . . ." etc.

"You don't see how everyone's jealous of the happiness I give you."

"I hit her, but let's say I did it tenderly. She screamed, I closed the shutters."

Ditto with the girl friend.

He wants her to be the one who comes back. Tragic character in this desire to humiliate her. He's going to take her to a hotel and call the "vice."[56]

Story about some friends and beer. "You all say you're connected to the underworld." "They told me they'd mark her if I wanted."

Story about the car coat. Story about the matches.

"You'll understand the happiness I gave you."

She's Arab.[57]

Theme: the universe of death. Tragic work; happy work.

---

54. In *The Stranger*, much of this background is given to Meursault's neighbor, Raymond Sintès. This entry begins a series of entries that alternate between material for *The Stranger* and material for *The Happy Death*.

55. The French phrase here, *un sentiment pour son coït*, which Camus would also use in *The Stranger*, is an unusual pairing of a possessive (his) and a noun (coitus). It's both oddly formal and nonidiomatic. Similarly, in the next paragraph, *t'amuser avec ta chose* is also a nonidiomatic usage, though one more clearly linked to the standard *faire la chose* ("to do it" / "to have sex"), but with the emphasis on the woman's enjoyment of the act, rather than on the act itself (i.e., the emphasis is on her having "fun getting off"). Both phrases, which appear as bits of dialogue, likely originate in the Cagayous dialect of Camus's youth. See p. 98n89.

56. In French, Camus has written *mœurs*, shorthand for *brigade des mœurs* (vice squad).

57. In the handwritten notebook, this last line is in much tinier print than the rest of the entry.

... "But this life doesn't seem to satisfy you, Mersault, judging by your tone."

"It doesn't satisfy me because it's going to be taken away from me—or rather, it's because it satisfies me too much. That's why I feel all the horror of losing it."

"I don't understand."

"You don't want to understand."

"Maybe."

After a little while, Patrice goes to leave.

"But there is love, Patrice."

He turns back, his face wrecked by hopelessness.

"Yes," Patrice says, "but love is of this world."

Nursing home (the old man crossing the field). Burial. The sun melts the road tar—feet sink into it, leaving the black flesh torn open. You can see a resemblance between this black mud and the coachman's cuir-bouilli hat.[58] All this black, the sticky black of the open tar, the faded black clothes, the black-lacquered car—the sun, the scent of leather and manure, of varnish, of incense. The exhaustion. And the other man, crossing the field.

He's going to the burial because she is his only friend. At the home, they used to say to him, as people say to children: "Oh, she's your fiancée?" And he laughed. And he was happy.

Characters.

A) Étienne,[59] "physical" character; the attention he pays to his body:

1. watermelon
2. illness (sharp pains)
3. biological needs—Good—Hot, etc.
4. He laughs with pleasure when eating something good.

B) Marie C.[60] Her brother-in-law and their life together, "he pays the rent."

C) Marie E.'s childhood. Her position in the family. Her virginity, which everyone talks about. Saint Francis of Assisi. Suffering and humiliation.

D) Mme Leca. Cf. above.

---

58. *Cuir-bouilli* (boiled-leather) is a leather-tanning technique dating back to the Middle Ages in which the product is soaked in wax and hardened, often to be used as armor.

59. A sketch of Camus's uncle, who would appear as a character in *The First Man*, where he is also referred to as Ernest.

60. Likely Marie Cardona, Meursault's mistress in *The Stranger*.

E) Marcel, the chauffeur—and the old woman from the café.

———

We don't have feelings that transform us but feelings that suggest the idea of transformation to us. In this way, love doesn't purge us of selfishness, but makes us feel our selfishness and helps us to imagine a distant homeland where such selfishness would no longer have a place.

———

Resume work on Plotinus.[61]

Theme: Plotinian Reason.

I) Reason—the concept isn't unambiguous.

Interesting to consider its role in history at a time when it has to adapt or perish.

Cf. Diplôme.

It's the same reason and it's not the same.

That's for two reasons:

one ethical, the other aesthetic.

Dig into: the Plotinian image as the syllogism of this aesthetic reason.

(The image as parable: an attempt to cast indefinable feeling into the discernible, indefinable concrete.)

As in all descriptive sciences (statistical—collecting facts—) meteorology's great problem is a practical problem: replacing absent observations. The methods of interpolation that have substituted for them have always relied on the concept of the average and from it suppose the generalization and rationalization of an experience whose rational aspect is precisely what we're trying to discern.

———

Belcourt. The sugar speculator who commits suicide in the bathroom.

———

The German family in '14. Four months reprieve. They come to look for the father. Concentration camp. Four years without news. Life during this time. He returns in '19—tubercular. Dies a few months later.

The little girls at school.

———

61. In 1936, Camus completed a thesis on Plotinus for his Diplôme d'études supérieures. A critical edition of the text appeared in English in 2015, translated and annotated by Ronald Srigley, as *Christian Metaphysics and Neoplatonism*.

Some of the ideas expressed here would appear in *The Myth of Sisyphus*, toward the end of the section titled "Philosophical Suicide."

Artist and work of art. The true work of art is the one that says less. There's a certain relationship between an artist's global experience, his thought + his life (his system, in a sense—omitting from the word any implication of the systematic), and the work that reflects that experience. The relationship is bad when the work of art adds a literary fringe around all his experience. The relationship is good when the work of art is a piece cut from experience, the facet of a diamond whose inner brilliance crystallizes without being constrained. In the first case, you get overwriting and literary pretension. In the second, a fertile work emanating from a whole subtext of experience whose richness we're able to feel.

The problem lies in acquiring that knowledge of life (having lived, rather), which goes beyond knowing how to write.[62] In the end, the great artist is, above all else, great at living (it being understood that, here, living is also thinking about life—that it's the same subtle relationship as between the experience and the awareness of it).

Pure love is a dead love if love implies a love life, the creation of a certain way of living—in such a life, love is nothing but a perpetual point of reference and coming to an understanding about everything else is what must be done.

Thought is always ahead of things. It sees too far, further than the body, which is in the present.

To take away hope is to bring thought back to the body—and the body must rot.

Lying in bed, he smiled awkwardly and his eyes sparkled. She felt all her love welling in her throat and tears coming to her eyes. She threw herself on his lips and crushed the tears between their faces. She cried in his mouth and he, nibbling those salty lips, tasted all the bitterness of their love.

The creator's cold heart.

"If only I knew how to read! I can't knit by the light in the evening. So, all I can do is lie down and wait. It's a long time, two hours like that. Ah! If my

---

62. In French, the comparison between *savoir-vivre* and *savoir-écrire* is a little more direct. Something like "life-knowledge" vs. "writing-knowledge."

This entry appears, with some editing, in *The Myth of Sisyphus*, in the section on "Absurd Creation," under the heading "Philosophy and Fiction."

granddaughter were here with me, I'd talk with her. But I'm too old. Maybe I smell bad. My granddaughter never comes. So, that's how it goes, and all alone."[63]

2P[64]

Today, Maman died. Or maybe yesterday, I don't know. I got a telegram from the home. "Mother passed. Burial tomorrow. Sincerely yours." That doesn't mean anything. Maybe yesterday . . . [65]

As the caretaker said: "Out on the plains, it's hot. Burials happen quicker. Especially here." He told me he was from Paris and that he'd had a hard time getting used to things here. Because in Paris, you stay with the dead two, three days sometimes. Here, you don't have the time. You've hardly gotten used to the idea and already you're running after a hearse.

. . . Even the procession moved too fast. The thing is, the sun was beating down like a big bully, and as the head nurse correctly pointed out: "If you go slowly, you risk sunstroke, and if you go too fast, you get covered in sweat and catch a chill in the church."[66] She was right. There was no way out.

The person from the undertaker's office said something to me that I didn't hear. He was holding his cap up for a second and, with his other hand, running a handkerchief underneath it to dry off his skull. I said to him, "What was that?" He repeated himself, pointing at the sky: "It's scorching hot." I said, "Yes." A little later, he asked me, "That's your mother over there?" I said, "Yes."

"She was old?"

---

63. Under this entry, Camus drew a large line and arrow pointing to the next page.

Over twenty years later, a fleshed-out version of this entry would appear in *The First Man*, at the beginning of chap. 6, "The Family."

64. The official French edition of the notebooks records this as "22," but the handwritten notebook seems to read "2P." On the initial typescript, it appears Camus corrected the printed "22" to "2P," and this correction does then appear integrated in print on the final typescript.

65. The first formulation of *The Stranger*'s opening lines. There are three very small changes between this initial version and the final version: In the final version, rather than a period after "home," there is a colon; the penultimate sentence begins with *Cela* rather than *Ça*; and the last sentence begins with *C'était* (imperfect past) rather than *C'est* (present). All the rest remains the same.

66. In French, the nurse's comment has a little more symmetry. The clauses translated here as "you risk sunstroke" and "you get covered in sweat" rhyme in the French, and the final clause, translated here as "you catch a chill"—which literally translates as "you catch a hot and cold"—brings together the intense heat outside and the cold inside the church.

I replied, "Something like that," because I didn't know the exact number. After that, he didn't say anything else.

———

December '38.

For *Caligula*: Anachronism is the most annoying thing you can introduce in the theater. That's why Caligula doesn't say the one reasonable thing he could have said in the play: "~~You miss~~ a single person who thinks and the whole world empties."[67]

Calig = "I need the people around me to be quiet. I need the people's silence and for that awful uproar in my heart to be quiet."[68]

———

15

Labor camp. Cf. article.[69]

———

At the meeting. The old railroad worker, neat, clean-shaven, a carefully folded, tartan-lined raincoat over his arm with the lining facing out—shoes polished—asks if "this is where" the meeting is taking place, and tells me how worried he gets when he thinks about what will become of the worker.

———

At the hospital. A tubercular patient is given five days to live by the doctor. The patient takes the initiative and slits his throat with a razor. Obviously, he couldn't wait the five days.

To a journalist who comes: "Don't mention it in your paper," the nurse says. "He's suffered enough as it is."

———

67. In the handwritten notebook, Camus copied out Lamartine's famous quote, "You miss a single person and the whole world empties," then put his own twist on it, crossing out "you miss" and adding "who thinks."

68. In the handwritten notebook, there is a numbered entry after this one, which Camus has drawn a box around and scratched out.

69. In the December 1, 1938, issue of *Alger républicain*, under the headline "Men Stripped of Their Humanity," Camus wrote of the *La Martinière*, a ship used to transport convicts to slave labor camps in Guyana, arguing that the ship itself was a "Floating Labor Camp." Not long after the article appeared, the ship was sold to the French Navy. See p. 562.

The man who loves *here on earth* and the woman who loves him with the certainty that they'll be together again in the afterlife. Their love is not of the same magnitude.

———

Death and a body of work. Near to death, he has his last work read to him. It's still not what he wanted to say. He has it burned. And he dies without consolation—something in his chest ripped up like a broken agreement.

———

Sunday.

The storm winds in the mountain were keeping us from making progress, gagging us, screaming in our ears. The whole forest twisted from top to bottom. Above the valleys, red ferns were flying from one mountain to the next. And that beautiful orange bird, too.

———

Story about a legionnaire who kills his mistress in a stockroom, and then takes the corpse by the hair and drags it out into the dining area, then out into the street where he's arrested. He has a stake in the café-restaurant and the owner had forbidden him from bringing his mistress around. She came anyway. He ordered her to leave. She refused. That's why he killed her.

———

The little couple on the train. Both ugly. She clings to him, laughs, plays the coquette, seduces him. He, eyes empty, is embarrassed that everyone can see him being loved by a woman he's not proud of.

———

High-society types or the two old journalists bawling each other out in the middle of the police station, surrounded by a circle of laughing officers. A senile fury unable to be expressed in blows flows from them in an astonishing excess of profanity: "Bastard."

"Cuckold."

"Filthy piece of shit."

"Dirty-ass impostor."

"Pimp."

"Me? I'm a respectable guy."

"There's a difference between us."

"Yeah, a big one. You're the dumb fuck to end all dumb fucks."

"Say another word and I'll break your face and shove my foot up your ass."

"The tip of my dick's harder than you are. Because I'm a respectable guy."

———

—Spain. The guy and the party. Wants to enlist. After questioning, it's due to personal grievance. *They don't want him.*

———

In each life, there are a small number of great feelings and a great number of small feelings. If you choose: two lives and two literatures.

———

But *in fact*, they are two monsters.

———

The pleasure of male relations. A subtle pleasure that consists of giving or asking for a light—a complicity, a freemasonry of the cigarette.[70]

———

P., who declares he's prepared to offer "a miniature of the pregnant virgin in a frame made of toreador clavicles."

Notice posted at the barracks: "Alcohol extinguishes the man and inflames the beast"—which only helps him understand why he likes alcohol.

"Earth would be a splendid cage for animals with nothing human about them."

———

Some of my purest joys are linked to Jeanne.[71] She'd often say to me: "You're ridiculous." That was her word, one she said with a laugh, and always when she loved me most. We both came from poor families. She lived a couple of streets past mine, on the Rue du Centre. Neither of us ever left that neighborhood, to which everything pointed back. The same sadness and sor-

70. There is an entry after this one in the handwritten notebook and typescript, likely someone's name, which appears to read "D. Amsellem."

It was around this time Camus met Pascal Pia (1903–1979), a French writer and journalist who would serve as a friend and mentor to Camus at the short-lived "workers' newspaper" *Alger républicain*, which began publication October 6, 1938, and was shut down in 1939. The two would work together again at *Combat* but would drift apart not long after, with Pia heavily criticizing Camus later in life.

71. This entry, which appears almost unchanged in the first draft of *The Plague*—and which appears in revised form in the published version, in part 2, section 2—is the first in the notebooks that can be definitively linked to the novel. In the published version, Jeanne is Grand's wife.

After being held in a private collection for many years, Camus's handwritten first draft of *The Plague* was acquired by the Bibliothèque nationale de France in 1983. In 2020, the French press Les Saints Pères put out a limited-edition facsimile, presenting the manuscript to the general public for the first time.

did life that hung in her home hung in mine, as well. Our meeting was a way of escaping all that. And yet, as I turn back now to look at that tired child's face, back across so many years, I understand we weren't really escaping that life of poverty, and that, in truth, it was loving each other right there amid its shadow that turned our feelings into something no amount of money could ever buy.

I think I truly suffered when I lost her. And yet, I didn't rebel at the time. It's because I've never been very comfortable with possession. Regret has always seemed more natural to me. And, though I've a pretty good sense of my own inner workings, I've never been able to help believing that Jeanne is more alive inside me at times like this, today, than when she was standing there on her tiptoes, lifting herself up a little so she could put her arms around my neck. I can no longer remember how we met. But I do know that I used to go see her at her place. And that her father and mother would laugh when they saw us together. Her father was a railroad worker, and when he was at home, we'd always find him sitting in a corner, pensive, staring out the window, his huge hands pressed against his thighs. Her mother was always cleaning. Jeanne was, too, but to see her going about it, laughing and lighthearted, I didn't think of her as doing work. She was an average size, but she seemed small to me. And because she seemed so slight, so weightless, my heart skipped a beat when I saw her step into the street and cross in front of some trucks. I can see now she probably wasn't so smart. At the time, the thought never occurred to me. She had this way of playing at being angry that filled my heart with teary delight. That secret move of hers, the one where she'd turn and throw herself into my arms as I begged for her forgiveness, how could it not, all these years later, still touch my heart, closed as it is to so much else. I don't remember now if I desired her. I know everything was all mixed up and confused. I know only that my troubles dissolved into affection. If I did desire her, I forgot about it the first time, in the hallway of her apartment, she gave me her mouth as a thank you for a little brooch I'd given her. With her hair pulled back, her teeth a little too big for her mouth, her light eyes and straight nose, she seemed like a child that night, a child I would've brought into the world just to receive the kisses and affection she gave. I've long had that impression, and it's one Jeanne helped create, always calling me her "best friend."

We shared some moments that can never be repeated. When we got engaged, I was twenty-two and she was eighteen. But it was the official nature of the thing that filled our heart with a joyful, solemn love. When Jeanne was presented at my home, when Maman hugged and kissed her and said, "My little one," the myriad joys were so ridiculous we didn't even try to hide them.

But my memory of Jeanne is linked to an impression that seems inexpressible today. I can still conjure the feeling if I'm a little sad and I encounter, within minutes of each other, a woman with a face that touches me and a glowing storefront window; this, with a painful feeling of reality, conjures Jeanne's face turning to me and saying, "Look how pretty." It was the holiday season, then, and the shops in our neighborhood spared neither lights nor decorations. We would stop in front of the pastry shops. Chocolate figures, pebbles made of silver-and-gold paper, snowflakes made of waterproof cotton, gilded plates and rainbow-colored pastries, all of it enchanted us. I was a little ashamed. But I couldn't contain the joy that filled me and caused Jeanne's eyes to sparkle.

If I try to explain that unrepeatable feeling now, I see many things in it. Of course, the joy came to me, first and foremost, from Jeanne—from her perfume and her hand squeezing my wrist, from those pouts I expected, but also from the sudden brightness of the shops in a neighborhood that was usually so black, the hurried air of passersby weighed down with their purchases, the joy of the children in the streets, all of it contributed to the feeling of being pulled out of our solitary world. The silver paper those chocolates were wrapped in signaled that a confused, noisy, golden period was opening up for simple hearts, and Jeanne and I, we pressed a little closer together then, one against the other. Maybe in some vague way we could feel that unrepeatable happiness, the kind felt by those whose outer life is in harmony with their inner self. Usually, we walked the enchanted desert of our love in a world where love no longer had a place, yet on days like these it seemed as if the flame rising within us when our hands were clasped together was the same as the one dancing in the shop windows, in the hearts of workers turned to their children, and in the depths of the icy, raw December sky.

———

December.

Faust in reverse. The young man asks the devil for worldly goods. The devil (who wears a sport coat and happily declares that cynicism is the intellect's great temptation) says to him, gently: "But you have worldly goods. God's the one you have to ask for whatever it is you're lacking—if you believe you're lacking something. You'll be able to make a deal with God. You'll be able to sell him your body in exchange for the next world's worldly goods."

After a moment's silence, the devil lights an English cigarette and adds: "And that will be your eternal punishment."

———

Peter Wolf. Escapes from a concentration camp, kills a guard, and manages to cross the border. Takes refuge in Prague, where he tries to start a new life. After the annexation of Munich,[72] is extradited by the Prague government. Delivered to the Nazis. Sentenced to death. Executed with an axe a few hours later.

On a door: "Come in. I've hanged myself." They go in and it's true. (He says "I," but it isn't an "I" anymore.)[73]

Javanese dances. Slowness, a principle of Hindu dance. An unfolding. An efflorescence of detail in the movements of an ensemble, like the accumulation of details in architecture. A proliferation of gestures. Nothing is hurried, everything unfurls. It's not an act or a gesture. It's a participation.

In comparison, tragedy in the leaps of certain cruel dances. The use of silence in the accompaniment (which, incidentally, is music's ghost). Here, the music doesn't define the pattern the dance follows. It forms a background. It encompasses gestures and music. It flows around the bodies and their imperceptible geometry.

(Othello in the dance of the heads.)[74]

For the end of *Noces*.

Earth! That great temple deserted by the gods. Man's task is to people it with idols made in his own image, expressionless faces of love with feet of clay.

. . . those monstrous idols of joy, face of love and feet of clay.

The deputy from Constantine is elected for the third time. On election day, at noon, he dies. In the evening, the people come to cheer for him. His wife comes out on the balcony and says he's a little tired. Not long after, the corpse is elected deputy. That's the way it goes.[75]

---

72. Camus is undoubtedly referring to the Munich Agreement, though he doesn't use the standard "Accords de Munich" here.

73. In the first draft of *The Plague*, Stephen is the one who hangs himself. In the final version, it's Cottard.

74. This entry calls to mind Camus's discussion of theater in *The Myth of Sisyphus*. Several words and phrases that appear in this entry, and in the one that follows, appear in the section titled "Drama" and rarely anywhere else in Camus's work.

75. There is an arrow after this entry pointing to the next page.

About the Absurd?[76]

There's only one case in which hopelessness is pure. The case of the person sentenced to death (which gives us an opportunity for a little evocation). You could ask a man whose lost all hope of love if he wants to be guillotined the next day, and he'd refuse. Due to the horror of the torturous proceedings? Yes. But the horror here is born of certainty—or, rather, of the mathematical element that makes things certain. Here, the Absurd is perfectly clear. It's the opposite of irrational. It bears all the characteristics of the obvious fact. What's irrational, what would be irrational, is the fleeting, moribund hope that the situation will change and that death might be avoided. But not the absurd. The obvious fact is that they're going to cut the man's head off and that he'll be fully conscious when it happens—that it'll happen right as his entire consciousness is focused on the fact that they're going to cut his head off.

Kirilov is right. To commit suicide is to prove you're free. And the problem of freedom has a simple solution. People have the illusion of being free. Those sentenced to death don't have such illusions. The whole of the problem is in the reality of this illusion.

Before: "This heart, this soft sound that's been with me for so long, how could I imagine it stopping, how could I imagine it especially at the very second . . ."

"Oh, prison! The paradise of prison."

(the Mother: "Now they'll give him back to me . . . Look what they've done to him . . . They're giving him back to me in two pieces.)

"It got to the point where I could only sleep a little during the day, where I'd patiently wait each night for the light to come and, with it, the truth of a new day. For that whole uncertain hour, the hour I knew *they* usually came . . . in those moments, I was like a wild animal . . . Afterward, I had one more day . . .

I calculated. I tried to control myself. I filed an appeal. And I always imagined the worst: it was rejected. Well, then I was going to die. Maybe sooner than others. But my life had often seemed absurd to me when I thought of dying. If you're going to die, the how and the when don't matter. So then, I have to accept it. And only then, at that moment, do *I have the right* to consider

76. This entry makes clear Camus was now working on *The Myth of Sisyphus*. The first paragraph of the entry would be further developed there (as well as in "Reflections on the Guillotine"). The comment about Kirilov would be fleshed out in the chapter on Absurd Creation.

the second possibility: I'd be pardoned. I tried to tamp down the fiery rush of blood surging through my body, stinging my eyes with a mad and senseless joy. I stifled the cry, its importance, so my resignation to the first hypothesis would feel more plausible. But what was the point? Those dawns came, and with them, that uncertain hour . . .

. . . It's them. But it's still really dark out. They've come early. I've been robbed. I've been robbed, I tell you . . .

. . . Run away. Smash it all. But no, I stay. Cigarette? Why not? Still time. But at the same time, he's cutting off my shirt collar. At the same time. It's the same time. I haven't saved any time. They're robbing me, I tell you.

. . . This hallway is so long, but these people walk so fast . . . As long as there are a lot of them, as long as they welcome me with cries of hatred. As long as there are a lot of them and I'm not alone . . .

. . . I'm cold. It's so cold. Why'd they leave me in shirtsleeves? It doesn't matter anymore, that's true. There's no more getting sick for me. I've lost the paradise of suffering, I am losing it, losing the joy of coughing my lungs out or being eaten up by cancer while a loved one watches.

. . . And this starless sky, these unlit windows, that bustling street and that man in the front row, the foot of that man who . . ."[77]
END

The Absurd. Gurvitch.[78] Treatise on hopelessness. Power of the bosses . . .

Mersault.
Caligula.

---

77. This final image would also return in Camus's play *The Just.*

78. Georges Gurvitch (1894–1965) taught at a variety of universities, including the Sorbonne, where he specialized in the sociology of law and the sociology of knowledge. In 1960, he signed the Manifesto of the 121, which denounced France's use of torture during the Algerian War and called on the government to recognize the conflict as a "war of national liberation." In *The Myth of Sisyphus,* Camus seems to borrow from Gurvitch's book *Current Trends in German Philosophy,* a study of Husserl, Heidegger, and others, with the line, "But it's claimed they are directly present in all data of perception," a sentence that is only a shade off from one Gurvitch wrote: "They are directly present in the real world and, in general, in all data of perception and imagination."

Special edition of *Rivages*[79] on the theater. Relocate stage direction. Commentary about Miquel's plan.[80] Introduction. Everything with regard to the theater.

The Mirabel Garden in Salzburg.

The troupe on tour in Bordj-bou-Arreridj.

———

1939.

Burning is my rest. Joy isn't the only thing that burns. But never-ending work, never-ending marriage or never-ending desire.

———

Order of work:

Talk on theater.

Reading for the Absurd.

Caligula.

Mersault.[81]

Theater.

Rivages at Charlot's Monday.

Lesson.

Journal.

———

February.

Lives death doesn't surprise. Which have prepared for it. Which have accounted for it.

———

Just as a writer's death leads us to exaggerate the importance of his work, an individual's death leads us to overestimate his place in our life. In this way, the past is made entirely from death, which peoples it with illusions.

———

79. *Rivages* was an Algerian literary magazine published by Edmond Charlot, who would also publish Camus's first two essay collections, *L'envers et l'endroit* and *Noces*. The magazine only lasted two issues, the first of which included an introduction by Camus and the second of which contained Camus's essay "Summer in Algiers."

80. Louis Miquel, an Algerian architect and friend of Camus, was one of the original members of the Théâtre du Travail. See p. 569n63.

81. After "Mersault," there is an arrow pointing back up at "order of work."

A love that can't bear being confronted with reality isn't one. But then, being unable to love is the privilege of noble hearts.

———

Novel. Those nighttime conversations side by side, those confessions endlessly spoken . . .

"And this life of waiting. I wait for dinner and I wait for sleep. I think about waking up with the vague hope—of what? I don't know. When the time to wake comes, then I wait for breakfast. And on and on until the next day . . . Endlessly telling myself: Now he's at his office, he's having lunch, he's at his office, he's free—and then I have to imagine that unfilled space, I do imagine it, and it hurts so bad you could scream . . ."[82]

". . . Come filled with joy only to leave the next day—and how close hopelessness is to joy! We look back on those two days. They were beautiful and they're wrapped in tears."

———

Algeria, a country at once bounded and boundless. Bounded in its lines, boundless in its light.

———

Death of "Caporal." Cf. paper.

———

The crazy man in the bookstore. Cf. paper.

———

Tragedy is a closed world—where we trip over, where we collide with each other. In the theater, tragedy has to be born and die within the confined space of the stage.[83]

———

Cf. Stuart Mill: "Better to be Socrates dissatisfied than a pig satisfied."[84]

———

This sun-filled morning: the streets warm and filled with women. People selling flowers on every street corner. And those girls with smiles on their faces.

———

82. This idea would reappear in *The First Man*.

83. This entry was added by hand to the typescript; it does not appear in the handwritten notebook.

84. In the original English, "It is better to be a human being dissatisfied than a pig satisfied; better to be Socrates dissatisfied than a fool satisfied."

March.

"When I found myself in that heated, well-lit first-class compartment, I closed the door behind me and lowered all the blinds. And then, sitting there in the middle of that extraordinary silence so suddenly welcoming me, I felt delivered. Delivered, first and foremost, from all those dizzying days that had just passed, from the effort of trying to take control of my life, from all those tumultuous difficulties. All of it went silent. The train car gently rumbled. If beyond the windows I heard the cold patter of the rainy night, I nevertheless heard it as a silence. For a couple of days, I didn't have to think anymore, only go. I was a prisoner of schedules, of hotels, of some human endeavor awaiting me. No longer belonging to myself, I finally belonged to myself. I closed my eyes, relishing the peace I felt rising alongside this peaceful universe that had just been born, a universe without tyranny, without love, and beyond just me.[85]

———

Oran. Mers-el-Kébir, the bay above the little garden of red geraniums and freesia. It's only half-nice out: clouds and sunshine. A balanced country. A small stretch of open sky is enough to bring calm back to hearts run ragged.[86]

———

April '39.

In Oran, a "sufoco" is an affront. A sufoco can't stand. It must be handled, and right away. Oranians are hot-blooded.

A landscape can be magnificent without being grand. It can even lack the grandeur of something more modest. That's how the Bay of Algiers lacks grandeur, through an excess of beauty. On the other hand, Mers-el-Kébir, seen from Santa Cruz, shows what grandeur's really like. Magnificent and devoid of tenderness.[87]

———

In the banlieues just outside Oran, a few meters past the last houses, are endless stretches of land left uncultivated, covered in vibrant broom shrub this time of year. The first village settled by the colonizers is a little farther

85. At the end of February 1939, Camus returned to Oran to cover Michel Hodent's trial for *Alger républicain*. Parts of this entry would appear in *The Happy Death*.

86. The beginning of the last sentence could also be read as "a little slice of heaven."

87. In the handwritten notebook, the entry continues for several lines, which Camus crossed out on the typescript.

along. Soulless, a single street running through it, a symbolic bandstand setup there.

———

The Hautes Plaines and the Djebel Nador.[88]

Endless stretches of wheat fields devoid of trees and people. Here and there, a gourbi and a silhouette timidly making its way along the crest, clearly visible against the horizon. A few crows and silence. Nowhere to take refuge—nowhere to hang a moment of joy—or a melancholy that might bear fruit. What's cultivated on this land is anguish and sterility.

In Tiaret, a couple of teachers told me they were "bored shitless."

"And what do you do when you're bored shitless?"

"Get hammered."

"And after that?"

"Go to a whorehouse."

I went to the whorehouse with them. It was snowing. A fine, biting snowfall. They'd all been drinking. A bouncer made me pay two francs at the door. It was a huge, rectangular room, oddly painted with oblique black-and-yellow stripes. People were dancing to a record player. The girls were neither beautiful nor ugly.

One of them said: "You come to fuck?"

The man half-heartedly protested.

"I'd really like you to put it in me," the girl said.

When we left, it was still snowing. From a vista, we could see the countryside. Still the same desolate stretch, but white this time.[89]

———

88. The Hautes Plaines are a region of the Atlas Mountains in northern Algeria. Djebel Nador is located in Constantine, where Camus was born.

89. Much of the dialogue in this entry, as well as in the entry below about Tolba and in various other spots throughout the notebooks, is written in Pataouète, a French dialect largely spoken by poor white Europeans who settled in the cities of Algeria. Within Pataouète, the specific regional dialect Camus uses is often referred to as Cagayous, so named after a character popularized by Musette (Auguste Robinet). A collection of Musette's Cagayous stories, published by Gallimard in 1931—and edited by a friend of Camus's—featured a Pataouète lexicon to help guide readers of "standard" French.

About Musette's character, Camus writes that the "language used by Cagayous is often a literary language, which is to say a reconstruction. 'Ordinary' people don't go around speaking entirely in slang: they use slang words and phrases, which is different." This explanation, which comes at the end of the essay "Summer in Algiers," is followed by a similar scene to the one with Tolba that ap-

In Trezel—Moorish café. Mint tea and conversation.

The street where the girls walk is called "Rue de la Vérité." Three francs a pop.

Tolba and his brawls.

"Not a bad dude, just a sparkplug. Over here one second, there the next. This other guy, he says to me: "If you're a man you'll come down off that tram." I say to him: "All right, take it easy." He says to me: "You're no man." So, I step down and I tell him: "Best to let it go, or I'm gonna give you a beat down."

"Excuse me?"

So, I knock him one. He hits the ground. Me? I go over to help him up. Then this guy starts kicking me from the ground. So, I give him a knee and a couple'a smacks. His face is all bloody. So, I say to him: "Well, you had enough?" He says: "Yes."[90]

Mobilization.

The eldest son is heading out. He's sitting in front of his mother and he says: "It'll be no big deal." The mother doesn't say anything. She picks up a newspaper lying on the table. She folds it in half, then in quarters, then in eighths.[91]

At the train station, the accompanying crowd. The men are piled in the cars. A woman is crying. "I never thought it would be like this, as bad as this." Another woman: "It's funny how people run off to die like this." A girl cries on her fiancé's chest, his face grave. He doesn't say anything. Smoke, cries, jolts. The train is leaving.

Women's faces, the pleasures of sun and water, that's what we're murdering. If you don't accept such murder, then you'll have to bear this in mind.

---

pears here. Tasked with translating the essay into English, Justin O'Brien wrote to Camus to say that he was afraid he'd only be able to create, at best, an approximation of the dialect, to which Camus replied to remove the part in the Algerian language, which he deemed untranslatable in French. O'Brien did, in fact, take out that section of the essay, which has never appeared in English.

90. This entry would also be used in Raymond's first encounter with Meursault in *The Stranger*, part 1, chap. 3.

91. Camus's older brother, Lucien, was called up in 1939.

We're at the center of the contradiction. Our whole age is up to its neck in contradiction, suffocating and living it without a tear to deliver us.[92]

Not only are there no solutions, there are no problems.

92. Camus has crossed the first five lines of this entry out in the handwritten notebook.

Notebook III

APRIL 1939–FEBRUARY 1942

A common composition notebook widely used by schoolchildren at the time. It has the words "Le Calligraphe" and "Cahier" preprinted on a blue cover. At the top, Camus has written "Cahier no III," and below the preprinting he has written "April 1939," then drawn a line through the preprinted "belonging to," and, in a different color ink, written "to February 1942." In the top-right corner, someone has written and circled "28." The notebook is 22 × 13 cm, with eighty-three pages, six of which were left blank. The first two pages are joined to each other but loose from the rest of the binding, which is otherwise held together as a unified whole. Three pages—73, 80, and 81—were added from an outside source.

Whereas cypress trees are usually dark spots in the skies of Provence and Italy, the one here in the cemetery of El-Kettar was dripping with light, was awash with golden rays of sun. It seemed as if a golden juice was bubbling from its black heart out to the very tips of its short branches and flowing over its green foliage in long tawny strings.

———

. . . Like those books in which too many passages have been underlined in pencil so that you'll have a high opinion of the reader's taste and intellect.

———

Dialogue Europe-Islam.

"And when we think of your cemeteries and what you've made of them, we're gripped by a sort of pitiful admiration for you, a fright-filled respect for men who have to live with such an image of their death . . ."

". . . We also pity ourselves sometimes. It helps us to live. It's a feeling you'd hardly understand. It probably seems unmanly to you. Yet it's the most manly among us who feel it, for the people we call manly are those who are lucid, and we seek no strength divorced from clear-sightedness. For you, on the other hand, man's virtue is in commandment."[1]

———

During the war. People who rank the degree of danger of each front. "Mine was the most vulnerable." Even out of universal degradation, still they create hierarchies. That's how they make it through.

———

"Yeah," the sanitation worker said, "and if you only saw the johns 'they' made for them down there at the Navy yard! A shame to give johns like that to those sort of people."

———

A woman lives with her husband without understanding a thing about him. One day, he gives a talk on the radio. They put her behind a pane of glass, and she can see but can't hear him. All she knows is that he's gesturing. For the first time, she sees him in his body, as a physical being, and also as the puppet that he is.[2]

---

1. Philip Thody has noted the similarities between this entry and Malraux's *Temptation of the West*.

2. In *The Myth of Sisyphus*, Camus writes: "People also secrete inhumanity. In certain moments of lucidity, the mechanical aspect of their gestures, their meaningless pantomime, makes everything around them seem ridiculous. You see a man talking on a phone behind a glass partition, and you can't hear him, but you see his senseless gesticulating, and you wonder: why is he alive? This uneasi-

She leaves him. "It's that marionette that climbs on top of me every night."

Subject for a play. The Masked Man.[3]

After a long time away, he returns home wearing a mask. He wears it the rest of the play. Why? That's the subject.

He unmasks himself at the end. It was all for nothing. To see from under a mask. He would have kept it on for a long time. He was happy, if the word means anything. His wife's suffering is what forces him to unmask himself.

"Until now, I loved you with everything I had. Now, I'll love you only as you wish to be loved. It seems you'd rather be despised than love without understanding why. There are two important elements at play here."

(Or two women. One loves him masked because it intrigues her. Doesn't love him afterward. "You loved me with your brain. I *also* needed to be loved with your loins." The other loves him *in spite of* the mask and continues to love him afterward.)

In a strange yet natural reaction, she imagined precisely those reasons that hurt her most, and in doing so she caused the man she loved to suffer. She'd gotten so used to being deprived of all hope that the moment she tried to understand the man's life, she always saw in it only what was unfavorable to her. And that was precisely what irritated him.

Historical mind and eternal mind. One has a sense of beauty, the other of the infinite.

Le Corbusier. "What makes an artist, you see, are those moments when he feels he's more than a man."

Pia and the documents that'll disappear. Deliberate disintegration. In the face of nothingness, hedonism and continual displacement. Here, the historical mind becomes the geographical mind.

On the tram. The half-hammered guy who clings to me: "If you're a man, you'll give me twenty sous. You *are* a man. Look, I just got out of the hospital.

---

ness in the face of man's inhumanity, this unimaginable fall in the face of what we really are, this 'nausea,' as one of our modern writers calls it, this, too, is the absurd. In the same way, the stranger who occasionally greets us in the mirror, the familiar, and yet unsettling, brother we see in photographs of ourself, this, again, is the absurd."

3. An early sketch of *The Misunderstanding*.

Where am I going to sleep tonight? But if you're a man, I'll get a drink and forget it all. I'm miserable. That's what I am. I've got no one."

I give him five francs. He takes my hand, looks at me, throws himself against my chest, and bursts into tears. "Oh, you, you're a good guy. You understand me. I've got no one, you understand, no one." As I leave him, the tram starts up again and he stays on, lost and still in tears.

———

A man lives alone for many years, then adopts a child. He pours all his past solitude onto him. In the hermetic universe he creates, one-on-one with this other being, he feels himself master of the child and the magnificent kingdom he's captured. He tyrannizes him, frightens him, terrorizes him with his whims and exacting demands—And then one day the child runs away, and once again the man finds himself alone with his solitude, with tears in his eyes, and an awful surge of love for the toy he's just lost.

———

"I was waiting for the moment when, coming out onto the street, she'd turn and look up at me, and what she'd show me then was a pale, shining face, its makeup swept away by kisses, leaving only its natural appearance. Her face was bare. And for the first time, it was her I saw, after having pursued her through all those long, stifling hours of desire. The patience with which I'd loved her was finally rewarded. It was her I found deep down in that face with paler-than-usual lips and white cheekbones, that face my lips had exhumed from its layers of smiles and makeup."

———

Poe and the four conditions of happiness:

1) Living in the open air

2) Being loved by someone

3) Detachment from all ambition

4) Creation.[4]

———

Baudelaire: "We've forgotten two rights in the Declaration of the Rights of Man: the right to contradict oneself and to pick up and leave."

4. Toward the beginning of Poe's short story "The Domain of Arnheim," he writes: "He admitted but four elementary principles, or, more strictly, conditions, of bliss. That which he considered chief was (strange to say!) the simple and purely physical one of free exercise in the open air. 'The health,' he said, 'attainable by other means is scarcely worth the name.' He instanced the ecstasies of the fox-hunter, and pointed to the tillers of the earth, the only people who, as a class, can be fairly considered happier than others. His second condition was the love of woman. His third, and most

Id. "There are seductions so powerful they can only be virtues."[5]

On the scaffold, Madame du Barry: "One more minute, Mister Executioner."[6]

July 14, 1939. One year ago.

On the beach, the man, arms outstretched,[7] crucified by the sun.

With Pierre, obscenity is a form of hopelessness.

"Those terrible years of doubt during which he was waiting for marriage or anything else—during which he was already constructing the philosophy of renunciation that would justify his failure and cowardice."

"With his wife. The problem was knowing if it were possible for a man like him to live amid that woman's lies without demeaning himself."

August.

1) Oedipus overcomes the Sphinx and, if he dispels the mysteries, he does so through his understanding of man. The whole Greek universe is clear.[8]

---

difficult of realization, was the contempt of ambition. His fourth was an object of unceasing pursuit; and he held that, other things being equal, the extent of attainable happiness was in proportion to the spirituality of this object."

5. The quotes come from "Edgar Poe: His Life and Works," an introduction Baudelaire wrote for *Histoires extraordinaires,* the first of his French translations of Poe's stories. This entry, in combination with the previous one, indicate Camus was likely reading Poe's *Œuvres en prose,* which was published by Gallimard in 1932, and which collected all five volumes of Baudelaire's Poe translations. The first quote, as recorded here, is a shortened paraphrase, while the second records only part of the sentence.

6. Madame du Barry (1743–1793), mistress of Louis XV, was executed December 8, 1793, during the Reign of Terror.

7. In French, the second clause, *les bras en croix* (literally: arms cross-shaped), carries a stronger link to the final clause.

8. Camus and Francine Faure, his wife-to-be, had planned to take a trip to Greece at the end of the summer, but when the war broke out, the trip had to be cancelled. This entry begins a series of notes based on reading Camus was doing in preparation for the trip.

2) But this is the same man that fate so savagely tears to pieces, the implacable fate of blind logic. The shadow-free clarity of the tragic and the perishable.

———

See Epicurus (essay).

Aglauros's Grotto on the Acropolis. The Statue of Minerva stripped of its clothes once a year. Likely all Statues were dressed like this. The Greek nude is our invention.

———

In Athens, there was a temple dedicated to old age. Children were brought to it.

Coresus and Callirhoe[9] (play).

Sacrificed himself, sacrificed herself. Strikes herself down at such proof of love.

———

Legend about the gods dressing as beggars, inciting charity. It didn't come naturally.

———

In Sicyon, Prometheus tricked Zeus. Two cowhides, one filled with meat and the other with bone. Zeus chose the latter. That's why the use of fire was taken from man. Out of base revenge.

———

The potter Dibutades[10] had a daughter who loved a young man and used a stylus to trace the shadow his profile cast on a wall. Her father, seeing the drawing, discovered the ornamental style used on Greek vases. All things begin with love.

———

9. In Greek mythology, when Coresus's love for Callirhoe went unreciprocated, Coresus prayed to Dionysus, who in turn struck the city with a collective madness that would end only when the gods had been appeased through the sacrifice of either Callirhoe or someone willing to die for her. Coresus was given the task of sacrificing Callirhoe, but when the moment arrived, his love was such that he killed himself in her place. At this, Callirhoe was overcome with regret and slit her own throat.

10. The name is left as Camus recorded it, though it's now believed the name was Butades. His daughter, Kora, is also sometimes known as Callirhoe, linking this entry with the earlier note about Coresus and Callirhoe.

In Corinth, two neighboring temples: the temple of violence and the temple of necessity.

———

Dimetos's love for his niece crossed the line, and she hanged herself.[11] One day, on a beach of fine sand, small waves washed the corpse of a stunning young woman ashore. Dimetos saw it and fell to his knees, madly in love. But then, watching the beautiful body decompose, he went mad. It was his niece's revenge, and the representation of a condition we should try to define.

———

At Pallantion, in Arcadia, the altar to the "Pure Gods."

———

I'm willing to die for her, P. says, but I hope she doesn't expect me to live for her, too.

———

September '39. War.

The sort of people who arrange to have a reputable doctor in Algiers perform an emergency surgery because they're afraid he'll be mobilized.

Gaston: "The most important thing is that I have an opportunity to get lucky before being mobilized."

On the train-station platform, a mother to a young reservist (thirty years old): "Be careful."

On the tram: "Poland's not gonna roll over."

"The 'Anti-Comintern Pact's a goner."[12]

"Hitler, you give him an inch, you'll be dropping your pants in no time."

At the market: "We'll have an answer Saturday, you know."

"Whose answer?"

"Hitler's answer."

---

11. The term *amour coupable*, literally "guilty love," is used here, as in Beaumarchais's final play, *La mère coupable*, to refer to an incestuous love, and though the Beaumarchais play has been translated into English as *The Guilty Mother*, the closest English equivalent for the French term may be "forbidden love." That said, given that "forbidden love" is often associated with the steamy paperback novel today, it has been avoided here.

12. The Anti-Comintern Pact was signed by Germany and Japan in 1936 as a sort of unofficial alliance against the Soviet Union (officially, as a means of defending against Communism). In August 1939, Germany began negotiating with the Soviet Union as part of the Molotov-Ribbentrop Pact, thus breaking the original pact with Japan.

"And then?"

"Then we'll know if we're going to war."

"Wouldn't that be a shame!"

At the train station, some reservists were hitting the employees: "Draft dodgers!"

War's broken out. Where is the war? Aside from the news reports you have to believe in and the posters you have to read, what sign of the absurd event do we see? It's not in this blue sky over that blue sea, in these screeching cicadas, in those cypress trees on the hills. It's not this youthful surge of light in the streets of Algiers.

We want to believe in it. We look for its face and it refuses to show itself. The world alone is king, its faces magnificent.

To have lived hating this beast, and to have it in front of us now yet not be able to recognize it. So little has changed. No doubt the mud, the blood, and an immense nausea will come later. But right now, the beginning of war feels similar to the start of peace: the world and the heart are unaware of them.[13]

... Remember these first days of a war that's so likely to be disastrous as days of prodigious happiness, odd and instructive fate ... I'm looking for a way to legitimize my rebellion, which has, so far, not been substantiated by anything that has happened.

There are those who are made to love and those who are made to live.[14]

We always exaggerate the importance of an individual life. Yet so many people don't know what to do with their life that it's not absolutely immoral to deprive them of it. On the other hand, everything takes on a new value.[15] But that's already been said. That this catastrophe is fundamentally absurd doesn't change anything about it, rather it generalizes the somewhat more

---

13. Camus told Roger Quilliot he'd originally intended to use this entry in *The Plague*. As the novel evolved, the entry no longer fit.

14. The rest of the page after this entry was left blank in the original notebook.

15. Taken in isolation, the thought appears incomplete, but in the context of the preceding entries, and in the rest of the entry to follow, what is really being said here is: *in the face of war* everything takes on a new value.

fundamental absurdity of life. It makes it more immediate and more relevant. If this war is to have any effect on humanity, it'll be in solidifying what we already believe about our existence and the way in which we judge it. From the moment this war "is," any judgment that fails to integrate it is false. A thinking man generally spends his time adapting the idea he's formed of things to the new facts that contradict it. It's in this slanting, in this warping of thought, in this conscious correction, that truth resides, which is to say in a lifetime's education. That's why, no matter how ignoble this war may be, we can't stand outside of it. Especially not me—someone who can risk his life, betting on death, without the least fear. And not all those who, anonymous and resigned, are heading toward this inexcusable slaughter—and with whom I feel true brotherhood.

———

A cold wind comes through the window.

Maman: "The weather's starting to change."

"Yes."

"Are they going to keep the lights dimmed throughout the war?"

"Yes, probably."

"It'll be a sad winter."

"Yes."[16]

———

They've all betrayed, those who pushed for resistance and those who spoke of peace. And they are, in this regard, just as docile, and even more guilty, than the others. Never has the individual been more alone in the face of the lie-making machine. But he can still feel contempt and use his contempt to fight. If he doesn't have the right to stand aside with his contempt, he still has the right to judge. Nothing can come from humanity, from the crowd. The betrayal was believing otherwise. We die alone. We're all going to die alone. At least let the man who is alone hold onto the power of his contempt and the ability to choose what in this awful ordeal serves his own greatness.

---

16. This dialogue occurs at the beginning of *The Plague*, part 2, section 7, where Rieux is speaking with his mother. In thinking about the evolution of the novel, it's of note that in this entry Mme Rieux asks about the war, whereas in the final version she asks about the plague.

In the handwritten notebook, this is the only entry on the page.

Accept the ordeal and all it entails. But in the least noble tasks, swear to perform only the most noble gestures. Nobility, at bottom (true nobility, nobility of the heart), is contempt, courage, and profound indifference.

———

To be made for creating, loving, and winning matches is to be made for living in times of peace. But war teaches us to lose everything and become what we weren't. Everything becomes a question of style.

———

I dreamed we entered Rome victorious. And I thought of the Barbarians entering the Eternal City. Only I was among the Barbarians.

———

Reconcile the work that describes and the work that explains. Give description its true meaning. When left on its own, description is admirable but carries nothing further. In which case, we only need to make it clear that such constraints were intentionally set. Like this, the constraints disappear and the work "resonates."

———

"On the one hand," the medically unfit man called before the medical board says, "it really pisses me off. On the other hand,[17] I've heard more than enough punning insinuations. 'You haven't left yet?' 'You're still here.' In our building, there are forty-four men. I was the only one who didn't go. So then, I'd come home late at night and leave early in the morning."[18]

———

The other reservist whose stomach they X-rayed:

"They made me drink at least three liters of barium chalk. I used to shit black, now I shit white. That's war."

———

September 7.

We wondered where the war was—wondered what was so ignoble about it. Now we realize that we know where it is, that it's inside of us—that it is, for most people, this embarrassment, this obligation to choose, that leads us to ship out while feeling remorse for not having been brave enough to abstain

17. Camus has drawn an arrow from this phrase to a line on the recto page (the September 7 entry below) that begins "while feeling remorse."

18. Camus had twice tried to enlist, in 1939 and 1940, but both times he was declared unfit for service on account of his health.

or that leads us to abstain with the regret of not having shared in death with the others.

That's where it is, where it really is, and we'd been looking for it in the blue sky and the world's indifference. It's in that awful solitude felt by combatant and noncombatant alike, in that humiliated hopelessness we all feel, in the shame that becomes clearer on our faces with each passing day. The reign of beasts has begun.

———

You can already feel the hatred and violence rising up in people. Nothing is pure in them anymore. Nothing sets them apart anymore. They think together. All you come across is beasts, bestial European faces. This world is nauseating: this universal rise of cowardice, this mockery of courage, this counterfeit grandeur, this degradation of honor.

———

It's shocking to see how easily some people's dignity crumbles. On second thought, it's only natural, seeing as the dignity in question is only maintained by an incessant effort against their own nature.

———

There's only a single inevitability, which is death, and beyond that nothing else is inevitable. In the span of time between birth and death, nothing is set in stone: we can change everything—we can even stop the war, we can even maintain the peace—if only we want it enough, want it so much and for so long.

———

Rule: look first for what is valuable in each person.

———

Cf. Groethuysen with regard to Dilthey: "So then, having recognized the fragmentary nature of our existence and what is accidental and limited in each life taken on its own, we'll look to the collectivity of lives for what we'll no longer find in ourselves."[19]

———

If it's true that the absurd has run its course (or rather, become evident), then it's true that no experience has value in and of itself, and that all actions are equally capable of teaching. The will is nothing. Acceptance, everything.

---

19. Bernard Groethuysen (1880–1946) was a French writer, philosopher, and Kafka specialist, whose preface to *The Trial* Camus cited in *The Myth of Sisyphus*. In February 1939, Camus wrote to Jean Grenier to say he'd almost finished an essay he was writing about Kafka. According to Christiane Galindo, Camus then sent the text to Jacques Heurgon, an editor at *Rivages*, who sent it

Provided that, in even the most humbling or heartrending experience, the individual remains always "present"—and bears the experience without giving up the fight, outfitted with all their lucidity.

It's always futile to try to disengage,[20] even if it's from other people's stupidity and cruelty. You can't say, "I don't know." You collaborate or you combat. Nothing is less excusable than war and the appeal to national hatreds. But once war arrives, it's futile and cowardly to try to stand apart from it on the pretext that you're not responsible for it. The ivory towers have fallen. Complacency is forbidden, your own and that of others.

Judging an event from the outside is impossible and immoral. It's by remaining within this absurd misfortune that you bear the right to look down on it.

An individual's reaction holds no importance in and of itself. It may serve some purpose but it justifies nothing. To want, by way of dilettantism, to glide above and stand apart from your environment is to make a mockery of freedom. That's why I had to try to serve. And if they don't want me, then I have to accept the role of disdained civilian. In either case, my judgment can remain absolute and my disgust unreserved. In either case, I am in the midst of the war and I have the right to judge it. To judge it and to act.

Accept. And, for example, see the good in the bad. If they don't want me for combat, it's because my role is always to stand at a remove. And it's from this struggle to remain an ordinary man amid exceptional circumstances that I've always drawn my greatest strength and my greatest usefulness.

Goethe (to Eckermann): "If I'd wanted to let myself go unchecked, I would be the only one responsible for thoroughly ruining myself and all those around me . . ."

---

to Groethuysen. The essay, "Hope and the Absurd in the Work of Franz Kafka," would eventually be published as an appendix to later editions of *The Myth of Sisyphus*.

The passage Camus cites here comes from Groethuysen's "Introduction à la philosophie allemande depuis Nietzsche."

20. In French, the term used here, *se désolidariser*, is clearly linked to *se solidariser* (show solidarity), an important concept for Camus.

The first thing is to learn to control yourself.[21]

About Goethe: "He is tolerant without being indulgent."

A Prometheus—as a revolutionary ideal. "Whatever doesn't kill me makes me stronger" (Nietzsche).

"The will to a system is a loss of loyalty" (*Twilight of the Idols*).[22]

"The tragic artist isn't a pessimist. He says yes to everything that is problematic and terrible" (*Twilight of the Idols*).[23]

What is war? Nothing. It makes no difference at all if you're a civilian or soldier, if you make it or fight it.[24]

Man as seen by Nietzsche (*Twilight of the Idols*).

"G. conceived a strong man, highly cultured, skillful in all areas of physical life, having clear control of himself, respecting his own individuality, able to risk fully enjoying the whole breadth of the natural world in all its richness, strong enough for freedom; a tolerant man, not out of weakness but out of strength, because he always knows how to reap the benefits of what would be a loss for the average person; a man for whom there is nothing, nothing any longer forbidden, except the least weakness, be it called vice or virtue. . . . Such a mind, liberated, appears at the center of the universe, in a happy and confident fatalism, with the faith that there is nothing reprehensible except that which lives in isolation, and that, on the whole, everything resolves and affirms itself. *He no longer denies . . .*"[25]

Overcome even this? I'll have to. But this endless effort is not without sadness. Couldn't we have at least been spared this? But even this weariness must be overcome. Nothing will be lost in doing so. One evening, as you

---

21. This comment is reported in *Conversations of Goethe*, vol. 2, in an entry dated March 21, 1830. John Oxenford's translation of the original German reads: "The most important thing is to learn to rule oneself. If I allowed myself to go on unchecked, I could easily ruin myself and all about me."

22. Richard Polt's translation of the German reads: "The will to a system is a lack of integrity." Nietzsche, *Twilight of the Idols*, trans. Richard Polt (Hackett, 1997), no. 26.

23. Polt's translation of the German reads: "Tragic artists are *not* pessimists—in fact, they say *yes* to everything questionable and terrible itself." Nietzsche, *Twilight of the Idols*, no. 6.

24. The rest of the page after this entry was left blank in the original notebook.

25. The above translation is from the French, as Camus recorded it. See Polt for a translation from the German.

approach the mirror, a slightly deeper crease will curl your lips. What is it? It's what I've made my happiness overcome.

That story about Jarry being asked on his deathbed what he wanted.[26] "A toothpick." He got it, put it in his mouth, and died satisfied. O, misery, we laugh about it and no one sees the terrible lesson. No more than a toothpick, nothing other than a toothpick, may as well be a toothpick—there you have all the value there is in this inspiring life.

"But the boy's very sick," the lieutenant said. "We can't take him." I'm 26 years old, I have a life, and I know what I want.

After so many others have already done so, Paulhan marvels in the N.R.F. that the war of 1939 didn't begin in the same climate as in '14.[27] Naive people who believed horror always wears the same face; naive people who can't see beyond the images on which they've lived.

Springtime in Paris: a chestnut bud, or the promise of one, and the heart skips a beat. In Algiers, the transition happens quicker. It's not one rosebud but a thousand rosebuds suddenly suffocating you one morning. And it's not a subtle quality of feeling that comes over you, but the enormous, innumerable influx of a thousand fragrances and a thousand brilliant colors. It's not the senses awakening, it's a body under assault.

November '39.

What we make war with:

1) with what everybody knows:

2) with the hopelessness of those who don't want to fight it;

3) with the self-esteem of those not forced to ship out but who ship out so as not to be alone;

4) with the hunger of those who enlist because they no longer have a job;

---

26. In *The Rebel*, in the section titled "The Rebel Poet," Camus gives a less upbeat assessment of Jarry, writing in a footnote: "Jarry, one of the masters of Dadaism, is the last incarnation of the metaphysical dandy—though more an oddity than a genius."

27. Jean Paulhan (1884–1968) was a French writer and the director of *Nouvelle revue française* during much of Camus's lifetime. During the war years, when the *NRF* became a collaborationist publication, Paulhan continued working for Gallimard—though no longer as director of *NRF*—while also secretly writing articles for *Résistance* slamming the *NRF* and its writers. Along with Pascal Pia, he played an instrumental role in getting *The Stranger* published by Gallimard.

5) with a lot of noble feelings such as:

a) solidarity in suffering

b) contempt that can't be expressed

c) absence of hatred

All of this is used in the basest of ways and all of this leads to death.

Death of Louis XVI. He asks the man leading him to the guillotine to deliver a letter to his wife. Response: "I'm not here to run your errands, I'm here to lead you to the scaffold."[28]

In Italian museums, the little painted screens the priest held in front of the condemned's face so they didn't see the scaffold.

The existential leap is the little screen.[29]

Letter to a Man without Hope.[30]

You write to me that you're overwhelmed by the war, and that you'd be willing to die, but that you can't bear the universal stupidity, the bloodthirsty cowardice, and the criminal naivety that still believes bloodshed can solve human problems.[31]

I read what you wrote and understand where you're coming from. I especially understand that conflict, that opposition, between your willingness to die and your disgust at seeing other people die. Such feelings prove a man's quality. They place him among those people with whom discussion is still possible. So then, how can we avoid hopelessness? The fate of those we love has too often been threatened—by sickness, by death, by madness—but we, and what we believe in, have still remained! The values we've built our life around have too often come close to collapsing. But never has the fate of those we love and the values we've built our life around been threatened in

---

28. Camus would use this entry as the opening sentence of his essay "Intelligence and the Scaffold," originally published in the July 1943 issue of *Confluences*, which featured work on the theme "Novel Problems."

29. An idea Camus would expand on in *The Myth of Sisyphus*, where he discusses the need to maintain an awareness of the inevitability of death, something, he says, "existentialist" thinkers who take a "leap of faith" do not do.

30. In the handwritten notebook, Camus wrote this entry over the course of four recto pages, seemingly going back to use the verso pages at a later point.

31. The form of this entry calls to mind Camus's *Letters to a German Friend*, while the content shares much in common with the journalism Camus produced for *Alger républicain* and *Le soir républicain*.

their entirety and all at once. Never have we been so totally delivered unto annihilation.

I understand where you're coming from, but I can't go along with you when you claim to fashion a code of conduct out of such hopelessness, and then, judging that everything is pointless, retreat behind your disgust. For hopelessness is a feeling and not a state of being. You can't remain inside of it. And a feeling has to give way to a clear view of things.

You say: "And anyway, what's to be done? And what can I do?" But you can't start out by putting the question like that. Of course, you still believe in the individual, because you feel the good in those around you, and in yourself, but there's nothing those individuals can do, and so you despair for society. But don't forget that you'd already repudiated that society long before the catastrophe came, that you and I both knew such a society would end in war, that you and I both denounced it, and, finally, that we both felt we shared nothing in common with it. That society is the same today. It's come to its natural conclusion. And in truth, if you look at things objectively, you have no more reason for hopelessness now than you had in 1928. Indeed, you have just as much.

Really, all things considered, those who waged war in 1914 had more reason to be hopeless because they understood things less clearly. But then you'll tell me that knowing 1928 was as hopeless as 1939 gets you nowhere. But it only appears that way at first, for you weren't totally without hope in 1928, whereas now everything seems futile to you. If things haven't changed, then it's your judgment of things that's wrong. It's like this every time a truth, rather than appearing to you in the light of reason, is embodied in the flesh. You foresaw the war but thought you could prevent it. That's what kept you from total hopelessness. Today, you don't think you can prevent anything anymore. Therein lies the crux of the reasoning.

But first you have to ask yourself if you really did everything that could be done to prevent the war. If you did, then it may seem to you as if war were inevitable and you may judge that there's nothing more to be done. But I'm sure you didn't really do everything that could be done, any more than the rest of us did. You couldn't have prevented it? No, that's not true. This war, as you know, wasn't inevitable. If the Treaty of Versailles had been revised in time, that would have been enough. But it wasn't. So, there you have it. You can see that things could have been different. And that treaty, or any other cause, can still be revised. What Hitler says, we can still ensure its irrelevant whether he sticks to it or not. All these injustices that have called forth further injustices, we can still reject them and ask that any response to them be rejected, too. There's still a useful task to be done. You assume your role as an individual is practically nonexistent. Then I'll reverse my previous reasoning and tell you that your role is neither greater nor lesser than it was in 1928. In any case, I know you're not so settled on this notion of pointlessness, for I don't believe you really approve of conscientious objection, and if you don't approve of it, it's not for lack of courage or admiration but because you believe it's pointless. So then, you've already formed an idea of a certain type of utility, which allows you to follow what I'm saying.

You have something to do, no doubt about it. Each of us has some zone of influence, owing to our faults as much as to our qualities. And whatever the case may be, within this zone, you have immediate utility. Don't incite anyone to rebellion. We have to be careful with the blood and freedom of others. But you can persuade 10, 20, 30 people that this war wasn't and isn't inevitable, that ways of stopping it that haven't yet been tried can be tried, that we must say this, write it out when we can, shout it out if that's what it takes. These 10 or 30 people will in turn tell ten others who will keep the process going. If laziness stops them, never mind that, start over with other people. And once you've done what you had to do in your zone, on your home turf, then you can stop and be as hopeless as you like. Understand that we can be hopeless about the meaning of life *in general,* as we have no power over life in general, but not about the specific forms it takes, in actuality, and not about history, where the individual is capable of anything. It's individuals who are killing us today. Why couldn't individuals also bring the world peace? We need only get started without thinking about such grand goals. We need to understand that war is waged as much with the enthusiasm of those who want it as with the hopelessness of those who repudiate it with all their soul.

———

A bit quoted by Green in his Journal:
"We mustn't be afraid of death—it does him too much honor."[32]

———

Green and his Journal.

32. Julien Green (1900–1998), born to American parents living in France, was a novelist and essayist who wrote primarily in French. He is perhaps most notably remembered for his nineteen-volume diary, in which he credits the above quote to Marie-Laure de Noailles. In an interview published in *The Paris Review* many years later, Ned Rorem, a friend of Green and Marie-Laure, describes her as being the opposite of Julien: "French, half-Jewish, unimaginably rich, Catholic but communist and a nonbeliever, odd-looking but forceful, like George Washington in a Dior gown."

Records a lot of dreams. Hearing about dreams always bores me.

Death of Le Poittevin, Flaubert's friend.[33]
"Close the window! It's too beautiful."

Bordeaux Cathedral. In one corner:
"Great Saint Paul, let me be among the first ten."
"Great Saint Paul, let him come for our meeting."

Montherlant uses a lovely quote from Monsignor Darbout as an epigraph for *Useless Service*: "Your mistake is in believing man was put on Earth to do something." And from this he draws some lovely, bitter lessons about heroism. But you could draw the exact opposite teachings from it and justify Diogenes or Ernest Renan. Only great thoughts are capable of such fruitful contradiction.[34]

Always struck by the "jokey" approach Algeria takes with things concerning death. That seems perfectly legitimate to me. You can't overemphasize the ridiculous nature of an event that usually takes place amid gurgles and sweat.

Compare with a quote attributed to French philosopher Théodore Jouffroy (1796–1842): "To be afraid of death does too much honor to life."

33. In his essay "The Minotaur, or, The Stop in Oran," Camus writes: "It seems the people of Oran are like that friend of Flaubert's who, as he died, gave a last look at the earth that would never again be, and cried out: 'Close the window, it's too beautiful.' They have closed the windows; they have walled themselves in; they have exorcised the landscape. But Le Poittevin died, and, after him, one day continued after the next."

Camus returns to Le Poittevin in *The Rebel*, in the section titled "The Dandies' Rebellion," where he quotes from the last stanza of Le Poittevin's poem "Satan," which reads:

Then you will descend upon your glorious throne;
The few scattered just receiving the crown
  For having put your law into practice;
But quivering with rage and cherishing their crimes,
The rest of humanity, writhing in the depths of despair,
Will come with me to curse you there

34. *Useless Service* (*Service inutile*) is a collection of essays by Montherlant, about which he wrote that "all of these writings say: 'I judge this to be good. I judge that to be bad.' So then, all of these writings seek to serve; that's what unties them. To the word *service*, which describes the character of these texts, it was essential to add *useless*. The soul says: service, and the mind as a whole: useless."

Though the quote is attributed to Monsignor Darbout, the correct attribution is to Georges Darboy, Archbishop of Paris, who was executed in 1871 as the Paris Commune reached its conclusion. Camus has also misquoted Darboy. The original quote, as cited by Montherlant, reads: "Your mistake is in believing man has anything to do with this life."

By the same token, you can't overly degrade the sacred aura with which we surround it. Nothing is more despicable than respect based on fear. In this regard, death is no more deserving of respect than the Emperor Nero or my local police chief.

———

Lawrence: "Tragedy ought really to be a great kick at misery." (Cf. his aristocratic communism.)[35]

Id. "The Revolution shouldn't be carried out to give power to a class but to give a chance to life."

———

M.[36] "Men are not my people. They're the ones who look at me and judge me; my people are the ones who love me and don't look at me, who love me despite it all, who love me despite loss, despite unworthiness, despite betrayal, who love me and not what I've done or will do, who would love me as much as I would love myself—up to and including suicide."

. . . "it's only with her (May) that I share this love, broken or not, as others have children together who are sick and may die."

———

Absurd characters.[37]

Caligula. The sword and the dagger.

---

35. The quote is from *The Letters of D. H. Lawrence*. It appears in a letter to A. W. McLeod dated October 6, 1912. It seems likely Camus read the letters in French, though there are differences between the quotes as recorded here and as they appeared in the French edition then available to Camus. The original English is given here, as the French isn't substantially different. The quote also appears in Camus's essay "The Almond Trees," written in 1940 and included in his 1954 collection *Summer*.

The second quote appears in a letter to Charles Wilson dated December 28, 1928. Unlike the previous quote, the French cited by Camus is quite different from the source, which reads: "It's time there was an *enormous* revolution—not to install soviets, but to give life itself a chance."

36. The "M." refers to Malraux. The two quotes that follow are from *Man's Fate*, which Camus was rereading at the time. In the second quote, May is the protagonist's wife, and this line occurs after he has learned she was unfaithful.

37. The plural "characters" would seem to indicate that, though this particular entry only covers Caligula, the entries that follow—about Ptolemy, Don Quixote, and La Palice—were also part of the "absurd characters." At the beginning of *The Myth of Sisyphus*, Camus writes: "About all the essential problems, by which I mean those that might lead to death or a tenfold increase in the passion for living, there are probably only two ways of thinking: Palice's and Don Quixote's. Only a balance between the obvious and the lyrical can allow us to access emotion and clarity at the same time. With a subject that's simultaneously so humble and so filled with pathos, the learned and classical dialectic has to then give way, you would think, to a more modest attitude of mind, which proceeds simultaneously from common sense and sympathy."

"I don't think they really understood me the other day when I knocked the priest out with that mallet he was about to use to slaughter the heifer. And yet, it was all very simple. For once, I wanted to change the order of things—just to see, really. And what I saw, well, it was that nothing changed. A little fear and amazement among the onlookers, but for all that, the sun set at the same time. So then, what I've concluded is that changing the order of things makes no difference."

But why shouldn't the sun one day rise in the West?

———

Id. (Ptolemy). I had him killed because there was no reason for him to go and make a prettier coat than mine. Absolutely no reason at all. Of course, there's no reason my cloak should be the prettiest one either. But he didn't know that, and as I was the only one who saw things clearly, it's only natural that I should be the one to benefit.

———

Don Quixote and La Palice.

La P: "A quarter of an hour before my death, I was still alive. That was enough to ensure my glory. But that glory was usurped. My true philosophy is that a quarter of an hour after my death, I will no longer be alive."

Dq: "Yes, I've tilted at windmills. For it makes no difference whatsoever if one tilts at windmills or at giants. So little difference that it's easy to confuse them. My metaphysics are shortsighted."

———

Vedas. What a man thinks, he becomes.

———

Gisèle and the war. "No, I don't read the papers. What I'm interested in is the weather. I'm going camping on Sunday."

———

"Do you know what I admire most in the world, Fontanes? The powerlessness of force to hold onto a thing. There are only two powers in the world: the sword and the mind. In the long run, the sword is always defeated by the mind." Napoleon.[38]

———

38. Camus would use Napoleon's famous remark at the beginning of his essay "The Almond Trees."

Louis XIV. "You're going to be a great king, my child. Don't take after me in my taste for war. Try to alleviate the suffering of your people . . . something I'm rather unhappy I was unable to do."

Oran.[39]

Le Tlélat as a preparation for Oran. Stripped and receptive before plunging into the senses, contemplative before descending into those delicious hells.

To get to Oran, you either have to travel by day or by night. During the day, I don't know. But going at night, I know you arrive in Sainte-Barbe-du-Tlélat in the early morning, after having passed the trembling eucalyptus trees in Perrégaux at an hour that's not yet day but no longer night. In Tlélat, there's a little train station with green shutters, a large clock . . .

. . . Now, Tlélat when it rains . . .

. . . Sainte-Barbe du Tlélat, you who are indifference, equivalence, and receptiveness, save us from hasty choices and leave us that indivisible freedom we call naked destitution. In a few minutes, we'll be in Oran, bearing the weight of a hopeless life of flesh. Santa-Cruz will be still and the streets of Mers-el-Kébir will smell of anisette. There we'll be served "Vieilles Cures" over crushed ice at Café Cintra—there will be the Oranian women whose ankles are a little thick and who always go bareheaded. Preserve these Oranian women, Sainte Barbe, until they should reach the threshold of old age, and then replace them with many other Oranians like them who will take walks beneath the trees of the old prefecture. O, Sainte Barbe, don't let the Oranians think of Algiers and Paris. Teach them the truth about the world, which is that it has none. You who are like that quay where we smoke a cigarette and dream, waiting for the whistle that will return you to being just another of the earth's landscapes, you know I'm not often religious, but if it happens that I be so, you know I have no need of God, that I can only be religious when I want to play at being so, because a train is about to head out and my prayer will have no tomorrow.[40] Sainte Barbe, you who are a point

39. Many of these notes on Oran would be used in "The Minotaur, or, The Stop in Oran" (Oued Tlélat, previously Sainte-Barbe-du-Tlélat, is an Algerian municipality about fifteen miles southeast of Oran), but readers can also see the beginnings of *The Plague* forming in the contrasting depictions of Oran as being at once an "indifferent" and an "extravagant" city.

40. In a previously unpublished notebook that Camus had left in Oran (see appendix II), the fifth page bears the title "No Tomorrows" (*Sans Lendemains*), plural, whereas when the title appears

in space on the Oran-Algiers line, closer to Oran, very close to Oran, and a stop in time that carries me toward Oran, you, so of the flesh and so precise, so terrestrial and cardinal, be for a few seconds a non-believer's saint and an innocent's counselor.

Oran. Extravagant city where shoe shops display awful plaster models of deformed feet, where gag novelties are displayed in storefronts side by side with tricolor wallets—where you can still find extraordinary cafés that have grime-varnished counters sprinkled with fly parts, a leg, a wing, and where you're served in chipped glasses. Happy cafés in a happy country where a small coffee costs 12 sous and a large 18. In an antique shop, an ignoble wooden sculpture of the virgin, her smile indecent, signed by a famous unknown. Beneath it, so as not to be missed, the proprietors have placed a sign: "Wooden virgin by Maya." The photographers' studios exhibit astonishing faces, from the Oranian sailor leaning an elbow on a console table to the poorly dressed girl-to-be-married standing before a sylvan backdrop, and on through Oran's authentic product, the handsome young man, hair slicked back, with a mouth like a trench made for passive defense.

An unparalleled, easygoing city with a parade of imperfect, touching girls, their faces without makeup, unable to feign an emotion, faking coquetry so poorly the trick immediately falls flat.

Café d'Apollon, Milo's, small bars, trams shaped like gondolas, 18th century pastels leaning against a mechanical stuffed donkey, eau de Provence for making green olives, florists' patriotic bouquets, Oran, the Chicago of our absurd Europe!

Santa-Cruz carved from the rock, the mountains, the flat sea, the violent wind and sun, the great cranes and gigantic ramps that climb the city's rock, the trams, the bridges and sheds—yet you can feel there's greatness here.

I've often heard Oranians complain about their city. "There's no interesting society life here!" Egad! You wouldn't want such a thing.[41] A certain sort of grandeur doesn't lend itself to elevation. It's sterile by nature. It holds a

---

in these pages, it's in the singular, "No Tomorrow."

41. These first lines are used verbatim (punctuation aside) in "The Minotaur, or, The Stop in Oran."

person before their condition. So then, forget about society life and go out into the streets. (But Oran isn't made for Oranians.)

———

Oran. Canastel.[42] The motionless sea at the foot of the red cliffs. Two massive, sleepy capes in the clear water. The soft sound of a motor lifting toward us. A coastguard boat imperceptibly advancing in the sparkling sea, bathed in a radiant light. An excess of indifference and beauty—the call of inhuman and glittering forces. On the plateau, exquisitely colored crocuses, their bodies nervous.

———

The bay in Mers-el-Kébir and the path beneath the flowering almond trees; the bay's perfect design—it's *average* size—the water like a plate of blue metal. Indifference.

Id. above the tile factory. Red and blue. Transparency of things. Indifference.

———

November

When Borgia is elected pope, a straw fire is lit in front of him three times, a reminder to this master of the world that the world's glory is something that passes.

He dispensed justice in an "admirable" way (Burchard).[43]

A Jewish medium had Innocent VIII drink breastmilk mixed with human blood.

Ferdinand of Naples embalmed the corpses of his tortured enemies to "decorate his apartments."

Alexander and Lucretia Borgia protected the Jews on all occasions. Alexander divided the world between the Spaniards and Portuguese by tracing a

42. When this was written, Oran was divided into eighteen areas, much like the arrondissements of Paris or the boroughs of New York City. The division of Oran has since changed, most recently in 2017, and Canastel is today known as El-Menzeh.

Parts of this entry would appear in *The Stranger*, part 1, section 6, where Camus writes: "Before we even reached the edge of the plateau, we could already see the motionless sea and, farther off, a massive, sleepy cape in the clear water. The soft sound of a motor rose toward us through the still air. And, far away, we saw a little trawler moving, imperceptibly, over the sparkling sea."

43. The commentary on the Italian Renaissance that follows is derived from Jean Burchard's *Journal*.

straight line from the Azores to the South Pole. The world's worth no more than that.

———

According to Burchard.

After the murder of the Duke of Gandia, his son.[44]

Alexander VI remained in a stupor, fiercely pained. He'd stared at the inert and bloody corpse, his eyes fixed—and then he locked himself in his room, where he could be heard sobbing.

Remained there from Thursday to Saturday without eating or drinking and didn't sleep until Sunday.

Cesare Borgia. Robust, had some "health mishaps," abscesses that kept him in bed, "funerary visons mixed with young glory." So would cut his work short to indulge urgent pleasures. Slept through the day—worked through the night.

"Aut Caesar aut nihil."[45]

———

NOVEMBER 29. Novel. He doesn't accomplish anything and won't accomplish anything because he spreads himself thin, because he doesn't know how to choose among his obligations, and because a person only creates a work of art if . . .

He is explained entirely by his habits. His deadliest habit: staying in bed. It's stronger than he is. Yet what he wants to become, what he dreams of, what he admires is just the opposite. He wants a work born from the opposite of habit—the resolutions he makes.

———

November 29.

The exaltation of diversity, of quantity, of, in particular, the life of the senses and the surrender to deep stirrings, is only legitimate if you can demonstrate your disinterestedness with regard to the object.

There's also the leap into the material—and many men who exalt the senses do so only because they're enslaved by them. Here, too, they're kissing the vulture.

44. Juan Borgia, the second duke of Gandia and son of Pope Alexander VI, was assassinated in June of 1497, at which point his son took over as duke.

45. Literally, "Caesar or nothing," but in colloquial usage, "All or nothing."

That's why it's absolutely necessary to have tested, for example, chastity, to have treated yourself rigorously. Before any theoretical undertaking aimed at the glorification of the immediate, impose *a month* of asceticism, in all senses.

Sexual chastity.

Mental chastity—forbidding desires to go astray, thoughts from wandering.

A single subject—constant—for meditation—refuse the rest.

Work at a set time, without stopping, without failure, etc., etc. (moral asceticism also).

A single failure and it all falls apart = practice and theory.

In Ferrara, the palace of Schifanoia is built by Alberto d'Este to "dodge boredom."

The Estes.

Ippolito had his brother Giulio's eyes gouged out because the woman he loved said she "preferred Giulio's eyes to Ippolito's body."

Giulio and Ferrante wanted to assassinate Ippolito and Alfonso d'Este. Found out, sentenced to death, sadistically pardoned while on the scaffold. 35 years in the dungeon for Ferrante, who dies there, 54 for Giulio, who has gone mad by the time he gets out.

Alfonso d'Este has a statue of Jules II by Michelangelo melted and made into a cannon.

Cf. Gonzague Truc. "They built only for themselves and, failing to step aside and let the work itself shine through, failing to humbly situate it among the world's mysterious works (?), failing to nourish it on eternal values (?), they condemned it to disappear as soon as it was born. Of themselves, all that remained were their haughty and cursed names." *Precisely.*[46]

Borgia Bibliography.

Louis de Villefosse (*Machiavel et nous*, 1937).

---

46. It seems Camus may have been reading Truc's *Rome et les Borgia*, which was published in 1939 and which won the 1940 Prix Alfred-Née, then given by the Académie-Française. Of note is the strong similarity between the quote cited here and a bit of Camus's own short story "Pride," which remained unpublished during Camus's lifetime, and which, as a result, is hard to date. In the story, Camus writes: "It's all well and good to build, but it's wrong to want to deify man's name. I'm delighted every time I see a beautiful man-made work without a signature, made for the thing itself and not for its author."

Rafaël Sabatini (*César Borgia*, 37).
Fred Bérence (*Lucrèce Borgia*, 37).
Gab. Brunet (*Ombres vivantes*, 36).
L. Collison-Morley (*Histoire des Borgia*).
Charles Benoist (*Machiavel*).
Le *Journal* de Jean Burchard (ed. Turmel, 1933), etc. etc.

———

1940.

Evenings on the Deux Merveilles' terrace. A swaying sea that can only be felt in the hollow of night. Trembling olive trees and the scent of smoke rising from the earth.

Rocks in the sea covered with white seagulls, their gray mass lit up by the whiteness of their wings, floating out there like luminous cemeteries.

———

Novel.

The story begins on a burning, blue beach, with the brown bodies of two young people—swimming, playing in the sun and water—summer evenings on beach roads, the scent of fruit and smoke in the shade—the body relaxing in lightweight clothes. The attraction, the secret and tender drunkenness, in a heart at seventeen.

—Ends in Paris with the cold or gray sky, the pigeons among the Palais-Royal's black stones, the city and its lights, the hurried kisses, the irritating and unnerving tenderness, the wisdom and desire that rises up in the heart of a man at twenty-four—the "let's keep in touch."

Id. The other story began on a cold and stormy night, back against the ground, surrounded by cypresses, beneath a sky streaked with stars and clouds;

—continued on the hills of Algiers or in front of the wide and mysterious harbor.

—the destitute, magnificent Casbah, the El-Kettar cemetery spilling all its tombstones toward the sea, warm, soft lips between the pomegranate flowers and a tombstone—trees, hillsides, climbing toward the parched and pure Bouzaréah, and, turning toward the sea, the taste of lips and eyes filled with sunlight.

It doesn't begin with love but with a desire to live. Love. Is it so far away when, in the large square house above the sea, after having climbed up through the wind, two bodies come together and hold each other close while, from deep down at the horizon, the sea's muffled breathing reaches up to them in that room isolated from the world? Wonderful evening where love's hope is inseparable from the rain, the sky, the earth's silences. The perfect balance of two beings physically united, mirroring each other in their shared indifference to everything that isn't this one moment in time.

The other moment is like a dance, she in a stylish dress, he done up like a dancer.

The first almond trees to flower along the road, facing the sea. All it takes is a single night, and like that they're covered in a fragile snow that you can hardly imagine resisting the cold and rain that will come to soak their petals.

In the trolleybus.

An old lady who has a madam's face but who wears a cross between nonexistent breasts:

"Respectable women know how to control themselves. Not like those women who use the war to their advantage. Their husband's away, they get the pension, and then they go and cheat on him. Listen, this one woman I know, she says to me, 'He may as well die at the front. He was a nasty piece of work before the war, and the war's not about to change anything.' So then, I tried to tell her, 'Now that he's at the front, you have to forgive him,' but it was no use. Well, you see, Monsieur, that's how bad women are. It's in their blood, it's in their blood, I tell you, it's in their blood."

February.

Oran. From as far off as Valmy, from inside the train, the Santa-Cruz mountain can be seen, its deep notch in the ground, the cathedral itself like a stone finger drawn up in the blue sky.

You have to try getting your shoes shined at 10 in the morning on the corner of Boulevard Gallieni. A cool breeze, bright sun, men and women rushing about, and, perched up high in that chair, the extraordinary contentment you feel watching the bootblacks work. Everything is carried out with the greatest care and most exacting detail. At a certain point, seeing them apply the soft brushes, noticing that ultimate gleam, you may think the impressive process is winding down. Then that same ferociously determined hand passes the wax once more over the gleaming surface, dulls it, scrubs it, presses the wax into the depths of the hide and makes a second, truly ultimate shine burst forth from beneath the brush, from deep inside the leather.

———

The Maison du Colon simultaneously expresses a metaphysic, a moral, and an aesthetic. A layered cake topped with an Egyptian Pschent.[47] A curious mosaic, and who knows why it's done in the Byzantine style, with charming nurses wearing sandals carrying straw baskets filled with grapes while an entire cortege of slaves dressed in ancient clothing rush over to a graceful colonist wearing a pith helmet and bow tie.

———

The Rue d'Austerlitz and its century-old Jews. Each action: a small theatrical scene.

———

Tailors like Marie-Christine are "not only fashionable but always up to date." Laxatives "are only a last resort. Compelling a bowel movement doesn't fix the problem."[48]

———

From the top of the coastal road, the cliffs are so massive that, by its very nature, the landscape becomes surreal. Humanity is so completely cast out of it that such an immense load of beauty seems to come from another world.

———

Place de la Perle, a little square where children play at 2:00 in the afternoon. A mosque, some minarets and benches, and a little bit of sky. A tinny voice from the Spanish radio. It's not the hour at hand that I like here but

---

47. The French *pièce montée* (layered cake) refers to an elaborate confectionary that's sometimes seen as not only a pastry-baking feat but also an architectural feat. In the early 1800s, Marie-Antoine Carême, one of the first famous haute cuisine chefs, said, "There are five fine arts: painting, sculpture, poetry, music, and architecture, the main branch of which is pastry work." Today, the term is largely associated with the dessert known as croquembouche.

A Pschent was a crown worn by a pharaoh who ruled over both Upper and Lower Egypt.

48. In the handwritten notebook, the first quote is in English and was likely copied out of a newspaper, while the second quote is a word-for-word transcription of a French newspaper advertisement for "Petites Pilules Carters." Camus liked cutting humorous ads from the paper, a habit he first gave to Mersault in *The Happy Death*, part 1, chap. 2, where he writes: "When he went back upstairs, he did two crosswords, carefully cut out an ad for Kruschen salts, and then glued it in a notebook already filled with funny old grandfathers sliding down banisters." Camus would give the same habit to Meursault in *The Stranger*, part 1, chap. 2: "I cut out an ad for Kruschen salts and glued it in an old notebook where I keep things from the paper that amuse me."

the one I imagine, the summer sky emptied of its warmth, the small square softening in the evening, the soldiers and women circling around it as the scent of anisette draws the men to the bars.

Women's novel. A single theme: sincerity.

"O, my soul, don't aspire to immortality but exhaust all the possible" (Pindar—*Pythian 3*).[49]

Characters.

The old man and his dog. Eight years of hatred.

The other and his verbal tics: "He was charming. I'll go one better. Pleasant."

"A deafening noise. I'll go one better. Thunderous."

"It's eternal. I'll go one better. Human." A.T.R.[50]

A morning in the sun, bodies naked. Shower, then light and heat.

February.

This Florentine face that speaks of love and its painful past. How much of it's an act? How much of it's genuine emotion, so great, so overwhelming at certain moments, so tenuous at others?

Maria—like the soul of Paris. This morning in the sun, the city full of lights—her eyes like the city and this easygoing life.

"O dolore dei tuoi martiri,

---

49. Camus would use Aimé Puech's French translation of the quote as the epigraph for *The Myth of Sisyphus*. L. Faucon, editor of the first Pléiade edition of *The Myth of Sisyphus*, points out that Paul Valéry had previously used the quote as an epigraph for *Le cimetière marin*, though he'd used it in the original Greek.

50. The two characters indicated here are Salamano and Masson from *The Stranger*. It seems the latter's manner of speaking may have been based on André Thomas-Rouault, a painter and merchant who often contested Camus's leadership of the Théâtre du Travail. In *The Stranger*, Camus describes Masson as follows: "He spoke slowly, and I noticed he was in the habit of finishing everything he said with 'and I'll go one better,' even when, really, it didn't add any more meaning to what he was saying. Talking about Marie, he said to me, 'She's stunning, and I'll go one better, charming, too.' After that, I didn't pay any attention to the tic, because I was too busy experiencing how good the sun felt.'"

O diletto del tuo amore."[51]

"It's not love she represents but a chance to live—everything that's not exile, everything that consents to life. And never has a chance to live had such a moving face. Who can be sure of their love? But everyone knows how to recognize the feeling. This song, that face, this deep and supple voice, that clever and free life, that's all I hope for, all I expect. And if I give them up, they nevertheless remain as so many promises of freedom, as that image of myself that I can't let go of."

———

March.[52]

What does this sudden awakening mean—in this dark room—amid the sounds of a city that's all at once become strange? Everything is strange to me,[53] everything, without anyone who belongs to me, without anyplace to heal this wound. What am I doing here, what rhyme or reason is there for these gestures, these smiles? I'm not from here—not from anywhere else, either. And the world is now but an unknown landscape where my heart no longer finds its bearings. Stranger—who can know what the word means?

———

Stranger, admit that everything is strange to me.

Now that it's all clear, wait and spare nothing. Work in such a way as to at least hone silence and creation. For all the rest, for all the rest, whatever happens, happens.

———

51. Roughly: "O sorrow of your martyrs, O pleasure of your love."

52. In mid-March 1940, Camus moved to Paris to take a job as an assistant editor with the newspaper *Paris-soir*. He started out renting a room at the Hôtel du Poirier, 16 Rue Ravignan, Montmartre.

53. This entry, which brings out both the mood and title of *L'Étranger*, also exemplifies some of the challenges in translating the title. An American traveling to France to meet an old friend would say, for example, that she is "going abroad" (*aller à l'étranger*), which is to say that she is going to "a foreign country" (*un pays étranger*). Technically, then, her friend is, to her, a "foreigner" (*étranger*), but her friend is certainly not a "stranger" (*étranger*), nor is she necessarily "a strange person" (*une personne étrangère*). As with so much of translation, then, context is key. Yet with Camus's single-word title, *L'Étranger*, there is no immediate context, leaving any translation to depend on a given translator's interpretation of the novel as a whole, at which point personal experience, geography, language variant, and other factors come into play. That said, the French phrase *quelqu'un de l'extérieur* is used to make it clear that a person is from another community, which is to say "an outsider," though given the context of Camus's sudden move to Paris, a strong argument could be made that the word is used in this entry, as well as in the novel's title, with the meaning "foreign" and "foreigner."

Evening: Events. Characters. Personal reactions.

Trouville. An asphodel-filled plateau facing the sea. Small villas with green or white fences, with verandas, some of them buried beneath the salt cedars, some standing naked amid the stones.[54] Down below, the sea softly rumbles. Yet the sun, the light wind, the whiteness of the asphodels, the already steel-blue sky, all of it conjures the summer, its golden youth, its brown girls and boys, the blossoming passions, the long hours in the sun and the sudden mildness of its evenings. What other meaning can be found in our days beyond the one found here, the lesson of this plateau: a birth, a death, and between the two, beauty and melancholy.

R.C. One of those guys who feels the need to slip off to the bathroom unseen. But then they have to go and make a theory out of it: man's greatness lies in his ability to smell what brings him down a notch.[55] And just like that, it's the rest of us who are disgusted.

S. wants to write a diary for a novel that its author didn't write.

More and more often, when faced with the world of man, the only reaction is individualism. Man is his own end, in and of himself. Everything we try to do for the common good ends in failure. Even if we want to try anyway, we should do so with the appropriate level of contempt. Withdraw completely and run your own race.[56]

The man receives a letter from his lover's husband. In the letter, the husband declares his love and says he'd like to speak directly to his rival before giving in to his anger. It's the anger that the man fears. That's why he admires the

54. Camus would use this part of the entry in *The Stranger*, part 1, section 6, immediately preceding the description given a few pages back, in the entry on Canastel: "[The plateau] was covered in yellowish stones and pure white asphodels set against an already steel-blue sky. Marie was having fun scattering the petals with great swoops of her oilskin bag. We walked between rows of small villas with green or white fences, some of their verandas buried beneath the salt cedars, some standing naked amid the stones."

55. Camus is indulging in a little wordplay here. This passage could also be read as "his ability to sense what diminishes him."

56. In the original notebook, Camus wrote "IDIOT" over this entry in bold red letters. Interestingly, in 1933, seven years before this entry was made, Camus wrote an essay titled "Art in Communion," in which he said of Paul Claudel: "He understood that man is nothing in and of himself and that he must give himself to something higher."

husband's show of generosity. The more afraid he is, the more he says so. He emphasizes it. So then, he gets to play the good guy. He'll give it all up, solely in recognition of this show of generosity, he'll sacrifice himself—without so much as a word—as he's so much less worthy. All of this, he actually believes, at least in part. But let's not forget the part played by his fear of being hit.

———

A dog in the villa. S. takes it in, despite his mother. The dog steals two anchovies. The mother chases after it and the dog runs away, terrified, while S. says: "Come back, come back. Don't be scared."

Afterward:

S. "That poor dog. He'd already begun to believe in heaven."
The mother: "I did, too. I believed in heavens and I've never seen any of them, not once in my whole life."
S. "Yes, but he'd already passed through the gates."[57]

———

Descending to the sea from above Mers-el-Kébir. The line of hills and cliffs surrounding the bay. Heart walled up.

———

Marseille. The circus freak: "Life? Nothingness? Illusions? But the truth all the same." Bass drum. Boom, boom, enter into Nothingness.

———

At the dawn of modern times: all is consummated?[58] Okay, then let's start living.

———

Paris, March 1940

What's loathsome in Paris: the endearment, the sentiment, the hideous sentimentality that sees what's beautiful as pretty and what's pretty as beautiful. The endearment and hopelessness of these cloud-smudged skies, of these gleaming roofs, of this endless rain.

In French, the final phrase extends Camus's use of the word "play." A more literal translation of *et jouer son jeu* might read "and play your own game."

57. The timing of this entry, the initial S., and the mention of the dog all bring *The Stranger*'s Salamano to mind.

58. Perhaps a reference to Heidegger's claim that Nietzsche was "the consummation of metaphysics," as well as, given the entry that follows, a reference to John 19. A less formal rendering might be "everything has run its course."

What's exhilarating: the terrible solitude. As a remedy for life in society: the big city. It's the only feasible desert these days. The body no longer holds a special place here. It's covered up, hidden beneath shapeless skins. There's nothing but the soul, the soul with all its excesses, it's drunkenness, its tearful, emotional intemperance, and all the rest. But the soul with its sole greatness, too: silent solitude. When you see Paris from the top of the Butte, a monstrous bed of steam beneath the rain, a formless, gray swelling of the earth, if you turn toward the Calvary of Saint-Pierre de Montmartre,[59] you can feel the kinship between a country, an art, and a religion. Every line of these shuddering stones, every crucified or flagellated body, permeates the soul with the same distraught and defiled emotion as the city itself.

On the other hand, though, the soul's never right, and even less here than in other places, for the most splendid faces given to this religion so preoccupied with the soul are carved in stone, in the image of the flesh. If this god touches you, he does so through a human face. A curious limitation of the human condition is its inability to get past the human, its need to give the likeness of the body to those of its symbols that wish to deny the body. They do deny it, but it gives them their special place. Only the body is generous. This Roman legionary, we feel he's alive on account of that extraordinary nose or that bulging back, this Pilate on account of the ostentatious expression of boredom the stone has for centuries preserved on his face.

In this regard, Christianity understands how things stand. If, previously, it made a deep impression on us, it did so by making God a man. But his truth and his greatness stop at the cross, at the moment he cries out that he's been forsaken. Let's tear the last pages of the Gospel out and, there, a humane religion, a cult of solitude and grandeur, will be offered to us. Its bitterness, of course, makes it unbearable. But in this is its truth and the lie of all the rest.

This is where knowing how to live alone in a poor man's room in Paris for a year teaches you more than a hundred literary salons and forty years' experience of "Parisian life." It's a tough, awful, sometimes torturous thing, and always so close to madness, but it's in this arena that a man's quality must be forged and established—or perish. But if it should perish, it'll be because it wasn't strong enough to live.

———

59. Saint-Pierre de Montmartre is one of the oldest churches in Paris, having been consecrated in 1147, while the Calvary Cemetery alongside it is one of the smallest in Paris.

Eisenstein and the Mexican Festival of the Dead.[60] Macabre masks to amuse the children, sugar skulls they nibble with delight. The children laugh along with death. They find it cheerful. They find it gentle and sweet. Also, the "dead pups." Everything ends with "Our friend Death."

———

Paris.

The woman on the floor above committed suicide by throwing herself out onto the hotel courtyard. She was 31 years old, one of the tenants said, which is enough to have lived, and, if she'd lived a little, to die. The shadow of the drama still hangs over the hotel. Sometimes, she'd go down and ask the proprietress to save her a place at dinner. She'd suddenly embrace the woman—out of a need for contact and warmth. It ended with a six-centimeter split in her forehead. Before dying, she said: "At last!"

———

Paris. Black trees in a gray sky with sky-colored pigeons. The statues in the grass and this melancholy elegance . . .

A flight of pigeons snapping like laundry on a line. Cooing in the green grass.

Paris. The small cafés at 5:00 in the morning—condensation on the windows—coffee boiling—the people who work in Les Halles and the deliverymen—a little drink in the morning, Beaujolais.

La Chapelle. Haze—elevated tracks and lampposts.[61]

———

Léger. This intellect—this metaphysical painting that rethinks the material. Curious: as soon as you rethink the material, the only permanent thing is precisely the thing that made it *appear* as it did: color.[62]

———

60. The history of the film that would become known as *¡Que viva México!* is long and circuitous, but, given the date of this entry, it's likely Camus is referring to *Time in the Sun*, Marie Seton's 1939 version of the film, which she put together using Eisenstein's raw footage. Seton, an actress and film critic, was a close friend of Eisenstein's, as well as his biographer. The film ends with the celebration of the Day of the Dead.

61. During Camus's lifetime, Les Halles was still Paris's central food market, or, as Émile Zola dubbed it, "The Belly of Paris." La Chapelle is a Métro station to the north (and just slightly east) of Les Halles.

62. In *The Myth of Sisyphus*, Camus clarifies this entry about French painter Fernand Léger when he writes: "It's curious to see that the most intellectual types of painting, the kind that seek to reduce reality to its essential elements, are only, when all is said and done, a visual delight. The only thing they hold onto is the world's color. (This is especially noticeable in Léger.)" In 1953, on the occasion of a hardback reprinting of the book, Camus would review and revise the manuscript, at which point

The guy at the brasserie who hears a lady phoning, calling his name and number. *He* picks up the phone and answers. She speaks to *him* as if he were there (family, specific details, etc.). He doesn't understand. That's how it goes.

———

No Tomorrow

"The works J.M. is referring to here were burned, but it's clear he could just as well have published them and that there would have been nothing but indifference or contradiction, which amounts to the same thing." *N.T.*[63]

To provide punctuation and space to breathe, take note throughout my life. "Today, I'm 27 years old," etc.

Create a system of notes made by a commentator (or a preface summing things up).[64]

———

The little Spanish soldier at the restaurant. Not a word of French when he speaks to me but a desire for human warmth. Peasant from Extremadura, Republican fighter, Camp de concentration d'Argelès, joined the French army.[65] When he pronounces the name Spain, its wide-open sky fills his eyes. He on a week's leave. He came to Paris, which crushed him within only a couple of hours. Without a word of French, wandering through the Métro, a stranger, a stranger to everything that isn't his land, he'd be happy if he could find his friends from the regiment again. Then, even if he has to die under a low sky, in a thick sludge, at least it'll be side by side with the men of his country. ~~This city is a serious maneater.~~

———

he removed the reference to Léger. This final version of *The Myth of Sisyphus* has not appeared in English.

63. The N.T. written here (S.L. in French) likely stands for "No Tomorrow" (*Sans Lendemain*), but it's unclear to whom J.M. refers. One possibility is John Stuart Mill, who let Carlyle's book be burned. Another possibility is J. M. Querard, writer of *La France littéraire*, with the reference being to Jeanne de Valois-Saint-Rémy's memoir, which was burned during the Revolution.

64. Camus drew an arrow from this last sentence to the word "indifference" in the first paragraph.

65. The Camp de concentration d'Argelès-sur-Mer was set up in February 1939 to hold Spanish Republicans, both civilians and soldiers, fleeing the end of the Spanish Civil War. The exodus, known as *La Retirada* (the retreat), saw more than 450,000 Spaniards cross the border from Spain into France. The French government's main concern was controlling, rather than aiding, the refugees, and the conditions in the camps, complete with barbed wire and armed guards, was despicable. When the Germans occupied France, many of the refugees were executed, some in the Nazi gas chambers. Despite the haunting treatment they received, a good number of Spanish refugees would go on to join the French Resistance.

The last line of the entry is crossed out on the typescript.

April.

In The Hague. A man lives in a pension not knowing it's a brothel. Never anyone in the dining room. He comes down in his bathrobe. A gentleman in a jacket and top hat enters. He's stiff, meticulous, and Black. He asks to have a very good meal. The dove in the dining room coos. Then the man withdraws, leaving payment for the price of the meal on the table. Sudden silence. The waiter returns and begins to panic. The Black man carried the dove off beneath his opera hat.

Novel (Part 2—consequences).

The man (J.C.) has set a certain day to die—fairly soon. His astonishing and immediate advantage over all social and other such forces.

The little soldier in the Métro. About forty years old. Wants to arrange a tryst with a fairly young girl. "Perhaps I could come to see you if I were passing by your way one of these days."

"No, my brother would have it out with me."

"Oh, yes, obviously, that's only natural, you're right. But maybe I could write to you then?"

"No, I'd rather just have a fling with you."

He's flustered by her direct acquiescence to the thing he was trying to approach in a more roundabout way. "Oh, well, right, right. Yes, you're right, absolutely right, that's much better. Well, let's see then. Tomorrow's Monday. Yes, Monday. Let's see. Around what time? I'm trying to think it through, because, you know, in these matters . . . Let's see, yes, tomorrow's Monday. Well, how about 5 o'clock?"

She (still direct): "Can't you do it after dinner?"

He (still flustered): "But of course, of course, you're right as usual."

She: "At 8 o'clock."

He: "Yes, yes, at 8 o'clock. At Terrasse, if that works for you?"

She: "Yes."

He goes quiet. But then, suddenly, he panics, not wanting to let on why. He has to make sure such an easy and precious opportunity for an affair doesn't slip away. "And if something should come up, I could write to you?"

"No, I'd prefer not."

"Well, then, we could set up another rendezvous, in case something should come up."

"Okay, Thursday at 8 o'clock at the same place."

He's happy for a second, but then suddenly worries this new rendezvous will somehow make tomorrow's seem less important. "Tomorrow, though, at 8 o'clock, for sure, right? The other's only in case of a mishap."

"Yes," she says.

She gets off at Concorde and he at Saint-Lazare.

———

A painter goes to Port-Cros to paint. Everything's so beautiful there he buys a house, puts away his canvases, and never touches them again.[66]

———

Can feel Paris's beating heart at *Paris-soir*, its wretched midinette mentality. They've turned Mimi's garret into a skyscraper, but it's still the same at heart.[67] Rotten. The sentimentality, the picturesque, the complacency, all those slimy places a person takes refuge to protect themselves in a city that's so hard on them.

———

You wouldn't write so much about solitude if you knew how to make the most of it.

———

"I am," he said, "an olfactory man, and there's no art addressed to that sense. There's only life."

———

Short Story. A priest happy with his lot in the Provençal countryside. By chance, attends to a condemned man in his last moments. Loses his faith as a result.

———

April.

Preface for Terracini[68]

---

66. Port-Cros is a small island in the Mediterranean, one of the four islands collectively known as the Îles d'Hyères. During Camus's lifetime, it was privately owned, but shortly after his death it was willed to France on the condition that a national park be established there.

67. *Midinette*, originally a term for a Parisian shopgirl, is often used pejoratively to refer to a starry-eyed, fashion-conscious person who tends not to think about things very deeply.

"Mimi's garret" is a reference to *La bohème*.

68. Jeanne Terracini was a friend of Camus's from Algiers. At the time of this entry, she lived in Paris, and Camus often visited her. She would go on to become a literary translator, working on books by Arthur Koestler, such as *The Yogi and the Commissar*. In 1940, she translated a book by her husband, Enrico, *D'un soir, d'un pays lointain*, which this entry seems to reference.

"... Many of us also feel this sense of exile as nostalgia. The lands of Italy and Spain have formed so many European souls that they also in some small way belong to Europe, to that Europe of the mind that will prevail over all those that are forged by weapons. In this, perhaps, lies the importance of these pages. These current events were already current 200 years ago. They still are today. But we must not lose hope—they'll still be alive and full of youth the day the flowers are finally reborn atop the ruins."

2nd cycle. For Don Juan. See Larousse: the Franciscan monks killed him and made it look as if he were struck down by the Commander. Final act. The Franciscans' speech to the people: "Don Juan has been converted," etc. "Glory to Don Juan."

Penultimate act: challenges the Commander, who doesn't show. Bitterness of being right.[69]

2nd cycle. For Don Juan.

(The Father and Don Juan enter Don Juan's vestibule and he escorts the monk to the door.)

Beginning of 1st.

The Franciscan Father: "So then, Don Juan, you believe in nothing?"

Don Juan: "No, Father. In three things."

The Father: "Might we know what they are?"

Don Juan: "I believe in courage, in intelligence, and in women."

The Father: "Then we have no choice but to see you as hopeless."

Don Juan: "Yes, if you must feel sorry for a happy man. See you later, Father."

The Father (at the door): "I'll pray for you, Don Juan."

---

69. From an early age, Camus envisioned writing a play about Don Juan—initially as part of his second cycle of works—making it a curious fact that no such play was ever written. One possible explanation may be derived from this entry, where some of what is planned for the Don Juan play would show up in other works that Camus did complete. For example, this last line would be turned into a bit of dialogue spoken by Caligula at the beginning of act 4, scene 14: "You can clearly see Helicon hasn't come, and I will not be getting the moon. But how bitter it is to be right and to have to follow things through to their logical conclusion." Of course, Camus would also incorporate much of his research on Don Juan into *The Myth of Sisyphus*, where Don Juan is studied as one of the "Absurd Men" and where the same line that appears in this entry and in *Caligula* also appears: "Above all else, I believe that the evening Don Juan waited at Anna's, the commander didn't show up, and that the impious one must have felt, as midnight came and went, the terrible bitterness of those who've been right."

Don Juan: "I appreciate that, Father. I'd like to think of it as a form of courage."

The Father (gently): "No, Don Juan, it's two feelings you insist on ignoring: charity and love."

Don Juan: "I understand only tenderness and generosity, the masculine forms of those feminine virtues. In any case, goodbye, Father."

The Father: "Goodbye, Don Juan."

———

May.

The Stranger is finished.[70]

———

The Misanthrope is worthy of admiration, with its crude contrasts and set character types.

Alceste and Philinte

Célimène and Éliante

Alceste's monotony—the absurd consequence of an individual's character taken to extremes—which is the whole point. And the verse, "the bad verse," which is barely punctuated, has the same monotony as the individual's character.[71]

———

Exodus.[72]

Clermont. The insane asylum and its strange clock. Messy early mornings at 5:00 A.M. The blind people—the mental patient who lives on the hall and screams all day long—a scaled down version of this earth of ours. The entire body turned toward two poles, the sea or Paris. It's in Clermont you can begin to understand Paris.

———

70. In the early morning hours of May 1, Camus signed the final handwritten page of *The Stranger*, adding: "Paris, May 1940."

71. In *The Myth of Sisyphus*, in a footnote in the section on drama, Camus writes: "Here I'm thinking of Molière's Alceste. Everything is so simple, so obvious, and so crude. Alceste against Philinte, Célimène against Éliante, it's all about the absurd consequence of an individual's character taken to the extreme, and the verse itself, the 'bad verse,' barely punctuated, monotonous as the individual's character."

72. In June 1940, the German advance forced *Paris-soir*, and thus Camus, to move to Clermont-Ferrand, then to Bordeaux, then back to Clermont-Ferrand, and finally on to Lyon, where Camus would get married, lose his job, and then move back to Oran with his new wife.

September.

Finished Part I of the Absurd.[73]

The man who razes his house, burns his fields, and then covers them with salt so no one else can use them.

———

Little man from Banque de France. Transferred to Clermont, tries to keep up the same routines. Almost succeeds in doing so—but there's an imperceptible shift.

———

October 1940. Lyon.

Saint Thomas (himself Frédéric's subject) recognized the subject's right to rebel. Cf. Baumann: *Politique de saint Thomas*, p. 136.

———

The last Carrara, a prisoner in Padua—ravaged by the plague, besieged by the Venetians—roamed the halls of his palace screaming: he called out to the devil, asking him for death.[74]

In Siena, there's no question a condottiere saved the city. He asks for everything. The people reason: "Nothing will ever be enough to repay him, not even absolute power. Let's kill him. Then we can worship him." So that's what they did.

Machiavelli says that Gian-Paulo Baglioni, in missing the chance to assassinate Pope Julius II, missed his chance at immortality.

---

73. By this, Camus means *The Myth of Sisyphus*. On December 12, he wrote to Claude de Fréminville: "Soon, I'll have finished what I consider to be the 'first *stone*.'"

The second part of the entry would resurface nearly twenty years later as an anecdote told in *The First Man*.

74. In *The Myth of Sisyphus*, in the section "The Conqueror," Camus writes: "At the end of all this, despite all this, is death. We know that. We also know that it ends everything. That's why those cemeteries that cover Europe, and that obsess certain among us, are hideous. We only ornament and beautify what we love, and death repulses and wearies us. It, too, is to be conquered. The last Carrara, a prisoner in Padua, which had been ravaged by the plague and besieged by the Venetians, roamed through the halls of his deserted palace crying out: he called to the devil and asked him for death. It was a way of overcoming it. And it's still a mark of the West's courage that they made so dreadful those places where death thinks it's being honored. In the rebel's universe, death glorifies injustice. It's the ultimate abuse."

Burchard: "Villainousness, impiety, military talent, and intellectual culture were all brought together in J. Malatesta (died in 1417).

Filippo Maria Visconti, a Milanese condottiere, never wanted to hear talk of death and asked that even his favorite people be taken from his sight when they were dying. And yet, Burchard: "He died with nobility and dignity."

In Ravenna, the people took the candles from the altar to Dante's tomb to honor him: "You're worthier than the other, the one who was crucified."

———

Short story: Follow the Rhône and the Saône along their course, the one leaping forward, the other hesitating before eventually joining back up with the first and getting lost in its rush. Two people floating down them: parallel.

———

Short story: Y's story.

———

Ternay. Cold, deserted little village hanging over the Rhône. Gray sky and wind as icy as a silk dress. The uplands left uncultivated. A few black furrows and flights of crows. Small cemetery open to the sky: they were all good husbands and fathers. They all leave eternal regrets.

———

The old church with a copy of a Boucher.[75] The church marm who took care of the seating: she was so scared when the German bombardiers came. Thirty people from the commune had already been killed in the last war. Now, there are only eighteen prisoners, but it's tough all the same. Soon, there will be a marriage, two young people. The primary school teacher is an Alsatian refugee; she's had no news of her parents. "Do you think it'll stop soon, Monsieur?" Her son died in '14. When he was wounded, she went to get him, and ended up near the Retreat from Mons. She brought him back, he died at home. "I'll never forget what I saw."

Outside, the same sky, the same cold. The plowed fields are lukewarm, the shiny river below smoothly flowing, with only the occasional ripple. A little farther on, the waiting room at the small train station in Serresin. War lighting—shadows on the posters inviting you to live happily in Bandol. The stove is out, the morning water sprinklers leave trails of figure 8s on the cold

75. François Boucher (1703–1770), a French painter, enjoyed considerable success during his lifetime.

stones. An hour waiting with the distant rumbling of trains and the evening wind over the valley. So isolated and so close. Here, you can touch your freedom, and how awful it is! Solidarity, solidarity with this world where the flowers and wind will never make up for all the rest.

———

—DECEMBER (Egypt)

The Greeks—The Etruscans—Rome and its decadence—The Alexandrians and the Christians—Holy Roman Empire and audacious thinking—Provence and Provençal schisms—Italian Renaissance—Elizabethan period—Spain—From Goethe to Nietzsche—Russia.

India, China, Japan.

Mexico—United States.

Styles—from the Doric column to the cement arch through the Gothic and the Baroque.

History Philosophy Art Religion
P.S.M.

———

DEC. The Greeks. History—Literature—Art—Philosophy.

———

Consciously or not, women always use that feeling of honor, and of honoring your word, that men feel so sharply.

———

Cain's sons—au naturel.[76] The father watches Abel's murder and does nothing to prevent it. But Cain's suffering grows, as does his strength. The father offers forgiveness, but Cain refuses it: "I don't want to see your face anymore."

(Or a poem—*id.* Judah.)

Oran. January '41.

Story of P. The little old man who tosses scraps of paper from the second floor to attract the cats. Then he spits at them. When he hits one of the cats, the old man laughs.[77]

———

76. Philip Thody suggests Camus meant "Adam's sons" rather than "Cain's sons," and that this is a simple mistake. He further notes that the dialogue here attributed to Cain may find reference in Genesis 4:14.

77. This anecdote is retold in *The Plague*.

There isn't anywhere the Oranians haven't defiled with some hideous construction that would crush the life out of any landscape. A city that turns its back to the sea and builds itself around itself, like a snail. You wander around this labyrinth looking for the sea as for a sign from Ariadne,[78] but in these unsightly, ugly streets, you only go around in circles. Eventually, the Minotaur devours the Oranians—and the Minotaur is boredom

But it's all in vain: this, one of the strongest lands in the world, breaks through the misguided backdrop with which they've draped it, its violent cries heard between every house and above every rooftop. Beyond the boredom, the life you can lead in Oran is worthy of the land. Oran proves there's something stronger in people than their works.

You can't know what stone is if you haven't visited Oran. In one of the dustiest cities in the world, the pebble and stone are king. In other places, Arab cemeteries are well-known for their gentleness. Here, above the Raz el-Aïn ravine, facing the sea, flattened against the blue sky, they are fields of chalky, crumbling stone, of blinding whiteness. Amid these bones of the earth, from time to time a red geranium fresh as blood and life.

We write books about Florence and Athens. Those cities have formed so many European minds that they must hold some meaning. There's something about them that moves or excites us. They sooth a certain spiritual hunger, the kind nourished on memory. But nobody would think to write about a city where nothing appeals to the mind, where ugliness takes up a disproportionate amount of space, where the past is reduced to nothing. And yet, sometimes it's very tempting.

What is it that makes a person become attached to and interested in something that has nothing to offer? The emptiness, the ugliness, the boredom beneath a merciless and magnificent sky, what is it that makes these things seductive? I have a response: the human animal. For a certain tribe, the human animal, wherever it may be beautiful, is a homeland with a thousand capitals. Oran is one of them.

---

78. Ariadne appears throughout these pages, and throughout Camus's larger body of work, first being mentioned in his thesis *Christian Metaphysics and Neoplatonism*, then in a review of Jean-Paul Sartre's *The Wall*, and on through *The Myth of Sisyphus* and other works. The passage above, as well as the one below, would be expanded in "The Minotaur, or, The Stop in Oran." Usually, Camus refers to "Ariadne's string," whereas here he mentions only a "sign."

Café. Langoustines, kebabs, snails in a sauce that sets your mouth on fire. You have to drink a sickly-sweet Muscat to calm it. You can't make this stuff up. On one side, a blind man sings "flamenco."

———

The hills above Mers-el-Kébir offer a perfect landscape.

———

Servitude et Grandeur militaires.[79] An admirable book you have to reread as an adult.

"After Turenne was killed, Montecuculli withdrew, not deigning to face off against an ordinary player."

Honor "is a completely human virtue, one we can imagine is born of death, without heavenly accolades after death; it's a virtue of life."

———

Oran. Noiseux Ravine: long path between two dry and dusty slopes. The earth cracks under the sun. The lentisk shrubs are the color of stone. The sky above steadily pours forth its supply of heat and fire. Little by little, the lentisks fatten and turn green. The vegetation thickens, at first imperceptibly, then suddenly. At the end of a very long road, the lentisk shrubs slowly turn into oaks, growing and thinning all at once, and then, at a sharp turn, a field of flowering almond trees: like fresh water for the eyes. A small valley like a paradise lost.

The hillside road overlooking the sea. Passable but abandoned. It's covered in flowers now. A white-and-yellow road made of daises and buttercups.

———

February 21, 1941.

Finished *Sisyphus.* The three Absurds are complete.

Beginnings of freedom.[80]

---

79. Although Alfred de Vigny's book has appeared in several English translations since its original publication in 1835, each has carried a different title, the first being 1840's *Lights and Shades of Military Life,* the next *The Military Necessity,* then *The Military Condition, The Servitude and Grandeur of Arms,* and, in 2013, *The Warrior's Life.* Throughout his life, and throughout these pages, Camus would return to de Vigny's work.

80. The three Absurds being *The Stranger, The Myth of Sisyphus,* and the initial version of *Caligula.* Camus drew an arrow down from this entry and through the next two pages of the notebook, which, aside from the arrow, remain blank, perhaps as a means of emphasizing the completion of one cycle of his work and the beginning of the next (the next entry he makes would appear in *The Plague*). Ten years later, March 7, 1951, Camus would record a very similar entry in these pages with regard to his second cycle.

March 15, 1941.

On the train. "You knew Camps, right?"

"Camps? The tall skinny guy with the black mustache?"

"Yeah, the one who was at the switch in Bel Abbès."

"Yes, of course."

"He died."

"Oh! Of what?"

"The ol' ticker."

"Never would have known looking at him."

"Yeah, but he was a musician, at the Orphéon. Always blowing away at his instrument. That's what killed him."

"That must be it. When you're sick, you have to take care of yourself. You can't go blowing a gasket."[81]

———

The lady who looked as if she were suffering three years of constipation: "These Arabs, covering their daughters' faces. Ah! They're just not civilized yet!"

Little by little, she reveals her ideal civilization: a husband who makes 1,200 francs a month, a two-room apartment, kitchen and full bath, the cinema on Sundays, and furnishings from Galeries Barbès for the rest of the week.

———

—The Absurd and Power: dig into this (cf. Hitler)

———

March 18, '41.

In spring, the heights above Algiers overflow with flowers. The honey scent of yellow roses flows through the small streets. The tops of enormous black cypresses are splashed with bursts of wisteria and hawthorn, their path to the top hidden somewhere inside. A gentle wind, the gulf immense and flat. A strong and simple desire—and the absurdity of leaving all this.[82]

———

81. In *The Plague,* this entry appears as a conversation Tarrou overhears between two tram conductors, which he then copies down in his notes. There, Tarrou wonders why Camps would risk his life just to play music.

The French word *orphéon* could refer to a specific place where music is played or to a male choir in general.

82. Although Camus lived in Oran at the time, he returned to Algiers regularly to visit his mother and his friends, as well as to look for work.

Santa-Cruz and the climb through the pines. The gulf continuously widening all the way to the top, where the view gets lost in its own immensity. Indifference—and I, too, have my pilgrimages.

———

M. 19.

Girls blossom on the beaches each year. They have but a single season. The next year, they're replaced by the faces of other flowers who, the season before, were still little girls. For the man looking at them, they're a yearly wave whose weight and splendor washes over the yellow sand.[83]

———

M. 20.

With regard to Oran, write an insignificant and absurd biography. With regard to Cain, the insignificant unknown who sculpted the insignificant lions of the Place d'Armes.

———

M. 21.

The icy water of spring dips. The dead jellyfish on the beach: a jelly that gradually melts back into the sand. The immense dunes of pale sand.

The sea and the sand, those two deserts.

—The weekly *Gringoire* calls for the Spanish refugee camps to be transferred to the extreme southern end of Tunisia.[84]

———

83. In *The Rebel*, in reference to Proust, Camus writes: "It's difficult to return to places of happiness and youth. The young girls in flower eternally laugh and chatter by the sea, but the person watching them slowly, little by little, loses the right to love them, just as the people the person loved lose the power to be loved. This is Proust's melancholy. It flowed with such force inside him that he rejected all existence. But his love of faces and light also, at the same time, attached him to the world. He didn't accept that such happy excursions could be forever lost. He took it upon himself to recreate them and to show that, despite death, the past could be regained at the end of time in an imperishable present, truer and richer than when it first occurred."

84. *Gringoire* was founded in 1928 as a weekly newspaper of the center-right, but by the mid-1930s, it had already begun to take on a an extreme-right, nationalist angle, featuring collaborationist writers such as Pierre Drieu La Rochelle, but also Jewish writers—albeit Jewish writers with conservative views—such as Irène Némirovsky. In 1943, in an essay on the politics of W. B. Yeats, George Orwell writes: "A year before the war, examining a copy of *Gringoire*, the French Fascist weekly, much read by army officers, I found in it no less than thirty-eight advertisements of clairvoyants. . . . The very concept of occultism carries with it the idea that knowledge must be a secret thing, limited to a small circle of initiates. But the same idea is integral to Fascism. Those who dread the prospect of universal suffrage, popular education, freedom of thought, emancipation of women, will start off

Give up the servitude that is female allure.

———

Rosanov:[85] "Michelangelo and Leonardo built. The revolution will exhaust them and slit their throats at the age of twelve or thirteen, as soon as they begin to display their personality, their very own soul."

———

"Deprived of what is sinful, man couldn't live, but he'd live only too well deprived of what is holy."

Immortality is an idea without a future.

———

Shakyamuni remained in the desert for many years, motionless, eyes lifted to the heavens. The gods themselves envied such wisdom, such a fate of stone. In his steady, outstretched hands, swallows made their nest. But one day they flew off, never to return, and he who'd killed off all the will and desire, all the glory and pain, inside himself, began to cry. This is how flowers are born from stones.[86]

———

"They may torture, but shall not subdue me."[87]

———

"The Abbot: 'But why not live with, why not act with, other men?'

---

with a predilection towards secret cults. There is another link between Fascism and magic in the profound hostility of both to the Christian ethical code."

85. Vasily Vasilievich Rozanov (1856–1919) may have led Camus to the writings of Nicolas Berdyaev, whose work seems to have been of greater interest to Camus.

The French phrase *tirer la langue* (exhaust) can also indicate "financial deprivation," as well as, more literally, "to stick out your tongue."

86. This entry is used at the end of "The Minotaur, or, The Stop in Oran."

87. This first quote, which is in English in the original notebook, is from Lord Byron's "Stanzas to Augusta," while the quote that follows, from *Manfred*, is in French, making it unclear if Camus was reading the text in French or in English. Given that the French version recorded here is fairly different from the English, it's possible Camus translated the text into French himself. The original English reads: "*Abbot*. And why not live and act with other men? / *Man*. Because my nature was averse from life."

Between the two works cited here and Camus's own work to this point, there is a shared theme of incest, which Camus touches on in *The Rebel*, when he writes: "Exquisite sensitivities bring out the brute's elementary fury. The Byronic hero, incapable of love, or capable only of an impossible love, suffers from melancholy. He's alone, languishing, and his condition exhausts him. In order to feel alive, he needs the terrible ecstasy of a brief, devouring act. To love what you can never love again is to love the fiery flames and the cry for ruin that they bring. You live only for and in the present moment, for that 'brief but vivid moment when a tormented heart unites with its torment' (Lermontov). . . . Wild drunkenness and, at the extreme, beautiful crime, instantly exhaust all sense of life."

Manfred: 'Their existence sickens my soul.'"

How should a heart govern itself? With love? Nothing is less certain. We can know what it is to suffer from love; we can't know what it is to love. Here, it's deprivation, regret, empty hands. I'll never have the urge; I'm left with the anxiety. A hell where everything assumes there's a heaven. Is nevertheless a hell. What leaves me empty, that's what I call life and love. Departure, constraint, rupture, this unlit heart scattered inside me, the salty taste of tears and love.[88]

The wind: one of the few clean things in the world.

April. *2nd Cycle.*

The world of tragedy and the spirit of rebellion—Budejovice (3 acts).[89] Plague or adventure (novel).

The liberating plague.[90]

Happy city. The people live according to different systems. The plague: breaks down all systems. But they die all the same. Twice as pointless. A philosopher living there is writing "an anthology of insignificant actions." He's keeping a journal about the plague from this perspective. (A second journal, but from a pathos-based perspective. A Latin and Greek teacher.

---

88. Camus was still torn between Yvonne Ducailar and Francine, and he wrote to Yvonne to say: "Even if I'm wrong and you are suffering, why should you care about that other stuff? I don't see anything vulgar in the situation because neither of us have made anything vulgar of it. If others judged it so, we'd know it wasn't. We still know it. You also know nothing's really been ruined or compromised. It'll never be absurd for you to write to me, never absurd to come see me, to call me or turn your face toward me." Then he and Yvonne spent a week camping together, a fact Francine's family did not take well, and which forced him to write to Yvonne: "I'll never see you again. . . . Forgive me for the absurdity of it all. I'm miserable and I love you, but even that's in vain."

89. There is also an illegible parenthetical after "rebellion."

Budějovice, a city in the Czech Republic, was the original title for what would become *The Misunderstanding.*

Though some scholars include *The Misunderstanding* among Camus's first cycle of work dealing with the absurd, this entry makes it clear that Camus saw the play as being part of his second cycle on rebellion.

90. These notes for *The Plague* would initially be published in *Symposium*. The parenthetically mentioned Latin and Greek teacher is Stephan, who would be cut from the second draft and replaced by the character Grand. The young parish priest who loses his faith is Paneloux, though he doesn't end up losing his faith in the final version of the book.

He understands that he hadn't understood Thucydides and Lucretius until now.) His favorite phrase: "In all likelihood." So, then: "The tramway company had only 760 workers available, rather than 2,130. In all likelihood, the plague is to blame."

A young parish priest loses his faith on seeing black pus ooze from plague sores. He anoints himself with his oils. "If I make it out of here . . ." But he doesn't make it out. Everything must be paid for.

The bodies are carried away on the trams. Entire cars filled with flowers and dead bodies run alongside the sea. Soon enough, they fire the conductors: the passengers are no longer paying.

The "Ransdoc—SVP" agency gives all available information over the telephone. "200 victims today, Monsieur. We'll debit two francs from your account." "Impossible, Monsieur. No hearses available for at least four days. Talk to the Tramway Company. We'll debit . . ." The agency advertises on the radio: "Would you like to know the daily, weekly, monthly number of plague victims? Call Ransdoc. five lines are open—dial 353-91 or any of the four digits that follow."

They close up the city. People die in crowded isolation. One gentleman, nevertheless, tries to keep to his normal routines. He continues to get dressed for dinner. One by one, the members of his family disappear from the table. He dies sitting in front of his plate, still dressed. As the maid says, "Well, we're halfway there. Least we won't need to get him all dressed up." Bodies are no longer buried but thrown into the sea. There are too many of them, though, and they ride like a monstrous spume on the blue sea.

A man loves a woman and reads the signs of the plague on her face. He'll never love her as much as he does then. But never has she disgusted him as much as she does then. There's a divorce inside him. But the body always prevails. Disgust carries the day. He takes her by the hand, drags her from the bed, through the main room, the entrance, the hallway of their building, two small side streets, and then the main street. He leaves her in front of a sewer. "After all, there are others."

At the end, the most insignificant character decides to speak: "In one sense," he says, "it's a curse."[91]

———

91. The word used here, *fléau*, could also be translated as "pestilence" or "scourge."

In the meantime: pamphlet about Oran. The Greeks.

———

Western art has put all its effort into offering the imagination types. And the history of European literature seems nothing more than a series of variations on these given types and themes. Racinian love is a variation on a type of love that perhaps doesn't exist in real life. It's a simplification: a style. The West doesn't record everyday life. It provides an endless stream of grand imagery, the kind that whips it into a frenzy. It chases after such images. It wants to be Manfred or Faust, Don Juan or Narcissus. But its approximation is always in vain. The frenzy for unity always drives everything. The movie hero was invented out of hopeless desperation.

———

The dunes facing the sea—dawn's early warmth, naked bodies facing the first waves, black and bitter still. The water's a heavy load. The body soaks it in, then runs along the beach beneath the first rays of sunlight. Each summer morning on the beach feels like the world's first. Each summer evening has the solemn look of the world's last. Evenings on the sea were immeasurable. Sun-filled days on the dunes were crushing. At two o'clock in the afternoon, a simple hundred-meter walk on the burning sand makes you feel drunk. In only a moment, you'll fall to the ground. It's a killer, this sun. But in the morning, the beauty of brown bodies on blond dunes. Terrible innocence of these games, of these naked bodies in this bounding light.

At night, the moon casts a white glow over the dunes. A little before, the evening had sharpened all the colors, deepened them, made them more intense. The sea is navy blue, the road a blood-curdled red, the beach yellow. All of it disappears as the sunset flashes green and the moonlight flows over the dunes. Nights of immeasurable happiness beneath a shower of stars. What we hold tightly to us, is it a body or the warm night? The night of the storm, the lightning flashed along the dunes, faded out, left an orange or whitish glitter on the sand and in our eyes. Such nuptials are unforgettable. To be able to write: I've been happy for a whole week.

———

We must pay, must dirty ourselves with the wretchedness that is human suffering. The dirty, disgusting, slimy universe of sorrow.

———

"A moan mingled with sobs reigns alone on the open sea, until the dark face of night comes to end it all." (The Persians—Battle of Salamis.)

———

In 477, to consecrate the Delian League, blocks of iron were thrown to the bottom of the sea. The oath of alliance was to be maintained as long as the iron remained at the bottom of the water.

When it comes to politics, we haven't quite caught on that a certain sort of equality is the enemy of freedom. In Greece, there were free men because there were slaves.

"It's always a great crime to destroy the freedom of a peoples under the pretext that they've put it to poor use." (Tocqueville.)

The problem in art is a problem of translation. Bad writers: those who write with contextual information in mind that the reader has no way of knowing. You have to be two people when you write: the primary thing is, again, to learn self-control.

War manuscripts, by prisoners, by fighters. They all witnessed unspeakable things and learned nothing from them. Six months in a post office would have taught them no less. They repeat what's in the papers. What they read there hits them harder than what they saw with their own eyes.

"This is the moment to let our actions prove man's dignity doesn't bow before the gods' grandeur." (Iphigenia in Tauris.)[92]

"I want empire, possession. Action is everything, glory is nothing." (Faust.)

For the wise man, the world is no secret, so why does he need to lose himself in eternity?[93]

Will is also a solitude.[94]

---

92. *Iphigenia in Tauris* is an Ancient Greek play by Euripides.

93. In French, the phrase *s'égarer dans* carries the sense of getting "sidetracked by" or "consumed by" something. It could also be translated as "to go astray" or "to get lost."

94. In the top right corner of this page, Camus has written the letters "BYW" and enclosed them in a box.

Liszt on Chopin: "These days, he only uses his art as a devotion to his own tragedy."

———

September

It's all settled: all very simple and obvious. But then human suffering intervenes and changes all our plans.

———

The dizziness of losing yourself and denying everything, of feeling like nothing, of forever shattering what defines you, of offering solitude and nothingness to the present, of rediscovering the only platform from which fates can begin again. It's a perpetual temptation. Should it be obeyed or rejected? Can the haunting desire to create be carried in the hollows of a routine and droning life or does a life, to the contrary, have to be equal to desire, to obey that flash of lightning? Beauty, my greatest concern, along with freedom.

———

J. Copeau:[95] "In periods of greatness, don't go looking for the dramatic poet in his study. He'll be in the theater, among his actors. He is an actor and director."

We're not in a period of greatness.

———

On Greek theater:

G. Méautis: Eschyle et la Trilogie

L'aristocratie athénienne.

Navarre: Le théâtre grec.[96]

———

95. Jacques Copeau (1879–1949), French playwright, actor, director, and producer, was one of Camus's earliest and greatest theatrical influences. In 1909, Copeau helped found the *Nouvelle revue française*, one of France's premier literary magazines, as a means of trying to bring literature and theater closer together, and in 1913 he founded the Théâtre du Vieux-Colombier in Paris. Copeau believed in the primacy of the script—the writing—over the staging and direction. In 1959, Camus would write a short text titled "Copeau: The Sole Master," in which he declares: "There are two periods in the history of modern French theater: before Copeau and after Copeau."

96. The first two works, *Aeschylus and the Trilogy* and *The Athenian Aristocracy*, are by Georges Méautis, and the last, *The Greek Theater*, is by Octave Navarre. All were published in the 1920s and '30s.

When putting on a pantomime, the Comédiens Routiers[97] use an incomprehensible language (a sort of farcical Esperanto) not to give meaning but to give life.

Chancerel rightly insists on the importance of mime. The body in theater: all contemporary French theater (Barrault aside) has forgotten it.[98]

———

Formation of Zibaldone in the Commedia dell'Arte. (Louis Moland: *Molière et la Comédie italienne.*) (Fabric curtains with appliqué trims.)

Molière, dying, asked to be carried to the theater, not wanting to deprive the actors, musicians, and stagehands, "who had nothing but their wages to live on," of their earnings from the performance.

Chancerel's book is interesting despite one flaw: it risks discouraging people. Also significant to see a man who's concerned with the moral influence of the theater nevertheless recommend a repertoire that includes the Elizabethans. We're not used to this sort of intelligence.

———

Louis XIV's librarian, Nicolas Clément, on Shakespeare: "The English poet had a rather lovely imagination, and he expresses himself with finesse, but these lovely qualities are obscured by the trash he adds to his plays."

That great century was great only through mutilation of the soul and the mind, Clément being a prime example. Meanwhile, the English poet wrote magnificently in Richard II:

"Let's talk of graves, of worms, and epitaphs." And Webster: "A man is like cassia: to free his odor, he has to be bruised."[99]

———

97. An amateur acting troupe formed within the Scouts de France (Boy Scouts) by Léon Chancerel in 1929. Chancerel was a disciple of Copeau's, and it is perhaps in this way that his work became known to Camus.

98. In 1953, Camus would publish his own mimodrama, *The Life of the Artist*, in a small Algerian journal. The play is not very well known—an English translation appeared in *The New Yorker* in 2013—and it doesn't appear to have been performed during Camus's lifetime.

99. The French translation of the first quote translates directly back to the original English with no change, but the French translation of the second quote, given above, differs from the English original, which reads: "Man, like to cassia, is proved best being bruis'd." This second quote is from John Webster's *The Duchess of Malfi*, act 3, scene 5.

Masques, entertainments for special occasions. The dancers use their steps out on the floor to trace the newlyweds' initials, the party being given in their honor.[100]

"O no, there is no end: the end is death and madness." (Kyd: *La Tragédie espagnole*)[101] and Marlowe died at thirty from a dagger to the forehead, murdered by a cop.

fifty-three manuscript plays from Warburton's collection (Philip Massinger and Fletcher) were burned by his top chef, who used them as kindling for his pies. That's how it ends.[102]

Cf. Georges Conne: *Le Mystère shakespearian* (Boivin)
État présent des études shakespeariennes (Didier).

~~Cf. The Battle of Le Mans.~~[103]

October

Plague. Bonsels, p. 144 and 222.

1342—Black Plague on Europe. They murder the Jews.

1481—Plague ravages Southern Spain. The Inquisition says: The Jews. But the plague kills an inquisitor.

In the second century, discussions about Jesus's personal appearance. Saint Cyril and Saint Justin: for the incarnation to carry its full meaning, it had to have a wretched, repulsive appearance. (Saint Cyril "the most frightful of man's sons.")

---

100. A masque was a type of court entertainment involving a dramatic performance with singing and dancing.

101. *The Spanish Tragedy* is an Elizabethan revenge play written by Thomas Kyd in the late 1500s. In the handwritten notebook, the quote is in English, but the title of the play is recorded in French.

102. John Warburton (1682–1759) was a dedicated collector of books and manuscripts. As the story goes, he left the stack of plays in the kitchen, forgot about them, and then came looking for them a year later, at which point his cook, Betsy Baker, had already used them to line pie pans and light cooking fires. Of the fifty-three plays that were burned, only five survived through other copies. A good number of the plays were by Philip Massinger, but among the lost works were also works by Shakespeare, Middleton, and Marlowe.

103. This entry is crossed out on the first typescript.

But to the Greek mind: "If he's not handsome, he's not God." The Greeks won.

———

On the Cathari: Douais, *Les Hérétiques du Midi au XIIIe siècle.*[104]

———

La hermosa Sembra.[105] Denounces her father, who's plotting against the Inquisition, because she has a Castilian lover and they're "conversos." She enters a convent. Consumed with desire, she leaves it. Has several children. Grows ugly. Dies while being looked after by a grocer—asks that her skull be placed over the door of the house as a reminder of her soiled life. In Seville.

———

Alexander Borgia was the first to oppose Torquemada. Too knowledgeable and "distinguished" to bear this fury.

———

See Herder. Ideas to use in a philosophy of the history of humanity.

———

Those who created in periods of great unrest: Shakespeare, Milton, Ronsard, Rabelais, Montaigne, Malherbe.

———

Originally, nationalistic feelings were lacking in Germany. What's come to stand in for them is a racial consciousness that German intellectuals created out of thin air. *Much more virulent.* What interests the Germans is foreign policy—the French, domestic policy.

———

On Monotony

---

104. The Cathari were a dualist Christian sect that believed the material world was evil. Around the mid-1100s, the group formally organized, with several bishops and churches in France and Italy. *The Heretics of the South in the 13th Century* is a collection of five plays by Célestin Douais.

105. The Spanish phrase *la hermosa Hembra* (literally: beautiful woman) is in reference to the legend of Susana Ben Susón (or La Susona), which Camus gives an account of in this entry. In 1478, the Spanish Inquisition was established, in large part to make sure that conversos—Spanish Jews who'd converted to Catholicism to avoid the 1391 pogroms—were actually practicing the Christian faith. La Susona's father, Diego Susón, was one of a group of Sevillian converso conspirators plotting to overthrow the state. When La Susona learned of this, she told her lover, a Christian, who then informed on Diego Susón, who was subsequently arrested by the Inquisition and executed. Weighed down with immense guilt, La Susona locked herself away in a convent. What happens next differs from one telling to the next, but all agree that upon her death, her head was hung above the entrance to her family's home in Barrio Santa Cruz. A tile featuring the word "SVSONA" and a picture of a skull can still be seen there today.

Monotony of Tolstoy's last works. Monotony of Hindu books—monotony of Biblical prophecy—monotony of the Buddha. Monotony of the Koran and of all religious texts. Monotony of Nietzsche—of Pascal—of Shestov—terrible monotony of Proust, of the Marquis de Sade, etc., etc. . . .

———

At the Siege of Sevastopol, Tolstoy leaped from the trenches and ran toward the bastion under heavy enemy fire: he was terribly afraid of rats and had just seen one.

———

Politics can never be the subject of poetry (Goethe).

Add Tolstoy quote to the Absurd as a model of illogical logic:

"If all the earthly goods for which we live, if all the joys that make up life, the riches, the fame, honor, power, are wrenched away by death, then these goods have no meaning. If life is not infinite, it's quite simply absurd, it's not worth living, and we must clear it away as quickly as possible by means of suicide." (*Confession.*)

But, later on, Tolstoy corrects himself: "The existence of death forces us either to give up on life voluntarily or to transform our life *in such a way as to give it a meaning death can't wrench away from it.*"

———

Fear and pain: the most fleeting of emotions, Byrd says.[106] In the absolute solitude of the North, he realizes the body's needs are just as demanding as the mind's: "It *can't do without* sounds, smells, and voices."

———

Using a false name, T. E. Lawrence reenlists after the war as a *private*. He needs to see if anonymity will bring what greatness could not. He refuses the king's decorations, gives his Croix de Guerre to his dog. He sends his writings to publishers anonymously and the publishers reject them. Motorcycle accident.

This is where A. Fabre-Luce's definition comes from: the superman can be recognized by the rigor with which he encloses himself in history and the inner freedom he maintains toward it.[107]

———

106. Richard Byrd (1888–1957), American explorer of the Antarctic.

107. Alfred Fabre-Luce (1899–1983) was a prolific French essayist who at first supported Marshal Philippe Pétain's Vichy France and its Compulsory Work Service plan, which deported approximately 650,000 French citizens into forced labor in Germany during World War II.

On rereading: The Notebooks of Malte Laurids Brigge is an insignificant book. The responsible party: Paris. It's a Parisian failure. A Parisian infection not overcome. Ex: "The world considers the loner an enemy." Wrong. The world doesn't give a damn, and that's certainly its right.

The only worthwhile part: the story about Arvers, who, as he's about to die, corrects a mispronunciation: "You mean to say 'corridor.'"[108]

As Newton says: by thinking about it all the time.[109]

Jean Hytier,[110] on the dramaturge: "He does what he wants as long as he does what he must."

For Montherlant (the decline of chivalry through women). Little John of Saintré, p. 108. MA. LF.[111]

Pierre de Larivey: translator. *Les Esprits*, translation of Lorenzino de Medici's drama—Saint-Évremond.[112]

All the headlands come together like a flotilla floating away. These vessels of rock and azure tremble on their keels as if preparing to sail off toward the isles of light. All of Oran is ready to depart, and every day at noon a shiver

---

108. *The Notebooks of Malte Laurids Brigge*, published in 1910, was Rainer Maria Rilke's only novel. In the book, as Félix Arvers, a poet, dies in a hospital, he is attended by a nun, who, being uneducated and never having seen the word "corridor" written out, thinks the word is pronounced "collidor," and so pronounces it that way when calling out instructions. With his last breaths, Arvers corrects her.

This same mispronunciation appears in *War and Peace*, where, in the French translation that would have been available to Camus, Tolstoy writes: "The door at the end of the corridor (which the uncle pronounced 'collidor') . . ." In Anthony Briggs's more recent English translation, a further clarification appears: "which 'Uncle' called a 'collidor,' like the peasants . . ."

109. This was Newton's response when asked how he discovered the law of gravity.

110. Jean Hytier was born in Paris and taught French literature at Columbia University in New York. He edited both Pascal's and Paul Valéry's works and wrote a book on André Gide that was initially published by Éditions Charlot.

111. *Little John of Saintré*, published in 1456, is a romance novel by Antoine de la Salle in which a young knight begins to learn the ways of chivalry just as it's dying out.

112. Pierre de Larivey (1549–1619) was a French playwright known for adapting Italian comedies into an energetic, colloquial French. *Les esprits* (The spirits) is his adaptation of de' Medici's *L'Aridosia*. Camus would later adapt de Larivey's *Les esprits* first for a performance in Algeria in 1946 and then for a reworked performance at the 1953 Festival de Angers.

of adventure runs through it. Maybe one of these mornings we'll float off together.

Out on the immense dunes at the height of the day's heat, the world closes up and narrows its horizons. It's a cage of blood and heat. It extends no further than my body. But let a donkey bray in the distance, and the dunes, the desert, and the sky recover their vastness. And it is infinite.

Essay on tragedy

I. Prometheus' silence
II. The Elizabethans
III. Molière
IV. The revolutionary mind.[113]

Plague. "I want something just."
"That's just what the plague is."

"Nowadays, how many people know the night, the 'real night'? The waters and the earth, the return of silence. 'And my soul, it, too, is a gushing fountain.' Oh, let the world grow distant, let the world fall silent. Over there, above Pollensa . . ."

Break up with this empty heart—refuse everything that dries it out. If the rushing waters are elsewhere, why stay here?

At a certain point, you can no longer feel the emotion of love. All that's left is the tragic. Living for someone or something no longer means anything. Only *in the thought* of dying for something can you find meaning.

A Spartan is publicly reprimanded by an ephor because his stomach is too fat.

An Athenian proverb relegates those who can neither read nor swim to the lowest rank of citizenry.

See Alcibiades, according to Plutarch: "In Sparta, he kept himself in shape, was frugal and austere; in Ionia, delicate and idle; in Thrace, in love with

113. This planned essay exists only as a series of "Notes on the Theater." No formal essay was ever written.

drink; in Thessaly, always riding horses; at the satrap Tissaphernes's home, he exceeded all Persian luxury in his expenditure and pomp."[114]

The day the people applauded him: "Did I say something stupid?" Phocion asked.

Decadence! Speeches about decadence! For Greece, the 3rd century BC is a decadent century. It gave the world geometry, physics, astronomy, and trigonometry via Euclid, Archimedes, Aristarchus, and Hipparchus.[115]

There are still people who confuse individualism and a taste for personality. They're mixing together two separate spheres: the social and the metaphysical. "You're spreading yourself too thin." To go from life to life is to have no face of your own. But having a face of your own is an idea particular to a certain form of civilization. To others, it may seem the worst of misfortunes.

Contradiction in the modern world. In Athens, the only reason the people could really exercise their power is because they devoted the great majority of their time to doing so, while the slaves spent all day doing the rest of the work that had to be done. As soon as slavery is abolished, everybody is put to work. It's in this period, when the proletarianization of the European is at its height, that the dream of popular sovereignty is strongest: when it's impossible.

Only three actors in the Greek theater: it's not about creating a *character*.

In Athens, a show is a serious thing: performances take place two or three times a year. In Paris? And they want to go back to what's dead. Create your own forms instead.

---

114. The French translation of Plutarch's *Alcibiades* differs a bit from John Dryden's standard English translation, which reads: "At Sparta, he was devoted to athletic exercises, was frugal and reserved; in Ionia, luxurious, gay, and indolent; in Thrace, always drinking; in Thessaly, ever on horseback; and when he lived with Tisaphernes the Persian satrap, he exceeded the Persians themselves in magnificence and pomp."

115. After this entry, Camus has inserted an outside sheet of paper, also handwritten, into the notebook. It is not reproduced here.

"There's nothing so innocent men can't add a little crime to it." (Molière, preface to *Tartuffe.*)

———

See *Tartuffe*, Act I, last scene: "cranks up the suspense and holds our interest." To be continued next Friday.

Solon does the work for which we know him and, in his old age, immortalizes the work through poetry.[116]

———

Thucydides has Pericles say that what's unique to the Athenians "is their ability to be extremely daring and, at the same time, to weigh their undertakings carefully."

The triremes that were victorious in Salamis were helmed by *the poorest Athenians.*

Cf. Cohen:[117] "Athens didn't have a theater worthy of the name until there was no longer a poet in Athens worthy of leading it."

———

O. Flake on Sade:[118] "No value is stable for the person who can't bow down before it. Sade can't see any reason to bow, has long searched for a reason, and hasn't been able to find it." According to Sade, the man without grace is without responsibility.

Cf. the mathematics of evil in Juliette.

A monomaniac in his revolt against basic law, recognizing the same raison d'être in both mind and sexuality. Ends up in Charenton Asylum, declared insane yet sound of mind, where he makes the mental patients play roles in performances he directs with complete control: Tableau.

"He made up cruelties he hadn't lived and wouldn't have wanted to live—to get in touch with great problems."

———

116. Solon (c. 630–c. 560 BC) was an Athenian lawmaker who turned to poetry as a leisure activity and as another form of activism. His poetry survives only in fragments.

117. Gustave Cohen (1879–1958), who fought with the French Army during World War I, later became a professor of medieval literature at the Sorbonne and then emigrated to the US when the Nazis came to power.

118. In 1933, Otto Flake's book *The Marquis de Sade* was translated into French by Pierre Klossowski. Ten years after Camus recorded this entry, he would devote a section of *The Rebel* to discussing Sade.

Moby-Dick and the symbol, p. 120, 121, 123, 129, 173–177, 191–193, 203, 209, 241, 310, 313, 339, 373, 415, 421, 452, 457, 460, 472, 485, 499, 503, 517, 520, 522.[119]

The feelings, the images, they multiply the philosophy tenfold.

———

In Athens, people only attended to the dead during Anthesteria.[120] Once it was over: "Go away, spirits, the days of Anthesteria are over."

Originally, in the Greek religion, everybody was in Hades. There was neither reward nor punishment—same in the Jewish religion. It's commercial interests that give rise to the idea of reward.

———

404. After Athens had signed the armistice with Lysander, the end of the Peloponnesian War was marked by Lysander's flute-filled assault on the walls of Athens.

———

The beautiful story of Timoleon, tyrant of Syracuse (he had his father captured so he could have him killed as a traitor to the country). (P. 251, 2, 3.)

———

In the 4th century, in certain Greek cities, the oligarchs took the following oath:

"I will always be the enemy of the people and I will recommend what I know to be harmful to them."

Darius flees, chased by Alexander (293–4).

The Susa weddings: 10,000 soldiers, 80 generals, and Alexander himself, all wed Persians.[121]

———

Demetrius Poliorcetes—sometimes sitting on the throne, sometimes wandering from village to village.

---

119. In 1941, Herman Melville's *Moby Dick* had just been translated into French by Jean Giono, Lucien Jacques, and Joan Smith. The pages Camus lists above refer to that edition, published by Gallimard. *Moby Dick* served as an influence on the narration style Camus ended up using in *The Plague*.

120. An Athenian festival honoring Dionysus, held for three days in the month of Anthesterion (February/March), likely centered around the full moon. The notes that follow indicate Camus was likely reading Plutarch.

121. The Susa weddings were a mass wedding ceremony that took place in 324 BC and was intended as a symbolic coming together of Greek and Persian culture.

Antisthenes: "It's the way of kings to do good and to hear bad things said of you."

Cf. Marcus Aurelius: "Wherever a person can live, a person can live well."
"What stops a work-in-progress becomes the work itself."
What bars the road creates the way.[122]

Finished February 1942.[123]

---

122. This last quote is attributed to Jean de La Bruyère.

123. Though the published French edition of the notebooks records this as "February 1942," on the cover of the following notebook, as well as in the first entry, Camus gives the opening date as January 1942. The word in the notebooks is not clearly written and may in fact read "January."

The rest of the page after this entry is left blank. The extant photocopy of the original notebook is missing the three pages that follow this one, very likely blank, as well. At the end of the journal, there are two more full pages, one of which was crossed out by Camus, as well as a third handwritten page inserted at the back of the notebook. None of these are reproduced here.

Notebook IV

JANUARY 1942–SEPTEMBER 1945

A pinkish composition notebook, 22 × 17 cm, with the preprinted letters "LF" circled on the cover. In the top-left corner Camus has written "Cahier IV," and toward the bottom center he has written the dates "January 1942" and below that "September 45." The notebook has eighty-four pages. Page 83 is blank, and pages 79–84 were crossed out by Camus and as such have not appeared in any published version of the notebooks.

January–February

"Whatever doesn't kill me makes me stronger." Yes, but . . . How hard it is to dream of happiness. The crushing weight of it all. Best to remain forever silent and turn toward all the rest.

———

A dilemma, Gide says: to be moral, to be sincere. And again: "The only beautiful things are those madness dictates and reason writes."[1]

———

Free yourself of everything. In absence of the desert, the plague or Tolstoy's little train station.

———

Goethe: "I felt myself God enough to descend onto the daughters of man."

———

There are no great crimes an intelligent man feels incapable of committing. According to Gide, great minds don't give in *because they'd limit themselves in doing so.*

———

Retz easily quells a first uprising in Paris because it's suppertime: "The ones who are most worked up don't want to, as they say, subvert their schedule."[2]

———

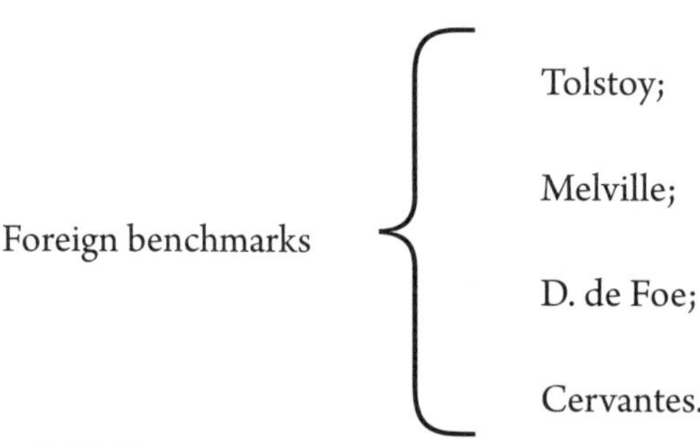

———

1. The references to Gide, as well as the Goethe quote, come from *The Journals of André Gide*, which was first published in France in 1939. The Goethe quote is itself a reference to Genesis 6:4.

2. The word *désheurer*, here translated as "subvert," is archaic and quite rare nowadays. The closest modern equivalent is probably *dérégler*, which means to "disturb" or "disrupt." The quote plays on the Parisians' revolutionary passion, their willingness to overthrow the government, but not their own schedule.

The following entry was added to the typescript; it doesn't appear in the handwritten notebook.

Retz: "Aside from courage, the Duc d'Orléans had everything a respectable man needs to have."

———

Coming upon a convoy during The Fronde, a group of noblemen charge the crucifix with swords drawn, screaming: "There's the enemy."

———

There are many reasons for the official hostilities with England (good or bad, political or not). But we're not mentioning one of the worst motives: rage, the base desire to see the one who dares to resist the power that's crushed you, crushed themselves.

———

The French have held onto the habits and traditions of revolution.[3] The only thing they lack is guts: they've become bureaucrats, petite bourgeois, midinettes. The stroke of genius was in making them Legal Revolutionaries. Now, they're formally authorized to conspire. They remake the world without lifting their ass from their armchair.

———

Epigraph for Oran, or The Minotaur.[4]

Gide. An Unprejudiced Mind. "I imagine him at the Court of King Minos, anxious to know what kind of unspeakable monster the Minotaur may be, if he is indeed as frightful as all that, or if really, maybe he's a little charming."

———

In ancient drama, the one who's made to pay is always the one who's right: Prometheus, Oedipus, Orestes, etc. But it makes no difference. They all end up in Hades anyway, right or wrong. There's neither reward nor punishment. That's why, in our eyes, shrouded by centuries of Christian perversion, those dramas seem so gratuitous—and full of pathos, too.

In contrast: "The great danger is in letting oneself be monopolized by an obsession" (Gide) and Nietzschean "obedience." Gide again, speaking of the less privileged: "Leave them eternal life or give them revolution." For my

3. The handwritten notebook has *grand pensée* (great thoughts) where the typescript has *révolution*.

4. When the essay was first published in Algiers in 1939, the epigraph appeared with it. When the essay was reprinted by Gallimard in 1954, in the collection *Summer*, the epigraph was removed. Gide's essay "An Unprejudiced Mind" explores Theseus's feelings about the Minotaur.

essay on rebellion. "Don't take me from my dear little grotto," the Sequestered Woman of Poitiers said, living there amid the shit and filth.[5]

The attraction certain minds feel for justice and its absurd functioning. Gide, Dostoyevsky, Balzac, Kafka, Malraux, Melville, etc. Find the explanation.

Stendhal. You could imagine the story of Malatesta or the House of Este told by Barrès and then by Stendhal. Stendhal would approach it as a chronicle, the reporting style of the "greats." It's in the disproportion between tone and story that Stendhal hid his secret (compare with certain Americans). Precisely the same disproportion that exists between Stendhal and Beatrice Cenci. Lost if Stendhal had employed a tone based in pathos (despite what literary histories say, Tyrtaeus is comic and hateful). *The Red and the Black* is subtitled "A Chronicle of the Nineteenth Century." *Italian Chronicles*. (Etc.)

March

Milton's Lucifer: "Farthest from Him is best. . . . The mind is its own place, and it can make a Heaven of Hell, a Hell of Heaven. . . . Better to reign in Hell, than serve in Heaven."

Psychology of Adam and Eve summed up: he formed for contemplation and courage, she for mildness and attractive grace; he for God alone, she for God in him.[6]

Schiller dies "having saved everything that could be saved."

Book X of *The Iliad*. The leaders, haunted by insomnia, by an unbearable defeat, turn in circles, wander, love one another, and come together to go on an adventure, a raid on the enemy for the sake of "doing something."

Patroclus's horses cry during the battle, their master having been killed. And (book 18) Achilles's three great cries on returning to the battle, camped out on the defense ditch, sparkling in his armor, fierce. And the Trojans retreat. Book 24. Achilles's grief, crying in the night after the victory. Crying

5. In reference to André Gide's *La séquestrée de Poitiers*, which lightly fictionalized the story of Blanche Monnier, a French woman kept locked in a small windowless room for twenty-five years.

6. The first set of quotes come directly from *Paradise Lost*, book 1. The second part of the entry, which comes from book 4, is a slight paraphrase.

out: "For I have done what no man on Earth has done: to bring to my mouth the hands of the one who killed my children."

(Nectar was red!)

The highest praise one could give The Iliad is to say that, knowing the outcome of the battle, we still share the Achaeans' agony as the Trojans force them back behind their own lines of defense. (Same goes for The Odyssey: we know that Ulysses will kill the Suitors.) What a feeling it must have been to hear the story told for the first time!

For a generous psychology.

We help a person more by giving him a positive image of himself than we do by constantly pointing out his faults. Everyone usually strives to be the best version of themselves. Can apply to pedagogy, history, philosophy, politics. We, for example, are the result of twenty centuries of Christian imagery. For 2,000 years, man has been presented with an abased image of himself. The result is clear. In any case, who can say what we would be now if the ancient ideal, with its beautiful human form, had lasted through those past twenty centuries.

To a psychoanalyst, the ego is always performing for itself, but the libretto's all wrong.

F. Alexander and H. Staub. *The Criminal.*[7] Centuries ago, hysterics were condemned; there will come a time when criminals will be treated.

"Live and die before a mirror," Baudelaire says. Too often we overlook "and die." Living, we all stand before it. But to become master of your own death, that's the hard part.

Arrest mentality.[8] He regularly frequented distinguished public establishments: concert halls, high-class restaurants. Building bonds, a solidarity with the people there, is a form of defense. And then there's warmth in rubbing elbows with others. He dreamed of publishing impressive books that would create a halo around his name and make him untouchable. As he saw it, it

7. *The Criminal, the Judge, and the Public,* written by Franz Alexander and Hugo Staub, originally appeared in German in 1929 and in a French translation in 1938.

8. An early sketch for the character Cottard. Pieces of this entry would appear in *The Plague,* part 1, in the final section.

would be enough if the cops read his books. They'd say, "But this man has such sensitivity. He's an artist. We can't condemn that kind of soul." But other times he thought a sickness, an infirmity, would protect him just as well. And just as criminals used to escape to the desert, he planned to escape to a clinic, a sanatorium, a nursing home.

He needed contact, needed warmth. He was going through his relations. "We're not doing that to Monsieur X's friend, Monsieur Y's guest." But there are never enough relations to prevent that calm, menacing arm from advancing. So, he'd consider epidemics. Imagine typhus, a plague, it happens, it has happened. In a way, it's plausible. Well, all that's changed. It's the desert that comes for you. No one has time to think about you anymore. Because that's just it: the idea that someone, without you knowing it, is thinking of you and you don't know where he's at—what he's decided, or if he's decided. So then, the plague—and I'm not talking about earthquakes.

So then, this wild heart called out to its fellow men and begged for their warmth. So then, this ravaged, shriveled soul asked the deserts for their freshness and made its peace with a sickness, a contagion, a catastrophe. (Expand on this.)

At 50 years old, A.B.'s grandfather decided he'd done enough. He lay down in his little house in Tlemcen and, until his death at 84, didn't get back up again, except to attend to essentials. He'd never wanted to spend the money to buy a watch. He kept track of time, and mealtimes in particular, by using two pots, one of which was filled with chickpeas.[9] With a steady, careful movement, he'd fill the other, and like that he'd keep track of his days, measured out in pots.

He'd already given hints at his vocation, in the sense that nothing interested him, neither work, nor friendship, nor music, nor the café. He'd never left the city he was from until he was forced to go to Oran, and then, frightened by the whole thing, he stopped at the first station outside of Tlemcen, and took the next train back. To those who were astonished he'd spent 34 years in bed, he said that religion stipulated that half a man's life was an ascent and the other half a descent, and that during the descent the man's days no longer belonged to him. Incidentally, he contradicted himself by pointing out that God didn't exist, because if He did, the existence of priests would have

9. This entry appears in *The Plague*, part 2, section 6, where it's attributed to an old asthmatic patient of Dr. Rieux's.

been pointless—but this philosophy can be attributed to how he felt about the frequent passing of the parish collection plate.

Completing the picture, his most profound wish, which he repeated to anyone who would listen: he hoped to die a very old man.

———

Is there a tragic dilettantism?

———

Having arrived at the absurd, and trying to live *accordingly*, the individual always realizes awareness is the most difficult thing in the world to maintain. Circumstances almost always get in the way. It's a matter of living lucidly in a world where fragmentation is the rule.

The real problem then, *even without God*, is the problem of psychological unity (working with the Absurd really only poses a problem with regard to the metaphysical unity of the world and the mind) and inner peace. This isn't possible without a discipline that's difficult to reconcile with the world. *That's where the problem lies.* Precisely in that it must be reconciled with the world. So then, it's a matter of realizing a *rule for living in our outer surroundings.*

The obstacle is the *life we've already lived* (work, marriage, past opinions, etc.), what's already happened. Don't evade any element of this problem.[10]

———

Despicable is the writer who speaks to exploit what he's never lived. But be careful: a murderer isn't necessarily the best person to speak about crime.[11] (But isn't he the best person to speak of *his* crime? Not even that is certain.) We have to imagine a certain distance between creation and action. The true artist finds himself halfway between his imaginings and his actions. He's the one who is "capable of." He could be what he describes, live what he writes. Only action itself would limit him; then he would be the one who *did*.

———

"Superiors never forgive their inferiors for possessing outward signs of greatness." (*The Village Priest*)[12]

---

10. At the top of the page on which this entry appears (but seemingly unconnected from the entry itself), Camus has drawn an arrow pointing toward the corner of the page, with the word "Italy," followed by two illegible words.

11. In legal terms, *assassin*, the word Camus uses here, designates premeditation, as opposed to *meurtrier* (murderer) or *tueur* (killer), though "assassin" is now often used in a broader, more general sense.

12. *Le curé de village* (*The Village Priest*) is one of the novels in Honoré de Balzac's multi-volume *La comédie humaine* (*The Human Comedy*). The novel is set in the southwest of France, in a real vil-

Id. "There's no more bread." Véronique and the Montignac Valley *grow* at the *same rate*. Same symbolism as in *The Lily*.[13]

For those who say Balzac's a bad writer, cf. the death of Mme Graslin: "Everything in her was cleansed and purified, her face full of light, reflecting the flaming swords of the guardian angels that surrounded her."

Study of Woman: The tale is impersonal—but Bianchon is the one telling it.

Alain[14] on Balzac: "His genius lies in presenting the ordinary and rendering it sublime without changing it."

Balzac and cemeteries in *Ferragus*.

Balzac's Baroque: the pages about the organ in *Ferragus* and *Duchess of Langeais*.[15]

The ardent, shadowy reflection of that flame the duchess sees at Montriveau's casts a red glow throughout all of Balzac's work.

There are two types of style: Mme de Lafayette's and Balzac's. The first is perfect in detail, the second works on a grand scale where four chapters are hardly enough to give an idea of its strength. Balzac is a good writer not *despite* but *with* his imperfect French.

—Secret of my universe: Envisioning God without human immortality.

Charles Morgan and the singleness of mind:[16] the felicity of a single intention—the firm talent of excellence—"genius is this power to die," in opposition to woman and her tragic love of life—so many themes, so much nostalgia.

Shakespeare's Sonnets:

---

lage, though Balzac spells the name Montégnac in the novel, not Montignac, as Camus has written it here and as it is spelled on maps.

13. The reference is to Balzac's *Le lys dans la vallée* (*The Lily of the Valley*), the novel preceding *The Village Priest* in the "Scenes from Country Life" segment of *The Human Comedy*.

14. Émile Chartier, pseudonym Alain (1868–1951), was a French philosopher and antiwar activist who, on one hand, argued extensively for the rights of the individual, the worker, against all forms of state power and then, on the other, privately expressed high praise for Hitler.

15. *Ferragus, Chief of the Devorants* and *The Duchess of Langeais* make up the first two parts of "The Thirteen" section of *The Human Comedy*. The third and final novel in the section is *La fille aux yeux d'or* (*The Girl with the Golden Eyes*).

16. Charles Langbridge Morgan (1894–1958), English novelist and essayist, whose 1938 play *The Flashing Stream* featured a long preface with the title "On Singleness of Mind."

"Looking on darkness which the blind do see."[17]
". . . call the fools of time,
Which die for goodness, who have lived for crime."

Countries that shelter beauty are the most difficult to defend—so difficult we'd like to spare them. So then, artistic peoples should be the chosen victims of ungrateful peoples—if, in the hearts of men, the love of freedom didn't take priority over the love of beauty. It's an instinctive wisdom—freedom being the source of beauty.

Calypso offers Ulysses the choice between immortality and his homeland. He rejects immortality. This may be The Odyssey's entire meaning.[18] In Book XI, Ulysses and the dead stand before the blood-filled pit—and Agamemnon tells him: "Be not too good to your wife and don't confide all your thoughts in her."

Note, too, that The Odyssey speaks of Zeus as the Father of Creation. A dove falls on the rock "and the Father creates another so their number may be complete."

XVII.—The dog Argos.

XXII.—They hang women who have given themselves—unbelievable cruelty.

Stendhal as ever the chronicler—See Journal, pp. 28–29.

"The most extreme passion may be killing a fly for one's mistress." "Only women of great character can make me happy."

And this little barb: "As often happens to men who have concentrated their energy on one or two vital points, he appeared indolent and unkempt."

Vol. II: "I felt so much this evening my stomach aches."

---

17. The first line comes from sonnet 27, the second and third lines are the last of sonnet 124.

18. This indeed seems to have been a crucial point for Camus, as the last paragraph of *The Rebel* begins: "At the high point of thought, the rebel refuses divinity, sharing instead the struggles and fate of the common man. We'll choose Ithaca, that faithful land, that audacious and frugal thought, that lucid action, and the generosity of the man who knows. In the light, the world remains our first and last love. Our brothers breathe beneath the same sky we do. Justice goes on living."

Stendhal, who never fooled himself about his own literary future, completely fooled himself about Chateaubriand's: "I'd be willing to bet that by 1913 no one will be talking about his writing anymore."

———

H. Heine's epitaph: "He loved the roses of the Brenta."[19]

———

Flaubert: "The sight of one man judging another would make me laugh myself to death if it didn't fill me with pity."

What he saw in Genoa: "A city made entirely of marble with gardens filled with roses."

And "Foolishness consists of wanting conclusions."

———

Flaubert's Correspondence.

Volume II. "Success with women is generally a sign of mediocrity" (?)

Id. "Live as a bourgeois and think as a demi-god" ?? cf. the story of the tapeworm.[20]

"Masterpieces are stupid: they have the untroubled look of large animals."

"If I'd been loved at 17, what an artist I'd be now!"[21]

———

"In art, you should never fear being *exaggerated* . . . but the exaggeration must be consistent—in proportion to itself."[22]

His goal: the ironic acceptance of existence and it's complete remaking through art. "Our business isn't living."

Explain the man through this keyword, which goes a long ways: "I maintain that cynicism is akin to chastity."

Id. "We wouldn't get anything done in this world if we weren't guided by false ideas" (Fontenelle).

---

19. The quote comes from Heinrich Heine's *Das Buch Le Grand*. The full sentence, translated by Charles Godfrey Leland, reads: "But when at a later day the lover has lost his love, then he will come again to the well-known linden, and sigh and weep, and gaze long and oft upon the stone until he reads the inscription, 'He loved the flowers of the Brenta.'"

20. In a January 1853 letter, Flaubert recounts the story of the family coachman who, believing he had a tapeworm that demanded constant feeding, struck upon the idea of killing the worm by drinking a bottle of sulfuric acid, which, of course, killed him.

21. The January 1853 letter referenced here reads: "what a dummy I'd be," not "what an artist I'd be."

22. In the original manuscript, Camus had written at the top of the page: "Cf. Berlioz correspondence. Theologico-political treatise." Flaubert, in his later letters, writes on multiple occasions how much he enjoys Berlioz's correspondence.

At first glance, a person's life is more interesting than his works. It's a tighter, more complete picture. Unity of mind rules over it. A single inspiration through all those years. The person *is* the novel. To be revised, obviously.

———

A lack of courage always finds its philosophy.

———

Art criticism, for fear of being labeled literature, tries to speak the language of painting, which is what makes it literary. We have to go back to Baudelaire. Human transposition, *but objective.*

———

Mme V. surrounded by the scent of rotten meat. 3 cats. 2 dogs. Holding forth on inner song. The kitchen is closed. It's dreadfully hot in there.

All the weight and heat of the sky lean atop the bay. Everything is glowing. But the sun has disappeared.

———

The difficulties of solitude are to be covered in their entirety.

———

Montaigne: A slippery, somber, and silent life.

———

Modern intelligence is in complete disarray. Knowledge has been stretched so thin that the world and mind have lost all bearing. It's a fact that we're suffering from nihilism. But what's really rich are those sermons on "turning back." Back to the Middle Ages, to their primitive mentality, to the earth, to religion, to that arsenal of old solutions. To give such balms the slightest hint of efficacy, we'd have to act as if accumulated knowledge no longer existed—as if we'd learned nothing—we'd have to pretend to erase what is, in short, inerasable. With the stroke of a pen, we'd have to cross out the contributions of several centuries and the undeniable achievements of a mind that's finally (as its last bit of progress) recreated chaos on its own terms. This is impossible. To heal, we have to come to terms with this lucidity, with this insight. We have to take into account what our exile has so suddenly illuminated for us. Intelligence isn't in disarray because knowledge has turned the world upside down. It's in disarray because it can't come to terms with the upheaval. It hasn't "gotten used to the idea." If it should do so, the disarray will disappear. The only thing left will be the upheaval and the clear knowledge the mind has of it. There's a whole civilization to be rebuilt.

———

All proofs must be tangible.

———

"Europe," Montesquieu said, "will be lost by its military men."

———

Who can say: I've had a perfect week. That's what my memory is telling me and I know it doesn't lie. Yes, this image is perfect, as those long days were perfect. Those pleasures were purely physical and had the mind's approval. There lies perfection, in harmony with our condition, the recognition and respect for mankind.

A long line of dunes, wild and pure! Feast of water, so black in the morning, so clear at noon, and warm and golden in the evening. Long mornings on the dune, among the naked bodies, the afternoons crushing, and it all has to be repeated, everything that's been said, said again. There was youth. There is youth and, at 30 years old, there's nothing I want more than for that youth to continue. But . . .

———

Copernicus and Galileo's books remained on the Index until 1822. Three centuries of pigheadedness, how very charming.

———

Death penalty. We kill the criminal because the crime completely exhausts a man's ability to go on living. If he's killed, he's lived all there is to live. He can die. Murder is exhaustive.[23]

———

What makes the literature of the 19th and especially the 20th century different from that of the classical periods? It's French, so it's moralist, too. But classical morality is a critical morality (an exception being made for Corneille)—negative. 20th-century morality, on the other hand, is positive: it defines *lifestyles*. Just look at the Romantic hero, Stendhal (he's clearly of his century but in just this way), Barrès, Montherlant, Malraux, Gide, etc.

———

Montesquieu. "Some kinds of idiocy are such that even greater idiocy would be preferable."

———

It's easier to understand "Eternal Return" if you think of it as a repetition of great moments—as if everything were geared toward reproducing or echoing humanity's highest moments. The Italian Primatives or the Passion

23. This idea would appear in *The Rebel*. See p. 194n53.

according to Saint John, reviving, imitating, endlessly commenting on the "It is finished" of that sacred hill.[24] Every defeat has an element of Athens being opened to the Roman barbarians, every victory calls Salamis to mind, etc., etc.

———

Brulard:[25] "My compositions have always inspired the same modesty in me as my loves."

Id. "A salon with eight to ten people, where all the women have had lovers, where the conversation is merry and anecdotal, where light punch is served at half-past midnight, that's the one place in the world I feel most at home."

———

Arrest mentality: as he's about to send his son his monthly allowance, he increases it by a hundred francs. He felt impelled to sentimentality, to generosity. Anxiety makes him altruistic.[26]

It's in this way that the two men who have been hunted through the city all day grow sentimental as soon as they have a chance to talk. One of them cries, talking about the wife he hasn't seen for two years. Imagine evenings in cities where the hunted individual wanders alone.

———

To J.T. about *The Stranger.*

It's a very carefully put together book and the tone . . . is on purpose. It heightens four or five times, it's true, but only to avoid monotony and to give structure. My Stranger doesn't justify himself to the chaplain. He gets angry, but that's a very different thing. So then, it's up to me to explain, you might say. Yes, and I've thought a lot about it. I did it because I decided I wanted my character to be carried toward a single big problem by way of normal, everyday events. That big moment had to stand out. Notice, though, that there's no break in my character's personality. In that chapter, as in the rest of the book, he limits himself to *responding to questions.* In the past, they were the questions the world asked us every day—in the present, they're the chaplain's questions. In this way, I define my character negatively.

With all of this, it is, of course, a matter of artistic means and not the end. The meaning of the book lies precisely in the parallelism of its two parts. Conclusion: society needs people who cry at their mother's funeral, other-

———

24. The reference is to John 19:30.

25. *The Life of Henry Brulard* (*Vie de Henri Brulard*) is Stendhal's unfinished autobiography, begun in 1836 and, as Stendhal himself assumed would be the case, not published until 1890, forty-eight years after the author's death.

26. This is used in *The Plague,* part 1, in the final section.

wise you're never condemned for the crime you think. That said, I can see ten other possible conclusions.

The great words of Napoleon: "Happiness is the greatest development of my faculties."

Before the Island of Elba: "A living lout is better than a dead emperor."

"A truly great man will always place himself above the events he has caused."

"You have to want to live and know how to die."

Criticisms of *The Stranger*. "Moral-arrhea" flows freely. Imbeciles who believe negation is a renunciation when it's a choice. (The writer of The Plague shows the heroic side of negation.) There's no other life possible for a person deprived of God—and everyone is. To imagine that virility lies in prophetic tremors, that greatness lies in spiritual affectation . . . ! But the struggle through poetry and its obscurities, the mind's supposed rebellion, is *the thing that costs the least*. It changes nothing and tyrants are well aware of it.

No tomorrow.[27]

"What am I meditating on that's greater than I am, what is this thing I feel without being able to define it? A kind of difficult march toward a holiness of negation—a heroism without God—a faithful man[28] at last. All human virtues, including solitude with regard to God.

What makes Christianity the superior *paradigm* (the only one)? Christ and his saints—the search for a *lifestyle*. This body of work will take as many forms as there are stages on the path toward a perfection without reward. The Stranger is the zero point. *Id*. The Myth. The Plague is progress, not from zero toward infinity, but toward a deeper complexity that remains to be defined. The end point will be the saint, but he'll have his arithmetic value—measurable as man."

On criticism.

---

27. "*No tomorrow*" was added to the entry at a later date, tying it to the earlier entries with the same title, as well as to the other notebook Camus had been keeping at the time.

28. *L'homme pur*, literally "pure man," could be used to indicate "clean," "innocent," or, as the case above seems to indicate, "faithful," though the implication is "faithful to man" not "faithful to God."

Three years to create a book, five lines to ridicule it—and with inaccurate quotations.

Letter to A.R.,[29] literary critic (destined never to be sent):

". . . One sentence in your critique struck me loud and clear: 'I'm not taking into account . . .' How can an enlightened critic, aware of the careful planning that goes into any work of art, not take into account, in the painting of a character, the *single moment* when that character speaks of himself and confides in the reader, revealing a part of his secret? And how could you not feel that this end was also a coming together, a privileged place where a being as fragmented as the one I described was finally gelling . . ."

". . . You assume my ambition to be realism. Realism is a word devoid of meaning (*Madame Bovary* and *The Possessed* are both realist novels and they have nothing in common). I was never concerned with it. If I had to describe my ambition, I'd speak of symbolism instead. Clearly, you were aware of this. But you assumed for this symbol a meaning it doesn't have and, to be completely honest, you've wantonly attributed a ridiculous philosophy to me. In fact, nothing in the book gives you grounds for saying I believe in the natural man, that I identify a vegetable as a human, that human nature is foreign to morality, etc., etc. The novel's main character never takes the initiative. You didn't notice he never allows himself to go beyond *responding to questions*, those of life or those of man. In this way, he never asserts anything. All I've given of him is a photo negative. Nothing that could lead you to make presumptions about his inner character, until, of course, the last chapter—but you're "not taking it into account."

The reasons for this determination to "say as little as possible" would be too long to give you, but, nevertheless, I regret that a superficial examination has led you to assume for me an armchair philosophy I'm not prepared to assume for myself. You'll have a better idea of where I'm coming from if I point out that the only quotation you give in your article is inaccurate (give it and correct it) and thus leads to unfounded conclusions. Maybe there was another philosophy there and you just barely grazed it when using the word "inhumanity." But what's the point of trying to prove it?

Maybe you'll think this is a lot of noise for a little book by an unknown writer, but I believe this situation goes beyond me, for you've taken a moral point of view that's prevented you from judging with the foresight and talent

29. Likely a reference to André Rousseaux's July 17, 1942, review of *L'Étranger* in *Le figaro littéraire*, as the complaints Camus lodges here line up with comments made in Rousseaux's review.

for which you're known. This position is unacceptable and you know it better than anyone. There's a very shaky border between your criticisms and those that could soon be made under a literary board of supervision (that were made not so long ago) about the moral character of this or that work. I say to you, without anger, that this is detestable. Neither you nor anyone else is qualified to judge if a work serves or doesn't serve the nation at the present moment or at any other time. In any case, I refuse to submit to such jurisdictions, and that's the reason for my letter. I hope you'll believe me when I say I would have accepted much harsher criticisms with equanimity if they'd been put forth in a less predetermined spirit.

I hope, in any case, that this letter hasn't given rise to any new misunderstandings. This isn't simply an unhappy author's reproach and I'd ask you not to publish any part of this letter. You don't often see my name in the popular press, easy as it may be to get into it, and that's because, having nothing to say that fits their needs, I'd rather not give in to self-promotion. At the moment, I'm publishing books that have taken me years of work, simply because they're complete and I'm moving on to those that follow. I don't expect any material profit or critical acclaim to come from them. I only hoped that they would be given the careful, patient attention given to any endeavor undertaken in good faith. I have to believe that even this was too much to ask. Please accept, nevertheless, my sincere regards and best wishes.

Three people figured into the composition of *The Stranger*: two men (one being me) and a woman.[30]

Brice Parain. Essay on the Platonic logos. Studies logos as language. Amounts to endowing Plato with a philosophy of expression. Traces Plato's efforts to find a reasonable realism. What is the "tragic" part of the problem? If our language has no meaning, nothing has any meaning. If the sophists are right, the world is nonsense. Plato's solution isn't psychological, it's cosmological. The originality of Parain's position: he considers the problem of language to be metaphysical, not social and psychological . . . etc., etc. See notes.[31]

---

30. In his biography of Camus, Olivier Todd notes that the woman was Yvonne Ducailar, whom Camus often referred to in letters and conversations as *l'étrangère*.

31. Brice Parain (1897–1971), philosopher and writer, as well as a principal partner at Gallimard. Camus wrote a long, positive review of Brice Parain's 1942 works *Essai sur le logos platonicien* and *Recherches sur la nature et les fonctions du langage* in *Poésie* 44, no. 17 (December 1943–February 1944),

French workers—the only people I feel at home with, that I'd like to know and "live" with. They are like me.

———

End of August '42.

Literature. Don't trust the word. Don't let it come from your lips too quickly. If we took literature from the great writers, we'd remove what is likely the most intimate part of them. Literature = nostalgia. Nietzsche's superman, Dostoyevsky's abyss, Gide's gratuitous act, etc., etc.

———

Noisy streams run throughout my days. They flow around me, through sun-filled meadows, then closer to me, so that soon the sound will be inside of me, that stream in my heart and that noisy fountain accompanying all my thoughts. This is forgetting.

———

Plague. Impossible to get it on track. Too many "coincidences" in its composition. Have to stick closely to the idea. *The Stranger* describes man laid bare before the absurd. *The Plague*, the fundamental equality of individual points of view faced with the same absurd. It's a progression that will be clarified in future works. What's more, though, *The Plague* shows that the absurd *teaches nothing*. It's the definitive progression.

———

Panelier.[32] Before sunrise, rising from the high hills, the fir trees are indistinguishable from the rolling hills on which they stand. Then the sun, far off in the distance, gilds the treetops from behind, bleaching the background so that it looks as if an army of feathered savages were surging up from behind the hill. As the sun rises and the sky lightens, the fir trees grow larger and the barbarian army seems to advance, massing together in a tumult of feathers, preparing for the invasion. Then, when the sun is high enough, it suddenly illuminates the fir trees pouring down the mountainside, as if in a savage race

under the title "Sur une philosophie de l'expression" (On a philosophy of expression). This entry would be used in several places throughout the essay.

32. In August 1942, Camus went to stay in Le Panelier with Francine's aunt's mother-in-law, Sarah Œttly, who had a boardinghouse there, in the Haute-Loire, at an altitude of almost three thousand feet. He'd stay through much of 1943, taking regular trips from Le Chambon-sur-Lignon to Saint-Étienne for medical treatment, during which he recorded the train observations that occur in the entries that follow.

to the valley below, the beginnings of a brief and tragic struggle in which day's barbarians will chase off night's fragile army of thoughts.

———

What's moving about Joyce isn't the work itself but the fact that he undertook it. In this way, distinguish the pathos of an undertaking—which has nothing to do with the art—and the artistic feeling itself.

———

Convince yourself a work of art is something human and that its creator shouldn't wait around for divine "dictation." *The Charterhouse*, *Phèdre*, *Adolphe* could have been very different—and no less beautiful. It all depended on their author—absolute master.

———

An essay about France, even many years from now, won't be able to go without mentioning the current moment. This thought came to me on a small, local train as I watched file past, massed in tiny stations, those French faces and silhouettes it'll be hard for me to forget: old peasant couples, she papery, he with a smooth face lit with two light-colored eyes and a white mustache—silhouettes wrung out by two winters of deprivation, dressed in glossy, patched-together clothing. Elegance has abandoned these people in whom poverty dwells. The briefcases on the trains are tattered, held shut with twine, patched up with cardboard. All French people look like emigrants.

Id. in industrial cities—that old workman seen at his window, wearing his spectacles, taking advantage of the last light of day to do some reading, his book wisely laid flat between his two spread out hands.

At the station, masses of hurried people down vile food without objection and then go out into the dark city, shoulder to shoulder without ever mingling, returning to their hotel, their room, etc. A silent and hopeless life the whole of France endures in suspended animation.

Around the 10th, the 11th, the 12th of the month, everyone smokes. By the 18th, it's impossible to get a light in the street. On the trains, people talk about the drought. It's less dramatic here than in Algeria but no less tragic. An old workman tells of his poverty: a two-room place an hour from Saint-Étienne. Two hours on the road, eight hours of work—nothing to eat at home—too poor to take advantage of the black market. A young woman does hours of washing because she has two children and her husband came back from the war with a stomach ulcer. "He's to be fed well-cooked white meat. Where are you going to find that? They gave him a diet certificate. So, they give him ¾ of a liter of milk, but they took away all the fats. Have you ever heard of keeping a man fed on milk alone?" Her clients' clothes are sometimes stolen from her and she has to pay for them.

All the while, the rain drowns the industrial valley's grimy landscape—the acrid scent of its poverty—the awful suffering of those lives. And the others, they're making speeches.

Saint-Étienne, there in the morning mist, sirens sounding the call to work, the call to the center of that jumble of towers, of buildings and tall chimneys carrying to their tops, toward a sky covered in shadows, their deposits of slag, the valley like a monstrous sacrificial cake.

Budejovice, Act III.[33] The sister comes back after the mother's suicide.

Scene with the wife: "What makes you think you can say that?"

"My love makes me think it."

"What's that?"

The sister walks out to end it. The wife screams and cries. The taciturn maidservant enters, drawn by the crying:

"Ah, you, at least you'll help me!"

"No." (Curtain.)

All great virtues have an absurd side.

Nostalgia for others' lives. It's because, seen from the outside, those lives appear whole, whereas our own, seen from the inside, seem fragmented. We're still chasing after an illusion of unity.

Science explains how things work, not how things *are.* Ex: why are there different types of flowers rather than just one?

Novel. "He'd wait for her in the morning at the corner of the meadow, under the tall hazel trees, in the cold autumn wind. Wasps buzzing without warmth, the wind in the leaves, a rooster obstinately crowing behind the hills, hollow barking, and, here and there, the cawing of a crow. Between the dark September sky and the damp earth, he felt as if he were waiting for winter as well as for Marthe."

---

33. These notes would be used for *The Misunderstanding*'s final scenes.

Coupling with beasts eliminates concern for *the other*. It's "freedom." That's why it's attracted so many minds, even Balzac.[34]

Panelier. September's first rains arrive with a light wind that lifts the yellow leaves into the downpour. They hover for a moment, then the weight of the water they retain suddenly flattens them to the ground. When nature is plain, as it is here, it's easier to notice the changing of the seasons.

Childhood poverty.[35] The overly large raincoat—the siesta. Canette Vinga—Sundays at the aunt's place. The books—the municipal library. Coming home on Christmas Eve and the dead body in front of the restaurant. The games in the basement (Jeanne, Joseph, and Max). Jeanne collecting all the buttons: "That's how you get rich." The brother's violin and singing lessons—Galoufa.

Novel. Don't put "The Plague" in the title. Something like "The Prisoners" instead.

Avakkum and his wife on foot in Siberia's frozen wasteland. The Archpriestess: "Have we long to suffer, Archpriest?" Avakkum: "Until death, Daughter of Mark." She, sighing: "Well, then we'd better get walking again, Son of Peter."[36]

I Corinthians, VII, 27: "Art thou bound unto a wife? Seek not to be loosed. Art thou loosed from a wife? Seek not a wife."

Luke, VI, 26: "Woe unto you, when all men shall speak well of you!"

As an apostle, Judas performed miracles (Saint John Chrysostom).

---

34. The remark is likely in reference to Balzac's *Une passion dans le désert* (*A Passion in the Desert*), in which a soldier falls in love with a panther.

35. Almost all the elements of this entry would be expanded on in *The First Man*. In chap. 4, "The Child's Games," for example, Camus describes "canette Vinga" as a "poor man's tennis." In chap. 6a, "School," Camus explains that Galoufa is the nickname Jacques and his friends give the municipal dog-catcher, whose efforts they try to thwart. For more on the events of Christmas Eve mentioned here, see p. 15n10.

36. Archpriest Petrovich Avvakum's (1620–1682) memoirs were translated into French by Pierre Pascal in 1938. Avvakum, a religious dissident and leader of The Old Believers, was exiled to Siberia several times before finally being burned at the stake. In 2021, the memoirs appeared in an English translation by Kenneth N. Brostrom as *The Life Written by Himself*.

Zhuang Zhou (the 3rd of the great Taoists—2nd half of the 4th century B.C.) shares Lucretius's point of view: "The great bird rises on the wind to a height of 90,000 stadia. What it sees from up there are galloping bands of wild horses."

———

Until the Christian era, Buddha is not represented because he's nirvanic, which is to say depersonalized.

———

According to Proust, it's not that nature imitates art, it's that great artists teach us to see in nature what their work, in its own incomparable way, has isolated from it. All women become Renoirs.

"At the foot of the bed, racked by those final agonized breaths, not crying but at times drenched with tears, my mother bore the unthinking desolation of a leaf whipped by the rain and thrown back by the wind." *Gu.*

"It's rare for those who have played an important part in our life to suddenly and definitively exit it." *Gu.*[37]

In Search of Lost Time is a heroic and potent work:

1) on account of the perseverance of creative will

2) on account of the effort it demanded of a sick man[38]

"When bouts of illness forced me not only to remain without sleep for several consecutive days and nights but without lying down, without drinking and without eating, at the moment the exhaustion and suffering became such that I thought I'd never escape them, I thought of a certain traveler washed up on shore, poisoned by inedible herbs, shivering with fever in his seawater-soaked clothes, who, all the same, felt better two days later, set back out at random, searching for any inhabitants whatsoever who might be cannibalistic. Their example invigorated me, gave me hope, and I was ashamed of having had a moment's despondency." (Sodom and Gomorrah).

———

37. The reference to Renoir, as well at the two direct quotes given here, appear in *The Guermantes Way*, the third volume in Proust's *In Search of Lost Time*.

38. As with the earlier comment about Joyce's work, Camus again makes a distinction here between the act of creation and the creation itself. In *The Rebel*, Camus writes: "Proust's true greatness is to have written *Time Regained*. . . . In its ambition, at least, *Time Regained* is eternity without God. In this regard, Proust's work seems one of the most immeasurable and significant ventures man has taken against its mortal condition. He's shown that the art of the novel recreates creation itself, such as it's imposed on us and as we reject it."

He doesn't sleep with a hooker who approaches him, whom he wants to sleep with, because he only has a thousand-franc note on him and wouldn't dare ask her for change.

Feeling opposite to Proust's: standing before each city, each new apartment, each person, each rose and each flame, marveling at their novelty while wondering what habit will make of them—looking for the future "familiarity" they'll bring, seeking out times yet to come.

Example:

Solitary arrivals in unknown cities at night—that feeling of suffocation, of being overwhelmed by an entity a thousand times more complex. All you have to do the next day is find the main street, see how everything is laid out in relation to it, and then you settle down. Collect nocturnal arrivals in foreign cities, living off the power of those unknown hotel rooms.

On the tram: "He was born normal, but a week later his eyelids glued shut. So, it was only natural his eyes rotted."

As when we're attracted to certain cities (almost always those where we've already lived) or certain lives by images of sex—and then find we've been duped, for even the less spiritual among us never live according to sex, or, at the very least, encounter too many things in everyday life that have nothing to do with sex. So that after having painfully incarnated one of these images, from time to time, or recalled one of those memories, long stretches of empty time begin to hang on life like dead skin. Then, off we go to desire other cities.

Critique of *The Stranger*: Impassivity, they say. The wrong word. Benevolence would be better.[39]

Budejovice (or God Doesn't Answer).[40] The taciturn maidservant is an old manservant.

---

39. By "they," Camus means Henri Hell (José Enrique Lasry), who reviewed *The Stranger* in the July 1942 issue of *Fontaine*, a magazine founded by Camus's friend Max-Pol Fouchet. In the review, Hell uses the word "impassive" on three separate occasions and, more generally, links Camus's ideas with those of Sartre, Kierkegaard, and Malraux.

40. A second version of *The Misunderstanding*'s final scene.

The wife in the final scene: "Lord, have mercy on me, turn to me. Hear me, Lord. Reach your hand out to me. Lord, have mercy on those who are in love and who are separated."

The Old Man enters.

"You called me?"

The Wife: "Yes . . . no . . . I don't know anymore. But help me, help me, for I need someone to help me. Have mercy and say you'll help me."

The Old Man: "No."

(Curtains)

Look for details to reinforce the symbolism.

———

How is it that her face, linked to so much suffering, is still the face of happiness for me?

———

Novel. By the dying body of the woman he loves: "I can't, I can't let you die, for I know I'll forget you. Then, I'll lose everything, and I want to keep you on this side of the world, the only side where I'm able to hold you tight," etc., etc.

Her: "Oh, it's awful to die knowing you'll be forgotten."

Always see and express both aspects *at the same time*.[41]

———

Clearly summarize my intentions with *The Plague*.

———

OCTOBER. In the still-green grass the leaves are already yellow. With a sonorous sun shining on the green anvil of the meadows, a quick and lively wind forges a bar of light through which a murmur of bees reaches out to me. Red beauty.

Splendid, poisonous, and solitary as red fly agaric.[42]

———

In Spinoza you can see the cult of what is and not what should or must be—the hatred of black-and-white values, of moral hierarchy—a certain equivalence between virtues and vices bathed in divine light. "People prefer

———

41. Parts of this entry would go on to appear not in a novel but in *State of Emergency*, part 3.

42. In French, Camus writes *rouge oronge*, which leaves some room for interpretation, as "fly agaric" is formally referred to as *fausse oronge*, while the term *oronge* on its own refers to "Caesar's Mushroom." Still, the description of the mushroom as being both "red" and "poisonous" would seem to indicate fly agaric.

order to confusion, as if order corresponded to something real in nature" (App., Bk. I).

What he'd find inconceivable isn't God having created imperfection and perfection at the same time, but not having created it. For having the power to create the whole gamut, from the perfect to the imperfect, he couldn't have failed to do so. From our point of view, this can only be seen as regrettable, but that's not the right way to look at it.

This God and this universe are stationary and their reasons are in harmony with them. Everything is given once and for all. It's up to us, if we so desire, to untangle the consequences and reasons (whence the geometrical form). But this universe tends toward nothing and comes from nothing because it already is, and always has been, complete. There is no tragedy in it because there is no history in it. It is as inhuman as could be. It's a world that requires courage.

[A world without art, as well—because without chance (book 1's appendix denies there's such a thing as ugly or beautiful).]

Nietzsche says mathematical form is only justified by Spinoza as a means of *aesthetic* expression.

See *Ethics*, Bk. I. Prop. XI gives four proofs of God's existence. Prop. XIV and the long Scholia in XV, which seems to negate creation.

Could justify those who speak of Spinoza's pantheism? There is, however, a postulate there (a word Spinoza avoids throughout *Ethics*): the void does not exist (demonstrated, it's true, in the preceding volumes).

You can juxtapose the XVII and the XXIV: the one proving necessity, the other serving to reintroduce contingency. Proposition XXV establishes the relationship between distance and modes. In XXI, at last, the will is constrained. God, as well, by his own nature. XXXIII further tightens this tightly bound world. It would seem that for Spinoza, God's nature is stronger than He is—though in prop. XXXIII he declares (in opposition to the partisans of Sovereign Good) that it's absurd to subject God to fate.

This world is given once and for all, it's a world in which "that's how it is"—in it, necessity is infinite—originality and chance play no part. In it, everything is monotonous.

Curious. Intelligent historians tracing the history of a country do everything they can to advance policies—realistic, for example—similar to those that brought about, it seems to them, that country's greatest period. Yet they themselves point out that such a state of affairs has never lasted very long, because soon enough another statesman or a new regime came along and spoiled everything. Nevertheless, they persist in defending policies that don't account for, that aren't resistant to, changes in leadership, even though politics is entirely based on changes in leadership. It's because they only think and write for the period in which they live. The historian's alternative: skepticism or political theory that doesn't depend on changes in leadership (?)

———

This lovely effort is to genius as the jerky flight of a grasshopper is to that of a swallow.

———

"Sometimes, after all those days commanded by will alone, when work was constructed hour by hour, when it allowed neither distraction nor weakness, when it wished to ignore feeling and the world, O, what abandon gripped me, with what relief did I throw myself into the heart of that distress that had accompanied me through all those days. What desire, what temptation to be nothing that had to be constructed, to abandon this work and this so-difficult face I had to model. I loved, I regretted, I desired, I was, in the end, a man . . .

. . . the deserted summer sky, the sea I loved so much, and those tender lips."

———

Maybe sexual life was given to man to turn him from his true path. It's his opium. Inside it, everything drifts off to sleep. Outside it, things come back to life.[43] At the same time, chastity extinguishes the species, which is maybe the truth.

———

A writer should never talk about his doubts with his creation in front of him. It would be too easy to say to him: "Who's forcing you to create? If it's such continual anguish, why do you keep doing it?" Doubts are the most intimate thing we have. Never talk about your doubts—*whatever they may be.*

———

Wuthering Heights is one of the greatest novels about love because it ends in failure and rebellion—by which I mean death without hope. The main

43. An extra bit of innuendo could be extrapolated here, as French nouns and pronouns, including those used for ideas and objects, are gendered, so that where English uses "it" to refer back to "sexual life" in the above entry, French uses *elle* (her).

character is the devil. Such love can only be sustained in the final failure that is death. It can only continue on in hell.

———

October.

The great red woods beneath the rain, the fields all covered in yellow leaves, the scent of drying mushrooms, the wood fires (the pine cones reduced to glowing-red embers, like diamonds from hell), the wind moaning around the house, where else is autumn as traditional as this. The peasants walk a little bent forward now—against the wind and the rain.

In the autumn forest, the beeches create golden-yellow spots or stand isolated at the edge of the woods like fat nests dripping with golden honey.

———

October 23. Beginning.

The Plague has a social meaning and a metaphysical meaning. It's exactly the same. This ambiguity is also present in *The Stranger*.

———

People say: he cares no more about it than about a fly—and that doesn't mean much. But watch a fly die stuck to that paper of theirs—the kind made just for them—and you'll realize the inventor of the thing thought long and hard about that awful and insignificant method of dying—that slow death that barely gives off the slightest whiff of putrefaction. It's genius that creates the commonplace.

———

Idea: He refuses everything that's offered to him, all the happiness that comes his way, on account of a deeper need. He ruins his marriage, engages in unsatisfying liaisons, waits, hopes. "I can't really define it, but I feel it." Continues like this until the end of his life. "No, I'll never be able to define it."

———

Sexuality leads to nothing. It's not immoral but it is unproductive. You can indulge in it as long as you don't wish to produce. But only chastity is linked to personal progress.

There's a time when sexuality is a victory—when you detach it from moral imperatives. But then it quickly becomes a defeat—and then the only victory conquers it in turn: chastity.

———

Think about a commentary for Molière's *Don Juan*.

November '42.

In autumn, this countryside blossoms in leaves—the cherry trees turning all red, the yellow maples, the beeches tanning. The plateau is covered in the thousand flames of a second spring.

The renunciation of youth. I'm not the one who renounces people and things (I couldn't), it's the things and people that renounce me. My youth escapes me: that's the meaning of being ill.

The first thing for writers to learn is how to transpose what they feel into what they want to make felt. The first few times they succeed by chance. But after that talent has to take the place of chance. So then, there's an element of luck at the root of genius.

He always says: "In my country, it's what we'd call . . ." and then he adds a banal phrase that doesn't come from any country at all. Ex: In my country, it's what we'd call perfect weather (or a dazzling career, or a model young lady, or fairytale lighting).[44]

NOVEMBER 11. Like rats!

In the morning, everything is covered in frost, the sky sparkling behind the garlands and banners of an impeccable country bazaar.[45] At 10:00, as the sun begins to warm, the whole countryside fills with the crystalline music of an overhead thaw: the crackling sighs of the trees, the frost falling to the ground like the sound of white insects thrown one atop the other, the late leaves weighed down with ice falling one after the next and barely bouncing against the earth as if they were weightless bones. All around, valleys and hills

---

44. A verbal tic Camus would give to Grand in *The Plague*. Earlier in these pages, Camus records verbal tics he would give to Masson in *The Stranger*.

45. Operation Torch was carried out by Allied forces, led by General Dwight D. Eisenhower, November 8–16, 1942. The operation, which began with invasions of Oran, Algiers, and Casablanca, cut Camus off from friends and family, including his wife, whom he wouldn't see again until October 1944.

vanish into smoke. If you look long enough, you can see that this country, in losing all its color, has suddenly aged. Over the course of a single morning, a very old country rises up through the ages . . . That tree-and-fern covered spur pushes forward like a prow at the confluence of two rivers. Cleared of frost by the sun's first rays, it's the only living thing remaining in the middle of this countryside white as eternity. In this spot, at least, the two stream's muddled voices join forces against the boundless silence that surrounds them. But little by little, even the waters' song is itself incorporated into the countryside. Without getting any quieter, it nevertheless grows silent. And the closer you get, the more you need the three smoke-colored crows passing overhead to return signs of life to the sky.

Sitting at the prow's summit, I continue on this motionless navigation through the land of indifference. No less than all of nature and that white peace that winter brings to overheated hearts—to soothe this heart devoured by a bitter love. I watch this swelling of light spread out through the sky, denying omens of death. A sign of the future at last, beyond me to whom everything now speaks of the past. Keep quiet, lungs! Suck down this pale and icy air that nourishes you. Be silent. Let me no longer be forced to hear your slow decay—let me finally turn toward . . .

———

Saint-Étienne

I know what Sunday is like for a poor working man. I know, especially, what Sunday evening is like, and if I could give meaning and form to what I know, then from a poor Sunday I could make a work of humanity.

———

I shouldn't have written: if the world were clear, there'd be no art—rather, if the world seemed to me to have meaning, I wouldn't write. There are cases when you have to be personal, out of modesty. Adding that phrase would have forced me to think a little clearer and, in the end, I wouldn't have written it. It's a brilliant truth, with no basis.[46]

———

46. The reference is to a line Camus wrote in *The Myth of Sisyphus*, which had just been published in October: "The absurd work illustrates the renunciation of thought's prestige, leaving it as nothing more than the intelligence that works up appearances and uses images to cover what has no reason. If the world were clear, there'd be no art."

Unbridled sexuality leads to a philosophy of the nonsignificance of the world. Chastity, on the other hand, gives meaning back to it (to the world).

Kierkegaard. Aesthetic value of marriage. Definitive views but too wordy.

Role of ethics and aesthetics in the formation of personality: a lot more solid and moving. Apologia for the *universal.*[47]

For Kierkegaard, the goal of aesthetic morality is originality—and in reality, it's a matter of getting back to the universal. *Kierkegaard is not mystical.* He criticizes mysticism because it separates itself from the world—precisely because it's not part of the universal. If there's a leap in Kierkegaard, then it's in the realm of intelligence. It's a leap in its pure state. That's at the ethical stage. But the religious stage transfigures everything.

At what point does life become fate? At death? But that's a fate *for others*, for history or for a person's family. Through consciousness? But it's the mind that creates an image of life as fate, that introduces coherence there where there is none. In both cases, it's an illusion. Conclusion?: there is no fate?

Excessive use of Eurydice in the literature of the '40s. It's because never have so many lovers been separated.[48]

Kafka's whole art consists of compelling the reader to *reread.*[49] His endings—or lack of endings—suggest explanations, but explanations that are never explicitly stated and that require the story to be reread from a different perspective in order to seem well-founded. Sometimes there are two or three possible interpretations, which in turn require two or three readings. But it would be wrong to try to do an in-depth interpretation of every detail in Kafka. A symbol is always general and the artist gives a rough translation

---

47. See Kierkegaard's *Fear and Trembling* and his concept of the "universal." His three "stages of life" are aesthetic, ethical, and religious.

48. Camus ends *The Plague*, chap. 4, sec. 1, with a staging of Orpheus and Eurydice. In 1941, French playwright Jean Anouilh had just written a play titled *Eurydice* (performed on Broadway, in English, as *Legend of Lovers*).

49. Camus's essay "Hope and the Absurd in the Work of Franz Kafka" was originally intended to be part of *The Myth of Sisyphus* but was removed because of the censors. It would first be published in 1943, in *L'arbalète*, a literary magazine featuring "contraband" writing, before finally being included as an appendix to *The Myth of Sisyphus* in 1945. The entry recorded here would become the essay's opening paragraph.

of it. There is no word for word. Only the gestures are sketched. And for the rest, we have to let chance play its part, a big part of any creator.

———

In this country where winter has suppressed all color, everything here being white, where the slightest sound is smothered by snow, where any fragrance is covered by cold, the first scent of Spring grass inevitably appears as a joyous call, a blaring trumpet, of sensation.

———

Illness is a convent that has its own rule, its asceticism, its silences, and its inspirations.

———

In the Algerian night, dogs' howls echo through spaces ten times larger than those in Europe. This endows them with a nostalgia unknown in those narrow countries. Today, it's a language I only hear in my memory.

———

Development of the absurd:

1. if the fundamental concern is the need for unity;

2. if the world (or God) can't satisfy it.

It's up to man to fabricate a unity for himself, either in turning away from the world or within the world. In this way, morality and asceticism, which remain to be defined, are restored.

———

To live with your passions is also to live with your suffering—which is the counterweight, the corrective, the balance, and the payment. As soon as a person has learned—and not on paper—how to be alone with the intimacy of their suffering, how to overcome their desire to run from it, the illusion that others can "share" in it, there remains little else for them to learn.

———

Let's suppose a thinker, after having published a number of works, declares in a new book: "Until now, I've been headed in the wrong direction. I'm going to start all over again. I realize now I was wrong." Nobody would take him seriously anymore. And yet he would be proving he's worthy of thought.

———

Woman, outside of love, is boring. She doesn't know. You have to live with one and be quiet. Or sleep with them all and be active. The most important things are elsewhere.

———

Pascal: error comes from exclusion.

Equivalence in Macbeth: "Fair is foul and foul is fair," but this has a diabolical origin. "And nothing is but what is not." And elsewhere, in act 2, scene 3: "for from this instant there is nothing serious in morality." Garnier translates "The night is long that never finds the day" as "Il n'est si longue nuit qui n'atteigne le jour" (?)[50]

M.[51]—"it is a tale told by an idiot, full of sound and fury, signifying nothing."

The gods have placed great and glittering virtues in man, putting him in a position to conquer everything. But, at the same time, they've also placed a more bitter virtue in man, one that causes him to look down on everything that can be conquered after it has been.

. . . To always enjoy is impossible, weariness eventually shows up—Perfect. But why? In reality, you can't always enjoy because you can't enjoy everything. You feel as much weariness in considering all the potential enjoyments that, no matter what you do, you'll never have, as you feel appreciation for the ones you've already had. If you could, in fact, truly embrace everything, would weariness still exist?

Question to ask: Do you love ideas—passionately, pulse pounding? Does the idea keep you up at night? Do you feel you're betting your life on it? How many thinkers would take a step back!

For publication of the plays: Caligula: *tragedy*—The Exile (or Budejovice): *comedy.*

---

50. It seems likely Camus was reading a bilingual edition of *Macbeth* put out by the French publisher Garnier, as all the quotes from the play appear in the original English in Camus's notebook. The translation discrepancy Camus points out toward the end of the entry—"The night is long that never finds the day" vs. "The night isn't so long that it doesn't find the day"—indicates that he was indeed reading the French and English together and, moreover, that he had a fairly strong grasp of written English.

51. In Camus's small, tight handwriting, it's hard to tell if this is simply the letter *M*, indicating that the line is spoken by Macbeth, or if it's *oui*, indicating Camus's agreement with the given quote.

December 15.

Accept the test, draw unity from it. If the other doesn't respond, die in diversity.

———

Beauty, Nietzsche says, echoing Stendhal, is a promise of happiness. But if it's not happiness itself, what can it promise?[52]

———

. . . It was when everything was covered in snow that I noticed the doors and windows were blue.

———

If it's true that crime exhausts a person's entire capacity to live (see above) . . . [53] Then that's the way Cain's crime (and not Adam's, which, next to this, seems a venial sin) drained our strength and our love of life. To the extent we share in his nature and his damnation, we suffer from that strange vacancy, that melancholy maladjustment, that follows overly large outpourings and draining gestures. With a single blow, Cain emptied all possibility of an effective life for us. That's how it is in hell. Though we can clearly see it here on earth.

———

The Princess of Clèves. Not so simple as that. It bounces back and forth between several storylines. It begins with complication, even if it ends with unity. Next to Adolphe, it's a complex serial.[54]

Its real simplicity is in its conception of love. For Mme de Lafayette, love is peril. That's her postulate. And what you feel all throughout her book, as in *The Princess of Montpensier* or *The Countess of Tende*, is a constant suspicion of love. (Which, of course, is the opposite of indifference.)

"A pardon was granted when the only thing he'd been expecting was the death blow. But fear had such a hold on him he lost consciousness and died a few days later." (*All* of de Lafayette's characters who die, die of *feeling*. It's understandable that feeling would cause her such fright.)

---

52. The reference is to Stendhal's *On Love*, chap. 17, "Beauty Dethroned by Love," where Stendhal writes: "Beauty is only the promise of happiness. A Greek's happiness was different from the happiness of a French person in 1822. Just look at the eyes of the Venus de' Medici and compare them to the eyes of the Magdalene of Pordenone."

53. See Camus's earlier entry, p. 174n23.

54. Camus expands on this entry in his essay "Intelligence and the Scaffold." In 1954, Camus would begin working on a film adaptation of *The Princess of Clèves*, and, though he never completed the project, pieces of the script can be found in his archives. Like *The Princess of Clèves*, Benjamin Constant's novel *Adolphe* also explores contemporary ideas about love.

"I told her that as long as his affliction had its limits, I accepted it and shared in it, but that I would cease to pity him if he drifted off into hopelessness and lost his mind." Magnificent. That's the modesty of our great age. It's manly. But it's not unfeeling. For the same man (the Prince of Clèves) who says this will then die precisely of hopelessness.

"The Chevalier de Guise . . . resolved never to think of being loved by Mme de Clèves. But to give up that endeavor that had seemed so difficult and glorious to him, he needed some other whose greatness could occupy him. He set his mind to taking Rhodes."

"What Mme de Clèves had said of his portrait brought him back to life by letting him know that it was him *she did not hate*." The word burns her mouth.

Poverty is a state whose virtue is generosity.

Childhood poverty. Essential difference when I went to my uncle's house: at home, things didn't have names. We'd say: the soup plates, the pot by the fireplace, etc. At his house: the glazed Vosges, the Quimper service set, etc.—I awoke to choice.[55]

Raw physical desire is easy. Desire and affection at the same time takes time. You have to cross all the countries of love before finding the flame of desire. Is that why it's always so difficult, at the start, to desire what you love?

Essay about rebellion.[56] Nostalgia for "beginnings." *Id.* the theme of the relative—but *passionately relative*. Ex: torn between a world that isn't enough

---

55. The uncle referred to here is Gustave Acault, who married Camus's aunt Gaby (née Antoinette Sintès) and worked as a butcher on Rue Michelet in Algiers. As a student, Camus lived with him for a period, as the family thought the less impoverished home environment, and the food it could provide, might help ameliorate Camus's tuberculosis. Though Camus looked up to his uncle as a father, the two had a falling out when Camus married Simone Hié against his uncle's wishes.

56. The first expression of an idea Camus would expand on in "La remarque sur la révolte," published in *L'existence* in 1945 and then in the first chapter of *The Rebel* in 1951.

In these early notebook entries, Camus uses only the word *Révolte* to indicate notes being made for *L'homme révolté*, just as he uses *Peste* to indicate entries being made for *La Peste*. When Camus uses *Révolte* in this way, indicating notes for the book to come, the translation given is "Rebellion," not *The Rebel*, as he hadn't yet included the word "homme." In the years since the book's English publication, some have questioned the translation of the title—as well as the translation of the book as a whole—but in a June 27, 1952, letter to Camus, Blanche Knopf, his American publisher, indicates that it was Camus himself who chose the English title *The Rebel*, as she had previously been referring to the book as "Man in Revolt." Blanche, who wrote to Camus mostly in English, felt, as she told

and a God that isn't there, the absurd mind passionately chooses the world. *Id*: split between the relative and the absolute, it ardently leaps into the relative.

Now that he knows the price, he's dispossessed. The condition for possession is ignorance. Even when it comes to the physical: you only really possess the unknown.

Budejovice (or *The Exile*).

I

The Mother: "No, not tonight. Let's leave him this bit of time and rest. Let's allow ourselves this window. Maybe we can be saved in that window."[57]

The Daughter: "What do you mean by be saved?"

The Mother: "Receive eternal forgiveness."

The Sister: "Then I'm already saved, because I've already forgiven myself in advance for all the times to come."

II

Id. see above.

Sister: "In the name of what?"

The Wife: "In the name of my love."

Sister: "What does that word mean?"

(Passage).

Wife: "Love is my past joy and my present grief."

Sister: "You certainly speak a language I don't understand. Love, joy, grief. I've never heard words like those before."

III

"Ah!" he says before dying. "Then this world isn't made for me and this house isn't my home."

The Sister: "The world is made for people to die and houses for people to sleep."

IV

2nd Act. Meditation on hotel rooms. He rings. Silence. Footsteps. The old mute appears. Stays by the door a minute, still and silent.

"Nothing," the other says. "Nothing. I wanted to see if anyone would answer, if the bell worked."

Konrad Bieber, that "Camus's English is much better than average." So much so that she suggested he should be the one to edit or do some of the English translations himself.

57. The numbered entries that follow would all, with some revision, be incorporated into *The Misunderstanding*.

The old man, still for a moment, goes on his way. Footsteps.

V

The Sister: "Pray that God turns you to stone. That's true happiness and that's what he's chosen for himself.

He's deaf, I tell you, and dumb as a rock. Be like him and you'll know nothing of the world but flowing water and the warming sun. Become one with stone while there's still time" (expand on this).

The absurd world receives only an aesthetic justification.

Nietzsche: "Nothing decisive is built but on a 'despite it all.'"

Maurice Blanchot's metaphysical novels

Thomas the Obscure.[58] What attracts Anne in Thomas is the death he carries inside him. Her love is metaphysical. That's why she lets go of him at the moment of death. For at that moment she *knows* and we love by not knowing. So then, only death is true knowledge. But at the same time, it's also what makes knowledge useless: its progress is sterile.

Thomas discovers death in himself, which prefigures his future. The key to the book is given in chapter 14. Then you have to reread and everything is illuminated—but in that flat light that bathes the asphodels of our mortal destination.[59] (Near the farm, a unique tree, formed from two married trunks, one of which, long dead, base rotted, no longer even touches the ground. It remains attached to the first one and the two of them together symbolize Thomas rather well. But the living trunk hasn't let itself be suffocated. It's thickened the bark embracing the dead trunk—it's spread its branches all around and over it—it hasn't let itself be dragged down.)

Aminadab, despite appearances, is more obscure. It's a retelling of the Myth of Orpheus and Eurydice (note that in both books the impression of weariness the character seems to feel, and that he simultaneously gives to the reader, is an *artistic impression*).

Plague: Second Draft

58. Maurice Blanchot (1907–2003), French writer and philosopher, whose first novel, *Thomas l'Obscur*, was published in 1941, and his second, *Aminadab*, in 1942.

59. In Greek mythology, the asphodel—which also appears in *The Stranger*—is closely associated with the land of the dead.

Bible: Deuteronomy 28:21; 32:24. Leviticus 26:25. Amos 4:10. Exodus 9:4; 9:15; 8:29. Jeremiah 24:10; 14:12; 6:19; 21:7 and 9. Ezekiel 5:12; 6:12; 7:15.[60]

"Each man seeks out his desert and, as soon it's found, recognizes it's too harsh. It will not be said that I cannot bear mine."

Originally,[61] the first three parts, composed of newspapers—notebooks—notes—sermons—treatises—and objective accounts were to suggest, intrigue, and open the depths of the book. The last part, composed solely of events, was to translate the general meaning through those events and only those events.

Each part was also to draw the links between the characters a little tighter—and was to make this felt + by the gradual merging of the diaries into a single one and was to tie it all together in the scenes making up the fourth part.

Second Draft

The Plague, picturesque and descriptive—short documentary segments and a disquisition on pestilence.

Stephan—chap. 2: He curses the love that's stripped him of everything else.

Put everything in indirect discourse (sermons—newspapers, etc.) and monotonous relief through portraits of the Plague?

It absolutely has to be an account, a chronicle. But how many problems this poses.

Maybe: completely rewrite Stephan, removing the love theme. Stephan lacks development. What followed gave a fuller picture.

Follow the theme of separation to the end.

Have a comprehensive report written on the plague in O?[62]

Those who find a flea on themselves.

A chapter on poverty.

For the sermon: "Have you noticed, my brothers, how monotonous Jeremiah is?"

---

60. Each of these references deal with God sending forth a plague. In Paneloux's first sermon in *The Plague,* he, too, will discuss God sending out plagues.

61. The rest of the entry (after the word "Originally") doesn't appear in the handwritten notebook; rather, Camus has written "see Notebook," referring to the set of notes he kept exclusively for *The Plague.* The words that follow have been restored from those notes.

62. Here, *O* stands for Oran.

Additional character: a man who's been separated, an exile who will do anything to get out of the city but can't.[63] His approach: he wants to be granted safe passage under the pretext "that he's not from here." If he dies, show that he suffers first and foremost from not having been able to get back to the other, and having left so many things hanging. That gets at what's worst about the plague.

Be aware: asthma doesn't justify so many visits.

Introduce Oran's atmosphere.

Nothing "forced," only natural.

Civilian heroism.

Expand the social critique and rebellion. What they lack is imagination. They settle into the epic as if at a picnic. They don't consider the scale of pestilence. The remedies they're able to imagine are hardly up to a head cold. They'll perish (expand).

A chapter on the disease. "They realized once more that physical pains never came all on their own but were always accompanied by moral suffering (family—loves stripped away), which gave the physical its depth. They realized, then—contrary to popular opinion—that if one of the human condition's atrocious privileges was to die alone, it was no less cruel and no less true an image that a person could never really die alone."

Morality of the plague: it serves nothing and nobody. Only those touched by death, personally or through loved ones, learn anything. But the truth that they've gained concerns only them. It has no future.

The events and chronicles have to give the Plague its social meaning. The characters give the deeper meaning. But all of this in broad strokes.

Social critique. When the administration, which is an abstract entity, and the plague, which is the most concrete of all powers, meet, the result can only be comic and scandalous.

The man who's been separated escapes because *he can't just wait until she gets old.*

A chapter on single parents *in the camps.*

End of the first part. The increase in cases of plague has to be based on the increase in rats. More. More.

A phony plague?[64]

---

63. In *The Plague,* this would become the journalist, Rambert.

64. The "Phony War" (literally: "strange" or "funny" war in French) originally referred to the initial eight-month period after France and the United Kingdom declared war on Nazi Germany but before major physical military action began. Over time, the term has come to refer to any situation

The first part is a part of the exposition that should move very quickly as a whole—even in the newspapers.

One of the possible themes: struggle between medicine and religion: the power of the relative (and how relative!) against those of the absolute. It's the relative that triumphs or, more precisely, that doesn't lose.

"Of course, we know the plague has its benefits, that it opens our eyes, that it forces us to think. In that regard, it's like all the world's evils and the world itself. But what's also true of the world's evils and of the world itself is also true of the plague. Whatever greatness individuals may draw from it, when we take our brothers' suffering into consideration, a person would have to be a madman, a criminal, or a coward to approve of the plague, and when faced with it, man's only rallying cry is rebellion."

Everyone searches for peace. Underscore this.

? Present Cottard *in reverse*: describe his behavior and *at the end* reveal that he was afraid of being arrested.

Newspapers no longer have anything to report but stories about the plague. People say: there's nothing in the paper.

They bring in doctors from the outside.

Separation is what seems to best characterize that period for me. Everyone was separated from everyone else, from those they loved or from their usual activities. And in this seclusion they were forced, those who were able, to reflect, the others to live the life of a hunted animal. In short, there was no middle ground.

At the end, the exile, infected with plague, runs to a high spot and calls out to his wife, great cries over the city walls, the countryside, three villages, and a river.

? A preface by the narrator with some thoughts on objectivity and eyewitness reports.

At the end of the plague, all the inhabitants look like emigrants.

Add "epidemic" details.

Tarrou is the one who can understand everything—and who suffers for it. He can't judge anything.

What ideal does the man who falls prey to the plague hold? I'm really going to make you laugh: honesty.

---

in which there is no clear, open sign of fighting despite a declaration of action. Camus, like Tolstoy, returns to the atmosphere of such times throughout his work.

Get rid of: "at the beginning—in fact—in reality—the first days—around the same time etc.

? Give clues throughout the novel that Rieux is the narrator. At the beginning: smell of cigarettes.

Both antisocial and in need of warmth. To reconcile this: the cinema – where people are pressed against each other without knowing each other. ~~(Expand at length)~~

In a dark city a shadowy people converge on isles of light like an assembly of paramecia falling prey to heliotropism.

For the exile: evenings in cafés where, to save on electricity, they delay turning on the lights as long as possible, where twilight invades the room like gray water, the flames of setting sun faintly reflecting in the windows, the marble tabletops and the backs of chairs faintly gleaming: this is the hour he lets himself go.

The Separated second part: "They were struck by the number of small things that meant so much to them but that didn't even exist for others. It was through this that they discovered private life." "They knew very well they had to end it—or at least they had to want the end—and so they wanted it, but without the fire they'd had at the beginning—with only the very clear reasons they had for wanting it. All that remained of the great outpouring they'd had at the beginning was a dull despondency that made them forget the very reason for their consternation. They appeared sad and unhappy but no longer felt the sharp edge of it. Deep down, that's precisely what unhappiness was about. Before, they were only prey to hopelessness. It was that which led so many to be unfaithful. For, from the suffering they felt on account of love, they held onto nothing but the taste and need for love, and so, gradually growing apart from the person who'd given birth to those feelings in them, they felt all the weaker for it and ended up giving in to the first promise of affection. In this way, they were unfaithful on account of love." "Seen from a distance, their life now seemed to form a whole to them. It was then they embraced it with a new strength. In this way, the plague reunited them. So then, we have to conclude these men didn't know how to live in unity, even though they had been—or rather, they were only able to do so after the possibility had been taken away from them."—"They occasionally realized they were still in the first phase of things when some day they planned to show such-and-such to such-and-such, a friend who was no longer there. They still had hope. The second phase really began when they could no longer think but in terms of pestilence."—"But sometimes in the middle of the night their wounds would open up again. And suddenly awoken, feeling those inflamed lips, they found their suffering all fresh and waiting, and with it the shattered face of their love."

Through the use of the plague, I want to express the suffocation we've all suffered and the atmosphere of threat and exile in which we've lived. At the same time, I want to extend this reading to the notion of existence in general. The plague will paint a picture of those whose share in this war has been reflection, silence—and moral suffering.

———

People here don't know the thirst, the feeling of dryness, that completely takes over you after a run beneath the sun, in the dust. The lemonade you swallow: you don't feel the liquid going down at all, only the thousand little burning pricks of carbonation.

———

Not made for dissipation.

———

January 15

Illness is a cross, but maybe also a safeguard. The ideal, however, would be to take its strengths and refuse its weaknesses. Let it be the retreat that makes us stronger *in due course*. And if we have to pay with suffering and renunciation as our currency, then let's pay.

———

Because the sky is blue, the snow-covered trees down by the river's edge, with their white branches reaching out just above the icy water, have the look of almond trees in bloom. In this country, the eyes are perpetually confused between spring and winter.

I've had an affair with this country, which is to say I have reasons to love it and reasons to hate it. With Algeria, on the other hand, it's unbridled passion, letting myself go to the pleasures of loving. Question: Can a person love a country like a woman?

———

Plague, Second Draft: The Separated.

The separated realize that in reality they never stopped hoping for something in that initial phase: that letters would arrive, that the plague would end, that the absent person would slip into the city. It's only in the second phase that they lose hope. But by that point they've fortunately gone blank (or life has given them new reasons to take interest). They have to die or betray.

Id.: those moments when they let themselves slip toward the plague and hope for nothing more from it than sleep. Cottard says: that must be nice, prison. And the residents: maybe the plague will deliver us from it all.

———

Kierkegaard's Purity of Heart—How verbose. Is genius really so slow?

"Hopelessness is the frontier where the outrage of a cowardly, frightened selfishness and the temerity of a pridefully obstinate mind meet in equal powerlessness."

"When the impure spirit is gone out of a man, he walks through dry places, seeking rest, and finds none" (Matth. XII: 43).

His distinction between men of action and men of suffering.

Id. for Kafka: "Earthly hope must be struck dead, for only then will you save yourself with true hope."

For K, purity of heart is unity. But it's unity *and* the good. There is no purity outside of God.[65] Conclusion: resign yourself to the impure? I'm far from the good and I thirst for unity. That's irreparable.

———

Essay about Rebellion. After having begun with a philosophy of anguish: bring forth one of happiness.

Id. To rekindle love in the absurd world is in fact to rekindle the most burning and ephemeral of human feelings (Plato: "If we were gods, we wouldn't know love"). But there's no value judgment to be made about a love that lasts (on this earth) and one that doesn't. A faithful love—*if it doesn't become impoverished*—is a way for mankind to maintain what's best in them for as long as possible. This is how fidelity regains value. But this love exists outside the eternal. It's the most human of feelings, with all the limitations and joys the word contains. That's why mankind only realizes itself in love, because it's in that dazzling form it finds its condition has no future (and not, as the idealists say, because mankind approaches a certain form of the eternal). The perfect example: Heathcliff.[66] All of this illustrates the fact that absurdity's

---

65. Throughout these pages, Camus often uses the phrase "outside of" in the sense of "fish out[side] of water." In other words, for Camus, "outside of" means suffocation and death. Though the phrase can sometimes read awkwardly in English, it has been carried over whenever possible.

66. The use of Heathcliff as an example would form the second paragraph of *The Rebel*, where Camus writes: "In *Wuthering Heights*, Heathcliff would kill every last person on the planet to possess Cathy, but it would never occur to him to say that killing is reasonable or that it can be justified by a system. He'd commit the act, but that's as far as his beliefs would go. Acting in this way requires the power of love, and of character, and given that such powerful love is rare, murder would remain an exception and would, on the whole, maintain its sense of violation. But the moment we, for lack of

signature expression is in the opposition between *what lasts* and *what doesn't last*. With the understanding that there's only one way to last, which is to last eternally, and that there's no middle ground. We are of a world that doesn't last. And everything that doesn't last—and nothing more than what doesn't last—is ours. So then, it's a matter of taking love back from eternity or at least from those who dress it up in eternity's image. I can already see the objection: you've clearly never loved. Let's set that aside.

———

Plague, 2nd draft.

The separated lose their critical faculties. The most intelligent among them can be found searching the newspapers or radio broadcasts for reasons to believe in a quick end to the plague, coming up with unfounded hopes, and experiencing gratuitous fear when reading a journalist's commentary, written with few facts at hand, the journalist yawning with boredom.

———

What lights up the world and makes it bearable is the familiar feeling we have of being connected to it—and more specifically the feeling of what unites us with others. Relationships with others always help us to keep going because they always imply development, a future—and also because we live as if our only task were precisely to have these relationships with others. But days when we become aware that this isn't our only task, especially when we understand that our will alone is what holds others close to us—stop writing or speaking to them, isolate yourself and you'll see the relationships melt around you—that in reality the majority have their back turned (not out of malice but out of indifference) and that it's *always* possible that the rest may turn their interest elsewhere, as soon as we consider how much of what we call a love or a friendship is, in this way, contingent, dependent on circumstance, then the world returns to its dark night and we to that immense cold from which human tenderness had momentarily removed us.

———

character, rush to create a doctrine, the instant crime is rationalized, it will begin to spread as reason itself, taking on all the features of a syllogism. Once as solitary as a scream, it will become as universal as a science. Yesterday it was judged, today it legislates."

February 10.

Four months of ascetic and solitary life. The will, the mind, they're better for it. But the heart?

———

The entire problem of the absurd should be able to be centered on a critique of value judgments and judgments of fact.

———

Odd passage in Genesis (III:22) "And the lord God said, 'Behold, the man has become like *one of us*, knowing good and evil, and now we must be careful that he doesn't reach out his hand and that he doesn't also take from the tree of life and eat from it and that he *doesn't live forever*."[67]

And the sword of fire that then chases man from Eden "turns this way and that to guard the path to the tree of life." It's a retelling of the story of Zeus and Prometheus. Man had the power to become God's equal, and God feared him and kept him in bondage. *Id.* Of divine responsibility.

———

Imagination. That's what gets in my way when I'm trying to think or disturbs the discipline necessary to create a work. My imagination leads me astray, knows no limits, is a little monstrous. Difficult to know how immense a role it's played in my life. And yet, I didn't recognize this personal peculiarity until I was thirty.

Sometimes, on the train, the bus, the hours drag and I have to stop myself from getting lost in imaginary games, in constructs that seem sterile to me. Tired of having to constantly straighten my sloping thoughts, to lead them back to where I need them most, a moment comes when I let myself go—sink would be more accurate—and the hours pass by in a blink and I've arrived before even knowing it.

———

Maybe it's an appreciation for stone that draws me so strongly to sculpture. It brings a weight and indifference back to the human form, and without these I can see no greatness in it.

———

67. The emphasis in the French, which has been preserved here, differs a little from the English. Robert Alter, who has produced a linguistically observant English translation of the Bible, renders the passage as follows: "And the Lord God said, 'Now that the human has become like one of us, knowing good and evil, he may reach out and take as well from the tree of life and live forever.'"

Essay: a chapter on "the fecundity of tautologies."

A mind somewhat steeped in mental gymnastics knows, like Pascal, that all error comes from exclusion. At the outer limits of intelligence, we know, with absolute certainty, that there's truth in every theory and that none of humanity's great experiences, even if they appear quite opposed, even if they're named Socrates and Empedocles, Pascal and Sade, is a priori insignificant. But circumstances force us to choose. That's why Nietzsche felt it necessary to attack Socrates and Christianity with such forceful arguments. But that's also why it's necessary for us to defend Socrates today, or at least what he represents, because the present age threatens to replace his ideas with values that are the negation of all culture and that would risk handing Nietzsche a victory he wouldn't want.

This would seem to introduce a certain opportunism into the life of ideas. But it only seems that way, as neither Nietzsche nor we ourselves lose sight of the *other side* of the matter and so it's only a defensive reaction. And in the end, Nietzsche's experience has added to ours, as Pascal's did to Darwin, Callicles's to Plato, and has restored the whole human register and returned us to our homeland. (Though all of this can only be true with a dozen further nuances.)

See, in any case, Nietzsche (Origin of Philosophy, Bianquis, p. 208): "Socrates, I have to confess, is so close to me I'm endlessly fighting against him."[68]

Plague, 2nd draft. The separated have difficulty with the days of the week. Sundays, of course. Saturday afternoons. And certain days previously devoted to certain routines.

Id. A chapter about the terror: "The people they came for at night . . ."

In the chapter about the quarantine camps: parents had already been separated from the dead—then, for sanitary reasons, they separated children from parents and men from women. This reaches the point *the separation becomes total.* Everyone is sent back to their own solitude.

So then make the theme of separation the novel's central theme. "They asked nothing of the plague. In the heart of an incomprehensible world, they patiently formed their own universe, a rather human one in which the days were shared between tenderness and routine. Lo and behold, it wasn't enough

68. Geneviève Bianquis's study *Nietzsche* was published in France in 1933.

to be separated from the world itself, the plague also had to separate them from their modest daily creations. After having blinded their mind, it tore out their heart." In practice: *all the men in the novel are solitary.*

Plague, 2nd draft.

We seek peace and go to others to find it. But in the beginning, all they can give is madness and confusion. We have to seek it elsewhere, but the heavens are silent. And it's then, and only then, we can return to others, as, in the absence of peace, we find they grant us sleep.

Plague, 2nd draft.

It's good that there are terraces above the plague.

They're all right, Rieux says.

Tarrou (or Rieux) forgives the plague.

Essay about Rebellion. *At first,* the absurd world isn't rigorously analyzed. It's evoked and it's imagined. So then, that world is the product of *thought in general,* which is to say of a specific imagination. It's the application of a certain modern principle to the conduct of life and to aesthetics. It's not an analysis.

But once this world has been sketched in broad strokes, the first stone (there is only one) laid, philosophizing becomes possible—or more precisely, if we've really understood—becomes necessary. Analysis and rigor are required and reintroduced. Detail and description prevail. From "nothing is interesting but . . ." we pull: "everything is interesting except . . ."—From which a precise and rigorous study—without conclusions—about rebellion.

1) the movement toward rebellion and external rebellion

2) the state of rebellion

3) metaphysical rebellion

Movement toward rebellion: Shared system of values[69]—the impression that this has gone on too long—that the other is overstepping his right (his father, for ex.) "Up to this point, yes, after this, no"—continue analysis.

---

69. The French phrase used here, *le bon droit,* refers to the idea of common values, or a shared value system, in terms of social justice. The similar phrase *à bon droit* means "justly" or "legitimately." In translation, the connection is lost between *droit* (right) as used in this first phrase and *droit* as used in the one that follows.

See notes Origin Philosophy and Man of Ressentiment in Essay.[70]

———

Essay about Rebellion: one direction of the absurd mind is poverty and destitution.

The only way not to be "possessed" by the absurd is not to make use of its benefits. No sexual dispersion without chastity, etc.

Id. Introduce theme of oscillation

Id. Contemplation as one of the absurd ends, insofar as it benefits without taking sides.

———

Let's imagine a thinker who says: "Well, I know that's true, but when I think about it, I find the consequences repulsive, so I take a step back. *The truth is unacceptable even to the person who discovers it.*" This is where we find the absurd thinker and his perpetual malaise.

———

The unusual wind that's always running along the edge of the woods. Man's curious ideal: to build an apartment in the very heart of nature.

———

We have to agree to introduce into the realm of thought the necessary distinction between a philosophy of evidence and a philosophy of preference. Put another way, we can end up with a philosophy the mind and heart find repulsive *but we can't avoid*. So then, the absurd is my philosophy of evidence. But that doesn't stop me from having (or more precisely from *understanding*) a philosophy of preference: Ex: a just balance between the mind and the world, harmony, plenitude, etc. . . . The happy thinker is the one who follows the slope of his thought—the exiled thinker the one who refuses to do so—out of truth—with regretful determination.

Can we push this separation between the thinker and his system as far as possible? Is it not in fact a return to a roundabout realism: truth exterior to man—constraining. Perhaps, but then it would be an unsatisfactory realism. Not an a priori solution.

———

70. Max Scheler's *Vom Umsturz der Werte* was published in France in 1933 as *L'homme du ressentiment*. In English publications, the French spelling of "resentment" is maintained to denote the philosophical concept.

Camus discusses Scheler and his definition of ressentiment in *The Rebel*, at the beginning of part 1.

The great problem to be solved "practically": can a person be happy and solitary?

———

Anthology of insignificance.[71] And first of all, what is insignificance? Here, the etymology is misleading. It's not what has no meaning. Then we'd have to say the world is insignificant. Meaningless and insignificant are not synonymous. An insignificant character may be quite reasonable. It's also not what's trivial. There are great deeds, serious and grandiose projects, that are insignificant. This, however, puts us on the road to progress, as these deeds don't appear insignificant to those who undertake them with official seriousness. So then, we have to add that they are insignificant for . . . that a character is insignificant with respect to . . . that a thought is insignificant in the context of . . . Put another way, and as with all things, there is a relativity to insignificance. Which isn't to say that insignificance is relative. It's related to something that isn't insignificant—that has meaning—a certain importance, that "matters," that deserves attention, that's worth stopping for, that should be cared for, that people should devote themselves to, that has its place and has it for good reason, that strikes the mind, that imposes itself on our attention, the leaps out before our eyes . . . etc. This thing is not well defined yet. Insignificance will only be relative if we can give several definitions of this standard measure of significance. Otherwise, it is, as all things, comparable to something bigger, drawing the little meaning it has from a more general significance. Let's linger on these words. To a certain extent, being very careful and calling for much nuance, we could say that an insignificant thing is not necessarily a thing that has no *meaning*, but a thing that doesn't have, in and of itself, general *significance*. Put another way, and according to the normal scale of values, if I marry, I perform an act that holds a general significance with regard to the species, another with regard to the society, with regard to religion, and perhaps a final type with regard to the metaphysical. Conclusion: marriage is not an insignificant act, at least with regard to commonly accepted values. For if the significance of the species, social or religious, is taken away from it, which is the case for individuals indifferent to these considerations, then marriage really is an insignificant act. In this example, in any case, we can see that insignificance is held in the significance it doesn't have.

71. In 1959, Camus would publish an expanded version of this entry as "De l'insignificance" in *Cahiers des saisons.*

To give a counter example, if, to open a door, I turn the latch to the right rather than to the left, I can't say this gesture comes from any commonly accepted general significance. The society, the religion, the species, and God Himself don't care the slightest bit if I flip the latch to the right or to the left. Conclusion: my action is insignificant, unless for me that habit comes from, for example, a desire to save energy, from a taste for efficiency that reflects a certain will, a way of life, etc. In that case, it would be, for me, much more important to turn my latch a certain way than to get married. So then, insignificance always has a context that determines what it is. The general conclusion is that there's uncertainty in the case of insignificance.

But as I'm proposing to put together an anthology of insignificant actions, that means I know what an insignificant action is. Probably. But knowing if an action is insignificant is not the same as knowing what insignificance is. And after all, I can, for example, put this anthology together to figure it out. All the same . . .

Outline.

1) insignificant acts: the old man and the cat—the soldier and the girl (note about this one. I hesitated to use this story in the anthology. It may have great significance. But I'm adding it anyway to show the extreme difficulty of my work. In any case, it'll *also* be possible to include it in an anthology of things that have meaning—in preparation), etc., etc.

2) Insignificant comments. "As they say in my country"—"As Napoleon said"—and, generally speaking, the majority of historical comments. Jarry's toothpick.[72]

3) Insignificant thoughts. Expect several enormous volumes.

Why this anthology? It's worth noting that, in the end, insignificance is almost always identified with the mechanical aspect of things and people—with habit, most often. That's to say that as everything ends up becoming habitual, we can be sure the greatest thoughts and actions end up becoming insignificant. Life's assigned goal is insignificance. That's where the interest of the anthology comes from. It describes in practical terms not only the largest part of existence, its little gestures, little thoughts, and little moods, but also

72. For "the old man and the cat," see *The Plague*, part 1, section 3. For the "soldier and the girl," see p. 136. For "Jarry's toothpick," see p. 114.

our common future. It has the extraordinarily rare advantage these days of being truly prophetic.

———

Nietzsche, having the most monotonous external life possible, proves that thought alone, carried out in solitude, is a tremendous adventure.

———

We accept that Molière had to die!

———

MARCH 9. The first periwinkles—and a week ago it was snowing!

———

Nietzsche also experiences nostalgia. But he doesn't want to ask anything of the heavens. His solution: what we can't ask of God, we ask of man: here we find the superman. Astonishing that, in revenge for such pretension, we didn't make him a God himself. Maybe it's just a matter of patience. The Buddha preached a wisdom without gods and a few centuries later we put him on an altar.

———

The European who turns courage into a pleasure: he admires himself. Disgusting. True courage is passive: it's indifference to death. An ideal: pure knowledge and happiness.

———

What better can a person wish for than poverty? I didn't say destitution or the hopeless work of the modern proletarian. But I can't see what more a person could wish for than poverty tied to active leisure.

———

We can't *completely* suppress value judgments. That denies the absurd.

———

The ancient philosophers (and for good reason) reflected a lot more than they read. That's why they stuck so close to the concrete. Printing changed this. We read more than we reflect. We don't have philosophies, only commentaries. That's what Gilson is getting at when he says that the age of philosophers who busied themselves with philosophy has been succeeded by the age of professors of philosophy who busy themselves with philosophers.[73] There's both modesty and impotence in this approach. And a thinker who would begin his book with the words: "Let's start from the beginning" would

73. Étienne Gilson (1884–1978), French philosopher specializing in medieval philosophy, as well as the history of philosophy.

face a few smiles. We've reached the point where a philosophy book published today that doesn't lean on any experts, quotations, commentaries, etc., wouldn't be taken seriously. And yet . . .

———

For *The Plague*: There are more things in man to admire than to look down on.[74]

———

When we choose renunciation despite the certainty of "Everything is permitted," something still remains: we no longer judge other people.

———

What attracts a lot of people to the novel is that it appears to be a form without a style. In fact, it demands the most difficult style, the kind that fully submits to the subject. In this way, we can imagine an author writing each of his novels in a different style.[75]

———

The sensation of death that's now familiar to me: it's deprived of pain's help. Pain is fastened to the present; it requires a struggle that *keeps you occupied*. But to sense death at the simple sight of a handkerchief filled with blood, without any effort, is to be vertiginously plunged back in time: it's the dread of becoming.

———

The thick clouds thinned out. As soon as the sun broke through, the plowed fields began to steam.

———

Death gives shape to love as it gives shape to life—transforming it into fate. The woman you loved died while you loved her, so now you have a love forever fixed—one that, without this ending, would have disintegrated. So then, what would the world be without death? A series of evanescent and renascent shapes, an anguished flight, an unfinishable world. But fortunately death is with us, steadfast death. And the lover crying over the remains of

---

74. This would be incorporated into the final lines of *The Plague*, where Camus writes: "Surrounded by joyous cries doubling in strength and duration, resounding all the way out to the foot of the terrace, as bouquets of multicolored light rose higher and higher into the sky, and in ever greater numbers, it was then Doctor Rieux decided to compose the narrative now completed, so as not to be one of those who remain silent, so as to bear witness on behalf of the plague victims, so as to leave behind at least some memory of the injustice and violence that had been done to them, and to say, simply, what it is we learn in the midst of an epidemic: that there are more things to admire in man than to look down on."

75. This entry would appear in Camus's essay "Intelligence and the Scaffold."

the beloved, René standing before Pauline, sheds tears of pure joy—it's all over now—those of the man who recognizes his fate has finally taken shape.

———

Mme de Lafayette's curious theory considers marriage as a lesser evil. It's better to be unhappily married than to suffer from passion. In this we recognize an ethic of *Order*.

(The French novel is psychological because it's wary of metaphysics. It constantly refers to the human as a *precaution.*) To see *The Princess of Clèves* as a classical novel would require a pretty poor reading of it. By contrast, it's very poorly put together.[76]

———

Plague. The separated: Journal of Separation? "The feeling of separation was abstract but it's possible to give an idea of it through the conversations, confidences, and news that appeared in the papers."

Id. The separated. That hour of evening that, for believers, is the hour of self-examination—that hour is hard for the prisoner—it's an hour stripped of love.

Plague. *Id.* Hunger forces some to reflect and others to make a run on supplies. So then, it wasn't just that what brought misfortune also brought good, but that what was misfortune for some was good for others. We couldn't tell which way was up.

? Stephan. Journal of separation.

Three strands of the novel:

Tarrou, who describes the details;

Stephan, who evokes the abstract;

Rieux, who reconciles through the greater efficiency of *relative diagnosis*.

———

The separated. *Id.* By the time the plague was coming to an end, they could no longer imagine the intimacy they'd once enjoyed, how they could have lived so close to someone that they could, at any given moment, reach out and touch them.

———

76. In French, *un moindre mal* (a lesser evil), *mal mariée* (unhappily married), *mal lu* (poor reading), and *fort mal* (very poorly) all use *mal*, whereas this connection can't be completely maintained in English.

Epigraph for *The Misunderstanding*? "What is born does not grow toward perfection, and yet never stops growing." Montaigne.[77]

———

We can easily imagine a European converting to Buddhism—because it assures him of survival—which Buddha considers an incurable misfortune—but which he desires with all his strength.

———

Saint-Étienne and its banlieues. A spectacle such as this is a condemnation of the civilization that gave birth to it. A world where there's no longer any place for people, for joy, for active leisure, is a world that has to die. No peoples can live outside of beauty. They can survive for a while but that's it. And Europe, which displays one of its most enduring faces here, is steadily drifting away from beauty. That's why it's convulsing and, if peace doesn't mean for Europe a return to beauty and restoration of its place in love, that's why it'll die.

———

Every life aimed at money is death. Rebirth is in selflessness.

———

The act of writing bears evidence of a self-confidence I'm starting to lack. The confidence that you have something to say and especially that something can be said—the confidence that what you feel and what you are is worth expressing—the confidence that you're irreplaceable and that you're not a coward. All of this is what I'm losing and I'm beginning to imagine the moment I'll stop writing.

———

Have the strength to choose what you prefer and stick to it. Otherwise it's better to die.

———

The separated: "They waited impatiently for the hour of unfounded jealousy so that they could relive their love."

———

Id. They're asked to register so that a list of the separated can be drawn up. They're amazed that nothing comes of it. But they were only asked so that there would be a record of the names of those who should be notified "in case." "So, we registered."

———

77. In its published form, *The Misunderstanding* does not bear an epigraph.

Id. 3rd p. "But when they'd found each other again, they still had a hard time replacing the person in their imagination with the one in real life . . . and you could say that the plague didn't really die until the day one of them was able to look again at the face across from them with boredom."

Every system of thought is judged by what it's able to pull from suffering. Despite my repugnance, suffering is a fact.

I can't live outside of beauty. That's what makes me weak before certain people.

When it's all over, *step aside* (God *or* woman).

Imagination. That's what most distinguishes man from beast. That's why our sexuality can't be truly natural, which is to say blind.

The absurd is the tragic man faced with a mirror (Caligula). Then he's *not alone*. There's the seed of satisfaction or self-indulgence. Now the mirror must be destroyed.

Time doesn't go so fast when you pay attention to it. It can feel it's being watched. But it takes advantage of our distractions. Maybe there are even two types of time: the one we pay attention to and the one that changes us.

Epigraph for Misunderstanding:[78] "That's why the poets claim that, having first lost seven sons and then as many daughters, that poor mother Niobe, overcome with loss, was finally transmuted into rock . . . so as to express that bleak, deaf, and dumb stupor that passes through us when adversities overwhelm us, beyond what we can bear." Montaigne.

Id. On sadness: "I am of those most free of this passion, neither having it nor holding it in high esteem, even though the world has taken, as if by common consent, to honoring it with special favor."

78. This first quote, like the one below it, comes from Montaigne's "On Sadness," while the third, as Camus indicates, is from "On Liars." The snippet that's been left out of the first quote is a citation from Ovid's *Metamorphoses*: "*Diriguisse malis*" (Petrified by Such Misfortunes).

Id. (On liars): "And nothing shows the strength of a horse so much as a clean and sudden stop."

Absurd. Restore morality through the informal You.[79] I don't believe there's another world where we'll be "held accountable." But we already have our accounts to hold here in this world—to all those we love.

Id. With regard to language. (Parain: the arguments proving man couldn't have invented language are irrefutable.) Everything, as soon as we start digging, leads to a metaphysical problem. So then, whichever way man turns, he finds himself as isolated on reality as on an island surrounded by a deafening sea of questions and possibilities. We can conclude from this that the world has a meaning, for it wouldn't have any, in the raw. Happy worlds have no reasons. So, it's ridiculous to say: "Is metaphysics possible?" Metaphysics is.

The consolation of this world is that no suffering lasts forever. Grief passes away and joy is reborn. Everything balances out. The world is offset. And if even our will draws a privileged suffering from becoming, one we raise to the level of a strength so as to endlessly experience it, there's proof in this choice that we take this suffering to be a good and that it's through suffering, in this case, that things are offset.

Untimely Meditations, Part 3.[80] "With a pained expression, Schopenhauer turned away from the picture of Rancé, the great founder of La Trappe, saying, 'This requires grace.'"

With regard to M. I don't refuse to move toward The Being, I just don't want a path that pushes other beings aside. To know if we can find God by pursuing our passions.

---

79. The English language doesn't use a formal and informal form of "you," as French does. One thing Camus seems to be expressing here is the idea that interpersonal formality might distance people from each other, allowing us to see and treat each other as less than human, whereas informality, addressing everyone in the personal form, as we would address family and friends, might help us treat each other in a more humane fashion.

80. Nietzsche's *Unzeitgemässe Betrachtungen* has also been translated into English as *Unfashionable Observations* and *Thoughts Out of Season*. It contains four essays written between 1873 and 1876.

La Trappe Abbey in Orne, France, is where the Trappist order was founded.

Plague: very important. "It's because they threw you some food and such, and from the grief of being separated, that they got you without rebellion."

———

May 10.

For the first time: strange feeling of satisfaction and fulfillment. Question I asked myself, lying in the grass, a hot and heavy evening in front of me: "If these days were the last . . ." Response: a calm smile inside of me. Yet nothing I can be proud of: nothing is resolved, even my behavior isn't so firm. Is this the hardening that ends an experience, or the gentleness of night, or, on the contrary, the beginning of a wisdom that denies nothing more?

———

June. Luxembourg.[81]

A Sunday morning full of wind and sun. The wind splashes water from the fountain all over the large basin, the tiny sailboats on the rippling water, and the swallows by the tall trees. Two young people having a discussion: "You who believe in human dignity."

———

Prologue: "Love . . ."
"Knowledge . . ."
"It's the same word."

———

Even though birds always seem directionless in their daytime flight, they always seem to find where they're going in the evening. They fly toward something. Maybe that's how it is in the evening of life . . .

Is there an evening of life?[82]

———

Hotel room in Valence.[83] "I don't want you to do that. How would I bear such a thought? How would I be able to face your mother, your sisters, Marie-Rolande? I'd promised myself I wouldn't tell you, you must know that.

---

81. The Jardin du Luxembourg in Paris.

82. This last line doesn't appear in the handwritten notebook. It was added to the typescript in pencil.

83. Camus went to Valence to see Blanche Balain. The two spent three days together, traveling north to Vienna. During the trip Camus asked Blanche if she wanted to work as his secretary, an offer she refused. Roger Grenier notes that Camus overheard the dialogue recorded here in the room next to his.

"I'm begging you not to do this. I needed these two days rest so much. I'm not going to let you do this. I'll go through with it. I'll marry you if that's what it takes. But I can't have this on my conscience.

"I'd promised myself I wouldn't tell you."

"That's all talk. It's actions that matter to me—"

"They'll think it was an accident. The train . . . etc."

(She cries. She shouts: I hate you. I hate you for doing this to me.)

"I know, Rolande, I know very well. But I didn't want to tell you. Etc., etc."

He promises. Duration: an hour and a half. Monotony. Stagnation.

Van Gogh is struck by one of Renan's ideas: "Let the self die, achieve great things, arrive at nobleness, and move beyond the vulgarity in which most people's existence drags on."[84]

"If a person continues to sincerely love that which is truly worthy of loving and *doesn't waste their love on insignificant and trivial and tasteless things*, they will gradually be enlightened and will become stronger."

"If one perfects oneself in one domain and understands it well, one acquires understanding and knowledge of many other things in addition."[85]

"I'm a faithful sort in my unfaithfulness."

---

84. The quotes that follow all come from Van Gogh's letters. The translations given above are from the French as recorded by Camus. In the case of this first quote, Camus has abridged what Van Gogh wrote, which itself was an abridgement of a passage from Ernest Renan's *Studies of Religious History and Criticism*. The quote, which Van Gogh includes at the end of a letter to his brother, Theo, on May 8, 1875, reads in full: "To act on the world one must die to oneself. The people that makes itself the missionary of a religious thought has no other country henceforth than that thought. Man is not placed on the earth merely to be happy; nor is he placed here merely to be honest, he is here to accomplish great things through society, to arrive at nobleness, and to outgrow the vulgarity in which the existence of almost all individuals drags on."

85. From a long letter to Theo, April 3, 1878 (as is often the case with Van Gogh's letters, parts of this one come from the Bible): "Love is the best and most noble thing in the human heart, especially when it has been tried and tested in life like gold in the fire, happy is he and strong in himself who has loved much and, even if he has wavered and doubted, has kept that divine fire and has returned to that which was in the beginning and shall never die. If only one continues to love faithfully that which is verily worthy of love, and does not squander his love on truly trivial and insignificant and faint-hearted things, then one will gradually become more enlightened and stronger. The sooner one seeks to become competent in a certain position and in a certain profession, and adopts a fairly independent way of thinking and acting, and the more one observes fixed rules, the stronger one's character becomes, and yet that doesn't mean that one has to become narrow-minded.

"It is wise to do that, for life is but short and time passes quickly. If one is competent in *one* thing and understands *one* thing well, one gains at the same time insight into and knowledge of many other things into the bargain."

"If I were to make landscapes, there would always be something of the figure about them."[86]

He quotes Doré: "I have the patience of an ox."

Cf. letter 340 on the trip to Zweeloo.

The bad taste of great artists: he makes equals of Millet and Rembrandt.

"I'm thinking more and more that we shouldn't judge the Good Lord by this world, because it's one of his sketches that turned out poorly."[87]

"In life and in painting, too, I can easily do without the Good Lord, but I can't, suffering as I do, do without something greater than myself, which is my life, the power to create."[88]

Van Gogh's long search wanders this way and that until at twenty-seven years old he finds his way and discovers he's a painter.

———

When you've done what's necessary to truly understand, truly acknowledge, and truly endure poverty, illness, and your own shortcomings, there's still another step to take.

———

Plague. Sentimental teacher concludes at the end of the plague that the only intelligent occupation is copying a book back to front (expand the text and the meaning).[89]

Tarrou dies in silence (wink, etc.).

Administrative quarantine camp.

Conversation at the end between teacher and doctor: They're reunited. But it's because they hadn't asked for much. Me? I haven't had, etc.

The Jewish quarter (the flies). Those who want to keep up appearances. They invite people over for a cup of chicory.

Separated. Second. And what was already so hard for them to endure themselves (old age) they now had to endure for two.

Yet routine business continues to be carried out. It was, in fact, at this time we learned the outcome of a case that had in those days aroused the curiosity of people in the know. A young murderer . . . had been pardoned.

---

86. Letter to Theo, March 1882. Camus has recorded the second half of the sentence here; the first half reads: "Theo, I'm certainly no landscape painter."

87. Letter to Theo, May 26, 1888. Camus would also reference this line in *The Rebel*.

88. Letter to Theo, September 3, 1888. Camus would also reference this line in *The Rebel*.

89. The reference is to Stephen, from the first draft of *The Plague*.

The newspapers thought he'd get off with ten years good behavior and that he could then resume his normal life. It really wasn't such a big deal.

———

Confidence in words is classicism—but to keep its confidence, it only uses them with caution. Surrealism, which misuses them, abuses them. Let's get back to classicism, out of modesty.

———

Those who love truth have to look for love in marriage, which is to say love without illusions.

———

"Of What Is Occitanian Inspiration Made?" A special edition of *Cahiers du Sud*.[90] In sum, we were worthless during the Renaissance, the eighteenth, and the Revolution. We only counted for something from the tenth to the thirteenth century, right when it was so difficult to speak of us as a nation—when all of civilization is international. So then, entire centuries of history, fame or misfortune, the hundreds of great names that they've left us, a tradition, a national life, love, all of that's in vain, all of that's nothing. And we're the nihilists!

———

Humanism doesn't bother me: it even makes me smile. But I find it falls short.

———

Brück, Dominican:[91] "These Christian Democrats annoy the heck out of me."

"G. has all the makings of a parish priest, a sort of Episcopal unction. And I can hardly bear it in the bishops as it is."

———

Me: "When I was young, I thought all priests were happy."

Brück: "Fear of losing their faith causes them to shrink their feelings. It's only a negative calling now. They don't look life in the face." (His dream, a great victorious clergy, but magnificent in poverty and audacity.)

Conversation about Nietzsche damned.

———

90. *Cahiers du Sud* 249 (August/October 1942) featured an article by Emile Novis (Simone Weil) with the title "En quoi consiste l'inspiration occitanienne?"

91. Father Raymond Léopold Bruckberger (1907–1998), French Dominican priest, member of the Resistance, writer. He and Camus had become friendly during the war years.

Barrès and Gide. Uprooting is an outdated problem for us. And when we're not so fired up about a problem, we say fewer stupid things. In short, we need a homeland and we need to travel.[92]

Misunderstanding. The wife, after her husband's death: "How I love him!"

Agrippa d'Aubigné.[93] Here's a man who believes and who fights because he believes. In short, he's happy. This can be seen in the satisfaction he takes in his house, his life, in his career. If he flies off in a rage, it's against those who are wrong—so he says.

What makes a tragedy is that each of the opposing forces is equally legitimate, has the right to live. Which gives us weak tragedy: which uses illegitimate forces. Which gives us strong tragedy: which legitimizes *everything*.

On the Mézenc plateaus, the wind whistles its sword through the air.

Living with your passions assumes you have them under control.

Eternal Return assumes deference to suffering.

Life is cluttered with events that make us wish we were older.

Don't forget: illness and the decrepitude it carries. There's not a minute to lose—which is perhaps the opposite of "we have to hurry up."

Moral: You can't live with people while knowing their ulterior motives.

92. See the series of articles written by André Gide and Maurice Barrès in 1897 (collected in *Pretexts*), in which Barrès highlights the importance of native roots and Gide the importance of nomadism. As French literature scholar David Carroll notes in *Albert Camus the Algerian*, Barrès, a hardcore nationalist, used the term *déracinés* (uprooted) to refer to those he felt were "French in name only and who share none of the authentically rooted cultural values that for him constitute the essence of 'Frenchness.'" In other words, for Barrès, "cosmopolitans, 'Orientals,' and especially Jews" weren't truly French.

93. Théodore-Agrippa d'Aubigné (1552–1630), French poet and advocate of Protestantism, wrote the epic *Les tragiques* over the course of three decades. In Camus's archives, there are three pages of notes made by Camus about d'Aubigné.

Persistently refuse any collective judgment. Bring innocence to the center of the "commentary" aspect of any society.

———

Heat ripens people like fruit. They ripen before having lived. They know everything before having learned anything.

———

B.B.[94] "No one realizes some people have to make a Herculean effort just to be normal."

———

Plague. If Tarrou's notebooks figure so strongly, it's because he happened to die at the narrator's home (at the beginning).

"Are you absolutely sure it's contagious, that quarantine is advisable?"

"I'm not sure of anything, but I am sure abandoned corpses, large gatherings, etc., are not advisable. Theories can change, but consistency is something that's always and at all times worth ensuring."

———

Amid their struggle, health facilities lose interest in news of the plague.

The plague suppresses value judgments. People no longer judge the quality of clothing, food, etc. They accept everything.

The separated man wants to ask the doctor for a certificate allowing him to leave (that's how he knows him) he explains the steps he's taking . . . He comes back regularly.

The trains, the stations, the waiting.

The plague highlights separation. But the reality of being joined together is only a lasting coincidence. The plague is the rule.

———

September 1, 1943

He who is hopeless about events is a coward, but he who places hope in humanity is a fool.

———

September 15

He drops everything, his own work, business letters, etc. to respond to a thirteen-year-old girl who wrote him a heartfelt letter!

———

94. This refers to Blanche Balain.

As the word existence does express something, which is our nostalgia, and as it can't help but simultaneously contain an affirmation of a higher reality, let's only hold onto it in converted form—let's call it inexistential philosophy, which doesn't entail a negation and attempts only to describe the state of "man deprived of . . ." Inexistential philosophy will be the philosophy of exile.

———

Sade: "We rail against the passions without considering that it's from their torch philosophy lights its own."[95]

———

Art shares modesty's tendencies. It can't say things directly.

———

In times of revolution, it's the best who die. The law of sacrifice ensures that it's always the cowards and cautious whose voices get heard at the end, as the others lose theirs while giving the best of themselves. Speaking always implies a betrayal by the speaker.

———

Only artists do good in the world. No, Parain says.

———

Plague. Everyone struggles—and each in their own way. The only cowardice is to get down on your knees . . . All these new moralists were coming out of the woodwork and their conclusion was always the same: you have to get down on your knees. But Rieux responded: you have to struggle in such and such way.

The exile spends hours in train stations. Reviving the dead station.

Rieux: "In any collective struggle there's a need for men who kill and for men who heal. I've chosen to heal. But I know I'm in the struggle."

———

Plague. At this very moment, there are far-off harbors where the water is pink at sunset.

———

"Coming to God because you've cast off the earth, because sorrow has separated you from the world, is futile. God needs souls attached to the world. It's your joy that pleases him."

———

95. The quote is from *Juliette*, part 1.

Reproducing this world may be a more certain betrayal than transfiguring it. The best of photographs is already a betrayal.

Against rationalism. If pure determinism made sense, it would only take a single true statement to reach, following one consequence to the next, the whole truth. This is not the case. So, then either we've never made a single true statement, not even in saying everything is deterministic, or else we've spoken the truth but *for no set reason,* and determinism is false.

For my "creation against God." It's a Catholic critic (Stanislas Fumet) who says art, *whatever its purpose,* is always in guilty competition with God. Likewise: Roger Secrétain, *Cahiers du Sud,* August-September '43. Péguy, too: "There's even a poetry that draws its brilliance from the absence of God, that doesn't gamble on any salvation, that relies on nothing but itself, human effort, rewarded here on earth, to fill the emptiness of space."[96]

There's no middle ground between a literature of apologetics and a literature of competition.

Duty is doing what we know to be just and good—"preferable." Is this easy? No, for even what we know to be preferable is difficult for us to do.

Absurd. If you kill yourself, you negate the absurd. If you don't kill yourself, the practical application of the absurd reveals a principle of satisfaction that itself negates it. This isn't to say that the absurd isn't there. It's to say that the absurd is *really* without logic. That's why we can't *really* live by it.

Paris, November 1943[97]

Surena.[98] During the 4th Act, all the doors are guarded, and Eurydice, who until now has so admirably expressed herself, begins to stop talking, to wring her heart dry without being able to utter the word that would deliver her. She'll remain silent through the end—at which point she dies for not having spoken. And Surena:

96. The ideas expressed here appear in *The Rebel,* chap. 4, "Rebellion and Art."

97. At the beginning of November, Camus moved to Paris to take a job as a "reader" at Gallimard. He initially lived in a hotel, then moved to 22 Rue de la Chaise in the seventh arrondissement.

98. *Suréna,* Corneille's final play, was first put on in 1674. It centers on the relationship between the Parthian spahbed Rustaham Suren and the Armenian princess Eurydice.

"O the sorrow that wrings me dry
Don't reduce it to affection for a guy."

Classical theater's admirable challenge is to have a series of coupled actors come on stage to tell the events without ever showing them—and yet the tension and action nevertheless continue to mount.

———

Parain. They've all cheated. They never got past the hopelessness that surrounded them. And that's because of literature. For him, a communist is someone who has renounced language and replaced it with *actually existing rebellion*. He's chosen to do what Christ didn't deign to do—save the damned—by damning himself.

———

In all suffering, emotion, passion, there's a stage where it belongs to man, even at his most individual and inexpressible, and a stage where it belongs to art. But in its first moments art can never do anything with it. Art is the distance time gives to suffering.

It's man's transcendence of himself.

———

With Sade systematic eroticism is one of the directions of absurd thought.[99]

———

For Kafka, death is not a deliverance. His humble pessimism according to Magny.[100]

———

Plague. In them, love took the form of stubbornness.

———

Add to proofs for Caligula: "Come then, the tragedy is over, the failure truly complete. I'll turn and go now. I've played my part in this fight for the impossible. Now we wait for death, knowing in advance death delivers from nothing."[101]

———

"Christ may have died for someone, but it wasn't for me."

---

99. Camus would dedicate a section of *The Rebel* ("A Man of Letters") to discussing Sade and the idea of absolute rebellion.

100. Claude-Edmonde Magny (1913–1966), French literary critic.

101. Camus didn't end up including this note in the proofs or in any of the later versions of *Caligula*.

Man is guilty, but what he's guilty of is not being able to get everything out of himself—it's a failing that's grown since the beginning.

———

On justice—the guy who stops believing in it the moment he gets roughed up.

Id. My problem with Christianity is it's a doctrine of injustice.[102]

———

Plague. End on a motionless woman in mourning whose suffering shows what men have given in life and blood.

———

Thirty years old.

Man's first faculty is forgetfulness—though it's fair to say he forgets even the good he's done.

———

Plague. Separation is the rule. The rest is chance.

—But people are always brought together.

—There are some chances that last a lifetime.

Bathing in the sea is banned. That's the sign. Forbidden to take delight in the body—to get back to the truth of things. But the plague will come to an end and there will be a truth of things.

The Separated man's journal?

———

The greatest intellectual economy that can be achieved is to accept the world's unintelligibility—and to make man your primary concern.

———

When, in old age, we reach a certain wisdom or ethic, how troubled we must be, and what regret we must feel, for all we've done counter to that ethic and wisdom. Too far ahead or too far behind. There is no middle ground.

———

I spend time with the X's because they have a better memory than I do. They make our shared past richer by recalling to my memory everything that had left it.

———

For a body of work to be challenging, it has to have an end (that's why "no tomorrow" is necessary). It's the opposite of divine creation. It has an

102. This idea appears again in both *The Rebel* and Paneloux's second sermon in *The Plague*.

end, a well-defined limit, is clear, and is shaped by human needs. Unity is in our hands.

Parain. Can the individual choose the moment he'll die for the truth?

In this world, there are the witnesses and the ruiners. As soon as a person who bears witness dies, the witness he's born is ruined through words, preaching, art, etc.

Success can improve a young man, as happiness can a grown man. His effort having been recognized, he can meet it with relaxation and a carefree approach, royal virtues.

Roger Bacon spends *twelve years* in prison for having asserted the primacy of experience in the realm of knowledge.[103]

A moment comes when our youth is lost. It's the moment we lose someone. And we have to know how to accept it. But it's a tough moment.

With regard to the American novel: it aims for the universal. As does classicism. But while classicism aims for an eternal universal, contemporary literature, on account of circumstances (interpenetration of borders) aims for a historical universal. It's not about a man of all times, but a man of all places.

Plague. "He liked to wake at 4 in the morning and think of her then. That's when he could hold her tight. At 4 in the morning, *no one's doing anything*. They're asleep."[104]

A theater troupe continues to perform: a play about Orpheus and Eurydice.[105]

The separated: the world . . . but who am I to judge them? They're all right. But there's no way out.

Conversation about friendship between the doctor and Tarrou: "I thought about it. But it's not possible. The plague leaves *no time*."

---

103. There is a significant amount of disagreement in current scholarship as to whether Roger Bacon ever was imprisoned, and, if he was, for what he was imprisoned.

104. In *The Plague*, this characteristic is given to Rambert, who wakes early to think of his mistress.

105. In *The Plague*, part 4, section 1, an actor performing in a production of Orpheus and Eurydice drops dead on stage, a victim of the plague.

Suddenly: "At the moment, we're all living *for* death. It makes you think about things."

Id. A guy who chooses *silence.*

———

"Defend yourself," the judges said.

"No," the Defendant said.

"Why? That's how it works."

"Not yet. I want you to take on all the responsibility you bear."

———

On the naturel in art. Absolute, it's impossible. Because the real is impossible (bad taste, vulgarity, inadequate to meet man's deeper needs). That's why human creation, made from the world, always ends up turning against the world. Serial novels are bad because for the most part they're true (either because reality has conformed to them or because the world is conventional). It's art and the artist that remake the world, but always with protest as an ulterior motive.

———

Portrait of S. by A: "Her grace, her sensitivity, that mixture of listlessness and resolution, of prudence and audacity, that naivety that doesn't keep her from being healthily sensible."

———

The Greeks wouldn't have understood anything about existentialism—whereas, *despite the scandal,* they were able to get into Christianity. That's because existentialism doesn't presuppose any *conduct.*

Id. There is no absolutely pure, which is to say impartial, knowledge. Art is an attempt to get at pure knowledge through description.

———

To raise the issue of the absurd world is to ask: "Are we going to accept hopelessness without doing anything?" I imagine no honest person can say yes.

———

Algeria. I don't know if I'm expressing myself clearly, but I get the same feeling coming back to Algeria as when looking at a child's face. And yet, I know it's not all pure.

———

My body of work. Finish cycle with book on the created world: "*Creation Corrected*."[106]

If the work, a product of rebellion, summarizes the entirety of man's aspirations, it's necessarily idealistic (?). In this way, the purest product of rebellious creation is the love story that . . .

The extraordinary confusion that leads to poetry being presented to us as a spiritual exercise and the novel as a personal asceticism.

Novel. Facing action or death, all the attitudes assumed by one man. But each time as if it were the right one.

Plague. We can't enjoy the calling birds in the cool evening—in the world as it is. For the world's now covered in a thick layer of history, which its language must pass through to reach us. This deforms it. Nothing of the world is felt for its own sake because every moment in it is linked to a whole series of images of death or hopelessness. There are no longer any mornings without death's rattle, no more evenings without prisons, no more afternoons without horrific carnage.[107]

Memoirs of an executioner. "I alternate gentleness and violence. Psychologically, it's a good thing."

Plague. The guy who wonders if he should join the health-and-safety units or save himself for his great love. Fecundity! Where is it?

Id. After curfew, the city is still stone.

---

106. This title will continue to appear throughout the notebooks, especially in the next notebook, where a subtitle, "The System," is added to it.

107. In *Letters to a German Friend*, Camus writes: "And for five years, it was no longer possible to enjoy the calling birds in the cool evening. We were forced to despair. We were separated from the world, because each instant of the world was attached to a whole host of mortal images. For five years, there has been no morning on earth without agony, no evening without prisons, no afternoon without massacres. Yes, we had to follow you. But our difficult task was to follow you into war without forgetting happiness. And through the clamors and violence, we tried to keep the memory of a happy sea in our heart, of a hill never forgotten, of a dear and smiling face. Especially because it was our best weapon, the one we'll never lower, for the day we lose it, we'll be as dead as you. Clearly, we now know that forging the arms of happiness requires a long time and too much blood."

Id. What troubled them was the insecurity. Every day, every hour, without respite, stalked, uncertain.

Id. I try to keep myself ready. But there's always an hour of day or night when man is a coward. That's the hour I fear.

Id. The quarantine camp. "I knew how it went. They'd forget me, that much was sure. Those who didn't know me would forget me because they were thinking of other things and those who knew and loved me would forget me because they would tire themselves out planning and thinking of ways to get me out. Either way, no one would think of me. No one would imagine what I'm doing minute by minute, etc., etc."

(Have Rambert visit.)

Id. The health-and-safety units or the men of atonement. All the men in the health-and-safety units seem sad.

Id. "It was on this terrace that Doctor Rieux came up with the idea of leaving a chronicle of the event, one that would clearly show the solidarity he felt with these men. And that testimony, which draws to a close here . . . etc."[108]

Id. During the plague people no longer live by the body, they become emaciated.

Id. Beginning: The doctor accompanies his wife to the train station. But he's forced to demand that it be closed.

Being and Nothingness (p. 135–136). Strange mistake about our lives because we try to experience them from the outside.

If the body is nostalgic for the soul, there's no reason the soul shouldn't suffer terribly in eternity for being separated from the body—and no reason, then, it shouldn't still yearn to return to the earth.

We write in moments of hopelessness. But what is hopelessness?

Nothing can be founded on love: it's escape, heartbreak, wonderful instants or an instant collapse. But it isn't . . .

Paris or the very backdrop of sensitivity.

---

108. This would be used in the final lines of *The Plague*. For the full quote, see p. 212n74.

Short stories. In the middle of the Revolution a guy promises to save the loves of his opponents. Then one of his party's courts sentences them to death. He helps them escape.

Id. A tortured priest betrays.

Id. Cyanide. He doesn't use it so he can see if he'll follow things through to the end.

Id. A guy suddenly joins the civil defense. He takes care of the victims. But he kept his armband. He's shot.

Id. The coward.

Plague. *After* the plague he *hears* the rain on the ground for the first time.

Id. Since he was going to die, seeing life as stupid was now a more urgent matter. He'd always thought it was, and at least the thought would serve him in this difficult moment. After all, he wasn't about to, just when he needed to be as positive as he could be, see smiles on a face that had always been closed off to him.

Id. The guy they put in the hospital by mistake. It's a mistake, he said. What's a mistake? Don't be stupid, there are no mistakes.

Id. Medicine and Religion: These are two professions that seem to be compatible. But today, when everything is clear, we understand they're incompatible—and that we have to choose between the relative and the absolute. "If I believed in God, I wouldn't nurse man. If I thought man could be healed, I wouldn't believe in God."[109]

Justice: the experience of justice *through sport.*

Plague. A guy who accepts others' illnesses philosophically. But let his best friend be the one who's sick—and then he does everything he can. So then, solidarity in the fight is in vain, individual feelings win.

Tarrou's Chronicle: a boxing match—Tarrou makes friends with a boxer. Clandestine matches organized—a soccer ball—a pitch.

That early morning hour when, after a good breakfast, you walk through the streets smoking a cigarette. There were still good moments.

Tarrou: "It's curious, you have a sad philosophy and a happy face."

"So then, you can conclude my philosophy isn't sad."

In the middle, all the characters come together in the same health-and-safety unit. A chapter about a big gathering.

---

109. In *The Plague*, Father Paneloux writes about whether priests should see doctors.

Sunday for a soccer player who can no longer play, link him to Tarrou: Étienne Villaplane is bored on Sundays because soccer matches are prohibited. What were his Sundays like? What are they like: he roams the streets, kicking pebbles, trying to sink them straight into a manhole ("One to nothing," he said. And he added that life is cruel). He slips into children's games if a ball's involved. He spits out his cigarette butts and kicks them in midair with his foot (early on, of course. Later on, he held onto the cigarette butts).[110]

Rieux and Tarrou.

Rieux: When people write what you write, they seem to have nothing to do with the needs of man.

"Come on," Tarrou said. "That's only the way it looks."

W. Anything she can define seems contemptible to her. She says: "It's sickening. It's the battle of the sexes." But the battle of the sexes exists and there's nothing we can do about it.

A person demands *the other* do everything and then lets go and lives passively, except when violently acting to persuade the other to continue to give and do everything.

Essay about Rebellion: "All rebels, nevertheless, act as if they believe in the end of history. The contradiction is . . ."

Id. Only a few minds wish for freedom. Many wish for justice—and many even confuse justice and freedom. But question: does absolute justice equal absolute happiness?—We come to the conclusion that we have to choose to sacrifice freedom to justice or justice to freedom. For an artist, this comes down to, in certain circumstances, choosing between one's art and the happiness of all man.

Can man create his own values on his own? That's the whole problem.

Are you relevant? But I never said man wasn't reasonable. What I want is to strip him of his illusory afterlife and make him understand that, with this being stripped away, he's finally clear and coherent.

110. Some of this entry appears in *The Plague,* where Gonzalez is a soccer player who helps Rambert try to escape.

Id. Sacrifice that leads to value. But suicide is selfish too: asserts a value—which seems more important to the suicide than his own life—and which is the feeling of that dignified and happy life of which he's been deprived.

———

Consider heroism and courage as secondary values—*after having given proof of courage.*

———

Novel about a planned suicide. To be carried out in a year—his formidable superiority drawn from the fact that death is of no concern to him.

Link him to the love story novel?

———

Crazy nature of sacrifice: the guy who dies for something *he will not see.*

———

It's taken me ten years to achieve what seems priceless: a heart without bitterness. And as often happens, once past the bitterness, I put it into one or two books. As a result, I'll always be judged by that bitterness, which means nothing to me anymore. But that's only fair. It's the price that must be paid.

———

The terrible and all-consuming selfishness of artists.

———

A person can only preserve a love for reasons outside of love. Moral reasons, for example.

———

Novel. What does love mean to her: that emptiness, that small hollow inside her since they first found each other, that call drawing lovers toward each other, shouting out each other's name.

———

A person isn't capable of being committed at every level. A person can choose, at least, to live at a level where commitment is possible. To live what is honorable in them and that alone. In certain cases this can lead to turning away from others, even (and especially) for a heart that feels passionately about others.

In any case, this opens a rift. But what does that prove? It proves that anyone who *seriously* addresses the moral problem ends up at extremes. Whether you're for (Pascal) or against (Nietzsche), you only have to be serious about it to see that the moral problem is blood, madness, and screaming.

———

Rebellion. Chap. 1. Morality exists. What's immoral is Christianity. Definition of a morality to counter intellectual rationalism and divine irrationalism.

Chap. X. Conspiracy as a moral value.

Novel.

The woman who inadvertently ruins everything:

"And yet, I loved him with all my soul."

"Well, then," the priest says, "it still wasn't enough."

Sunday, September 24, 1944. Letter.[111]

Novel: "Night of confessions, of tears and kisses. Bed soaked with tears, sweat, love. At the height of every heartbreak."

Novel. A handsome man. And he's forgiven for everything.

Those who love all women are those who are on the road to abstraction. They move beyond this world, whether it seems that way or not, for they turn away from the concrete, from the individual. The man who would run from all ideas and abstraction, the truly hopeless, is the man of one woman. Through stubborn commitment to that individual face that can't satisfy everything.

DECEMBER. This heart full of tears and night.[112]

Plague. Separated, they write to each other and he finds the right tone to keep her love alive. Triumph of language and good writing.

Justification for art: the true work of art helps with sincerity, reinforces the bonds of man, etc. . . .

---

111. The letter mentioned here, as well as the entry in general, may refer to an exchange with Maria Casarès. Camus and Casarès had been having an affair while Camus's wife, Francine, was stuck in Oran, but it was around this time that Francine was finally able to return to Paris and, as such, that Casarès, despite being very much in love with Camus, called off their relationship. This entry also appears in *The First Man*'s Jessica/Véra file.

112. After having separated from Casarès at the end of November, Camus wrote to wish her a happy birthday, but she didn't respond.

I don't believe in hopeless actions. I only believe in well-founded actions. *But* I believe it doesn't take much to find founding for an action.

The only objection to the totalitarian attitude is moral or religious objection. If this world has no meaning, they're right. I don't accept that they're right. So . . .

It's up to us to create God. He is not the creator. Here you find the whole history of Christianity, for we have only one way of creating God, which is to become him.

Novel about Justice.

At the end. Standing before the poor, sick mother.

"I am not worried about you, Jean. You are smart."

"No, Mother. That's not it. I've often been wrong and I haven't always been fair, but there's one thing—"

"Of course."

"There's one thing, and it's that I've never betrayed you. My whole life, I've been faithful to you."

"You are a good son, Jean. I know that you are a very good son."

"Thank you, Mother."

"No, I am the one who should thank you. You, you have to carry on."

There can be no freedom for man until he's overcome his fear of death. But not by suicide. To overcome, you can't give up. Be able to die facing reality, without bitterness.

Heroism and holiness, secondary virtues. But you have to have proven yourself.

Novel about Justice. A rebel who carries out an action he knows will get innocent hostages killed . . . [113] Then he agrees to add his signature to a pardon for a writer he despises.[114]

---

113. In French, *qui exécute une action* (who executes an action).

114. In January 1945, Camus signed a petition asking that the death sentence given to Robert Brasillach, a fascist French writer and editor, be commuted. To French writer Marcel Aymé, who'd

———

Reputation. It's given to you by mediocre people and you share it with mediocre people or rogues.

———

Grace?

We must serve justice because our condition is unjust, add to happiness and joy because the universe is unhappy. Likewise, we must not sentence to death as we have been sentenced to death.

The doctor, God's enemy: he struggles against death.

———

Plague. Rieux said he was God's enemy because he was grappling with death and that it was his job, even, to be God's enemy. He also said that in trying to save Paneloux he was simultaneously showing him that he was wrong and that by accepting being saved he was accepting the possibility of not being right. All Paneloux could say was that he'd end up being right, as he was certainly going to die, and Rieux responded that the most important thing was not to accept it and to struggle until the very end.

———

Meaning of my work: So many people are deprived of grace. How can we live without grace? We have to get down to it and do what Christianity has never done: take care of the damned.

———

Classicism is mastery of the passions. In the Grand Siècles,[115] passions were individual. Today, they're collective. We have to master collective passions, which is to say give them their form. But at the same time that we experience them we are devoured by them. That's why most works of the period are reportage and not works of art.

The reply: if we can't do everything at once, give up everything. What does that mean? It takes more strength and will than was needed. We'll get through it. Tomorrow's great classic is an unrivaled conqueror.

———

requested Camus's signature, Camus wrote that it wasn't for Brasillach "that I'm adding my signature to the others, it's not for the writer, who I take to be a nothing, or for the person, whom I despise with all my strength," rather, he said he was signing because "I've always been horrified by the death penalty, and as an individual I can at least choose not to support it, even by abstention." De Gaulle ignored the petition, signed by some of the most famous artists in France, and had Brasillach executed by firing squad on February 3.

115. Literally "great centuries," used to refer to seventeenth-century movements in art and culture, with a particular focus on style surrounding Louis XIV.

Novel about justice.

The guy who allies with the revolutionaries (Comm.) after having judged or been suspicious of them (because unity is needed) is immediately given a mission everyone knows will lead to his death. He accepts because that's the nature of things. He dies.

Id. The guy who applies the morality of sincerity to affirm solidarity. His enormous solitude at the end.

Id. We kill the most daring among them. They killed the most daring among us. That leaves the bureaucrats and the bullshit. What a wonder it is to have ideas.

Plague. A chapter about the fatigue.

Rebellion. Freedom is the right not to lie. True at the social level (subaltern and superior) and the moral level.

Creation corrected. Story of a planned suicide.

Plague. "Things that moan for being separated."

That guy (an S.N.C.F. inspector) lives solely for the railroads.[116]

The S.N.C.F. bureaucrat lives on the surface skin of things.

M.V.'s cousin. He collects hot-air balloons (made of porcelain, made into pipes, paperweights, inkwells, etc.).[117]

Universal novel. The tank that flips over and falls apart like a centipede.

Bob on the attack in the summer meadows, his helmet covered with wallflowers and wild grasses.

---

116. The state-owned Société nationale des chemins de fer (French National Railway Company) was founded six years before this entry was made.

117. M.V. may refer to Marie Viton, who designed costumes for the Théâtre de l'Équipe.

Creation corrected.

The tank that flips over and struggles like a centipede.[118]

Bob in the summer meadows of Normandy, his helmet covered in wild grasses and wallflowers.

Cf. the English commission's report about the atrocities in the *Times*.

Suzy's Spanish journalist (ask for his article) (children laugh while showing him the corpses).

An hourlong cold shower for the heart.

They talk all day about having milk soup in the evening because it makes you have to piss a couple of times during the night. How the W.C.s are a hundred meters from the building, how cold it is, etc.

—Women deported on entering Switzerland burst out laughing when they catch sight of a funeral: "That's how they treat the dead here."

—Jacqueline.

—Two young Poles who, at fourteen years old, had their house burned down with their parents inside. From fourteen to seventeen, Buchenwald.

—The Gestapo's caretaker is set up on two floors of a building on Rue de la Pompe. In the morning, she cleans up right there amid the tortured. "I never worry with what my tenants are doing."

—Jacqueline returning from Königsberg to Ravensbruck—100 kilometers on foot. In a large tent divided in four by a frame. So many women they can only sleep, on the ground, by fitting themselves together like puzzle pieces. Dysentery. W.C.'s a hundred meters away. But they have to step over and stomp on bodies to get there. They go where they are.

—Global dimension of the dialogue between politics and morality. Facing that conglomerate of gigantic forces: Sintes.[119]

—Rachel X. deported, liberated with a tattoo on her skin: served for a year in the S.S. camp in . . .

———

Show. That abstraction is the evil. It causes wars, torture, violence, etc. Problem: how the abstract view is maintained in the face of physical evil—the ideology in view of the torture inflicted in the name of that ideology.

———

118. In French, this iteration of the sentence is even closer to the previous iteration than in English, the interchanged words showing only a few letters difference: *se défait* and *se débat*.

119. There are a couple of illegible letters preceding "Sintes" in the original manuscript. Sintès was Camus's mother's maiden name, as well as Raymond's last name in *The Stranger*.

Christianity. You'd really be punished if we accepted your postulates, for then our sentence would be merciless.

Sade. Autopsy by Gall:[120] "The skull itself looked like any old man's skull. The organs of paternal tenderness and of love of children are clearly defined."

Sade on Mme de Lafayette: "And as she became more concise, she became more interesting."

Sade's passionate admiration of Rousseau and Richardson, from whom he learned "that it isn't always the triumph of virtue in which we're interested."

Id. "We only acquire understanding of man's heart" through misfortune and travel.[121]

Id. 18th century man: "When, following the Titans' example, he dares to raise his emboldened hand to the heavens and, armed with his passions,[122] he is no longer afraid to declare war on those who'd once made him tremble."

Rebellion. Eventually politics ends up with the parties that serve ~~communication~~ complicity.[123]

—And creation itself. What's to be done? The rebel is the one *least likely* to push aside his accomplices. But they will be.

Profound disgust with all society. Temptation to run away and accept the decadence of the times. Solitude makes me happy. But also the feeling that decadence begins the moment we accept. And we stay—so that man stays

120. Franz Josef Gall (1758–1828), German physiologist, pioneer of what would become phrenology. The quote about Sade appears in the 1835 book *Les fous célèbres*, though the quote found there is much longer and quite different from what Camus has recorded here.

The rest of the quotes in this entry, with one exception, come from "An Essay on Novels," collected in Sade's four-volume *The Crimes of Love*. Camus's quotes are not exact, and they often leave out punctuation present in the source text. With the exception noted below, none of Camus's adjustments substantially change the originals.

121. This quote is not from "An Essay on Novels." It's possibly in reference to the Bible, Proverbs 18:15, but the match is not exact.

122. Camus leaves a clause out here that reads: "as they were once armed with the lavas of Vesuvius." The reference is to the Titans' rebellion against the gods, during which the Titans layered piles of lava that, when cooled, formed mountains the Titans intended to climb to reach the gods. Zeus, of course, destroyed the mountains before they could be used.

123. In the handwritten notebook, the word "complicity" is written over the word "communication."

atop his rightful place. Precisely, so as not to contribute to bringing him down. But disgust, nauseating disgust at this fragmentation in others.

———

Communication. Obstacle for people because they can't reach outside the circle of those they know. Beyond, they make an abstraction of everything. Man *has to live* in the circle of flesh.

———

The aging heart. To have loved and still have nothing be saved.

———

The temptation of menial, daily tasks.

———

C. and P.G.: passion for the truth. Around them, everyone is crucified.[124]

———

The rest of us, the French, are now at the forefront of all civilization: we no longer know how to put people to death.

We are the ones who testify against God.

———

July '45.

Chateaubriand to Ampère[125] headed for Greece in 1841:

"Give my goodbyes to Mount Hymettus, where I left some bees; to Cape Sounion, where I listened to the crickets singing. . . . I'll have to give it all up soon. I'm still wandering through my memory, amid my recollections, but they'll fade away. . . . You'll find neither the leaf of the olive tree nor the seed of the grapes I saw in Attica. I'll miss even the grass from my time. I didn't have the strength to keep a heather alive."

———

Rebellion.

In the end, I choose freedom, for even if justice isn't achieved, freedom preserves the power to protest against injustice and upholds communication. Justice in a silent world, the justice of the mute, destroys complicity, denies rebellion, and restores consent, but in its lowest form this time. It's here we see the value of freedom gradually acquire its precedence. But the difficult thing is to never lose sight of the fact that freedom must *at the same time* demand

124. The initials may refer to Christiane and Pierre Galindo.

125. Jean-Jacques Ampère (1800–1864), French philologist, author of *Greece, Rome, and Dante*, as well as a three-volume *History of French Literature Before the 12th Century*, a four-volume history of Rome, and a history of the development of the French Language, among numerous other works.

justice, as has been said. That being the case, there's also justice, though a very different sort, in establishing the only consistent value in the history of those who have never really died for anything other than freedom.

Freedom is being able to stand up for what I don't think, even in a regime or world I support. It's being able to say the opposition is right.

———

"Great is the man who repents. But who today would want to be great without being seen?" (Life of Rancé)[126]

———

The man I'd be if I hadn't been the child I was.

———

Previously unpublished Ch.[127]

"I've never been held in a woman's arms with that full feeling of surrender, those double knots, that ardent passion I sought and whose charm would be worth an entire life."

"There are times when, character being without energy, vices produce only corruption and not crimes."

Id. "If there were no passion, there would be no virtue, and yet this century has reached such heights of misery that it is without passion and without virtue; it does good and evil, passive as matter."

"When you have a high mind and a low heart, you write great things and do only small ones."

———

Novel.

"I gave men what they deserved. That's to say I lied and desired alongside them. I ran from person to person, did what had to be done. That's enough, now. I've got a score to settle with this landscape. I want to be alone with it."

———

July 30, '45.

At thirty years old, a man should have himself under control, know the exact number of his faults and qualities, understand his limit, foresee his failures—be what he is—and above all accept them. We're moving in a positive

---

126. Chateaubriand's final work, *Life of Rancé* (*Vie de Rancé*), tells the story of Armand Jean de Bouthillier de Rancé, a seventeenth-century French aristocrat who withdrew from society and founded the Trappist order.

127. The "Ch" refers to Chateaubriand. The quotes are from *Pensées, réflexions, et maximes* and *Memoirs from Beyond the Grave.*

direction. Everything to do and everything to let go. Settle into your nature, but with your mask. I've known enough things to be able to let go of almost everything. What remains is a prodigious, daily, persistent effort. An effort of secrecy, with neither hope nor bitterness. No longer deny anything, given everything can be affirmed. Above tearing down.

Notebook V

SEPTEMBER 1945–APRIL 1948

A gray-green composition notebook, 22 × 17 cm, featuring more cover design than the others, with the word "L'iDÉAL" preprinted in large letters, with a circle and triangle design behind it. At the top-left side of the notebook, Camus has written "Cahier no V," and below the designs he has written the date "September 1945" and below that "to April 1948." The notebook is quite beaten up, with the outer edges chewed away. It contains eighty-six pages, all written on, though pages three and four have been torn out and are now missing. The notebook is otherwise complete.

The only contemporary problem: Can we transform the world without believing in the absolute power of reason? Despite rationalist illusions, even the Marxist kind, the whole history of the world is the history of freedom. How could the paths to freedom be determined?[1] It's probably false to say that what's determined is what's no longer living. But the only thing determined is what has been lived. God himself, if he existed, couldn't change the past. But the future belongs to him no more or less than to man.

———

Political antinomies. We're in a world where we have to choose to be victim or executioner—and nothing else. It's not an easy choice. It has always seemed to me that in fact there were no executioners, only victims. When all is said and done, of course. But that's a truth not commonly held.

I have a strong taste for freedom. And for any intellectual, freedom ends up being confused with freedom of expression. But I'm perfectly well aware that this isn't the primary concern for a very large number of Europeans, as only justice can grant them the basic material they need, and that, right or wrong, they would willingly sacrifice freedom for this elementary justice.

I've known this for a long time. If it's seemed necessary to me to defend the reconciliation of justice and freedom, it's because, in my opinion, doing so remains the West's last hope. But this reconciliation can only happen in a certain climate, one that seems practically utopian today. One or the other of these values will have to be sacrificed? What are we to think, in that case?

———

Politics (continued). Everything comes from the fact that those charged with speaking for the people don't have, have never had, real concern for freedom. When they're being honest, they even boast of the opposite. Yet the slightest concern would be enough . . .

So then, those—and they're rare—who live with this scruple will some day or other have to perish (in this respect, there are several ways to die). If they're proud, they won't do so without a struggle. But how could they really struggle against their brothers and all justice? They'll bear witness, that's all. And, two millennia from now, we'll see, repeated several times over, Socrates's sacrifice. On the schedule for tomorrow: the solemn and symptomatic putting to death of freedom's witnesses.

———

1. In 1945, the year this entry was made, Jean-Paul Sartre published the first volume of his unfinished tetralogy *The Paths to Freedom* (*Les chemins de la liberté*).

Rebellion: Create to connect with man? But creation gradually separates us from everyone and pushes us away without the shadow of a love.

People always think someone commits suicide for a reason. But you can very well commit suicide for *two* reasons.

We aren't born for freedom. But determinism is also a mistake.

~~What could~~ What does immortality mean for me?[2] To live until the last person has disappeared from the earth. Nothing more.

S. That strange character speaks to say nothing. But it's the opposite of nonchalance. She speaks, and then contradicts herself or acknowledges that she's undoubtedly wrong. All this because she considers it unimportant. She doesn't really think about what she says, preoccupied as she is with some other wound, infinitely more serious, which she'll drag around with her, unknown, until death.[3]

Aesthetics of rebellion.[4] If classicism is defined by the ability to control passions, a classical period is one whose art forms and formulates its contemporary's passions. Today, when collective passions have taken precedence over individual passions, it's no longer love that has to be controlled by art, but politics, in its purest sense. Man has been seized by a passion, hopeful or destructive, for his condition.

But how much more difficult the task is—1) because, if the passions have to be lived before being formulated, collective passion devours all the artist's time; 2) because the chances of dying are greater—and even so, the only way of living collective passion authentically is to be willing to die for it. Here, then, the greatest chance for authenticity is also the greatest chance for failure for art. For this reason, such classicism may be impossible. But if it were, it would be because in truth the history of human rebellion has had a mean-

2. In the original notebook, Camus wrote "What does" over "What could."

3. In *The First Man*'s Side Characters file, this entry is headed: "*Marie's Sister*." As Marie seems largely based on Francine, it's likely the "S." refers to Francine's sister, Suzy.

4. See Camus's preface for Chamfort's *Maximes et anecdotes*, as well as the last chapter of *The Rebel*.

ing, which was to lead to this boundary.[5] Hegel would be right and the end of history would be imaginable, but only in failure. And here Hegel would be wrong. But if, as we seem to believe, this classicism is possible, at least we see it can only be built by a generation—and no longer by a man. To put it another way, the chances of failure I'm talking about can only be counterbalanced by the chance of numbers, which is to say the chance that out of ten authentic artists, one survives and manages to find time in his life for passion and time for creation. The artist can no longer be a solitary individual. Or, if he is, it's a triumph he owes to an entire generation.

October '45[6]

Aesthetics of rebellion

Impossibility of man being completely hopeless. Conclusion: any literature of hopelessness is but a borderline case and not the most characteristic. What's remarkable about man is not that he can be hopeless, but that he overcomes or forgets hopelessness.—A hopeless literature will never be universal.—Universal literature can't stop at hopelessness (or at optimism either—we need only reverse the reasoning), it need only take it into account. To add: reasons literature is or is not universal.

Aesthetics of rebellion. High style and beautiful form, manifestations of the ultimate rebellion.

Creation corrected.

---

5. In J. B. Baillie's English translation of Hegel's *The Phenomenology of Mind*, both the terms "boundary" and "limit" are used throughout, sometimes even in the same sentence, such as when he writes: "Similarly, the distinctive difference of anything is rather the boundary, the limit, of the subject; it is found at that point where the subject-matter stops, or it is what the subject-matter is not."

Throughout *The Rebel*, and in the notebook entries concerning its creation, Camus uses the French word *limite*, which can be translated as either "limit" or "boundary." In some cases, such as in the notebook entry that follows, the word is used as part of a phrase, *cas limite* ("borderline" or "extreme" case) that asks for a particular English translation. In criticism, much has been made of Camus's use of these terms, as well as the term *mesure*, especially when in reference to Hegel, a philosopher who some of Camus's critics claim he doesn't understand.

6. The date is written in the top-left corner of the notebook. It doesn't appear attached to any entry in particular.

"Men like me aren't afraid of death," he said. "It's an accident that vindicates them."

———

Why am I an artist and not a philosopher? Because I think in words and not ideas.

———

Aesthetics of rebellion.

E. M. Forster: "(The work of art) is the only material object in the universe which may possess internal harmony. All the others have been pressed into shape from outside, and when their mould is removed they collapse. The work of arts stands up by itself, and nothing else does. *It achieves something which has often been promised by society, but always delusively.*"

"(. . .) It (art) is the one orderly product which our muddling race has produced. It is the cry of a thousand sentinels, the echo from a thousand labyrinths; it is the lighthouse which cannot be hidden: c'est le meilleur témoignage que nous puissions donner de notre dignité."[7]

———

Id. Shelley: "Poets are the unacknowledged legislators of the world."[8]

———

Tragedy.

C. and L: "I'm coming to you given the circumstances. I'm sending you into mortal danger."

"All of them are right," a character cries out.

C: "I'm sending you off to an almost certain death, but I need you to understand why I'm doing it."

"I can't understand what's inhuman."

"So, I'll have to give that up, too—being understood by those I love."

C: "I don't believe in freedom. That's my individual suffering. I'm uncomfortable with freedom today."

L: "Why?"

"It keeps me from establishing justice."

"I'm convinced they can be reconciled."

---

7. The two quotes are from E. M. Forster's essay "Art for Art's Sake," collected in *Two Cheers for Democracy*. Camus underlined the last sentence of the first quote; the last clause of the second quote appears in French in the original.

8. The final line of Shelley's "A Defence of Poetry."

"History shows your conviction is wrong. I don't believe they're reconcilable. That's my individual wisdom."

"Why choose one rather than the other?"

"Because I want as many people as possible to be happy—and because freedom is never the concern, the utmost concern, of but a few."

"And if your justice misses the mark?"

"Then I'll be sent to a hell you can't imagine, not even today."

"I'm going to tell you what'll happen" (tableau).

"Every man bets on what he believes to be the truth . . .

Once again, freedom makes me uncomfortable."

"We have to suppress freedom's witnesses."[9]

C: "What do you think, L?"

L: "What's it matter to you?"

C: "You're right. It's a weakness that makes no sense."

L: "All the same, it's what makes me continue to think highly of you. Goodbye, C. . . . Men like me always seem to die alone. That's what I'm off to do. But the truth is that I'll have done what had to be done for others not to be alone."

L: "Remaking the world is a task of no great importance."

C: "It's not the world that needs to be remade, it's man."

C: "There are fools everywhere, but everywhere else there are fools and cowards. Among us, you won't find a single coward."

L: "Heroism is a secondary virtue."

C: "You . . . you have the right to say it because you've proven yourself. But then what'll be the primary virtue?"

L. (looking at him): "Friendship."

L: "If the world is tragic, if we live in the rift, it's not so much because of tyrants. You and I know there's freedom, justice, a profound, shared joy, a community, really, in the struggle against tyrants. As long as evil's in control, there's no problem. When an opponent is in the wrong, those fighting against him are free and at peace. But rifts open when some of the people working for the good of man want it right away and others plan to have it three generations from now, and that's enough to separate them forever. When an opponent is

9. This section of dialogue dramatizes the earlier entry on "political antinomies." See p. 244.

also in the right, well, that's when we're headed for tragedy. And you know what lies at the end of tragedy?"

C: "Yes. Death."

L: "Yes. Death. And yet, I'd never agree to kill you."

C: "I'd agree if necessary. That's my sense of morals. And to me, it's a sign you're not living the truth."

L: "To me, it's a sign you're not living the truth."[10]

C: "I appear victorious because I'm alive. But I'm in the same darkness as you, having only my individual will to help me."

End. They bring L's body back. A partisan treats it flippantly. Silence. C: "This man died a hero for our cause. We must respect and avenge him."[11]

C: "Look. Look at this night. How vast it is. It wheels its silent stars over our awful human battles. For millennia, you've worshipped these heavens, no matter their stubborn silence, you've accepted that your impoverished loves, your desires, and your fears were nothing in the presence of divinity. You've believed in your solitude. And today, when the same sacrifice is asked of you, but in the service of man this time, are you going to refuse?"

C: "Don't think my soul's completely blind."

L. returns injured.

C: "We had to go through with it all the same."

L: "It wasn't possible."

C: "If you were able to come back, you were able to go through with it."

L: "It wasn't possible."

C: "Why?"

L: "Because I'm going to die."

X: "It's not up to you to go."

C: "I'm in charge here and I'm the one who makes the decisions."

---

10. Camus crossed out three lines at the end of this entry.

11. The handwriting in the notebook is difficult to decipher here. The last words, especially, are conjectural.

X: "That's just it—we need you. We're not here to make noble gestures, we're here to be effective. Being effective requires a good leader."

C: "That's well and good, X, but I'm not so big on truths that turn to my advantage. So then, I'll go."[12]

The F: "But who's right, then?"

The Lieut: "The one who survives."

A man enters.

"He . . . he died, too."

Oh, no, no! And I, I know very well who was right. He was, yes, he who'd asked for us to come together.[13]

Rebellion.

Collective passions take precedence over individual passions. People no longer know how to love. What interests them today is the human condition. They're no longer interested in individual fates.

Freedom is the last of the individual passions. That's why it's immoral today. Immoral in society, and, strictly speaking, in itself.

Philosophy is the contemporary form of shamelessness.

At 30 years old, almost overnight, I became famous. I don't regret it. I might have had bad dreams about it later. Now, I know what it amounts to—not much.

Thirty articles.[14] The reasons for praise are as bad as the reasons for criticism. Barely one or two authentic or passionate voices. Fame! In the best of cases, a misunderstanding. But I won't put on the haughty act of the person who looks down on it. It, too, is one of man's gestures, no more or less important than their indifference, friendship, or loathing. What does it all matter to

12. Of the dialogues recorded here, this is the only one that would end up in one of Camus's completed plays. It appears, in revised form, in *The Just*, act 2.

13. This section of dialogue was penciled in at a later date.

14. Camus's first major play, *Caligula*, had opened at the Théâtre Hébertot in Paris on September 26. This entry is in reference to its reception.

me anyway? This misunderstanding, for someone who knows how to take it, is a liberation. My ambition, if I have one, is of another order.

November, 32 Years Old

Man's most natural inclination is to ruin himself and everyone else with him. What excessive effort just to be normal. And what an even greater effort for those who aspire to take control of themselves and their mind. In himself, man is nothing. He is nothing but infinite possibility. But he's infinitely responsible for that possibility. Left to himself, man is ready to dilute himself. Only let his will, his conscience, his adventurous spirit prevail and the possibility begins to grow. No one can say they've reached man's limits. The five years we've just gone through taught me that. From the beast to the martyr, from the evil spirit to the hopeless sacrifice, not a single testimony has been less than shattering. We are each responsible for taking advantage of the greatest of man's possibility that we hold within ourselves, his definitive virtue. The day human limits mean something, then we can deal with the problem of God. But not before, never before the potential has been lived to its fullest. There's only one possible goal for great deeds and that's human fecundity. *But first we have to master ourselves.*

Tragedy is not a solution.

Parain. God didn't create himself. He's the son of human pride.

To understand is to create.

Rebellion. If man fails to reconcile justice and freedom, then he fails at everything—And religion is right? No, only if he accepts approximation.

It takes boatloads of blood and centuries of history to bring about an imperceptible change in the human condition. Such is the law. For years heads fell like hail, the Terror reigned, we cried out for Revolution, and we ended up replacing absolute monarchy with constitutional monarchy.

I lived my whole youth with the idea of my innocence, which is to say with no idea at all. Today . . . [15]

---

15. In *The Plague,* Tarrou tells Rieux: "When I was young, I lived with the idea of my innocence, which is to say with no idea at all. I'm not the tormented type. I got off to a good start in life. Had

---

I'm not cut out for politics given I'm incapable of wanting or accepting my opponent's death.

It's through continual effort that I'm able to create. My tendency is to roll to a standstill. My deepest, surest inclination is to silence and the daily routine. It's taken me years of persistent determination to avoid distractions, the draw toward autopilot. But I know it's precisely this effort that's kept me standing and that if I stopped believing in it for even a second I'd roll over the edge of the cliff. This is how I escape illness and renunciation, lifting my head up with all my strength, in order to breathe and overcome. This is my way of being hopeless and this is my way of being healed.

Our task: to create universality or at least universal values. Conquer for man his catholicity.

Historical materialism, absolute determinism, the negation of all freedom, that awful world of courage and silence, these are the most legitimate consequences of a philosophy without God. Parain is right about this. If God doesn't exist, nothing is allowed. In this regard, only Christianity is strong, for it will always, to the deification of history, argue for the creation of history, to the existentialist situation, ask its origin, etc. But its answers are not based in reasoning, they're based in a mythology that requires faith.

What to do between these two? Something inside of me says, persuades me, that I can't detach myself from the times without it being cowardly, without agreeing to be a slave, without disowning my mother and my truth. I couldn't do that, or agree to a commitment that's simultaneously sincere and relative, unless I were Christian. Not being Christian, I have to follow things through to the end. But following things through to the end means choosing history absolutely, and the murder of man along with it, if the murder of man is necessary for history. Otherwise, I'm just a witness. There's the question: can I be just a witness? Put another way: do I have the right to be just an artist? I can't believe that. If I don't choose, then I have to keep quiet and agree to be a slave. If I choose to be against God and history at the same

success with everything. I was comfortable with intellectual matters, and even more comfortable with women, and if I had any worries, they passed as quickly as they came. Then one day I started thinking about things. Now . . ."

time, I'm the witness of a pure freedom whose fate in history is to be put to death.[1] As things stand, my situation is one of silence or death. If I choose to go against my gut instinct and believe in history, my situation will be one of lying and murder. Outside of this, religion. I understand a person blindly throwing themselves into it to escape this madness, this atrocious (yes, really and truly atrocious) rift. But I can't do it.

Consequence: Do I have the right, as an artist, still committed to freedom, to accept the advantages, in money and recognition, that are linked to this position? My answer would be simple. It's in poverty that I have found and that I will always find the conditions necessary for my guilt, if it exists, at least not to be shameful, to remain proud. But must I reduce my children to poverty, refuse them even the very modest comforts I provide them? And under these conditions, was I wrong to agree to the simplest of human tasks and duties, such as having children? When it really comes down to it, does a person have the right to have children, to take on the human condition,[2] if the person doesn't believe in God (add the intermediary reasoning).

How easy it would be if I gave in to the horror and disgust with which this world fills me, if I could still believe man's task is to create happiness! Keep quiet, at least, keep quiet, keep quiet until I feel I have the right . . .

(1) Or to cheat by taking material advantage from being a privileged artist

(2) Besides, have I really taken it on when I feel such reluctance and have such a hard time doing so? Certainly, this heart that has such difficulty with faithfulness must deserve this contradiction?

Creation corrected.

Under the Occupation: those who shovel manure. Gardens in the banlieues.

Saint-Étienne Dunières: Working people in the same compartment as German soldiers. A bayonet disappeared. The soldiers don't let the workers off until Saint-Étienne. The tall guy who was supposed to get off at Firminy. His rage bringing him almost to tears. Over his face's weary exhaustion, the crueler exhaustion of humiliation.

We're being asked to choose between God and history. Which brings about this terrible desire to choose the earth, the world and the trees, were I not completely sure all mankind doesn't coincide with history.

———

Every philosophy is a self-justification. The only genuine philosophy would be one that justifies someone else.

———

Against committed literature.[16] Man isn't *only* social. His death, at least, belongs to him. We're made to live alongside others. But we only ever really die alone.[17]

———

Aesthetics of rebellion. Thibaudet on Balzac: "*The Human Comedy* is an imitation of the Holy Father."[18] The theme of rebellion, of the outlaw, in Balzac.

———

80% divorce rate among repatriated prisoners. 80% of human loves can't withstand five years separation.

———

Thomas: "Err . . . what was I saying? Well, it'll come back to me eventually . . . Anyway, Roupp, he says to me, 'Look, I manage a boxer. I'd like to deal for a painter, too. So then, if you want . . .' Me? I didn't want. I like freedom. And then Roupp, he suggests setting off for Paris. Naturally, I accept. I have meals at his place. He gets me a room at a hotel. He's the one paying for it. Now he's pushing me to get to work."

———

X: A modest and charitable satanism.

———

16. The French term *littérature engagée* is often used in English without any translation, though it's also sometimes rendered as "engaged literature" or "committed literature." At root, the term refers to the idea that an artist has a responsibility to society and not just to "art for art's sake." This entry, then, can be compared with the one a little earlier in which Camus quotes from E. M. Forster's essay "Art for Art's Sake."

17. The translation "die alone" is clear and readable at a sentence level but leaves room for misinterpretation. Translated more literally, the sentence ends: "but we really only die for ourself." The idea being that it's the individual who experiences death, not the group.

18. Albert Thibaudet (1874–1936), French literary critic, wrote books on Mallarmé, Valéry, Stendhal, Flaubert, Thucydides, and his former teacher, Henri Bergson, as well as being a regular contributor to *Nouvelle revue française*. The comment about Balzac would also appear in *The Rebel*, in the section "The Novel and Rebellion."

A tragedy about the problem of evil. The best of men must be damned if he serves only man.

"We love people less for the good they've done us than for the good we've done them." No, in the worst cases, we love them equally. And that's not a bad thing. It's natural that we be grateful to someone who at least once allows us to be better than we are. We revere and recognize a better image of man by doing this.

What right does a Communist or Christian (to take only the respectable forms of modern thought) have to reproach me for being pessimistic? I'm not the one who invented man's destitution or those terrible formulations of divine curse. I'm not the one who said man was incapable of saving himself on his own and that in the depths of his debasement he has no real hope beyond the grace of God. As for that famous Marxist optimism, you'll allow me to laugh a little. Few people have deepened mistrust of their fellow man more. Marxists don't believe in persuasion or dialogue. You don't make a worker from a bourgeois, and, in their world, economic conditions are more terrible fatalities than divine whims.

As for M. Herriot and the clientele of his *Annales*![19]

The Communists and Christians will tell me that their optimism takes the long view, that it's above everything else, and that God or history, accordingly, is a satisfactory culmination of their dialectic. I have the same reasoning to put forward. If Christianity is pessimistic with regard to man, it's optimistic with regard to human destiny. Marxism, pessimistic with regard to destiny, pessimistic with regard to human nature, is optimistic with regard to the march of history (its contradiction!). I'll say that, for my part, pessimistic with regard to the human condition, I'm optimistic with regard to man.

---

19. Édouard Herriot (1872–1957) served three terms as Prime Minister of France and sponsored *Annales*, an organization giving and publishing lectures on literature and politics. Camus had been critical of Herriot for some time, but his criticism came to a head in an article written for *Combat* on June 27, 1945.

Almost all of this entry, minus the line about Herriot, would appear with only minor changes as the third section of Camus's essay "The Unbeliever and the Christians," which itself was part of a speech Camus gave in 1948.

How can they fail to see that never has such a cry of confidence in man been let loose? I believe in dialogue, in sincerity. I believe they are the path to an unparalleled psychological revolution; etc., etc. . . .

———

Hegel: "Only the modern city offers the mind the grounds to become aware of itself." Significant. This is the time of big cities. We've amputated a part of the world's truth, what gives it its permanence and equilibrium: nature, the sea, etc. There is no consciousness but in the streets![20]

(Cf. Sartre. All the modern philosophies of history, etc.)

———

Rebellion. The human drive toward freedom and its *usual* contradiction: discipline and freedom die by their own hands. Revolution has to accept its own violence or be disavowed. So then, it can't be carried out in purity: but in blood or calculation. My aim: demonstrate that the logic of rebellion refuses blood and calculation. And that dialogue pushed to the absurd[21] gives purity *a* chance.—Through compassion? (suffering together)

———

Plague. "Let's not exaggerate," Tarrou says. "The plague's here. We have to protect ourselves from it and that's what we're doing. Really, it's no big deal, and in any case it proves nothing."

The airfield is too far from the city to establish regular service. Packages are only sent in by parachute.

After Tarrou's death, a telegram announcing Mme Rieux's death is received.

The plague follows the course of the year. It has its spring, when it germinates and blooms, its summer and its autumn, etc. . . . [22]

———

To Guilloux:[23] "All man's misfortune comes from not speaking plainly. If the hero of The Misunderstanding had said, 'Here I am. It's me. Your son,' then dialogue would have been possible and the awkward situation in the play would have ceased to exist. There would have been no tragedy left given

20. Camus would include this entry, with a few revisions and additions, in his essay "Helen's Exile." The quote from Hegel seems to be a loose translation or interpretation, perhaps second-hand, from *The Philosophy of Right.*

21. As in the phrase *poussé à l'extrême* (pushed to the limit, or taken to extremes).

22. Half of this entry was crossed out by Camus on the manuscript.

23. Louis Guilloux (1899–1980), committed socialist and writer of social realist novels. On December 7, 1945, he and Camus began a long-running correspondence. When Guilloux's first book, *La maison du peuple,* was reprinted in 1953, Camus provided a preface.

the climax of all tragedy lies in the hero's deafness. From this point of view, it's Socrates who's right, as opposed to Jesus and Nietzsche. Progress, true greatness, they lie in dialogue at a human level, not in the Gospel, monologued and dictated from atop a solitary mountain. That's where I stand. What balances the absurd is a community of individuals struggling against it, and if we choose to serve that community, we choose to serve dialogue to the point of the absurd, against any policy of lies or of silence. That's how a person is free with others."

The limits. It's with regard to this that I'll say there are some mysteries it's appropriate to enumerate and meditate on. Nothing more.

Saint-Just: "I think, therefore, we must be exalted; this doesn't preclude common sense or wisdom."[24]

For a thought to change the world, first it has to change the life of the one who has it. It has to be made into an example.

At 12 years old, she's taken by a hackney-coach driver. Once. The thought that she's in some way defiled stays with her until she turns seventeen.

Creation corrected. The two Jews in Verdelot during the Occupation.[25] The haunting dread of arrest. She loses her mind on account of it and goes to inform on him. Then she goes to tell him what she's done. They're both found hanged. The dog howls all night long, as in the most uninspired serial writing.

Creation corrected: "I'd always been told the first opportunity to escape should immediately be seized. Any risk was better than what would follow. But it's easier to stay a prisoner and give yourself over to the horror than to escape, because in the latter case, you have to take the initiative. In the former, others take it for you."

---

24. The quote appears in a posthumous collection of Saint-Just's writing titled *Fragmens sur les institutions républicaines,* third fragment, section 4, "Republic and Government." The lines preceding the quote read: "Just as a nation can be governed with the greatest degree of feeble opinion, so it can be governed with the highest degree of energy. Whatever tone you take can be made to work, so long as you're in harmony with it."

25. Verdelot is the town in the Seine-et-Marne where Camus hid out at the end of the Occupation after fellow editor Jacqueline Bernard was arrested.

Id. "If you really want to know, I never believed in the Gestapo. It's just we never saw them. Of course, I took precautions, but in an abstract way, if you will. From time to time, a buddy would disappear. This one day, in Saint-Germain-des-Prés, I saw these two big guys punching a man in the face and tossing him into a taxi. And nobody said a thing. A waiter at the café said to me: "Keep quiet. It's them." That made me think maybe they really did exist and that one day . . . but it only made me think it. The truth is I was never going to believe in the Gestapo until it was me getting kicked in the stomach. That's just how I am. That's why you shouldn't make too much of my courage for being in the Resistance, as they say. No, I don't deserve any credit, seeing as I don't have any imagination."

———

Politics of rebellion. "It's in this way the pessimistic revolution becomes the revolution of happiness."

———

Tragedy. C.L.C. "I'm right and that's what gives me the right to kill him. I can't dwell on the details. I think according to the world and history."

L: "When the detail is a human life, it is the entire world and the whole of history for me."

———

Origins of modern madness. It's Christianity that turned man away from the *world.* It reduced him to himself and his history. Communism is a logical follow-up to Christianity. It's a Christian story.

Id. After 2,000 years of Christianity, the body's rebellion. It took two thousand years for people to be able to expose their naked bodies on the beach again. That's where the excess comes from. Yet the body has once again found its place in everyday practice. It remains to give its place back to it in philosophy and metaphysics. That's one of the meanings of the modern convulsion.[26]

———

Albert Wild rightly criticizes the absurd: "The *feeling* of anguish is irreconcilable with the *feeling* of freedom."

———

The Greeks made sense of the divine. But *the divine wasn't everything.*

———

26. Camus later wrote over this last sentence, making it somewhat hard to decipher. The above reading is conjectural.

"But let your communication be, Yea, yea; Nay, nay: for whatsoever is more than these cometh of evil." Matth., 5:37.[27]

Koestler. Extreme doctrine: "Whoever enters into opposition against a dictatorship must accept civil war as a means. Whoever shies away from civil war must abandon opposition and accept the dictatorship." That's the typical "historical" reasoning.[28]

Id. "The Party denied the free will of the individual—and at the same time it extracted his willing self-sacrifice. It denied his capacity to choose between two alternatives—and at the same time it demanded that he should constantly choose the right one. It denied his power to distinguish good and evil—and at the same time spoke pathetically of guilt and treachery. The individual stood under the sign of economic fatality, a wheel in a clockwork which had been wound up for all eternity and could not be stopped or influenced—and the Party demanded that the wheel should revolt against the clockwork and change its course."[29]

Typical of the "historical" contradiction.

Id. "The greatest temptation for the like of us is: to renounce violence, to repent, to make peace with oneself.[30] The temptations of God were always more dangerous for mankind than those of Satan."

Love story: Jessica.[31]

An old actor's death.

A Paris morning full of snow and mud. The oldest and saddest neighborhood in the city, the one where they put La Santé, Sainte-Anne, and Cochin.[32]

---

27. Given the entry that follows, it's likely Camus was reading Arthur Koestler's *Darkness at Noon,* where Matthew 5:37 appears before the third interrogation.

28. The quote appears in *Darkness at Noon,* third interrogation, end of section 2.

29. The full quote, which comes in the last part of *Darkness at Noon,* finishes with one additional line: "There was somewhere an error in the calculation; the equation did not work out."

30. In *Darkness at Noon,* there's an additional line here that reads: "Most great revolutionaries fell before this temptation, from Spartacus to Danton and Dostoevsky; they are the classical form of betrayal of the cause."

31. The love story involving Jessica would go on to become part of Camus's plan for *The First Man.*

32. La Santé Prison, Sainte-Anne Hospital Center, and Hôpital Cochin are all grouped together along the border of Paris's thirteenth and fourteenth arrondissements. Seventy-plus years after this

Along the icy black streets, the mad, the sick, the poor, and the condemned. As for Cochin: the barracks of poverty and sickness, its walls sweating out the dirty dampness of misery.

It's there he died. At the end of his life, he was still playing bit parts (what terms theater people use), trading in the only suit he owned, its black tones yellowing, its fringes fraying, for the more-or-less sparkly getups that have to be worn even for secondary roles. He had to hang up his hat. He could no longer drink anything but milk and, at any rate, there wasn't any. They led him off to Cochin and he told his comrades he was going to be operated on and it would be over after that (I remember a line from his role: "When I was a small child," and when he was directed how to deliver it, "Ah," he said, "that's not the way it feels to me"). They didn't operate on him, rather they sent him packing, telling him he was cured. He even went back to playing the clownish little role he'd been playing at the time. But he'd lost weight. That's something that's always amazed me, how a certain amount of lost weight, a certain sharpening of the cheekbones and receding of the gums, are the obvious signs it'll all be over soon. It's only the one who's losing the weight who never seems to "be aware" of it. Or if he "becomes aware," the moment seems fleeting, though I, of course, have no way of knowing. All I know is what I see, and precisely what I saw was Liesse was going to die.

And die he did. He stopped working again. He returned to Cochin. They still didn't operate on him, but he didn't need to be operated on to die—one night without anyone noticing. In the morning, his wife came to see him, as she always did. Nobody on staff had let her know ahead of time because nobody knew ahead of time. The dead man's neighbors, they let the wife know ahead of time. "You know," they said, "it happened last night."

And there he was, that morning, in the little morgue overlooking Rue de la Santé. Two or three of his old comrades were there with the widow and the widow's daughter, who isn't the dead man's daughter. When I arrived, the director (why was he wearing a tricolor sash, like a mayor?) told me we could still see him. I didn't really want to, that leprous, never-ending morning stuck like a lump in my throat. But I went. All you could see was his head, the cloth that they'd used as a shroud having been pulled up to his chin. He'd lost even more weight. I didn't think someone in his condition could lose more weight. But, nevertheless, he had, and you could see how big his bones were

---

entry was made, all are still in operation. George Orwell's essay "How the Poor Die," which describes the author's stay at Cochin in 1929, furthers the details Camus provides here.

and in seeing them you understood that strong and gnarled head was made to bear a heavy weight of flesh. Without the flesh, the teeth protruded, terribly so . . . but am I really going to describe this? A dead person is a dead person, everyone knows that, and we have to let them be buried together.[33] What a pity, nevertheless, what an awful pity!

The men who were at his head, their hands on the rim of the coffin, as if presenting him to visitors, started up then. Started up is the right way of putting it, for those awkward, ill-at-ease automatons who'd been standing there in their shoddy clothes suddenly and at full speed threw themselves on the shroud, the lid, a screwdriver. The top was down in only a second and two of the men were tightening the screws, putting all their weight behind a brutal twisting of the forearm. "Ah-ha," they seemed to be saying, "you're not getting out of this one!" They, being alive, wanted to get on with it, that was clear right away. They carried him. We followed. The widow and the daughter climbed into the hearse along with the dead man. We squeezed into a car that followed. Not a flower, nothing but black.

We were going to the Cimetière de Thiais. The widow thought it a bit far but the authorities didn't give her a choice. We left through the Porte d'Italie. Never had the sky seemed so low over the Parisian banlieues. Bits of shanties, of beds,[34] of sparse, black vegetation peeked out from piles of snow and mud. Six kilometers through the center of this land and we pulled up to the monumental gates of the world's most hideous cemetery. A guard with a flushed face came out to stop the procession at the gate and to demand our entrance ticket. "Go on," he said once he had what he needed. We drove through piles of mud and snow for a good ten minutes and then we stopped behind another procession. We were separated from the burial grounds by a snowbank. Two crosses were planted sideways in the snow, one for Liesse, according to what I read, the other for a little eleven-year-old girl. The procession in front of us was the one for the little girl. The family was in the process of getting back in the hearse. They started up and we were able to move a couple of meters ahead. We got out. Tall men dressed in blue and wearing sewer boots put down the shovels they'd been holding and surveyed the scene. They stepped forward and began to pull the casket from the hearse. At that moment, a sort of mailman dressed in blue and red, wearing a crushed-in kepi, suddenly appeared

33. The last clause may be intended as a biblical reference, "let the dead bury the dead," though the wording Camus gives differs from standard French translations of the passage.

34. The word Camus uses here could be "stakes" or, colloquially, "beds."

with a pad of deposit slips, a sheet of carbon paper slipped between each page. Then the sewage workers read out a number engraved on the casket: 3237 C. The mailman followed along the lines of his pad with the tip of his pencil and said "Good" while pointing at a number. After that, they let the coffin through. We entered the grounds. Our feet sunk into the oily, elastic clay. The hole had been dug between four other graves, which surrounded it on all sides. The sewage workers slid the box in rather quickly, and we were all still a ways away from the hole because the graves prevented us from getting closer and the narrow paths between them were filled with tools and earth. When the casket reached the bottom, there was a moment of silence. Everyone looked at each other. There was no priest, no flowers, and not a word of peace or regret spoken. Everyone felt the moment should have more formality to it—that it should somehow be marked, but nobody knew in what way. Then one of the sewage workers said: "If the ladies and gentlemen would like to throw a little soil." The widow indicated they would. He put some soil on a shovel, took a scraper out of his pocket, and put a little of the soil on the scraper. The widow reached her hand out over a mound of soil. She took the scraper and threw the soil toward the hole, a little blindly. We heard the hollow sound of the box. The daughter, for her part, missed completely. The soil flew over and past the hole. She made a gesture that meant "oh well."

The bill: "And they lay him in the clay for an exorbitant price."

You know, this here's the cemetery for those sentenced to death.

Laval is a little farther off.[35]

———

America. Departure.[36] The bit of anxiety that accompanies all departures has passed. On the train, I run into R.,[37] a psychiatrist who's going over to

35. Pierre Laval (1883–1945), twice prime minister of France, started his political career as a socialist and ended it as a collaborationist. Charles de Gaulle's government tried, convicted, and executed Laval by firing squad. His body was initially placed in an unmarked grave in the Cimetière de Thiais before being moved to a family plot in Montparnasse right around the time this entry was made.

36. On March 8, 1946, Camus wrote to his friend Louis Guilloux: "I leave for America on Sunday. The departure is a bit rushed, and while I understand that all departures are a bit rushed, it keeps me from knowing if I'm happy or not." Two days later, Camus took the train from Paris to Le Havre, where he boarded the cargo ship *Oregon*, which set sail for New York the next day.

In the handwritten notebook, Camus didn't separate the entries he made during this trip from the entries he'd already been keeping at home: the trip to North America appears here in the middle of "Notebook V," as Camus recorded it, with less frequent spacing between the entries.

37. Pierre Rubé (1899–1991) had trained as a psychiatrist but served as a medical doctor during World War II. After several attempts to escape occupied France, Rubé finally made it into Spain, only

make contacts. We'll be sharing a cabin on the boat, which is fine by me, as I find him sharp and friendly. In my compartment: three kids who start out rather boisterous but then settle down, their little maid, their mother—a tall, elegant woman with light-blue eyes—and a blond, a little wisp of a woman, who starts crying right in front of me. An uneventful trip, with one exception. As I'm doing a few favors for the young blond woman, before we've reached Rouen, a tallish woman with flat features[38] and a long animal fur asks me if everyone in our car is going to America. If I'm going there. "Yes." She begs pardon and asks me if she can ask me what I'm going there to do. "Some talks."

"Literary or scientific?"

"Literary."

She gives a real theatrical cry, hand darting to her mouth. "Oh!" she says. "How wonderful!" And two seconds later, eyes lowered: "I'm a writer, too, you know."

"Ah!" I say.

"Yes, I'm about to publish a book of poems."

"Very good," I say.

"Yes, I've gotten Rosemonde Gérard to write the preface. She's written a rather beautiful sonnet for me."

"Bravo."

"Of course, it's only my first book, but to have a debut with a preface by Rosemonde Gérard . . ."

"Who's the publisher?"

She gives me a name I don't recognize. She explains that the poems are in regular verse "because I'm more the traditional type. The modern, I don't know what you think of it . . . but me, I don't like what I don't understand," etc., etc. She gets off in Rouen and offers to post a telegram for me that I want sent back to Paris because I forgot to bring R.'s address in New York.[39] She didn't post it as I haven't received a response.

I meet R. in the dining car and we have lunch sitting across from the little blond wisp who's having trouble cracking her walnuts. When we get to Le

---

to be arrested, jailed, and then sent to North Africa, where he was reenlisted in the French army. Shortly after Camus died, Rubé wrote a biographical remembrance of his friend, "Who Was Albert Camus?"

38. Eliette Boulen (1903–1997), author of *Montcalm: 1945, sonnet-préface de Rosemonde Gérard*.

39. Camus is likely referring here to a second person with R. as their first initial. This sentence may refer to Régine Junier, who will make her appearance later in the journals.

Havre, the little wisp, looking completely lost, asks if I might help her. We talk a little while waiting for the bus. She's going to Philadelphia. The bus is a dirty, dusty old police wagon. Le Havre, with its vast fields of rubble. The air is calm. When we arrive at the *Oregon*, I realize it's a cargo ship, a big cargo ship, but a cargo ship nonetheless. Customs, exchange, a police checkpoint with a little box of cards that one cop consults while another calls out your name—and that I know well thanks to a few cold sweats that boxes like this one gave me during the Occupation. And then we board.

The four-person cabin, with a shower and bathroom, has been turned into a five-person cabin, where it's impossible to sneeze without knocking something over. We're asked to head to the dining room to see the maître d', but what we really see is a comedy routine. The maître d' looks like one of those Frenchmen you see in American movies, on top of which he's afflicted with a number of tics that have him throwing winks and glances left and right. He's trying his best to arrange the tables harmoniously, consulting a layout he has, as all good maître d's do, that lists the titles of some of the notable passengers. Naturally, he wants to put me with another journalist who's on board.[40] I emphatically refuse, and in the end he puts me with R. and the little blond wisp, whose name, O wonder, is Jeanne Lorette. She's an elegant Parisienne who's in the perfume business and who was crying this morning because she'd just left her twin sister behind and because her sister is her whole world, though she's headed to Philadelphia now to reunite with an American man she's engaged to marry. R. is delighted by Lorette's lack of affectation, her discretion, and kindness. I am, too. We're a little less delighted with the cabin. The cot in the middle of the room is occupied by an old man, about 70. On the bunk above mine there's a middle-aged guy, a businessman, I assume. Above R. is a vice-consul who's on his way to Shanghai and who has an open, loud quality about him.[41] We settle in, and I decide to get to work.

At dinner, I meet R., Lorette, the tall woman from the compartment (she's not so tall—rather slim and elegant), and a Mexican couple who are

---

40. On official paperwork filled out for the trip, Camus wrote that he was traveling to North America as a journalist.

41. In his biography of Camus, Herbert Lottman recounts how the vice-consul refused to bathe, which, in such a tiny cabin, was hard for the others to bear. Camus and Rubé wondered how they might compel him to do so. "Rubé had an idea," Lottman writes. "He enlisted the help of their steward, with a tip, so the steward knocked at the door of their cabin the next morning to announce: 'Monsieur the Consul, your shower is ready.' The steward was carrying soap and a towel, and the strategy worked."

"in business."[42] The two women seem to regard our Lorette with a little suspicion. But she's so naturally at ease that she's the one who comes off as having more class. She tells us that her mother-in-law, who doesn't even know her, writes her the nicest letters and that it seems mothers-in-law in America are of truly superior quality. Her fiancé is very religious, doesn't drink or smoke. He asked her to take confession before leaving. The morning of the departure (she'd been getting things in order in the days leading up to it), she woke at six in the morning to go to church, but it was closed and the train was leaving early. She'll have to take confession when she gets there, and, she says in her slight Parisian accent (usually, she doesn't enunciate her words very clearly and she speaks very quickly and you have to lean in to catch what she's saying), "Anyway, I prefer it this way, because they won't understand me very well over there and so they'll give me absolution." We explain that absolution is always given in such cases. "Even for mortal sins." Of course, R. says, certain it's true. We point out that there's probably a chaplain aboard the ship.

By the end of dinner, R. and I agree that our charming Lorette is trying to calm her apprehension by presenting to others, and so to herself, a comforting image of her situation—which may in fact be comforting, but that's beside the point. Either way, we both wish this droll little creature all the happiness she deserves. Getting to sleep takes a little more work. The cabin's about as roomy as a barracks. The old man and the businessman are both snorers. What's more, R. and I had opened the porthole but the old man closed it during the night. I feel like I'm breathing other people's breath and have a furious desire to go sleep up on deck. Only the thought of the cold keeps me from doing so. Wake up at 7:30 because breakfast is served only until 8:30. Work in the morning. Lunch at 12:15. The Mexican man tells me he represents French perfumeries in Mexico City and he praises French quality. The handsome, pale eyes in front of me lose a bit of their pride, and it's clear now that it came mostly from shyness. Lorette assures us she'll never let anyone in her family speak ill of France. She draws us a remarkable portrait of Antwerpian judgment. (If they buy a piece of jewelry for their wife, it's an uncut diamond, never a finely crafted ring. That way, they'll have capital. Fur coats, too. Safe bets, either way.)

In the afternoon, we talk with the vice-consul. I'm not so surprised to learn he's from Oran. Naturally, we give each other a couple of slaps on the

42. Edmundo Detchart-Dartayet (1898–1987) and Margarita Berriozabal de Detchart (1901–1970).

shoulder. He's been to the most incredible countries, one being Bolivia, which he speaks of highly. La Paz is 4,000 meters above sea level. Automobiles lose 40% of their power, tennis balls barely bounce, and horses jump only over short obstacles. He kept his strength up by eating garlic. His wife, a witty Polish woman, tells R. stories filled with magic. 3:00 P.M. Departure. The sea is beautiful. A sailor's wife, in full lamentation, runs awkwardly along the length of the jetty, following the boat and waving goodbye. The last image of France is one of destroyed buildings hanging on the very edge of that wounded earth.

Off to work. At dinner, the Mexican man tells stories about going through customs. Only one is interesting: the case of an American who had a leg amputated in Mexico City after an accident and who wanted to bring his deceased leg back with him in a crystal box. Three days of discussion to determine if the thing fell into the category of objects prohibited in order to protect against epidemics. Then the American declared that he wouldn't leave his leg behind and that he'd rather stay with it in Mexico, and the United States, well, they didn't want to lose an upstanding citizen. Our Lorette coughs a lot and is worried about seasickness. R. wants to try to cure her with a course of autosuggestion. He does so quite deftly. After dinner, I have a drink with Mme D., the tall, pale-eyed woman.[43] Husband at the embassy in Washington.

TUESDAY, 10 A.M. A good night, if short. It's raining this morning and the seas are getting rough. The bar is practically empty. I work in peace. The Atlantic is the color of pigeon wings. I lie down before lunch, feeling a little nauseated, and sleep for a full half-hour before waking up fresh as a daisy. Some abstentions at lunch. Our Lorette doesn't leave her berth all day. The Mexican couple leaves the table before the end of the meal. Mme Douteau, R., and I enjoy a friendly chat. Then R. goes off to bed, looking a little green. Although feeling fine, I decide to do the same. My head's too foggy to work. But I'll read a little *War and Peace*. How I would have been in love with Natasha!

The day dragged on from there, heavy and monotonous. After dinner, the furrier from Revillon tells me about Eastern wisdom.[44] It's the type of

---

43. "Mme D," mentioned below by her full name, Paule Douteau (1913–?), traveled on a diplomatic passport with her three children to join her husband, Robert Douteau (1906–1997), who was posted at the French Embassy in Washington.

44. Jean Revillon (1885–1963) and his English wife, Margaret, were on board the ship with Camus. Jean had a home in New York, 210 West 90th Street, and served as "Manager of Commercial Banking" for the New York City office of Revillon Frères, then located at 260 West 30th Street.

conversation I've never been able to bear for more than five minutes. I go to bed with Natasha Rostov.

WEDNESDAY. Get up with a fever and slightly sore throat. A beautiful sun, despite the choppy sea. I spend the morning stretched out in the sun. In the afternoon, English with R. on deck and cocktails at the captain's with Mme D. After dinner, R. recounts stories of his time as a doctor. Dachau. The pile of dying people, diarrhea running all over each other.

THURSDAY. Rough day with chills from the flu. A little champagne in the evening with R. and Mme D. revives me. But my head's empty. English in the afternoon all the same.

FRIDAY. The flu is subsiding. But life's still monotonous. I work a little in the morning. The sea's still rough. In the afternoon, we receive Mme D. and L. in our cabin, along with the consul (Dahoui).[45] Enjoyable chat. The consul recounts (with Algerian eloquence) the story of a little vice-consul from Adrianople who couldn't make his first appointment with the consul because four orangutans were leashed in the consulate's antechamber. The vice-consul finally decides to go in but spends his days at the consulate in fear. In the end, having been told by the consul that one of the animals died after eating a box of matches, the vice-consul brings a box every day and affectionately feeds it to one of the animals until it dies. When all the beasts are dead and buried, then he breathes easy.

A classic story, as well, about 30-year-old consuls in Jeddah and other such places who drink themselves to death in solitude (for me).

We're to pass the Azores in the evening, so I go on deck after dinner, and in a corner sheltered from the gusty wind that's been blowing since we left, I enjoy a clear night, with a few sparse but very large stars streaking above the ship, each with the same rectilinear motion. In the sky, a sliver of moon casts a dullish light that reflects evenly on the turbulent waters. I gaze once again, as I have for years, at the drawings etched on the surface by the foam and wake, that lace made and unmade, that liquid marble . . . and once again

---

Though the company moved locations in the mid-1950s, two stone lions supporting an R. F. shield can still be seen above the doorway. At the time, Revillon Frères was the premier fur and luxury goods company in France.

45. Albert Dahoui, counselor at the French Embassy in New York and a French-Algerian like Camus. He was born in Ain El Arbu.

I search for a comparison exact enough to capture that marvelous blossoming of sea, of water and light, a comparison that has for so long escaped me. Still in vain. For me, it's a symbol that persists.

FRIDAY. SATURDAY. SUNDAY. Same schedule. The sea still too rough, we head south and pass the Azores. This microcosm of society is at once fascinating and monotonous. Everyone prides themselves on their elegance and savoir vivre. Like seals trained to do tricks. Some of them are opening up, though. The Revillon furrier is on the boat. We learn he has a magnificent porcelain service, some superb silverware, etc., but that he shows copies he's had made and keeps the originals locked away. Likewise, it seems he also has a copy of a wife with whom he's only ever made a copy of love.

3 or 4 passengers are obviously going to the USA for the export of capital.[46] I even let the scheme, quite crafty in itself, be explained to me. "You'll notice," one of them says, "that I'm not doing anything against the State. Its intentions are good, but it doesn't understand anything about business." These people here, they know about business. We agree with R., always the charming companion, that the only contemporary problem is money. Unpleasant characters rotted by greed and powerlessness. Thankfully, there's the company of women. The truth and the light. Mme D., more and more charming. L., too.

MONDAY. Beautiful day. The wind has died down. For the first time, the sea is calm. Passengers sprout up on deck like mushrooms after rain. We breathe easy. In the evening, a magnificent sunset. After dinner, moonlight on the sea. Mme D. and I agree most people don't lead the life they'd like to lead and that this is a matter of cowardice.

SUNDAY. They announce we'll arrive in the evening. The week passed in a whirlwind. Tuesday evening, the 21st, our table decides to celebrate the arrival of spring. Alcohol until 4 in the morning. The next day, too. Forty-eight hours of pleasant euphoria, during which all our relationships quickly deepen. Mme D. is rebelling against her class. L. confesses to me the marriage she's headed for is one of convenience. On Saturday, we exit the Gulf Stream,

46. In 1917, Vladimir Lenin published the pamphlet *Imperialism, the Highest Stage of Capitalism*, in which he argues that financial capital relies on imperialism and colonialism in order to generate larger and larger profits: "Typical of old capitalism, when free competition held undivided sway, was the export of goods. Typical of the latest stage of capitalism, when monopolies rule, is the export of capital."

and the temperature turns awfully chilly. Nevertheless, the time passes very quickly, and ultimately, I'm not in such a rush to arrive. I've finished preparing my talk. In the remaining time, I gaze out at the sea and chat, mostly with R., who's really quite smart—and with Mme D. and L., of course.

At 12:00 in the afternoon, we catch sight of land. Seagulls have been flying alongside the boat since morning, hanging above the decks as if suspended and motionless. Coney Island, which looks like the Porte d'Orléans, is the first thing we see. "It's Saint-Denis or Gennevilliers," L. says. It's absolutely true. In the cold, with the gray wind and flat sky, it's all rather gloomy. We'll anchor in the mouth of the Hudson but won't disembark until tomorrow morning. In the distance, Manhattan's skyscrapers stand against a backdrop of mist. My heart is still and cold, as it is when faced with sights that don't move me.

MONDAY. Went to bed very late last night. Got up very early. We sail through New York Harbor. A tremendous sight despite, or because of, the fog. Order, power, economic strength, they're all here. The heart trembles before so much remarkable inhumanity.

I don't disembark until 11 o'clock, after a long series of formalities where, out of all the passengers, I'm the one treated as suspect. The immigration officer ends up apologizing for having kept me. "I was required to do so, but I can't tell you why." A mystery—but after five years of occupation . . . [47]

Welcomed by C.,[48] E.,[49] and an envoy from the consulate. C. hasn't changed. E. either. With the whole circus over at immigration, the goodbyes with L., Mme D., and R. are quick and cold.

---

47. Unbeknownst to Camus, FBI director J. Edgar Hoover had ordered one of his special agents in the New York field office to begin an investigation of "Albert Canus," who was, Hoover noted, "reportedly the New York correspondent of 'Combat' . . . filing inaccurate reports which are unfavorable to the public interest of this country." Hoover was concerned that existentialism and absurdism might be nothing more than Communist fronts.

48. Nicola Chiaromonte (1905–1972) was an Italian antifascist author and activist. In 1934, he was forced to flee Italy for France. During the Spanish Civil War, he fought alongside André Malraux and later appeared as a character in Malraux's novel *Man's Hope*. When the Germans stormed Paris in 1940, Chiaromonte escaped to Marseille, and from there, after briefly being jailed, he crossed to North Africa. It was there, in Algeria, that he and Camus first met, when Camus offered to help Chiaromonte apply for passage to the US as a war refugee. Once in New York, Chiaromonte began to write for *The Nation*, *Partisan Review*, *politics*, and other leftist magazines and journals. The two friends would correspond and travel together throughout the rest of Camus's life.

49. Pierre-André Emery (1903–1982) was an acquaintance from Camus's early days in Algeria, where they were both involved with the Théâtre du Travail. Emery lived in New York at the time of Camus's visit and was part of the welcoming party sent by Claude Lévi-Strauss, who was then serving as the French Embassy's cultural attaché.

Tired. My flu is coming back. I catch my first glimpse of New York on shaky legs. At first sight, a hideous, inhuman city. But I know people can change their mind. Here are the details that strike me: the garbage collectors wear gloves,[50] the traffic is orderly, without the need for officers at the intersections, etc., no one ever has any change in this country, and everyone looks as if they've just stepped off a low-budget film set. In the evening, crossing Broadway in a taxi, tired and feverish, I'm literally staggered by the circus of bright lights. I've come from five years of night, and this intense and violent illumination is the first thing that gives me the impression of being on a new continent (a huge 15 m. billboard advertising Camels: a G.I., his mouth wide open, lets out huge puffs of *real* smoke. All of it yellow and red). I go to bed as sick at heart as in body but knowing perfectly well that I'll have changed my mind in two days.

TUESDAY. Get up with a fever. Unable to leave the room before noon. When E. arrives, I'm a little better, and I go with him and D., an adman originally from Hungary, for lunch at a French restaurant. I notice that I haven't noticed the *sky-scrapers*,[51] that they've seemed only natural. It's a question of overall scale. And in any case, you can't always walk around with your head turned up. A person can keep only so many floors in sight at once. Magnificent food shops. Enough to make all of Europe burst. I admire the women in the streets, the hues of their dresses, and the color of the taxis, which look like insects dressed in their Sunday best, red and yellow and green. As for the tie shops, you have to see them to believe them. So much bad taste hardly seems imaginable. D. assures me Americans don't like ideas. That's what they say. I don't really trust "they."

---

50. To Janine and Michel Gallimard, two of Camus's closest friends, Camus would write that upon arriving in the US, he wasn't sure if he were "among crazy people or the most reasonable of people, if life here is as easy as they say or if it's as ghastly as it seems, if it's only natural that they hire ten people where one would suffice and where doing so doesn't really improve the service, if Americans should be called moderates, liberals, or conservatives, if it's admirable or irrelevant that the garbagemen wear high-quality gloves."

51. Throughout his travels, both in North and South America, as elsewhere, Camus shows a fondness for picking up words and phrases in the local language and then using them in his journals and letters. Here, for example, *sky-scrapers* is written in English.

With regard to the English language in general, it seems Camus was able to read it proficiently and follow along with spoken conversations but preferred not to speak the language himself unless necessary.

At 3 o'clock, I go see Régine Junier.[52] Admirable spinster who sends me everything she can afford because her father died of tuberculosis when he was 27, and so . . . She lives in two rooms, amid a mountain of homemade hats that are exceptionally ugly. But nothing could overshadow the generous and attentive heart that shines through in everything she says. I leave her, devoured by fever and unable to do anything but go back to bed. Too bad for the scheduled meetings.—New York's smell—a perfume of iron and cement—the iron dominates.

In the evening, dinner at Rubens with L.M.[53] He tells me the very "American Tragedy" story of his secretary. Married to a man with whom she's had two children, she and her mother come to find out the husband's a homosexual. Separation. The mother, a puritanical Protestant, works on the daughter for months, instilling the idea in her that her children are going to become degenerates. The idiot ends up suffocating one and strangling the other. Declared not guilty by reason of insanity, she's set free. L.M. tells me his personal theory about Americans. It's the fifteenth one I've heard.

On the corner of East 1st Street, a small bistro where a screaming mechanical phonograph drowns out all conversation. To get five minutes of silence, you have to put in five cents.

WEDNESDAY. A little better this morning. Liebling,[54] from the *New Yorker*, visits. Charming man. Chiaramonte then Rubé. These last two and I

52. Régine Junier was a French milliner who'd moved to New York and begun a correspondence with Camus. During the war years, she sent him packages of food, as well as clothes and toys for his twins. "Please accept these things I send as with the kind heart of an older sister," she wrote. Camus tried to send her money for the items, about $200, but she rejected it, saying, "I'd prefer not to be responsible for such a sum given the current conditions." Later in his journal, in 1951, Camus notes that she'd sent him a letter saying she was going to kill herself—which she did.

53. Most likely Reuben's Restaurant and Delicatessen, which opened on Park Avenue in 1908, then moved to Broadway, then Madison Avenue, and was likely located on East 58th Street when Camus would have been there. On advertisements of the period, the name of the deli appears as one word with no apostrophe, as Camus has indicated, though he's misspelled the name here.

54. A. J. Liebling (1904–1963) wrote about Camus's visit in the April 20 issue of *The New Yorker*. According to Pierre Guédenet, then Claude Lévi-Strauss's deputy at the French Embassy, Liebling and Camus were first introduced on March 27, but it wasn't until after Camus's talk at Columbia University, Liebling and Camus having gotten on well, that Liebling decided to interview Camus for a "Talk of the Town" profile. The interview took place on either the 29th or 30th at the Embassy hotel on Broadway and 70th Street. Among other things, they discussed Camus's idea for a newspaper that would "take a lot of the fun out of newspapering." It would, Camus said, "be published one hour after the first editions of the other papers" and would "evaluate the probable element of truth in the other papers' main stories, with due regard to editorial policies and the past performances of the cor-

have lunch at a French restaurant. Ch. speaks of America as no one else does, in my opinion. I point out *Funeral Home* to him. He tells me how it works. One of the ways to understand a country is to know how people die there. Here, everything is planned. "*You die and we do the rest,*"[55] the promotional flyers say. Cemeteries are private property: "Hurry up and secure your spot." It's all bought and sold, the transport, the ceremony, etc. A dead man is a man who has lived a full life.—At Gilson's place, radio. Then at my place with Vercors, Thimerais, and O'Brien.[56] We discuss tomorrow's talk. At six o'clock, a drink with Gral at the Saint-Regis. I walk back to the hotel along Broadway, lost in the crowd and the enormous illuminated signs. Yes, there's an American tragedy. It's what's oppressed me since I arrived here, though I don't know what it's made of yet.

On Bowery Street, a street where the bridal shops stretch for more than 500 meters. I eat alone in the restaurant from this afternoon. And I come back to write.

The Negro Question. We sent a man from Martinique on assignment here. We put him up in Harlem. Vis-à-vis his French colleagues, he saw, for the first time, he wasn't of the same race.

An observation to the contrary: an average American sitting in front of me on the bus stood to give his seat to an older Negro lady.

Impression of overflowing wealth. Inflation is on the way, an American tells me.

THURSDAY. Spent the day dictating my talk.[57] A few jitters in the evening, but I head straight out, and the audience is "glued." But then, while I'm

---

respondents. . . . After a few weeks the whole tone of the press would conform more closely to reality. An international service."

Incidentally, the last piece Liebling ever wrote was a review of Camus's then newly published journals. "His energies," Liebling quipped, "were dissipated in creative writing and we lost a great journalist."

55. In this entry, both the words *Funeral Home* and the quotation are written in English in the original notebook.

56. French Resistance writers Jean Bruller and Léon Motchane wrote under the pseudonyms Vercors and Thimerais. On March 28, 1946, they joined Camus for an appearance at Columbia University, where Justin O' Brien, who would go on to translate several of Camus's books into English, worked in the French Department. Given Camus's difficulties with the FBI, it's interesting to note that O'Brien and Camus first met while O'Brien was in France working for the Office of Strategic Services, the precursor to the modern CIA.

57. Camus's talk, "The Crisis of Mankind," was given at Columbia University's McMillin Theatre (now Miller Theatre).

speaking, someone filches the cashbox, the proceeds of which were to go to French children. At the end of the talk, O'Brien announces what's happened, and someone in the audience stands up to suggest everyone give the same amount on the way out that they gave on the way in. On the way out, everyone gives much more and the proceeds are considerable. Typical of American generosity. Their hospitality and cordiality are also like this, immediate and without affectation. This is what's best about them.

Their fondness for animals. A multistory pet shop: canaries on the second floor, great apes at the top. A couple of years ago, a man was arrested on 5th Avenue for driving a giraffe around in his truck. He explained that his giraffe didn't get enough air out in the suburbs where he kept it and that he'd found this to be a good way to get it some air. In Central Park, a lady brought a gazelle to graze. To the court, she explained that the gazelle was a person. "Yet it doesn't speak," the judge said. "Oh, yes, it speaks the language of lovingkindness." Five-dollar fine. There's also the 3-kilometer tunnel under the Hudson and the impressive bridge to New Jersey.

After the talk, a drink with Schiffrin[58] and Dolorès Vanetti[59]—who speaks the purest slang I've ever heard—and with others, too. Madame Schiffrin asks if I was ever an actor.[60]

FRIDAY. Knopf.[61] 11 o'clock. Cream of the crop. 12. Broadcasting. Gilson's a nice guy. We'll go see the Bowery together. I have lunch with Rubé and J. de

58. When the Bolsheviks came to power, Jacques Schiffrin (1892–1950) fled his home in Baku, Azerbaijan, and settled in Paris, France, where he founded the Bibliothèque de la Pléiade. When Vichy came to power in France, he was forced to flee once more, this time settling in New York, where, along with German exile Kurt Wolff, he founded Pantheon Books.

Shortly after Camus returned to France, he and Schiffrin worked out a contract for Pantheon Books to publish a French edition of *L'Étranger* in America. Camus was paid an advance of $300 and given 8 percent of sales.

59. Dolorès Vanetti Ehrenreich (1912–2008) worked for the Office of War Information and had served as Jean-Paul Sartre's guide when he came to New York the year before Camus, in 1945. "Do you realize," she said, "I've slept with Napoleon!" Ehrenreich and Sartre would carry on their affair—Sartre enough in love to dedicate the first issue of *Temps modernes* to her—until 1950, when out of the blue Sartre informed her that he was no longer in love with her. Ehrenreich briefly served as Camus's guide, as well.

60. To Janine and Michel Gallimard, Camus wrote that he'd discovered that "the secret to all conversation here is to speak in order to say nothing." Then, in English, he demonstrated: "'Good morning.' 'Nice weather today, is it not?' 'It is.' 'The spring will be wonderful.' 'I think so. OK. How do you like America now, M. Camus?' 'OK! I like it very much.' 'You are right. It's a nice country, is it not?' 'It is.' 'Will you come back again?' 'Sure.' 'Etc. etc.'"

61. Although Jacques Schiffrin had acquired the French-language rights for a US edition of *L'Étranger*, it was Alfred A. Knopf—through his wife, Blanche—who acquired the English-language

Lannux,[62] who drives us around New York afterward. Beautiful blue sky that reminds me we're at the same latitude as Lisbon, which is hard to imagine. In tune with the flow of traffic, the gold-lit skyscrapers turn and spin in the blue above our heads. A moment of pleasure.

We go to Tryon Park above Harlem, where we tower over the Bronx on one side and the Hudson on the other. Magnolias blooming pretty much everywhere. I try a new type of these *ice-cream* that I enjoy so much.[63] Another moment of pleasure.

At 4 o'clock Bromley is waiting for me at the hotel.[64] We're off to New Jersey. Immense landscape of factories, bridges, and railroads. Then, all of a sudden, East Orange, the most postcard-perfect countryside there could be, with thousands of cottages, neat and tidy, set down like toys amid the tall poplars and magnolias. They take me to see the small public library, bright and cheery and used by the whole neighborhood—with its giant children's reading room. (Finally a country that really takes care of its children.) I look up philosophy in the card catalog: W. James and that's it.

At Bromley's, American hospitality (though his father is from Germany). We work on the translation of *Caligula*, which he's finished. He explains to me that I don't know how to handle my own publicity, that I have a "*standing*"[65] I should be taking advantage of and that *Caligula*'s success here will allow me—my children and me—to be free from want. According to his calculations, I'll earn $1,500,000. I laugh, and he shakes his head. "Oh, you have no *sense*." He's the best of fellows, and he wants us to go to Mexico together. (Nota: he's an American who doesn't drink!)

SATURDAY. Régine. I take over the gifts I brought for her, and she sheds tears of happiness.

---

rights. Knopf would go on to publish all of Camus's major works, maintaining copyright to the present day.

62. Pierre de Lanux (1887–1955) was a French writer and diplomat. He married the American artist Elizabeth Eyre in 1918. In Paris, they were part of the artistic and intellectual scene that included the writers Ernest Hemingway, André Gide, and Natalie Barney, with whom Eyre would have a long-term relationship.

63. The word "ice-cream" is written in English in the original manuscript, in the singular form, though the French determiner is plural.

64. Harald Bromley, an aspiring young producer when Camus met him, wanted to put *Caligula* on the American stage but was never able to do so.

65. In the original manuscript, both "standing" and "sense" are written in English.

A drink at Dolorès's, then Régine takes me to see some American department stores. I think of France. In the evening, dinner with L.M. From the top of the Plaza, I admire the island, covered in its stone monsters. At night, with its millions of illuminated windows and tall black building faces blinking and flashing halfway up to heaven, it makes me think of a gigantic blaze burning itself out, leaving thousands of immense, black carcasses along the horizon, studded with smoldering embers. The charming countess.

SUNDAY. A stroll to Staten Island with Chiaromonte and Abel.[66] On the way back, in Lower Manhattan, immense geological excavations between tightly packed skyscrapers. As we walk past, the feeling of something prehistoric overtakes us. We have dinner in China Town. For the first time, I'm able to breathe easy, finding real life there, teeming and steady, just as I like it.

MONDAY MORNING. Stroll with Georgette Pope, who came all the way to my hotel, God knows why. She's from New Caledonia. "What is your husband's job?"[67]

"Magician!"

From the top of the Empire State Building, in a glacial wind, we admire New York, its ancient waters and flood of stone.

At lunch, Saint-Ex's wife[68]—an exuberant person—tells us that back in San Salvador her father had had, alongside 17 legitimate children, forty bastards, each of whom received a hectare of land.

---

66. Lionel Abel (1910–2001) was a playwright, critic, and Jean-Paul Sartre's handpicked translator. In a 1963 essay in *The New York Review of Books*, Abel quotes Sartre as having told him, back in 1947, that "Camus is a very fine writer, but France has many other fine writers. Camus is not a great writer, not a genius." In 1949, Abel himself would go on to attack Camus, saying that his political writing had "become wordy, soft and vaguely noble" and that, moreover, Camus would "only raise his voice for what is clearly good." Given Abel's position as Sartre's personal translator, and the similarity of their arguments, it's hard not to see such words in light of the attack Sartre would later launch on *The Rebel*.

67. The question and response are written in English in the original manuscript. Georgette O'Connor Pope Day (1920–?) was performing with her husband, Glen Kent Pope, in a magic act when Camus met her. She also worked as a freelancer for *Paris-Presse* and *France-Illustration*.

68. Camus was meeting with Antoine de Saint-Exupéry's widow, Consuelo, because Saint-Exupéry's French publisher, Gallimard, for whom Camus worked, was suing Saint-Exupéry's American publisher, Reynal & Hitchcock, over rights to *The Little Prince* and *Flight to Arras*, rights that Saint-Exupéry had himself sold to the American publisher, even though the rights belonged to Gallimard.

Though Camus asserted Gallimard's rights in the case, when it came to his own work, he himself would engage in similarly questionable behavior. While in New York, not only was he discussing

Evening, interview at the École libre des Hautes Études.[69] Tired, I go to Broadway with J.S.

Rolley Skating on W. 52nd Street.[70] A huge velodrome covered in red velvet and dust. In a rectangular box perched close beneath the ceiling, an old woman plays a most eclectic mix of tunes on a pipe organ. Hundreds of sailors, of girls dressed for the occasion in jumpsuits, pass from arm to arm in an infernal racket of metal wheels and pipe organ. This description could be pushed further.

Then Eddy et Léon,[71] a charmless club. To make up for it, J.S. and I have ourselves photographed as Adam and Eve, like one of those photographs you find at fairs, where there are two completely naked cardboard cutouts with openings at the head where you can put your face through.

J., who has good things to say about American love, wants to introduce me to some taxi girls. A small, dusty room with dim lighting. Each ten-cent coin[72] gives you the right to a dance. But if you want to chat with the lady, you have

---

rights with Jacques Schiffrin while simultaneously being feted by Blanche Knopf, but he was also negotiating with James Laughlin, head of New Directions, to whom he wrote: "I'd be happy to work with you because I've had enough time to see that you're one of the rare men here who hasn't confused the editor's job with the shopkeeper's." The two discussed publishing *Letters to a German Friend*, some of Camus's plays, and the essay/speech on Chamfort. They even got so far as discussing who would translate what. "Please get back to me quickly," Camus closed his letter, "because I leave America at the end of the month, and I'd be happy to have successfully arranged things with you." Such negotiations earned a rebuke from Camus's American agent, Marion Saunders, who wrote to Laughlin: "I am amazed to see from your letter that it was Camus himself who discussed the LETTERS with you. When he was in New York, he told me that he . . . considered me the exclusive agent for all his work and . . . nothing would be done without consulting me. Oh! these French authors and publishers." These disputes between New Directions, Knopf, and various other agents and translators would continue on for years.

69. The École libre des Hautes Études (Free School of Advanced Studies) was founded by the Free French and Belgian governments-in-exile during World War II. Housed at the New School in New York City, it offered academic appointments to French scholars who'd fled Europe, such as Jean Wahl and Claude-Lévi Strauss. After the war, some of those who'd taught at the school helped establish a sister school in Paris, L'École des Hautes Études en Sciences Sociales (School of Advanced Studies in the Social Sciences), which continues to operate today.

70. "Rolley Skating" is written in English in the original manuscript. Given the address and the date, this must have been Gay Blades, which opened as an ice-skating rink in 1922 and was converted into a roller-skating rink in the 1940s. In 1946, the year Camus would have been there, it hosted the National Roller-Skating Championship. In 1956, the building became home to the famous Roseland Ballroom, which continued to operate until 2014.

71. Leon and Eddie's was a New York City nightclub that reached the height of its fame around World War II. It hosted burlesque shows, concerts, and comedy routines featuring such notable performers as Bob Hope, Red Skelton, Jackie Gleason, and Harry Belafonte.

72. In French, Camus has written *nickel de dix cents*, which translates as "ten-cent nickel," which seems to be a confusion of the American "nickel" and "dime."

to sit in the back of the room on either side of a small barrier and you're not allowed to get close. Feeling of repression and terrible sexual frustration. J. tells me about *V Day*[73] and the orgy-like scenes in Times Square.

TUESDAY. With charming Harold, who also tells about American women. In the evening, the irritating French Institute. But then we go to a Negro nightclub with Dr. Jerry Winter. Rocco, the Negro pianist, is the best I've heard in years.[74] He plays standing in front of a rolling piano that he pushes in front of him. The rhythm, the force, the precision of his playing, the way he puts his whole self into it, jumping, dancing, throwing head and hair right and left.

Impression that only Negroes give life, passion, and nostalgia to this country that they colonize in their own way.

Night in the Bowery. The poverty—which gives a European the urge to say: "At last, reality." The real wreckage. The twenty-cent hotels. Bowery Follies[75] where elderly singers perform for impoverished listeners in a space made up like a "saloon." And then, only steps away, the most splendid bridal shops you could ever see—all lined up—windows sparkling, etc. Yes, an astonishing night.

W. Frank.[76] One of the few exceptional men I've met here. He despairs a little for today's America and compares it to that of the 19th century. "The great minds (Melville) have always been solitary here."

Vassar College.[77] An army of young, long-legged starlets crossing on the lawns. What they do for young people here is worth remembering.

---

73. In English in the original manuscript.

74. Maurice Rocco (1915–1976) was a singer, composer, pianist, and actor, famous for his nightclub performances.

75. Sammy's Bowery Follies opened at 267 Bowery in 1934. Initially, it served as a dive bar for the down-and-out, but by the 1940s, having gained a reputation for its odd assortment of patrons, it began to attract more upscale clients who wanted, even if only for a night, to play at slumming it. The bar closed in 1969, a year after Sammy died.

76. Waldo Frank (1889–1967) was an American author and activist who wrote extensively about Latin American and Spanish literature. He told Camus that "to find great art—and great poetry—in America, you have to go to Hispanic America." In the 1930s, he was elected chairman of the League of American Writers, an organization created by the Communist Party, USA, and in 1937 he interviewed Leon Trotsky, then exiled in Mexico, which eventually led to Frank's break with the Communist Party, USA. Frank's first novel, *The Unwelcome Man*, followed the life of Quincy Burt, a character alienated from industrial society and contemplating suicide.

77. Officially, Camus's talk at Vassar, in Avery Hall, was billed as "French Theater Today," but the director of the French Department later recalled Camus's having given "The Crisis of Mankind" talk that evening.

SUNDAY. Long conversation with Ch. Could we remake the church as a secular institution?

With students in the afternoon. They don't feel the real problem and yet their yearning is clear to see. In this country where *everything* is put toward proving life isn't tragic, they feel as if something is missing. This great effort is moving, but we have to reject the tragic *after* having looked it in the face, not before.

MONDAY. Ryder and Figari.[78] Two truly great painters. Ryder's paintings, with their mystic inspiration and almost traditional technique (they're almost enamels), inevitably call Melville to mind, who was more-or-less his contemporary (younger). Yes, America's greatness is there. And now? Figari has it all: yearning, strength, humor.

Then Alfred Stieglitz, a sort of aged American Socrates. "The older I get, the more and more beautiful life seems—but the more and more difficult it is to live. Don't expect anything from America. Are we an end or a beginning? I think we're an end. We're a country that doesn't understand love."

Evening. Circus. Three-ring. Everyone doing something at the same time—and I can't follow a thing.[79]

Tucci:[80] How very easy human relationships are here because there are no human relationships here. They remain superficial. Out of respect and laziness.

Here in New York, thousands of would-be admirals and generals are doormen, captains, and boys. The elevator operators like so many bottled genies going up and down in their big boxes.[81]

---

78. At the Metropolitan Museum of Art, Camus saw the works of Albert Pinkham Ryder (1864–1946) and Pedro Figari (1861–1938).

79. In a letter to Janine and Michel, Camus clarified the point, writing "that the circus here simultaneously presents ten different attractions in four different rings, and in such a way that, interested in all of them, you end up seeing none of them."

80. Niccolo Tucci (1908–1999) was an Italian-American antifascist writer and friend of Nicola Chiaromonte.

81. To Janine and Michel, Camus wrote that "252,000 bison laughably dressed as admirals and generals stand by the front doors of the buildings, one group to stop the beetles with the blow of a whistle, another group to open the door for us, and a last group who go up and down like multicolored genies bottled in fifty-floor cages that the exegetes call elevators, in memory of the Virgin Mary, though the Virgin Mary didn't gather so many disciples here, being a virgin, which in a way is a blessing, because at the end of the day at least no one will get crucified."

APRIL 19.[82] Another night in the Bowery. The *elevated*—we're at the front—barrels along five stories up,[83] and the skyscrapers slowly bend around us and the engine swallows the little red and blue lights and then stops to digest for a moment at one of the small stations and then resumes its course through poorer and poorer neighborhoods where fewer and fewer cars drive.

Once again, the Bowery Follies and the old women who sing there at the end of their careers. Enormous, their makeup-caked faces oozing—suddenly starting to stamp their feet so that their rolls of blubbery flesh jiggle. "I'm a bird in a gilded cage."

"Me? I've got no ambition."

"I'm nobody's baby," etc.

The least ugly are a flop. They have to be either *very beautiful* or *very ugly*. Instructive. There's mediocrity even in ugliness. Then the night. Surrounded by squalor, a group of Romanians sing and dance until they're out of breath. Transported to the edge of an exalted land—and that unforgettable face.

When you look out from the heights of Riverside, the Highway, which runs along the Hudson, is an unbroken line of smooth-sailing, well-oiled cars letting loose a song both grave and distant, exactly like the sound of waves.

In Philadelphia, small cemeteries filled with flowers lie beneath enormous gas tanks.[84]

Gentleness of evenings out on the vast lawns of Washington, the sky turning red and the grass beginning to darken, throngs of Black children playing there, hitting a ball with a wooden stick and crying out in joy as Americans in rumpled shirts sit slumped on benches—having come straight from a saloon

82. After the previous entry, Camus traveled to Cambridge, Massachusetts, to celebrate the English-language publication of *The Stranger*, which was released on April 11. On the 15th, he gave the "Crisis of Mankind" talk at The New School for Social Research. Years later, Pierre-André Emery would tell biographer Herbert Lottman that Camus was heckled during the talk when he suggested that Russia's October Revolution had cost too many lives. On the 16th, Camus gave a talk at the French Institute and then participated, reluctantly, in a photoshoot at *Vogue*, where he met Patricia Blake, who would from then on become his guide to New York, as well as his lover. The two of them had formed, he said, "an island on the island of three rivers."

83. "Elevated" is in English in the original manuscript.

84. Camus was in Philadelphia to give the "Crisis of Mankind" talk at Bryn Mawr. Patricia Blake accompanied him on the trip.

like the kind you see in old movies—using their last bit of energy to suck on ice-creams molded into waxed-paper cups, while from under people's feet squirrels dig up treats only they know how to name and, in the hundred thousand trees of this city, against a still-light sky, a million birds salute the appearance of the first star above the Washington obelisk, while long-legged creatures stride along the grass paths, the grand monuments behind them, and, in a moment of relaxation, offer their splendid faces to the sky, their loveless gazes.[85]

———

Plague: it's a world without women and so a stifling one.[86]

———

The one who is right is the one who has never killed. So then it can't be God.

———

My curiosity about this country has suddenly ended. As with certain people whom I turn away from without being able to explain why and without being able to maintain interest (F.[87] reproaches me for this). Though I can see the thousands of reasons someone would have for being interested in this place, and I could defend and advocate for it, could reconstruct its beauty or its future prospects, still my heart has simply stopped speaking and . . . [88]

———

Chinese theater in China Town. A large hall, dusty and round. The show runs from 6:00 to 11:00 P.M. and takes place in front of 1,500 Chinese people,

85. Camus visited Washington, DC, on April 23 and 24, before visiting Philadelphia on the 25th and 26th, yet here in the journal he's written about the trip to Philadelphia before the one to Washington, a hint that the entries weren't always made chronologically.

When Camus later wrote his essay "The Rains of New York," he transposed these descriptions of Washington onto New York, such that, for example, "the Washington obelisk" becomes "the Empire State Building," but the rest of the details remain the same.

86. This entry was added in at the top of the page, with a box drawn around it.

87. Francine was an accomplished mathematician and pianist. On the boat to New York, Pierre Rubé would sit and play the piano while Camus worked on his speech. Once, as Rubé began a Bach concerto, Camus said: "Hey, you play that piece? My wife often plays it, too."

"Your wife's a musician?"

"Yes, she's the one who introduced me to Bach."

88. To Janine and Michel, Camus added: "So then here I am, ready, yes, to leave America . . . having already left it in spirit, having left nothing other than an empty, soulless husk, well-dressed, it's true, and continuing to move among those eight million dead who themselves also continue to pretend to live in this quite astonishing capital. This husk, no, it doesn't resemble that charming and exceptional fellow you had the good fortune of getting to meet. . . . After so many days, I myself still don't have a clear picture of New York, which continues to irritate and seduce me at the same time."

who eat peanuts, chatter, enter, exit, and follow the show with a sort of constant distraction. Children run around in the middle of the hall. Onstage, costumed actors perform alongside musicians in business suits and suspenders, who break off from time to time to have a sandwich or pull up a child's pants. Similarly, throughout the performance, stagehands in vests and shirtsleeves come and go, collecting a sword fallen from the hand of a dead man, setting a chair in place or removing one, all of it done for no particular reason. From time to time, actors waiting to make their entrance can be seen standing in the doorways that lead backstage, chatting or following the action.

As for the play itself, given the show is in Chinese, I try to conjure up the storyline. I suspect I've only misinterpreted things, though, for just as a brave man is dying onstage in a most realistic fashion, his wife and friends wailing around him, at that very moment, right when everything seems very serious, the audience laughs. Then, at the clownish entrance of a sort of foghorn-voiced magistrate, I'm the only one who laughs while the rest of the audience shows a sort of respectful attention. A sort of butcher covered in blood kills a man. He forces a Chinese boy to carry the body. The Chinese boy is so scared his knees knock together . . .

From New York to Canada[89]

Clean, wide-open countryside with houses small and large, the latter with white columns and tall, sturdy trees, with lawns that are never separated by fences, so that a single lawn belongs to everyone, a lawn where beautiful children and lithe adolescents laugh before a life filled with the good things, with rich crèmes. Here, nature contributes to those beautiful American fairy tales.[90]

A narrative about an American childhood in which the child searches in vain for his heart's calling. He gives up.

---

89. On May 1, at Brooklyn College, Camus gave his last official talk in the United States, "Are We Pessimists?" At the end of the month, he was due in Canada for one final talk before heading back to France. Camus and Harald Bromley—who'd gone out and bought a used car specially for the occasion—began the drive to Canada on May 24. They stopped at Camp Downey in the Adirondacks on the 26th, stopped in Québec on the 27th, and arrived in Montreal on the 28th, only to find out Camus's talk had been canceled due to threats of violence from Montreal's Pétainist faction.

90. One further sentence is crossed out here on the typescript.

The owl who was playing the drums at the Bowery Follies.[91]

Two people are in love with each other, but don't speak the same language. One speaks both languages but speaks the one they share imperfectly. For them, being able to love each other is enough. The one who knows both languages dies. Her last words are in her native tongue, which the other is helpless to grasp. He's trying to figure it out, trying to figure it out . . .

Small inn in the heart of the Adirondacks,[92] a thousand miles from civilization. Upon entering the bedroom, a strange feeling: a man arrives, on a business trip, with no preconceived notions, in the wilderness, in a remote inn. There, amid nature's silence, amid the room's simplicity, amid the remoteness from civilization, he decides to stay for good, to cut all ties with what his life was and never again let anyone know he's alive.

New England and Maine. Lands of lakes and red houses. Montreal and the two hills. A Sunday. Boredom. Boredom. The only amusing thing: the trams that look, in their shape and gilding, like carnival rides. This great country, calm and slow. You get the feeling it's completely unaware of the war. Europe, which was centuries ahead in knowledge, has just, in a few short years, gained several centuries in awareness.[93]

Remake and recreate Greek thinking as a rebellion against the sacred, but not a rebellion against the Romantic sacred—itself a form of the sacred—but a rebellion that puts the sacred in its place.

---

91. In "The Rains of New York," amid a lengthy description of the "café," Camus adds: "There's an old woman, too, who plays the drums, and she looks like an owl, and some evenings you feel like getting to know about her life."

92. In a letter to Patricia Blake, Camus wrote: "I think you'd like this place, lost in the Adirondacks, where we've landed after two days, where we've wandered in the surrounding mountains. It's an old, isolated house usually frequented by hunters and fishermen but deserted at the moment. I'm in the living room, sitting before a grand fireplace, beneath a wood-beam ceiling. A storm just passed through a little while ago and now the night's silence is filled with the calls of toads and birds and crickets."

93. To Janine and Michel, Camus wrote that he couldn't wait to get back to "Europe's flaws and defects. To conversations based on wit, even bad wit, on irony, haughtiness, on passion and its lies, to your kind French faces."

The idea of messianism is at the root of all fanaticism. Messianism in exchange for man. Greek thinking is not historical. The values are *preexistent. Against modern* existentialism.[94]

Plague. Tarrou spends most of his time with Spanish dancers. He loves only passion. Naturally, a man has to fight. "But if he's stopped loving other things, then what's the point of fighting?"

In the American newspapers: a weapon more terrible than the atomic bomb, "the Black Plague killed 60% of the population in some places during the Middle Ages. We don't know if American scientists have found ways to spread it, but the Japanese were unable to do so in China, where they'd sown the black plague in rice."

Québec's spectacular landscape. At the tip of Cap Diamant, facing the immense opening of the Saint Lawrence, air, light, and water come together in an infinite expanse. For the first time while on this continent, the real impression of beauty and true greatness. It seems I should have something to say about Québec, about its past, about men coming here to struggle in solitude, driven by a force greater than themselves. But what's the point? I know now there are many things, artistically speaking, I could *accomplish*. But this word no longer holds any meaning for me. The only thing I'd like to say I've so far been unable to say and I'll probably never be able to say.

Do a play about bureaucracy (as stupid in America as elsewhere).[95]

Even the Salvation Army advertises here. And in their advertisements, Army women have rosy cheeks and glittering smiles . . .

---

94. In other words, against Sartre's famous "existence precedes essence" proposition. In Camus's journals, interviews, and letters, he continually expresses frustration at being linked with existentialism, a philosophy he didn't believe in, one he would firmly push back against in *The Rebel*.

Only a couple of months before making this entry, in January 1946, Camus sent a "Letter to the Editor" of *La Nef* in which he writes, "I'm beginning to get a little (a very little) impatient with this continual lack of clarity that leads to me being mixed up with existentialism. . . . The only book of ideas I've ever written, *The Myth of Sisyphus*, was directed specifically against existentialist philosophies. A part of that critique still applies, in my mind, to Sartre's philosophy."

95. A theme that appears in *State of Emergency*, which Camus was working on at the time this note was made.

Zaharo's father.[96] Polish. At fifteen, slaps an officer. Runs away. Arrives in Paris during Carnival. Buys confetti with the few sous he has and resells it. Thirty years later, he has a huge fortune and a family. Completely illiterate. His son reads him things at random. Reads him the Apology of Socrates. "You don't have to read me any other books," the father says. "This one says it all." He's been having the same book read to him ever since. He hates judges and police.

Manhattan. Above the *sky-scrapers,* through hundreds of thousands of high walls, a tugboat cry sometimes turns up in the midst of your insomniac night, reminding you this desert of iron and cement is an island.

The guy in the Holland Tunnel in New York or the Sumner Tunnel in Boston. All day long on an elevated walkway, counting the cars that endlessly pass in a deafening racket, the length of the tunnel violently lit and too long for him to see any exit. A hero made for the modern novel.

B. as a superior American. His psychology: mariners love the mountains, and mountaineers love the sea.

Rain over New York. It falls tirelessly between tall cubes of cement. Odd feeling of estrangement in the taxi, its quick, monotonous windshield wipers sweeping away waters endlessly reborn. Impression that I'm trapped in this city, that I could escape the blocks immediately surrounding me and run for hours without finding anything other than new cement prisons, without the hope of a hill, a real tree, or a face overcome with emotion.

B.'s father. Supreme Court judge in Hamburg. His bedside reading is the German Indicateur Chaix, which lists the arrivals and departures of all the

96. Leon Zaharo (1898–?), whose father made his money in furs, attended one of Camus's talks, after which he phoned Camus at his hotel to explain that he, Zaharo, was going out of town on business and that Camus might be more comfortable moving to his apartment rather than remaining in the dank hotel room where he'd been staying. Camus initially declined the offer, but when Zaharo called back a couple of days later, Camus accepted, in part because he'd come down with a fever and thought the move might be good for his health. Zaharo's apartment was in The Century building at 25 Central Park West, then only about fifteen years old, now on the National Register of Historic Places.

world's trains.[97] He knows it practically by heart, and B. notes this oddity with an admiration completely devoid of irony.

Rains of New York. Incessant, sweeping over everything. The skyscrapers rise above the gray haze like the immense, whitish sepulchres of this city of the dead. Through the rain, you can see the sepulchres swaying on their foundations.

Terrible feeling of abandonment. Even if I were to hold everyone in the world tight against me, I still wouldn't be protected from anything.

Plague. To Tarrou: "So, then you believe you know all there is to know about life?"

Tarrou: "Yes."

Rebel. In-depth analysis of the Terror and its relationship with bureaucracy.

—Note that our age marks the end of ideologies. The atomic bomb prohibits ideology.[98]

Julien Green wonders (*Journal*) if it's possible to imagine a saint writing a novel. Of course not, because there can be no novel without rebellion. Or we'd have to imagine a novel that indicts the earthly world and man—a novel completely devoid of love. Impossible.

At sea[99]

The longueur of this return trip. Evenings at sea and the passage from sunset to moonrise are the only times I feel my heart relax a little. I always have and always will love the sea. It always has and always will soothe all the things inside of me.

97. Camus would later give this bit of backstory to Tarrou's father in *The Plague*.

98. This idea recurs throughout a series of essays Camus published in the Resistance newspaper *Combat*. Collectively, the articles have been titled "Neither Victims nor Executioners."

99. Camus sailed from New York back to Le Havre on the cargo ship *Fort-Royal*, June 10–23. In May, he had a package sent back home, via the French Consulate, which included "six pounds of sugar, six pounds of coffee, three pounds of powdered eggs, six pounds of flour, four pounds of rice, six pounds of chocolate, thirty pounds of baby food, twenty-eight pounds of soap," and an assortment of other items.

Terrible mediocrity of this environment. Until now, I've never once suffered from the mediocrity surrounding me. Until now. But here this intimacy goes too far. At the same time, in all of them there's something that could go far, if only . . .

Two young and beautiful people began a fling aboard the ship, and as soon as they did, a sort of nasty circle closed in on them. These beginnings of love! I love and approve of them from the bottom of my heart—with a form of gratitude, even, for those who, on this deck, in the middle of this Atlantic bursting with sun, midway between continents gone mad, sustain the truths of youth and love. So why not give a name to this longing that I, too, feel in my heart, to this tumultuous desire that leads me back to the restless heart I had at 20? But I know the remedy: I'll gaze out at the sea for a while.

Sad to still feel so vulnerable. In 25 years, I'll be 57. 25 years, then, to do my work and find what I'm looking for. Then, old age and death. I know what's most important to me. And I still find a way of giving in to those little temptations, of wasting time on pointless conversations or fruitless dawdling. I've mastered two or three things in myself. But how far I am from that excellence I'll need so much.

Wonderful night on the Atlantic. The hour between the sun disappearing and the moon barely emerging, between the still-luminous west and the already-dark east. Yes, I've truly loved the sea—that peaceful immensity—those wakes covered over—those liquid roads. For the first time, a horizon equal to human breath, a space as great as its audacity. I've always been torn between my appetite for people, the vanity of restlessness, and the desire to make myself measure up to those seas of forgetfulness, to those immeasurable silences that are like death's enchantment. I have a taste for the world's vanities, for my fellow man, for faces, but unlike this century, I have a rule I live by, which is the sea and everything in this world that resembles it. O sweet night, when all the stars spin and streak above the masts, and this silence in me, this silence at last delivers me from everything.

———

Novel. When the evening soup was late, it meant an execution was taking place the next morning.

———

V. Ocampo goes to Buckingham Palace. At the entrance, the guard asks her where she's going. "To see the queen."

"Carry on."

The Swiss Guard (?) *Id.* "Carry on."

The Queen's apartments. "Take the lift." Etc. She's received without any further questioning.

———

Nuremberg. 60,000 corpses under the rubble. Drinking the water is forbidden. No one wants to bathe in it either. It's Morgue water. Above the putrefaction, the trial.

On the lampshades made of human skin you can make out a very old dancer with a tattoo between her breasts.

———

Rebellion. Opening: "The only truly serious moral problem is murder.[100] The rest comes afterward. But knowing if I can kill this other person standing in front of me, or accept the person being killed—knowing I know nothing until I know if I can take a life—that's what we need to figure out."

People want to push you toward *their* conclusions. If they judge you, it's always with their own principles as ulterior motives. But I don't really mind if they think this or that. What matters to me is knowing if I can kill. Because this brings you to the boundary that all thought bumps up against, and here you'll find them rubbing their hands. "Now what's he going to do?" And they've got their own truth all ready. But I don't really mind being in a contradictory position; I have no desire to be a philosophical genius. I don't really want to be a genius at all, seeing how hard it is just to be a man. I'd like to reach an agreement, and, knowing I can't kill myself, know if I can kill others or let others be killed and then, knowing this, draw all my conclusions from it, even if doing so leaves me in a contradictory position.

———

It seems I still have to find a humanism. I have nothing against humanism, of course. I just find it falls short, that's all. And Greek thought was, for example, quite different from a humanism. It was a way of thinking that was open to everything.

———

100. This opening line demonstrates Camus's explicit attempt to link *The Myth of Sisyphus* and *The Rebel*. The structure of the first clause here is only slightly different from the first clause of *The Myth of Sisyphus*, and it's possible Camus thought he was using the same structure: *Il n'y a qu'un problème* vs. *Le seul problème* ("There's only one problem" vs. "The only problem"). The full first line of *The Myth of Sisyphus* reads: "There's only one truly serious philosophical problem: suicide." The language used throughout the rest of the two opening paragraphs continues this mirroring. For example, *Le reste vient après* vs. *Le reste . . . vient ensuite*. *The Rebel* went through several drafts and versions before publication, and, in the end, the above opening was not used.

The Terror! And already they forget.

———

Justice novel.

1) Poor childhood—injustice is natural.
At the first show of violence (beating up) injustice
and adolescent rebellion.
2) Policy toward indigenous population. Party (etc.).
3) Revolution in general. Doesn't think about principles.
War and resistance.
4) Purge. Justice can't go with violence.
5) That truth can't go without a true life.

Loves

6) Return to the mother. Priest? "It's not worth the trouble." She didn't say no, just that it wasn't worth the trouble. He knew she never thought it was worth the trouble of bothering someone for her. And even her death . . .[101]

———

Rebellion and Revolution.

The revolution as myth is the definitive revolution.

Id. Historicity leaves the phenomena of beauty unexplained, which is to say our relationships with the world (feeling for nature) and with people as individuals (love). What to make of a supposedly absolute explanation that . . .

———

Id. The whole aim of German thought has been to substitute the notion of human situation for human nature and thus History for God and modern tragedy for ancient balance. Modern existentialism pushes this aim even further and introduces the same uncertainty into the idea of situation as into the idea of nature. All that remains is a gesture. But like the Greeks, I believe in nature.

———

Plague. In all my life, never such a feeling of failure. I'm not even sure I'll make it to the end. Yet, at certain times . . .

———

101. This entry was inserted back into the text as the notebooks were being prepared for publication.

Blow it all up. Write rebellion as a pamphlet.[102] Revolution and those who will never kill. Preaching rebellion. Not a single concession.

———

"What a madness & anguish it is, that an author can never—under no conceivable circumstances—be at all frank with his readers." Melville.[103]

———

From the point of view of a new classicism, *The Plague* should be the first attempt to form a collective passion.

———

For *The Plague*. Cf. Defoe's Preface to the 3rd volume of *The Life and Strange Surprizing Adventures of Robinson Crusoe*: "It is as reasonable to represent one kind of imprisonment by another, as it is to represent anything that really exists by that which exists not. [. . .] Had the common way of writing a man's private history been taken [. . .] all I could have said would have yielded no diversion. . . ."[104]

———

The Plague is a *pamphlet*.

———

How to learn to die in the desert!

———

Lourmarin.[105] First evening after so many years. The first star above the Lubéron, the incredible silence, the tip of the cypress tree trembling in the depths of my exhaustion. Solemn and austere country—despite its overwhelming beauty.

———

Story about the former deportee who comes across some German prisoners in Lourmarin. "The first time he'd been hit was during his interrogation.

---

102. In this entry, "rebellion" seems to refer to *The Rebel*, the specific book Camus was working on, and not the general concept. A literal translation of the line would be: "Give to rebellion the form of a pamphlet." In French, the word "pamphlet" covers not only the physical object (a short text) but also its content (a fiery critique).

In the French, *La prédication révoltée* (Preaching rebellion), has the same structure as what would become the book's title, *L'homme révolté*.

103. The quote comes from a letter Melville wrote to American publisher Evert Augustus Duyckinck, dated December 14, 1849. Camus cited the excerpt in French, but it is given here in its original English.

104. Camus would use the first part of the quote as an epigraph for *The Plague*, though the epigraph doesn't appear in all editions.

105. French writer Henri Bosco had invited Camus, along with several other writers, to come to Lourmarin.

But that was sort of normal given the exceptional nature of things. At the camp, he'd been given two hard smacks for some small bit of misconduct, and that's when everything began. For then he understood that in the eyes of the one who'd hit him this was just an everyday, normal, natural thing . . ." He tries to talk to the German prisoner to explain all of this. But he's a *prisoner,* and you can't talk to him about such things. In the end, the prisoner disappears without him ever having spoken to him. When he thinks about it, he feels no man is ever free enough to be able to clarify this sort of thing. They're all prisoners.

Another time, in the camp, the guards got a kick out of making them dig their own graves and then not executing them. For a good two hours they'd sifted through the black earth, seen the roots, etc., in a whole new light.

———

"It's dying without death and getting nowhere
Swinging here and there
In the dark womb of narrow disaster."
Agrippa d'Aubigné.

———

Rebellion. Chap. 1 on the death penalty

Id. end. So then, setting out from the absurd, it's not possible to live rebellion without at some point arriving at an experience of love that remains to be defined.

———

Novel. Poor childhood. "I was ashamed of my poverty and my family (But they're monsters!) And if I can speak about it in a straightforward way today it's because I'm not ashamed of that shame anymore and because I no longer look down on myself for having felt it. I'd never known that shame until I was sent to the lycée. Before then, everyone was like me and poverty seemed to be the very air the world breathed. At the lycée, I learned about comparison.

A child is nothing in himself. His parents speak for him. And to have become a man without having known such ugly feelings is a lot less advantageous, for by then you're judged on who you are and you even go so far as to judge your own family on what you've become. Now I know I would have needed a heart of heroic and exceptional purity not to have suffered on those days when I read the poorly hidden surprise on a more fortunate friend's face as we arrived at the house where I lived.

Yes, my heart was weak, which is quite common. And if, until I turned 25, I could only bear the memory of that weakness with rage and shame, it's because I refused to be common, whereas now I know I am and, no longer finding it either good or bad, I take interest in other things . . .

I hopelessly loved my mother. I've always hopelessly loved her.

———

Idea of resistance in the metaphysical sense.

———

Dealing with the wrong the world does me. It makes me disparaging when I'm not . . . A sort of fugue state . . .

———

Machado:[106] "The sound of the casket in the ground is a very serious thing."

———

"Lord, we are alone, my mother and my heart."
"As soon as the day of my final travel arrives,
When sets sail the vessel that never sets back
You will see me on board, a man of meager baggage,
Practically naked, like the sons of the sea."

———

Translate Juan Mairena's Speeches.[107]
——An African romancero?

———

Saint Augustine is the only great Christian thinker to have looked the problem of evil *directly in the face*. He drew the terrible "Nemo Bonus" from the experience. Ever since then, Christianity has sought to provide temporary solutions to the problem.[108]

---

106. This entry, as well as the one that follows, refer to Spanish poet Antonio Machado. The first quote is from *En el Entierro de un amigo*, poem 4, and the next two are from *Poesias completas*, poems 119 and 97. The poems are quoted in French, although it doesn't appear an official French edition existed at the time this entry was written, and Camus may have done the translation himself. In the original Spanish, the line Camus quotes as "Lord, we are alone, my mother and my heart," actually reads "my heart and the sea" (that is *mar/mer*, not *mère*).

107. Juan de Mairena is a heteronym used by Antonio Machado, as well as the title of one of his books.

108. Some of the ideas here, as well as the mention of the Nemo Bonus, would appear in "The Unbeliever and the Christians," in the same section as the earlier entry. See p. 255n19.

The result is clear, for it is the result. Men took their time, but now they're suffering the effects of an intoxication that began 2,000 years ago. They're overwhelmed by evil or resigned to it, which amounts to the same thing. At least they can no longer put up with lies about it.

———

February 19, 1861. Acts abolishing serfdom in Russia.[109] The first shot (from Karakazov) comes April 4, 1866.

See Herzen's novel *Who is to Blame?* (1847).[110]

and *id. On the Development of Revolutionary Ideas in Russia.*

———

I prefer committed people to committed literature. A little courage in life and a little talent in work, that's not so bad. Then a writer can be committed on his own terms. His virtue is in his flexibility. If commitment is put in place by law, profession, or terror, where exactly is the virtue in that?

Today, it seems that to write a poem about spring is to serve capitalism. I'm not a poet, but I'd gladly enjoy such a work, if it were beautiful, without a second thought. You serve all man or no man. And if man needs both bread and justice, and if what has to be done has to be done to satisfy this need, he also needs pure beauty, which is his heart's bread. The rest isn't a big deal.

Yes, I'd like them to be less committed in their works and a little more so in their everyday life.

———

Existentialism has retained Hegelianism's fundamental error, which is to reduce man to history, but it hasn't retained the consequence, which is in fact to refuse man any freedom.

———

OCTOBER 1946. 33 years old in a month.

For the past year, my memory's been slipping. Currently unable to retain a story told—to recall whole sections of the past, which were once so alive. While waiting for this to get better (if it gets better) it's clear that I have to record more and more things here, even personal things, unfortunately. For everything eventually lands on this hazy plane of forgetfulness, which even

---

In 1936, Camus wrote a thesis, *Christian Metaphysics and Neoplatonism*, that focuses in part on Saint Augustine.

109. The reference is to the Emancipation Manifesto issued by Russian Emperor Alexander II and its seventeen acts known as the Statues Concerning Peasants Leaving Serf Dependence.

110. Alexander Herzen (1812–1870) advocated a sort of agrarian socialism while rejecting larger socialist metanarratives. These readings would serve as influences for *The Just* and *The Rebel*.

blankets my heart. It experiences only short-term emotions, deprived of the long reverberations memory brings. That's the way dogs feel things.

———

Plague . . . "And whenever I read a story about plague, from the depths of a heart poisoned by its own rebellion and others' violence, a clear cry rose up saying there were still more things to admire in man than to look down on."

. . . "And how each one of us carries it, the plague, because nobody, no, nobody in this world, is untouched by it.[111] So, we have to keep a close and constant watch on ourselves so as not to allow a moment's distraction, to breathe in someone else's face and pass the infection on to them. Germs are the natural state of things. The rest—health, integrity, purity, if you will—comes from an application of will, a will that must never let up. The honorable citizen,[112] the one who doesn't infect anyone else, is the one with the fewest possible distractions.

Yes, it's exhausting being a bastard. But it's even more exhausting wanting not to be a bastard. That's why everyone's exhausted, because everyone's a little bit of a bastard. But that's also why some people experience an extreme form of exhaustion from which nothing will deliver them so much as death."

———

Of course, what interests me, personally, isn't so much being better but being accepted. And nobody ever accepts anyone. Has she accepted me? No, obviously not.

———

In the doctor's waiting room, people have the look of sad animals.

———

Jacques Rigaut:[113] "The example comes from above. God created man in his image. What a temptation for man to conform to that image."

"The solution, the response, the key, the truth, is the death sentence."

———

111. An idea expressed by Tarrou in the penultimate section of *The Plague*.

112. The term Camus uses here, *honnête homme*, has a long history in France. In *French Literature: A Very Short Introduction*, John D. Lyons writes that the "polite and decorous 17th-century French" placed "great emphasis on avoiding highly visible partisanship and zealotry, and on being a reasonable person, an amusing, sensitive, and accommodating companion—in short, an *honnête homme*. This term is not easily translated, and it is important to note right away that it does not mean 'honest man.' . . . The *honnête homme* is someone who 'fits in,' who is not notably eccentric."

113. Jacques Rigaut (1898–1929), French surrealist poet, committed suicide November 6, 1929, leaving behind his *Papiers posthumes*, from which these quotes are taken. In *The Rebel*, Camus writes that the surrealists "spoke of suicide as a solution, and Crevel, who considered that solution 'the most realistically just and definitive,' killed himself, as did Rigaut and Vaché." Surrealism, Camus adds, "justified Rigaut's heartrending cry: 'All of you are poets, and me, I am on death's doorstep.'"

"Filled with pride, of nothing would he be afraid."

"And the greater my selfless disinterest, the more genuine my interest."

"One of two things. Don't speak, don't remain silent. Suicide."

"I'm well aware that, as long as I haven't overcome the taste for pleasure, I'll remain susceptible to the dizzying thought of suicide."

———

Conversations with Koestler. The end only justifies the means if there's a reasonable relationship in magnitude. Ex: I can send Saint-Exupéry on a life-threatening mission to save a regiment, but I can't deport millions of people and suppress all freedom for a quantitatively equivalent result that assumes the sacrifice of three or four generations as part of its initial calculations.

"Genius. There's no such thing."

"Once the creator's talent is recognized, that's when the great misery begins (I no longer have the courage to publish my books).

———

There are times I don't think I'll be able to bear the contradiction any longer. When the sky is cold and nothing in nature sustains us . . . Oh, maybe it's better to die.

———

Following on the previous. Wrenching feeling at the thought of doing these articles for Combat.[114]

———

An essay about the feeling for nature—and pleasure.

———

Art and rebellion. Breton is right. I don't believe in the split between the world and man either. There are moments of harmony with raw nature. But nature is never raw. Yet landscapes slip away and are forgotten. That's why there are painters. Surrealist painting, for example, is *inclined to* express this rebellion of man against Creation. But its mistake lays in wanting to preserve

114. Most likely in reference to the series of articles titled *Neither Victims nor Executioners*, published in *Combat* from November 19 to November 30. To Patricia Blake, Camus wrote: "Europe's getting heavier and heavier. . . . The fear is everywhere. I just took a stand in a series of articles, 'Neither Victims nor Executioners.' I understood how you could be left on your own the moment you decide to use a certain sort of language"—a reference, it seems, to being abandoned by the political left for pointing out the atrocities committed in the name of Communism—"You can't desert, and yet playing the victim doesn't appeal to me."

or imitate only the miraculous part of nature. The true rebel artist doesn't deny miracles but tames them.

Parain. How the essence of modern literature is the palinode.[115] The surrealists becoming Marxists. Rimbaud devotion. Sartre morality. And how the day's great problem is the conflict. Human condition, Human nature.

"But then, if there's a human nature, where does it come from?"

Obvious I should cease all creative activity until I know. What's made my books successful is what makes them feel like a lie to me. In fact, I am an average man + a demanding nature. The values I should defend and illustrate today are average values. The talent required for this has to be so pure I doubt I have it.

The goal of rebellion is to bring peace to the people. Every rebellion reaches and is carried on by asserting a human limit—and by centering a community of all people, whoever they may be, within those limits. Humility and genius.

OCTOBER 29. Koestler, Sartre, Malraux, Sperber and I. Between Piero della Francesca and Dubuffet.[116]

K.—Need to define a minimum political morality. So then, the first thing is to clear away a certain number of false scruples ("fallacies," he calls them) a) that what a person says can serve causes the person can't serve. b) Soul-searching. The order of injustices. "As for me, when the interviewer asked if I hated Russia, something shut down inside me right then and there. I made an effort, though. I said I hated the Stalinist regime as much as I hated the Hitlerian regime and for the same reasons. But something came undone then." "So many years of struggle. I lied for them . . . and now, like that buddy of mine who'd bang his head against my wall and say, with his bloody face turned to me: 'There's no hope left.'"—Course of action, etc.

M.—Momentary impossibility of reaching the proletariat. Is the proletariat the highest historical value?

115. A palinode is a poetic ode that retracts an earlier stated belief. The larger reference here is to an article Brice Parain published in the November 11, 1946, issue of *Combat*.

116. On October 29, 1946, Camus, Koestler, Sartre, Sperber, and Malraux took part in a meeting to try to define a minimum for political morals.

C.—Utopia. Today, a utopia will cost them less than a war. War is the opposite of utopia. For one thing. And for another: "Don't you think we're all responsible for the absence of values, and that if those of us who have our roots in Nietzscheism, nihilism or historical realism were to make a public statement saying that we were mistaken and that there are moral values and that from now on we were going to do what it takes to establish[117] and illustrate them, don't you think that would be the beginning of hope?"

S.—"I can't turn my moral values solely against the U.S.S.R., for while it's true that the deportation of several million people is more serious than the lynching of a single Negro, the lynching of a Negro is the result of a situation that's been going on for over a hundred years and that eventually, over the years, comes to represent the plight of as many millions of negros as there were millions of deported Circassians."

K.—It should be said that history will see us writers as traitors if we don't denounce what must be denounced. A conspiracy of silence[118] would condemn us in the eyes of those who come after us.

S.—Yes. Etc., etc.

And all the while, the impossibility of defining the role of fear or truth in what each person says.

If you believe in moral value, you believe in all morality up to and including sexual morality. The reform is comprehensive.

Read Owen.[119]

Write the story of a contemporary cured of his heartbreak by nothing other than the long contemplation of a landscape.

Robert, a conscientious objector with Communist sympathies, in '33. Three years in prison. When he gets out, the Communists are for the war, the pacifists are for Hitler. He no longer understands anything about this

117. The word is hard to make out in the original manuscript. It may be *garder* (preserve) rather than *fonder* (establish).

118. Alex Weissberg's 1952 book about Stalin and the show trials, printed in English as *Conspiracy of Silence*, featured an introduction by Arthur Koestler. The term "conspiracy of silence" previously appeared in Camus's "Neither Victims nor Executioners" articles in *Combat*.

119. Robert Owen (1771–1858), utopian socialist, author of *A New View of Society*.

world gone mad. He enlists with the Spanish Republicans and *he goes to war*. He's killed on the Madrid front.

———

What is a famous person? A person whose first name doesn't matter. With everyone else, a first name has a meaning all its own.

———

Why do we drink? Because in drinking everything takes on importance, everything takes place in a heightened state. Conclusion: we drink out of powerlessness and condemnation.

———

Universal order can't be created from above, which is to say by an idea, but from below, which is to say by the common ground that . . .

———

Put together a book of political texts centered on Brasillach.[120]

———

Guilloux. The only point of reference is pain. So that even the guiltiest retain a connection with the human.

———

Ran into Tar. coming out of the session about dialogue. He seemed reticent but still had the same look of friendship he had when I helped him break into the Combat organization.

"You're a Marxist now?"

"Yes."

"So then, you'll be a murderer?"

"I already have been."

"So have I. But I don't want to be one anymore."

"And you were my sponsor."

It was true.

"Listen, Tar. Here's the real problem: no matter what happens, I'll always defend you from the firing squad, but you, you'll be obligated to approve of me being shot down. Think about that."

"I'll think about it."

———

Unbearable solitude—which I can't believe in or resign myself to.

———

120. See p. 235n114.

What makes a man feel alone is other people's cowardice. Should I try to understand that cowardice, too? But I don't have the strength for it. And yet, I can't be someone who looks down on others.

———

If everything can truly be reduced to man and history, I'd like to know where—nature—love—music—art—fit in.

———

Rebellion. We don't want just any hero. The reasons for heroism are more important than the heroism itself. So then, the value of consequences comes before the value of heroism. Nietzschean freedom is an exaltation.

———

Creation corrected. The terrorist character (Ravenel).

———

Relationship between the absurd and rebellion. If the final decision is to reject suicide so as to maintain the confrontation, this implicitly recognizes life as the only de facto value, the one that allows for the confrontation, that *is* the confrontation, "the one without which nothing." From which it follows that to obey this absolute value, whoever rejects suicide also rejects murder. Our era, having pushed nihilism to its extreme conclusions, has accepted suicide. This is borne out in the ease with which it accepts murder, or with which it justifies murder. The man who kills only himself still upholds a value: the life of others. The proof is in that he *never* uses his freedom, the terrible strength his decision to die gives him, to reign over others: every suicide is in some way illogical. But men of terror have pushed the values of suicide to their extreme consequence, which is legitimate murder, which is to say collective suicide. Illustration: the Nazi apocalypse in 1945.[121]

———

Briançon. January '47.[122]

The evening flowing over these cold mountains ends up freezing the heart. I've never been able to bear this hour of night except in Provence or on the beaches of the Mediterranean.

———

121. A revised version of this entry would be used in *The Rebel*'s introduction.

122. On January 16, Camus left Paris, on doctor's orders, for a three-week stay at the Grand Hôtel in Briançon, the highest city in France, sitting at an altitude of 4,350 feet.

G. Orwell. Burmese Days. "Most people can be at ease in a foreign country only when they are disparaging the inhabitants."

". . . that inordinate happiness that comes of exhaustion and achievement, and with which nothing else in life—no joy of either the body or the mind—is even able to be compared."[123]

———

Read Georg Simmel[124] (*Schopenhauer and Nietzsche*). Commentary on Nietzsche translated into English by Berneri[125] (killed by the Communists in Spain during the liquidation of the Anarchists). Develops Nietzsche's desire for God. "Though this may seem to us fantastic and excessive it reveals under the form of an extreme personalism, a feeling which, in another form, is not very distant from the Christian conception of the inner life. In Christianity, in fact, as well as in our infinite distance and smallness before God, there is the idea of becoming equal to him. The mystic of every age and every religion gives rise to this aspiration to become one with God or, more audaciously, to become God. The scholastics talk of deificatio, and for Meister Eckhart man can shed his human form and become God again, as he is by his proper and original nature, or, as Angelus Silesiu expressed:

I must find my ultimate end and my beginning
I must find God in me and me in God
And become what he is . . .

This same passion was felt by Spinoza and Nietzsche: *they could not accept not being God.*"

---

123. Camus recorded the title, *Burmese Days*, in English, but the quotes in French (the first quote is from chap. 10, the second from chap. 14). The book had just been translated into French in 1946, with the title *Tragédie birmane*. The quotes are given here in the original English.

In one of history's great literary misses, Orwell and Camus had planned to meet at Les Deux Magots in Paris in February 1945, and, in fact, Orwell showed up for the meeting, but Camus, sick, never did. Shortly after, Orwell's wife died, and the two were never able to reschedule their meeting.

124. Georg Simmel (1858–1918), antipositivist sociologist, author of the 1908 essay "The Stranger," in which Simmel lays out the differences between a "stranger," an "outsider," and a "wanderer," an argument of interest in relation to the title of Camus's *L'Étranger*.

125. Camillo Berneri (1897–1937) was an Italian professor and militant Anarchist who was, as Camus notes, assassinated in Barcelona, presumably by Italian Communists.

Camus recorded the whole quote in English, and it's given here as he wrote it, though the available English translation—by Helmut Loiskandl and Deena and Michael Weinstein—differs from the version here.

Nietzsche says: "There can be no God as, if there were one, I couldn't accept not being Him."

———

—There's only one freedom: coming to terms with death. After that, everything is possible. I can't force you to believe in God. Believing in God is accepting death. When you've accepted death, the problem of God will be resolved—and not the other way around.

———

Radici, a member of the Milice,[126] joined the Waffen SS, prosecuted for having had 28 inmates at La Santé shot (he watched each group be executed), a member of the Humane Society for the Protection of Animals.

———

Rebatet and Morgan.[127] To the right and to the left—or universal definition of fascism: Having no character, they established a doctrine.

———

Title for the future: System (1,500 pp.).[128]

———

As human works have finally, little by little, covered the vast spaces where the world lay slumbering—to the point that the very idea of untouched nature now pertains to the myth of Eden (there are no more islands)—peopling the deserts, parceling out the beaches, and striking out the sky with the broad brush strokes of airplanes, leaving intact precisely and only those places where man can't live, in the same way, and at the same time (and because of it), a sense of history has little by little covered over the sense of nature in man's heart, taking back from the creator what had until then belonged to him so as to give it to his creatures, and all of this with such a powerful and irresistible momentum that we can foresee the day when silent natural creation will be entirely replaced by human creation, hideous and swift, reverberating with revolutionary and warlike commotions, buzzing with factories and trains, at

---

126. The Milice Française (French Militia) was a paramilitary organization funded by the Germans and run by Vichy France to fight against the French Résistance.

127. Lucien Rebatet (1903–1972), fascist, antisemitic French journalist. His 1946 death sentence for having collaborated with the Germans was commuted, and he was released from prison in 1952.

Claude Morgan (1898–1980), militant French Communist, led the underground newspaper *Les lettres françaises*.

In *The Fall*, Clamence says: "75,000 Jews deported or murdered in cold blood, well, that's a real housecleaning. I admire such diligence, such patience. When you have no character, you certainly have to have a method."

128. An alternative title Camus was considering for *Creation Corrected*.

last definitive and triumphant in the course of history—having completed its task on this earth, which was perhaps to demonstrate that all the grandiose and astonishing things man could do over thousands of years wasn't worth the fleeting scent of a wild rose, a valley of olive trees, a beloved dog.

———

1947.[129]

———

Like all weak people, his decisions were brutal and unreasonably firm.

———

Aesthetics of rebellion. Painting makes a choice. It "isolates," which is its way of unifying. A landscape isolates in space what normally gets lost in perspective. A painting of a scene isolates in time a gesture that normally gets lost in another gesture. The great painters are those who give the impression that the fixation has *just taken place* (Piero della Francesca), as if the projector had just stopped that very moment.

———

A play about a government of women. The men decide they've failed and that they should turn the government over to the women.

Act I—My Socrates arrives and decides to hand over power.

Act II—The women want to do what the men did—failure.

Act III—Well-advised by Socrates, they reign as women.

Act IV—Conspiracy.

Act V—The women give it back to the men.

Pretend to declare war. "Now do you understand what it means to the one who stays behind—to see everyone you love in this world going off to be butchered?"

We can go now. We've done everything we could hope to do in this world faced with human stupidity.

"And what's that?"

"A little education."

"As stupid as we are but not as cruel."

A one-year experiment.

If all goes well it will be extended.

All goes well but it's not extended. They lacked the hatred.

---

129. This date and the one below are written in the top left corner of their respective pages. They do not appear to be linked to a given entry.

We're going to start all over again, Socrates says. They're laying the groundwork. Grand ideas and historical perspectives. In ten years, mass graves.

Listen:

A town crier.

Article I—There's no longer any rich or poor.

Article II

"You're going out again?"

"Yes, I have a meeting."

"I could use a good distraction—get my house in order . . ."

1947.

Vae mihi qui cogitare ausus sum.[130]

After a week of solitude, again a sharp feeling of inadequacy about a work I began with the maddest ambition. Temptation to give up. This long struggle with a truth stronger than I am required a purer heart, a broader, more powerful intellect. But what to do? I'd die without this.

Rebellion. Freedom with regard to death. Faced with the freedom to murder, the only other possible freedom is to die, which is to say to suppress the fear of death and to reestablish this accident as part of the natural order of things. Strive for this.

Montaigne. Change of tone in Chap. XX of Bk. 1. On Death. Astonishing things he says about his fear in the face of death.

Novel.—Twinkie:[131] "When I arrived, I was drained by anxiety and fever.

130. Woe unto thee who dared to think.

131. The word "novel" was added to the entry after the fact. This first word after that is hard to make out in the original notebook, and while Camus's hand correction on the typescript appears to read "Twinkle," given that the entry is in reference to Mamaine Paget (who married Alfred Koestler in 1950), the word is more likely "Twinkie," which is how Camus addressed her in letters (an address only one letter off from "Twinnie," which is how Mamaine and her twin sister, Celia Kirwan née Paget [who later married Arthur Goodman in 1954]—whom Camus also knew—addressed each other in correspondence). Before taking the train to meet Mamaine in Avignon, Camus wrote to her that he was "devoured by flu and fever." After the trip, lamenting her return to England, he wrote: "That week, you made me as happy and unhappy as a man can be made."

I went to check the schedule to see when she'd be getting in, if, by chance, she wasn't already there. It was 11 at night. The last train from the west would arrive at 2:00 A.M. I was the last one out. She was waiting for me at the exit, alone, two or three other people nearby, a wolfdog she'd taken in with her. She came over to me. I gave her an awkward kiss, but I was happy as could be. We headed out. Above the ramparts, the Provence sky glittered with stars. She'd been there since 5 in the afternoon. She was already there when the 7:00 train arrived, but I wasn't on it. She was afraid I wouldn't come, because when she gave my name at the hotel, her papers didn't match. They'd refused to let her sign-in and she didn't dare go back again. When we reached the ramparts, she threw herself against me, there in the middle of a passing crowd that turned to look, and squeezed me in an explosive fit of relief, not love, but the hope of love. As for me, I wanted to be strong and handsome, but my fever was weighing on me. At the hotel, I set the record straight and everything went well. I wanted to have a fine[132] before we went up to the room. And there, in the well-heated bar where she kept me drinking, I felt my confidence return and a wave of relaxation completely wash over me."

———

His upper lip was completely split open, teeth visible as high as the gums. It seemed as if he were always laughing. But his eyes were serious.

———

What's man worth? What is man? After what I've seen, I'll continue, all my life, to hold a deep distrust of and worry for him.

———

Cf. Marc Klein in *Études germaniques*. "Observations and Reflections on the Nazi Concentration Camps."[133]

———

Creation Corrected novel. "He put the spade against the man's neck the second the man hit the ground. And, foot on the spade, with the same motion used to break up clumps of loam, he drove it in."

———

132. The term "fine" was a common way of referring to high-quality French brandy.

133. Marc Klein, a doctor who was himself sent to Auschwitz, later wrote the above-mentioned essay, which would go on to become part of the Holocaust Revisionism movement. It is still cited today.

Nemesis—goddess of balance.[134] All who tip the scales of balance will be mercilessly destroyed.

———

Isocrates: There's nothing in the universe more divine, more august, more noble than beauty.

Aeschylus, about Helen: "Soul as serene as calm seas, beauty of the richest finery, kind eyes that pierced swiftly as a bolt, flower of love fatal to hearts."

Helen isn't guilty but a victim of the gods. After the catastrophe, she resumes her life.

———

La Patellière.[135] The moment (the last canvases) when the seasons burst forth—when mysterious hands spread their flowers in every corner of the picture. A quiet tragedy.

———

Terrorism.

The great purity of terrorists like Kalyayev is that for them murder coincides with suicide (cf. Savinkov: *Memoirs of a Terrorist*).[136] A life is paid for with a life. The reasoning is faulty, but respectable. (A life taken is not the equivalent of a life given.) Today, murder by proxy. Nobody pays.

1905 Kalyayev: sacrifice of the body. 1930: sacrifice of the mind.

———

Panelier, June 17, '47.

Wonderful day. A frothy light, shimmering and soft, above and around the tall beech trees. As if secreted by all the branches. Bouquets of leaves slowly stir in that blue gold like a thousand multi-lipped mouths drooling an ethereal, golden, sugary juice—or maybe a thousand little waterspout mouths, green, bronze, and contoured, endlessly irrigating the heavens with a resplendent blue water—or maybe . . . but that's enough.

———

134. A more literal, less contextual, translation might read: "All those who have exceeded the limit [*la mesure*] will be mercilessly destroyed." For more about the translation of the term *mesure* as "balance," see p. 72n34.

This entry, as well as the one that follows, would be used in Camus's essay "Helen's Exile."

135. Amédée Dubois de La Patellière (1890–1932), French painter.

136. Boris Savinkov (1879–1925) played a lead role in the assassination of Grand Duke Sergei Alexandrovich. Camus would make extensive use of Savinkov's memoirs in the writing of *The Just*.

Ivan Platonovich Kalyayev (c. 1877–1905), Russian poet and member of the Socialist Revolutionary Party, is discussed in *The Rebel* and features as the main character in *The Just*.

How impossible it is to *say* that anyone is absolutely guilty and, consequently, impossible to pronounce total punishment.

Critique of the idea of efficacy—a chapter.

German philosophy added movement to matters of reason and the Universe—whereas the ancients added fixity to them. We won't get past German philosophy—and we won't save man—until we define what is fixed and what is movable (and what we don't know whether to class as fixed or movable).

The aim of the absurd, rebellion, etc., and, consequently, the aim of the contemporary world, is compassion in the original sense of the word, which is to say, ultimately, love and poetry. But this requires an innocence I no longer have. All I can do is correctly recognize the path that leads to it and let the time of innocents arrive. To see it, at least, before dying.

Hegel against nature. Cf. Grande Logique, 36–40.[137] Why nature is abstract.—What's concrete is the mind.

This is the intellect's great adventure—the one that ends up killing everything.

To put in the Plague archives:[138]

1) Anonymous letters denouncing families. Bureaucratic form of interrogation.

2) Form of decrees.

No tomorrow.

1st cycle. Absurd: *The Stranger*—*The Myth of Sisyphus*—*Caligula* and *The Misunderstanding*.

2nd—Rebellion: *The Plague* (and appendixes)—*The Rebel*—Kalyayev.

---

137. In English, the book is most often titled *Science of Logic*, but it has also been called *Greater Logic*, which is closer to the French title Camus gives here.

138. In April 1947, Camus published "Les archives de la Peste" ("The Plague Archives") in *Cahiers de la Pléiade*, though the items listed above do not figure in the publication. The translation of the second item is contextual; it could equally be translated as "form of shutdown," "form of regulation," "form of order," etc.

3rd—Judgment—The First Man.[139]

4th—Love Torn Asunder: The Pyre—On Love—The Seducer.

5th—Creation Corrected or The System—major novel + major meditation + unperformable play.

June 25 '47.

Sadness of success.[140] Opposition is necessary. If everything were more difficult for me, as before, I'd have much more right to say what I say. Nevertheless, I can still help a lot of people—in the meantime.

Distrust of formal virtue—that's the explanation for this world. Those who have felt this distrust in themselves and who have extended it to everyone else have, in so doing, become endlessly suspicious of all professed virtues. It's only a small step from there to suspecting virtuous *actions*. So then, they choose to call virtue whatever serves to bring about the society they desire. The deeper motive (that distrust) is noble. Whether the logic is sound, that's the question.

I, too, have a bone to pick with this idea. Everything I've ever thought or written is related to this distrust (it's the subject of *The Stranger*). As long as I don't accept pure and simple negation (nihilism or historical materialism) of the "virtuous conscience," as Hegel calls it, I have a middle ground to find. Being in history by referring to values that are beyond history, is that possible? Legitimate? Doesn't the very value of ignorance drape a convenient refuge over itself? Nothing's pure, nothing's pure, there you have the cry that's poisoned this century.

The temptation to go along with those who negate and act! There are some who retreat into lies the way others retreat into religion. And with the same admirable inclination, that's for sure. But what is an inclination? By what, whom, and why should we judge?

---

139. This line doesn't appear in the handwritten notebook. Camus later added it to the typescript by hand.

The Judgment was a working title for *The Fall*.

140. *The Plague* was published June 10, 1947. Four days later, Camus was awarded the prestigious Prix des Critiques. But, as Camus told Louis Guilloux, that wasn't the only cause of his distress: "There's also *Combat* and its unhappy ending, *The Plague* being released, and that stupid prize I tried, until the last second, to refuse. Ultimately, I'm paying for everything with a brutal depression, fainting spells included. . . . The book's success leaves me a little disconcerted. There are certain accolades that aren't so pleasing. In any case, I think I know the book's flaws pretty well."

If this is really the march of history, if there is no freedom but only unification, am I not one of those holding history back? No freedom without unification, they say, and, if that's true, then we're backward. But to be forward we'd have to prefer a hypothesis that's barely probable—one that's already obtained a few terrifying *historical* refutations—to the reality of misfortune, murder, and two or three generations of exile. So then, the choice is based on a hypothesis. It's not been proven that freedom first requires unification. It's also not been proven that it can do without it. But nowhere does it say unification must be accomplished through violence—violence generally tears apart under the guise of unity. It's probable that unification, that freedom, is necessary, and possible this unification could take place through *knowledge* and preaching. Words would then be acts. At least then you'd have to give yourself completely to the task.

Oh, how these hours are filled with doubt. And who can carry the whole world's doubt all on their own.

I know myself too well to believe in pure virtue.

Play. The Terror. A nihilist. Violence everywhere. Everywhere lies.[141]
Destroy, destroy.
A realist. He has to get into the Okhrana.[142]
Between the two, Kalyayev: "No, Boris, no."
"I love them."
"Why do you make it sound so terrible?"
"Because my love is terrible."

Id. Yanek and Dora.
Y (gently): "And love?"
D: "Love, Yanek? There is no love."
Y: "Oh, Dora, how can you say that? You. You whose heart I know."

---

141. Early ideas for *The Just*. The dialogue between Dora and Kalyayev would be incorporated into act 3, scene 1, with very few changes. Of the changes that were made, only one is substantive: "we cut them [heads] off" vs. "we have stiff necks." The rest of the changes are matters of punctuation and style.

142. The Department for Protecting the Public Security and Order, abbreviated as Okhrana, was a secret police division founded in Russia in 1881 to defend the monarchy, disrupt terrorism, and dispense with leftist revolutionary groups.

"There's too much blood, that's how, too much hardened violence. Those who love justice too much have no right to love. They stand perfectly straight, as I do, head held high, eyes fixed and staring. What role could love have in a heart so proud? Love gently bows heads, Yanek, and we, we cut them off."

"But we love our people, Dora."

"Yes, we love them with a great and unhappy love. But the people, do they love us and do they know we love them? The people stay quiet. What a silence, what a silence . . ."

"But that *is* love, Dora. To give everything and sacrifice everything without hope of getting anything in return."

"Maybe it is, Yanek. It's a pure, eternal love. It's the kind that burns inside me, to be sure. But sometimes I wonder if love isn't something else, if it could cease to be a monologue and if there isn't sometimes a response. I imagine it, you know: heads gently bowing, the heart letting go of its pride, the eyes beginning to squint, and the arms opening up a little. To forget the world's atrocious misery, Yanek, and just let yourself go for once, for one hour, one small little hour of selfishness, can you imagine such a thing?"

"Yes, Dora, it's called tenderness."

"You see everything, my darling. It's called tenderness. But do you love justice with tenderness?"

Yanek remains silent.

"Do you love your people with that same abandon or with the fiery flames of vengeance and rebellion?"

Yanek remains silent.

"You see. And me? Do you love me with tenderness, Yanek?"

"I love you more than anything in the world."

"More than justice?"

"I don't divide you up like that—you, the Organization, justice."

"I know. But answer me. Answer me, I beg you, Yanek, answer me. Do you love me in your solitude, tenderly, selfishly?"

"Oh, Dora, I'm dying to say yes."

"Say it, my darling, if you really mean it and if it's true. Say it here before the Organization, before justice, before the world's misery, before the people in chains. Say it, I beg you, here before children living in agony, before the endless prisons, despite people being hanged and whipped to death."

Yanek turns pale.

"Quiet, Dora. Quiet."

"Oh, Yanek, you still haven't said it."

A silence.

"I can't say it. And yet you fill my heart."

She laughs as if she were crying.

"But that's all right, my darling. You see, that was unreasonable. I couldn't have said it either. I love you with that same single-minded love, alongside justice and prisons. We're not of this world, Yanek. It's blood and the cold rope for us."

Rebellion is a mad dog's barking (*Antony and Cleopatra*).[143]

I reread all these notebooks—beginning with the first. What jumped out at me: little by little, the landscapes are disappearing. The modern cancer is eating away at me, too.

The most serious problem facing contemporary minds: conformity.

For Lao-Tzu: The less you act, the more you control.

G.[144] lived with his grandmother, who sold funeral products in Saint-Brieuc: did his homework on a tombstone!

Cf. Crapouillot:[145] Anarchy. Tailhade: Memoirs of committing magistrate. Stirner: The Ego and Its Own.

G: Irony doesn't necessarily come out of malice.

M: It certainly doesn't come from kindness.

143. In act 4, scene 15, of Shakespeare's play, Cleopatra says: "It were for me / To throw my sceptre at the injurious gods; / To tell them that this world did equal theirs / Till they had stol'n our jewel. All's but naught; / Patience is scottish, and impatience does / Become a dog that's mad; then is it sin / To rush into the secret house of death, / Ere death dare come to us?" In an early manuscript version of *The Rebel*, Camus uses Gide's French translation of this passage as an epigraph.

144. Jean Grenier.

145. *Le Crapouillot* was a muckraking French magazine that was founded in August 1915 and ran, in its original form, until 1996. In 2016, it was revived under new direction and in a new format. Over the course of its original run, and especially after World War II, it became less a magazine of "arts and letters" and more an outlet for right-wing propaganda. Here, Camus is referencing the January 1938 issue dedicated to "Anarchy," which featured Victor Serge as one of its editors.

Laurent Tailhade (1854–1919), French anarchist poet, essayist, and translator, who, after Auguste Vaillant's attack on the French Chamber of Deputies, is supposed to have said: "What does the victim matter so long as the act is beautiful?" (though different versions of the statement exist).

G: No, but maybe from grief, which we never think about *in others.*

In a Moscow threatened by the White Army, to Lenin, who'd decided to mobilize ordinary convicted criminals:

"No, not *with* them."

"*For* them," Lenin said.

Kalyayev play: Impossible to kill a man in the *flesh,* we kill the autocrat. Not the guy who shaved in the morning, etc., etc.

Scene: they execute the subversive.

The great problem of life is knowing how to move between men.[146]

Grenier. "I'm a man who believes in nothing and loves no one, at least not at first. There's an emptiness inside me, a terrifying desert."

Marc sentenced to death at the Prison de Loos.[147] Refuses to have his chains removed during Holy Week so as to appear more like his Savior. There was a time when he used to fire his revolver at crucifixes he came across on the road.

Happy Christians. They kept grace for themselves and left us charity.

Grenier. On proper use of freedom. "Modern man no longer believes there's a God to be obeyed (Hebrew and Christian); a society to be respected (Hindu and Chinese) a nature to be followed (Greek and Roman)."

Id. "He who loves a value deeply is for that very reason an enemy of freedom. He who loves freedom above all else either negates values or only holds them temporarily. (Tolerance coming from the erosion of values)."

Max Stirner's classic anarchist text *The Ego and Its Own* (literally: The unique and its property) was republished in French in 1948, around the time of this writing. Camus would discuss it in *The Rebel,* in a section titled "The Ego" ("L'Unique").

146. The letters "A.F." were later added to the typescript in parenthesis.

147. The Prison de Loos is a now-shuttered penitentiary outside Lille, France. Originally the site of the Notre-Dame de Loos Abbey, built in 1146, the structure was nationalized during the French Revolution, converted into a poorhouse for manual labor, transformed into a full-scale prison in the early 1800s, and taken over by the Nazis during World War II. It closed in 2011.

"If we stop ourselves (on the path of no), it's not so much to spare others as to spare ourselves." (No for oneself, yes for others!)

———

Play.

D: "The sad thing, Yanek, is that all of this is aging us. Never again, never again will we be children. We can die now. We've seen all there is to see of man. (Murder is the limit.)"

"No, Yanek. If the only solution is death, then we're not on the right track. The right track is the one that leads to life."

"We've taken the world's misery upon ourselves, and that type of pride will be punished."

"We went straight from childish loves to that first and last mistress that is death. We moved too quickly. We're not human."[148]

———

This century's misery. It wasn't so long ago that bad actions needed to be justified. Today it's the good ones.[149]

———

Novel. "If I love her, I want her to know me as I was, for she believes this admirable benevolence . . . But no, she's exceptional."

———

Reactionary? If it means taking history backward, I'll never go as far as they do—all the way back to Pharaoh.

———

Defoe: "I was born to destroy myself."

Id. "I have heard talk of a man who, taken with an extraordinary disgust for the unbearable conversation of some of those closest to him . . . suddenly decided he would stop talking . . ." (Play.)

---

148. Seven lines of dialogue preceding the start of the entry as included here were crossed out on the typescript. One line from that section would go on to be used in *The Just*, in the scene with the Grand Duchess. The dialogue that was left intact here would be used at the end of the play, where it occurs between Dora and Annenkov, not Dora and Yanek, as written here.

149. Camus expands on this idea early in *The Rebel*, where he writes: "In simpler times, when the tyrant razed cities for his own greater glory, when the slave was chained to conquering chariots and dragged through celebrating cities, when the enemy was thrown to the beasts right before the assembled masses, before such guileless crimes, a conscience could be firm, its judgement clear. But slave camps beneath banners of freedom, massacres justified by love of man or a taste for the superhuman, these have a way of disorienting our judgement. The day crime drapes itself in the spoils of innocence, by a curious reversal peculiar to our times, it's innocence that's called to furnish its reasons."

Marion[150] on Defoe (p. 139) 29 years of silence. His wife goes crazy. His children leave. His daughter stays. Fever, delirium. He speaks. Thereafter, speaks often, but little with the daughter "and very rarely with anyone else."

Ps. 91: "The Lord is my refuge and my fortress. For he will deliver thee from every snare of the fowler, from the deadly plague [. . .] Thou shall not be afraid for the terror by night, nor for the arrow that flieth by day, nor for the plague that walketh in darkness, nor for the epidemic that ravages in the light of midday."

Perfect solitude. In the urinal of a major train station at 1:00 in the morning.[151]

A man (a Frenchman?), a holy man who lived his whole life in sin (never approaching the Lord's Supper Table,[152] never marrying the woman with whom he lived) because, unable to bear the idea that only one soul was damned, he wanted to be damned too.

"It was a type of love greater than all others: the love of a man who gives his soul for a friend."

Merleau-Ponty. Learn to Read.[153] He complains he was misread—and misunderstood. It's the kind of complaint I would have once been inclined to make. Now I know it's unjustified. There is no misinterpretation.

Scoundrels virtuous in their principles. True. But practically speaking, and at the current moment, I prefer a debauched person who doesn't kill anyone to a puritan who kills everyone. And what I've never been able to stomach, above all else, is the debauched person who wants to kill everyone.

---

150. Denis Marion, who Camus knew from his days at *Combat*, had just published a biography of Defoe. In the summary Camus records here, we can see hints of Camus's later story "Jonas, or The Artist at Work" and his play *The Life of the Artist*.

151. This entry was added to the typescript by hand.

152. The Lord's Supper, or the Lord's Table, is more often referred to as Communion or the Eucharist.

153. Maurice Merleau-Ponty (1908–1961), French philosopher, editor of *Les temps modernes*. His July 1947 essay "Learn to Read," published in *Les temps modernes*, was an attempted defense of his recently published book *Humanism and Terror*, which had come under fire for supporting the Soviet prison camps. In *Situations IV*, Sartre tells of a fight that took place between Merleau-Ponty and Camus at this time, with Camus accusing Merleau-Ponty of irresponsibly justifying the Moscow Show Trials. Merleau-Ponty's stance ended their friendship.

M.P. or the typical contemporary man: the one who keeps track of every blow. He explains how no one's ever right and how it's not so simple as all that (I hope he's not going to the trouble of trying to show this on my account). But a little further on he argues Hitler is a criminal against whom all forms of resistance will always be right. If no one is right, then we must not judge. But *today*, we must be against Hitler. Every blow has been tracked. On we go.

Action, from here on out, only seems justifiable for limited objectives. So says contemporary man. There's a contradiction.

Dwinger[154] (in a Siberian camp): "If we were animals, everything would have been over long ago, but we're men."

Id. A lieutenant, a pianist who lives for his art. He makes a silent piano with boards from a crate. He plays six to eight hours a day. He hears every note. At certain passages, his face begins to glow.

It's what *all of us* will do, if the worst comes to pass.

Id. During the Italian Front.[155] In a train behind enemy lines. D. and a comrade enter a compartment where they find a tall captain with feverish eyes. In front of him, someone, a coat-covered form, is stretched out on a bench. Night is falling. The moon lights up the compartment. "Open your eyes, brothers. You're about to see something special. You've earned it." He slowly lifts his coat: a naked young woman, incredibly beautiful and naturally so . . . "Look," the officer says. "It'll renew your strength and remind you why we fight, for we're also fighting for beauty, aren't we? *It's just that nobody ever says so.* ~~The 'reds' fight to transform these 'whites' by force, who then go and fight their former comrades.~~"[156]

With regard to Bataille on *The Plague*.[157] Sade also called for an end to the death penalty, *legitimate* murder. Reason: the murderer's excuses lie in nature's passions. In the law, no.

154. Edwin Erich Dwinger (1898–1981), Russian-German writer, author of *My Siberian Journal* and *Between the Reds and Whites*.

155. In the original French, Camus uses the term *guerre blanche* to refer to the Italian Front, a series of battles that lasted several years during World War I and took place high in the Alps, where the winters could be cold and snowy.

156. The last sentence is crossed out on the typescript.

157. Georges Bataille (1987–1962) reviewed *The Plague* for *Critique*'s July–August 1947 issue. He titled the review "*The Plague*: The Moral of Tragedy."

Sade's rejection of the death penalty occurs in *Philosophy in the Bedroom*.

Study on G:[158] G. as a thinker contrasted with Malraux. Both are aware of the temptation of the other's way of thinking. The world today is a dialogue between M. and G.

Play. Yanek to another person, who is the Killer.

Yanek: "Maybe, but that'll rob us of love."

The K: "Says who?"

Yanek: "Dora."

The K: "Dora is a woman and women don't know what love is . . . That terrible explosion I'll annihilate myself in is the very outpouring of love."

Days of our Death. 72–125–190.

W.C.C. 15–66.[159]

Retain violence's character as a *breakdown,* as a crime—which is to say only accept it when linked to *personal* responsibility. Otherwise, it's *by order,* it's *in order*—either law or metaphysics. It's no longer a breakdown. It eludes contradiction. It represents, paradoxically, a leap into comfort. *They've made violence comfortable.*[160]

M.D.'s friend who goes, as he does every day, to the little café on Rue Dauphine, where he follows his normal routine—sits at the same table to watch the same people play belote. The player he's sitting behind has nothing but diamonds. "A shame," M.D.'s friend says, "it ain't chosen for trumps." And he suddenly drops dead.

Id. The old spiritualist who lost her son in the war: "Wherever I go, I have my son behind me."

Id. The old colonial governor who holds himself ramrod straight and expects to be called Monsieur le Gouverneur. He's conducting research to try to establish a correlation with the Gregorian calendar. The only subject that inspires him, his age: "80 years old! Never an aperitif and look at me!" He jumps in place several times, kicking his heels up against his rear.

---

158. Jean Grenier.

159. David Rousset's *Days of Our Death* and *The World of the Concentration Camp* were published in France in 1947 and 1946, respectively. The page numbers Camus gives here refer to those editions.

160. The ideas expressed here would go on to form *The Rebel*'s opening paragraphs.

Palante (I.S.)[161] "Humanism is an invasion of the priestly mind into the field of feeling . . . It's the icy coldness of the Mind's reign."

We're reproached for making men into abstractions, but it's because the man who serves as our model is abstract—for being ignorant of love, but it's because (the man who serves as our model) is incapable of love, etc., etc.

Lautréamont:[162] All the water in the sea wouldn't be enough to wash away an intellectual bloodstain.

Justice short story or novel. Tortured, five days standing upright, with neither food nor water, forbidden to lean over, etc., etc. They come to break him free. He refuses; he doesn't have the strength. Staying put requires less effort. He'll be tortured again and he'll die.

L'Isle-sur-Sorgue.[163] Large room open to autumn. Autumnal itself, with its furniture made of contoured trees, the dead leaves from the plane trees slipping into the room, blown beneath the windows by the wind, past curtains embroidered with ferns.

In May '44, as R.C.[164] was leaving the Maquis for North Africa, a plane was leaving the Basses-Alpes and flying over the Durance at night. And that's when he noticed, all along the mountains, the fires his men lit as a farewell salute.

---

161. Georges Palante (1862–1925), French philosopher and sociologist, friend of Jean Grenier and Louis Guilloux. "I.S." is an abbreviation of Palante's 1909 book *The Individualist Sensibility* (*La sensibilité individualiste*). Many of the quotes that follow, from Bayle and Sainte-Beuve and Stendhal and Benjamin Constant, come from Palante's text rather than from their original source.

162. Comte de Lautréamont (1846–1870), pen name of Isidore Ducasse, French poet, author of *Les chants de maldoror* and *Poésies*, the first of which fully embraces a violent, nightmarish revolt against norms, the second of which fully embraces standard moral values. Camus would discuss the significance of this switch in *The Rebel*, in the section titled "Lautréamont and Banality."

163. On September 20, 1947, Camus traveled to Avignon, staying at the Hôtel de l'Europe, with the dual purpose of visiting René Char in L'Isle-Sur-la-Sorgue, about twenty miles east of Avignon, as well as going house hunting in the surrounding area.

164. René Char (1907–1988), French poet, served in the French Resistance as commander of the Durance drop zone under the name Captain Alexandre. Char, who was also friends with Martin Heidegger, Georges Bataille, Pablo Picasso, and many other well-known artists of the period, formed a close friendship with Camus, the two exchanging letters and seeing each other regularly throughout the rest of Camus's life.

In Calvi, he goes to sleep (awash with dreams). In the morning, he wakes and sees a terrace littered with the fat butts of American cigarettes. After four years of struggle and clenched teeth, the tears burst forth, and for an hour, there before the cigarette butts, he cries.

The old Communist militant who sees what he sees and never gets used to it: "I can't be cured of my heart."[165]

Bayle: Various Thoughts on the Occasion of a Comet.[166]

"We mustn't judge a man's life either by what he believes or by what he publishes in his books."

The informant who keeps his records up to date. Several types of ink. Lines traced. Names written in ronde script.

How to make it clear that a poor child can feel ashamed without feeling envious.

An old beggar to Eleanor Clark: "It's not that we're bad, it's just our light's gone out."[167]

Sartre or nostalgia for the universal idyll.[168]

---

165. In the playbill accompanying *The Just*, Camus would write that it was a story about "men and women who, in the midst of the most unforgiving of tasks, were unable to shake off their own hearts."

166. Pierre Bayle (1647–1706), French philosopher and lexicographer, author of *Various Thoughts on the Occasion of a Comet*, which argues that celestial occurrences, such as comets, have a natural basis and are not signs from God. Further, Bayle, who fled his homeland due to religious persecution, implies that atheists may in fact be more virtuous than the religious. Bayle is discussed in Palante's *The Individualist Sensibility*, and the quote Camus gives here is, as Palante notes, actually a heading in Bayle's table of contents. It's possible Camus went on to read Bayle's book, as well, as it shares much in common with *State of Emergency*, the play Camus was working on at this time.

167. Camus would later utilize this entry in *The Fall*, where Clamence says: "I'm like that old beggar who, one day out on some café patio, didn't want to let go of my hand: 'Oh, Monsieur,' he said, 'it's not that we're bad men, it's just that our light's going out.' Yes, our light has gone out, as our mornings have, as the saintly innocence of those who forgive themselves has."

168. In *The Rebel*, Camus writes: "No doubt, Saint-Just was sincere in his desire for a universal idyll. He really dreamed of a republic of ascetics, of a humanity reconciled and given over to the chaste games of original righteousness, watched over by those old wise men he decorated from the outset with a tricolor sash and a white plume. We also know that, at the start of the Revolution, Saint-Just pronounced himself, alongside Robespierre, against the death penalty. His only suggestion was that murderers be dressed in black for the rest of their lives. He wanted a justice that didn't seek

———

Ravachol (interrogation): "Faced with those who bring truth, proof, and human happiness, every obstacle, every single one, must disappear, and if, afterward, there were only a few people left on earth, at least they would be happy."

Id. (Declaration to the Assizes) "As for the innocent victims I've affected, I sincerely regret having done so. I regret it all the more because my life's been full of bitterness."

Witness deposition (Chaumartin): "He didn't love women and drank nothing other than water, with a little lemon."[169]

———

Vigny (correspondence): "The social order is always bad. From time to time, it's just barely tolerable. The argument about the difference between bad and tolerable isn't worth a drop of blood."[170]—No, the tolerable deserves, if not blood, at least the effort of a lifetime.

Misanthropic in a group, the individualist forgives the individual.

———

Saint-Beuve: "I've always believed that if we spent even a single minute saying what we think, society would collapse."[171]

———

'to find the accused guilty, but to find him weak,' and that's admirable. He also dreamed of a republic of forgiveness, which recognized that if the tree of crime was hard, the root was tender."

The problem, Camus notes—and here finds the connection with Sartre—is that, as in the Revolution, factions always develop within a movement, and one of these will, like Saint-Just and Robespierre, end up demanding an "absolute virtue" that's impossible to live. It's in trying to enforce this absolute virtue that "the implacable logic of the republic of forgiveness leads to the republic of guillotines."

169. François Claudius Koenistein (1859–1892), pseudonym Ravachol, was guillotined for his role in multiple anarchist bombings. Auguste Vaillant's later bombing of the Chamber of Deputies was carried out to avenge Ravachol's murder. The quotes Camus gives here come from the "Assizes" (court hearings) printed in the aforementioned issue of *Crapouillot* on Anarchism. See p. 309n145.

170. Quoted in Palante, originally from Vigny's *Journal d'un poète* (*A Poet's Journal*). Later, on the boat to South America in 1949, Camus will begin to read the *Journal* itself. Here, in Palante, the quote is preceded by the following: "We see that individualism is essentially a form of social pessimism. In its most moderate form, it acknowledges that, if life in society isn't an absolute evil and completely destructive of individuality, it is, at least for the individual, a restrictive and oppressive condition, a sort of forced hand, a necessary evil, a last resort.

"The individualists who meet this description form a morose little group in which the words rebellion, resignation, or hopelessness contrast with optimistic sociologists' future-looking fanfares."

171. Quoted in Palante—though in Palante, as well as in Sainte-Beuve, instead of the word *cru* (believed), as Camus has written here, the word used is *vu* (seen).

B. Constant (prophet!): "A person has to go to almost as much trouble to live in peace as to govern the world."[172]

———

To devote yourself to humanity: means wanting, according to Sainte-Beuve, to play a role that's applauded to the very end.[173]

———

Stendhal: "I'll have done nothing for my personal happiness as long as I'm not accustomed to suffering from a soul thinking ill of me."[174]

———

Palante rightly says that if there's a single and universal truth, freedom has no reason to exist.

———

OCTOBER 14, '47. Running out of time. Alone, all energy extended into dry air.

———

OCTOBER 17. Beginning.

———

It's as if man had to make an absolute choice between abasement and punishment.

At the Children's Hospital.[175] Small room with a low ceiling, completely closed up, overheated—filled with the odor of oily broths and bandages . . . blackout.

———

There are messianic actions and considered actions.

———

Write it all—as it comes.

———

172. Quoted in Palante, originally from Benjamin Constant's *Personal Diary*.

173. Quoted in Palante, originally from Sainte-Beuve's *Volupté*. The last clause is in fact a direct quote, not a paraphrase.

174. Quoted in Palante, originally from Stendhal's *Journals*, in which Stendhal attributes the thought to Pascal. Palante precedes the Stendhal quote by writing that "the most moderate and frequent form of individualistic contempt is indifference to people's judgements. . . . Stendhal regards this feeling as a primary condition of happiness and independence."

175. Likely the Hôpital des Enfants Malades in Paris, which is the oldest pediatric hospital in the Western world, having been founded in 1801.

We can do everything to better ourselves, understand everything and then master everything, but we'll never be able to find or create for ourselves the power of love that's been taken from us forever.

Death penalty. They say I'm opposed to all violence, no matter what. That would be about as smart as being opposed to the wind always blowing in the same direction.[176]

But no one is absolutely guilty, so no one can be absolutely condemned. Nobody is absolutely guilty 1) in the eyes of society 2) in the eyes of the individual. Some part of the individual shares in the sorrow.

Is death the absolute punishment? Not for Christians. But the world isn't Christian. Is forced labor not worse? (Paulhan). I really don't know. But prison leaves the chance to choose death (unless, *out of laziness*, you'd prefer that others do the work for you). Death leaves no chance to choose prison. Finally, Rochefort: "You would have to be bloodthirsty to ask that the death penalty be abolished."[177]

Generation of old men. "A young man so thrown into the world, rich on the outside but poor on the inside, tries in vain to replace inner wealth with outer, wants to receive everything *from the outside*, similar to those old men who look to draw new strength from young girls' breath. (The Wisdom of Life).[178]

Socrates on being kicked. "If it had been a donkey, would I have filed a complaint?" (Diogenes Laërtius, II, 21.)

---

176. The "they" referred to here is Emmanuel d'Astier de La Vigerie, who, in the March 1948 issue of *Caliban*, published an article accusing Camus of being a pacifist whose only concern was "saving bodies," a position that left Camus, so d'Astier claimed, as one of capitalism's accomplices. In an article titled "Where's the Mystification?" Camus gave a furious reply, accusing d'Astier of being a Communist tool. D'Astier replied once more, as did Camus.

177. An entry that followed this one with dialogue intended for *The Just* was crossed out.

178. The quote given in Arthur Schopenhauer's *The Wisdom of Life*, in T. Bailey Saunders's translation, is much longer and fairly different. In part, it reads: "A young man of rich family enters upon life with a large patrimony. . . . He was sent into the world outwardly rich but inwardly poor, and his vain endeavor was to make his external wealth compensate for his inner poverty, by trying to obtain everything *from without*, like an old man who seeks to strengthen himself as King David or Maréchal de Retz tried to do. And so in the end one who is inwardly poor comes to be also poor outwardly."

The Socrates quote also comes from *The Wisdom of Life*, from a section in which Schopenhauer assails the modern fixation on "personal courage."

Heine (1848): "What the world pursues and hopes for has now become completely foreign to my heart."[179]

———

Courage, according to Schopenhauer, "merely a second lieutenant's virtue."

———

In *Emile*, Book IV, Rousseau advocates murder (note 21) for reasons of honor.

"To receive and endure a slap in the face and a betrayal has civil effects that no wise man can foresee and that no court can avenge for the wronged individual. In this respect, the inadequacy of the laws returns his independence to him; he is then the sole magistrate, the sole judge, between the wrongdoer and himself; he is the sole interpreter and minister of the natural law; he owes himself justice and he alone can render it [. . .]. I'm not saying he has to go out and fight—that's a bit excessive—I'm saying that he owes himself justice and that he's the only one who can dispense it. Without so many vain edicts against duels, if I were sovereign, I would declare that neither slaps nor betrayals would ever be given in my states, and this would be upheld *through a very simple means that wouldn't involve the courts*. In any event, Emile knows the justice he owes himself in such a case and the example he owes to the security and protection of honorable people. Not even the toughest man can prevent himself from being insulted, but he can prevent the person who insulted him from going on about it for long."

———

For Schopenhauer: the objective existence of things, their "representation," is always pleasant, whereas the subjective existence, the will, is always painful.

"All things are beautiful to the eye and awful in their being, from which we get the widespread illusion, which always strikes me, of the outer unity of others' lives."

———

Schopenhauer. "To have fame and youth at the same time is too much for a mortal."

179. Heinrich Heine (1797–1856), German poet, spent the last years of his life in Paris. The quote recorded here comes from Palante's *The Individualist Sensibility*.

Id. "In this world, you really can find education, but not happiness." So then, "limiting yourself makes you happy."

His son being sick, David hounds Jehovah for help. But as soon as his son dies, he snaps his fingers and thinks no more of it.[180]

Voltaire: "One only succeeds in this world at the point of a sword and one dies with weapons in hand."

Pecherin,[181] a 19th century Russian émigré who became a monk abroad, cried out: "What an exquisite pleasure it is to hate one's homeland and feverishly await its annihilation."

The intelligentsia and the *totalitarian* interpretation of the world.

Petrashevsky's conspirators: idyllic. (Emancipation of the serfs without revolutionary action—George Sand's influence.) Love of what's far off, not what's next door. "Finding nothing worthy of my affection, neither among men nor among women, I hereby devote myself to the service of humanity." (Petrashevsky) (Except Sprechner, model for Stavrogin.)

Belinsky's[182] individualistic socialism. Against Hegel, for the individual person. Cf. Letters to Botkin: "The fate of the subject, of the individual, of the person, is more important than the fate of the entire world and the health of the Emperor of China, which is to say the Hegelian Allgemeinheit."

Id. "I bow before your philosophical nightcap (to Hegel), but with all due respect to your philosophical philistinism, I have the honor of informing you that, if I ever managed to climb to the highest rung of the ladder of development, even from there I'd demand an account of all the martyrs of the conditions of life and of history, of all the victims of chance, of superstition,

180. Both this entry and the Voltaire quote that follows come from the Schopenhauer text.

181. The quotes from Father Vladimir Sergeyvich Pecherin (1807–1885) and Mikhail Petrashevsky (1821–1866), as well as the rest of the information in this entry, come from Nicolas Berdyaev's *The Origin of Russian Communism*. The name of the model for Stavrogin has been left as Camus wrote it, "Sprechner," though it seems he's referring to Nikolai Alexandrovich Speshnev (in French transliteration, Nicolas Alexandrovitch Spechnev, which is the spelling given in the French edition of Berdyaev's *The Origin of Russian Communism*).

182. Vissarion Belinsky (1811–1848), influential Russian literary critic. This entry is composed of excerpts from Belinsky's famous March 1, 1841, letter to Botkin, which Dostoyevsky, among others, hailed and which is quoted in Berdyaev's *The Origin of Russian Communism*. Camus will return to the letter in *The Rebel*, but the version he'll use there comes from Benoît P. Hepner's *Bakounine et le pansalvisme révolutionnaire*, not Berdyaev.

of the Inquisition, of Philip II, etc. . . . Otherwise, from these lofty heights, I would throw myself down headfirst. I want none of the happiness granted me if I'm not first reassured about each of my blood brothers, bone of my bones, flesh of my flesh . . ."

"They say disharmony is the condition of harmony; well that may be very beneficial and delightful for the music lovers,[183] but certainly much less so for the person whose role it is to suffer the disharmony."

———

Petrashevsky and the idyllics.

Belinsky and individualistic socialism.

Dobrolyubov—ascetic, mystical, and scrupulous.

He loses his faith *in the face of evil* (Marcion).

Chernyshevsky: "What's to be done?"[184]

Pisarev. "A pair of boots is worth more than Shakespeare."

Herzen—Bakunin—Tolstoy—Dostoyevsky.

The sense of guilt among intellectuals separated from the people. The "repentant gentleman" (for social sin).

———

Nechayev and the revolutionary catechism[185] (centralized party prefigures Bolshevism).

"The revolutionary is a marked individual. He has neither private interests nor affairs, neither personal sentiments nor ties, nothing that is his alone, not even a name. Everything in him is seized by a single exclusive concern, by a single thought, by a single passion: the Revolution."

Everything that serves the revolution is moral.

Resemblance to Dzerzhinsky, creator of the Cheka. Bakunin: "The passion for destruction is creative."

---

183. In French, the word is *mélomane* (music lover), which, given the context of the letter, brings the word *mégalomane* (megalomaniac) quickly to mind.

184. Chernyshevsky's novel *What Is to Be Done?*, written in 1863, would go on to inspire both Tolstoy in 1886 and Lenin in 1902 to write pamphlets with the same title. Of the novel, Lenin said: "It completely reshaped me. This is a book that changes one for a whole lifetime." Joseph Frank, author of a five-volume biography of Dostoyevsky and his times, has said: "Chernyshevsky's novel, far more than Marx's *Capital*, supplied the emotional dynamic that eventually went to make the Russian Revolution."

185. Although Camus hasn't capitalized it here, *The Revolutionary Catechism* (sometimes rendered *Catechism of a Revolutionary*) is the title of Nechayev's most famous pamphlet. The passage Camus cites comes from the start of the text, which Camus has quoted from Berdyaev's *The Origin of Russian Communism*. The quote from Mikhaylovsky below, as well as the discussion of "transition," all come from the Berdyaev text.

Id. Three principles of human development:
animal man
thought
rebellion

The '70s. Mikhaylovsky, individualistic socialist.

"If those revolutionary people burst into my bedroom with the intention of shattering the bust of Belinsky and destroying my library, I'd struggle against them to the last drop of my blood."

The transition problem. Did Russia have to pass through the stage of bourgeois, capitalist revolution, as the logic of history would have it? On this point only Tkachev (along with Nechayev and Bakunin) is Lenin's predecessor. Marx and Engels were Mensheviks. The only thing they had in sight was the coming bourgeois revolution.

The constant discussions among the first Marxists about the necessity of capitalist development in Russia and their willingness to welcome such a development. Tikhomirov, a longtime member of the People's Will,[186] accuses them of being "the champions of the first capitalizations."

Lermontov's Prediction.

But already rising from immense mass graves
The plague comes to haunt those sinister merchants

Cf. Berdyaev, p. 107.[187]

Dostoyevsky's spiritual communism is: everyone's moral responsibility.

Berdyaev: "There can be no dialectic of matter; dialectic presupposes Logos and Thought; the only dialectic possible is of thought and mind. Marx transferred the properties of mind into the realm of matter."

---

186. As Camus has pointed out with other intellectuals, Lev Alexandrovich Tikhomirov (1852–1923) swung from being a revolutionary thinker, even serving on the People's Will (Narodnaya Volya) Executive Committee, to being a critic of liberal democracy and an advocate of monarchism.

187. These lines from Lermontov's poem "Prediction" were taken from Berdyaev's *The Origin of Russian Communism*. R. M. French's 1948 translation from the Russian gives the lines as: "Plague will ride / From stinking corpses through the grief-struck land." A contemporary, uncredited transla-

In the end, it's the will of the proletariat that transforms the world. So then, there's *really* an existential philosophy in Marxism that denounces the lie of objectification and affirms the triumph of human activity.

———

In Russian, *volia* means *both* will and freedom.

———

Question for Marxism:

"Is Marxist ideology the reflection of economic activity, as all other ideologies, or does it claim to uncover absolute truth independent of historical forms of economy and economic interests."[188] In other words, is it a pragmatism or an absolute realism?

Lenin asserts the primacy of politics over economics (despite Marxism).

———

Lukács: the revolutionary sense is the sense of totality. Conception of the total world in which theory and practice are identified.

Religious sense according to Berdyaev.

———

What exists in Russia is a collective, "total" freedom, not personal freedom. But what is a total freedom? A person is free *from* something—in relation to. Clearly, the limit is freedom in relation to God. So then, we can clearly see it means enslavement to man.

———

Berdyaev puts Pobedonostsev (Ober-Procurator of the Most Holy Synod, the ideological director of the Russian Empire) in touch with Lenin. Both of them *nihilists*.

———

Vera Figner:[189] "Bring words and actions into agreement, demand that others bring words and actions into agreement . . . that was to be my life's motto."

Id. "I found the formation of a secret association within an already secret society intolerable."

---

tion from the Russian reads: "When the plague of stinking, dead bodies / Begins to walk among the unfortunate villages."

188. The passage comes from Berdyaev's *The Origin of Russian Communism*.

189. Vera Figner (1852–1942), Russian revolutionary, who, as a member of People's Will, helped plan the assassination of Alexander II, for which she was eventually arrested and sentenced to death. The sentence was commuted to twenty years in prison, after which Figner was released in exile, and she wrote her immensely popular *Memoirs of a Revolutionist*.

80 to 90% of the Czar's budget is supplied by the lower classes.[190]

———

Every member of the "People's Will" solemnly pledged to devote their strength to the revolution, to forget their blood relationships for it, their personal sympathies, love, and friendship . . .

———

Play *Dora*: If you love nothing, this isn't going to end well.

———

How many members were in the "People's Will"? 500. The Russian Empire? More than a hundred million.

———

Sophia Perovskaya, stepping onto the scaffold with her comrades in arms, embraces three of them (Zhelyabov, Kibalchich, and Mikhaylov) but not the fourth, Rysakov, who, though he'd fought hard, had, in order to save his own life, provided an address that caused the loss of three other comrades. They hanged Rysakov, who died in solitude.[191]

Rysakov's the one who threw the bomb at Alexander II. Uninjured, the Czar said: "Thanks to God, everything's all right." "We'll see if everything's all right," Rysakov replied. And a second bomb, Hryniewiecki's, strikes the emperor down.

———

Cf. Vera Figner, p. 190 on the denunciation.

Id. Marie Kaluzhnaya.[192] Freed, she's accused of betrayal. To wash herself of the accusation, she shoots at a police officer. Sentenced to a labor camp. She, along with two comrades, commits suicide in Kara as a protest against the corporal punishment inflicted on a third (p. 239).

———

190. The French *alimenté*, figuratively "supplied," is more literally "fed," a double sense that's lost in English.

191. This entry is incorporated into *The Rebel*, in the section titled "The Sensitive Murderers." Sophia Perovskaya was the first woman officially executed in Russia for political actions.

192. The incident referred to here, and which Camus alludes to early in *The Rebel*, is known as "The Kara Katorga Tragedy." Following two unsuccessful hunger strikes against the mistreatment of women in the prison camp, and following Nadezhda Sigida being transferred to the criminal block for slapping one of the abusive prison commandants, on September 1, 1889, Marie Kaluzhnaya, Marie Kavelefskaya, and Nadezhda Smirnitskya went on a third hunger strike that resulted in the three of them being transferred to the criminal block as well. It was then that Nadezhda Sigida was given twenty lashes with a birch rod, an incident that she and the other women mentioned above, as well as twenty others, protested by taking poison. The incident led to the closing of the prison and a law abolishing the death penalty for women.

To remind Christians. "The Christian Brotherhood." A call to "those who venerate Christ's holy teachings." "The existing government, all of its laws being founded on lies, oppression, and the banning of the free pursuit of truth, should be considered illegitimate, contrary to the divine will and the Christian spirit."

———

Vera Figner: "I had to live, to live to be judged, for it's the trial that crowns the revolutionary's activity."[193]

———

A man sentenced to death: "In all my life, however short, I've seen nothing but evil . . . In such conditions, and with such a life, can a person love anything at all, *even what is good?*"

———

In the '80s, a soldier who'd killed a noncommissioned officer was executed. Before it happened, turning in each direction, he cried out: "Goodbye North, Goodbye South . . . East, West."

———

Nobody was as sure as I was of conquering the world by way of the straight and narrow. And now . . . So then, where was the flaw? What so suddenly gave way and determined all the rest . . . ?

———

Tidbit: people often believe they "have met me before."[194]

———

Paris-Algiers.[195] The plane as an element of modern negation and abstraction. There's no nature anymore: the deep gorge, the true relief, the impassable torrent, all gone. What remains is *a blueprint*—a map.

Man, in short, gazes down as God, and it's then that he recognizes God can only see things in the abstract. A raw deal.

———

193. In *The Just*, Dora expresses similar sentiments when she tells Kalyayev that to kill the Grand Duke *and* be tried and sent to the gallows would be like giving your life twice for the cause. Shortly after, when she believes Kalyayev has been captured before he could kill the Grand Duke, she says she knows Kalyayev wanted to go to prison and have a trial, but that he wanted it after having killed the Grand Duke. At the end of the play, Dora says of Kalyayev: "He wanted purity, it's true. But what an awful crowning achievement."

194. Camus would use this entry in *The Fall*, where he writes: "For example, people often believed they had already met me."

195. Camus returned to Algiers in November 1947, where he gave an interview to Emmanuel Roblès on Radio-Alger.

Polemics—as an element of abstraction. Every time we decide to take an individual as an enemy, we make him an abstraction. We move further from the person. We no longer want to know he has a boisterous laugh. He becomes a *silhouette*.

Etc., etc. . . .

If, to overcome nihilism, we have to return to Christianity, then we can clearly continue on and overcome Christianity with Hellenism.

Plato goes from nonsense to reason and from reason to myth. He covers it all.

Glorious morning on the port of Algiers. The landscape, ultramarine blue, penetrates the windows and spills all over the room.

Socrates: "I have no sympathy for you."

Returning from the camp.

End of II. He shows the marks:

"What's that?"

"The marks."

"What marks?"

"The marks of man's love."[196]

Reproached because my books don't draw enough attention to the political element. Translation: they want me to depict political parties. But I only depict individuals, opposed to the machinery of the State, because I know of what I speak.

The world will be more just insofar as it will be more chaste (G. Sorel).[197]

In the theater: the need, for variety, to load syntactic constructions.

Play. Dora or another woman: "Condemned, condemned to be heroes and saints. Heroes by force, because such things don't interest us, you under-

196. Parts of this dialogue would be used in *The Just*, act 3.

197. From Sorel's *Matériaux d'une théorie du prolétariat*, where the line reads: "We can assert that the *world will only become more just insofar as it becomes more chaste*; I don't think there's any truth more certain."

stand, they don't interest us at all, the filthy dirty affairs of this stupid, poisoned world that sticks to us like glue.

"Admit it, admit that what interests you are individuals, their faces . . . and that, claiming to seek some truth, in the end you're really only waiting for love."[198]

———

"Don't cry. This is the day of justification. Something is rising up at this moment. It's our testimony, our testimony as rebels."

———

Novel. A man is caught by the secret police because he was too lazy to worry about having a passport arranged. He knew it. He didn't do it, etc. . . .

———

"I've had every luxury, and here I am, forever a slave . . . etc."

———

Rousset. What keeps my lips sealed is that I wasn't deported. But I know what a scream I'm suffocating in saying this.[199]

———

It's Christianity that explains Bolshevism. Let's keep the balance so as not to become murderers.

———

Contemporary literature. Easier to shock than to convince.

———

R.C. On a train during the Occupation, the day breaking. The Germans. A woman drops a gold coin. C. covers it with his foot and returns it to her. The woman: thank you. She offers a cigarette. He accepts. She offers some to the Germans. R.C: "On second thought, Madame, you can have your cigarette back." One of the Germans looks at him. Tunnel. A hand grips his. "I'm Polish." As they exit the tunnel, R.C. looks at the German. His eyes are full of tears. At the train station, the German, as he exits, turns to him and winks. C. responds and smiles. "Bastards," a Frenchwoman says of them, having seen the exchange.

———

Form and rebellion. Giving form to what doesn't have any is the goal of any work. So then, there's not only creation, but correction (see earlier).

---

198. Snippets of this entry show up in *The Just*, though the overall form is different. The next entry is spoken by Dora in act 5.

199. See Camus's earlier reference to Rousset's *The World of the Concentration Camp*.

Which is why *form* is so important. Which is why a certain style is needed for each subject, one not completely different, because the author's language is their own. It's precisely this language that will reveal not *the unity* of this or that book but of the body of work as a whole.

———

There is no justice, there are only limits.

———

The Tolstoyan anarchist during the Occupation. He wrote on his door: "Wherever you come from, you're welcome here." It was the miliciens who came in.[200]

———

Dictionary. *Umanity*: begins with an *H* and is finished off with an *atchet*.[201] But here we're against. . . . Secondary meaning: *pretext*. Synonyms: Straw Mattress—Straw Doormat—Stepping Stone—Mouthwash—Terminus.

Palinode: Haute literary exercise in which the flag is raised to the top of the pole after having spit on it, in which morality is recovered by way of the gang bang, and in which slippers are put on former pirates. They start out playing the raider and end up with the Legion of Honor. *Hist*: 80% of 20th century authors, if only they could avoid signing their name, would write and salute

---

200. In *The Fall*, Clamence says: "I knew a pure-hearted guy who refused to be suspicious. He was a pacifist, a libertarian socialist, he loved all humanity, all its animals, with a single, encompassing love. An exceptional soul, yes, that's for sure. Well, during the last wars of religion in Europe, he retired to the countryside. On the threshold of his house, he wrote: 'Wherever you come from, please come in, you're welcome here.' Who do you think responded to that lovely invitation? The miliciens, who came in, made themselves at home, and gutted him."

201. In French, the letter *h* and the word *hache* (axe) are pronounced the same way, allowing Camus to create a pun that doesn't translate directly into English. A literal translation of the line might read: "*Umanity*: written and generally executed with an *h*."

The list of synonyms poses its own translation problems, as a word like *paillasse* (which is sometimes used in British English) could refer to a "straw mattress" or a "lab bench" or a "drying rack," but it's also just two letters off of *paillasson*, which refers to a doormat, which itself is one derivation of *marchepied*, generally used, in the figurative sense, to mean "steppingstone."

In his "Notice" for *State of Emergency*, David H. Walker points out that, though Camus doesn't often indulge in this sort of wordplay in his essays and personal writings, he does occasionally allow his fictional characters, such as The Plague in *State of Emergency*, to do so. In that play, which Camus was just finishing up when this entry was made, The Plague does, in fact, make several puns with the word "execute."

God's name. *Natural sciences*: Process of transformation by which a pinstriped resistant becomes a garden variety servant to the high altar.[202]

———

Tragedy. He's *suspected* of treason. That suspicion is enough to get him killed. It's the only possible explanation.

———

Leysin.[203] Snow and clouds fill the valley to the peaks. Over that still and cottony sea, the jackdaws skim the surface like a flock of black seagulls, snow spray speckling their wings.

———

Tolstoy: "A strong westerly wind lifted columns of dust from the roads and fields, bent the tops of the garden's tall lime and birch trees, and carried far away the falling yellow leaves" (*Childhood*).

Id. "If in those sorrow-filled hours of life I could see that smile (his mother's) once again, even if for only a second, I would know no sorrow."

———

I withdrew from the world not because I had enemies but because I had friends. Not because they did me any of the usual wrongs, but because they believed me to be better than I am. It's a lie I couldn't bear.

———

202. In *The Fall*, Clamence says that "80% of our writers, if only they could avoid signing their name, would write and salute God's name. But they sign, according to my friend, because they love themselves, and they salute nothing at all, because they detest themselves. But they just can't help but judge, so they make up for it with morality. In short, their Satanism is virtuous. What a funny time we live in, really! Little wonder these are troubled minds and that a friend of mine, an atheist when he was a perfect husband, converted when he became an adulterer."

Like the opening of the entry, the last sentence relies on several word-level usages that don't translate directly into English. The term *réfractaire*, often left as such in English-language histories of World War II, and translated here as "resistant," refers specifically to those French citizens who refused the *service du travail obligatoire* (compulsory labor service), which saw approximately 650,000 French citizens sent to do forced labor in Germany. The point Camus is making, as he has in different ways throughout these pages, and as he will more forcefully in *The Rebel* and more humorously in *The Fall*, is that those who start out as resistants often end up as bureaucrats, as enforcers of the system.

When reviewing the first typescript, Camus initially wrote "in which one succeeds in the world" before changing it to "in which morality is recovered." Likewise, he had first written "killer" before changing it to "raider."

203. Almost a year to the day after his stay at the Grand Hôtel in Briançon, Camus went for a stay at the Grand Hôtel in Leysin, Switzerland. To Jean Grenier, Camus wrote that he'd been having trouble working in Paris and that he'd "fled to Switzerland to see Michel Gallimard and to begin work on my play about the Russian terrorists in 1905. To rest, also, despite, or because of, how much I hate the mountains." Camus would remain at the sanatorium through February 7.

An extreme virtue that consists of killing one's passions. A deeper virtue that consists of balancing them.

———

Everything currently worthwhile in the contemporary mind is embedded in the irrational. And yet everything that prevails in politics professes, kills, and rules in the name of Reason.[204]

———

Peace would be to love in silence. But there's the conscience, and the person; you have to speak. Loving becomes hell.

———

P.B., the actor, lazy and religious, listens to mass on the radio from his bed. He doesn't even have to get up. He's covered his bases.

———

Ludmilla Pitoëff: "It's more like the audience makes me uncomfortable. When they're not there, it's just perfect." Speaking of G.P: "He's never ceased to surprise me."[205]

———

According to the Egyptians, after a just person dies, he has to be able to say: "I haven't caused anyone to suffer." Otherwise, there's punishment.[206]

———

The conclusion is that history can only find its ends by means of crushing spiritual conquest. We're reduced to this . . . [207]

———

For Christians, Revelation is at the beginning of history. For Marxists, it's at the end. Two religions.

———

Small bay before Ténès, at the foot of the mountain chains. Perfect semi-circle. As night falls, an anxious fullness hovers above the silent waters. You

---

204. On the typescript, Camus wrote, "Everything currently worthwhile in the contemporary mind is found in the individual. Ultimately, everything . . ." before changing it to the above.

205. Ludmilla Pitoëff (1895–1951), Russian-born, French theatrical actress. G.P. refers to her husband, Georges Pitoëff (1884–1939), also an actor and director.

206. In a speech given December 13, 1948—alongside Richard Wright, Jean-Paul Sartre, André Breton, and others—which was then printed in *La Gauche* 10 as "Freedom's Witness," Camus writes: "Deaf is the one who wishes to dominate. Faced with such a person, your only option is to fight or die. And that's why people today live in terror. In *The Book of the Dead*, it says that to earn forgiveness, the just Egyptian must be able to say: 'I haven't caused anyone to be afraid.' Given such terms, on the day of the last judgment, we'll search in vain for our great contemporaries among the line of the blessed."

207. Camus added this last sentence by hand on the typed version.

understand, then, that if the Greeks formed the idea of hopelessness and tragedy, they always did so *through* beauty and the oppressiveness it bears. It's a tragedy that reaches its peak. Whereas the modern mind has made its hopelessness out of ugliness and mediocrity.[208]

Probably what Char means. For the Greeks, beauty comes at the start. For a European, it's a goal, rarely achieved. I'm not modern.

Truth of the century: As a result of living through major events, you become a liar. Finish with all of that and say what I really have to say deep down.[209]

---

208. Camus and his wife, Francine, visited friends and family in Algeria from March 2, 1948, through March 13. Ténès is a town approximately 125 miles west of Algiers.

The commentary about the Greeks would reappear in "Helen's Exile."

209. Only the last sentence of this entry appears in the original notebook, written on the top line of the last page. Camus added the preceding lines to the typescript by hand.

Notebook VI

APRIL 1948–JUNE 1949

A plain, light orange composition notebook, 22 × 17 cm, with the word "Cahier" preprinted on the cover, after which Camus added "no. VI." On the line below that he wrote "from April 1948" and below that "to March 1951." Camus only used the first half of the notebook (sixty-nine pages, with pages 4, 6, 28, and 32 left blank), though he did scrawl a series of notes on three pages at the end, one of which he tore out, none of which have appeared in the published notebooks.

At the end of the 19th century, Antoine Orly,[1] an attorney in Périgueux, suddenly left home and headed for Patagonia, where he settled. He found a way of ingratiating himself with the local Indians, and simply by being likable, he had himself named, after several years, emperor of Araucania. He had coins minted, issued postage stamps, and eventually began to exercise the prerogatives of a legitimate sovereign. So much so that the Chilean government, to which those distant lands belonged, had him brought before a special court of law, which sentenced him to death. His sentence was commuted to ten years in prison.

Freed after ten years, he returned to Patagonia, where his subjects once again welcomed him as their emperor and he again accepted the title. But, beginning to feel age creep up on him, he started thinking about a successor and bequeathed the throne of Araucania to his son, Orly Louis, who, under the name Louis I, was to become emperor. But Orly Louis refused. So, Antoine abdicates in favor of his nephew, Achille Orly of Périgueux, and dies honored by his subjects. But Achille I wouldn't have dreamed of living among his subjects. He returned to Paris, gained a foothold in society, lived the high life, entertaining as an emperor. His income came from doling out, in exchange for money, consulate posts in Araucania. His needs having grown, he also put in place a system of donations to extend the Christian religion through the construction of churches and cathedrals. In doing so, he made a lot of money, so much that the Society of Jesus grew troubled and appealed to the Pope. They then noticed that not a single church was being built in Patagonia, and Achille I appeared before the courts, which sentenced him. Ruined, the emperor finished out his days in Montparnasse, frequenting the same cabaret where it's believed Queen Ranavalona came to visit him.

All sacrifice is messianic. Prove sacrifice can be imagined at the level of reflective thought (which is to say non-messianic).[2] The tragedy of balance.

---

1. Antoine Tounens (1825–1878) proclaimed himself Orélie-Antoine de Tounens I, King of Araucania and Patagonia, in 1860. He was arrested by the Chilean army in 1862, declared insane by a court in Santiago, and sent back to France. He made three more attempts to regain his kingdom, each of which was unsuccessful.

2. The term "reflective thought" is explained in John Dewey's *How We Think*, where he introduces the concept as follows: "No words are oftener on our lips than *thinking* and *thought*. So profuse and varied, indeed, is our use of these words that it is not easy to define just what we mean by them. . . . In some cases, a belief is accepted with slight or almost no attempt to state the grounds that support it. In other cases, the ground or basis for a belief is deliberately sought and its adequacy to support the belief examined. This process is called reflective thought; it alone is truly educative in value."

Modern art. They rediscover objects because they ignore nature. They remake nature, and they have to do so, because they've forgotten it. *When this work has been carried out,* the greatest years will begin.[3]

"Without unlimited freedom of the press, without absolute freedom of assembly and association, the rule of the broad masses of the people is inconceivable" (Rosa Luxembourg, *The Russian Revolution*).[4]

Salvador de Madariaga:[5] "Europe will only return to its senses when the word revolution evokes shame and not pride. A country that boasts of its glorious revolution is as vain and absurd as a man who boasts of his glorious appendicitis."

True in a sense. But open for discussion.

Stendhal (Letter to Di Fiore, 34): "But my own soul is a fire that suffers if not ablaze."

Id. "Every novelist must try to make readers believe in *burning passion* but never name it: that would work against modesty" (Letter to Mme Gaulthier, 34).

Id. Against Goethe: "Goethe gave Doctor Faust the devil as a friend and, with such a powerful assistant, Faust does what we all did at twenty: he seduces a milliner girl."[6]

---

3. After this entry, which is at the bottom of a notebook page, there are two brief, illegible entries crossed out on the next page, the rest of which is left blank, and then a third, longer entry crossed out on the next page.

4. The difference between Luxemburg's text and the French translation of it are minor but may have been important to Camus. The original quote is: "It is a well-known and indisputable fact that without a free and untrammeled press, without the unlimited right of association and assemblage, the rule of the broad masses of the people is entirely unthinkable."

After this entry, there is an entry crossed out in the handwritten notebook.

5. Salvador de Madariaga y Rojo (1886–1978), Spanish ambassador to the United States and France, took refuge in England during the Spanish Civil War and spoke out against Franco. In the April 1956 issue of *Monde nouveau,* Camus published an essay titled "Homage to Salvador de Madariaga."

6. The letters Camus cites here were all written in 1834 and appear in the third volume of the Bosse edition of Stendhal's *Correspondance.*

London. I remember London as a city of gardens where the birds would wake me in the morning. London is the opposite, and yet my memory is accurate. The flower carts in the streets. The docks, prodigious.

N. Gallery. Wonderful Piero and Velasquez.

Oxford. The finely groomed stud farm. The Oxford silence. What would people go there to do?[7]

Early morning on the Scottish coast. Edinburgh: swans in the canals. The city around a false acropolis, mysterious and misty. The Athens of the North has no north. Chinese and Malayans on Princess Street. It's a port.

According to Simone Weil,[8] thoughts relating to the spiritual nature of work, or an intuitive sense of it, scattered throughout Rousseau, Sand, Tolstoy, Marx, Proudhon, are the only original thoughts of our times, the only ones we haven't borrowed from the Greeks.

Germany: Misery that's bitten too deeply arouses a disposition to misery that drives people to plunge themselves and others into it.[9]

According to Richelieu, and all else being equal, rebels are always half as strong as the official system's defenders. On account of a guilty conscience.

Father de Foucauld, a witness of Christ among the Tuaregs, found it only natural to provide France's Deuxième Bureau with information about the *state of mind* of those same Tuaregs.[10]

---

7. Camus had been invited by the French Institutes of the United Kingdom to attend a conference in London and Edinburgh. He and Francine stayed in Great Britain from May 4 to May 10.

8. Simone Weil (1909–1943), French mystic, anarchist, and activist, who, like Camus, lodged a left-wing critique of the Communists, claiming they made life just as awful for the working class as capitalists. Camus would edit and publish seven of Weil's books, helping to popularize her work.

The above entry is a paraphrase from Weil's *The Need for Roots*: "Our era has as its own mission, as its vocation, the constitution of a civilization founded on the spiritual nature of work. Thoughts having to do with an intuitive sense of this vocation, and which are scattered throughout Rousseau, George Sand, Tolstoy, Proudhon, Marx, in the papal encyclicals, and elsewhere, are the only original thoughts of our times, the only ones we haven't borrowed from the Greeks."

9. Two entries in the handwritten notebooks have been crossed out after this one.

10. Two entries in the handwritten notebooks have been crossed out after this one.

S.W. Contradiction between science and humanism. No. Between the so-called modern scientific spirit and humanism—for determinism and force deny man.

"If justice can't be wiped from man's heart, it has a reality in this world. So then, it's science that's mistaken."

———

S.W.: It was the Romans who debased Stoicism by replacing a powerful love with pride.[11]

———

G. Greene:[12] "In a happy life the final disillusionment with human nature coincided with death. Nowadays they seemed to have a whole lifetime to get through somehow after it" . . . "You learned too much in these days before you came of age."

Id. Devotion . . . "What a world to let such qualities go to waste!"

Id. "He (the secret agent) promised rashly, as if in a violent world you could promise anything at all, beyond the moment of speaking."

Id. "But he hadn't that particular faith.[13] Unless people received their deserts, the world to him was chaos, he was faced with despair.

———

The writer sentenced to *understanding*. He can't be a killer.

———

Fondness for prison in those who struggle. So as to be delivered of their loyalties.[14]

———

Epigraph for The Stake.[15]

---

11. A paraphrase of Weil's statement in *The Need for Roots*: "Of course, when the Romans believed it necessary to dishonor Stoicism by adopting it, they replaced love with a callousness based on pride. This is where the preconception, still common today, that there's an opposition between Stoicism and Christianity comes from, even though they're two twin modes of thinking."

12. The passages Camus quotes in this entry come from Marcelle Sibon's 1948 French translation of Graham Greene's *The Confidential Agent*. The quotes are given here in the original English.

13. In the French translation, the quote is a single sentence, and the first clause begins: "For the person who didn't believe in God."

14. Two entries written in Spanish, covering half a page in the handwritten notebooks, have been crossed out after this one.

15. Throughout these pages, Camus considers a story, or section of a larger work, with the title "Le Bûcher," a term that refers to the stake used to burn people alive. In *The First Man* files, there's a folder titled The Stake, Unknown to Himself, Etc, and in one of the entries in the folder, Camus writes, in part: "Then, once again, it would have been Jessica's time, and probably her triumph, since it would have been the time for what was most secret in my heart and in my flesh, and in my incapac-

"Men afflicted with deep sadness betray themselves the moment they're happy: the way they seize on happiness, it's as if they wanted to squeeze and suffocate it out of jealousy . . ."[16]

———

July '48—Como:[17]
"What will we do with a heaven bereft of our love
We'll remain all alone before the horror of our real life."[18]

———

Play. Pride. Pride is born in the open country.

———

Provence funeral.[19]

———

Responsibility to history dispenses with responsibility to human beings. That's its convenience.[20]

———

The stars twinkle in tune with the cicadas' chirp. The world's music.

———

C.'s friend: "We die at forty from a bullet we shot into our heart at twenty."

———

ity to form some grand resolution. . . . I would have likely decided to die in the flames of regret, bound to the stake of that irreplaceable love."

The epigraph Camus quotes here comes from Nietzsche's *Beyond Good and Evil*, no. 279. The final clause, not recorded here, reads: "—ah, they know only too well that it will flee from them!"

16. An entry written in Spanish, running almost a full page in length, has been crossed out here. The following page, written in French, has also been completely crossed out.

17. It's not clear what "Como," which was originally written in the top-right corner of the notebook page, refers to here, as Camus was in Isle-sur-la-Sorgue at the time (see below). One possibility is that Camus was reading Stendhal's *The Charterhouse of Parma*, part of which takes place on Lake Como, as he references the book not long after this entry, and he was reading other works by Stendhal during this period.

18. The poem, "Sans passé" by Armand Robin, was first published in *Cahiers du Sud* 189 (December 1936), then collected in his first book of poetry, *Ma vie sans moi* (Gallimard, 1940). As was his way, Camus left out some of the punctuation in the section he cites here. Robin, a member of the Fédération Anarchiste, came to work for *Combat* at Camus's request and published his only novel, *Le temps qu'il fait*, the same year Camus published *The Stranger*.

19. From July 25 to September 10, Camus rented Le Domaine de Palerme, a bastide just outside Isle-sur-la-Sorgue, which was renovated and opened to the public in 2016. While there, Camus worked on revisions of *State of Emergency*, as well as working on his essay "Helen's Exile," the manuscript of which he gave to René Char and which bears the date August 30, 1948.

20. An entry is crossed out in the handwritten notebook after this one.

We live too long.[21]

The dialogue between the Laws and Socrates in the *Crito* could be read against the Moscow Trials.

Butterflies the color of rock.

Wind running through the valley, a sound like cool and turbulent waters.

La Sorgue adorned with flowery trains.

A madness for virtue shakes this century. Turning its back on skepticism, which is in part made of humility, humanity becomes inflexible in its search for a truth. It will loosen up as soon as society finds a mistake it can live with.

Artists want to be saints not artists. I am not a saint. We want universal approval and we're not going to get it. So, then?

Play title. The Inquisition in Cadiz. Epigraph: "The Inquisition and the Society are the two scourges of the truth." Pascal.[22]

Heartbreak of having increased injustice while believing you were serving justice. At least recognize it, and then discover that even greater heartbreak: recognizing that total justice doesn't exist. At the end of the most terrible rebellion, recognize that you're nothing. There you have true sorrow.

The luck of my life is to have only met, loved (and disappointed) exceptional people. I've known virtue, dignity, naturalness, nobility, in *other people.* An admirable experience—and painful, too.

Gobineau. We didn't descend from monkeys, but we're catching up with them as fast as can be.[23]

It's the pleasure of living that distracts, that submerges concentration, that stops any drive toward greatness. But without life's pleasures . . . No, there is

21. An entry covering a quarter of a page has been crossed out after this one.

22. *The Inquisition at Cadiz* was one of the early working titles for *State of Emergency*. The epigraph comes from Pascal's *Pensées*, no. 920.

23. Arthur de Gobineau (1816–1882), author of the book *An Essay on the Inequality of the Human Races,* one of the urtexts of "scientific" racism and the belief in an Aryan master race.

no solution. Unless the solution is to root yourself in a great love and find the source of life in it without being punished by distraction.[24]

———

September 1, 1948.

———

"I'm close to having completed the series of works I'd intended to write ten years ago. They've helped me develop a better understanding of my craft. Now that I know my hand won't shake, I'll be able to let my madness loose."[25] So said the person who knew what he was doing. After all is said and done, the stake.

———

Can a man having consciousness, Dostoyevsky writes, have the slightest respect for himself?[26]

———

D: "And what if it so happens that, sometimes, man's profit not only can but even must consist precisely in desiring a loss and not a profit?"[27]

———

"We only really live a few hours of our life . . ."[28]

———

Night on the heights of the Vaucluse. The Milky Way runs all the way down into the valley's nests of light. Everything swirls together. There are villages in the sky and constellations in the mountain.

———

You have to find love before finding morality. Otherwise, heartache.

———

There's not a single thing you do for one person (you really do) that doesn't deny another. This is a law that, when you can't resign yourself to denying people, forever sterilizes. Taken to extremes, to love one person is to kill all others.[29]

———

24. An entry after this one has been crossed out on the manuscript.

25. In *The Just*, Stepan implies that Kalyayev shouldn't be the one to throw the bomb because doing so "requires a steady hand," which for Stepan means absolute faith in the cause, something he doesn't believe Kalyayev possesses. At the end of the play, after Kalyayev has been executed for assassinating the Grand Duke, Dora asks Stepan, "Did he shake?" to which Stepan replies, "No."

26. The quote appears in *Notes from Underground*, at the end of chap. 4.

27. The quote appears in *Notes from Underground*, chap. 7.

28. On the typescript, someone has written "Goethe?" which Camus crossed out.

29. This last line opens the first complete draft of *The Rebel*.

I chose creation to escape crime. And their respect! There's a misunderstanding.

———

H.C.[30] "You have coffee in the evening?"
"Generally, no, never."
"10 doses of sulfonamides a day."
"10? Isn't that a lot?"
"It's take it or leave it."

———

André B. and his aunt, who'd given him a scarf that was too heavy and too flashy. She checks every morning to see if he's wearing it when he leaves, so he goes in his shirtsleeves to say goodbye to her, then quickly slips on his jacket and overcoat in the front hall, as he's on his way out.

———

Aunt sick.[31] Bowel cancer. "I'd built myself a nice little customer base" (she was a butcher). And all around her, everything being said is far from her abiding concern.

"The Xs would prefer to have water soup for dinner if it allowed them to show off a little. A nice handbag and no cheese. I mean, when you owe money, you don't go out and buy a radio set. The husband needs a good meal. But no, they'd rather be sick, so long as they can go to the movies."

For her part, she didn't go to the movies, and this is how she's going to die. But it won't be without recrimination.

The cousin (who watches over her at night): "The stench, Hélène, the stench! I can take care of any patient at all, so long as they don't smell."

The Aunt says, speaking of the thermometer: "Look, I've got a candy cane."

As a butcher, her nails were never clean. Little bits of meat, probably. They're still there, even after ten days in bed.

---

30. Most likely Camus's mother, Catherine-Hélène, who was referred to as Hélène within the family.

31. The editors of the original French edition of the *Notebooks* had removed this entry, which has now been restored.

On December 26, 1948, Camus flew to Algeria to see his maternal aunt Antoinette Acault, who had undergone an operation. To Maria Casarès, Camus wrote: "Spent the whole day at the clinic, with an elderly woman who didn't realize how close she was to death. . . . I'll be staying here until the next operation, in ten days or so."

Someone comes to see her, barely knows her, but because the other person has heart damage, that damage reveals an awful sort of solidarity between them.

You begin by creating in solitude and you think doing so is difficult. But then you write and create in company. Then you know the whole business is madness and that happiness was back where you started.

End of the novel.—"Man is a religious animal," he said. And over the cruel earth fell a sweeping rain.

Creation corrected: He's the only representative of that religion old as man and everywhere he's hunted.

I've tried with all my strength, knowing my weaknesses, to be a moral person. Morality kills.

Hell is a special favor reserved for those who've insistently sought it out.

A man shouldn't be judged by what he says or writes, according to Beyle.[32] I'll add: or by what he does.

Bad reputations are easier to bear than good ones, for good ones are heavy to haul around, you always have to measure up to them, and any failure to do so is held against you as a crime. With bad ones, failings are taken as part of the charm.[33]

Dinner Gide. Letters from young authors who ask if they should keep writing. Gide responds: "What's that? You can keep yourself from writing and you hesitate to do so?"

You begin by loving no one. Then you love everyone as a whole. After that, you no longer love but a few people, then a single person, and then the one.

Algiers after ten years. The faces I recognize, after some hesitation, and

32. Bayle's name is correctly spelled earlier but misspelled here.

33. In the handwritten notebook, there are two letters, initials of some sort, preceding this entry, and there is another entry after this one that has been crossed out.

which have aged. It's the soirée at the Guermantes' house.[34] But scaled up to the size of a city in which I'm lost. There's no going back to who I was. I'm part of that vast crowd restlessly marching toward the hole where all will fall, one atop the other, pushed on by a new crowd behind them, which itself . . .

From the airplane in the middle of the night, the lights of the Balearics, like flowers on the sea.

M: "They're disappointed when I seem happy. They question me, wanting to get me to admit it's fake, to pull me toward them, to bring me back to their world. They feel betrayed."

To live is to verify.

Grenier. Nonaction is acceptance of the future—but with dismay about the past. It's a philosophy of death.[35]

Talk on *Don Juan* or *The Charterhouse of Parma*. And French literature's continual demand, which is to maintain the elasticity and resistance of the individual mind.

Alexander Blok.[36]

---

34. In the final volume of Proust's *In Search of Lost Time*, the narrator, after having been away for many years, returns to Paris and attends a party held by the Prince de Guermantes, where he finds that not only has the house itself changed, but so have the people. This leads to the narrator's realization that he can now step outside time.

To Maria Casarès, Camus wrote: "It's late and I'm oddly tired, rather worn out from a whole day of coming face-to-face with memories, the neighborhood where I grew up, forgotten parents, a childhood friend with whom I just had dinner." The description in the next entry also appears in the letter to Maria.

35. On January 15, 1949, Camus wrote to his former teacher Jean Grenier to ask if he'd be interested in directing the philosophy column for *Émpedocle*, a magazine Camus and Char were then preparing to launch. Camus asked if, in addition, Grenier might be interested in writing the first column himself. As a subject, Camus suggested Lao-Tzu. In the *Tao Te Ching*, a work generally credited to Lao-Tzu, "non-action," or *wu wei*, is one of the fundamental principles. Grenier would go on to write several articles, as well as a book, on the subject.

In a footnote to *The Rebel*, Camus writes that Grenier's book shows "absolute freedom is the destruction of all values; absolute value the suppression of all freedom."

36. Alexander Blok (1880–1921), Russian poet, ardent supporter of the Russian Revolution of 1905, with which, in his later years, he would become disillusioned. In a December 1957 speech given at the University of Uppsala and later printed as "Create Dangerously," Camus mentions Blok as

"O if you knew children
The dark and cold of days to come."[37]

and again:

"How painful it is to walk among men,
Pretending to still exist."[38]

and again:

"We're all unhappy. Our homeland has prepared for us a land ready for anger and quarrels. We each live behind a Wall of China mutually despising each other. Our only real enemies are the priests, vodka, the crown, the police, hiding their faces and inciting us against each other. I'll try to forget . . . this whole quagmire so as to become a man and not a machine made to hatch hatred . . .

I love only art, children, and death."

Id. Faced with the ignorance and exhaustion of the poor:

"My blood runs cold with shame and hopelessness. All is but emptiness, wickedness, blindness, misery. Only total compassion can bring about change. . . . I react like this because my conscience is not clear. . . . I know what I have to do: give away all my money, ask everyone's forgiveness, distribute my goods, my clothes. . . . But I can't do it . . . I don't want to do it . . ."

"O my darling, my beloved riffraff!"

"What lies at the far reaches of art can't be loved" and yet: "We all die, but art remains."

Prokosch.[39] *The Seven Who Fled*. "Everyone hated him, but they all coveted his sparkling smile, and he more than suspected that all that most people

being among those great Russian artists who produced the "beautiful, tragic works of the early years of the Russian Revolution."

37. These are the last lines in Blok's "Voice from Choir." Lyudmila Purgina translates them from the original Russian as: "Oh, if you could foresee, children, / The future cold, the future dark!"

38. These are the first lines in Blok's "How Difficult to Wander in the Crowd . . ." Tatiana Tulchinsky, Andrew Wachtel, and Gwenan Wilbur translate them from the original Russian as: "How difficult to wander in the crowd / Pretending every day to be alive."

39. Frederic Prokosch (1906–1989) was an American writer and translator. His novel *The Seven Who Fled* appeared in the United States in 1937 and in a French translation by Rose Celli and Joan

long for in their heart of hearts, is the unattainable and fleeting glow of personal beauty."

"Watchers; the rocks; below them the enormous plateau and above them the stars. Nothing if not strong, and what they refused to condone in this place, so assiduously observant, was weakness; that is, impurity and frailness of spirit."

". . . those who have lost, somewhere among the ardors of childhood and youth, all power to love."

Wonderful p. 106.

". . . his mother—the only being for whom he had ever felt what might be called, maybe not love, but a certain loyalty of heart."

"High society! They talk of war and money and starvation and injustice and all the rest. But the reality is far bigger, more profound, and more terrible than those things. Do you want to know what it is? It's this. The love of death."

"I predict a great fire. . . . Everything will be consumed. Everything. Except those who are purified and made eternal by the fire of the spirit. By love."

"What sort of love?"

"By the love that destroys. Love without appeasement or end."

A short story that will take place on a day of yellow fog.

It's in rejecting a part of the world that the world becomes livable? Against Amor fati. Man is the only animal that refuses to be what it is.

"Oh, I'd certainly kill myself if I didn't know that death itself provides no rest and that a terrible anguish awaits us even in the grave."

The prosecutor enters the condemned man's cell. He's a young man, the guy in the cell. He smiles. The prosecutor asks if he wants to write. Yes, he says. And he writes "victory day!" He smiles the whole time. The prosecutor asks him if he'd like anything. Yes, the young man says. And he smacks the

---

Smith in 1948. Camus quotes from the French edition, but the original English has been restored here.

prosecutor as hard as he can. Others rush over. The prosecutor wavers. The whole of a hatred as old as the world floods back—but he remains motionless, an idea slowly rising up inside him. *There's nothing we can do to him.* The young man smiles and looks at him. No, he says joyfully, there's nothing you can do. The prosecutor back home with his wife. But, she says, what did you do? Didn't you—

"What?"

"It's true. There's nothing we can do."

Trial after trial, the prosecutor pursues the official line, and does so with hatred. With each of the defendants he faces, he waits for the accused to break. But it doesn't happen. They are united.

So then, he judges with too much hatred. He goes off course. He becomes heretical. They condemn him. Then the tide comes in: this is freedom. He goes to smack the prosecutor. Same scene. Only he doesn't smile, the face of the other man there before him. "Is there anything you'd like . . ."

He looks at the prosecutor: "No," he says. "Let's go."

The limit of rebellious reasoning: agreeing to kill yourself in order to refuse complicity with murder in general.

The duties of friendship help to bear the delights of society.

Stake. "What struck me in that 2nd period was just how unknown she'd been to me in the first, even though she'd filled and colored my life forever."[40]

Id. "I could picture her. I knew those mornings when the image of the person met the night before, and the somewhat blurred pleasures we'd found in those first outpourings, suddenly becomes clear and the somewhat hazy drunkenness of the night before becomes a solar joy, the kind belonging to the purest of conquests."

Char. Calm block fallen to earth from some dark disaster.[41]

---

40. These notes for "The Stake" reflect Camus's recent reuniting with Maria Casarès, as can be seen in their correspondence. In *The First Man*'s Jessica/Véra folder, there is another line that reads: "And in the third period, she again becomes unknown to him."

41. Stéphane Mallarmé (1842–1898) begins the last stanza of his poem "Edgar Poe's Tombstone" with the line Camus cites here. In 1875, Mallarmé translated Poe's *The Raven* into French in an edition illustrated by Édouard Manet.

I have two or three passions for which I can be judged guilty, for which I consider myself to be so, and of which I try to cure myself through an application of will. I succeed sometimes.[42]

Max Jacob:[43] "A person produces early experience through a strong memory." Cultivate your memory, set all else aside.

"Brevity and rigidity are the effects of laziness."

Don't look down on the little people, *or the bigshots* (for me).

Novel. Back from the camp. He arrives, having recovered a little, out of breath, but straight to the point. "Let me satisfy your curiosity once and for all. But after this, I'd prefer not to be questioned." A cold account follows.

Ex. {

I got out.

The words came out, hard, straightforward. There were no more nuances.

I'd like a smoke.

First puff. He turns around and smiles.

Excuse me, he says, in the same quiet, closed-up way.

Then he never speaks of it again. He lives the most ordinary life. Only one thing: he doesn't touch his wife anymore. Until the breaking point and the explanation: "Everything human horrifies me."

Schedule February–June.

1) The Rope.[44]

2) The Rebel

---

42. In the handwritten notebook, there is an entry crossed out after this one.

43. Max Jacob's letters to Jean Grenier, as well as Camus's own letters to Grenier, indicate that Camus and Jacob shared an early correspondence, one that was likely lost when Camus destroyed parts of his personal papers in 1939.

44. *La Corde* (The Noose / The Rope) was the original title for what would become *Les Justes* (*The Just*).

Finalize the 3 volumes of essays:

1) Literary essays. *Preface*—The Minotaur + Prometheus in the Underworld, + Helen's Exile + Cities of Algeria + . . .

2) Critical essays. *Preface*—Chamfort + Intelligence and the Scaffold + Agrippa d'Aubigné + Preface for The Italian Chronicles + Commentaries on *Don Juan* + Jean Grenier.

3) Political essays. *Preface* 10 editorials + Intelligence and Courage + neither victims nor executioners + Responses to d'Astier + Why Spain + The Artist and Freedom.

February 18–28: Finish Rope 1st draft

March–April: Finish Rebel. 1st draft

May: Essays

June: Revise Rope and T.R. drafts.

Get up early. Shower *before* breakfast.

No cigarettes before noon.

Strict work routine. It overcomes shortcomings.[45]

Portraits. From behind her half-veil, both her beautiful eyes look out. Understated beauty, a little bit like a farm girl. Suddenly she speaks and her mouth tightens into a parallelogram. She's ugly. A socialite.

You're having a conversation with him. He's talking. All of a sudden, he's still speaking, but his gaze is elsewhere, still on you due to the circumstances, but already wandering. Ladies' man.[46]

Last words of Karl Gebhardt, Himmler's former doctor (and he knew about Dachau):

---

45. In a February 16, 1949, letter to Janine and Michel Gallimard, Camus writes with a humor characteristic of their correspondence: "I've set myself the task of submitting to my contractual exploiter five volumes before I leave for South America. That's to say, 'The Rope,' a play in five acts, 'The Rebel,' a 250-page essay, a volume of critical essays, a volume of political essays, a volume of literary essays about the Mediterranean. So then, it's only a matter of clearing away everything else I've been dragging around for a couple of years now, and then, for a few months, writing nothing else, and getting going on my second cycle, which will lead me to universal fame. Until then, these five volumes should bring me enough money—if Gallimard's lion's share doesn't eat too much more—to allow me to live modestly. But to accomplish what I'd like to between now and June, I'll have to work my butt off, not be hassled by anyone, and apply a considerable pressure to my natural nonchalance."

46. In *The Fall*, Clamence will assume the role of the "ladies' man" who loses the thread of the conversation when an attractive woman walks past.

"I regret that there's still injustice in the world."

Giving yourself only means something if you have mastered yourself.—Otherwise, you're giving yourself to escape your own misery. You can only give what you have. Be your own master before laying down your arms.

Amélie: "That was the year I had peritonitis.

It was just after I had a perforated . . ." etc., etc. Visceral calendar.

Trial—When you think of a big heart's irreplaceable experience, of the sum of knowledge such experience supposes, of the many great battles fought and won against itself and the heavens' hardness, and that, nevertheless, all it takes is three court lackeys . . .

In a world that no longer believes in sin, it's the artist who's responsible for preaching. But if the priest's words once carried weight, it's because they were inspired by example. So then, the artist tries to be an example. That's why, to his great indignation, he's shot or deported. And anyway, virtue isn't learned as quickly as the handling of a machine gun. The battle is unequal.

After Alexander II's assassination, the Executive Committee addressed Alexander III:

". . . Better than anyone else, we understand how sad is the loss of so much talent, of so much energy in the work of destruction . . ."

". . . A peaceful struggle of ideas will come to replace the violence that is more repugnant to us than it is to your minions and that we practice only by virtue of a sad necessity."[47]

---

47. The quotes are drawn from "Letter of the Revolutionary Committee to Alexander III," the full text of which appears in Robinson and Beard's *Readings in Modern European History*. There, the passage Camus cites reads: "A dispassionate glance at the grievous decade through which we have just passed will enable us to forecast accurately the future progress of the revolutionary movement, provided the policy of the government does not change. The movement will continue to grow and extend; deeds of a terroristic nature will increase in frequency and intensity. Meanwhile the number of the discontented in the country will grow larger and larger; confidence in the government, on the part of the people, will decline; and the idea of revolution—of its possibility, and inevitability—will establish itself in Russia more and more firmly. A terrible explosion, a bloody chaos, a revolutionary earthquake throughout Russia, will complete the destruction of the old order of things. Do not mistake this for a mere phrase. We understand better than anyone else can how lamentable is the waste of so much talent and energy—the loss, in bloody skirmishes and in the work of destruction, of so

—See Rysakov's curious deposition, ready to serve as an informant to save his own life. But he *rationalizes* doing so (p. 137 of *Les Procès célèbres de la Russie*).[48]

Lieutenant Schmidt.[49] "My death will finalize everything and, crowned with torture, my cause will be blameless and perfect."

G.[50] That mouth scraped clean by the dirty erosion of pleasure.

Rebellion. Chapter on appearances (to oneself and to others). Dandyism, driving force of so many actions, even revolutionary ones.

As long as man hasn't dominated desire, he's hasn't dominated anything. And he almost never dominates desire.

Vinaver.[51] Ultimately, the writer is responsible for what he contributes to society. But he has to accept (and this is where he has to show great modesty, to ask very little) that he can't know his responsibility ahead of time, that he will be unaware, *for as long as he writes,* of the terms of his commitment—has to accept taking a risk.

Essay. Introduction. If we're neither Christians nor Marxists, why reject denunciations, police, etc. We have no system of values for doing so. Until we've found a basis for these values, we're condemned to choose the good

much strength which, under other conditions, might have been expended in creative labor and in the development of the intelligence, the welfare, and the civil life of the Russian people."

48. Camus gives the source reference as Soukhomline's *Les procès célèbres de la Russie* (*Famous Russian Trials*), but the details Camus notes in the entry appears on page 137 of Maurice Laporte's *L'histoire de l'Okhrana*, another text Camus was reading as background for *The Just*.

49. Pyotr Schmidt (1867–1906), who took a lead role in the Sevastopol Mutiny during the 1905 Russian Revolution, was executed by firing squad. Boris Pasternak wrote a long poem about him titled "Lieutenant Schmidt."

50. J.G. in the handwritten notebook.

51. Michel Vinaver (1927–2022), novelist and playwright, joined the Free French Army in 1944. He and Camus met while Vinaver was a student at Wesleyan University and Camus was on his North American speaking tour. The two exchanged letters for many years afterward, and Camus helped him get his first novel, *Lataume*, published.

(when we choose it) in a way that's unjustifiable. Until that day arrives, virtue will always be illegitimate.

———

1st Cycle. From my first books (*Nuptials*) up through *The Rope* and *The Rebel*, all my effort has in fact gone toward depersonalization (each time, in a different tone). After this, I'll be able to speak in my own name.

———

I'm interested in great souls—and only them. But I'm not a great soul.

———

Preface for collected articles.[52] "One of my regrets is having sacrificed too much to objectivity. Sometimes, objectivity is complacency. Today, things are clear, and a person has to call a concentration camp a concentration camp, even with socialism. In a sense, I'll never again be so polite."

I've striven for objectivity, contrary to my nature, because I didn't trust freedom.

———

Zhelyabov,[53] who organized the assassination of Alexander II, arrested 48 hours before the events unfolded, asked to be executed at the same time as Rysakov, who threw the bomb.

"Only the government's cowardice could explain erecting one gallows instead of two."

———

Zybine, the Okhrana's unbeatable decoder, is kept in his post by the S.P.D. *Id.* Kommissarov, organizer of pogroms on behalf of the Okhrana, goes to the Cheka. "Go underground" (illegality).

"The terrorist attacks must be carefully organized. The Party will assume moral responsibility. That will provide the struggle's heroes the necessary peace of mind."

Azef—grave number 10 466 in a cemetery in the suburbs of Berlin.[54]

A few days before Plehve[55] was attacked, he gave a "general" warning to Lopukhin, of the Okhrana, and asked for a raise. He denounced the South-

52. This entry, intended as part of a preface for *Actuelles I*, was not used.

53. Andrei Ivanovich Zhelyabov (1851–1881) was a member of the Executive Committee of People's Will.

54. Yevno Fishelevich Azef (1869–1918), a double agent who served both the Russian Secret Police and the Socialist Revolutionary Party. He's buried in an unmarked grave in Wilmersdorf, Germany.

55. Vyacheslav von Plehve (1846–1904), reactionary Russian minister of the interior, was assassinated in large part thanks to Azef's efforts.

ern terrorists so that those in Petersburg would have a free hand. Plehve is killed; what Azef had said: "It's not from this side (Gershuni)[56] that you have something to fear."

———

Director Zubatov.[57] Pleaded on behalf of the accused before a fake investigative body. And turned him into an informant.

9 times out of 10 the revolutionary took passionately to the job of being an informant.

———

The 1905 revolution began with a strike at a Moscow printing press where the workers had asked that periods and commas be counted as characters in "by the word" calculations.

In 1905, the Saint Petersburg Soviet called for a strike with cries of *Down with the death penalty.*

———

During the Moscow Commune, a plate with a piece of human flesh on it is displayed in Trubnaya Square, in front of a building destroyed by cannons, with a sign that says: "Give your obols for the victims."[58]

———

Provocation. The Malinovsky case, cf. Laporte, pp. 175–176.

———

Interview. Burtsev—Azef, in Frankfurt—after the sentencing. Cf. p. 221, Laporte.

———

Dmitry Bogrov, Stolypin's assassin, was granted the privilege of being hanged in a tailcoat.

———

Finish June 1st. Then travels. Diary.[59] Life force. Never get bogged down.

———

An essay on alibi.

---

56. Grigory Gershuni (1870–1908), founding member of the Socialist Revolutionary Party.

57. Sergei Zubatov (1864–1917), head of the Moscow Okhrana, advocated a sort of trade-union-based "police socialism" for which Plehve fired him and banned him from living in St. Petersburg.

58. The obol (or obolus) was the Ancient Greek coin paid to the ferryman, Charon, for safe passage to the underworld across the rivers Styx and Acheron.

59. With rare exception, Camus referred to these writings as his *cahiers* (notebooks), not *carnets* (journals) and not *journaux intimes* (diaries), the latter being the term he uses here, thus distinguishing ahead of time that the notes he will keep on the upcoming trip to South America will be of a more personal nature.

The entire history of Russian terrorism can be seen as a struggle between intellectuals and absolutism, carried out before a silent population.

Novel. Amid the camp's endless misery, an instant of indescribable happiness.

In short, the Gospel is realistic, even though people believe it impossible to practice. It knows man can't be pure. But he can make the effort to recognize his impurity, which is to say, to forgive. Criminals are always judges . . . Only those who are absolutely innocent can condemn absolutely . . . That's why God has to be absolutely innocent.

To put a person to death is to take away his chance to grow and develop.[60]

How to live without a few good reasons for hopelessness!

Preface.—To call yourself a revolutionary while also rejecting the death penalty (quote Tolstoy preface—that preface I'm old enough to read with veneration isn't well enough known), the limitation of freedoms, and wars, is meaningless. So then, you have to declare you're not a revolutionary—rather, more modestly, a reformist. An uncompromising reformism. In the end, *all things considered,* you can say you're rebellious.[61]

(You're going to lose your credibility, I'm told.
"I hope so, if it's built on such shaky ground.")

---

60. This could be read more literally as: "To put a person to death is to suppress his chance at perfection."

61. This passage shows up not in the preface to *Actuelles* but in an interview included toward the end of the collection, labeled "III," where Camus says: "Of course, to call yourself revolutionary while also rejecting the death penalty, the limitation of freedoms, and wars, is meaningless. So then, we can only say, provisionally, that to call yourself revolutionary while extolling the death penalty, the suppression of freedoms, and war means only that you're reactionary, in the most objective, least comforting sense of the word. And it's because contemporary revolutionaries have accepted this language that we are today living a universally reactionary history. For a still unknown span of time, history is made by the powers of police and money against the people's interest and against man's truth."

Tchaikovsky had a habit of absentmindedly eating his papers (even very important ones, at the Ministry of Justice, for example).

"Such a violent desire to create rose up in him that only his immensely powerful work ethic could satisfy it" (N. Berberova).[62]

"If that emotion of the artist we call inspiration were never interrupted, we wouldn't be able to live" (Tchaikovsky).

"In moments of idleness, the anxiety of never being able to attain perfection takes over me, the dissatisfaction, the hatred of myself, the thought that I'm good for nothing, that it's only my great ability to keep at it that mitigates my faults and elevates me to the rank of man, in the deepest sense of the word, it harasses me, torments me. It's work that saves me" (Tchaikovsky).

And yet his music, more often than not, is mediocre.

Recruitment. Most failed writers become Communists. It's the only position that lets them judge artists from on high. From this point of view, it's the party of thwarted callings. A lot of recruitment, you'd suspect.

MAY '49. And now: give up "the human," as they say.

I gave myself subjects as so many pretexts to force myself to speak.

Preface book political essays. From this point of view, the last essay expresses rather well what I think, namely that modern man is forced to take up politics. I take it up reluctantly and because I've never, as a result of my defects more than my qualities, been able to refuse the obligations I've encountered.

We can't believe in generosity, morality, and selflessness, on account of psychology, but we can't believe in evil, etc., on account of history.

Novel. The stone lovers. And now he knew what he'd suffered throughout the whole of that love, what could only have been resolved if . . . at that precise moment . . . a wind come from the heavens had petrified them in the very rush of their love and they were from then on forever fixed face-to-face, finally wrenched from this cruel earth, unaware of the desires furiously swirl-

62. It seems Camus was reading Nina Berberova's *Tchaïkovsky, histoire d'une vie solitaire*, published in French in 1948.

ing around them, turned one toward the other as toward the resplendent face of a love made whole.[63]

We don't say a quarter of what we know. Otherwise, everything would founder. The little we do say, and just listen to them howl.

When once we've seen that radiant happiness on the face of someone we love, we know a man can have no other calling than to kindle that light in the faces that surround him . . . and we're torn up by the thought of the unhappiness and gloom we cast, simply by living, into the hearts of those we meet.

When the barbarians from the North had destroyed the fair kingdom of Provence and made us into Frenchmen . . . [64]

In "Esprit," Mounier[65] advises me to turn away from politics, not having a head for it (that much, in fact, is obvious), and to content myself with the rather more noble role, such a lovely fit for me, of harbinger. But what is a head for politics? Reading *Esprit* doesn't help me understand that. As for the "noble" role of harbinger, it would require a spotless conscience. And the only calling I feel is to telling consciences they're not spotless and telling reasons they're missing something.

See South American Journal.
June to August 1949.

---

63. After this entry, Camus has written "July 49" in large print, with an arrow pointing to the recto page, where there is one entry written at the top, which wasn't carried over to the published edition, and then the "See South American" entry, as printed below.

64. In the handwritten notebook, this entry and the one that follows it actually come after the "See South American Journal" note. They are the only two entries on the page.

65. Emmanuel Mounier (1905–1950) was founder and editor of the magazine *Esprit*, which served as a mouthpiece for his "personalist" movement. While critical of certain elements of Stalinism, such as the Moscow Trials, he let other elements pass in silence. Less than a year after this entry was made, in March 1950, Mounier would die at age 44, even younger than Camus.

Travels in South America

JUNE–AUGUST 1949

June 30.

At sea.[1] Exhausting day. R.[2] and I drive as fast as possible to make it to Marseille on time. Desdemona gets the job done.[3] In Marseille, scorching heat and a wind strong enough to carve your face. Even nature is an enemy. Single room. I walk through the corridors and decks while waiting for departure. Feeling of shame on seeing the passengers in 4th class, housed in steerage, in berths stacked on top of each other, like in a concentration camp. Dirty diapers hung out to dry. Children are going to live in this hell for 20 days, and I . . . The boat weighs anchor two hours late. Dinner. At my table, G., a history of philosophy professor at the Sorbonne—a short young man who's going to see his family in Argentina—and Mme C., who's going to see her husband. She's from Marseille, a long, brunette girl. She says whatever

---

1. When Camus traveled to North America in 1946, he didn't separate the entries he made during the trip from the entries he'd been keeping back home. That trip to North America appears in "Notebook V" with no page breaks or discontinuities. But when he traveled to South America only three years later, in 1949, he did precisely the opposite, using a separate notebook to record his observations, giving the notebook a title—*Travels in South America*—and making a notation in his regular journal, as seen above, to indicate the discontinuity.

One possibility for why he chose to use a separate notebook for the trip to South America but not the one to North America can be found in his letters to Maria Casarès. On June 6, 1948, she and Camus ran into each other on Boulevard Saint-Germain, completely by chance, and rekindled the affair they'd begun exactly four years earlier, June 6, 1944. By the time Camus was getting ready to leave for South America, he and Maria had only been back together for less than a year, and Camus was terrified of what might happen to their relationship while he was away. The two of them agreed—though it's not clear whose idea it was—that they would exchange journals when he returned from South America, so that they could each see how the other had spent their days. Perhaps it is with this in mind that Camus decided to keep a separate journal.

2. Robert Jaussaud was an old friend of Camus's from his days in Algeria. They met in one of Jean Grenier's philosophy classes and worked together on the Théâtre du Travail and the Théâtre de l'Équipe. Jaussaud was an early influence on Camus's political thought, discussing with him issues such as income inequality and the variety of difficulties faced by Algeria's Arab population.

Jaussaud and Camus were having lunch together on September 3, 1939, the day France officially declared war on Germany, and the two friends got into a heated argument over the news. Despite the fact that Camus had tried to enlist—in solidarity with those who had no choice, he said—he believed France was entering the war for the wrong reasons. Jaussaud, on the other hand, believed the war to be an antifascist conflict and thus justified. For a long time after, they refused to speak to each other but eventually reconciled and again became the close friends they'd been before. When Camus died, it was Jaussaud, along with Camus's brother, Lucien, and wife, Francine, who picked out Camus's tombstone.

3. On June 23, 1949, Camus and Jaussaud set out in Camus's car (a black Citroën 11 CV that he'd named Desdemona) for Isle-sur-la-Sorgue in the South of France, where he'd planned to spend a couple of days with his wife and kids at Palerme, a rustic and isolated country home he'd first rented the summer before, while working on *State of Emergency*. The *Campana* didn't set sail for South America until the 30th, though here Camus has placed the trip down from Paris and the departure side by side, as if they happened on the same day.

pops in her head—and sometimes it's entertaining. Other times . . . In any case, she's alive. The others are dead—and so am I, after all. After dinner, G., who's made some allusions to having experienced the plague, introduces me to a Brazilian professor and his wife as "the author of *The Plague*." I must look *really* good! In the "music hall" (where half the emigrants currently in 4th class could be comfortably housed), G. plays us some trivial little snippets on the ship's piano, which seems to have blown all its gaskets. Conversation follows. The Brazilian professor praises Salazar. Mme C. makes two huge blunders in trying to convince the Brazilians that a revolution's happening every day in South America. I hear, "She's low class, the lowest of the low," and other such pearls. I say goodbye and go on my way. In the rear of the boat, where I go to take refuge, some emigrants are drinking wine from a wineskin and singing. I stay with them, unknown and happy (for ten seconds). Then I go gaze out at the sea. A crescent moon rises above the masts. As far as the eye can see, in a still-clear night, the sea—and a feeling of calm, a powerful melancholy, rises from the waters then. I've always been able to make peace with things out at sea, and for a moment the infinite solitude does me good, though I can't help but feel all the world's tears are rolling atop the sea now. I return to my cabin to write this—as I'd like to do every evening, without getting into personal details, but forgetting none of the day's events.[4] With an anxious heart, my thoughts turn back to what I've left behind, and yet, still, I'd like to get some sleep.[5]

---

4. In a letter to Maria Casarès, Camus elaborated: "In the evening, I summarize the day in my notebook. Summarize what, though? As a journal is only a journal of events, and as there are no events, it'll seem to you a rather poor one."

In the first part of the sentence, as in most other places, Camus refers to his notebooks as *cahiers*, not *carnets*, while in the second part, in saying what his notebooks are not, he uses the term *journal*. For Camus, there is a clear distinction between these terms. His *cahiers* are a place to take notes, as one would take notes in school—and the physical objects he used were quite literally the kind issued to grade-school children—whereas a *journal* or *carnet* would be more for recording daily events. For an American reader, a *cahier* might best be thought of as a sort of "marble" or "spiral" notebook, and a *journal* or *carnet* as more of a daily log, though not one of a highly personal nature, such as a *journal intime* (diary).

5. On the car trip down, Jaussaud thought Camus looked lower than he'd ever seen him before. Camus said that he felt as if an evil spell had been cast on him and said that he shouldn't have agreed to the trip. The thought of leaving Maria Casarès alone for the summer filled Camus with dread. He feared that, without his physical presence, she would move on with her life and leave him behind. In the less than a week he spent at Palerme, with his wife and kids around him, before even leaving for South America, Camus wrote Casarès two full letters, one follow-up letter, and a telegram. In his first letter, he writes: "Love me, love me against the whole world, against you and against me—that's the way I love you. I thirst for you so! And for the moment, this love is but burning and passion. . . . I'm kissing you, I'm kissing you, my love, as I begin the wait for you, with anguish, with ardor—with

July 1

Waking with a fever, I stay in bed, dreaming and dozing for part of the morning. At 11:00, I feel better and go out. G. on deck. We talk philosophy. He wants to do a philosophy of the history of philosophy. He's quite right. But, according to him, he's young at heart and likes to live. Right again. Lunch with my three musketeers. Mme C. makes another blunder, asking G. if he's a middle-school teacher, when really he teaches at the Sorbonne. But she doesn't realize her mistake. I note the way men act with her. They think she's flighty because she's cheery. A mistake, of course. In the afternoon, I read an account of the Brazilian revolutions—Europe's got nothing on them. At five o'clock, I go work in the sun. The sun beats down on the sea, which is barely able to breathe, and the boat is weighed down with silent people from fore to aft. Unlike the people, the ship's record player screams its tunes out in every direction. I'm introduced to a young Romanian who's leaving England to go live in Argentina. A passionate woman—neither beautiful nor ugly, with a hint of a mustache. Then I go to my cabin to read, then get dressed again for dinner. Sad. I drink some wine. After dinner, conversation, but I'm gazing out at sea, trying once again to fix that image I've been seeking for twenty years, the patterns and drawings etched on the sea by waters cast aside by the bow. When I find it, it'll all be over.

Twice, the thought of suicide. The second time, still gazing at the sea, a frightful burning rises in my temples. Now I think I understand *how* a person kills himself.[6] Return to the conversation—jaw-dropping. After having made

---

my whole entire being." His second letter begins: "Two days closer to being cut off in a way I can't even imagine. Two difficult days cut from wretched nights filled with wicked images. I'm suffocating. Literally. . . . At certain moments, I'm consumed with desire, but a desire that doesn't end only at surface enjoyments, that goes deeper, deeper down toward that which is most secret and greatest in you, that for which I perpetually thirst."

6. Camus kept with him a copy of Adolf Abramovich Joffe's suicide letter, dated November 16, 1927, and addressed to Leon Trotsky. In the wake of Vladimir Lenin's illness and eventual death, Joffe, Trotsky, and other old guard Bolsheviks came together as the Left Opposition, which fought against Stalinist policies. Little by little, the group began to compromise and capitulate to Stalin and his supporters, eventually expelling Trotsky from the Party. Joffe refused to abandon his values and beliefs. "All my life," he wrote in the letter, "I've believed that a man of politics should know when it's time to go." The only meaning he'd found in life, he said, was working and struggling for the good of his fellow humans, but by that point Joffe was gravely ill, and in order to keep fighting, he needed medical care outside of Russia—a request that, as political payback, was denied. "So now," he wrote, "it seems the time has come where my life has lost its meaning and, as a consequence, it appears I have an obligation to leave it, to put it to an end." Joffe assured Trotsky that his political positions were sound but

some decisions about work, I climb, in the dark, to the upper deck and finish my day out in front of the sea, the moon, and stars.—The surface of the water is barely illuminated, but you can feel the depths of its darkness. That's how the sea is, and that's why I love it! The call of life and an invitation to death.

———

July 2

Monotony has set in. A little work in the morning. Sun on the upper deck. Before lunch, I end up being introduced to all the passengers. We're not spoiled with pretty women, but I say that without bitterness. All afternoon in view of Gibraltar, the sea suddenly calmed by that enormous rock of sloping cement, its face hostile and abstract. These are the trappings of power. Then Tangiers, with its comfortable white houses. At six o'clock, as the day comes to an end, the sea rises a little, and the ship's speakers boom the *Eroica*[7] as we pull away from the high, forbidding banks of Spain and leave Europe for good. My eyes never leave that land, my heart heavy.

After dinner, a movie. A high-octane American dud, of which I can only swallow the first few images. I go back to the sea.

———

July 3

The days all blend together. This morning, a dip in the pool (the water comes up to my stomach) and some ping-pong to finally stretch the muscles. This afternoon, horse racing (dice game) with my usual bad luck. We're on the Atlantic, and the boat's rolling a lot due to some large swells. Tried to work, but without much success. In the end, I read de Vigny's Journal,[8] a lot of which is delightful, except that part of him that's like a constipated swan.[9] To all of that I prefer this clean and narrow cabin, this hard berth, and this destitution. Either this solitude without the superfluous or the storm of love, no, nothing else in the world interests me. Have I forgotten anything? I don't

lightly chastised him for being too willing to negotiate and compromise on them. The reason Lenin had been so successful, Joffe said, was that he never compromised, that he was completely and totally intransigent when it came to his beliefs.

7. Beethoven's *Symphony No. 3*, also known in Italian as *Sinfonia Eroica* (*Heroic Symphony*).

8. Alfred de Vigny (1797–1863), French poet, novelist, dramatist, and translator. The work referenced here is his *Journal d'un poète* (A poet's journal).

9. Alfred de Musset (1810–1857) may be responsible for this image. In 1834, de Musset drew a caricature of de Vigny as "an old, constipated swan about to birth a proverb after a painstaking effort."

think so. I finish the day, as usual, in front of the sea, sumptuous this evening, beneath a moon that writes Arabic characters in phosphorescent lines atop the slow-moving swells. The sky and water are never-ending. What good company sadness finds there!

July 4

Same sort of day. Aggravated by lethargy—as if the endless series of insomnia-filled nights has suddenly come calling. I lie down several times during the day and drift off each time even though I had a pretty good night. Other than that, work, pool, sun (at 2 o'clock, since the rest of the time it's like a frog pond), and de Vigny. A lot of what's written speaks to my current state of mind. This, again: "If suicide is permissible, it's in one of those situations where a man is too much in his family's way and where his death would bring peace to all those whom his life troubles." I should say, however, that tanned, rested, with a full stomach, and dressed in light-colored clothes, I have all the air of life in me. I could please someone, it seems—but whom?

Facing the sea, before going to bed. This time the moon illuminates an entire corridor of sea that, with the ship's movement, seems, on the dark ocean, like a full and milky river flowing tirelessly toward us.[10] I'd already tried, during the day, to make some notes about the sea, which I'll return to now:

Morning sea: Enormous fishpond—heavy and wriggling—scaly—sticky—covered in fresh slime.[11]

---

10. Like several of the entries Camus made on the trip to South America, this one would go on to be incorporated into his essay "The Nearby Sea," in which he writes: "Finally at its zenith, it illuminates an entire corridor of sea, a rich river of milk that, with the movement of the ship, flows down toward us, tirelessly, overtop the dark Ocean."

In both the journal entry above and this passage from the finished essay, the syntax of the two French sentences has been strictly maintained in order to give the reader a glimpse of how Camus went about editing and polishing his writing.

11. In "The Nearby Sea," the passage reads: "So, all morning long, our sails clap above a joyous fishpond. The waters are heavy, scaly, covered in fresh drool."

Afternoon sea: pale—a wide, white-hot sheet of metal—sizzling, too—it'll flip over to offer its wet face, now in the shadows, to the sun . . . etc.[12]

Goodnight.

July 5

Morning swim, then sun, then to work. At noon, we pass the Tropic of Cancer, beneath a vertical sun that kills all shadows. Still, it's not overly hot. The sky is filled with a bad fog, though, and the sun looks like a sickness. The sea looks like a great swell, with the metallic radiance of decomposition. In the afternoon, the big event: we pass an ocean liner traveling the same route as us. The salute the two boats give each other—three great cries from some prehistoric animal—the waving of passengers lost at sea, awakened by the presence of other people, and the final separation of those green, malevolent waters—all of this is a little heartrending. Afterward, I stay facing the water for a long time, full of a strange and good exhilaration. After dinner, I head to the fore. The emigrants are playing accordion and dancing in the night, and already the heat seems to be rising.

July 6

The day dawns on a steel sea, choppy and covered in blinding scales. The sky is white with fog and heat, with a dull but unbearable brightness, as if the sun had liquefied and spread through the thick layers of cloud, over the entire expanse of the heavenly crown. As the day progresses, the heat climbs in the pallid air. All through the day, the bow flushes clouds of flying fish from their wavy bushes. At 7 P.M., the coast comes into view, gray and leprous. At night, we disembark in Dakar. Two or three cafés violently lit with neon, tall Black men admirable in dignity and elegance in their long white boubous, Black women in traditional, brightly colored dresses, the scent of peanuts and dung, dust and heat. Only a couple of hours, but enough to pick up the scent of my Africa, the scent of poverty and dereliction, a virgin yet strong

---

12. In "The Nearby Sea," the passage reads: "An hour of cooking and the water pales, a large piece of sheet metal worn white and sizzling. It sizzles, smokes, and finally burns. In a moment, it will turn to offer its wet face to the sun, now that it's in the waves and shadows."

scent whose seduction I know. When I return to the boat, a letter.[13] For the first time, I go to bed somewhat calmed.

July 7

Night of insomnia. Heat. Pool and then I go to stretch out in my cabin. I finish Vigny. After lunch, I try to sleep, in vain. I work until 6 P.M., with good results. Then I'm out on the promenade deck with this strange character I've been seeing since we first set out. Always dressed, even at the Tropic, in a suit of gray-black wool, stiff collar, traveling cap, black footwear, 60 years old. Short, thin, the look of a headstrong rat. Alone at a table, his deckchair always in the same place on the promenade deck, he reads nothing but *Les Nouvelles littéraires,* of which he seems to have an inexhaustible supply and which he reads from the first line to the last. He smokes cigar after cigar and doesn't talk to anyone. The only conversation I've heard him engage in was to ask a sailor if porpoises are fat or thin. He also sometimes has a drink (pastis) with a young Swiss-German man who doesn't speak French. He himself doesn't speak German. It makes for a conversation of deaf-mutes. This evening, following him four laps around the promenade deck, I noticed he didn't look at the sea a single time. Nobody onboard knows what he does for a living.

Before dinner, I watch the sun set. It's absorbed by the fog long before it reaches the horizon. At that moment, the sea is pink on the port side, blue on the starboard. We set out over a boundless expanse. There'll be no land until Rio. The evening hour grows suddenly wonderful. The water thickens, tarnishes a little. The sky stretches itself thin. At this hour of such great peacefulness, hundreds of porpoises rise from the water, prance and turnabout for a moment, and then flee toward a horizon without man. When they've left, the silence and anguish of primitive seas. After dinner, I return to the front of the boat, facing the sea. It's sumptuous, heavy, and embroidered. The wind whips

---

13. Maria Casarès's June 30 letter in which she writes: "My love! What are you afraid of? Your letters are so filled with pain, so feverish and overflowing with anguish. . . . Sit still, and there, in the middle of that immense sea that surrounds you—my sea—listen. I love that ocean too much for it to betray me, for it to remain deaf to my cry, and if you'll only clear away all those thoughts that I've, by some misfortune, provoked in you, if you'll cast off all those horrible visions with which I've peopled your imagination, if you'll only shut your ears to all those dreadful things I've said, if, finally, naked, you turn yourself toward those waters where I live, you'll hear me cry my love out to you as I've never cried it out in front of you, beside you. Stop tormenting yourself, my darling. I know all too well the hell where such awful images lead to be able to bear the thought that you might be living through it."

my face with brutal force, coming at me head-on, having crossed stretches of space whose immensity I can't even imagine. I feel alone and a little lost, but ultimately enraptured, feeling my strength reborn little by little before this unknown future, this greatness that I love.

———

July 8

Night of insomnia. The whole day, I walk around with a hollow head and an empty heart. The sea is rough. The sky overcast. The decks are deserted. In fact, since Dakar, there are only about twenty passengers left. Too tired to describe the sea today.

———

July 9

Better night. In the morning, I walk on the large, empty decks. The trade winds we're encountering now have cooled things off. A clipped, heavy wind vigorously brushes the sea, which rolls back in small, foamless waves.

A little work, a lot of dawdling. I realize I haven't been writing down conversations with other passengers. Some of them are interesting, like the one with the publisher Delamain and his wife.[14] Read a charming novel by him about fidelity. I'll come back to it. Also because my current interest isn't really in people but in the sea and this profound sadness in me that I'm not used to.

At 6 P.M., at sunset, recordings of the great works are played, as they are every evening. Suddenly, Toccata,[15] just as the sun disappears behind the clouds accumulated along the horizon line. In this operatic sky, immense streaks of red gather with black stuffed animals, with fragile structures that seem to be made of wire and feathers, in a vast arrangement of red, green, and black—covering the entire sky, evolving with the oft-changing light, in step with the most majestic choreography. *Toccata,* over this sleeping sea, under this royal sky's celebrations . . . the moment is unforgettable. So much so that the whole ship goes silent, the passengers pressed onto the decks, along the western edge, brought back to silence and what is truest in them, lifted for an instant from the misery of days and the pain of being.

———

14. Maurice Delamain (1883–1974) took over Éditions Stock in 1921, along with Jacques Chardonne. In 1945, he wrote *La double ascension: Une aventure de la fidélité* (Double ascension: An adventure in fidelity).

15. Most likely J. S. Bach's famous *Toccata and Fugue in D Minor, BWV 565.*

July 10

We cross the equator in the morning, the weather as in the Seine-et-Oise[16]—brisk, a little cutting, the sky filled with sheep, the sea a little prickly. The ceremony in honor of crossing the equator having been canceled, for lack of passengers, we replace those rites with some games in the pool. Then, a moment with the emigrants playing the accordion and singing at the front of the ship, facing toward the deserted sea. I again notice a woman with them, already graying but high class, a beautiful face, proud and gentle, hands and wrists like stems, and a look like no other. Always followed by her husband, a tall, taciturn blond man. Information gleaned: she's fleeing Poland and the Russians and is taking exile in South America. She's poor. But, looking at her, I think of those well-dressed maritornes[17] occupying a couple of the first-class cabins. I haven't dared speak to her yet.

A calm day. Aside from the grand champagne dinner in celebration of our having crossed the equator. Social gatherings of more than four people are hard for me to bear. A story from Mme C: Her grandmother: "Oh, me? Well, in my life, you see, I've only skimmed the surface of things." Her grandfather: "Go on, my love, don't forget you've given me two sons!"

After dinner, the passengers are treated to some Laurel and Hardy, but I run off to the bow to contemplate the moon and the Southern Cross toward which we're endlessly sailing. Surprised by how few stars there are in this southern sky and how practically anemic they look. I think of our swarming Algerian nights.

Remained in front of the sea for a long time. Despite all my efforts and reasoning, impossible to shake this sadness that I no longer even understand.

July 11

The day dawns, in the middle of the Intertropical Convergence Zone,[18] beneath a battering rain. Buckets of water wash over the decks, but the temperature remains stifling and dead. In the middle of the day, the sky clears,

---

16. From 1790 through 1968, the Seine-et-Oise was a *département* (administrative division) of France covering, roughly, the western half of Paris, with Versailles as its *préfecture* (capital).

17. The term originates with Maritornes, a character in *Don Quixote*. In chap. 16, Maritornes, a hunchbacked, half-blind servant at an inn where Quixote and Sancho are staying, is, in the dark of night, confused with the innkeeper's beautiful daughter and thus welcomed into Don Quixote's bed.

18. The Intertropical Convergence Zone is more commonly referred to as "the doldrums," in reference to the lack of wind.

but the sea is rough, and the ship pitches and rolls. Some defections from the dining room. Worked. Poorly. Toward the evening, little by little, the sky again fills with clouds, growing more overcast by the minute. Night falls fast over a sea of black ink.

July 12

Rain, wind, furious sea. People are sick. The ship sails forward, surrounded by a sea-spray smoke. Slept and worked. Toward the end of the afternoon, the sun makes its appearance. We're already at the latitude of Pernambuco[19] and are heading toward the coast. In the evening, the sky again grows overcast. Dramatic clouds come to greet us from the continent—messengers from a frightening land. That's the thought that suddenly comes to me and reawakens the absurd premonition I had before the trip. But the sun will dispel all of that.

July 13

A radiant sun endlessly floods the surface of the sea. The whole boat is bathed in a dazzling light. Pool, sun. I work all afternoon. The evening is cool and gentle. We arrive in two days. All of a sudden, the thought of leaving the boat, this narrow cabin where, during these long days, I've been able to shelter a heart turned away from everything, the thought of leaving this sea that's helped me so much, it frightens me a little. Beginning to live again, to speak. People, faces, a role to play, it'll require more courage than I feel. Fortunately, I'm in good shape, physically. But there are times when I'd like to avoid the human face.

Late at night, on a boat fast asleep, I gaze out at the night. The curious southern moon, pressed flat at the top, illuminates the waters to the south. You can imagine those thousands of kilometers, those solitudes where the thick, shiny waters are like an oily glebe. That, at least, would be peace.

July 14

Perpetual good weather. I finish up my work, or at least the work I've been able to carry out on the boat, having given up on the rest. In the afternoon, a few hundred meters out in the water, an enormous black beast rises to the

19. Pernambuco, a state in Northeast Brazil, is just south of the Equator.

surface, rolls atop a couple of waves, and sprays two jets of mist into the air. The busboy next to me claims it's a whale. Probably, given the size, the awesome force of its stroke, the solitary air surrounding the beast . . . but I remain skeptical. In the afternoon, mail and suitcases. In the evening, the captain's reception and the 14th of July dinner.[20] For the first time, sunset without fog. Brazil's first foothills, black and silhouetted, surround the sun, right and left. We dance, sign menus, exchange cards, and we all promise to see each other again, we give our word. Tomorrow, everyone will have forgotten everyone else. I go to bed late, tired and telling myself to approach this country in a more relaxed state of mind.

July 15

At four in the morning, a commotion on the upper deck wakes me. I leave my cabin. It's still dark out. The coast is very close, though: a continuous line of rolling black hills, sharply silhouetted, yet the silhouettes are rounded, too—the aged edges of one of the oldest lands on Earth. In the distance, some lights. We follow along the coast as the night begins to lift, the water barely rippling, and we tack, the lights in front of us now, but still far away. I return to my cabin. When I go up again, we're already in the bay, immense and steaming as the day breaks, the light suddenly condensing into islands. The fog quickly dissipates. We can see the lights of Rio running along the coast, the "Sugarloaf," four lights on its summit and, on the highest of the mountain's summits, which seems to lord over the city, an immense and regrettable Christ stands illuminated. As the day breaks, we can see the city better, huddled between the sea and mountains, stretched out lengthwise, spreading out endlessly. In the center, huge buildings. Every other minute, a rumbling sounds above us: an airplane taking off in the dawning day, blending in with the land at first, then rising up in our direction and passing over our heads with a great clamor of elytra. We're in the center of the harbor, and the mountains form an almost perfect circle around us. Eventually, a blood-red light comes to announce the rising sun, which emerges from behind the eastern mountains, facing the city, and begins to climb into the pale, cool sky. The richness, the sumptuousness of the colors that then play on the harbor, the

---

20. Bastille Day (officially, "le 14 juillet") serves as France's national day of celebration, much like the Fourth of July in the United States. It commemorates the Storming of the Bastille on July 14, 1789, and the unity celebrations that took place one year later, July 14, 1790.

mountains, and the sky cause everyone to fall silent once more. A minute later, the colors are about the same, but it's a postcard now. Nature abhors miracles that go on too long.

Formalities. Then disembarkation. Instantly, it's the whirlwind I'd feared. Some journalists had already come aboard. Questions, photos. No better or worse than anywhere else. As soon as I reach Rio, though, where I'm welcomed by Mme M.[21] and a great Brazilian journalist—already met in Paris, very nice—the real ordeal begins. Amid the confusions of this first day, a couple of random notes:

1. They ask me to choose between a room at the embassy, which is deserted, and a room at one of the luxury hotels, which are everywhere. I run from the luxury hotel's ugly facade and am grateful to find one of the most basic, most charming rooms in a completely empty embassy.

2. Brazilian drivers are either pleasure-seeking lunatics or cold sadists. The chaos and anarchy of the traffic know only one law: get there first, no matter the cost.

3. A most striking contrast is displayed between the luxuriousness of the hotels and modern buildings and, sometimes only a hundred meters from the luxurious, the favelas, a sort of shantytown hanging on the sides of the hills, with neither water nor light, where an impoverished population lives, Black and White. The women go to fetch water at the foot of the hills, where they line up and load their provisions into scrap-metal containers that they carry on their heads like Kabyle women. While they wait, an unbroken line of the silent, nickel-plated beasts of the American automobile industry passes in front of them. Never have luxury and misery seemed to me so insolently thrown together. It's true that, according to one of my companions, "they have a lot of fun, at least." Regret and cynicism—B. alone is generous. He's going to take me to the favelas, which he knows well: "My beat as a reporter was the criminal and communist," he says. "Both good ways of getting to know the slums."

4. People. Lunch with Mme M., B., and a sort of thin, well-read, and witty lawyer, whose first name, Annibal,[22] is all I can remember, and for good

21. Gabrielle Mineur worked at the French Embassy in Brazil and helped Camus arrange his visit. In January, before embarking on the trip, he wrote to her: "May I ask only that I not give too many talks and say that I'd be grateful to avoid as many official functions as possible."

22. Anibal Machado (1894–1964) was an award-winning Brazilian novelist and poet and was elected president of the Brazilian Association of Writers in 1945. He organized the first Brazilian congress of writers in São Paulo.

reason, as we were in a country club that lives up to his name: tennis, lawns, young people. Annibal has six daughters, all pretty. He says the mixture of love and religion in Brazil is quite interesting. To a Brazilian hack who'd translated Baudelaire, he telegraphed: "Please translate me back to French immediately. Signed, Baudelaire." He reminds me of those many elegant Spaniards you meet deep in the provinces.

5. One of the three or four Brazilian warships I've been shown, and which seems somewhat obsolete, is called Terror do Mondo. It's been through several revolutions.

6. People. After lunch, reception at Mme M.'s. Beautiful apartment on the harbor. The afternoon on the water is pleasant. Lots of people, but I've forgotten their names: a translator of Molière, who, a dear colleague tells me, added an act to *The Imaginary Invalid*, because it wasn't quite long enough to be performed; a Polish philosopher, from whom the heavens, if they be merciful, will protect me; a young French biologist on assignment, incredibly nice; most important, some young people from a troupe of Black actors who want to put on *Caligula*. I promise to work with them. Then, a side conversation with one of them who speaks Spanish, during which, with my dreadful Spanish, we arrange for me to attend a Black ball with him on Sunday. He's delighted with this little prank we're going to pull on the officials and repeats: "Segreto. Segreto."[23]

7. When I think we're wrapping up, Mme M. announces I'll be dining with a Brazilian poet. I don't say a word, promising myself that, starting tomorrow, I'll cut out everything that's inessential. I resign myself. But I didn't expect the ordeal that was to follow. The poet arrives, huge, indolent, squinty-eyed, mouth hanging open.[24] From time to time, agitation, a sudden stirring, and then he spills himself back into his armchair and sits there panting a little. He gets up, pirouettes, and falls back into his armchair. He talks about Bernanos, Mauriac, Brisson, Halévy. He knows everyone, apparently. They didn't treat him well. He doesn't take part in Franco-Brazilian politics, but he's founded

23. In 1944, Abidas do Nascimento (1914–2011), the Spanish-speaker mentioned here, founded the Teatro Experimental do Negro. He would go on to have a long and successful career as a writer, filmmaker, painter, and politician in Rio de Janeiro's Democratic Labor Party, fighting for the human and civil rights of Brazilian Black people, winning many international awards for his work, and twice being nominated for the Nobel Peace Prize—though all of this recognition came only after he'd faced years of governmental persecution, jailing, and exile.

24. Augusto Frederico Schmidt (1906–1965) was a Brazilian modernist poet and the founder and editor of Schmidt Editora, a publishing house important in the intellectual life of Rio between 1930 and 1939.

a fertilizer plant with some French people. Anyway, he's never been honored. In this country, they honor all of France's enemies, but not him, no, etc., etc.

He momentarily drifts into dreams, visibly suffering from who knows what, then yields the floor to the señorito, who greedily takes it up, for this señorito is like those who proudly walked their long-legged dogs on the Calle Major in Palma de Mallorca[25] before setting out like connoisseurs to watch the executions of '36. This one here's the arbiter of all things: I just have to go see this, go do that, Brazil is a country where all we do is work, no vices, because who has the time, we work, we work, and Bernanos told him, and Bernanos created a lifestyle in this country, and oh how we love France so much . . .

Frightened by the prospect of this event, I enlist the young biologist to come have dinner with us. In the car, I ask that we not go to a fancy restaurant. The poet emerges from his 330 pounds of weight to tell me, finger raised: "There is no luxury in Brazil. We're poor here, impoverished," he says, affectionately patting the tasseled shoulder of the chauffeur driving his enormous Chrysler. Having said this, the poet wearily sighs and returns to the recesses of his flesh, where he begins to absently gnaw at one of his complexes. The señorito shows us Rio, which is at the same latitude as Madagascar, yet so much more beautiful than Antananarivo.[26] "All workers," he repeats, sprawled in his cushioned seat. The poet has his driver stop in front of a pharmacy, laboriously pulls himself from the car, and asks us to hang tight a few minutes while he goes to get an injection. We wait, and the señorito comments: "Poor guy's diabetic." Letarget[27] politely asks: "It's getting worse?" Indeed. "Getting worse." The poet returns, whimpering, and collapses onto his poor cushioned seat, in his sad impoverished vehicle. We end up in a restaurant near Halles—where all you can get is fish—in a quadrangular room with a very high ceiling, the space so brutally lit with neon we look like pale fish gliding through irreal waters. The señorito wants to order for me. But, feel-

25. Roger Quilliot, an early Camus scholar and friend of the author, notes that this simile likely comes from a combination of personal experience, a trip Camus took to Mallorca in 1935, and literary experience, his reading of Bernanos's *Les grands cimetières sous la lune* (The great cemeteries beneath the moon), an eyewitness account of the violent nationalist repression that took place in Mallorca during the years of the Spanish Civil War.

26. Antananarivo is the capital of Madagascar.

27. Raymond Latarjet (spelled "Letarget" by Camus) (1911–1998) was a French biologist who made important discoveries in oncology, virology, and radiobiology. He was a professor at the French National Institute for Nuclear Science and Technology and was elected to the French Academy of Sciences in 1976.

ing drained, I'd prefer to eat lightly and so refuse everything he suggests. The poet is served first and he begins eating right away, without waiting for us, his fat and stubby fingers sometimes taking the place of his fork. He talks about Michaux, Supervielle, Béguin, etc., interrupting himself from time to time to turn his nose up and spit bits and pieces of bone and fish out onto his plate. This is the first time I've seen such a maneuver done without a person bending forward. He's so skilled at it, in fact, he misses his plate only once. Then the rest of us are served, and I see that the señorito ordered fried shrimp for me, which I turn down, explaining to him, in what I believe to be a friendly manner, that I'm familiar with the dish, a common one in Algeria. Hearing this, the señorito turns an angry red. We're only trying to make you happy, that's all. Humbly, in fact, humbly. You don't have to go looking all over Brazil for what you have in France, etc., etc. Fueled by my fatigue, a ridiculous anger washes over me, and I push my chair back to leave. A gentle intervention by Letarget, as well as the sympathy I feel, despite it all, for this curious character, the poet, holds me back, and I make a great effort to calm myself down. "Ah," the poet says, sucking his fingers, "Brazil requires a lot of patience, a lot of patience." All I say, as a retort, is that it didn't seem I'd been lacking it so far. Hearing this, the señorito calms down as quickly and senselessly as he'd gotten angry and, to try to make up, overwhelms me with compliments that leave me speechless: all Brazil feverishly awaits me, my visit to the country is the most important thing that's happened here for a long time, I'm as famous here as Proust . . . There's no stopping him. He concludes with: "That's why you have to be patient with Brazil. Brazil needs your patience. Patience, well, that's what Brazil requires . . ." and so on. Despite it all, the rest of the meal goes smoothly, though the poet and señorito continue to make asides in Portuguese, in which I believe they're complaining about me a little. In fact, these rude manners are spread out so naturally they become almost pleasantries. Leaving the restaurant, the poet declares that he needs a coffee and that he'll drive us back afterward. We go to his club, which is a copy of an English club, where I resign myself to drinking a "real" cognac, which I don't want at all. The señorito takes the opportunity to explain Figaro's administrative difficulties to us, which I know well, but of which he gives us an absolutely false, peremptory description. Chamfort's right, though: if you want to succeed in society, you have to let yourself learn a lot of things you already know from people who don't know anything about them. Nevertheless, I let them know I'm ready to go, but not before the señorito has said, triumphantly, gesturing at the poet, who's completely laid out in his armchair, his arm held up like a periscope, gripping a monstrous cigar: "S. is Brazil's greatest poet." To which the poet, faintly waving the periscope, responds in a weary voice: "Brazil doesn't have a greatest poet." I think I've made it through when, in the hall, the poet suddenly finds his second wind, violently grabs me by the arm, and says: "Don't move a muscle. Pay close attention. I'll show you a character for one of your novels." We notice a small, skinny man on the sidewalk, fedora askew, features sharp. The poet hurries toward him, swallows him in a long Brazilian embrace, and says to me: "Now this is a man. A minister of the interior. But a man." The man responds that Federico is excessively kind. The señorito joins the show. Another embrace, on an even footing this time, the señorito being a featherweight. The señorito pulls the minister's jacket open: "Look." The minister is carrying a revolver in a beautiful holster. We go on our way. "He's killed some forty men," the poet says, filled with admiration. "Why? They were enemies."

Ah!

"One time, he killed a guy, then used the body as a shield and killed the others."

"He's allowed to carry a weapon," Letarget says, without flinching.

"Because he's a minister." Turning to me: "Is he not the perfect character for you?"

"Yes," I say. But he's wrong—he's the one who's the character.

July 16

Get up early. Work. I put my notes in order. Conversation with the waiter serving me. From Nice, wants to go to North America because he found the G.I.s friendly. He couldn't get an immigration visa, so he came to Brazil, thinking it would be easier to get the required visa here. It wasn't easier. I ask him what he wants to do in the U.S.A. He's hesitating between boxing and singing. For the time being, he's training to be a boxer. I'll go to the gym with him Monday.

Lunch with Barleto[28] at a Brazilian novelist and translator's place. She has a charming house hanging on a hill. Of course, there are a lot of people there, one of them a novelist who's supposedly written the Brazilian Buddenbrooks,

---

28. João Batista Barreto Leite Filho (1906–1987), referred to as "B." or "Barleto" by Camus, was a Brazilian journalist and activist. He led the Union of Workers in Books and Newspapers (UTLJ) and was a member of the Brazilian Communist Party (PCB), though he challenged and criticized the Party for straying from Marxist principles to seize power. Between 1946 and 1949 he lived in Paris

but who exhibits a curious case of half-formed cultural awareness. If I'm to believe B., the novelist was heard saying, "English authors like Shakespeare, Byron, or David Copperfield." Yet the novelist's clearly well-read, and as I couldn't care less if he mistakes David for Charles, I find him to have a rather good head on his shoulders. At lunch, a Brazilian couscous that turns out to be fishcakes. The guests are excited when I ask to attend a soccer match and absolutely ecstatic when they find out I had a long career playing soccer. I've inadvertently stumbled upon their true passion. But no, the hostess translates Proust, and everyone present has a truly deep understanding of French culture. Afterward, I ask B. if he wants to go for a walk with me in the city.

Traffic is forbidden on the smaller streets, cheerfully lit by multicolored signs, which are havens of peace next to the main thoroughfares of roaring traffic. It would be as if cars were forbidden on Rue Saint-Honoré between Concorde, Madeleine, and Avenue de l'Opéra.[29] The flower market. The little bar where you drink "little coffees" sitting on tiny chairs. Moorish houses next to skyscrapers. Then Barleto makes me take a small "garden"-style tramcar, which climbs a steep path along the city's hills. We arrive in a neighborhood that's both poor and luxurious and that overlooks the city. In the dying light, the city stretches all the way to the horizon. A multitude of multicolored signs stand smoking above it. The outline of palm-tree-topped hills stands out against the calm sky. There's a tenderness in this sky, a fierce and barely concealed nostalgia. We take the stairs back down, and then walk through small and sloping streets, to reach the city itself. In the first real street that greets us, a positivist temple. They worship Clotilde de Vaux here, and it's in Brazil that the most disconcerting thing Auguste Comte left behind survives.[30] A little farther along, a Gothic church made of reinforced concrete. The temple itself is Greek, but for lack of money, the columns remain without capitals. We chat with B.N. in a little bistro. A charming man, sometimes deep ("there's an innocence that's lost by sitting out in the sun and darkening the

---

and Berlin as a war correspondent for the Associated Diaries, a conglomerate of Brazilian newspapers and radio stations.

29. Place de la Madeleine, Place de la Concorde, and Avenue de l'Opéra form, roughly, a rectangular space right in the center of Paris, directly north of the Louvre and the Tuileries Garden. Rue Saint-Honoré runs through the center of the space, parallel to the Tuileries.

30. In 1844, Auguste Comte fell in love with Clotilde de Vaux, a committed Catholic who died a year later from tuberculosis. In the wake of her death, Comte created what he called the Religion of Humanity or the Positivist Church, a fully formulated secular religion. It failed to catch on in France but found some success in Brazil. The temple Camus mentions here is likely the Positivist Chapel in Porto Alegre.

skin"), who lives the drama of the times with, it seems to me, great dignity. I leave him to meet up with Abidas, the Black actor, at Mme Mineur's. We'll leave for the *macumba* from there.

A macumba, in Brazil[31]

When I arrive at Mme M.'s, there's an air of anxiety. The father of the saints (the priest and principal dancer), who was to organize the *macumba*, consulted the saint of the day, who didn't give his permission. Abidas, the Black actor, thinks it's mostly a matter of money, that he didn't promise enough to earn the saint's goodwill. He thinks we should still take a trip to Caxias, a village outside the city, 40 km from Rio, where we might be able to find a macumba at random. During dinner, they explain the macumbas to me. There seems to be a consistent aim to the ceremonies: to coax the god down into the body by means of song and dance. The goal is a trance. What distinguishes the macumba from other ceremonies is its mix of Catholic religious practices and African rites. As far as gods or saints, they have Echou, an evil spirit and African god, as well as Ogoun, who is our Saint George. They have saints, too: Cosme and Damien, etc., etc. Here, the worship of saints is integrated with rites of possession. Each day has its own saint who's not celebrated on any other day, except with special permission from the principal "father of the saints." The father of the saints has his daughters (and his sons, I suppose), and he's responsible for making sure they've reached a trance.

Armed with this basic information, we head out. 40 km in a sort of fog. It's 10 at night. Caxias reminds me of a country fair composed of stands. We stop at the village square where there are already some twenty cars and a lot more people than we'd imagined. We have barely come to a stop when a young

31. The descriptions of the macumba that follow would go on to form the basis of Camus's short story "The Stone That Grows," which appears in the collection *Exile and the Kingdom*. In preparation for the English translation, Camus told Justin O'Brien that "the Stone that Grows is very important to me and I confess that it's the story I care about most." Though the two discussed how best to translate the title of one of the other stories in the collection, "L'Hôte"—"it obviously has to be the Guest," Camus wrote, giving the English title himself, because "the French word hôte is ambiguous, and naturally I've played with that ambiguity, but as English doesn't permit this, we have to clarify things and denote the Arab"—unfortunately, they didn't discuss the title of "La pierre qui pousse," which O'Brien would go on to translate as "The Growing Stone," a fluid title that reads well in English and that translates the French structure in the standard way, but one that deemphasizes the inherent strangeness of the original. One of the story's main themes is that of the foreign versus the familiar (the stranger versus the community), an idea that a more literal translation, such as "The Stone That Grows," helps to center. In a letter to Maria Casarès, Camus referred to the title object as the "miraculous stone."

mulatto man hurries over to offer me a bottle of aguardiente,[32] asking if I've brought Tarrou with me. He has a good laugh—just kidding—and introduces me to his friends. He's a poet. Finally, they let me in on the fact that everyone in Rio knew I was going to be brought to see a macumba (I'd been told to keep it a secret and innocently did so) and that a lot of them wanted to come enjoy it. Abidas inquires about something, then sits still. We stay there, in the middle of the square, endlessly discussing this and that. No one seems to have a care in the world, everyone has their head in the stars. All of a sudden: a general hustling and bustling. Abidas tells me we have to go into the mountains. We set out, rolling along for a couple of kilometers on a bumpy road full of potholes, and then we suddenly stop for no clear reason. We wait, no one seeming to have a care in the world. Then we set out again. The car suddenly veers off at a forty-five-degree angle and takes a mountain trail. It climbs, with difficulty, then stops: the path is too steep. We get out of the car and walk. The hill is smooth, the vegetation sparse, but we're up in the open sky, amid the stars, it seems. The air smells like smoke. It's so thick it almost feels like it's pressing against your forehead. When we reach the top of the hill, we can hear drums and singing off in the distance, but they stop almost immediately. We walk toward where we heard them. With neither trees nor houses, the place is a desert. But in a hollow we notice a sort of shed, rather spacious, without walls, its framework visible. Paper garlands are strung up along the shed. Suddenly, I notice a procession of Black girls climbing toward us. They're wearing white, dropped-waist dresses of coarse silk. A man dressed in a sort of red tabard, wearing necklaces of multicolored teeth, follows behind them. Abidas stops him and introduces me. The greeting is earnest and friendly. But there's a complication. They're going to join a different macumba that's a twenty-minute walk from here, and we'll have to follow them. We head out. At an intersection, I catch sight of a lit candle stuck in the ground, in a sort of niche where statues of saints or devils (quite crude, by the way, and in the style of Saint-Sulpice) are gathered in front of a tallow candle and a bowl of water. They point Echou out to me, red and fierce, with a knife in his hand. The path we're following snakes through the hills beneath a star-filled sky. The dancers, male and female, are in front of us, laughing and joking. We go down

32. *Aguardiente* has traditionally been used in Latin America as a generic term for distilled alcohol. The word is etymologically similar to the English language's "firewater." In Portuguese, for example, the word is derived from *água* (water) and *ardente* (fiery).

a hill, cross the trail by which we came, and climb back up another hill. Huts made of branches and clay, filled with whispering shadows. Then the head of the procession comes to a halt in front of a raised platform, surrounded by a partition of reeds. We can hear drums and singing inside. When we're all together, the first women climb onto the platform and step backward through the reed door. Then the men. We enter a courtyard filled with junk. Singing escapes a small house of cob and straw in front of us. We enter. It's a very basic hut, the walls roughcast nevertheless. The roof is supported by a central mast, the floor is clay. A small lean-to in the back shelters an altar with a chromo print of Saint George above it. Similar chromos decorate the partitions. In one corner, on a small dais adorned with palm leaves, some musicians: two short drums and one tall drum. There were about forty dancers, men and women, when we arrived. Now there are so many of us we can hardly breathe, packed so tightly together. I back against one of the partitions and watch. The dancers, men and women, spread out into two concentric circles, the men on the inside. The two fathers of the saints (the one who received us is dressed, like the dancers, in a sort of white pajamas) face each other in the center of the circles. They take turns singing the first notes of a song everyone instantly takes up in chorus, the circles turning clockwise. The dance is straightforward: the double beat of a rumba played alongside a stomp. The "fathers" barely keep the rhythm. My Portuguese translator tells me these songs entreat the saint to allow newcomers to stay. The breaks between songs are rather long. Near the altar, a woman sings and shakes a bell so that it almost never stops. The dance is far from frenetic, its regular pattern fixed and heavy. In the still-increasing heat, the breaks are hard to bear. I notice:

1) that the dancers don't sweat the slightest bit;

2) a White man and two White women who dance much worse than the others.

At one point, one of the dancers comes over and speaks to me. My translator tells me the dancer's asking me to uncross my arms. The posture prevents the spirit from descending on us. Compliant, I let my arms drop. Little by little, the pauses between songs grow shorter and the dancing grows more spirited. A lit candle is brought to the center of the room and stuck in the ground, near a glass of water. The songs invoke Saint George.

"He arrives in the light of the moon
He departs in the light of the sun"

and then:

"I am the god's battlefield."

Indeed, one or two of the dancers already seem to be in a trance, but, if I may say so, a calm trance: hands on their lower back, standing straight, eyes blank and staring. The red "father" pours water around the candle in two concentric circles, and the dancing resumes with almost no transition. From time to time, one of the dancers, male or female, leaves the circle to dance in the center, right by the circles of water, but never crossing them. Their rhythm increases, they go into convulsions, and they begin to cry out inarticulately. Dust lifts from the ground, suffocating, thickening air that already sticks to the skin. The dancers increasingly leave their circles to dance around the fathers, who themselves dance more quickly (the White father, admirably). The drums are raging now and the red father suddenly lets loose. Eyes ablaze, his four limbs whirling around his body, he lands on each leg in turn, knees bent, his rhythm accelerating until the dance ends and he stops, gazing at the witnesses with a blank and terrible expression. Just then, a dancer emerges from a dark corner, kneels, and holds a sheathed sword out to him. The red father draws the sword out and twirls it around his body in a threatening manner. A huge cigar is brought to him. Little by little, everyone lights cigars and smokes them while dancing. The dance resumes. One by one, the witnesses come and lie down before the father, head between his feet. He strikes them on each shoulder, in a diagonal, with the flat of the sword, lifts them up, touches their left shoulder with his right shoulder and vice versa; he pushes them violently into the ring, a movement that, two out of three times, sets off a fit, different for each dancer: a fat Black man stands on his heels, gazing at the central mast, a blank expression on his face, the only movement a shiver continually running the nape of his neck. He looks like a *knock down*[33] boxer. A thick White woman, face animalistic, barks continuously, shaking her head from right to left. But the young Black women enter the deepest trances, their feet glued to the ground, their entire body twitching with convulsions that grow more and more violent as they rise toward the shoulders. Their heads jerk back and forth, completely decapitated. Everyone whoops and screams. Then the women begin to fall. They're picked up, their foreheads are touched,

33. The phrase "knock down" is written in English in the original manuscript, though "punch-drunk" would be the more colloquial term.

and they're set loose until they fall again. The peak is reached when all cry out in strange, hoarse sounds reminiscent of barking. They tell me it'll keep going as it's been going all the way until dawn. It's 2 in the morning. The heat, the dust, the cigar smoke, and the human smell make the air unbreathable. I stagger outside, delighted to finally be breathing fresh air. I like the night and sky more than the gods of man.

July 17

Work in the morning. I have lunch with G. and two Brazilian professors. Three professors in all, but nice. Then, joined by Lucien Febvre,[34] a rather taciturn old man, we set out for a drive through the mountains surrounding Rio. Seen a hundred times, the Tijuca Forest, the Mayrink Chapel, the Corcovado, Guanabara Bay, every angle is completely different. The immense beaches of the South, with white sand and emerald waves, stretching across thousands of deserted kilometers, all the way to Uruguay. The rainforest and its three levels. Brazil is a land without people. Everything that's created here is created through excessive effort. Nature suffocates man. "Is space enough to create culture?" the nice Brazilian professor asks me. It's a meaningless question. But only these spaces measure up to technological progress. The faster the plane flies, the less importance France, Spain, and Italy hold. They were nations, are provinces, and tomorrow will be the world's villages. The future's not on our side, and there's nothing we can do about this irresistible trend. Germany lost the war because it was a nation and modern warfare requires the means of empires. Tomorrow, it'll require the means of a continent. So now the two great empires set out to conquer their continent. What's to be done? The only hope is that a new culture will be born and that South America may help to temper this mechanistic foolishness. So that's what I poorly expressed to my professor friend as we stood before the whistling sea, letting the sand run through our fingers.

I head back—having caught a chill while in the car and while under Christ the Redeemer—to wait for faithful Abidas, who's going to take me to dance the samba after dinner. Disappointing evening. In a neighborhood way on the outskirts, a sort of working-class dancehall brightly lit with neon, of course. There are, for the most part, only Black people—but that means a great variety

---

34. Lucien Febvre (1878–1956) was a French historian and one of the original editors of the *Encyclopédie française*.

of color here. Surprised by how slow they dance, with a sloshy sort of rhythm. But then I consider the climate. The manic dancers in Harlem would be duller here, too. Even so, nothing differentiates this dancehall from a thousand others around the world, except skin color. About that, I notice I have to fight a sort of reverse prejudice. I like Black people *a priori* and am tempted to find qualities in them that they don't have. I wanted to find the people here beautiful, but if I imagine their skin being White, what I find is more a pretty collection of calicos[35] and dyspeptic employees. Abidas confirms this. An ugly bunch. That said, among the mulatto women who come straight over to our table to have a drink, not because it's ours but because that's where you drink, one or two are pretty. I'm even sweet on the one who's losing her voice, dance a little bit of a samba with another woman, slap myself on the thighs to get myself going, and then suddenly realize I'm not into it. Taxi. I return to the room.

July 18

It's pouring rain over the steaming bay and over the city. Quiet morning of work. I go have lunch with Lage, in a cozy restaurant overlooking the harbor. At 3 o'clock, I meet up with Barleto to go visit the working-class suburbs. We take the commuter train. *Méier. Todos os santos. Madureira.*[36] What strikes me is its Arab feel. Shops without storefronts. Everything out in the street. Saw a hearse: an Empire cenotaph with huge gilded bronze columns on a delivery van painted black. For the rich, it's horses. Striking fabrics on display. We take a bumpy tramcar that cuts through endless faubourgs that are empty most of the time, and sad (the tribes of workers camped at the entrance of the housing projects make me think of B.),[37] but as we get closer, they begin to coagulate around a central point, a square bright with neon, with red and green lights (in broad daylight), engulfed by a multicolored crowd at which a loudspeaker occasionally blares soccer scores. You can't help but think of these ceaselessly increasing crowds that'll end up covering the world's surface and suffocating. Here, I understand Rio better, better than in Copacabana, in any case, it's oily stain spreading infinitely in all directions. On the way back, in a *lotação*, a sort of public-transport taxi, we witness one of the many acci-

35. In colloquial French, *calicot* is used to refer to someone who works in a fabric shop.

36. Méier and Madureira are neighborhoods in the North Zone of Rio de Janeiro.

37. Roger Quilliot notes that this is likely a reference to Belcourt, the impoverished neighborhood in Algiers where Camus was raised.

dents occasioned by the unbelievable traffic. A poor old Negro man makes the mistake of trying to cross an avenue glittering with lights and is hit by a bus going full speed, is sent ten meters through the air, tossed like a tennis ball, and the bus just goes around him, fleeing the scene. It does so because of a stupid flagrante-delicto law on account of which the driver would have been taken to jail. So instead he flees, there's no longer any flagrante delicto, and he won't go to prison. The old Negro man lies there, not a single person coming to help him. But the blow would have killed an ox. Later, I learn a white sheet will be put over him, and it will grow soaked with blood, and candles will be lit around it, and the traffic will continue around him, bypassing him until the authorities arrive to reconstruct the scene.

In the evening, dinner at Robert Claverie's.[38] Only French people, which gives me a chance to relax. When you speak a foreign language, there is, Huxley says, someone inside of you who automatically says no.

July 19

Magnificent weather. A charming and myopic journalist. Mail. Lunch with the Delamains, in a sort of train-station buffet—neon lit, of course. Meal. Dark ruminations. As the afternoon comes to a close, I visit a drama school. Interview with students and teachers. Dinner at the Chapasses' with the national poet, Manuel Bandeíra,[39] a small, extremely sharp man. Kaïmi,[40] a Black man who composes and writes all the sambas sung in the country, sings and plays guitar after dinner. They are the saddest, most moving songs. The sea and love, longing for Bahia. Little by little, everyone begins to sing, among them a Black man, a deputy, a college professor, a notary public, all naturally and gracefully singing along with these sambas. Totally seduced.

July 20

Morning in a motorboat on Guanabara Bay, the weather wonderful. Only a small, crisp wind lightly brushes over the water. We pass along the islands; some small beaches (two twins named Adam and Eve). Finally, a dip in the

---

38. Jean Robert Claverie was head of the import-export company Maison d'importation Claverie and director of the Alliance Française in Rio.

39. Manuel Bandeira (1886–1968) was a very popular Brazilian poet at the time of Camus's visit.

40. Dorival Caymmi (1914–2008) was, as Camus indicates, one of the most well-respected composers of popular Brazilian music.

water, pure and fresh. Afternoon, visit from Murilo Mendès—poet, ill.[41] Shrewd mind, resistant spirit. One of the two or three I've actually seen here. In the evening, a talk.[42] When I get there, the crowd is bottlenecked at the entrance. Claverie and the ravishing Mme Petitjean are already on their way out, not having been able to find seats.[43] I find a pair for them, not without some difficulty. In the end, the auditorium, made to hold 800, is overflowing with listeners standing or sitting on the floor. Society people, diplomats, etc., arriving late, naturally, have to choose between standing or leaving. The Spanish ambassador sits on a riser behind the podium. In a few minutes, he'll learn a thing or two. Ninu, a Spanish refugee I knew back in Paris, bumps into me. He's head of the *campeones* on a fazenda 100 km from Rio. He came those 100 km to hear "*su compañero*." He heads back tomorrow morning. When you consider what coming 100 km from the middle of nowhere means . . . I'm moved to tears. Then he takes out a pack of cigarettes, the kind most like "*gusto frances*," he says, and offers me one. I keep him close, happy to have such a friend in the auditorium, thinking it's for people like him I'll give this talk. So that is how I talk,[44] and I've got men like N. on my side and, it seems, the other young people, too—but I doubt I have the society people on my side. Then, the mad dash. I collect a couple of sincere congratulations. The rest is playacting. Go to bed at midnight, having to get up at 4:30 A.M. to catch my flight to Recife.

July 21

Wake at 4:00 A.M. It's pouring rain. I get soaked just going from the embassy door to the taxi. At the air terminal, formalities, during which I'm asleep on my feet. Long way to the airfield. In this climate, you get soaked twice: first by the rain, then by your own sweat. At the airport, long wait. It turns out we won't take off until 8:30, and I again rage against the plane. While

41. Murilo Mendes (1901–1975) was a modernist poet who later converted to Catholicism and wrote mystic verse.

42. The talk was given at the Itamaraty Palace, which housed the Ministry of Foreign Affairs.

43. In a December 1991 interview with Dr. Paula Willoquet-Maricondi, Mme Yvette Petitjean gave the following impression of her time spent with Camus: "I found him extremely charming, a charmer, but also truly good, profoundly good, not full of himself. Albert Camus had the look of a little boy crossed with a Mandarin: young, good, and wise." She and Camus kept in contact for a couple of years after his trip to South America. In November 1953, they met one last time in person.

44. In the handwritten notebook, Camus wrote: "So, in fact, that's how I do talk, with greater clarity and intensity than I ever have before."

I wait, I look at a chart showing the distances between Rio and the world's capitals. Paris is almost 10,000 km away. Two minutes later, the radio plays *La vie en rose* for us. The plane takes off, heavy with rain, the sky low. I try to sleep but am unable to do so. When we land in Recife, four and a half hours later, the airplane door opens on a red land devoured by heat. It's clear we're at the equator again. Suffering from insomnia, vaguely feverish with some sort of cold I caught this morning, I stagger under the weight of the heat. Nobody is waiting for me. But it seems the plane is ahead of schedule, so it's not surprising. I wait in an empty hall, blazing air circling the room, and from afar contemplate the coconut forests surrounding the city. The delegation arrives. All nice. The three Frenchmen are all over six feet tall. We're well represented here. We get on our way. Red land and coconut trees. Then, the sea and its immense beaches. Hotel on the quay. Masts rising above the parapets. I try to sleep. In vain. Four hours. They come get me. The editor of the oldest newspaper in South America, *Le journal de Pernambouc,* is here. He's the one who's going to show me around the city. Admirable colonial churches dominated by white, the Jesuit style enlightened and lightened by roughcast. The interior is baroque, but without the excessive weight of the European Baroque. The Golden Chapel, in particular, is admirable. The *azulejos* are perfectly preserved here. As with the paintings, it's only the "wicked" Judases, the Roman soldiers, etc., that the people have disfigured. All of their faces are chewed and bloody. I admire the old town, the small red, blue, and ocher houses, the streets paved with large, pointed stones. The square of the church of San Pedro. The church, set next to a coffee factory, is completely blackened by smoke from the roasters. It's literally patinaed in coffee.

Dinner alone. The sound of an orchestra dying in the distance. Exile has its contentment. After dinner, a talk in front of a hundred or so people who appear exhausted as they leave. I like Recife, to be sure. A Florence of the Tropics, between its coconut-tree forests, its red mountains, its white beaches.

July 22

Get up with flu and fever. Legs unsteady. I get ready and wait at the hotel for three intellectuals who want to see me. Two likable. We go see Olinda, a small, historic city with old churches, across from Recife, out on the bay. The Saint Francis convent is quite beautiful. On the way back, I shake with fever and swallow some aspirin and gin. Lunch at the consulate. After lunch, stroll along the sea, through a coconut-tree forest, where, through the openings, you can see, out on the sea, the sails of the *jangadas,* a type of narrow raft made from the trunks of a very light wood that's tied together with rope. These fragile assemblages take to the sea for days and days, I'm told. Straw huts scattered about. In the bright and suffocating air, the shadows of the coconut trees wobble before my eyes. The flu is getting worse, and I ask to rest before the interview at 5 o'clock. Impossible to sleep. A roundtable that I make it through thanks to two whiskeys. Afterward, head over to a folk festival organized for me. They give me a flu shot. Uninteresting songs and dances. A phony macumba. But the *bomba-menboi,* extraordinary show.[45] It's a sort of grotesque ballet danced by masked figures and totem-representations, the theme of which is always the same: the killing of an ox. The characters partly improvise on this theme and partly recite a text written in verse, all while dancing. The part I see goes on for an hour, but I'm told it could go on all night. The costumes are extraordinary. Two red clowns, the "cavalier marin," a merry-go-round horse costume draped from his shoulders, a stork, a braggart dressed as a cowboy, two Indians, the ox, of course, and a "dead person carrying a live one," a sort of double-bodied mannequin controlled by a single actor, the *cachaça* (or drunkard), the horse's son, a prancing colt, a man on stilts, a crocodile, and, hanging over everything, death, at least three meters tall, looking out over the scene, its head high in the night sky. As an orchestra, a drum and rumba box. The religious origin is obvious (a few prayers still linger in the text), but it's all drowned in a frenzied dance, a thousand graceful or grotesque feats that conclude with the killing of the ox, which is reborn shortly afterward and gallops off carrying a little girl between its horns. The grand finale: a great cry, "Long live Señor Camus and the hundred *kings* of the Orient." I go back to the hotel, dazed by the flu.

———

45. The performance Camus attended in Recife was a *bumba meu-boi,* from *bumba* meaning a "call to action" (but alluding also to the bomba drum) and *meu-boi* meaning "my ox." The performance tells the story of life on the sugar plantations and features the captain, a member of the Euro-Brazilian ruling class, who comes to take the property of the workers, men of color, by force. The dancing is frenzied, and the figures—ox, stork, cowboys, Cavalier Marin—wear elaborate costumes, mixing the animal and the human. In the grand finale, the performers would have cried out, "*Viva Senhor Camus e o Santo Rei do Oriente,*" meaning "Long live Mr. Camus and the Holy King of the East" (i.e., Jesus Christ), which Camus and his party hear as "Camus and the Kings of the Orient."

July 23

9 o'clock. Depart for Bahia. My flu is a little better. But I'm still feverish and stiff. It's cold in the plane, God knows why? And it shakes terribly. Three hours in the air, then short hills covered in snow appear over a great stretch of land. At least that's the impression the white sand, so widespread here, gives me, its immaculate waves seeming to surround Bahia in an untouched desert. From the airfield to the city, six kilometers of winding road running between banana trees and dense vegetation. The land is completely red. Bahia, where you see only Black people, seems like an immense and bustling casbah, impoverished, dirty, and beautiful. Excessively large marketplaces made of torn sails and old boards, of short, old houses plastered with red, green-apple, and blue lime, etc.

Lunch on the harbor. Large boats with ocher and blue lateen sails unload bunches of bananas. We eat dishes spicy enough to cause miracles in paralytics. The bay, which I can also see from my hotel window, stretches out beneath a gray sky, round and clear, full of a strange silence, while the motionless sails you see out there look as if they're imprisoned in a suddenly frozen sea. I prefer this bay to the one in Rio, too spectacular for my taste. This one, at least, has its limits and its poetry. Since morning, downpours, one after the other, brutal and abundant. They've turned the potholed streets of Bahia into torrents. We drive between two great blades of water that continuously cover the car.

Visit some churches. They're the same as in Recife, even if these are supposedly more famous. Church of the Good Jesus with its votive offerings (casts, pair of buttocks, X-ray, brigadier stripes). Suffocating. This harmonious baroque is repeated again and again. In the end, it's the only thing to see in this country, and it's seen quickly. Real life is what remains. But in this immeasurable land that holds the sadness of wide-open spaces, life is lived close to the ground and it would take years to become a part of it. Do I wish to spend years in Brazil? No. At six o'clock, I take a shower, fall asleep, and wake up a little better. Dine alone. Then a talk given to a patient audience. The consul escorts me and slips, under the table, after the last drink, an envelope containing around 45,000 fr in Brazilian currency. It's the honorarium given by the University of Bahia. The consul is surprised by my refusal. He explains to me that "others demand such an honorarium." Then he accepts my position. Still, I know he won't be able to help thinking: "If he needed it, he'd accept it." And yet . . .

Before finishing, I copy down a couple of passages from the Palace Hôtel de Bahia's rules and regulations, which are written in French: "Everybody speaks French in Brazil," the propaganda says.

"Failure to pay bills, as stipulated in par. 3 and 4, will oblige management to withhold luggage as a guarantee against debt, and accordingly the client will immediately unoccupy the occupied room."

"It's forbidden to possess birds, dogs, or other animals in your room."

"On the ground floor of the hotel, you will find a well-stocked American bar and a spacious reading room."

And here's the one they end with:

"On the ground floor of the hotel, there is a barbershop and nail salon. Clients may request the use of these services in their own room."

July 24 (Sunday)

At ten o'clock, a charming Brazilian, Eduardo Catalao,[46] polite as can be, takes me to Itapoa beach by way of a potholed road. It's a fishing village made up of straw huts. The beach is beautiful and wild, the sea frothy at the foot of the coconut trees. This never-ending flu brings me to my knees and prevents me from swimming. We come across a group of young French filmmakers living in a straw hut so they can make a film about Bahia. Surprised to see me in this lost corner of the world. They have an air of Saint-Germain-des-Prés about them.

Scathing lunch at three o'clock. From 5:00 to 7:00, I work. Dinner at the consul's. Then we go see a candomblé, a new ceremony belonging to that curious Afro-Brazilian religion that, here, is Black Catholicism. It's a sort of dance performed in front of a table loaded with food, to the sound of three increasingly large drums and a flattened funnel struck with an iron rod. The dances are directed by a sort of matron, who takes the place of the "father of saints," and are performed only by women. The costumes are much richer than in Bahia. Two of the dancers, who are, by the way, enormous, have their faces covered with a curtain of raffia. Still, not much of this is new to me until a group of Black girls enters the scene in a semihypnotic state, eyes practically closed, yet standing upright, swaying on their feet, back and forth. I'm taken with one of them, tall and thin, wearing a blue huntress's hat with musketeer

46. Eduardo Catalão (1912–2004) was a Brazilian agronomist and politician who served as minister of agriculture between 1955 and 1956.

feathers, its brim turned up, and a green dress, while holding in her hand a green and yellow bow equipped with an arrow, a multicolored bird skewered on its tip. This beautiful, sleeping face reflects a symmetrical and innocent melancholy. This Black Diana is of infinite grace. When she dances, that extraordinary grace is undeniable. Still asleep, she staggers as the music stops. The rhythm alone acts as a sort of invisible stake around which she winds her arabesques, occasionally uttering a strange birdcall, piercing yet melodious. The rest isn't that great. Watered-down rites expressed in mediocre dances.[47] We leave with Catalao. In this remote neighborhood, as we stumble through the potholed streets, through the heavy, aromatic night, the cry of the injured bird still reaches out to me, reminding me of my sleeping beauty.

I'd like to go to bed, but Catalao wants to have a whiskey at one of those sad-as-death nightclubs you find all over the world. Without my knowing, he asks for some French music, and for the second time, I hear *La vie en rose* in the Tropics.

July 25

Wake up at 7 o'clock. Have to wait for a plane that may not come. Then, it's confirmed. I'll leave at 11:00. My flu's getting better, but my legs are still cottony. Furious desire to go home. Two hours lost at the airfield. We leave. It's 1:30, and we won't arrive in Rio before 7 o'clock. I'm writing all of this on the plane, where I feel quite lonely.

Evening. Flu and fever return with a vengeance upon arrival. This time, it seems serious.

July 26

In bed. Fever. Only the mind stubbornly persists. Awful thoughts. Unbearable feeling of walking step by step toward an unknown catastrophe that will destroy everything around and inside of me.

Evening. They come get me. I'd forgotten that the Black troupe was going to put on an act from *Caligula* for me tonight. The theater has already been reserved, there's nothing to be done. I wrap myself up as if I were going to the North Pole and take a taxi to the theater.

---

47. As with the earlier notes from the macumba, these notes from the candomblé are also incorporated into "The Stone That Grows."

Odd to see Black Romans. Then, what I'd seen as a cruel and intense way of acting becomes a slow, tender, vaguely sensual flirtation. After this, they put on a short Brazilian play that's just perfectly to my taste. I'll give the gist of it:

"A man, used to taking part in macumbas, is visited by the spirit of love. He then throws himself on his wife, who's transported and falls in love with the spirit. So she provokes, with the same song, the coming of the spirit as often as she can, which gives a pretext for putting some lively bacchanals on stage. In the end, the husband understands that it's not him she's in love with but the God, and he kills her. She dies happy, however, because she's certain she's going to the God she loves."

The evening ends with some Brazilian music that seems mediocre. Important, still, because Brazil may be the only predominately Black country that continuously produces new tunes. The highlight is a *frevo*,[48] a dance from Pernambuco, in which the audience themselves take part and which is really the most frenzied contortion I've seen. Charming. Barely back to my room, I hit the bed and sleep like a rock, not waking until 9 o'clock in the morning, infinitely better.

———

July 27

Brazil, with its thin framework of modernity laid over this immense continent teeming with natural and primitive forces, makes me think of a building slowly chewed, bite by bite, by invisible termites. One day the building will collapse, and a small and teeming people, Black, red, and yellow, will spread out over the surface of the continent, masked and brandishing spears, ready for the victory dance.[49]

Lunch with the poet Murilo Mendès—a sharp and melancholy mind—his wife, and a young poet who's collected 17 fractures and a pair of crutches thanks to Rio's intelligent traffic system. After lunch, they take me to Sugarloaf. But the morning is spent waiting in line only to get no closer, in the end, than the first piton—to the great dismay of Mme Mendès, who's afraid

48. The term *frevo* is used to describe the various styles of music and dance most traditionally associated with Brazilian Carnival.

49. On August 8, 1949, Camus wrote to René Char: "It's too hot here, in this country where nature will one day eat the fragile setting that's been erected, this setting with which man tries to surround himself. The termites are going to devour the skyscrapers, sooner or later, and the virgin vines will hold the others back, and Brazil's true self will finally burst forth. But what do you need my travel opinions for?"

I'm bored, even though, in their friendly company, I'm in a good mood. M. knows and quotes Char, whom he finds to be our most important poet since Rimbaud. I'm happy to hear that.[50]

———

July 28

The Embassy of Montevideo complicates my stay by wanting to change the previously arranged dates. In the end, I'll be staying in Rio until Wednesday before going to São Paulo. Lunch with Simon and Barleto, whom I like more and more each day. The afternoon is spent working. In the evening, a reception at the embassy, which, however charming, bores me. I take French leave, as they say here, and go to bed.

———

July 29

The days in Rio have little rhyme or reason and pass both fast and slow. Lunch with Mme B. and her sister-in-law. French women make for good company. Lively, witty, the time passes quickly. Stroll afterward, along the bay, the day marvelous and relaxed. It's difficult to tear myself away from these easy, natural moments only to have to run off to the embassy to find Mendès and his wife, who are going to take me to Corrêa's, the ex-publisher, where I have to meet with a student who . . . , etc. What I've persistently refused my whole life, I accept here—as if I'd agreed in advance to do everything on this trip I don't want to do. I get out in time to meet up with Claverie, Mme B., and her sister-in-law,[51] whom I've invited to dinner. After dinner, Claverie takes us for a ride on roads that cut through the mountains and into the night. The warm air, the stars, so many tiny specks, the bay far below . . . but it all makes me more melancholy than happy.

———

July 30 and 31

Weekend at Cl.'s in Teresópolis.[52] 150 km from Rio, up in the mountains.

---

50. On the typescript, there is another paragraph that follows this one, which was crossed out by Camus.

51. Mme Jeannette Besse ("Mme B") and her sister-in-law, the previously mentioned Mme Yvette Petitjean.

52. Camus spent the weekend in Teresópolis at the "Casa da Usina" with Claverie, Mme Petitjean, Mme Jeanette Besse, and Mme Yvonne Perririn.

The route is beautiful, especially between Petrópolis and Teresópolis. From time to time, an ipe[53] covered in yellow flowers jumps out from around a corner, against a horizon of mountains following one after the next, all the way out to the horizon. It's easy to again understand here what first struck me in the plane while I was flying over the country. Immense stretches, virgin and solitary, out of which the cities, hung on the coast, appear as nothing but unimportant dots. At any moment, this enormous, unpaved continent, entirely given over to natural wilderness, could turn and take back these cities of false luxury. The weekend is spent walking, swimming, and playing ping-pong. I can finally breathe out here in the countryside. The air at 800 m. helps me get a better sense of Rio's climate, truly exhausting. When we head back down on Sunday, it's without joy that I return to the city. On top of that, I'm greeted in front of the embassy by one of those scenes that are all too frequent in Rio. Again, a woman lying bloodied in front of a bus. A crowd looking on in silence, without trying to help her. This barbaric custom is revolting. A long time passes before I hear an ambulance siren. The whole time, they left the poor, moaning woman out there to die. Yet they turn around and make a big pretense of adoring children.

August 1

Difficult waking up. To live is to hurt—to hurt others and yourself through others. Cruel land! How not to touch anything? What permanent exile is there?

Lunch at the embassy. I'm told the death penalty is unheard of in Brazil. In the afternoon, a talk about Chamfort.[54] I always wonder why I attract socialites. All those hats! Dinner with Barleto, Machado, etc., in a nice Italian restaurant. In the afternoon, we visit a favela. A number of long negotiations before entering the city, a genuine city, made of wood and tin and reeds, clinging to the side of a hill above Ipanema beach. Finally, we're told we can go for a consultation (as a letter of introduction, we have, it's true, two good bottles

---

53. The most likely interpretation here is that Camus has abbreviated the French *ipéca,* itself an abbreviation of *ipécacuanha,* the name of the plant from which ipecac syrup is derived.

54. In 1944, Camus had written an introduction for Nicolas de Chamfort's *Maximes et anecdotes,* parts of which he adapted for the talk, which was delivered at the Ministry of Foreign Affairs in Rio. The talk has sometimes been titled "Chamfort: Moralist of Rebellion" and sometimes "Rebellion and the Novel," the latter title also being given to a section of *The Rebel,* in which the central ideas of the talk are expanded.

of cachaça) with one of the ladies of the place. We enter at night, between shacks emitting the sounds of either radios or snoring. The ground is completely vertical in spots, slippery, cluttered with garbage. It takes a good fifteen minutes to reach, out of breath, the Pythia's shack.[55] But as we stand on the platform in front of the shack, our effort is rewarded: beneath a half-moon, the beach and the bay stretch out before us, still and motionless. It seems the Pythia is asleep. Then she opens up for us. The shack is like a lot of others I've seen, with multicolored strips of cloth hanging from the ceiling. In one corner, a bed with someone asleep in it. In the middle, a red curtain covers a table with laundry on it, making it look like there's a dead body underneath. In an alcove with an altar, all the statues of saints that Saint-Sulpice has exported throughout the world are gathered. Also, a Red-Skin statue, lost there, who knows how. The Pythia seems like a fine homemaker. She's just finished the day's consultations, which she gives only when the saint is in her. The saint is gone now. It'll have to wait until next time. It's hot. Still, the Black people here are so welcoming and affable that we stay and chat a while longer. The descent, a real race toward death. Imagine what it's like for the women who go two or three times a day to fetch water, a bucket atop their head as they climb back up. Imagine what it's like on rainy days. As it is, Barleto takes a one-way ticket to the ground floor. I reach the bottom, safe and sound, and we end the evening at Machado's. He tells me about death's assistants out in Minas.[56] In some cases, when the agony goes on too long, these licensed gentlemen are summoned. They arrive, dressed as funeral directors,[57] nod, take off their gloves, and go to the dying person. They ask the person to pray "Mary-Jesus" and not to stop, while they place a knee on the person's stomach and their hands over the person's mouth and apply pressure until the sufferer drifts over the edge. They step back, put their gloves back on, receive fifty cruzeiros, and leave surrounded by a general sense of gratitude and respect.

August 2

Tired of making notes about nothing. (I'm writing this in the plane to

55. The Pythia was the name given to the priestess serving as Oracle of Delphi.

56. Minas Gerais is a large state at the southern end of Brazil and is the country's central hub of coffee production.

57. In French, Camus has written only *ordonnateurs* (directors), though in the given context the word clearly evokes the term *ordonnateur des pompes funèbres* (funeral director).

São Paulo.[58] Yesterday was a whole lot of nothing. Even a conversation with Mendès about the relationship between culture and violence, which helped me sharpen my thinking, seemed like another nothing.)

Haunted, in reality, in the glorious light of Rio, by the thought of the harm we do to others the moment we look at them. Causing suffering has long been a thing of indifference to me, I have to admit. It's love that's enlightened me about this. Now, I can no longer bear it. In a way, it's better to kill than to cause suffering.

What finally seemed clear to me yesterday is that I wish to die.

August 3

Night falls fast in São Paulo, bright signs atop thick skyscrapers lighting up one by one while thousands of birds greet the end of the day from the royal palms that stand tall between the buildings, the steady birdsong covering the deep bass of the car horns that announce the return of the businessmen.

Dinner with Oswald de Andrade,[59] a remarkable character (expand on this later). From his point of view, Brazil is peopled with primitives and is all the better for it.

The city of São Paulo, a strange city, an outsized Oran.

I stupidly forgot to note the thing that touched me most. A radio show in São Paulo where poor people come on to discuss their needs given their current situation. This evening, a tall, poorly clothed Negro man, a 5-month-old little girl in his arms, baby bottle in his pocket, came on to explain that, quite simply, his wife had abandoned him and he was looking for someone who could take care of the child without taking it away from him. An ex-fighter pilot, out of work, looking for a job as a mechanic, etc. Then, in the offices, we wait for listeners' phone calls. Five minutes after the end of the broadcast, the phone rings off the hook. Everyone offers themselves or offers something. While the Black man is on the line, the ex-pilot holds the child and cradles her. And the best part: a tall, much older Negro man enters the office half-dressed. He was sleeping and his wife, who was listening to the show, woke him and told him: "Go get the child."

---

58. In the previous entry, Camus uses the French name for São Paulo (Saint-Paul), but here he uses the Portuguese.

59. Oswaldo de Andrade (1890–1954) was a poet and Brazilian modernist intellectual.

August 4

Press conference in the morning. Lunch standing up at Andrade's. At 3 o'clock, they take me, I don't really know why, to the city penitentiary, "the most beautiful in Brazil." It is, in fact, "beautiful," like a penitentiary in an American film. Except the smell, the awful smell of man that lingers in every prison. Bars, iron doors, bars, doors, etc. And as you get deeper inside, signboards: "Be good" and above all "Optimism." I'm ashamed standing there in front of one or two of the prisoners, who are themselves among the privileged, and who are doing some work for the prison. The doctor-psychiatrist then begins to check off all the categories of mental perversity, and in doing so drives me up a wall. Someone tells me, as we're leaving, the standard slogan: "Here, you're at home."

I forgot. On our way there, we passed through a street filled with prostitutes. They stand behind doors with vertical blinds, the gaps between the slats wide enough to see them, charming for the most part, in any case. You discuss the price through the slats, which are painted in all imaginable colors, green, red, yellow, sky blue. They're caged birds.

Then, a steep climb up a small skyscraper. São Paulo at night. The fairytale side of modern cities, glittering roofs and avenues. Cafés and orchids all around. It's hard to imagine, though.

Then Andrade tells me about his theory: cannibalism as a vision of the world.[60] Faced with Descartes's failure and the failure of science, a return to primitive fertilization: matriarchy and cannibalism. Given that the first bishop who landed in Bahia was eaten there, Andrade dates his manifesto Year 317 of the Swallowing of Bishop Sardine (for his name was Sardine).

Last hour. After my talk,[61] Andrade tells me that in that model penitentiary, you see prisoners commit suicide by smashing their head against the walls or closing a drawer on their throat until they suffocate.

———

60. Andrade's *The Cannibalist Manifesto*, published in 1928, criticizes Europe's destructive influence on Brazil and argues that by "cannibalizing" other cultures—which is to say assimilating them—Brazil would create its own unique, postcolonial identity. Some saw the theory as one of reclamation, others as one of erasure.

61. This was "The Age of Murderers" talk, which Camus gave several times during his tour of South America and which served as a sort of preparatory step toward *The Rebel*.

August 5, August 6, August 7 (Trip to Iguape)[62]

We leave for the religious festivals in Iguape, but at 10 o'clock instead of at 7, as we'd planned. In fact, we were supposed to drive through the interior, on Brazil's pothole-filled roads, during the day, as it's best to arrive before night. There was a delay, though, the car wasn't ready, etc. We leave São Paulo and begin the drive south. The roads, whether of earth or stone, are consistently covered in a red dust that blankets all the vegetation for a kilometer on either side of the road in a layer of dry mud. After a couple of kilometers, we ourselves—which is to say the driver, who looks like Auguste Comte, Andrade and his son, who's responsible for philosophers, Sylvestre, the French cultural attaché, and myself—are covered in the same dust. It seeps in through every crack and crevice of our big Ford truck and little by little fills our mouths and noses. Overhead, a ferocious sun roasts the earth, bringing all life to a halt. Fifty kilometers on, a sinister noise. We stop. One of the front springs is broken, very clearly having escaped from its housing and now rubbing against the wheel rim. Auguste Comte scratches his head and declares that we'll be able to get it fixed in about twenty kilometers or so. I advise him to remove the casing now before it gets caught against the tire. He's an optimist, though. Five kilometers farther and we have to stop, the spring being caught. Auguste Comte decides to get a tool, which is to say he takes a tire iron from the trunk and uses it like a hammer, repeatedly striking the casing, claiming that it'll come off with a little force.

I explain there's a nut that needs to be removed and then there's the wheel itself. Then I finally realize he's set out on this long journey over pothole-filled paths without even a monkey wrench. We wait there, beneath a sun that could slay an ox—and finally a truck drives by and the driver, thankfully, has a monkey wrench. The wheel removed, the nut loosened, the casing is finally removed. We set off again between the pale, furrowed mountains, encountering, sometimes, a starving zebu, escorted at other times by sad black-vultures. At 1 o'clock, we arrive in Piédade, an unsightly little village where we're warmly welcomed by the innkeeper, Dona Anesia, whom Andrade must have courted at one point. Served by a Métis Indian, Maria, who ends up offering me artificial flowers. An interminable Brazilian meal that we get through thanks to pinga, which is what they call cachaça here. We set off again, the spring having been repaired. We're continually ascending and the air is getting very dry. There are immense expanses of uninhabited,

62. Camus would go on to use Iguape as the setting for "The Stone That Grows."

uncultivated land. The terrible solitude of this outsized stretch of nature goes a long way in explaining things about this country. Arrived in Pilar at 3 o'clock. Once we're there, August Comte realizes he's made a mistake. We're told we've gone 60 kilometers too far. On these roads, that means two or three hours of driving. Aching from all the bumping and shaking, covered in dust, we set back out to find the right path. In reality, we don't begin to descend the Serra until the end of the day. I have time to see the first kilometers of the rainforest, the thickness of that vegetal sea, to imagine the solitude that exists in the center of that unexplored world, night falling as we sink deeper into the forest. We roll on for hours, pitched this way and that on a narrow road running between high walls of trees, surrounded by a faintly sugary scent. In the thick of the forest, lightning bugs—illuminated flies—flicker here and there, and red-eyed birds come and beat against the windshield for only a second. Aside from this, the stillness and silence of this terrifying world are absolute, even if Andrade sometimes claims to hear a leopard. The road twists and turns, passing wobbly-planked bridges stretched across small rivers. Then the mist comes and a fine rain dissolves our headlights. We're no longer driving, but literally creeping. It's almost 7 in the evening, we've been driving since 10 in the morning, and our fatigue is such that we welcome, with fatalism, the hypothesis Auguste Comte presents: we may run out of gas. Nevertheless, the forest begins to thin a little—and slowly, the landscape begins to change. Finally, we come out into the open air and arrive in a small village where we're stopped by a large river. Light beacons from the other side and then we see a large ferry arriving, the oldest system there is, with poles steered by mulattos in straw hats.[63] We embark and the ferry drifts slowly over the Ribeira River. The river is wide and flows gently toward the sea and night. On both banks, the forest remains thick. In the soft sky, stars enveloped in mist. Everyone aboard goes quiet. The absolute silence of the hour is disturbed only by the river lapping at the sides of the ferry. At the front of the ferry, I watch the river flow, the scene strange yet familiar. From both banks, weird bird cries and cane-toad croaks. It's midnight in Paris, at this exact moment.

Debarking. Then we continue to creep toward Registro, an authentic Japanese capital in the center of Brazil, where I get a chance to glimpse a few delicately decorated houses and even a kimono. We're told, then, that Iguape is only 60 km away.

---

63. The arrival of the ferry would go on to be incorporated into "The Stone That Grows."

We set out again. A humid breath of air and incessant drizzle tell us we're not far from the sea. The road itself turns to sand—more difficult and dangerous than it was before. It's 12:00 A.M. when we finally arrive in Iguape. Not counting all our stops, it took us ten hours to travel the 300 km now separating us from São Paulo.

The hotel is all closed up. A prominent citizen we run into in the night takes us to the mayor's house (the prefect, they say here). The mayor informs us, through the door, that we're to sleep at the hospital. Off to the hospital. Despite the exhaustion, the city seems beautiful, with its colonial churches, the nearby forest, the low, bare houses, and the mildness of the dripping-wet air. Andrade claims he can hear the sea. But it's far away. At the "Happy Memory" hospital (that's its name), the friendly prominent citizen leads us to an unused ward, which smells like fresh paint, even from a hundred yards away.[64] He tells me that, in fact, it's been repainted in our honor. But there's no light, as the country's power plant stops running at 11 o'clock. Nevertheless, in the glow of our lighters, we glimpse six clean and rustic beds. This is our dormitory. We set our bags down. The prominent citizen wants us to have a sandwich at the club. Completely worn out, we go to the club. The club is a sort of bistro on the second floor where we meet other prominent citizens who shower us with respect. I once again note the Brazilians' exquisite politeness, a little ceremonious perhaps, but still so much better than the Europeans' boorishness. Sandwich and beer. A tall beanpole of a man who can barely keep himself upright has the bright idea of coming over to ask me for my passport. I show it to him and it seems he's saying my papers aren't in order. Exhausted, I tell him to take a hike. The prominent citizens, indignant with the man, hold a sort of board meeting, after which they tell me they're going to put the policeman (for he is one) in prison and that I have to choose what charges to press. I ask them to please set him free. They explain that the great honor I'm doing Iguape hasn't been properly recognized by this loudmouth and that such a lack of manners must be sanctioned. I protest. But they're determined to do me this honor. The whole thing goes on until the next evening when I finally find the right way of putting it to them, asking if they'd do me the exceptional, personal favor of sparing this thoughtless individual. They buzz about my chivalry and tell me things will be taken care of according to my wishes.

---

64. The "Happy Memory" hospital and many of the details surrounding it would later be incorporated into "The Stone That Grows."

In any case, the night of this drama we set off for the hospital, surrounded by kindness, and halfway there we run into the mayor, who got up and came over to personally lead us to our beds. He's also woken the power plant's personnel and now we have light. They get us settled in, they practically tuck us in, and finally, at 1 o'clock, completely worn out, we all try to go to sleep in unison. I say try because my bed tilts a little and my neighbors turn back and forth and Auguste Comte snores ferociously. At last, I drift off, late at night, to a dreamless sleep.

August 6

Wake up very early. Unfortunately, no water in the hospital. I shave with mineral water and do a little washing up in the same way. Then the prominent citizens arrive and lead us to the main ward to have something to eat. Finally, we head out into Iguape.

In the small Fontaine Garden, mysterious and gentle, with bunches of flowers between banana and pandan trees, I'm able to relax a little and find some calm. Some Métis, some mulattos, and the first gauchos I've seen are waiting patiently in front of the entrance to a grotto where they'll receive shards of the Stone That Grows. In fact, Iguape is the city of the Good Jesus, whose effigy was found out on the waves by some fishermen who washed it in this grotto. Since then, a stone has continued to grow there, and they chip pieces of it off, highly beneficial. The city itself, between the forest and the river, is gathered around the Church of the Good Jesus. A few hundred houses, but with a unique style, low, roughcast, multicolored. Beneath a fine rain soaking the poorly paved streets, with the motley crew filling it—Japanese, Indians, Métis, elegant prominent citizens—Iguape bears the colonial stamp. You breathe a very particular melancholy there, the melancholy of the far ends of the world. Aside from the heroic route we took, the only thing linking Iguape and the rest of the world is two weekly planes. You can withdraw from the world here.

Throughout the day, our hosts' kindness never wavers. But it's the procession we've come to see. As soon as afternoon arrives, firecrackers begin to go off everywhere, causing the hairless vultures perched on the rooftops to fly off. The crowd thickens. Some of these pilgrims have been traveling the pothole-filled paths of the interior for five days. One of them, who has the look of an Assyrian, with a beautiful black beard, tells us that the Good Jesus saved him from a shipwreck, after he'd spent a day and night out on the raging waters, and that he's vowed to carry a 60 kg stone on his head throughout the procession.[65] The hour draws near. From the church come Black penitents, then White, wearing surplices, then angel-children, then something like the Children of Mary, then the effigy of the Good Jesus himself, behind which the bearded man moves forward, torso naked, carrying an enormous slab on his head. Finally, the orchestra comes out playing "double time," and then to finish up, the crowd of pilgrims, the only interesting group, really, the rest being rather sordid and ordinary. The crowd lining the narrow street, overflowing it, is really the strangest gathering you could find. Ages, races, clothing color, classes, disabilities, all mixed together in a swaying and colorful mass, starred, sometimes, with tapers, above which firecrackers continually explode and, every now and again, a plane passes, unusual in this ageless world. Mobilized for the occasion, the planes roar at regular intervals above the elegant prominent citizens and the Good Jesus. We go to another strategic position to wait for the procession, and as it passes in front of us, the bearded man appears tensed with exhaustion, his legs trembling. Nevertheless, he makes it to the end safely. The bells ring, the houses and shops along the processional route that had closed their doors and windows reopen them—and we go for dinner.

After dinner, some gauchinos sing in the square and everyone sits around them. The firecrackers continue and a child blows off a finger. He screams and cries as he's led away: "Why'd the Good Jesus do this?" (They translate this soul-cry for me.)

To bed early because we leave early the next day. But the firecrackers, as well as Auguste Comte's terrific sneezing, keep me from falling asleep until late at night.

August 7

Same route, except we avoid the other day's detour and cross three rivers. Saw some hummingbirds. I again gaze, for hours, at the monotonous nature and immense spaces, which you can't quite call beautiful but which stick to the soul in an insistent way. A country where the seasons blend together, one with the other, where the vegetation is so tangled as to become shapeless, where blood is mixed to the point the soul has lost its limits. A heavy

65. The bearded man would go on to form the basis of the character The Cook in "The Stone That Grows."

swishing sound, the forest's murky blue-green light, the varnish of red dust covering everything, time melting, the slow pace of rural life, the brief and senseless excitement of big cities—this is a land of indifference and bloodshed. No matter how it tries, the skyscraper hasn't yet conquered the forest's spirit, its immensity, its melancholy. It's the sambas, the real ones, that best express what I mean.

The last fifty kilometers are the most exhausting. August Comte, cautious, lets everyone else pass. But then each car lifts so much red dust into the air that the headlights are no longer able to penetrate the mineral fog and the car has to stop sometimes. We don't know where we are anymore, and my mouth and nostrils feel like they're stuffing up with a suffocating mud. I welcome, with relief, São Paulo, the hotel, a hot bath.

———

August 8

All these degrees of longitude and latitude still to go nauseate me. Dreary, hectic day (I'm writing this on the plane taking me to Porto Alegre). At 11 o'clock, a visit from some Brazilian philosophers, who've come to ask me for a couple of "clarifications." Lunch with a young couple, French professors. Charming. Then a visit to the Alliance Française. Stroll with Mme P. through the streets of São Paulo, where I come across a photo of myself that humbles me. Cocktail at Valeur. Dinner at Sylvestre's. A talk. The lecture hall is again overflowing, with some people standing. A kind Frenchwoman brought me some Gauloises. After the talk, I'm taken to a theater to hear a Brazilian singer. Then champagne at Andrade's. I return totally worn out, tired of the human face.

———

August 9

Leave for Porto Alegre, Andrade and Sylvestre are emotional, etc. Lunch on the plane. For the first time, a little coughing fit. But nobody notices. In Porto Alegre, I disembark into a biting cold. Four or five frozen French people are waiting for me at the airport. They tell me I have to give a talk that evening, which isn't something we'd agreed to. Saw some capotes[66]—The light is quite

66. In the original manuscript, the word is hard to make out, though it seems reasonable that Camus was referring to "capotes," the warm, poncho-like coats worn in the region.

beautiful. The city ugly. Despite its five rivers. These islets of civilization are often hideous. In the evening, the talk. They have to turn people away. The press exaggerates the whole thing. That rather amuses me, though. My main concern is to get going and to finish, to finish this once and for all. They realize I don't have a visa for Chile. We have to stop in Montevideo, telegraph, etc.

———

August 10

Stroll in the city. Plane at 2:00 P.M., where I'm writing this and what preceded it. Terrible sadness and feeling of isolation. My mail hasn't caught up with me and I'm moving farther away from it.

The welcome given by the French officials in Montevideo lacks warmth. The dates for my talks have already been changed several times. Though I had nothing to do with it. They even neglected to reserve a room for me. I end up in a sort of comfortless storage room—where, all the same, I feel better than in the company of my forced hosts. It takes me a while to fall asleep, tossing and turning, focusing my willpower on not falling to pieces before the end of the trip.

Forced to admit to myself that, for the first time in my life, I'm in the midst of a psychological meltdown. That stable poise that's withstood everything else has now collapsed, despite all my effort. Murky waters inside me, hazy shapes passing in them, sapping all my energy. This depression is hell, so to speak. If the people welcoming me here could only feel the effort I'm making just to appear normal, they'd at least make an effort to smile.

———

August 11

Get up early, write some letters. Then, still without news from my chaperones, I go out into a beautiful, icy day in Montevideo. The tip of the city is bathed in the yellow waters of the Rio de la Plata. Spacious and orderly, Montevideo is surrounded by a necklace of beaches and a maritime boulevard that seems beautiful. There's a relaxed quality to this city, which seems easier to live in than the others I've seen here. Mimosas in the beachfront neighborhoods, palm trees reminiscent of Menton. Relieved, also, to be in a Spanish-speaking country. Return to my room. My chaperones are waking up. I'll leave by boat this evening, from Rio de la Plata to Buenos Aires. Lunch at the attaché's. Quai d'Orsay and flowery nonsense. He's a good guy, nonetheless. In the evening, the boat leaves Montevideo. I again gaze at the moon on the silty waters—but my heart is colder now than it was on the *Campana*.

———

August 12

In the morning, Buenos Aires. Huge cluster of houses pushing outward. W.R. is waiting for me. We discuss the matter of giving talks. I hold my ground, adding that my talk, if I were to give it, would focus in part on freedom of expression. Given, moreover, that he assumes the censor would be able to request a transcript of the talk to be read ahead of time, I warn him that I would categorically refuse. He's of the opinion, then, that it would be best not to go looking for trouble before it finds you. Same with the ambassador. Tour of the city—a rare degree of ugliness. Lot of people in the afternoon. Finally, I get to V.O.'s.[67] Nice, large house like the kind in *Gone with the Wind*. Grand, old luxury. I'd like to lie down and sleep there until the end of the world. I do drift off to sleep, in fact.

———

August 13

Good night. I wake to a cold and foggy day. V. sends me letters from her room. Then the papers. The Peronist press quietly ignored or softened the statements I made yesterday afternoon. Lunch with the editor of *Prensa* (opposition), the police beat, etc. Afternoon, forty people. After getting out of that, dinner with V. and we talk until midnight. She has me listen to Britten's *Rape of Lucretia* and the recorded poems of Baudelaire—very nice. First real night of relaxation since I set out. I'd like to stay here until it's time to go back home—to avoid the continual struggle that drains all my energy. There's a temporary peace in this house.

———

67. Victoria Ocampo (1890–1979) was an Argentinian writer and founder of the influential literary magazine *Sur*, which published authors such as José Ortega y Gasset, Jorge Luis Borges, and Julio Cortázar, as well as Camus. She and Camus—and, separately, she and Camus's wife, Francine—maintained an intermittent correspondence throughout the rest of their lives. In 1953, when Ocampo was arrested for her anti-Perónist political positions, Camus sent a letter, signed by a group of well-known French writers, to the Argentinian ambassador seeking her freedom.

August 14

At 9 o'clock, no news of the plane that's supposed to take me to Chile. At 12 o'clock, we call. Day spent at V's waiting to depart. Rafael Alberti[68] is there, with his wife. Likable. I know he's a communist. I end up explaining my point of view to him. He agrees with me. But some slander will eventually come to separate me from this man who is and should remain a comrade. What's to be done?[69] We're in the age of separation. The plane finally takes off, at sunset. We pass over the Andes at night—and I can't see a thing—which just about sums up the trip. If anything, I glimpse a few snowy ridges in the night. But before night had completely fallen, I had the chance to see the immense and monotonous pampas—which have no end. The descent on Santiago happens in a flash, through a velvety sky, with a forest of winking stars at our feet. The gentle caress of these cities stretched out along the ocean at night.

August 15

On the Pacific with Charvet and Fron. Ch. tells me how earthquakes influence the way Chileans comport themselves. Five hundred shocks a year—several of them catastrophic. It creates a psychology of instability. Chileans are gamblers, spending everything they have and doing politics day by day.

We ride on: the long white breakers riding atop the Pacific. Santiago huddled between the water and the Andes. Intense colors (marigolds the color of rust), the blossoming plum and almond trees etched against a white background of snowy peaks—an admirable country.

Afternoon: drudgery. At six o'clock, a forum.[70] I'm feeling good. Dinner at Charvet's. I'm in the midst of depression. I drink too much, due to exhaustion, and don't get to sleep until late. Time lost.

August 16

Hellish day. Radio, sightseeing. Lunch with Vincent Anidobre's son in a little house at the foot of the Andes. Colloquium with the local theater

---

68. Rafael Alberti Merello (1902–1999) was a Spanish surrealist poet and dramaturge.

69. The phrase *Que faire?* (What's to be done?), discussed in earlier notes, is used twice in the South American journal. In both cases it follows discussion of either Communism or the Soviet Union.

70. Camus discussed contemporary French literature at the Instituto Chileno-Francès de Cultura in Santiago, Chile.

people. At 7 o'clock, a talk in a room so packed it's exhausting.[71] Dinner at the embassy, a flood of boredom. Only the ambassador is amusing; yesterday, he took his jacket off and danced.

August 17

Day of unrest and riots. Protests were already taking place yesterday. But today it feels like an earthquake. The cause: an increase in the "micro" fare (Santiago's subway system). Buses are overturned and burned. Glass is shattered on the ones that pass through. In the afternoon, I'm told that the university, where the students protested, is closed—and that my talk won't be able to take place there. Within two hours, the French department has arranged for a talk at the French Institute. When I leave there, the shops have lowered their gates and the armed-and-helmeted troops literally occupy the city. They fire a blank every now and then. It's a state of emergency.[72] During the night, I hear shots fired here and there.

August 18

Plane delayed until nighttime. Bad weather in the Andes. I sleep poorly here, if at all—and I'm tired. The Charvets come get me at 11 o'clock, and I'm asleep on my feet. That's how bad my night went. But their kindness isn't a burden, and we drive through the Chilean countryside. Mimosa trees and weeping willows. Beautiful, hearty nature. At our next stop, an excellent lunch in front of an open fire. Then, we branch off toward the Andes and stop for a bite in a mountain lodge, in front of a beautiful fire, once again. I'm doing well in Chile and I could see myself living here for a little while, if circumstances were different. When we get back, we learn that the plane won't be ready until the next morning. The rain's coming down in buckets. Dinner at

---

71. On August 16, Camus gave "The Age of Murderers" talk at the University of Chile. On August 17, he was supposed to give a second talk at the university, the one on Chamfort, but, as he notes in the entry that follows, the talk was moved to the French Institute due to unrest at the university.

72. Here, Camus uses the term *l'état de siège,* which he'd also recently used as the title for one of his plays, written in 1948, less than a year before this entry was made. When the play appeared in English in the 1950s, its title was transparently translated by Stuart Gilbert as *State of Siege,* which doesn't collocate highly in American English, which prefers "state of emergency" or, as in the case of the specific incident Camus witnessed in Chile, "martial law."

the Charvets'. Bed at midnight. At the hotel, I find some parting gifts. It takes me a long time to fall asleep.

———

August 19

At 4:30 A.M., the company calls. I'm to be at the airfield at 6 o'clock. At 7:00 A.M., the plane takes off. But then, after it seemed the path had been set, the plane heads south and follows another path, after having gone 200 km out of the way. The Andes: prodigious, shattered ranges tearing through mountains of clouds—but the snow is dazzling. We're constantly pitching and rolling, and to make matters worse, I have a coughing fit. I just manage to avoid the worst—and pretend to be asleep.

We don't reach Buenos Aires until noon. By that point, the lack of sleep overwhelms me. V.O. came to get me but nobody from the embassy came and they also haven't gotten me a ticket to Montevideo, though I have a talk there at 6:30 P.M. Thanks to V., we hustle to Buenos Aires, then to the seaplane airport. There are no open seats. V. telephones a friend. Everything is taken care of. I leave at 4:45 P.M., the weather bad, a yellow sky over yellow waters. At 5:45, Montevideo. The embassy sent someone to tell me they decided to cancel the talk and to take me to the French high school instead. There, the principal tells me that some people have shown up anyway and that he doesn't know what to do. I suggest a debate, even though I'm running on empty. They agree and reschedule my two talks for the next day, one at 11:00 A.M., the other at 6:00 P.M. Debate. Then to bed, drunk with exhaustion.

———

August 20

Brutal day. At 10:00 A.M., journalists and C. At 11:00 A.M., first talk, in a hall at the University. In the middle of the talk, a curious character enters the hall. A cape, a short beard, a cold look in the eye. He finds himself a spot at the back, standing up, opens a journal and ostensibly reads it. From time to time, he coughs loudly. At least the guy livens up the auditorium. A minute with José Bergamín,[73] a refined man with the worn, deeply lined face of a Spanish intellectual. He doesn't want to choose between Catholicism and

73. José Bergamín (1895–1983) was a Spanish writer and activist who spent long periods of his life living in Latin America and France.

Communism until the Spanish Civil War is over. A hypotensive man whose energy is solely spiritual. My kind of guy.

Bergamín: my deepest temptation is suicide. A dramatic suicide. (Return to Spain at the risk of being jailed, resist, and die.)[74]

Lunch with some nice couples, French professors. At 4 o'clock, press conference. At 5 o'clock, I see the director of the theater that's going to stage *Caligula*. He wants to throw in some ballet. It's all the rage internationally. At 6 o'clock, Mlle Lussitch and the charming cultural attaché from Uruguay take me for a short ride through the gardens near the city limits. The evening is gentle, quick, and a little tender. This country is beautiful and easygoing. I'm able to relax a little. At 6:30, the second talk. The ambassador felt obliged to come with his better half. In the first row, the sinister faces of boredom and vulgarity. After the talk, I go for a walk with Bergamín. We end up in a packed café. He doubts the effectiveness of what he's doing. I tell him that maintaining an uncompromising refusal is a positive act, with positive consequences—Then dinner at Suzannah Soca's. A crowd of society women who, after a third whiskey, become a little much. A couple of them literally offer themselves to me—but that's not such a compliment. A Frenchwoman standing right in front of me finds a way to be an apologist for Franco. Exhausted, I go for it—and then realize I'd better take my leave. I ask the cultural attaché if she'd like to come have a drink with me, and we make our escape. At least this pretty face makes it easier to live. The night hangs gentle over Montevideo. A clear sky, the rustling of dry palm leaves above the Place de la Constitution, flights of pigeons, white in the black sky. The hour would be relaxing, and this solitude I feel, without news for 18 days, without confidence,[75] might be eased, but then the charming attaché begins to recite for me, in the middle of the square, some French poems she's written, miming their tragic nature, arms thrust out at her sides, voice rising and falling. I sit tight. Then we go for a drink and I take her home. I go to bed and the anxiety and melancholy return, keeping me from sleeping.

———

74. Bergamín did return to Spain in 1958 and, as he'd expected, was arrested. In 1963, he went back into exile and then returned to settle in Spain for good in 1970.

75. Four days earlier, on August 16, Camus wrote to Maria Casarès: "It's been fourteen days since I heard from you and I don't know if you can imagine what that means to me. I want to believe with all my strength that my mail's been held up in Rio for reasons I don't understand, but I can't help imagining, sometimes, that maybe you haven't written to me, and then I sink into a state it would be better not to tell you about."

August 21

Up at 8:00 A.M. I slept 3 or 4 hours But the plane takes off at 11 o'clock. Beneath a tender sky, freshly fluffed and cloudy, Montevideo unfurls its beaches—a charming city where everything requires happiness—and a witless happiness. Stupidity of traveling by plane—a retrograde and barbaric way of getting around. At 5 o'clock, we're flying over Rio, and on descent, I'm greeted by that dense and humid air, its consistency like cotton wool, which I'd forgotten about and which is particular to Rio. The garish, multicolored parrots, too, and a peacock with a discordant voice. Barely able to get to bed, with no news, not a single piece of mail waiting for me at the embassy.

August 22

My mail is brought to me. It's been sitting around in some office for 18 days. Tired, I don't leave my room all day. In the evening, a talk, after which a drink with Mme Mineur. To bed with a fever.

August 23

Get up a little better. My departure approaches. It'll be Thursday or Saturday. I think of Paris as of a monastery. Lunch in Copacabana, in front of the sea. The waves are high and gentle. Watching them calms me down a little. Back to my room. I sleep a little. At 5 o'clock, public debate session with Brazilian students. Is it the fatigue? I've never felt so loose and easy. Dinner at the Claveries' with Mme R., a ravishing woman, but without much depth, it seems.

August 24

I get up a little better still. Departure is now set for Saturday. Sightseeing in the morning and the exhaustion returns. So much so I decide not to have lunch. At 1:30, Pedrosa and his wife come get me so we can go see some paintings done by the insane, out in the banlieues, in a hospital of modern lines and ancient grime. It's heartbreaking to see faces behind those tall window bars. Two interesting painters. The others surely have what it takes to send our forward-thinking Parisians into fits of rapture—but what they have, in fact, is ugliness. Even more striking in the sculptures, ugly and vulgar. It terrifies me to recognize that one of the institution's young psychiatric doctors is the boy who, at the beginning of the trip, asked me the most asinine question anyone has asked me in all of South America. He's the one deciding the fate of these unfortunate people. Quite touched himself, really. But I'm even more terrified when he tells me he'll be making the trip to Paris with me on Saturday; 36 hours locked up in a metal box with him, that's the final straw.

In the evening, dinner at Pedrosa's with some intelligent people. Pouring rain on the way back.

———

August 25

Flu. Clearly, this climate doesn't agree with me. I work a little in the morning, then go to the zoo to see the sloth.

The sloth is free-roaming and you have to try to find it among the park's thousands of trees. I give up. At least the leopards are splendid—the lizards terrible and the anteater, too. Lunch with Letarget in Copacabana. Rio is veiled in an incessant rain that pools in the holes of the pavement and sidewalk, dissolving the thin veneer they've used to try to cover up the problem. The colonial city shows through, and I have to say that it's much more attractive like this, covered in mud, trampled over, its sky filled with mist. Shopping in the afternoon. Everything I find in this country comes from somewhere else. In the evening, at 5 o'clock, Mendès's place. Another crazy crowd, where I'm bored and no longer have the strength to hide it. Physically, I can no longer bear large gatherings. Same thing at dinner, where there were seven of us when I thought it would be only Pedrosa and Barleto, where everyone cuts each other off while speaking, and at the top of their voice, too. Fueled by my flu, the ordeal becomes hellish. I'd like to go back, but I don't dare let them know. At 1:00 A.M., Mme Pedrosa notices that I can barely keep myself upright, and I go to bed.[76]

———

August 26 and 27

Two awful days dragging about with my flu, to different places with different people, numb to all I see, concerned only with regaining my strength, amid people who, in their friendship or hysterics, notice nothing of the state

76. To Maria Casarès, Camus wrote: "For eighteen days I've fought the fatigue, a frightful depression that's gotten worse, the sleepless nights, exhausting work, the crowds of people who speak, challenge, ask, pressure. . . . This trip has been exhausting. Plane, talk, reception, journalists, hysterical society women, and then the whole thing over again the next day."

I'm in and so make it that much worse. Evening at the consul's where I hear comments about the necessity of corporal punishment in our colonial armies.

Saturday 4:00 P.M. I'm informed that the plane's motor has broken down and the plane won't be leaving until tomorrow, Sunday. The fever's getting worse and I'm beginning to wonder if it's not something more than the flu.

———

August 31

Sick. Bronchitis, at the least. They call to tell me we'll be leaving this afternoon. Glorious day. Doctor. Penicillin. The trip finishes in a metal coffin, between a mad doctor and a diplomat, heading for Paris.

Notebook VI

SEPTEMBER 1949–MARCH 1951

September '49.[1]

To finish, readjust the value of murder so as to oppose it to anonymous, cold, and abstract destruction. To defend and glorify the murder of man by man is one of the stages on the road to rebellion.

My life's only effort, the rest having been given to me, and generously so (aside from wealth, which I don't care about): to live the life of a normal man. I didn't want to be a man of the abyss. The excessive effort has been for nothing. Little by little, instead of getting better and better at what I do, I see the abyss getting closer.

Gheorghiu rightly notes that Christ's sentencing (and torture) was intertwined with that of the two thieves.[2] The technique of amalgamation was already being practiced in year zero.

The only progress, according to G: today, ten thousand innocents are surrounded by two guilty.

. . . the village facades erected by Potemkin along the routes Catherine the Great used while visiting her empire.

Czapski (*Inhuman Land*) tells how Russian children would sprinkle water over the corpses of German soldiers they found in the snow and, in the morning, use their frozen bodies as sleds.

We have to love life before loving the meaning of it, Dostoyevsky says. Yes, and when the love of life disappears, no amount of meaning will console us.

The great Imam Ali: "The world is a rotting carcass. Whosoever desires a piece of this world will live with the dogs."

Stendhal. "The difference between Germans and other peoples: they're exhilarated by meditation instead of calmed by it. Second nuance: they'd kill for a little character."[3]

---

1. In the original manuscript, notebook VI continues uninterrupted after the note to see the South American journal.

2. Constantin Virgil Gheorghiu (1916–1992), Romanian writer whose novel *The 25th Hour*, about a young man sent to various labor camps, had just been published in French.

3. The first part of the Stendhal quote would go on to be incorporated into *The Rebel* at the beginning of the chapter on "Individual Terrorism."

———

Sperber. "Let God punish the devout who instead of going to church enter a revolutionary party so as to make a church of it."[4]

—Communism, skeptical fanaticism.

—Speaking of a master (Grenier?): "Meeting that man was a great pleasure. Following him would have been bad, never abandoning him will be good."

———

Id. Rosa Luxembourg's death: "To others, she'd been dead for twelve years. To them, she'd been dying for twelve years."

———

"There are no isolated sacrifices. Behind each individual who sacrifices himself there stand others whom he sacrifices with him without asking their opinion."

They want what's good for the people, but they don't love the people. They don't love anyone, not even themselves.

———

October '49.

Novel. "Somewhere, in some far corner of his soul, he loved them. They were truly loved, but from such a distance that the word love took on a new meaning."

"He wished for two things, the first of which was absolute possession. The second was the absolute memory he wanted to leave her. Men are so well aware that love is doomed to die that they work at creating a memory of it the whole time they're living it. He wanted to leave her with a grand idea of himself so that their love would be grand, always and forever. But now he knew he wasn't grand, knew she would know it one day, sooner or later, and that in place of absolute memory would be, at least for him, absolute death. The victory, the only victory, would be to recognize that love can be grand even when the lover isn't. But he wasn't yet prepared for that terrible modesty."

"He carried inside him, seared with a red-hot iron, the memory of her face consumed with pain. . . . It was around that time that he lost the self-esteem

4. Manès Sperber (1905–1984), writer, disciple of Alfred Adler, and friend of Malraux, attended meetings at which Camus, Sartre, and Koestler were present.

that had always sustained him until then. . . . No match for love, she was right."

"A person can love in chains, through stone walls several meters thick, etc., but let the slimmest little section of the heart be subject to responsibility and true love is impossible."

"He imagined a future of solitude and suffering, and he found a sort of difficult pleasure in those imaginings, because he supposed suffering to be noble and harmonious. So then, what he really imagined was a future without suffering. When the grief arrived, it was quite the opposite: there was no more life."

"He told her that's how men love, through will, not grace, and that he had to conquer himself. She swore to him that wasn't love."

"He'd lost everything, even solitude."

"He cried out to her that this would be the death of him and that she didn't seem affected by it. For with such high expectations, she found it only natural that, having failed, he should die."

"Everything is to be forgiven, existing first and foremost. Existence always ends up being a misdeed."

"That was the day he lost her. Apparently, the unhappiness only came later. But he knew that was the day. If he'd wanted to hold onto her, he should have never faltered. Her expectations were such that he couldn't make a single mistake, show a single sign of weakness. From anyone else, she would've accepted such things, had accepted them and would accept them again. Not from him. Such are love's privileges."

"There's honor in love. Once it's lost, love is nothing."

———

"I was small before having loved, precisely because I was sometimes tempted to see myself as great" (Stendhal, *On Love*).

———

Of fine mind and mediocre heart. Or her virtues were of the mind, not the heart. What he liked in her was her outer life, the storybook romantic, the gameplaying and playacting.

———

Hopelessness is not knowing your reasons for being in the struggle and if being in the struggle is even necessary.

Walking through Paris, this memory: fires in the Brazilian countryside and the aromatic scent of coffee and spices. Then, cruel, sad nights falling on that boundless land.

———

Rebellion. The absurd supposes an absence of choice. To live is to choose. To choose is to kill. Murder is the objection to the absurd.

———

Guilloux. The artist's difficulty is that he's neither entirely a monk nor a layman—and that he's inclined to both.

———

The real problem of the moment: punishment.

———

Who can say the distress of the man who has sided with the creature against the creator and who, in losing the idea of his own innocence and that of others, judges the creature, and himself, as criminal as the creator.[5]

———

Monnerot. "The fecundity of a producer of ideas (he's talking about Hegel) is displayed in the wide range of possible *translations* (interpretations)."[6]

Of course not. That's true of an artist, absolutely false of a thinker.

———

Novel. Sentenced to death. But someone gets a cyanide capsule through to him . . . And there, in the solitude of his cell, he began to laugh. An immense relief filled him. He was no longer climbing the walls. He had all night. He *could choose* . . . Could say to himself, "Time to go," and then, "No, another minute," and savor that minute . . . What revenge! What a rebuttal!

———

For lack of love, we can try to have honor. Sad honor.

———

5. Camus crossed this entry out on the manuscript, but it nevertheless appears in the published French edition.

6. Jules Monnerot (1909–1995), French sociologist and author of *Sociologie du communisme*. Camus cites Monnerot, though not this passage, in *The Rebel*, "The Failing of the Prophecy."

F: Crazy to base anything on love, crazy to break anything for love.[7]

It's because he was jealous of our suffering that God came to die on the Cross. That strange look not yet his own . . .

End of October '49. Relapse.[8]

A sick person has to be clean to be forgotten, to be forgiven. And yet. Even his cleanliness is strange. It's suspect—like those overly large rosettes[9] you see swindlers wear in their buttonholes.

After such a long period of health, this relapse should devastate me. It does indeed devastate me. But coming in the wake of a steady stream of devastation, it makes me laugh. In the end, it frees me. Madness is also freedom.

"So sensitive that he could have touched pain with his hands" (about Keats—by Amy Lowell).

Keats again. "There is no greater Sin after the seven deadly than to flatter oneself into an idea of being a great Poet. How comfortable a feel it is to feel that such a Crime must bring its heavy Penalty?"[10]

"Get thee to a nunnery, Ophelia!"[11] Yes, indeed, for there's no other way to possess her than to ensure that nobody else possesses her. Aside from God, whose favors are easily accepted: they don't touch the body.

---

7. This entry also appears in Marie's *The First Man* file, with the name *Marie* in place of *F*.

8. The "flus" Camus had been experiencing throughout the South American trip would turn out to be a product of his tuberculosis. To Louis Guilloux, Camus wrote: "I'm dictating this letter because it's much easier. In fact, I'm in bed, and probably for a long time. What I came down with, and what you witnessed, was a return of my old sickness. The verdict, for the moment, is five weeks in bed, taking streptomycin and company, followed by several months in the mountains. I'd be lying if I told you I wasn't a little concerned about all this."

9. In France, several of the more prestigious medals, such as the Médaille de la Résistance, which Camus may have had in mind, feature a rosette on the accompanying ribbon.

10. The quote is from a May 10, 1817, letter to Benjamin Robert Haydon (postmarked May 13, 1817). There are some differences between the French rendition of Keats that Camus quotes and the English original, which has been used here, the most significant being that, in English, the quote is one sentence connected by: "—or one of those beings who are privileged to wear out their Lives in the pursuit of Honor—".

11. In an August 8, 1820, letter, as Keats began his final fight with tuberculosis, he wrote to his fiancée Fanny Brawne: "If my health would bear it, I could write a Poem which I have in my head, which would be a consolation for people in such a situation as mine. I would show some one in Love as I am, with a person living in such Liberty as you do. Shakespeare always sums up matters in the

———

If there is a soul, it's a mistake to believe that it's given to us fully formed. It's formed here, over the course of a life. And that long, torturous labor[12] is all there is to living. When the soul is ready, formed by us and by suffering, then comes death.

———

"I am glad there is such a thing as the grave" (Keats).

———

Chesterton. Justice is a mystery, not an illusion.

———

With regard to Browning: the average man—as far as he concerns me.

———

Kleist burns his manuscripts twice . . . Piero della Francesca, blind at the end of his life . . . Ibsen an amnesiac at the end, relearning the alphabet . . . Chin up! Chin up!

———

Beauty, which helps to live, also helps to die.

———

For millennia, the world has been like those Italian Renaissance paintings in which some men are tortured on a cold tile floor while others look around as if simply passing the time. The number of people who were "disinterested" is staggeringly high compared to those who were interested. What characterized history was the amount of people who weren't interested in the plight of others. At times, the disinterested had their turn—but it was while the others were just passing time, and this made up for that. Today, everybody pretends to be interested. In the courts,[13] the witnesses suddenly turn toward the one being whipped.[14]

———

Peer Gynt tells his fellow citizens how the devil had promised the crowd that he would do an impeccable imitation of a pig's squeal. He appears and does it. But after his performance, the critics all have something to say. Some

---

most sovereign manner. Hamlet's heart was full of such Misery as mine is when he said to Ophelia 'go to a Nunnery, go, go!' Indeed I should like to give up the matter at once—I should like to die."

The Keats quote that follows the next entry is also from this same letter.

12. The French word *accouchement* is used for "labor" in the sense of "childbirth."

13. The French *salles du palais* also means "palace halls," an image that calls back to the opening of the entry.

14. This entry is crossed out on the manuscript but was published in the French edition nevertheless.

think the voice was too thin, others too polished. All feel the effect was exaggerated. And yet what they'd heard were the cries of a piglet that the devil had held beneath his coat and pinched.

———

The end of Don Giovanni: the voices of damnation, silent until then, suddenly fill the world's stage. They were there, a secret multitude, more numerous than the living.

———

Rajk trial:[15] The idea of the objective criminal who bridges the divide between two aspects of man is a common idea in legal procedure, but *overstated.*

———

Marxism is a procedural philosophy, but one without jurisprudence.

———

Of note: throughout the trial, Rajk tilted his head to the right, which he'd never done before.

———

Id. The ones who are sentenced to death but *not actually executed* and who live, in Siberia or some other place, *another life* (heroes for a novel).

———

Against the death penalty. Fichte. "System of natural right."[16]

———

Novel (*end*). He remembered a time when he devoured biographies of famous men, rushing through the pages to the moment of their death. What he wanted to know back then was what genius, greatness, and sensitivity could offer in the face of death. But now he knew that such rage was in vain, that those great lives bore no lessons for him. The genius doesn't know how to die. The poor woman does.

———

Greatness is in trying to be great. There's no other way. (That's why M. is great.)

———

15. László Rajk (1909–1949), a Hungarian Communist politician, was falsely accused of being a spy for Tito and executed after a show trial.

16. J. G. Fichte's text, usually translated into English as *Foundations of Natural Right* and translated into French as *Fondement du droit naturel,* discusses the death penalty in part 2, or Applied Natural Right, "Second Section of the Doctrine of Political Right: On Civil Legislation."

Wherever you want slaves, as much music as possible is needed. At least that's what a German prince thought, as Tolstoy reports it.

Obey, Frederick of Prussia said. But then, dying: "I'm tired of ruling over slaves."[17]

Novel. "I was looking for a way not to die if he had his freedom. If I'd found one, then I would have given freedom back to him."

Gorky, speaking of Tolstoy: "He's a man seeking God, not for himself but for others, so that He might leave him, a man, in peace, alone in the desert that he's chosen."

Id. "I am not an orphan on the earth so long as this man is alive."[18]

When they burned Jan Hus, a sweet little old lady brought her bundle of sticks to add to the pyre.[19]

Those moments you give in to suffering as to physical pain: stretched out, motionless, with no will or future, listening only to the long, throbbing pain.

Overcome? But that's precisely what suffering is: the thing we're never above.

Novel. "When she was there and we were tearing each other apart, my suffering, my tears, they made sense. *She could see them*. When she left, the suffering was in vain, with no future. And true suffering is suffering in vain. Suf-

---

17. Reportedly Frederick the Great's last words, they are more likely to have their origin in a letter left for Count von Golz in which Frederick writes: "Peasants who settle on the newly dried swamplands, must be sole owners of all their property, they must not be people in servitude or subjugation."

18. From Maxim Gorky's *Tolstoy and Other Reminiscences*. The first quote comes amid Gorky's anxiety that when Tolstoy dies, he will be turned into a "myth": "They will be creating just what he wanted but what we do not need—the story of a holy man and a saint. In fact he is great and holy because he is a man, an insanely and maddeningly beautiful man, a man of all mankind."

The second quote comes after Gorky learns that Tolstoy has in fact died, amid a lyrical passage in which Gorky describes having once seen Tolstoy sitting out by the sea and having experienced a moment of the sublime.

19. Jan Hus (1372–1415) was a Czech religious reformer and rector of Charles University in Prague. In 1415, he was brought before the Council of Constance and condemned as a heretic. Asked to recant, he replied, "I would not for a chapel of gold retreat from the truth!"

fering beside her was a delicious happiness. But suffering alone and unseen, that's the cup that's constantly presented to us, the cup from which we obstinately turn away, but from which we must one day drink, a day more terrible than the day we die."

Nights of suffering leave a hangover—like others.[20]

Novel. "A last word. It's not a question of engaging in a delicious, bitter dialogue with a pretty picture no longer present. It's a question of diligently, ruthlessly destroying it deep inside of me, of disfiguring that face in order to protect my heart from those hopeless leaps memory brings . . ." "Kill that love, O my love."

Id. "It had been ten years since he'd been able to go into a theater . . ."

Essay about The Sea.[21]

The hopeless have no homeland. Me? I knew the sea existed and that's why I lived amid these mortal times.

So then, those who love each other and are separated can live with sorrow. But, whatever they may say, they don't live without hope: they know that love exists.

We insist on confusing marriage and love on the one hand, happiness and love on the other. But they have nothing in common. That's why it happens that, the absence of love being more prevalent than love, some marriages are happy.

Involuntary commitment.

Physical jealousy is in large part a judgment on yourself. It's because you know what you're capable of thinking that you imagine the *other person* is thinking it, too.

Days at sea, this life "rebellious to forgetting, rebellious to reminiscing," according to Stevenson.[22]

---

20. Camus crossed out one-quarter of a page here that was not carried over to the typescript.

21. See "The Nearby Sea," published in *Summer*.

22. This entry is used in Camus's essay "The Nearby Sea." The quote is likely a reference to Robert Louis Stevenson's book *In the South Seas*, where he writes: "There are elements in our state and

---

Lambert. "At the moment, I'm keeping all my pity for myself."[23]

Guilloux. "In the end, we don't write to speak, but so as *not to speak*."

Novel. "When those exhausting sufferings were over, I turned to that part of myself that loves no one and sought refuge there. I took a little breather. Then I returned, head lowered, to the thickets and thorns."

Virtue is praiseworthy today. Great sacrifices are unsustainable. Martyrs are forgotten. They rise up. We look at them. As soon as they fall, the newspapers move on.

Merle,[24] a blackmail journalist, couldn't get a thing from X., whom he libeled year-round in his paper. Merle, changing tactics, openly praised his victim, who paid immediately.

Tolstoy, during the Chibunin Affair, pleads before the court on behalf of a poor fellow, guilty of striking his captain—lodges an appeal for him after the death sentence is given—writes to his aunt asking her to intervene with the Minister of War. The latter says only that Tolstoy forgot to provide the regiment's address, which prevents him from intervening. The day after Tolstoy received the letter asking him to fill in the necessary information, Chibunin was executed *on account of Tolstoy's mistake.*

Tolstoy's last work, found unfinished on his writing desk: "*In this world, there are no guilty people.*"

He was born in 1828. He wrote *War and Peace* between 1863 and 1869. Between 35 and 41 years old.

---

history which it is a pleasure to forget, which it is perhaps the better wisdom not to dwell on."

23. Edmond Lambert, a friend of Jean Grenier and Louis Guilloux, died in 1940 without having published, though those who knew him considered him a great thinker.

24. Eugène Merle (1884–1946) was a legendary figure in the prewar French press, having founded *La guerre sociale* in 1905, *Le bonnet rouge* in 1913, *Le merle blanc* in 1919, and *Paris-soir* in 1923.

Life's too long, according to Greene. "Couldn't we have committed our first major sin at seven, have ruined ourselves for love or hate at ten, have clutched at redemption on a fifteen-year-old death-bed?"[25]

Scobie, an adulterer. "Virtue, the good life, tempted him in the dark like a sin."

Id. ". . . in human love there is never such a thing as victory: only a few minor tactical successes before the final defeat of death or indifference."

Id. "Love was the wish to understand, and presently with constant failure the wish died, and love died too perhaps . . ."

Marie Dorval to Vigny: "You don't know me! You don't know me!" After so long apart, she no longer recognizes herself. "Tell me, is it true that lust wrenches the cries from within me?"

Her passport issued by Toulouse: "Bone-thin, hair disheveled, past glory."

"I didn't separate from M. de Vigny, I tore myself from him!"[26]

Now Christ's death throes take place in the courts. Knout in hand—he sits enthroned behind the bank counters.

Strepto—40 grams from November 6 to December 5, '49.

P.A.S. 360 grams from November 6 to December 5, '49

+ 20 gr. Strepto from November 13 to January 2.[27]

Novel. "By questioning him about his love, and especially by bringing such anxiety to her questioning, she made him begin to doubt things, and as his doubts grew, his will to love hardened, so that the more she appealed to his heart, the more abstract his love became."

---

25. This quote, and those that follow, come from Graham Greene's *The Heart of the Matter*, which Camus quotes in French. The original English is used here. Interestingly, Greene writes not that life is "too long," as Camus notes, but that it's "immeasurably long."

26. Marie Dorval (1798–1849), a French actress, had an intimate relationship with Alfred de Vigny, which lasted from 1831 to 1838.

27. Camus's medical regiment for treating his tuberculosis. P.A.S. refers to *para*-aminosalicylic acid. Both medicines had just come into use around the mid-1940s.

Any murder that wishes to be justified must be balanced by love. For the terrorists, the scaffold was irrefutable proof of such love.[28]

———

In 1843, the Americans liberate Hawaii, which the English had taken by force. Melville was there. The king invites his subjects to "celebrate the joy they feel by ceasing to observe any moral, legal, or religious restrictions for ten days straight; for that period, he solemnly declared, all the laws of the territory were suspended."[29]

———

Mistakes are joyful, truth infernal.

———

This sacred uncertainty Melville speaks of always leaves people and nations in limbo.

———

Melville jots notes in the margins of Shelley's Essays: "Milton's Devil as a moral being is as far superior to his God as one who perseveres in a purpose which he has conceived to be excellent, in spite of adversity and torture, is to one who in the cold security of undoubted triumph inflicts the most horrible revenge upon his enemy—not from any mistaken notion of bringing him to repent of a perseverance in enmity, but with the open and alleged design of exasperating him to deserve new torments."[30]

———

Bitter are the waters of death . . .

———

Melville at 35 years old: I've accepted annihilation.

———

28. Camus crossed out three-quarters of the page following this entry, though there are only a few words on each line, for the most part.

29. This quote, a paraphrase of Melville, comes from Pierre Frédérix's biography, *Herman Melville*, which was about to be published by Gallimard and which Camus was reading. What Melville actually writes in the epilogue for *Typee* is: "Royal proclamations in English and Hawaiian were placarded in the streets of Honolulu, and posted up in the more populous villages of the group, in which His Majesty announced to his loving subjects the re-establishment of his throne, and called upon them to celebrate it by breaking through all moral, legal, and religious restraint for ten consecutive days, during which time all the laws of the land were solemnly declared to be suspended."

30. The wording of this entry allows for some confusion. Melville made a note on Shelley's essay "On the Devil, and Devils," but the quote given here is not Melville's note, rather the portion of Shelley's essay that Melville was making a note about. Camus returns to these thoughts in "The Dandies' Rebellion" section of *The Rebel*.

Hawthorne, on Melville: “He didn’t believe and he couldn’t be content with disbelief.”

———

L.G.—rather beautiful, but, as Stendhal says, leaves a bit to be desired in terms of ideas.

———

The day he separated from his wife, he had a serious craving for chocolate and gave in to it.

———

Story about M. de Bocquandé’s grandfather. In high school, he’s accused of having done something inappropriate. He denies it. Three days detention. He denies it. “I can’t confess a mistake I didn’t make.” His father is notified. He gives his son three days to confess. If he doesn’t, he’ll be sent off as a cabin boy (the family is rich). Three days detention. He’s let out. “I cannot confess to what I haven’t done.” His father, uncompromising, ships him out to be a cabin boy. The child grows up, spends his life on boats, becomes a captain. His father dies. He grows old. And on his deathbed: “It wasn’t me.”

———

During the Paris insurrection, as the bullets whistled, Gaston Gallimard cried out, Ah! Ah! Robert Gallimard rushed over to him, panicked. Then Gaston sneezed.

———

She flattered his vanity. And that’s why he was faithful to her.

———

F: “I’m a twisted person. I can only understand my ability to love through my ability to suffer. Until I suffer, I don’t understand.”[31]

———

Preface for *L’envers et l’endroit*.

There’s an artistic resistance in me, as there’s a moral or a religious resistance in others. The forbidden, the idea that there are “things you don’t do,” which is foreign to me as an independent child, is native to me as a slave (and an admiring one) of strict artistic tradition. (The only time I overcame such taboos was in *State of Emergency*, which explains my tender feelings for the play, generally disparaged.)

---

31. This entry appears in Marie’s *The First Man* file with an *M* instead of *F*. Camus crossed out the whole notebook page following this one.

. . . Maybe this distrust is also directed at my deep-seated anarchy and, in that regard, remains useful. I understand my disorder, the violence of certain instincts, the graceless surrender into which I can throw myself. The work of art to be raised (I'm speaking in the future) must utilize these unpredictable human strengths—but not without surrounding them with barriers. At the moment, my barriers are still too strong. But what they had to hold back was strong, too. The day balance is achieved, that very day, I'll try to write the work of my dreams. It will be similar to *L'envers et l'endroit*, which is to say that a certain form of love will guide me.

It seems I can do it. The range of my experience, the understanding of my craft, my violence and my submission . . . I'll place at its center, as here, a mother's admirable silence, a man's quest to find another love similar to that silence, finally finding it, losing it, and returning, through wars, the madness of justice, and sorrow, to the solitary, quiet being whose death is a happy silence. I'll place . . .

Maritain.[32] Rebellious atheism (absolute atheism) puts history in God's place and replaces rebellion with absolute submission. "For him, duty and virtue are nothing but a total submission to, and total immolation of himself in, the sacred voracity of becoming."

"Sanctity is also a rebellion: it's refusing things as they are. It's taking the world's misfortune upon yourself."

Band attached to *The Just*: Terror and justice.[33]

Novel. "She had a way of repeating 'I love you' three times in a whispered, breathless voice, as if the credo had worn a little thin."[34]

"Despite appearances, my main occupation has always been love (for a long time, its pleasures, and, finally, its most heartbreaking displacements).

---

32. Jacques Maritain (1882–1973), a French Catholic philosopher, helped write the Universal Declaration of Human Rights.

33. New books in France often come with a red band wrapped around the book, which highlights the author's name, if sufficiently well known, or provides a tagline, as in the case above. Camus's *The Just* premiered at Paris's Théâtre Hébertot on December 15, 1949. It was published in book form a few months later, March 5, 1950.

34. Camus uses the word *traquer* (hunt) fairly often in the notebooks, beginning with the reference to Montherlant's *The Hunted Travelers*. Here, in this entry, the last phrase, *comme un credo un peu traqué*, has no clear, definite meaning, leaving any English translation to be interpretative.

I have a romantic soul and I've always had a very hard time interesting it in other things."

———

In spring, when all of this is over, write *everything I feel*. Random little things.

———

Novel. "With most women, he'd been able to fake it, successfully. With her, never. She had a sort of brilliant intuition that revealed what was going on in his heart, that exposed him."

———

Criticism of *The Just*: "No idea what love is." If I were unfortunate enough not to know what love is and wanted to make a fool of myself learning about it, I wouldn't come to Paris or look in the tabloids for lessons.

———

The end of a cold day, a twilight of shadows and ice . . . more than I can bear.

———

Preface for Political Essays. "After the fall of Napoleon, the writer of the following pages, thinking it foolish to waste his youth on political hatreds, set out to see the world." Stendhal: *Life of Rossini*.

———

Id. Stendhal (*On Love*): "Man is not free to avoid doing what gives him more pleasure than any other possible action."

Id. "Extraordinarily beautiful women are less astonishing the second day. It's a great misfortune . . . etc."

The Duc de Policastro, who "every six months traveled the hundred leagues to Lecce to see, for a quarter of an hour, an adored mistress guarded by a jealous man."

Cf: Dona Diana's story. Play's end scene (p. 108 Garnier).[35]

———

In *The First Man*'s Jessica/Véra file, the words "On the telephone" are added to this entry.

35. In *On Love*, Stendhal tells the story of Dona Diana, who, upon hearing of the death of an officer whom she was ostensibly in love with, says only, "What a pity—so young." Stendhal then remarks that they'd been reading a play with a very similar ending that very day.

When all of this is over: write a montage. Everything that goes through my head.

———

Rebellion: rebellion without God ends in philanthropy. Philanthropy ends in trials. Chap. The Philanthropists.

———

Atheist when he was a perfect husband, converted after becoming an adulterer.[36]

———

Poor and free rather than rich and enslaved. Of course, people want to be both rich and free, and sometimes that's what leads them to be poor and enslaved.

———

Delacroix. "What's most real in me are the illusions that I create with my painting. The rest is quicksand."[37]

———

MOGADOR.[38]

———

Delacroix. "What makes men of genius . . . isn't new ideas, it's the idea, which possesses them, that what's been said hasn't yet been said enough."

Id. "The look of that country (Morocco) will always be present in my eyes. The men of that strong race will always be active, so long as I live, in my memory. It's in them that I truly rediscovered ancient beauty."

Id. ". . . They're closer to nature in a thousand ways: their clothing, the design of their footwear. So then, beauty comes together in everything they do. The rest of us, in our corsets, our narrow footwear, our ridiculous encasements, we're pitied. Grace takes revenge on our science."

PP. 212–213 (Plon), v. 1, admirable pages about talent.

---

36. Camus would give this line to Clamence in *The Fall*. See p. 330n202.

37. The citations are from Plon's 1932, three-volume edition of Eugène Delacroix's *Journals*, which, along with Stendhal's *On Love*, Camus was reading while in Cabris.

38. The reference is to Delacroix's trip to Morocco in 1832. Mogador is the Portuguese name for Essaouira, a city in western Morocco. The word is written in large letters in the handwritten notebook.

He classifies Goethe (with reasonable justification for his judgment) "among the petty and affectation-tainted minds."

"That man who's always sees himself as doing . . ."

———

January 10, 1950.

Ultimately, I've never seen very clearly inside myself. But I've always followed, on instinct, an invisible star . . . [39]

There's an anarchy inside me, an awful disorder. For me, creating costs a thousand deaths, for it's a matter of order and my entire being rejects order. But without it, I'd die unfocused.

———

In the afternoon, the sun and light streaming into my room, the sky blue and hazy, the sound of children climbing up from the village, the song of the garden pond . . . these are the hours that bring Algiers back to me. Twenty years ago . . .

———

L., about Maman: "An angel sent straight from above!"[40]

———

Bespaloff.[41] "From rebellion to rebellion, from revolution to revolution, we believed we were increasing freedom and we ended up with Empire."

———

Rebellion. Achilles defying creation after Patroclus's death.

———

Chap. We Nietzscheans.

———

39. The idea of "the star" plays a central role in Camus's "The Artist at Work."

40. The line, spoken by Camus's older brother, Lucien (whose full name is given in the handwritten notebook), literally reads: "She's bread, and what bread she is!" though the reference is likely to the expression *c'est du pain bénit* (she's a godsend).

41. The January 1950 issue of *Esprit* opens with Rachel Bespaloff's "Le monde du comdamné à mort," a study of Camus's work in which Bespaloff proposes that all of Camus's writing to that point responds to the question: "What values remain for a person condemned to death, one who refuses supernatural consolations?" The quotation Camus cites here, which occurs on page six, follows the statement: "We may wonder if rebellion isn't a phenomenon of decadence." Shortly before this piece was published, Bespaloff committed suicide, leaving a note that said she was "too tired to carry on" and that "we can imagine Sisyphus happy, but joy is forever beyond his reach."

Henry Miller: "I am dazzled by the glorious collapse of the world."[42] But there's a type of mind that's not dazzled by the collapse. More sordid than grandiose.

———

Get control of the work but don't forget the *audacity*. Create.

———

Couvreux.[43] Arrives, asks if they'd be so kind as to tune the radio to the B.B.C. news hour, which, according to him, is always interesting, sits down, and falls asleep.

———

Family. "You shouldn't have gone out of your way."
"You're putting yourself out."
"It comes from in here."

———

Topics. Hôtel de Province. Attraction of people.

———

Sea. Climate injustice. Trees in bloom in Saint-Étienne. Even more awful. In the end, I would've liked a completely black face. So then, the Northern peoples . . . [44]

———

February 1950.

Disciplined work until April. Then a blaze of work. Be quiet. Listen. Let overflow.

———

42. The quote comes from Henry Miller's *Black Spring*.

43. Emmanuel Couvreux was a friend of Camus's publisher, Gaston Gallimard. During the Occupation, Camus spent time at his home in Neuilly, a wealthy suburb of Paris, where Couvreux also welcomed Malraux's partner, the writer Josette Clotis, and their two sons, all of whom would die in transportation-related accidents.

44. Camus's concept of "climate injustice" is fleshed out in the 1958 preface to *L'envers et l'endroit*, where he writes: "We find many injustices in this world of ours, but there's one we never talk about, which is climate. Of that injustice I've long been, without knowing it, a beneficiary. . . . But it's when poverty is combined with a life with neither hope nor sky—something that, when I reached adulthood, I discovered in our cities' horrible suburbs—that the last and most revolting injustice is consummated, and we absolutely have to do everything we can so that these men may escape the double humiliation of misery and ugliness. Born poor, in a working-class neighborhood, I still didn't know what real misery was until I got to know our cold banlieues. . . . Once you've gotten to know the industrial suburbs, you'll feel forever soiled by them, and, I think, responsible for their existence."

The concept (and the reality) of the intellectual dates from the 18th century.

———

Write essay later, with no concerns or reservations, *about what I know to be true* (doing what we don't want to do, wanting what we don't do).

———

The original night.

———

I'm reading a life of Rachel.[45] Faced with history, it's always the same disillusion. All those words she spoke, in private for example, now join the dizzying mass of lost words nobody will ever know. Compared to that mass, what history carries down to us is but a drop of water lost in the sea.

———

In Delacroix's Journal, a comment (reported) about critics who allow themselves to create. "A person can't both hold the stirrup leathers and show their behind."[46]

———

Delacroix—on distances in London.

"You have to count in leagues: this disproportion alone, between the immensity of the place where these people live and the naturally cramped nature of human proportions, is cause for me to declare them enemies of true civilization, which brings people closer to that Attic civilization that made the Parthenon as big as one of our houses and that contained such intelligence, life, strength, and grandeur within the narrow limits of its borders that it makes you smile at our barbarity, so restricted in its immense States."

———

Delacroix. "In music, *as in all other arts no doubt*, as soon as style and character, in a word, seriousness, takes over, the rest disappears."

---

45. Rachel Félix (1821–1858), known as Mademoiselle Rachel, was a prominent Jewish-French actress and muse to many powerful French leaders.

46. The lead-in to this: "We [Delacroix and Jules-Joseph Arnoux] were speaking of artists who find themselves in the position of writing about their colleagues, and he told me what a M. Gabriel, a vaudeville performer, had to say on the subject."

Id. What revolutions have wiped out as far as monuments and artwork goes—the specifics, Delacroix says, are frightening.

Against progress. V. 1, p. 428: "We owe to antiquity the little we're worth."

———

Delacroix.

The great artist has to learn to avoid *what shouldn't be attempted*. "Only the mad and the powerless torture themselves over the impossible. And yet, *you have to be quite audacious*."

Id. "It takes great audacity to dare *to be yourself*."

Id. "We work not only to produce art but to put a price on time."

Id. "The satisfaction of someone who has worked and wisely used their day is immense. When I am in such a state, I deliciously enjoy the slightest bit of relaxation. I can even, without the slightest regret, be out among the most boring society people."

Id. ". . . not so much for the continuation of things that are mere wind but for the enjoyment of the work itself and the delicious hours that follow it . . ."

Id. "How happy I am no longer being forced to be happy as back then (the passions)."

Italy's great schools "where naivety is blended with the greatest of knowledge."

Id. Speaking of Millet. "He's of that squad of bearded artists who carried out the Revolution of '48 or at least applauded it, believing it would bring about equality in talent as well as in fortune."

Id. Against progress, p. 200 in its entirety ". . . What a noble sight in the best of centuries, that mass of human livestock fattened up by philosophes."

Id. Russian novels "have an astonishing aroma of reality."

P. 341. ". . . imperfect Creation . . ."

Original talent "timidity and drought in the beginning, breadth and neglect of details in the end."

———

The peasant who, during a prayer that brought everyone else to tears, remained indifferent. He told the people who reproached him for his coldness that he didn't belong to the parish.

———

February '50.

Memory lapsing more and more. Should bring myself to keeping a journal. Delacroix's right: every day that isn't recorded is like a day that never was. Maybe in April, when I'll have a little freedom.

———

Volume: matters of art—where I'll summarize my aesthetics.

———

Literary society. We imagine dark intrigues, great ambition-driven schemes. There's nothing but vanity, bought off for so little.

———

A little pride helps you keep your distance. Don't forget it, *despite everything*.

———

Pleasure that ends up as gratitude: the days' corolla. But at the other extreme: bitter pleasure.

———

The mistral's scoured the sky down to a new skin, blue and bright as the sea. Bird song bursts forth on all sides, strong, jubilant, joyously discordant, an infinite delight. The day streams out, resplendent.

———

Not morality but fulfillment. And there is no other fulfillment than the one found in love, which is to say the denial of the self, dying to the world. Follow it through to the end. *Disappear*. Dissolve in love. Then it will be the power of love that creates, not me. Deteriorate. Dismember. Be annihilated in truth's fulfillment and passion.

———

Epigraph: "Nothing's better than a humble, ignorant, obstinate life" (*L'Échange*).[47]

47. This quote and the one that follows, both very roughly recorded here, are from Paul Claudel's *The Exchange*, act 3. The play was produced by Jean-Louis Barraut at the Théâtre Marigny in

---

Id. "There was a way of loving you and I haven't loved you that way."

Adolphe. Rereading. Same feeling of burning drought.
"They examined her (E) with interest and curiosity, like a beautiful storm."
"This heart (A) foreign to all the world's interests."[48]

"The moment I saw that pained look upon her face, her will became mine: I was only at ease when she was happy with me."

". . . Those two unfortunate souls who on the whole of the earth knew only each other, *who were the only ones who could do each other justice,* could understand and console each other, seemed two irreconcilable enemies, bent on tearing each other apart."

Wagner, the music of slaves.

Novel. "He wanted her to suffer, but far away from him. He was a coward."

Constant. "We have to study the miseries of man but count among those miseries the ideas they come up with to combat them."

Id. "Appalling danger: that American business politics and a fickle intellectual civilization could join forces."

Solar essays title: Summer. Noon. Celebration.[49]

February '50.

Mastery: Not speaking.
Note: experience is a memory, but the inverse is true.

1951. This first quote would also appear, attributed, at the start of the Yellow Notebook, as well as, unattributed, in the text of *The First Man.*

48. (E) stands for Ellénore and (A) for Adolphe, two characters from Benjamin Constant's novel *Adolphe.*

49. The handwritten notebook reads "Mediterranean essays," not "Solar essays." The change was made on the typescript. Camus would eventually settle on *Summer* as the title for the essay collection, but he continues to refer to the collection as *Celebration* throughout these notebooks.

Return to the specifics now. Prefer truth to all else.

———

Nietzsche: "I was ashamed of that false modesty."[50]

———

The rosemary has bloomed. At the foot of the olive trees, wreaths of violets.

———

March '50.

Philanthropic religious zealots deny everything outside of reason, as reason, the way they understand it, can make them masters of everything, even nature. Of everything except Beauty. Beauty escapes such logic. That's why it's so difficult for an artist to be a revolutionary, however rebellious he may be as an artist. That's why it's impossible for him to be a killer.

———

Wait, wait for the garland of illuminated days still ahead of me to be snuffed out one by one. The last is finally snuffed out and it's pitch black.

———

March 1, '50.

A month of absolute mastery—on all fronts. Then start fresh—(but without losing *the truth, the reality* of prior experiences, and so *accepting all the consequences* with the *determination* to overcome them and transfigure them in the creator's ultimate (but informed) attitude. (Refuse nothing).

———

(Be able to say: it was difficult. I didn't succeed at first and I struggled a long and tiring struggle. But in the end, I prevailed. And this hard labor makes the success all the more clear, all the more humble, but also all the more resolute.)

———

Rebellion. After having completed a draft, rethink the whole thing *based on* how the documentary evidence and ideas are ordered.

———

In art, the absolute realist would be the absolute divinity. That's why attempts to deify man wish to perfect realism.

———

50. The quote comes from *Ecce Homo*, "Human, All-Too-Human," section 3.

The sea: I didn't lose myself there, I found myself there.

Vivet's friend who had stopped smoking begins smoking again when he learns the H-bomb has just been discovered.[51]

Family.

The carters are the ones who made Algeria.

Michel. 80 years old. Upright and strong.

Denise, his daughter. Leaves them at 18 years old to "make a life of her own." Returns at 21 flush with money and, selling her jewelry, replenishes her father's entire stable, wiped out by an epidemic.

Gurdjieff's "sly man."[52] Focus. Self-remembering (seeing yourself through the eyes of another).

Jacob Genns, dictator of the Vilna Ghetto, accepts a position with the police in order to limit the damage done. Little by little, three-quarters of the ghetto (48,000) is exterminated. In the end, he himself is shot. Shot for nothing—dishonored for nothing.[53]

Title: The Evil Genius.

She had to die. Then an atrocious happiness would begin. But that's what suffering is: "they" don't die in a timely fashion.

According to the Chinese, empires on the verge of collapse have a great many laws.

Radiant light. It seems as if I'm emerging from a ten-year sleep—still tangled up in the bandages of misfortune and false morality—but stripped naked

---

51. Jean-Pierre Vivet was a journalist at *Combat*. Camus would use this entry in *The Fall*, where he writes: "It was easier for me to understand that friend of mine who'd gotten it in his head to stop smoking, and, through sheer willpower, had succeeded. One morning, he opened the newspaper, read that the first H-bomb had been set off, learned about its admirable effects, and promptly took himself to a tobacco shop."

52. George Ivanovich Gurdjieff (1866/77–1949), Russian mystic and creator of the "Fourth Way" school of self-development.

53. In 1942, Jacob Genns (1903–1943) was appointed head of both the Jewish ghetto in Vilnius and its police force, positions he took because he ostensibly believed that in working with the Ger-

once again and stretched out toward the sun. Shining, steady strength—and sparing, sharp intelligence. I am reborn as a body, too . . .

———

Comedy. A man is formally recognized for a virtue he'd been exercising instinctively until then. From that point on, he exercises it consciously: catastrophes.

———

17th-century style according to Nietzsche: clean, precise, and free. Modern art: the art of tyrannizing.

———

After a certain age, the dramas between people are exacerbated by a race against time. Insoluble then.

———

As if love's first light slowly began to melt the snow accumulated inside her so as to let loose joy's irresistible, surging waters.[54]

———

March 4, 1950.

And openly I pledged my heart to the grave and suffering earth, and often, in the sacred night, I promised to love it faithfully until death do us part, without fear, with its heavy burden of fatality, and not to look down on any of its mysteries. In this way, I bound myself to it with a mortal bond. (*Empedocles*, Hölderlin.)[55]

———

It's only after the fact that we have the courage of what we know.

———

Artists and ideas *without sun*.

———

"Misunderstanding of affection," Nietzsche says. "A servile affection that submits and debases itself, that idealizes and deceives itself—but a divine affection that looks down on and loves, that transforms and elevates what it loves."[56]

---

mans he could slow the extermination process, though there is much debate about his motivation.

54. This entry is written in very tiny print at the top of the page, whereas the one that follows is written in larger print than usual.

55. Friedrich Hölderlin (1770–1843), German poet, suffered with severe mental illness the latter half of his life. Camus would use this quote as *The Rebel*'s epigraph.

56. The quote comes from *The Will to Power*, book 4, *Discipline and Breeding*, section 964 (1884).

The world in which I'm most *comfortable*: Greek myth.

The heart isn't everything. It *must be,* for without it . . . But it must be mastered and transfigured.

My whole body of work is ironic.

The most consistent temptation for me, the one against which I've never stopped waging an exhausting battle: cynicism.

Paganism for yourself and Christianity for others, that's every individual's instinctive desire.

Not the difficulty, but the impossibility of being.

Love is injustice, but justice isn't enough.

There's always a part of man that refuses love. It's the part that *wants* to die. That's the part that asks to be forgiven.

Title for "Stake": Deianira.[57]

Deianira. "I would've liked to freeze her in time, in that already distant day in the Tuileries when she showed up in front of me wearing that black skirt of hers and that white blouse rolled up on those golden arms, her hair loose, her feet unadorned, and her face leading the way."[58]

"What I'd been wanting to ask her for so long, I did ask her that last night: to swear never to belong to another man. I didn't want to live if human love

---

57. Camus continued to think about a story, or collection of stories, titled "The Stake." In Greek mythology, Deianira was tricked into believing a certain potion would make her husband, Heracles, stop cheating on her, but it wasn't until Heracles fell in love with Iole that Deianira tried the potion, which ended up burning Heracles so severely he committed suicide by throwing himself on a funeral pyre.

58. This last phrase, *visage de proue,* literally "face of a ship's prow," is used figuratively to mean that someone is a "leading light" or that something is a "flagship" item.

In *The First Man*'s Jessica/Véra folder, this entry appears with the following additions: she "showed up in front of me on a bicycle" and her "black hair" was loose.

couldn't produce, couldn't make possible, what religion can. She did promise, and without asking me to make any commitment of my own—but in the grip of love, amid its terrible joy and pride, I joyously promised anyway. It was a matter of killing her, and killing myself, in a way."

There where love is a luxury, how could freedom not be a luxury? All the more reason, it's true, not to give in to those who make a mockery of both love and freedom.

Voltaire was suspicious of almost everything. He only developed only a very few things, but well.

Novel. Male characters: Pierre G., Maurice Adrey, Nicolas Lazarevitch, Robert Chatté, M.D.b., Jean Grenier, Pascal Pia, Ravanel, Herrand, Oettly.

Female — : Renée Audibert, Simone C., Suzanne O., Christiane Galindo, Blanche Balain, Lucette, Marcelle Rouchon, Simone M. B., Yvonne, Carmen, Marcelle, Charlotte, Laure, Madeleine Blanchoud, Janine, Jacqueline, Victoria, Violante, Françoise 1 and 2, Vauquelin, Leibowitz.

Michèle, Andrée Clément, Lorette, Patricia Blake, M. Thérèse, Gisèle Lazare, Renée Thomasset, Évelyne, Mamaine, Odile, Wanda, Nicole Algan, Odette Campana, Yvette Petitjean, Suzanne Agnely, Vivette, Nathalie, Virginie, Catherine, Mette, Anne.[59]

"The sea and sky draw toward marble terraces hosts of young and powerful roses." A. Rimbaud.[60]

Those who write abstractly are rather lucky: they will have commentators. Others only have readers, which, it seems, is to be looked down upon.

---

59. The list, likely for *The First Man*, is made up entirely of people from Camus's life. He will return to certain of these "characters" later in these pages. Of note, many of the "male characters" listed here were only casual acquaintances or were people Camus had grown apart from by this point, whereas many of the women were people with whom he was close. Camus added some of these names on the typescript (they do not appear in the handwritten notebook), as he had yet to meet some of the people named here.

60. These are the final lines of Rimbaud's poem "Flowers."

Gide comes to the U.S.S.R. because he thinks *about joy*.

Gide: Only atheism can pacify the world today (!).

Dialogue between Lenin and a Russian concentration camp inmate.

In the beginning, Paris serves a work of art, pushing it forward. But once it's established, that's when the real fun begins. Then it's a matter of destroying it. In Paris, as in certain Brazilian rivers, there are thousands of little fish ready for the task. They're tiny but innumerable. Their whole head, I dare say, is in their teeth, and they can strip a man completely bare in less than five minutes, leaving nothing behind but clean white bones. Then they swim off, sleep a little, and begin again.[61]

From Bossuet: "The only character most men are capable of is rebelling when someone denies them that very character." He'd lost even that.

Like those elderly people who, in a big house once boisterous and full of life, retreat to a single floor, then to a room, then to the narrowest room, in which they gather up all of life's daily activities—cloistered and waiting for that even narrower, more confined space.

APRIL '50. Cabris, once again.[62]

All in all, we manage. It's difficult, but in the end we manage. Oh, they're not a pretty sight. But we forgive them. As for the two or three people I love, they're better than I am. How can I accept that? Come on, let's skip all that.

Hot and foggy night. In the distance, lights on the coast. In the valley, a great concert of toads whose voices, at first melodious, seem to grow

61. In *The Fall*, Camus writes: "From time to time, these gentlemen play around with knives or revolvers, but don't you believe they care for it. Their role requires it, that's all. They are dying of fear as the last cartridge falls. That said, I find them more moral than the others, the ones who do their killing within the family, through wear and tear. Haven't you noticed how our society has organized itself for just this sort of liquidation? Of course, you've heard talk of those tiny fish living in Brazilian rivers, the ones that attack unwise swimmers by the thousands, one little bite after another, a body stripped clean in an instant, leaving only an immaculate skeleton behind. Well, that's how their organization works. . . . The little teeth tear the flesh all the way to bone."

62. On March 29, Camus returned to Paris, only to be ordered back to Cabris by his doctor on April 14.

hoarse. These villages of light, of houses . . . "You're a poet and I'm on death's doorstep."[63]

———

A's suicide. Shaken because I loved him very much, of course, but also because I suddenly understood I wanted to do what he did.

———

At least women aren't obligated, as we are, to greatness. For men, even faith, even humility, are tests of greatness. Grueling.

———

A time always comes when people stop struggling and tearing each other apart, finally letting themselves love each other for what they are. That's the kingdom of heaven.[64]

———

Enough with the guilt—with the repentance.

———

Claudel. That greedy old man scurrying over to the Lord's Supper Table to stuff his face with graces . . . Wretched![65]

———

Short story. A good day. The middle-aged woman arrives alone. Cannes.

———

In big novel. Lazarevitch. Adrey. Chatté (and the acts he puts on with chance acquaintances).[66]

———

To grow old is to pass from passion to compassion.

---

63. See p. 293n113.

64. In *The First Man*'s Jessica/Véra folder, the last word is given as *vieux* (old people), not *cieux* (heavens).

65. On April 29, 1949, Paul Claudel was received by Pope Pius XII, at which time several of Claudel's poems were read to the pope. On February 25, 1951, in a letter to Jean Grenier, Camus expresses sadness about André Gide's death, then adds: "Note that I won't cry for Paul Pilate, I mean, Claudel."

66. Nicolas Lazarevitch (1895–1975) was a libertarian-anarchist activist who helped Camus with his research for *The Just*. Like Camus, he worked against the French Left's attempts to valorize the Soviet Union. On April 5, 1950, Camus's "Espoir" series at Gallimard published a book coauthored by Lazarevitch, *Tu peux tuer cet homme*.

Adrey is, perhaps, a reference to Françoise Adrey who, on July 15, 1950, in Oran, Algeria, married Jean Roméo, a socialist who, like Camus, supported Garry Davis and signed on to his cause (though Mamaine Koestler wrote to her sister that Camus "is only 10 per cent pro Garry Davis, and seemed uninterested in it. If so why does he make speeches for him?").

Robert Chatté was a bookseller and friend of Pascal Pia.

All three of these names appeared in Camus's earlier list of characters for the "big novel."

———

The lady who takes calcium phosphate. At the dinner table. "This poor dog (a marvelous red spaniel), after all his acts of bravery in Indochina, you'd think they'd give him a medal, but no. It appears we don't give medals to dogs here. You'll notice that in England they give medals to dogs who've conducted themselves well in war. But here! This fellow may well have foiled countless Chinese ambushes, but no, nothing for him. Poor beast!"

———

Bargirl. "Mail? Uh, no thanks. Personally, I don't like headaches."

———

The 19th century is the century of rebellion. Why? Because it was born of a failed revolution that only delivered the fatal blow to divine principle.

———

May 27, 1950.

Solitary. Love's fires set the world ablaze. They're worth the pain of being born and growing up. But do we have to go on living after them? Then any life is justified. But any survival?

———

After *The Rebel*, create freely.

———

How many nights in a life where you are no longer!

———

My body of work through these first two cycles: people who don't lie, so not real people. They are not of this world. That's probably why, so far, I haven't been a novelist in the traditional sense of the word but rather an artist who creates myths to match his passion and anguish. That's also why those who've carried me through this world are always those who had the strength and exclusivity of these myths.

———

The crazy thing about love is that we'd like to hurry through and *lose* those days of expectation. In doing so, we'd like to get to the end. In doing so, one of love's aspects comes to coincide with death.

———

Camp. An illiterate guard goes to town on an intellectual. "Here's to books! Look how smart we are . . ." etc. In the end, the intellectual asks for forgiveness.

———

Men have the hardened face of their knowledge (those knowing faces we sometimes encounter). But sometimes, beneath the scars, the adolescent's face still shows through, giving thanks to life.

With them, I didn't feel poverty, or deprivation, or humiliation. Why not say it: I felt, and I still feel, my nobility. Standing before my mother, I feel I'm of a noble race: the one that envies nothing.

I've taken more than my share of beauty: bread eternal.[67]

For most men, war is the end of solitude. For me, it's the ultimate solitude.

The bull's intercourse, quick as lightning, a single, searing stab, is chaste. It's a god's intercourse. Not enjoyment but a burning, sacred annihilation.[68]

Vosges. Thanks to the red sandstone, the churches and calvaries are the color of dried blood. All the blood of conquests and power has run over this land and dried on its sanctuaries.[69]

Useless morality: life is moral. He who doesn't give everything doesn't get everything.

When you're lucky enough to live the life of the mind, how foolish it is to wish for passions' horrible house of screams.

I love everything or I love nothing. So then, I love nothing.

End of Deianira. He kills her carefully, slowly (she slowly faded away right in front of him, and he watched as her features dried out, with an awful hope and a torturous sob of love). She dies. He rediscovers the other, young

67. Though Camus has written only *pain éternel* here, it's possible the reference is to Exodus 16:15: "It is the bread that the Lord has given you to eat" ("*le pain que l'Éternel . . .*").

68. For an expanded version of this entry, see p. 507.

69. From July 23 to August 28, Camus and Maria Casarès traveled through the Vosges region of France, spending two days at the Hôtel des Roches before going on to Gérardmer and then Le Grand Valtin.

again, and beautiful. A delicious love again rose in his heart. "I love you," he says to her.

Spiritual Exercises of Saint Ignatius—to keep somnolence at bay while you pray.[70]

Today, all of science's power is aimed at consolidating the State. Not a single researcher has imagined turning their work toward the defense of the individual. Yet this is where freemasonry would make sense.

If the times were simply tragic! But they're foul. That's why they have to be indicted—and pardoned.

I. The Myth of Sisyphus (absurd).
II. The Myth of Prometheus (rebellion).
III. The Myth of Nemesis.

J. de Maistre: "I don't know the scoundrel's soul, but I think I know the upstanding citizen's soul, and it's enough to make me shudder."[71]

The prisons should be liberated or your virtue demonstrated.[72]

Maistre: "Woe betide the generations that seek the ages of the world." Like that Chinese sage who, in wishing someone ill, hoped the person would live in "interesting" times.[73]

---

70. *The Spiritual Exercises of Saint Ignatius* is a day-by-day, morning, afternoon, and evening prayer book intended to be used over the course of a month. Camus, then, is having a little fun with words here.

Part of the entry following this one was crossed out in the handwritten notebook, while another part, which was not crossed out, was nevertheless also left out of the published French edition.

71. Joseph de Maistre (1753–1821), writer and politician who opposed the Revolution and supported the return to monarchy and the restoration of the House of Bourbon.

72. In French, Camus is juxtaposing *ouvrez* and *prouvez*, rendered here as "liberate" and "demonstrate." A more literal translation of the entry: "Open the prisons or prove your virtue."

73. This seems to be a slight misquote. In 1794, in *Discours à la marquise de Costa* (*Speech to the Marquise de Costa*), de Maistre says, "We must have the courage to admit, Madame, that for a long time we haven't quite understood the revolution for which we are the witnesses; for a long time, we took it to be an event. We were mistaken: it's an age; and woe betide the generations that witness the ages of the world!"

Baudelaire. The world has developed such a thick layer of vulgarity that it gives the spiritual man's contempt the ferocity of a passion.[74]

———

Unterlinden: "All my life I've dreamed of the convent's peace." (And I probably wouldn't have lasted there more than a month.)[75]

———

Europe of shopkeepers—hopeless.

———

Commitment. I have the highest, and most passionate, concept of art. Far too high to agree to subject it to anything. Far too passionate to want to separate it from anything.

———

"Love was impossible for him. He was only capable of lies and adultery."

———

Claudel.[76] Vulgar mind.

———

Savoie. September '50.[77]

People like M., eternal emigrants seeking a homeland, end up finding one, but only in sorrow.

———

Sorrow and its sometimes ugly face. But you have to pay the price by sitting with it and living through it. Destroy yourself with it for having dared to destroy others.

———

Novel. "He remembered one day, during one of those atrocious scenes, as the foreboding feeling of some awful future was growing inside him, she told him she'd sworn never to belong to anyone but him, and that never more, were he no more, would there be anyone else for her. And right then, when she thought she was showing him the soaring heights, the unbreakable nature

---

74. A direct quote from Baudelaire's draft preface for the second edition of *The Flowers of Evil*. Baudelaire's editor did not ultimately print the preface. The line Camus gives here is preceded by: "I would have never believed our country could move so quickly down the paths of progress."

75. Unterlinden, now a museum, was originally a thirteenth-century Dominican convent in Colmar, France.

76. In both the handwritten notebook and the typescript, there is a sentence crossed out between these two, indicating that it was crossed out in the notebook after the typescript was made.

77. After having spent a month traveling with Maria Casarès, likely the *M* referred to here, Camus met Francine and their kids in Saint-Jorioz for a week's vacation.

of their love, as she was, in fact, showing it, right when she thought she was binding him, melting him into her, the opposite thought came to him, the thought that he'd been released, that now was the time to make his escape, to leave her there, certain of her absolute fidelity and sterility. But he stayed that day—as on the others."

———

Paris. September '50.[78]

What I have to say is more important than what I am. Step aside—be an *aside.*

———

Progress: stop trying to tell a loved one the suffering he causes us.

———

The fear of suffering.

———

Faulkner. To the question: What do you think of this young generation of writers, he responds: It will leave nothing of value. It has nothing more to say. To write, you need to have the big basic truths rooted in yourself and to turn your work toward one of them or all of them at once. Those who don't know how to speak of pride, of honor, of pain, are writers of no consequence, and their work will die with or before them. Goethe and Shakespeare have endured because they believed in the human heart. Balzac and Flaubert, too. They are eternal.

"What's the reason for this nihilism that's invaded literature?"

"Fear. The day men stop being afraid, then they'll start writing masterpieces again, which is to say works that last."[79]

———

Sorel: "Disciples summon their master to close the age of doubts by providing final solutions."[80]

———

78. When Camus and his family returned to Paris on September 7, they moved to a new apartment on Rue Madame, near the Jardin du Luxembourg.

79. Camus added this entry to the typescript at a later date. It does not appear in the handwritten notebook.

80. The quote is from the beginning of Georges Sorel's *Reflections on Violence* ("Letter to Daniel Halevy").

There's no doubt every moral requires *a little* cynicism. Where's the limit?

Pascal: "I've spent a good part of my life believing there's such a thing as justice; and in this I wasn't mistaken; for there is such a thing insofar as God has wished to reveal it to us. But that's not the way I thought of it and that's where I was mistaken; for I believed that our justice was essentially just and that I had what it takes to understand and judge it."[81]

N. (The Hellenes). "Audacity of the noble races, mad, absurd, spontaneous audacity . . . their indifference and their contempt for all the body's safety, for life, for comfort."[82]

Novel. "Love is fulfilling or degrading. The more abortive the love, the more mutilation it leaves behind. If love isn't creative, it forever prevents any true creation. It's a tyrant and a mediocre one. So, then, P.[83] felt saddened for having gotten himself into a situation of loving without being able to give everything to that love. In that senseless waste of time and soul, he recognized a sort of justice that, in the end, was the only sort he'd ever really come across on earth. But to recognize that justice was also to recognize a duty: the duty to raise that love, and themselves, above mediocrity, to accept the most awful but most sincere suffering, the kind he'd always backed away from, heart pounding, filled with a frantic cowardice. He couldn't do more or be otherwise, and the only love that would have saved everything was a love in which he would have been accepted as he was—but love can't accept what is. That's not why it cries out across the earth. It cries out to reject kindness,

---

81. The quote, from Pascal's *Pensées,* is usually classified as no. 375, though not always. A clear link can be drawn between this entry and *The Fall,* especially in the lines that follow those recorded here: "But I've so often found myself in error of right judgement that I finally began to distrust myself and then others. I've seen that all countries and peoples change. And in this way, after real changes of judgement that touch on true justice, I've come to understand that our nature is but one continual change, and I haven't changed since; and if I changed, I would confirm my opinion. / The Pyrrhonian Arcesilaus becomes dogmatic once more."

82. It was around this time that Sartre publicly accused Camus of not reading and understanding primary source material (Hegel, in particular) and relying on other thinkers' interpretations. This entry, as well as many others throughout these pages, shows that, whether Camus went back to the primary source material or not, he often quoted from secondary sources. The quote in this entry, which he attributes to Nietzsche, almost certainly comes from Georges Sorel's *Reflections on Violence,* chap. 7, "The Ethics of the Producers," where Sorel abridges a much longer quote from Nietzsche's *On the Genealogy of Morality* ("First Essay") in precisely the same way Camus has recorded it here.

83. P. may stand for Pierre, a character intended for *The First Man.*

compassion, intelligence, all the things that lead to compromise. It cries out for the impossible, the absolute, the fiery heavens, the endless spring, life surpassing death, and death itself transfigured into eternal life. How could he, himself, have been accepted in love, he who was, in a way, nothing but misery and awareness of that misery. He alone could accept himself—in accepting the long, never-ending, excruciating pain of losing love and knowing it was his own fault he'd lost it. That's where he'd find his freedom, dripping with an awful blood, it's true. But that's also the condition that allows for at least something to be created, something within his own limitations, in the consecration of his own misery, the misery of every life, but also in the striving for that greatness that alone justified living.

Anything less than this torture, any weakness makes love look childish and stupid, makes it into a vain, crazed constraint at which even a slightly demanding heart balks. Yes, that's what he had to say: 'I love you—but I'm nothing, or so little, and you can't really accept me despite all your love. In the depths of your soul, at the root of your being, you demand everything, and I neither have nor am everything. Forgive me for having less soul than love, less luck than desire, and for loving above and beyond my reach. Forgive me and don't humiliate me any further. When you're no longer capable of loving me, you'll be capable of justice. On that day you'll measure my hell, and then you'll love me beyond what we are, with a love that will never be enough for me either but that I'll deposit in life's account anyway, to again accept it, in suffering.' That was it, yes, but the hardest part had only just begun. With her gone, the days cried out, and each night was an open wound."

The 20th century's strongest passion: servitude.[84]

In Brou, the recumbent statues of Margaret of Austria and Philibert of Savoy, instead of looking to the heavens, eternally look to each other.[85]

Those who haven't demanded absolute virginity from other beings and the world, and wailed with nostalgia and impotence at its impossibility, those who haven't destroyed themselves trying to love, half-heartedly, a face that

84. See *The Fall*, where Clamence says: "In me, dear friend, you will find an enlightened advocate of servitude."

85. The Royal Monastery of Brou, located in Bourg-en-Bresse, France.

can't inspire love but only echo it, they can't understand the reality of rebellion and its destructive fury.[86]

Action Française. Mentality of history's pariahs: resentment. Political ghetto's racism.[87]

I don't like other people's secrets. But I'm interested in their confessions.[88]

Play: A man with no personality. He changes according to the image of himself others project onto him. Pathetic wet blanket with his wife. Intelligent and brave with the woman he loves, etc. A day comes when the two images are in conflict. Ultimately:

The Maid: You're very kind, Monsieur.

The Man: Here, Marie, this is for you.

Few people capable of *understanding* art.

In Rembrandt's day, assembly-line artists were the ones who painted battles.

Paris. The wind and rain tossed the autumn leaves across the avenues. We walk on a damp and tawny fur.

Taxi driver, Negro, unusual level of courtesy for 1950s Paris, says to me as we pass the Théâtre-Français, all lined with cars: "Molière's House is packed tonight."

For 2,000 years, we've witnessed a constant, steady slandering of Greek values. In this regard, Marxism has taken over from Christianity. And for

---

86. This entry appears, with slight changes, in *The Rebel*, in the section titled "Rebellion and the Novel." A more personal version appears in the Yellow Notebook, where Camus writes: "Loves: he would have wanted them all to be virginal, with no past and no men. And the only person he ever met who was, he devoted his life to her, though he'd never been able to be faithful himself. So, he wanted women to be what he was not. And what he was sent him back to women like himself, women he loved and took with rage and fury."

87. *Action française* is both an extreme right-wing political movement and a magazine, today published under the title *Le bien commun* (The Common Good).

88. See *The Fall*, where Clamence says: "You can be sure I'll listen to your own confession with a great feeling of fraternity."

2,000 years, Greek values have been so resistant that the 20th century, beneath its ideologies, is more Greek and Pagan than Christian and Russian.

———

Intellectuals make up theories, the masses make up the economy. In the end, intellectuals use the masses and through them theory uses the economy. That's why they have to maintain a state of emergency and economic enslavement—so that the masses remain massively disposable.[89] It really is true that the economy is the material from which history is made. Ideas are happy to lead the way.

———

From then on, I knew the truth about myself and about others. But I couldn't accept it. I writhed beneath it, burned red-hot.

———

Creators. When disaster strikes, the first thing they'll have to do is fight. If it's defeat, those who survive will return to those lands where it'll be possible to reassemble culture: Chili, Mexico, etc. If it's victory: the greatest danger.

———

18th century: Judging that man is perfectible is already up for debate. But judging, after having lived, that man is good . . .

———

Yes, I have a homeland:[90] the French language.

———

Novel.

1) The taking of Weimar, or the equivalent, by those struck from the list.[91]

2) In the camp, a proud intellectual is subjected to the spitting cell.[92] His whole life from that moment on: survive so as to be able to kill.

———

89. *Masses de manœuvre* could also be translated as "a mass of laborers."

90. In the handwritten notebook and the typescript, the line continues: "and what sometimes saves me from everything, just when, apparently, I've lost everything."

91. In *State of Emergency*, Camus uses this same term, *rayés*, to refer to the people the Secretary has infected with the plague. Here, he's likely using it in reference to those deported to the concentration camps. In both cases, the idea is that they have been "struck" from the list of life.

92. In *The Fall*, Clamence says: "Have you at least heard of the spitting cell, that creation one of our nations came up with to prove it was the greatest on earth? It's a concrete box that keeps a prisoner upright but unable to move. The heavy door that locks the prisoner in his cement shell comes up to chin level, so that all you can see is the prisoner's face, and every time a guard passes, he spits on it. The prisoner, stuck in his cell, can't wipe his face, though it's true he's allowed to close his eyes. Well now that, my dear friend, was invented by man. They didn't need God for that little masterpiece."

Dissolution of the group.[93] Lazarevitch: "We love each other, that's the truth. Unable to lift a finger for what we love. No, we're not powerless. But we refuse to do even the little we could do. Even a meeting is too much, if it's raining out, if we got into an argument at home, etc., etc."

———

The artist's dishonesty when he pretends to believe in the democracy of principles. For he denies, then, his most basic experience and art's great lesson: hierarchy and order. That this dishonesty is sentimental doesn't change anything. It leads to slavery, in factories or in camps.

———

S. Weil is right: it's not the individual who needs to be protected but the possibility contained within her. And then, she says, "we don't come to truth without having passed through our own annihilation: without having spent a long while in a state of total and extreme humiliation." The misfortune (chance can do away with me) is this state of humiliation, not the suffering. And yet "the spirit of justice and the spirit of truth are but one."[94]

———

The revolutionary mind rejects original sin. In doing so, it drowns in it. The Greek mind doesn't think about it. In doing so, it escapes it.

———

Crazy people in the concentration camps. Roam freely. Objects of cruel jokes.

———

While being beaten in Buchenwald, an opera singer is forced to sing his great arias.

———

Id. The Jehovah's Witnesses in Buchenwald refused to take part in collecting woolen clothing for the German army.

———

In Hinzert,[95] French inmates wore two uppercase letters on their clothes: HN. Hunde-Nation: Nation of Dogs.

---

93. The Groupes de Liaison Internationale, which Camus helped found in 1948, was a left-wing collective opposed to all forms of totalitarianism, including Communism, and it was also where Camus first met scientist Jacques Monod.

94. This citation, from Simone Weil's essay "La personne et le sacré" (translated as "Human Personality"), shares much in common with the citation from Gandhi that Camus would use as an epigraph for his unpublished short story "Pride."

95. A Nazi concentration camp close to Germany's border with Luxembourg.

———

It's because France is a military nation that Communism has a chance there.

———

Play.

"There's honesty for you. She does bad things, thinking she's doing good."

"But she distinguishes."

———

The principle of law is the principle of the State. Roman principle that '89 reintroduced to the world by force, against the right. We have to return to the Greek principle of autonomy.

———

Text about the sea. The waves, the gods' saliva. The sea monster, the sea to be conquered, etc. My untidy taste for pleasure.[96]

———

Alexandre Jacob: "A mother, you see, is humanity."[97]

———

Leibniz: "I look down on almost nothing."[98]

———

January 23, '51—Valence.[99]

I've shouted, demanded, rejoiced, despaired. But at 37 years old, one day I met with misfortune and I understood what, despite appearances, I hadn't known until then. Toward the middle of my life, I had to painfully learn to live alone again.

———

Novel. "I, who'd been living for so long, moaning and groaning, in the world of the body, I admired those who, like S.W.,[100] seemed to escape it.

96. The word Camus uses here, *désordonné* (disordered), appears throughout his work, often with the sense of physical or political disorder, but also with the sense of excessive or uncontrollable desires.

97. Alexandre "Marius" Jacob (1879–1954), a French anarchist, served as a model for Maurice Leblanc's "gentleman thief" Arsène Lupin.

98. It seems likely Camus took the quote from Nietzsche's *Beyond Good and Evil*, section 6, "We Scholars," no. 207, where he writes that the objective person "no longer knows how to affirm, no longer how to deny; he does not command, neither does he destroy. 'Je ne méprise presque rien,' he says with Leibniz, and we should not ignore or underestimate that 'presque'!"

99. Camus stopped over in Valence on his way back to Cabris, where he was returning to treat his tuberculosis.

100. Simone Weil.

For my part, I couldn't imagine a love without possession and so without the humiliating suffering that's the lot of those who live according to the body. I went so far as to prefer that a person who loved me be faithful in body rather than in heart and soul. I knew very well that for a woman the latter was a condition of the former, and so I demanded it, but only as a condition of that exclusive possession that was more important to me than all the rest, that was my personal salvation, the deprivation of which was an infinite source of torture. My paradise was in others' virginity."

———

Grasse, capital of apprentice barbers.

———

Revisit the passage from Hellenism to Christianity, the only true turning point in history. Essay about fate. (Nemesis?)

———

Collection philosophical essays. Philosophy of expression + commentary Ethics Book 1 + reflections on Hegel (lectures on the philosophy of history) + Grenier essay + commentary Apology of Socrates.[101]

———

"Freedom is a gift from the sea." Proudhon.

———

What I've so long sought finally appears. Dying becomes consent.

———

FEBRUARY 5. To die without having resolved anything. But who dies having resolved everything, if not . . . ? Resolve at least to bring peace to those you've loved . . . Nothing is owed to you, not even, especially not, a peaceful death.[102]

———

101. In the original notebook, Camus has capitalized both *Ethics* and *Apology of Socrates* but not Hegel's *Lectures on the Philosophy of History*. None of the texts are italicized or underlined.

102. At the end of the night on February 2, Camus wrote to Maria Casarès: "Things aren't going as well this evening. For the first time in ten days, I put my work down and went to bed without picking it back up until 11:00 a.m. It's true that, my fire having gone out, I caught a cold this afternoon and am a little out of it. I hope that also explains the black waves that surged in as soon as I put my work down. I feel like throwing everything in the air and running to find you."

The two entries following this one were crossed out on both the manuscript and typescript and do not appear here.

FEBRUARY 1951.[103] The Rebel. I wanted to speak the truth while still being gracious. That's my justification.

———

Work, etc. 1) Essay on the sea. Gather together a book of essays: Celebration. 2) Preface for the American edition of the plays. 3) Preface for the American edition of the essays. 4) Translation of Timon of Athens. 5) Love of the distant. 6) The eternal voice.

———

Ignatius of Loyola. "Conversation is a sin if it's disorderly."

———

After *The Rebel.* Aggressive, obstinate rejection of the system. Aphorisms from now on.

———

Loyola. The human race: "That mass of man marching to hell."

———

Short story. The dread of death. And he commits suicide.

———

Petty breed of Parisian writers who cultivate what they believe to be insolence. Domestic servants who simultaneously ape the greats and ridicule them when back in the pantry.

———

I sometimes wished for a violent death—the type of death that would excuse a person for screaming as their soul is torn out. At other times, I dreamed of a long, ever lucid ending so that at least it couldn't be said I was taken by surprise—in my absence—to know, at last . . . But you suffocate, in the ground.

———

March 1st '51.

It's by holding back his conclusions, even when they seem obvious to him, that a thinker progresses.

———

A spectacular virtue that leads to denying your passions. A deeper virtue that leads to balancing them.

———

My powerful system for forgetting.

---

103. In both the handwritten notebook and the initial typescript, the date is given as 1950.

If I were to die unknown to the world, in a cold prison basement, the sea, at the last moment, would fill my cell, would come to lift me above myself and help me to die without hatred.[104]

March 7, 1951.

Finished the first draft of The Rebel. With this book, the first two cycles are complete. 37 years old. And now, can creation be free?

Every achievement is a servitude. It compels to greater achievement.[105]

---

104. Toward the end of "The Nearby Sea," Camus writes: "What does the wave say? If I were to die, surrounded by cold mountains, ignored by the world, disowned by my people, finally having exhausted my strength, the sea, at the last moment, would fill my cell, would come to lift me above myself and help me to die without hatred."

105. The last three pages of the notebook have a series of jottings written over them. It appears one additional page was torn out and is no longer present.

Notebook VII

MARCH 1951–DECEMBER 1953

A well-worn, white notebook with "Cahier VII" written at the top-center in thick ink and the dates "Mars 51–Decembre 53" written below it and to the right. In the very top-right corner, "38 bis" is written and circled in a different hand. This is the only one of the notebooks that is not an ordinary composition notebook of the sort used by schoolchildren in France. It is larger than the others and made of a nicer, unlined and unsquared paper. One result of this is that the handwriting, spacing, and location of the entries is more erratic than in most of the other notebooks. In addition, Camus seems to have skipped many of the verso pages in this notebook.

The French edition of the *Carnets* gives the cover dates as March 1951–July 1954, which is incorrect. The most likely explanation for the discrepancy is that when Camus was nearing the end of notebook VII, sometime in December 1953, as noted on the cover, he likely began writing in a new notebook, which he then abandoned several months later, mid-August 1954, in favor of the extant version of notebook VIII (Camus traveled from Paris to Marseille and then on to Oran mid-December 1953, and it is possible that he simply left or forgot notebook VII in Paris and began a new notebook for that reason). So as not to lose the entries he'd recorded in the new notebook, he likely tore them out—as he did on several other occasions—and placed them at the start of the extant notebook (see below). After his death, these looseleaf entries—many of which deal with Francine's mental health, his own mental health, and his children's physical health—were probably mixed up with a series of random letters and articles Camus had tucked in at the back of the notebook (some of these letters would go on to be published as an appendix in the French edition). Given that the starting date Camus wrote on the cover of the extant version of notebook VIII is December 1953 and that the first entry recorded in the notebook proper is dated August 15, 1954, it seems likely Camus intended these torn-out pages, which cover that exact period, December 1953–August 15, 1954, to be used as the start of notebook VIII when an eventual typescript was made.

Notes kept by Francine Camus in the wake of her husband's death give the correct dates for notebooks VII and VIII and indicate that the torn-out pages were indeed found tucked in the front of notebook VIII. These pages, which are present in the Camus Archive at the Bibliothèque Méjanes in Aix-en-Provence, France, have yet to be transcribed and published.

For related dating issues at the end of notebook VII, see p. 532n204.

Begun in March 1951
Finished in December 53

He who has conceived what is noble must also live it.
NIETZSCHE.[1]

1. Camus wrote the beginning and ending dates on the first page of the notebook (confirming the accuracy of the dates given on the cover), as well as a citation that he scratched out and beneath which he wrote the Nietzsche citation that appears here. He then drew an arrow from the citation to the edge of the page, indicating that it should be inserted at the start of the notebook proper. A couple of illegible words also appear on this first page.

Preface for E. and E.[2]

"... it was then I began to love art with that fiery passion that age, far from diminishing, makes ever more exclusive.... That disease added other constraints, the hardest ones, to those I already had. But in the end, it's also fostered this freedom of heart, this slight distance from human affairs, that's always saved me from bitterness and resentment. Living in Paris, I understand that this privilege (for it is one) is the kind enjoyed by kings. But the fact is that I've enjoyed it without being constrained by it. As a writer, I began to live in admiration, which is, in a sense, an earthly paradise. As a man, my passions have never been 'against.' They've always been addressed to those bigger or better than myself."

———

Madness of the 20th century: vastly different minds confuse the desire for the absolute and the desire for logic. Parain and Aragon.

———

JUNE 11, 1951. Letter from Régine Junier telling me that she's going to commit suicide.[3]

———

The creator. His books have enriched him, but he doesn't like them, so he decides to write his masterpiece. He works on nothing else, endlessly revising it. And little by little, malaise then misery settle over the household. Everything crumbles, and he lives with an alarming happiness. The children are sick. He has to rent the place out, live in a single room. He writes. His wife becomes neurasthenic. The years pass and, neglecting everything else, he continues working. The children flee. The day his wife dies at the hospital, he sets down the final period, and the only thing the person who comes to tell him the unfortunate news hears him say is: "Finally!"[4]

———

2. An unused portion of the preface Camus was writing for the publication of *L'envers et l'endroit* in France. The collection, Camus's first, was originally published by Edmond Charlot in a small print run in Algeria.

In the second sentence, the word *maladie* (disease) is used in the sense of "obsession" or "addiction."

3. See p. 271n52. Camus wrote on the typescript of the notebooks that he was going to attach Régine Junier's letter, which he did. Whether he somehow meant for it to be further incorporated into the entry is unclear. Régine Junier did, in fact, commit suicide.

4. An idea that would form the basis for both the short story "Jonas" and the play *The Life of the Artist.*

Novel. "His death was far from romantic. Twelve of them were put in a cell made for two. He started to choke and then fainted. He died, pressed against the grimy wall, while the others turned their backs on him and faced the window."

———

N.R.F. Curious environment intended to inspire writers, and where, instead, they lose the joy of writing and creating.

———

Her happiness demanded everything, even killing.

———

Naturalness isn't a virtue we have, it's one we acquire.

———

Response to the question about my ten favorite words: "World, pain, earth, mother, men, desert, honor, poverty, summer, sea."

———

The eternal voice: Demeter, Nausicaa, Eurydice, Pasiphaë, Penelope, Helen, Persephone.

———

O light! In Greek tragedies, this is the cry of those thrown before death or a dreadful fate.[5]

———

Man of 1950: he fornicated and read newspapers.[6]

———

I've always felt as if I were on the high seas: threatened in the heart of a royal happiness.[7]

———

Grenier or the faker: Believing only in what is not of this world, he pretends to be in this world. He plays the game, but openly, so that no one believes he's playing it. He fakes it twice over. And then one more time: a part of him really is attached to the flesh, to pleasures, to power.

———

5. A slight variation of this entry would appear in "Return to Tipasa," where it's followed by the oft-quoted lines: "Their last resort was also ours, and now I knew it. In the midst of winter, I finally learned that there was an invincible summer in me."

6. Clamence expands on this thought in *The Fall*: "I sometimes wonder what future historians will say about us. A single sentence will suffice for modern man: he fornicated and read newspapers. After that potent definition, the subject will be, dare I say, spent."

7. With one small change—"lived on" replaces "were on"—this would become the final line of "The Nearby Sea," the final essay in *Summer*.

Is the acceptance of what is a sign of strength? No, it leads to servitude. But the acceptance of what has been. In the present,[8] the struggle.

Truth is not a virtue but a passion. Which is why it's never charitable.

Tics of M.'s[9] language . . . : "And all," "All in all," "So many . . . ," "You know, right, you know . . . ," "I didn't find her interesting," "She doubts everyone, it's irritating." "It's one thing to say it, but you have to see it to believe it," "She's special," "When she was about to be operated on . . . ," "Scattered utensils (mismatched)," "It's all just to say, well, hold on now, I'll make you pay," "Remember now, you know she had a knack for . . . ," "And so on and so forth," "Which just goes to show . . ." "You're acting like a weirdo (to her husband who goes out without a sweater)."

Id. Augusta, to whom a soldier—whom she'd adopted as a son during the war—expressed his gratitude as follows: "For me, Madam Pellerin, you were worse than a mother." She recounts the bombing of Nantes.[10] Caught by surprise in the streets, she and a friend took shelter under a doorway. "I was wearing a new outfit and a fox fur. When it was over, I was wearing a slip." The friend disappeared under the rubble. "I pulled her by the hair. She had only one finger left . . ." "And all the while, my husband was loving life, not even wondering if I'd made it out of the wreckage . . . The day before, I'd gotten an identity card. Distinguishing Features, I wrote None. The next day, that face was gone."

A Baptist who spent fifty days and nights in Buchenwald's black dungeon: "When I got out, the concentration camp seemed as beautiful to me as freedom itself."

"They live as a single person, those who at any given moment, by their own will, choose separation." Hölderlin. The Death of Empedocles.

---

8. In the handwritten notebook, Camus wrote: "Until then, the struggle."

9. In *The First Man*'s Side Characters folder, the full name is given as Mauricette, and several different examples appear there.

10. In June 1940, Nantes was captured by the Nazis. In 1941, and again in 1942, the British bombed the city. Most likely, the reference here is to the surprise American bombing on September 16 and 23, 1943, which devastated the city center and killed over a thousand civilians.

Id. "But you, you were born for a limpid day."[11]

Id. "Before him, at the happy hour of death, on a sacred day, the Divine casts off the veil."

According to Victor Serge, the atrocities committed by Admiral Kolchak are what gave the Chekists in the Russian C.P. the edge over all those who wanted greater humanity.[12]

1920. Abolition of the death penalty. The night before the law is enacted, the Chekists massacre the prisoners. A few months later, the penalty is reinstated. Gorky: "When will we be through with the killing and bloodshed?"[13]

Victor Serge: "Everything done in the U.S.S.R. would have been done far better by a Soviet democracy."

Preface for E. and E.[14]—My uncle—"A Voltairean, as one was in his time, he professed the utmost contempt for people in general and for his bourgeois clients in particular. But when it came to satire and anathema, he was brilliant. And he had a strong personality, too. Being around him wasn't always easy. Now that he's dead, and I'm in Paris, I get homesick when I think about him."

How 20th-century socialism was spread through war: the war of '14 ignited the revolution of '17. Foreign wars, on top of the civil war in China, gave us Mao Zedong. 1939 Sovietized Polish Ukraine and Belarus, the Baltic States and Bessarabia. The war of 1941–45 brought Russia across the Elbe.

---

11. Camus would use this quote as the epigraph for his essay collection *Summer*, just as he'd recently used a quote from the same text as an epigraph for *The Rebel*.

12. Alexsandr Kolchak (1874–1920), a Russian naval officer, worked with the White Army against the Bolsheviks.

Victor Kibalchich (1890–1947), better known as Victor Serge, was a Russian-Belgian writer and revolutionary. It seems likely, based on the notes recorded here, that Camus was reading his *Memoirs of a Revolutionary*.

13. On January 17, 1920, the Bolshevik government abolished the death penalty. The Cheka, the Soviet state security force, answered this action by senselessly slaughtering hundreds of prisoners before the new law took effect. In his *Memoirs of a Revolutionary*, Victor Serge writes: "While the newspapers were printing the decree, the Petrograd Cheka were liquidating their stock! Cartload after cartload of suspects had been driven outside the city during the night, and then shot, heap upon heap. In Petrograd, between 150 and 200; in Moscow, it was said between 200 and 300."

14. The uncle referred to here is Gustave Acault. See p. 195n55. The preface is for the reissue of *L'envers et l'endroit*.

The war with Japan gave them Sakhalin, the Kuriles, and North Korea. We'll see what happens with Finland and South Korea.

Novel character. Ravanel. Pure intelligence. Accounting for terrorism. World-weariness. Militancy. Police. Prosecutor. See earlier, new prosecutor.[15]

We have to apply our principles in large matters. For little ones, mercy will suffice.

Cynical and realist positions allow us to dismiss and despise. Others force us to understand. That's why intellectuals hold cynical and realist positions in such high regard.

We work in our time without hope of true reward. They courageously work for their own immortality.

Whatever it may claim, this century is in search of an aristocracy. But it doesn't see that finding one would require giving up the goal it has so proudly assigned itself: well-being. The only way to aristocracy is through sacrifice. An aristocrat is first and foremost someone who gives without receiving, someone who *commits* themself. The Ancien Régime died for having forgotten this.

Wilde.[16] He wanted to place art above everything else. But art's grandeur doesn't come from hanging above everything. On the contrary, it comes from being immersed in everything. Wilde eventually came to understand this thanks to sorrow. But the age we live in is to blame for the fact that it always

15. Serge Asher (1920–2009), codename Ravanel during World War II, led the United Movements of Resistance, then became regional leader of the French Forces of the Interior in the later stages of the war.

"See earlier, new prosecutor" refers to notes made in these pages during the fall and winter of 1948–49. In the Pléiade edition of Camus's *Complete Works*, Alain Schaffner suggests that "new prosecutor" is an early reference to *The Fall*.

16. Camus's preface for the French edition of Oscar Wilde's *The Ballad of Reading Gaol* appeared in English in the March 1954 issue of *Encounter* magazine with the title "The Artist in Prison."

In the Yellow Notebook, Camus writes: "Perhaps what's helped me to deal with an adverse fate will help me to receive a fate too favorable—and what's helped me to deal with it is, first and foremost, the grand vision, the truly grand vision, that I have of art. / Not because I see it as being above everything, but because it doesn't exclude anyone."

takes sorrow and servitude to catch sight of a truth that's also found in happiness, when the heart is worthy of it. Servile century.

Id. There's not one talent for living and another for creating. The same talent covers both. And you can be sure that a talent that is only capable of producing an artificial work is only capable of sustaining a frivolous life.[17]

Novel. C.[18] and her floral dress. The prairies at night. The oblique light.

I started with works in which time was rejected. Little by little, I regained the source of time—and maturity. The work itself will take a long time to mature.

They sought to repudiate beauty and nature solely for the benefit of the intellect and its conquering powers. Faust wanted to have Euphorion without Helen. The wondrous child is nothing but a deformed monster, a homunculus in a jar. For Euphorion to be born, neither Faust without Helen nor Helen without Faust.[19]

Rebellion, the true crucible of the gods. But it also forms idols.

Revolting reality of death.[20] The history of mankind is the history of the myths in which we've cloaked this reality. Over the past two centuries, the loss of traditional myths has sent history into seizures, as death has lost all sense of hope. And yet, there is no human truth if there is no acceptance of

---

17. In the handwritten notebook, this entry is written in a bracket squeezed alongside the Wilde entry.

18. In both the handwritten notebook and the typescript, the letter given here is "F," not "C," "C" being the letter that appears in the published French edition.

19. The reference is to Goethe's *Faust* and *Faust II*. Jonathan H. King notes in his edited volume of Camus's *Selected Political Writings* that "Goethe envisioned the ideal marriage of modern man's ceaseless striving (Faust) with classical beauty and repose (Helen). From this marriage would be born human well-being (Euphorion)." The above entry would be incorporated into Camus's unpublished essay "In Defense of *The Rebel*," where he writes: "Neither Faust without Helen, nor Helen without Faust, that's just the truth of it. Goethe, who had his prophetic moments, had Euphorion die, too beautiful for this world's misery. For my part, all I believe, and it's *The Rebel*'s main idea, is that it's up to us to ensure Euphorion lives." See, also, Camus's related essay, "Helen's Exile."

20. In French, Camus writes only *Mort révoltante* (Revolting death) here, but the sense of the phrase is as given above.

death without hope. Accepting the limit—without blind resignation—while maintaining this tension at the core of being is what leads to equilibrium.

Novel. A nice day. "She wobbled along the Croisette on her high heels. She'd looked herself over in the mirror before leaving the room. Of course, her soft flannel pants were a little too tight. And her hips were clearly wider than her shoulders. But so what: real women are like that. Too much chest, too. But that's not such a big deal, and anyway, it's more feminine. Those bodies playing volleyball down there on the beach, you had to look closely just to figure out if they were men or women.

The little black silhouette was walking in front of the sea. Between the headscarf and sunglasses, all you could make out were two brushstrokes where eyebrows had once been and an oily, white forehead vainly trying to furrow beneath the glaring sun."

A short play about the seducer.[21]

No, I only drink water.

"Something to eat?"

"I don't eat much. If I have a drink on occasion, it's for my health."

What does love add to desire? Something invaluable: friendship.

I don't seduce, I surrender.

Why women? I can't stand the company of men. They flatter or they judge. I can't stand either of the two."

At midnight, nothing. The commander didn't come. The seducer is sad. He's leaving.

"Come," Anna says.

"No, you can't be happy and right on the same day . . ." (he changes his mind). "And yet, if you're right, all that's left is happiness."

"All that's left is the love you never believed in, never having stopped believing in your own dreams, the ones you called God."

He looks at her.

"So then, is this love, what I feel rising inside of me?"

"It must be. Now gently push aside everything else surrounding that fragile plant. Gently, gently make way for happiness at last."

---

21. A scene for the long-planned play about Don Juan. See p. 138n69.

Novel. One of B's[22] secrets . . . is that she's never been able to accept or deal with, or even simply forget, sickness and death. That's where her inability to focus comes from. As it is, she exhausts herself simply trying to live like everyone else does, feigning the sort of nonchalance and innocence necessary to go on living. But deep inside, she never forgets. She doesn't even have enough innocence for sin. Life for her is nothing but time, which itself is sickness and death. She doesn't accept time. She digs her heels in for a battle already lost. When she gives in, she finds herself adrift in the current, wearing the face of a drowning woman. She's not of this world because she rejects it with all her being.[23] Everything starts from this.

———

Dordogne.[24] Here, the soil is pink, the pebbles the color of flesh, the mornings red and wreathed in clear songs. Flowers die in a single day, ever reborn beneath the slashing sun. At night, sleeping carp float down the oily river; flares of mayflies blaze around the bridge lamps, casting a living plumage on the hands and covering the ground with wings and wax, from which fleeting life will gush. What dies here cannot pass. Asylum, faithful land, it is here, traveler, that you must return, to the house where hints and memories are kept, and that which doesn't die with man but is reborn in his sons.

———

It's not true that the heart wears out—rather the body, which creates the illusion.

———

Those who prefer their principles to their happiness refuse to be happy outside the conditions they've previously set for their happiness. If happiness

22. In the handwritten notebook, there is no initial given, only a series of dots. In the typescript, Camus inserted the letter "F." The "B" comes from the French edition.

23. This entry appears in *The First Man*'s Marie file, but with two key differences. In the file, the entry begins, "Panelier. M. and her floral dress. The prairies at night. The oblique light" (see p. 460n18), and the penultimate line seen above continues, "with all her being, except in those *blazes* of beauty or glory."

According to Pierre-François Astor, Blanche Balain believed this entry referred to her. See p. 222n94.

24. On July 26, Camus left Paris with Maria Casarès for a brief getaway in Sainte-Foy-la-Grande in Southwest France, after which he would join his wife and children in Chambon-sur-Lignon, where he would stay until the end of August while he revised and corrected the proofs for *The Rebel*.

While much of the poetry in this entry can be carried over into English, the phrase *torches d'éphémères*, here given as "flares of mayflies," loses the double sense of "ephemeral," short-lived, and "Ephemera," a genus of mayflies.

catches them by surprise, then they're at a loss—unhappy to be deprived of their unhappiness.

———

A tragedy about chastity.

———

Just as the absurd wasn't in the world or in us but in the contradiction between the world and our experience, so, too, is balance not in reality or desire but in . . . Balance is a process, a transposition of the absurd effort.[25]

———

Novel. M. (and she was conveying my truth at the same time): I desire nothing other than what I have. My curse, and my punishment, is not to be able to enjoy what I have.

———

Id. As a teenager, and even long after, the only thing about love that interested him was the unknown, and thus discovery.[26] That's what led to his affairs. But affairs don't just come out of nowhere; they always have a beginning, no matter how brief it may be. Quite often, the beginning was enough to satisfy discovery, when little was known, and so he would agree to the tryst, certain that it was nothing more than that.

In this way, those who confuse love and discovery have enough pride to believe, correctly or incorrectly, that they're self-sufficient. Others recognize their limits, and the being rather than the discovery, which makes their love unique, because it demands everything.

———

Novel. A.W.,[27] a young American who came to Paris after having fought in the war (into which he, a happy, conformist student, had been thrown), lives in Paris, cursing America and passionately pursuing the reflections of grandeur and wisdom that he still reads on old Europe's face. He lives a bohe-

25. The editors of the official French edition of the *Carnets* place this entry later in the notebook and note that it was written on a separate sheet of paper inserted into the notebook, but photocopies of the original notebook, which is now in a private collection, appear to show that the entry was written in the notebook proper, on its own page, in the spot where it is here located.

The essence of the entry would be incorporated into the opening of *The Rebel*, where Camus uses the French word *mouvement* (movement) in the sense of a "process" or an "action," which is how it is given here. For more on the translation of *la mesure* as "balance," see p. 72n34.

26. In French, the word used throughout the entry is *la connaissance*, usually translated as "knowledge" (or "acquaintance" if used in terms of a relationship).

27. In *The First Man*'s Side Characters file, the name of the young American who comes to Paris is given as Anstryn Wodcut. In the handwritten notebook, Camus wrote "Anustryn Woodcut," which he then crossed out on the typescript in favor of the initials A.W.

mian life. He's lost the shine of American faces. He doesn't look well—his eyes have circles under them. So there he is, sick and dying in a filthy hotel, and he cries out for that America he's never stopped loving: for the fields of Harvard University in Boston, for the sound of bats and late-evening laughter around the river.

Novel. Part One: football match. Part Two: bullfight.

Those evenings whose gentleness goes on. They help us die, knowing that such evenings will return to the earth after we're gone.[28]

A woman who truly loves, with all her soul, in total devotion, grows so disproportionately that there isn't a single man who, in comparison, is anything but mediocre, miserable, and without generosity.

Novel. In an unlit room, a child, nose next to the glowing radio dial, listens to music.

Novel. Two characters: the German friend. —Marcel H.

Countess Tolstoy's Journal.[29]

P. 45 about T.'s work routine.

T: "Writing is so boring."

The Countess, October 9, 1862 (the wedding was on Sept. 23): "All carnal relationships are disgusting" and in December, the true feminine cry: "If I could kill him and create another person just like him, I would do it with pleasure."

April '63. "The physical part of love plays a very big role for him, whereas for me it plays none whatsoever."

'63. "What's left of the man I was?" T. says.

Sept. '67. "I'm nothing but a wretched reptile that's been crushed, I'm

---

28. This line appears at the end of "The Nearby Sea," where Camus adjusts it as follows: "Those nights whose gentleness goes on, yes, they help us die, knowing they'll return after we're gone, there on the land and sea."

29. The page numbers Camus cites here refer to the two-volume French edition published by Plon in 1930 and 1931. In English, the diaries appeared in three volumes.

This entry appears on its own page in the handwritten notebook.

good for nothing, nobody loves me, I'm nauseated, have two rotten teeth, bad breath, am pregnant . . . etc."

'78. We learn Tolstoy read at the dinner table.

'87. He howls that he's constantly thinking of leaving his family.

'90. She secretly reads her husband's journal, which he keeps under lock and key.

Dec. '90. He writes: "Love doesn't exist. There's the physical need to unite with another person and the reasonable need to have a life companion."

'91. "'It's torture for me,' he says, 'to be surrounded by servants.'"

'91. The Countess writes about how she can never get used to the Count's filth and odor. *Id.* P. 283 ('97).

'92. The Countess reveals that L.T. is only ever cheerful in the glow of physical love.

Everyone, according to her, pities her and considers her "a victim."

Then the squabbles over royalties p. 81 and 97, 131–137, 216, 145.

P. 88. Confession of double love.

"People who have taken the wrong path in life, weak and foolish people, throw themselves on Lev Nikolayevich's pamphlets."

"These stilts on which he climbs in the presence of the dark unknown."

'97. He leaves the house and doesn't return until morning.

'97. He plays tennis every morning.

At 70 years old, after 35 versts on horse, in the snow, he shows his passion for the Countess, who notes it with amazement.

———

The nickname Stalin's comrades gave him (in '17): the gray blur.[30]

———

On the heights of happiness—and night came to find me.

———

No one more than I has longed for harmony, abandonment, and definitive equilibrium, but to try to reach them, I've always had to travel the steepest paths, through unrest and struggle.

———

"'Of course,' he says, 'I'm afraid of not being dead enough in death and of not having enough air to breathe underground. But I reason with myself: if

30. In *The Russian Revolution, 1917: A Personal Record,* Nikolai Sukhanov writes that Stalin "gave me the impression . . . of a gray blur that dimly flickered and left no trace. There's really nothing more to be said about him."

I'm afraid of not having enough air to breathe, it's because I'm afraid I'll die on account of it. So then there are only two options: either I really won't have enough air to breathe, but I'll have enough to survive, in which case I'll no longer be anxious about it, or, I'll die, and why the anxiety then?"

Novel. Jeanne P. and her unconscious movements.

Id. The military cemeteries of the East. At the age of 35, the son goes to his father's grave and realizes the person buried there died at the age of 30. He *is already older than that.*[31]

The Arabs laid to rest here—and forgotten by all.

Novel. Daydreams in the car on the road to Bérard.

M. I realized it was true that some people are greater and truer than others. And that they formed an invisible and visible society that stretched across the globe and justified living.

M.[32] Pathetic death at the end of a pathetic life. Only the death of big hearts is not unjust.

Novel. The Spanish refugees. Domenech (civil war—war '39, résistance, Buchenwald—unemployed) Garcia (for whom A.B.[33] forgave a debt of 140,000 F. "Ah, you, you're like me. You'll never be rich") Gonzales (there are classes—and they can never work together—Rejects all the boss's kindness—He wants to be treated tough) Bertomeu: The choir (and then he grills sardines in the office).

---

31. In 1947, at the age of thirty-four, Camus saw his father's grave in Saint-Brieuc for the first time. His father, Lucien, had been mortally wounded in the Battle of the Marne, not yet twenty-nine. This would go on to become a key scene in *The First Man*.

32. In *The First Man*'s Side Characters folder, this entry, also identified as Mauricette, follows the earlier entry. See p. 457n9. In the handwritten notebook, as well as on the typescript, the abbreviation "Maur." is given.

33. André Bénichou, a friend from Oran, was one of the few male friends with whom Camus openly spoke about his personal life.

James (The Am.).[34] "What I hate is myself—when I think that one has to take so much, to be happy, out of the lives of others, and that one isn't happy even then."

Mauriac. Admirable proof of the power of his religion: he arrives at charity without passing through generosity. He's wrong to send me endlessly back to Christ's agony. It's as if I have greater reverence for him than he does, never having believed I was entitled to exhibit my savior's suffering on the front page of a bankers' newspaper twice a week. He calls himself an opinion columnist. Indeed. But those opinions have an overwhelming tendency to use the cross as a projectile weapon.[35] Which makes him a first-rate journalist and a second-rate writer. The Dostoyevsky of the Gironde.

Novel. "In those moments, eyes closed, he received the shock of pleasure like a sailboat suddenly accosted in the fog, struck from hull to keel, the shock of the impact causing everything inside him to reverberate, from deck to foresail to the thousand ropes and ribs running through the ends of the ship, which then quivered for a good while before slowly rolling over on its side. After that, the shipwreck."

Novel. What struck him then was how few things there were in his home. The necessary. Never had a word been better illustrated. When his mother lived in a room, she left no trace, aside from the occasional handkerchief.[36]

"I desired, I called on the greatest suffering, certain I'd now find the happiness it contained (that I'd be able to taste happiness . . .)."

To start giving is to condemn yourself to never giving enough, even if you give everything. And do we ever give everything—[37]

---

34. "The Am." is written in English in the original. The quote comes from Henry James's *The Ambassadors*, book 12, chap. 2.

35. In the typed version of the notebooks, Camus crossed out a similar line about Mauriac that appeared between the entry about a "terribly hot day" and the one about the deportee.

36. On November 19, 1951, Camus flew home to Algiers to be with his mother, who had broken her leg. He would return to Paris on December 1.

37. In *The First Man*'s The Stake, Unknown to Himself, Etc. file, there is a similar entry that reads: "You probably haven't been loved enough. A person has to give everything. But it's true that I gave everything and that it didn't help. That's because you know nobody can give everything and it showed in who you were. You pay for everyone's condition." In the margins, Camus added: "I said

———

Never say of a man that he's dishonored. Actions, groups, civilizations can be. Not the individual. For if he's not aware of dishonor, he can't lose an honor he's never had. And if he does have it, the terrible burn it causes is like a hot iron on wax. The fire from the unbearable pain melts and blisters the individual at the same time as it regenerates him. This fire is the fire of an honor that rightly balks at, and affirms itself through, the very extent of its pain. At least that's what I felt the day, the exact second when, as a result of a misunderstanding, I believed I was guilty of having done something really low. It wasn't true, but in that single second I came to understand all those who've been humiliated.

———

December '51.

I patiently await a catastrophe that's slow in coming.[38]

———

My statements on the radio—Hearing them, I find myself exasperating. Paris makes me this way, despite my best efforts. Alone too often since the demise of *Combat*, with nowhere to discuss, defend, expose, or occasionally justify. Never relieved by the warmth of others, or at least not by the spectacle of their generosity, I end up freezing, and it's precisely this frozen voice that comes out of me, too contemptuous to really express contempt, but nonetheless exasperating to hear. If I felt true confidence, for just one second, I'd laugh and everything would be okay.[39]

———

I owe my idea of vulgarity to a few *grande bourgeoisie*, who, like Mauriac, reveal how proud they are of their culture and privileges the moment they make a show of their wounded vanity. So then, they try to wound at the same level at which they were wounded, and in doing so discover their true stature

---

that I gave everything. And that inevitably committed me to giving everything. You can't go looking for proof of love in a person's heart, a place where proof is unfathomable."

38. *The Rebel* was published on October 15, 1951. By December, the reviews were beginning to trickle in, but Sartre's magazine, *Les temps modernes*, had yet to publish one. In the copy of *The Rebel* Camus gave to Sartre and Simone de Beauvoir, he wrote: "To Beaver, To Sartre, from their friend, A. Camus." It appears Sartre gave the book away shortly after, adding his own inscription beneath Camus's: "and n[ot] l[ong] after, to Sveto Radeff, his best Annie."

39. Likely in reference to the BBC program "Albert Camus Talks About the General Election in Britain," which had been broadcast several times, first in French, then in English, then a third time with a response from Raymond Aron.

in the world. It's then that the virtue of humility triumphs in them for the first time. Poor things, indeed, but full of spite.

———

I've never felt the need to conform to the world, to opinion. Yet I have, even if only a little. But I've just made the ultimate effort. In this respect, I truly believe my freedom is total. Free, and therefore benevolent.[40]

———

I have the most awful impression of myself, for days on end.

———

Life of Velázquez. Commentary on Velázquez.

———

Balance. They consider it a resolution of the contradiction. It can be nothing but a confirmation of the contradiction and the heroic decision to stick with it and survive it.

———

In publicly condemning the atomic bomb, the U.S.S.R. is attempting to develop and appeal to international morality, which is its best chance at protection. So then, it compensates for its only inferiority by resorting to a moral judgment it nevertheless rejects in its official philosophy.

———

Hypocritical injustice leads to wars. Violent justice precipitates them.

———

Marxism reproaches Jacobin and Bourgeois society for the same reason Christianity reproaches Hellenism: intellectualism and formalism.

———

Play. He comes back from the war. Nothing's changed except that he only speaks poetically.

———

Emerson: every wall is a gate.[41]

———

40. See, for reference, the March 7, 1951, entry on p. 452. A more literal translation of the first line might read: "I've never been very submissive to the world, to opinion."

41. Notes occurring here and elsewhere indicate Camus was reading Ralph Waldo Emerson's *Journals*. The passage cited above appears in an entry from 1844, where Emerson writes: "The ground of Hope is in the infinity of the World, which infinitely reappears in every particle. I know, against all appearances, that there is a remedy to every wrong, and that every wall is a gate." Camus would use this quote from Emerson in the final paragraph of "Create Dangerously."

Never attack anyone, especially not in writing. The time for criticism and polemics is over—Creation.[42]

Completely eliminate criticism and polemics—From now on, only steadfast affirmation.

A bad temper is the worst of fates. I know from experience. After years of radiance and strength, that was what tempted me most. I gave in to it long enough to be educated by it, and then I got out.

Understand them all. Love and admire but a few.[43]

Overbeck[44] had the impression Nietzsche was faking his madness. An impression I've always gotten from the insane, no matter the individual. Maybe love is like that, too. Half faked.

The "limit" has to be everyone's truth. It's mine insofar as I am a part of everyone. But only for me is it a truth that one is not allowed to speak.

Guilloux, on Chamson: "For him, the other is only a possible switch."[45]

All over the world, from millions of marvelous machines, come torrents of sad music.

Judas turns treason and hatred into a principle so as to bear witness, at least indirectly, for Christ. Result: the 20th century. For lack of love, the camps.

Journalism, according to Tolstoy: an intellectual bordello. He wanted to

---

42. Though certainly stirred by reactions to *The Rebel*, this note and the one that follows may also have roots in one of Emerson's 1870 journal entries in which he writes: "How dangerous is criticism. My brilliant friend cannot see any healthy power in Thoreau's thoughts. At first I suspect, of course, that he oversees me, who admire Thoreau's power. But when I meet again fine perceptions in Thoreau's papers, I see that there is defect in his critic that he should undervalue them."

43. The entry is placed here as it appears in the handwritten notebook. When the typescript was made, both this entry and the one before it were accidentally left off, and Camus handwrote them in, but in reverse order.

44. Franz Camille Overbeck (1837–1905), German theologian and professor at the University of Basel, where he and Nietzsche lived in the same building.

45. The reference is most likely to French writer André Chamson.

write a novel "where no one was guilty." Letter from a dying Turgenev to Tolstoy: "I was happy to be your contemporary."

———

Novel (or play)—Character: Ellan. Fur.—cf. Heliosang.[46]

———

The myth of Euphorion. The child of contemporary titanism and ancient beauty. Goethe made him die. But he can live.[47]

———

Ran into P. Viannay yesterday,[48] not seen since the Occupation and the wonderful days of the Liberation of Paris. And all at once, immense nostalgia for our *comrades*, tears in our eyes.

———

Man of Aran.[49] Terrible life of these fishermen. Far from pitying them, you admire and respect them. It's not poverty or endless work that degrades a person but the sordid enslavement to the factory and life in the banlieues.

———

Two in the morning. Two favorite dreams, for years now, one of which, in different forms, always involves an execution. Jolted awake at night, I'm able to jot down many of the details.

I'm walking to the scaffold. Scotto-Lavina (a friend from Algiers whom I see very rarely but whom I like a lot) is with me. He whispers in my ear (the group's pace quickens): "My wife told me about X. and X. again yesterday." And I: "No proper names, absolutely no proper names." He, very gently, as if to a sick person: "Ah, forgive me." Someone in the group (there are guards whose presence barely registers, and A.,[50] who is by turns there and not) asks me why and I say, as we arrive at the foot of an immense staircase: "I want to keep to the heart of common nouns," a sentence I repeat to myself with a sort of peace. My children are at the top of the staircase I'm climbing,

46. According to Pierre-François Astor, the reference here is to a poem by Blanche Balain, "The Fortress," in which she creates an imaginary city named Heliosang and a character named Ellan Fur. Balain would later use the poem as the basis for a script.

47. Incorporated into "In Defense of *The Rebel*." See p. 460n19.

48. Philippe Viannay (1917–1966), journalist and founder of *Défense de la France*, an underground French Resistance newspaper. He also cofounded the Centre de formation des journalistes, one of the top journalism schools in France.

49. *Man of Aran*, the title of Robert Flaherty's 1934 film, is written in English in the original notebook.

50. On the typescript, Camus has scratched out what appears to be "Francine," leaving only a handwritten "F," not an "A" as given in the Pléiade. This is the case for all occurrences of the letter "A" in this entry.

still encircled, still quickly, and with hands bound, I think. (The sense, also, of being pushed, all of us pushed—walking with our backs bent forward.) Jean heads for a corner and on seeing him I say (though the feeling isn't fully formed inside of me, more like something dawning, a sort of delightful, agonizing discovery): "And then it will begin again." For the first time, I hug them and cry. They say goodbye to me as they usually do, no different, it seems. We move away from the staircase and pass through a sort of train station from which I exit alone with A. and Vera. Vera has been with me for a while—I don't know her during the dream, but when I wake up I think of her as S.[51] She's dressed as a peasant, vaguely Central European, like everyone around me. The surroundings are modern—train stations, construction sites—the night filled with a light wind. As we exit the train station, I head, with determination and without guards, toward where the scaffold is setup, the anxiety increasing and becoming unbearable. But I get the feeling Vera's carrying a gun, an old-fashioned one, that she stole from the train station (from whom?). As soon as I'm sure of it, I let out a joyous cry: "Oh, Vera! I knew it . . . (insinuation: that you'd do whatever it takes). How I love you so." I take the gun and we continue on our way. We approach a group of men doing some work. I seem to hesitate a bit, as if I wanted to wait a little longer, to live a little longer. But the others have gotten ahead of me. And I'm having a hard time holding the gun, which is too long, against my temple. I quickly pull the trigger, thinking that I didn't say goodbye to A. or anyone else. A terrible explosion in my head. And I hear a sentence, a sort of protest spoken by one of the workmen (the boss, I think), that I forget the moment the dream ends.[52]

———

Picaresque novel. Journalist—From Africa to the entire universe.

———

Play about love.

———

51. Part of this line was added by hand to the typescript, where the letter given is "M" not "S," as appears in the Pléiade.

52. This entry, which does not appear in the handwritten notebook and which Camus marked as pages "21 bis" and "21 ter." (21a and 21b) on the typescript, shares some similarities with Berlioz's "March to the Scaffold," the fourth section of his *Symphonie fantastique: Episodes from the Life of an Artist.*

In his own notebooks, Jean Grenier records that Camus's wife, Francine, told him that Camus talked about the dream often: "Always the same dream for Albert Camus: he is led to the guillotine with a woman named Vera. Francine joins him and gets him a revolver. He says to her: 'I knew you'd be there to help me.'"

Your morals are not mine. Your conscience is no longer mine.

———

M. "If a cure for death were found today, I wouldn't want it. My sorrow (the death of her father and mother) my happiness (her love) have no meaning unless I have to follow the same path, as well."

———

Emerson. "It can happen that the very same person who supported this doctrine (that man has a soul) takes flight in the face of a newspaper composed overnight by some dark reprobate who knows not what he writes and drenches his quill in mud and shadows."

———

Id. "What remains but to acquiesce in the faith that by not lying, nor being angry, we shall at last acquire the voice and language of a man."[53]

———

Id. "It's not through scruples that a man will become great. Greatness comes at God's pleasure, like a beautiful day."

———

Novel. During the Occupation, the St. Étienne–Dunières train, one winter's evening. The train is crowded, two compartments having been reserved for the German army. Shortly before the stop in Firminy, a German soldier notices that someone stole his bayonet while he was in the restroom. Howls of rage. Two workmen about to disembark and head home, their workday finished, are seized and held in the corridor as the train departs the station. They protest, weakly, their innocence obvious. At the next stop, the soldiers force them to disembark. They can be seen walking off in the icy mist, resigned to the worst.

The witness also disembarks, unhappy. He can't follow them. He doesn't know how to save them. He spends the night in the waiting room, thinking of them. Nothing to do but continue on in such a way that this doesn't happen again. But they'll be beaten by then, and dying maybe.[54]

———

53. This appears amid a long entry in Emerson's 1841 journal. The passage cited by Camus is preceded by the following: "Too feeble and faint fall the impressions of Nature on the sense. Let us not dull them by intemperance and sleep. Too partially we utter them again: the symbols in which I had hoped to convey a universal sense are rejected as partial."

54. This same story is told earlier in the notebooks, under the heading "Creation Corrected." See p. 253.

Thoreau. "As long as a man stands in his own way, everything seems to be in his way, governments, society, and even the sun and moon and stars."[55]

Id. Emerson. "For the obedience to a man's genius is the *particular* of Faith."[56]

Nietzsche to his sister, with regard to the situation with Lou:[57] "No, I am not made for enmity and hate. . . . Until then, I'd never hated anyone. It's only now that I feel humbled."

Necessity according to him of the "counter-Alexanders," of those "who will retie the Gordian knot of Greek culture after it has been cut."[58]

What I said, I said for the benefit of everyone and from that part of me that sides with the everyday. But another part of me knows a secret that's not meant to be revealed—one with which I'll have to die.

"A labyrinthine man never seeks the truth but always and only his Ariadne."[59]

---

55. While visiting Thoreau, Emerson noted in his journal: "Henry made last night the fine remark that 'as long as a man stands in his own way, everything seems to be in his way,—governments, society, and even the sun and moon and stars, as astrology may testify.'" Camus would use the Thoreau quote in his essay "Create Dangerously," though it seems either Camus himself, if he read Thoreau in English, or the French translator, if Camus read Thoreau in translation, has misconstrued the quote, reading "stands in his own way" as "remains faithful to himself." The original English is given above.

56. The full quote reads: "This is belief too, this debility of practice, this staying by our work. For the obedience to a man's genius is the *particular* of Faith: by & by, shall come the *Universal* of Faith." Camus would use the Emerson quote in his essay "Create Dangerously."

57. Lou Andreas-Salomé (1861–1937), Russian psychoanalyst and author, had close relations with Nietzsche, Freud, Wagner, and Rilke. Nietzsche twice proposed marriage and was twice rejected. In part, he blamed his sister, who had sent meddling letters to Lou's family. In November 1882, Nietzsche wrote to Malvida von Meysenbug: "My sister considers Lou a poisonous reptile who must be destroyed at all costs, and she acts accordingly."

Nietzsche's letter to Lisbeth seems to have been written around 1883 and reads, "Your brother is really quite unhappy. No, I am not made for enmity and hate: and since this matter has gone too far for a reconciliation with those two to be possible any more, I no longer know how to live; it is on my mind continually. Enmity is incompatible with my whole philosophy and way of thinking: to have entered the lists of the hostile (and against such poor folk) drags down my every aspiration. Until then, I'd never hated anyone—not even Wagner, whose perfidy went well beyond Lou's. It's only now that I feel humbled."

58. The quote comes from Nietzsche's *Ecce Homo*. Camus would use a slightly modified, uncredited, version of the quote in his essay "Create Dangerously."

59. The mention of Ariadne in Nietzsche's *Ecce Homo* seems to be the source of this quote, though the match is not perfect.

At the clinic in Jena, Nietzsche has long, lucid conversations with Overbeck about everything—*except his own work.*

Genius is health, superior style, good temperament—but on the brink of a breakdown.

Creation. The more it gives, the more it receives—Devotion for enrichment.

He only is rightly immortal to whom all things are immortal (E.).[60]

According to Emerson, Americans are such prodigious mechanics because they fear fatigue and pain: out of laziness.[61]

Every writer, well-known or not, feels the need to say or write that genius is always hissed at by his contemporaries. Naturally, this isn't true, or is only sometimes, often by chance. But this need in the writer is telling.

Emerson 1848. "How, then, have we managed for the progress of mechanization to serve everyone except the worker? He has been fatally wounded by it."

---

60. In 1846, Emerson wrote in his journal: "To the youth the hair of woman is a meteor. I think that he only is rightly immortal to whom all things are immortal; he who witnesses personally the creation of the world; he who enunciates profoundly the names of Pan, of Jove, of Pallas, of Bacchus, of Proteus, of Baal, of Ahriman, of Hari, of Satan, of Hell, of Nemesis, of the Furies, of Odin, and of Hertha;—knowing well the need he has of these, and a far richer vocabulary; knowing well how imperfect and insufficient to his needs language is: requiring music, requiring dancing, as languages; a dance, for example, that shall sensibly express our astronomy, our solar system, and seasons, in its course." Fourteen years later, in 1860, Emerson wrote: "That only which we have within, can we see without. If we meet no gods, it is because we harbor none. If there is grandeur in you, you will find grandeur in porters and sweeps. He only is rightly immortal, to whom all things are immortal. I have read somewhere, that none is accomplished, so long as any are incomplete; that the happiness of one cannot consist with the misery of any other."

61. The passage Camus refers to here comes from Emerson's 1847 journal: "They are an ardent race, and are fully possessed with that hatred of labor, which is the principle of progress in the human race, as any other people. They must and will have the enjoyment without the sweat. So they buy slaves, where the women will permit it; where they will not, they make the wind, the tide, the

Id. "It is the right of every man to see himself judged and characterized according to his foremost influence."

The Early and Classical periods feminized nature. We came along. Our painters made it masculine. Nature enters our eyes, practically tearing them out.

"No psychology in art." "That's what you're missing." "Maybe, but such is the law of creation: make do with what you have. Then you'll have to judge not what I have but what I have done."

To remain a man in the world today, you need not only unflagging energy and constant pressure, you also need a bit of luck.[62]

Novel. "The issue isn't that love is no longer possible between us. The issue is that it never was. From the depths of my being, I cried out for your love for years on end—and then I cried out for nothing more than your *attention*. I got neither of the two."

Play. D. Haughty, contemptuous, desperate, categorical.[63]

G.'s wife has it out with him, interrupting work on his novel. He comes to Paris to write but is unable to get going. In truth, he *doesn't want* to pick up where he left off, wants to hold onto the argument and keep his resentment intact.

He executed them with his own hands. "You have to be willing," he said, "to get a little dirty."

To the few men who've allowed my admiration, I owe a debt of gratitude, the deepest of my life.

At least sexual liberation gave us this: that chastity and superiority of will are now possible. All experiences—women reserved or liberated, passionate

waterfall, the steam, the cloud, the lightning, do the work, by every art and device their cunningest brain can achieve."

62. The rest of the page after this entry was left blank in the original notebook.

63. This entry and the one that precedes it appear on their own page in the original notebook.

or reflective, and you yourself, unbridled or cautious, triumphant or incapable of desire—that's all there is to it. There's no more mystery or inhibition. The mind is nearly liberated, mastery almost entirely possible.

———

Plan. Perpetual dictionary (for Chronicles). Write *Caprices* (à la Goya).[64]

———

Deep inside me, a Spanish solitude. Man only emerges from it for a few "*moments*," then returns to his island. Later (beginning in 1939), I tried to get back to it, I retraced all the steps of the time, but at breakneck speed, on the wings of commotion, under the whip of wars and revolutions. Today, I'm at the end—and my solitude is filled with shadows and works that are uniquely my own.

———

Iguape. A man at the front of the ferry. The city, the procession. The stone falls, the man collapses. The visitor picks up the stone but goes past the church and walks toward the river. He loads the stone onto a long boat and sets out on the river, toward the rainforest where he disappears.[65]

———

Even my death will be contested. Yet what I desire most today is a silent death that would leave those I love in peace.

———

One evening, absentmindedly leafing through an agreeable book, I read the following without blinking: "As with many passionate souls, the time had come when his faith in life was wavering."[66] A second later, the sentence rang out in me, and I dissolved into tears.

———

A part of me has utterly despised this age. Even amid my worst failings, I've never lost my sense of honor, and my heart has often faltered when faced

---

64. "Chronicles" may refer to Camus's third collection of journalistic essays, *Actuelles III: Chronique Algérienne* (*Current Affairs: Algerian Chronicles*).

The reference is to Goya's *Los Caprichos*, a series of eighty prints created between 1797 and 1798, which served to condemn the various "foibles and follies" of Spanish society.

65. A note for "The Stone That Grows." See the earlier entries made during Camus's travels in South America for more.

66. The "agreeable book" from which Camus quotes is Swiss author Guy de Pourtalès's *La vie de Franz Liszt*, published by Gallimard in 1925.

with the degree of decline this century has reached. But another part of me wanted to assume the decline and the common struggle . . . [67]

Comedy About the Press

"Nuance? If I find another word like that in your vocabulary, I'll throw you right out the door."

(To the drama critic) that author has no friends here. So then you'll try to say it's a question of ideas. In France today, the slightest suspicion of intelligence is enough to sink a man. But you'll take every opportunity to write that we're the most intelligent people on Earth. The public no longer accepts intelligence unless it's packaged in stupid clichés.

The End. The next day he'll write an article that reveals everything.

The public has no memory—We are its memory. Scene with reader.

La Revue des Journaux:[68] the one that parades Christ on the front page of a newspaper for the fat and happy. A progressive friend of the camps, etc.

3rd Act at his home. Ascetic.

To the idealistic copy editor

"Your paper isn't visible enough."

"It's read."

"A newspaper's meant to be read, sure, but from a distance. You have to be able to read your neighbor's copy on the Métro."

"A person reading their neighbor's copy isn't buying their own."

"No, but they're talking about it."[69]

FEBRUARY 28, 1952. Discovery of Brazil, of Villa-Lobos—with him, greatness returns to music. Masterpiece—in my eyes, only Falla is as good.[70]

If I were to die tonight, I'd die with an awful feeling, one previously unknown to me, and yet one that pains me tonight. The feeling that I have

---

67. The rest of the page after this entry was left blank in the original notebook.

68. *La revue des journaux*, a section in the magazine *Revue Pleyel*, aggregated performing-arts reviews from a variety of papers, presenting the differing critical opinions as being in conversation. For the comment on Christ, see the entry on Mauriac, p. 467.

69. This is the only entry on the page in the original notebook.

70. Heitor Villa-Lobos (1887–1959), Brazilian composer and musician. Manuel de Falla (1876–1946), Spanish composer.

helped and that I am helping a lot of people—and yet no one is coming to help me . . . Not proud of myself.

Medea—put on by the Théâtre Antique.[71] I can't listen to the dialogue without crying, like someone who's finally found his homeland. These words are mine, mine are these feelings, mine this belief.

"What misfortune is that of the man without a city." "O, please don't let me be without a city," the Chorus says. I am without a city.

Nemesis. Drunkenness of body and soul isn't madness but comfort and numbness. True madness blazes on the brink of an interminable lucidity.

A paper isn't truthful because it's revolutionary. It's only revolutionary because it's truthful.[72]

Ibsen (*Emperor and Galilean*).[73] After Olympus and Calvary, the Third Empire.

Polemic against T.R.[74] The mass mobilization[75] of darklings. I look up "Darkling" in Littré. 1) friend of intellectual darkness. 2) genus of beetles of

---

71. The Théâtre Antique d'Orange (Roman Theatre of Orange), located in the Vaucluse region of France, is one of the world's best preserved Roman theaters.

72. In February 1957, the socialist weekly *Demain* (no. 63) published an interview with Camus—conducted in written form by his friends Nicola Chiaromonte and Ignazio Silone—under the title "Le socialisme des potences." In it, Camus writes: "A paper, a book, isn't truthful because it's revolutionary. It has a chance of being revolutionary only if it tries to tell the truth. You have the right to think capital-T truth is relative. But facts are facts. And anyone who says the sky is blue when it's gray is prostituting words and preparing the way for tyranny." The British magazine *Encounter* published an English translation of the interview in April 1957 under the title "Parties and Truth" (though the table of contents gives the title as "Truth and Politics"). The interview was later collected as "Socialism of the Gallows" in *Resistance, Rebellion, and Death*.

73. Ibsen's *Emperor and Galilean* poses the question: How do we reconcile will and morals on one hand, and love and freedom on the other?

74. Abbreviation of *The Rebel*. In May 1952, *Les temps modernes* (no. 79) published Francis Jeanson's review of *The Rebel*, which set off the polemic that would lead to the break between Camus and Sartre.

75. In French, Camus uses the term *levée en masse*, which is sometimes transparently rendered in English as "levy en masse" and which refers to the practice of conscription during the French Revolutionary Wars, with particular emphasis placed on the idea of shared nationality and duty to protect the nation.

Littré is shorthand for Émile Littré's well-known French dictionary, *Dictionnaire de la langue française*, originally published in four volumes (1863–1873).

which one species, in its larval state, lives in flour. Also called the cockroach. Amusing.[76]

———

Our poètes maudits[77] have two laws: malediction and strategy.

———

Apparently God's love is the only love we can bear given we always want to be loved in spite of ourselves.

———

Cf. Romain Rolland. *The Life of Tolstoy*. P. 69. "Life" of the novel.[78]
Id. "It's difficult to love a woman and do anything worthwhile."

———

The Bacchantes.[79] Pentheus should say: "I don't want your excessive behavior. But I'd like to die of my own."

———

They are the rebellion, the pride, the inflexible wall that stands up to rising servitude. They'll leave the role to no one else—and anyone who claims to rebel some other way will be excommunicated.

So how does it go? One of them waits to see the most upstanding newspaper these times have ever known, created by the sacrifice and labor of hundreds of men, he waits, I say, for this newspaper to pass into the hands of a shady financier, for all the free men to leave the building, before he runs off to loan his services to the businesspeople. The other one, while supporting and applauding his old friend against me, writes to me to say that one mustn't put too much stock in what the old poet says, and then, suddenly worried, writes again to beg me not to make his letter, his little act of treason, public. Then another comes to ask me for a favor, receives it, and, back home, writes an article insulting me, and then writes to me to try to soften the effect. Yet another, afraid of being misjudged for having long represented a publishing house that abused my trust, asks to explain himself to me in person, receives

---

76. The last word of the entry, "Amusing," does not appear in the handwritten notebook. It was written in on the typescript.

77. The term *poète maudit* (accursed poet), likely coined by Alfred de Vigny, was popularized by Paul Verlaine. *Britannica* defines the term as "an outcast of modern society, despised by its rulers who fear his penetrating insights into their spiritual emptiness." Camus will return to the term in the long entry below.

78. In *The Life of Tolstoy*, Romain Rolland writes that Tolstoy's descriptions of Natasha in *War and Peace* are full of "life." See pp. 266–67 for Camus's own comments about Natasha.

79. Throughout these pages, Camus makes notes for a stage adaptation of *The Bacchante.* Camus was likely aware of Nietzsche's treatment of Euripides's play *The Bacchantes* in *Birth of Tragedy*.

a letter that, out of pure generosity, refuses to conflate him and his employer, and, without missing a beat, grinds out an essay lamenting the fact that moralists like me always end up turning into policemen.

There you have our heroes, our *maudits* lounging beneath the cozy tent of malediction, coming out only when it's strategic. They're the ones who'll ensure our freedom, declaring that they'll hold the standard firm before the advancing storm. Yeah, and the second some beat cop lays a finger on them, they'll fall to their knees!

Fragment from a Letter about T.R.

There are so few of us. But truth comes before efficacy. We have to define the former before worrying about the latter. Of what use would it be to be a million strong if the first commandment given by our "church" were: Thou shalt lie? This is certainly not to say that efficacy has no meaning. Its meaning is secondary. The survival of truth is no less important a problem than truth itself. It's just that it's a problem that comes *after*. Still, it'll need to be figured out . . . The Christians began as twelve—the Marxists two.

Letter to A. Maquet[80]

It seems I'm advancing at the same rate as both an artist and a man. And that's not by design. It's due to the trust I place, humbly, in my calling . . . My next books won't turn away from our current problem. But I'd like them to take it as a subject rather than be subjected to it. In other words, I dream of a freer creation, with the same content . . . Then I'll know if I'm a real artist.

According to Melville, *remoras*, fish found in the South Seas, are poor swimmers. That's why their only chance of getting ahead lies in attaching themselves to the back of a bigger fish. There, they plunge a sort of tube into the shark's stomach, pump their food out, and propagate by living off the

80. Albert Maquet's study of Camus's work *The Invincible Summer* would go on to be published in 1958.

beast's hunting and effort without doing anything themselves. Such is the custom in Paris.[81]

A certain type of man knows with whom he can let his guard down. Primarily, with those who practice as much generosity and loyalty as they can—and whom decency prevents from exploiting all their privileges.[82]

The Bacchante. Two Dionysus: 1) God of the earth. Black God, virile God. Iacchus, a cry personified.[83]

2) The decadent Asian: wine and sensual pleasure, gossip. The one Pentheus rejects.

In Eleusis, they didn't initiate murderers (Nero didn't dare) or those "whose voice isn't just."

Second day of mysteries: "Mystes, to the sea."

To crossover to Hell, Dionysus has to row himself.

3 gods in Eleusis: Iacchus, Demeter (the mother), Triptolemus.

Meaning: death isn't unpleasant. It's earthly life that's death—death is liberation.

Vestige in Luke: Let the dead bury the dead and you go proclaim the Kingdom of God.[84]

1st Dionysus will reassemble Pentheus:[85] "Behold your God, rejoice, but only worthy of worshipping me is the one who has shown he will never succumb to debauchery of the soul and flesh, to the false god I always precede. Wisdom now opens before you."

"Oh, how I burn to know it!"

"It is this—you have now earned the right to madness . . ."

Pentheus and the Bacchante howl on and on as the curtain falls.

---

81. An idea later incorporated into *The Fall*. See p. 437n61.

82. In September 1952, with the fallout from *The Rebel* yet to settle, Camus writes to Francine: "What's striking is this eruption of a detestation so long suppressed. It proves those people were never my friends, that I've always irritated or offended them in some way, and that that's where this nasty display comes from, this inability to be generous."

83. In Euripides's *The Bacchantes*, Iacchus is linked with Bromius, which is another name for Dionysus (and "Iacche" is the word cried out during the Eleusinian Mysteries). Several black-figure lekythoi from the fifth century BC also show Dionysus with the name Iacchus written on them.

84. The reference here is to Luke 9:60. See p. 261n33.

85. Pentheus, who'd been strongly against the cult of Dionysus, was torn apart by the Bacchantes, who'd been instructed to do so by Pentheus's own mother, Agave, and his aunts.

Or else . . . "Wait until everyone's asleep. Listen. Everything's gone quiet. It's now that you have the right to madness. You, alone. In solitude. So that it kills only you."[86]

Enter Dionysus II, followed by Dionysus I disguised as a dilettante skeptic (Silenus?) "Enjoy, enjoy!"

Beginning: the old men run to the Bacchantes.

A philosopher (Does he kill? How does he kill? Does he kill well, etc. He who kills so well and I who reason so powerfully . . . We'll do wonders. I'll lend him my reason and he'll kill for me.)

A poet

A priest: What are you going to do with those, Priest?

A merchant.

Nihilists.

The Bacchante: She wants to go. Pentheus is opposed. "We must hold the city. It cannot be sacrificed to love." "It cannot sacrifice love."

Dionysus I and Pentheus: Who are you to proclaim such virtue?

"I have no virtue."

"Have you not coveted women?"

"Yes."

"Have you not taken them?"

"Yes."

"Have you not been violent?" (He hits him.)

Pentheus is quartered. Dionysus II and the Bacchantes celebrate the sacrifice.

Dionysus I arrives and silences them.

II "Who can silence the cries of madness?"

I "He who knows madness and controls it."

Id. A man like me, a slave, if you had any idea what he holds inside him. I'm angry enough to smack the gods' faces, desirous enough to . . . to force my best friend's wife . . . But these dogs who chase after each other disgust me, each of them seeking the other's desire only to relieve their own. Me, virtuous!

---

86. In the handwritten notebook, the entry up to this point appears where it is currently placed, on the recto page, with an arrow pointing toward the verso, where the rest of the entry from this point on appears as the only entry on the page. It seems Camus initially left this verso page, which follows the "Fragment from a Letter about T.R." entry, blank and then went back and used the page when he ran out of space on the recto.

(He bursts out laughing.) I'd like to be so, to tell the truth, but my blood's on fire and my intelligence, having all the strength, can conceive of anything.[87]

At forty years old,[88] you accept the annihilation of a part of yourself. Let the heavens at least put all this unused love toward setting right and making shine a work for which I currently no longer have the strength.

... Everyone, man and woman, all over me,[89] to destroy me, relentlessly demanding their share without ever, ever lending me a hand, coming to help me, loving me, in the end, for what I am, so that I may remain what I am. They think my energy is limitless and that I should dole it out to them and keep them alive. But I've put all my strength into the grueling passion to create, and for all the rest I'm the most impoverished and needy of souls.

Novel. "He no longer had the strength to love her. The capacity to suffer because of her was all that was alive in him, all those parts of love that are lack or deprivation. The only thing she could give him now was suffering. As for the joy, it was dead."

Id. "You might think she was all about insubordination, and it's true that she was crowned with flames and burned like rebellion itself. But above all, she was about acceptation. "I'd accept dying today (at thirty years old) because I've had enough happiness. And if I had to do it all again, I'd want the same life, despite its extreme hardships."

I don't believe those who say they rush headlong into pleasure out of hopelessness. Real hopelessness never leads anywhere but sorrow or stasis.

Well then, here you are, a whore like all the rest!

He who gives nothing has nothing. The greatest misfortune is not to not be loved, but not to love.[90]

---

87. On the page following this entry, Camus wrote only: "Correct on next edition T.R: p. 58 l. 26., the most profound," which he then scribbled out.

88. This entry was made a little over a year before Camus turned forty on November 7, 1953.

89. In the handwritten notebook, "line up against me" rather than "all over me."

90. In "Return to Tipasa," Camus writes: "At noon, on the half-sandy, heliotrope-covered slopes, which look as if they've been left coated in foam by the retreat of the furious waves we've had these last days, I gazed out at the sea, barely moving at that hour, exhausted, and I quenched those two

---

Divided between a person who completely rejects death and a person who completely accepts it.

Too many white blood cells, not enough red blood cells, and as one eats the other, France grows sick with leukemia. It's no longer capable of waging a war or producing a revolution. Reforms, yes. But it's a lie to promise the country anything more. First, a blood transfusion.[91]

Style. Be careful with slogans. Sometimes they're like thunder: they strike but illuminate nothing.

Boghari—Djelfa[92]—The small erg.[93] The extreme, arid poverty—and the royalty of it. The nomads' black tents. On the arid, hard land—and I—who owns nothing and will never own anything, similar to them.

Laghouat. Standing before the rocky hill covered in folded leaves of flint—the vast expanse—night falls from the horizon like a black wave, while the west turns red, pink, green.

The tireless dogs of night.

In the oasis, golden fruit gleams above mud walls. Silence and solitude. Then you emerge on a square. Swarms of jubilant children whirl like little dervishes, laughing so all their teeth show.

So then maybe it's time to talk about the desert from which I found the same escape—From beyond the horizon . . . I'm also waiting to see fabulous

---

thirsts you can't betray for very long without your inner being drying up: loving and admiring. For not being loved is only a mishap, but not loving a misfortune. Today, we're all dying of misfortune."

91. A more literal translation, one that captures Camus's use of the phrase *état de* (state of), might read: "France is in a state of leukemia. It's no longer in a state to . . ."

92. This entry does not appear in the handwritten notebook. After the previous entry, which appears at the bottom of a notebook page, the following page has five entries in very small print, written across the page, sometimes sideways, such that no definitive ordering of the entries can be established. When the typescript was made, these entries would be placed a little further on, where they now appear. Read from left to right, top to bottom, the entries are: the "Brazil Short Story" entry (three parts), the "Novel—Deportee" entry, the "Europe . . . dogs" entry, the "That Europe inhabited by dogs" entry (see p. 487n100 below), and the "Play About Returning and Truth" entry.

Laghouat would serve as an inspiration for the setting of the short story "The Adulterous Woman," which appears in the collection *Exile and the Kingdom*. Camus would travel through the southern part of Algeria in December 1952.

93. When small in size, as Camus indicates here, an erg may also be referred to as a "dune field" or "sand sea."

beasts emerge out there and to find, quite simply, a silence no less fabulous, and this fascination . . .

Mme V.R. on Malraux, who's going to Japan: "He goes only to come back again." But we're all a little like that.[94]

Naivete of the 1950s intellectual who believes a person has to be inflexible to flex their intellect.[95]

Summer solstice. Short story that takes place on the longest day of the year.

In Algiers, flowers hang above high walls in the neighborhood with the villas. Another world from which I felt exiled.

Death of the concierge.[96] His wife is sick, lying on a large bed. Next to her in their one room, the dead man is laid out on a small cot, and can be seen twice a day while getting the mail.

"Goodbye," she said, "my darling, my sweet love. Oh, how big he is! How big he was . . ." We passed the casket "narrow side first," and upright. Only the neighbors followed the procession. "To think only three days ago I was drinking mint lemonade with him." "All I wanted was for him to replace the gas pipe."

There are four of us at the cemetery. A sanitation worker gives us each a carnation that we'll soon throw atop the beautiful indifferent one.[97]

Arriving at Buchenwald, a little Frenchman asks to speak privately with the official, a prisoner himself, who welcomes him. "Well, you see, my case is exceptional. I'm innocent."[98]

---

94. This last line does not appear in the handwritten notebook; it was added to the typescript.

95. The aphoristic quality of the French sentence derives from the *-dir* suffixes in *se raidir* (to stiffen) and *se grandir* (to grow), which, used figuratively, mean to be overly formal and hardened and to increase one's stature or prove one's worth.

96. This story is told at greater length in the first part of *The Fall.*

97. It's possible that the phrase used here, *le bel indifférent* (the beautiful indifferent), is in reference to Jean Cocteau's 1940 play *Le bel indifférent,* starring Edith Piaf.

98. Clamence relates this same story in *The Fall,* after which he says: "We're all exceptional cases. We all want to appeal to something. Everyone demands to be seen as innocent, at all costs, even if they have to indict heaven and earth to be so."

Short story about a terribly hot day, in Paris.[99]

Novel—Deportee. Wife and children also deported. They die as a result. When he returns, the man, wonderfully intelligent and gentle, devotes himself to finding the murderers . . . He pushes him into a room. Says to him: "I learned this over there—you don't kill in the same place you humiliate. Things are cleaner that way. Here's the phone. Call. You have time.[100]

Play about Returning and Truth.

Scene I—Wife and friend are waiting for him.

Scene II—He returns and with the friend standing there reveals to his wife that the friend is his mistress.

Brazil Short Story.[101] An Urubu snorts, opens its beak, seems to be getting ready to take flight, flaps its dusty wings twice against its body, lifts two inches above the edge of the roof, settles back down, and falls asleep almost immediately.

One by one, the stars fell into the sea, the heavens' last lights dripping away.

In the end, he carries the stone into the most impoverished hut. Without a word, the natives huddle together to make room for him. In the silence, the whisper of the river is the only sound.

99. Camus crossed out the entry that follows this one; it is very similar to some of his earlier comments about Mauriac. After the crossed-out entry, which is at the bottom of a notebook page, the next page has several lines in tiny, illegible print (though one of the few legible words is "Sartre"), which Camus also crossed out before moving on to the next page, which begins with the "If you lie" entry below. The intervening entries up to the "Hautes Plaines" entry occur earlier in the handwritten notebook; the "Hautes Plaines" entry and the four that follow it do not appear in the handwritten notebook.

100. Between this entry and the one that follows, Camus crossed out a passage on the typescript that reads: "That Europe inhabited by dogs. They bark and nip at each other, then sniff each other. Occasionally, they fornicate."

101. This entry, as well as the two that follow it, are notes for "The Stone That Grows," collected in *Exile and the Kingdom.*

An urubu is a black vulture.

"Here we are the last, the last place among the last."

"Europe . . . Dogs."
"I'm a dog, too. I've sniffed and fornicated."
"There's no difference."
"A small difference. I'm ashamed."
"Ah! You're rich."
"No, not really. But even very poor, I've always lived like a rich man."
"And that's what you're ashamed of?"
"Of that—and of having lied, sniffed, and fornicated."
"Well, good. There's nothing to be done."
"No."
Id. "We can't help ourselves. We can't help ourselves. And then a time comes when we can no longer."

Hautes Plaines Short Story.[102] The man arrives and explains the crime he's committed.

"Over here, this is the way to Djelfa. You'll come across a motorcar. You'll stop it. In Djelfa you'll find the police station and the train. That trail over there, that one crosses into the Hautes Plaines. A day's walk from here you'll come across the first pastures and nomads. They will welcome you. They're poor and impoverished, but they give everything to a guest."

The man, who'd been silent since the previous night, says only:
"They're kings?"
"Yes," Pierre says. "They're kings."

The Voiceless Short Story.[103]

After the strike fails, the workers return to the factory (cooperage). They remain silent. The day at the workshop.

---

102. Ideas used in "The Guest," collected in *Exile and the Kingdom*. This entry and the four that follow it do not appear in the handwritten notebook; Camus added them at a later date and then, when reviewing the typescript, added additional information, writing "Hautes Plaines Short Story" at the top of the entry. He also crossed out a line after "They will welcome you," which reads "When you arrive, say this."

103. The short story referenced here, "Les Muets," was originally published in English as "The Silent Men."

In the afternoon, the boss's hemiplegia. The foreman tells one of the workers. He doesn't say anything. Shortly after work, he cries, his arms on the table. "Even that, even that."

Short story told in a single, intense stroke.

On the Pacific. Young mute girl. She didn't know how to tell him she was pregnant. He runs with her in his arms. She dies.

Short stories collected under the title: Stories of Exile.[104]

1) Laghouat. The Adulterous Woman.

2) Iguape—human warmth, the black cook's friendship.

3) The Hautes Plaines and the condemned man.

4) The artist who withdraws (title: Jonas).

Then he no longer paints. Hands on his knees. Now I'm happy.

5) The intellectual and the jailer.

6) A Confused Mind—the progressive missionary goes to civilize the savages, who cut off his ears and tongue and enslave him. He waits for the next missionary and, filled with hatred, kills him.

7) Short story about madness.

---

104. Although this entry does not appear in the handwritten notebook, several changes were nevertheless made to it when Camus reviewed the typescript. The original version reads as follows:

3 short stories collected under the title: ***Love of Life***.

1) **Laghouat and** the adulteress.

2) Iguape—human warmth, the black cook's friendship.

3) The Hautes Plaines and the **doukhobor**

4) The artist who withdraws (title: Jonas). Then he no longer paints. Hands on his knees. Now I'm happy.

5) The intellectual and the jailer

6) **The** Confused Mind—**the professional**—the progressive missionary goes to **civilize. The** savages cut off his ears and enslave him. He waits for the next missionary and, filled with hatred, kills him.

7) Short stor**ies** about madness.

Five of the seven stories listed here went on to appear in *Exile and the Kingdom*: (1) "The Adulterous Woman," (2) "The Stone That Grows," (3) "The Guest," (4) "The Artist at Work," and (6) "The Renegade." Number five may refer to *The Fall*, as there is a scene in the novel with an intellectual being spit on by a jailer, while number seven was never written. "The Voiceless," which is mentioned on the previous page, would also appear in *Exile and the Kingdom* but is left off the list given here.

A Confused Mind.[105] "O liars, O liars! Oh, I knew him, I did. He'd trip the blind, and yes, dirty wretches he'd call the beggars. We nailed him to a barrier, O liar, and the earth trembled. A righteous one, the one we just killed." Morality was safe. There he was, head against the barrier. When they nailed him up, there was a nail behind his head, and in it went, like it's in mine now. Brains go squish! Brains go squish! And to top it off, we cut out his tongue. That was after he'd said, "Why have you forsaken me?" We weren't going let him go on like that, no, we weren't going to let him sit at the table, make confessions . . .

Hatred, that I discovered. Hatred makes me think of a mouth-icing mint lozenge, biting stomach a little burned. Must be wicked, must be wicked. I'm a slave, I am, all right. But if I'm wicked, I'm no longer a slave. Their loving kindness, I spit on it.

. . . There he is. In the desert, the detonation erupts, immense. He fell, nose in the stones, brains gone squish, all curled up. Arms out like a cross, I cried out, arms out like a cross. But just then, geysers of gray and black birds erupted into an inalterably blue sky. In the distance, far off in the distance, a jackal sniffed the wind and then trotted off toward the dead man.

In the end, he's crucified. Our father, who art in . . .

———

If you lie, how can you ever be forgiven, given the other person doesn't know there's something to forgive. Then, you must tell the truth at least once before dying—or accept dying without ever being forgiven. But could there be any lonelier death than that of the person who dies closed up in their lies and crimes.

———

Anti-Europe. On Chile's Pacific Coast. A 15-year-old girl follows him around with her eyes. She's alone in a sort of shack. He questions her. She doesn't respond, only looks at him. She's mute. Their silent love before the sea.

———

105. The only part of this entry that appears in type on the typescript is the title. The rest was added by hand. "A Confused Mind" would become the subtitle for "The Renegade." Of all Camus's writings, "The Renegade" is the most stylistically experimental, at times relying more on rhythm and association than strict literality. To give just one example, *mur* (wall) and *menteur* (liar) are here rendered as "barrier" and "liar" to maintain a hint of rhythmic texture.

Parts of this entry would also be used in several places in *The Fall*, which was originally intended to be one of the stories, alongside "The Renegade," in *Exile and the Kingdom*.

Novel. "For a long time, I'd believed, seeing how she let herself go, that we were complicit in desire, and it took me many years to understand that she, and most women, are never complicit in anything but love."

———

I'd always loved the way the sea washes over the beach. And then, over those deserted beaches of my youth, the boutiques began to proliferate. Now I only love the middle of the ocean, out where the existence of a shore seems unlikely. But on the beaches of Brazil one day, I once again understood that there is no greater joy for me than treading virgin sand and encountering a resonant light filled with the whistling of waves.

———

Novel. During the Occupation, realized just how nationalistic he'd become due to his bitterness on seeing a stray dog happily following a German soldier.[106]

———

G. Hard to guess, beneath his great kindness, how sensitive he is. It takes time to notice. And all the while, you risk hurting him.

———

Novel. Different rhythms for different people, as well as different rhythms within the same person. D. drags his feet in an ongoing seduction. Then all at once he calls, travels 1,500 km, takes her out to dinner, and takes her that night.[107]

———

Solitary from now on, yes, but by my own doing.

———

We want to live sentiments before feeling them. We know they exist. Both tradition and our contemporaries are constantly telling us about them, and not accurately. So then, we live them vicariously. And we wear them out without having felt them.

———

Novel. "It was precisely because of the immense wrong he was doing her that he searched out every little instance in which her attention, if not love, seemed to be lacking. And then he gave her a hard time about it, not because

---

106. Camus crossed this entry out in the handwritten notebook but not on the typescript. An expanded version of the entry appears in *The Fall*.

107. This entry also appears in *The First Man* files, where the *D* is changed to *J*.

he could ever hope to alleviate his own guilt, but to drag her down with him while keeping her by his side, only now in a deserted land deprived of love."

What always saved me from the depths of despair is that I never stopped believing in what, for lack of a better term, I'll call "my star." But today I no longer believe in it.[108]

Sachs (*Behind 5 Bars*).[109] "You can live well without Catholicism; I can barely live without thinking of Christ."

Montesquieu quote: "If men were perfectly virtuous, they'd have no friends."[110]

Balzac quote: "Genius is seen in everyone and no one is seen in it."[111]

"We only betray those we love."

"We get the death we deserve."

"It's not the people we've wronged who give us the most trouble, but those who witness the events and then voluntarily offer themselves up as judges."[112]

The tragedy isn't that we're alone but that we can't be. Sometimes I'd give the entire world to be totally untied from the universe of men. But I'm a part of that universe, and the bravest thing is to accept it and the tragedy of it at the same time.

Write an adaptation of Molière's *Don Juan*.

Play. A man who *cannot hate*.

People learn how to live little by little. And I, to whom life came so naturally, I little by little forgot how to live, so that each of my thoughts and actions

---

108. This is the only entry on the page in the handwritten notebook. On the "star," see p. 426n39.

109. Maurice Sachs (1906–1945), a French Jewish writer, was imprisoned at the Fuhlsbüttel concentration camp in Hamburg, Germany, from 1943 to 1945, during which time he wrote *Derrière cinq barreaux*. There is some disagreement about how he died, whether he was shot by the Gestapo or killed by other prisoners. *Derrière cinq barreaux* was published by Gallimard in September 1952.

110. From Montesquieu's *Mes pensées* (*My Thoughts*), no. 1253.

111. From, respectively, *The Village Priest* and *Pensées, sujets, fragmens*. Some of these quotes would go on to appear in Camus's speech "Create Dangerously."

112. An early formation of *The Fall*'s "judge-penitent."

now add to my own suffering or the suffering and discomfort of others, add to the unbearable weight of this world that I'd initially enjoyed so much.

———

Packs of dogs assembled in cities, gnawing away at thought.

———

Vaucluse. The evening light becomes fine and golden as liquor, comes to slowly dissolve those painful crystals that sometimes wound the heart.

———

Couple. Only a demanding nature restrains a demanding nature. She demanded nothing more than not to die, whereas I, I was crying out to live.

———

He usually placed his hat askew, on account of his limp.

———

The Russian critic Razumnik on Mayakovsky's play *Mystery-Bouffe*: "In the future, historical Socialism and historical Christianity will link up."[113]

———

As a motto, Char proposes: Liberty, Inequality, Fraternity.[114]

———

Advances in material conditions greatly enhance human nature, more than strictly necessary. But beyond this point, with the accumulation of wealth, human nature is harmed. Morality's true balance is found on the border.[115]

———

Century of serenity. The danger of catastrophe is now so widespread that it's intertwined with any possible conditions of future survival. That's why coming to terms with the times today is nothing other than coming to terms with death. This century of the most extreme danger is also the century of the greatest serenity.

———

113. Razumnik Ivanov-Tazumnik (1878–1946), a Russian writer and literary critic who took part in and wrote on the Russian Revolution, was very critical of Mayakovsky's play.

Vladimir Mayakovsky (1893–1930) was a Russian poet and playwright. *Mystery-Bouffe*, first written in 1918, then rewritten in 1921, is a play about a great flood and the subsequent warring between the "unclean" working class and the "clean" upper class. Mayakovsky committed suicide on April 14, 1930.

Se rencontrent, translated above as "link up," is also used in the sense of the saying *les grands esprits se rencontrent* (great minds think alike).

114. "Liberty, Equality, Fraternity" is the French national motto.

The rest of the page after this entry was left blank in the original notebook.

115. This is the only entry on the page in the original notebook.

Temps modernes. They accept sin and reject grace. Thirst for martyrdom.[116]

Hell is Heaven plus death.

Hell is here, to live. Only those who extricate themselves from life escape.

Who will bear witness for us? Our works. Alas! Who else, then? No one, no one other than those friends of ours who saw us in that second of sacrifice when the whole of our heart was devoted to another. That is, those who love us. But love is silence: every man dies unknown.

SEPTEMBER '52. Polemic with T.M. Attacks in "Arts," "Carrefour," "Rivarol." Paris is a jungle of mangy beasts.[117]

The nouveau riche, revolutionary mind's parvenus, the Pharisees of justice. Sartre, the man and the mind, *disloyal*.

The Best Friend. One act. X at the Zs' house. They're talking about Y, X's best friend, who's running late. His virtues are expounded by X. The Zs make known certain reservations Y has about X. The same virtues are little by little denounced by X as faults. The Zs mention that Y has a favorable judgment of X. X begins to backpedal. Y arrives. X hurries over to give a hug. "Ah," Y says, "it's so nice to be among friends again!"

The Doukhobors.[118] Christianity is within. It dies and resurrects inside us. Every Christian has two names. One is corporeal, the other spiritual, given

---

116. In *The Fall*, Clamence says that "our moral philosophers" and, in particular, atheist-novelists "only believe in sin, never grace."

117. The polemic surrounding *The Rebel*, already heated, reached its boiling point with *Les temps modernes* 82 (August 1952), in which Sartre took on a condescending tone of superiority in order to attack Camus not only intellectually but also personally. In the same issue, Francis Jeanson, who wrote the original review of *The Rebel*, added a searing second piece titled "To Tell You Everything." The September issue of *Arts* followed up with further negative coverage, as did *Carrefour*, a right-wing weekly, and *Rivarol*, an extreme-right weekly.

In French, the word *miteux*, here translated as "mangy," carries the literal meaning "moth-eaten" or "flea-bitten" and the figurative meaning of "pathetic" or "narrow-minded."

118. The Doukhobors were a Russian sect formed in the eighteenth century under the Western influence of the Quakers, Masons, and Protestants. They were oppressed by religious authorities and Tsarists. The information contained in this entry comes straight from pp. 25, 27, and 30 of *Tolstoï et les Doukhobors*. The entry that follows this one is drawn from p. 12. For more on Camus's use of this text,

by God upon spiritual birth, according to a person's deeds. The latter name is known to no one here on earth; it'll be known in the afterlife.

Not our brother died, but our brother changed.

———

Doukhobors. In Russian: those who wrestle the spirit.

———

Property is murder.[119]

———

Practical Morality

Never appeal to the courts.

Give money away—or lose it. Never try to grow it, or seek it out, or crave it.

Title: A Short Treatise on Practical Morality—or (to provoke) Everyday Aristocracy.[120]

———

T.M. polemic[121]—Backstabbers. Their sole excuse is in this terrible era. Something inside of them, in the end, aspires to servitude. They dreamed of getting there by some noble path, filled with thoughts and ideas. But there is no royal route to servitude. There's cheating, insulting, and denouncing one's brother. After that, the sound of thirty deniers.[122]

———

Oran's fresh water. Africa's light: a voracious blaze that burns the heart. I was too young.

———

Sometimes, late in those celebratory evenings, when alcohol, dancing, and our reckless abandon so quickly led to a sort of happy lassitude, it seemed to me, at least for a second, on the brink of exhaustion, that I finally under-

as well as an additional entry that appears in this spot in the handwritten notebook, see the introduction to the present volume.

119. This entry is also drawn from *Tolstoï et les Doukhobors*, 209 (as is the entry that follows this one, p. 56). Camus would go on to use the line in *The Fall*, where Clamence exclaims: "Property, gentlemen, is murder!"

120. In the handwritten notebook, this entry is followed by the outline for the play about Lespinasse that now appears on p. 497 below.

121. *Temps modernes*. See pp. 468n38, 479n74, and 494n117.

122. The Frankish, or French, denier appeared in the Middle Ages and marked the move from gold coinage to silver. This last sentence, then, is in reference to the thirty pieces of silver for which Judas sold out Jesus.

stood the secret of beings and that I'd one day be able to tell it. But then the exhaustion passed, and with it, the secret.[123]

———

Brunetière[124] already argued, like Sartre, for the theater of situations over the theater of characters. Copeau settled the question with a single sentence: "The situation is worth whatever the characters are worth."

Id. Copeau on "craft," on the "well-made" play. Don't confuse "revenue" and "craft." Cf. Speech on Corneille's Dramatic Poem.

———

Every society, and particularly its literature, aims to shame its members for their extreme virtues.

———

"Love at a distance" in commedia dell'arte. Princess of Clèves,[125] romantic.

———

Novel. "In those days, it wasn't her he hated. There was nothing in her to hate and nearly everything to love. It was himself he hated in her—his own inadequacy, his poverty, his impotence to love what should be loved, to live in a way that he knew was dignified, for her and for him . . ."

———

The type of people who have financial difficulties and heart problems.

———

"Wandering in love, loving in various places, is as monstrous as injustice in the mind." Pascal.[126]

———

Id. "Love and reason are but one and the same."

———

123. This entry appears, with slight revisions, in the second part of *The Fall*.

124. Ferdinand Brunetière (1849–1906), conservative French writer, teacher, and critic.

125. In May 1954, Camus wrote to René Char to say that he'd begun work on a film adaptation of Madame de Lafayette's 1678 novel. The work was so "ridiculous," he said, that it was making him stupid. But he needed the money, and the project paid well. The one bright spot, he told Mamaine Koestler, was that he was "learning a craft I didn't know before." Still, he couldn't stand the director, Robert Bresson—today considered one of the all-time greats—and he wrote to Michel and Janine Gallimard that "time's slipping away, that is, my time. I'm doing nothing. I spent a month working on *The Princess*, and then Bresson was such a pain (he's a crazed maniac) that we had to drop the whole thing."

126. This quote and the one that follows come from Pascal's *Discourse on the Passion of Love*. In the handwritten notebook, there is a series of very tiny, illegible lines in the margin, circled with an arrow pointing toward this entry.

To the beggar who was making a nuisance of himself, the owner of the restaurant, pointing to the customers eating lobster: "Put yourself in the place of these fine people."[127]

Novel. Mother ill. It was then he threw himself against that crippled woman's breast and cried on her. It had been years since he'd let go like this with another person—he'd never asked anyone else for protection. A few people had let go in a similar way with him, but for his part, he'd never managed to let his guard down. And as a result, he chose the same weakness and unhappiness.

Play: Lespinasse Élisa.[128]

Act I:

1. Élisa and d'Alembert (she tells him she loves Gonzalve).
2. Élisa and Guibert (love at first sight).
3. Guibert's declaration to Élisa (in a cold tone of voice).
4. It's announced that Gonzalve is returning.
5. Gonzalve and Élisa.

Act II:

1. D'Alembert and Gonzalve
2. Élisa and Gonzalve (receives letter and has to leave—farewell scene)
3. D'Alembert and Élisa
4. Guibert and Élisa. She gives in to the love that sweeps her away:

"Have you lost your mind?"

"You really think so?"

She turns, hears someone running toward her, and falls against him.

---

127. This entry was published among a dozen other notes in the October 15, 1953, issue of *Démenti*, in Liege, Belgium, then incorporated into *The Fall*, where Clamence says: "All the same, the very word 'justice' threw me into strange fits of rage. I continued, out of necessity, to use it in my pleadings before the court, but I got my revenge by publicly maligning the humanitarian spirit; I heralded the publication of a manifesto denouncing the oppression that the oppressed were inflicting on noble people. One day, while I was eating lobster at a sidewalk table, a beggar kept bothering me, and I called the manager over to get rid of him and loudly applauded the words of that dispenser of justice: 'You're embarrassing everyone,' he said. 'Put yourself in the place of these fine people, won't you.'"

128. Though Camus never completed the play, we can see the outline of Julie de Lespinasse's life here: a man, Mora, dies of his love for Julie, who will in turn die of her love for Guibert, author of *General Essay on Tactics*, while d'Alembert, waiting in the wings, remains eternally in love with Julie.

Act III. Love torn apart—Gonzalve's death. She's in Guibert's arms, d'Alembert returns with a letter: "He's dead." She reads and cries out: "Do you know what he said to me? That he can die happy knowing I loved him."

Scene with Guibert-Élisa: "Oh! How I love you now," she says.

Act IV. Misunderstanding love. She wants to be loved by Guibert as by Gonzalve. You don't love me. Guibert's marriage.

Act V. D'Alembert and Guibert. Ill. Forbidden to see her. She's deformed. He confesses he loves Élisa. D'A: "You've come too late. As do all those who are incapable of love. Their extraordinary passion consists in loving when there's nothing to work for, when it no longer matters."

Final scene: Élisa's death. "Didn't he also deserve to be loved?"

"Yes, Élisa, but you deserved to be loved, as you were."

"Was I? Was I really?"

Guibert enters. "Gonzalve!" she says.

Or I'm going to die without him having forgiven me.

Who, Guibert?

No. Guibert introduced me to the sort of love that leaves you with something for which to be forgiven. But the other one didn't know, never knew. How could he have forgiven me?

When my mother's eyes were turned away from me, I was never able to look at her without tears in my own.[129]

R: Marries a woman who's already had a lover (her fiancé). She loyally admits it to him. He says he loves her and that it's no big deal. Retrospective jealousy. Nights of interrogation and questioning. The day after the wedding, he gets tickets to the city where her ex-fiancé lives so he can "mark his face" (razor blades pushed into a cork). Years pass like this. He writes angry letters (Mrs. X. to Mrs. A.). Then he forces her to ask a friend to sleep with him. "I've been wronged," he says, then forces her to ask her sister to do the same

129. This entry, the only one on the page, is written in very tiny print in the left corner.

thing, etc. (forbidden from the country where she grew up, where she knew X.) etc. etc. Until she's on the verge of madness.[130]

———

Poems about Algerian regret.

———

That first morning, more damp than rainy, had given Marseille's cobblestone streets a Parisian feel, and only the mixed crowd served as a reminder that another world began here. But all at once, the flower market on Canebière Street, its stalls drowning in fat, glittering December flowers beaded with water. Anemones, marigolds, daffodils, gladioli . . . [131]

———

At sea. The sea beneath the moon, its silent expanses. Yes, it's here I feel the right to die a peaceful death, here I can say, "I was weak, but I did what I could."

———

Tipasa. See notes.

———

From Laghouat to Ghardaïa. The daïas and their ghostly trees. The tormented chebka.[132] A kingdom of stones that burns by day and freezes by night—and ends up bursting into sand under such terrible weight. Even in the Laghouat cemetery, covered in shards of schist, the dead get mixed up beneath the confusion of stones. Even these lean plots sometimes found in the desert, plowed and tilled, even these serve only to turn up a certain type of stone used in construction. When you plow in this country, you plow for stones. The land is so precious you scrape the few shavings and chips that accumulate in the hollows and transport them in straw bassinets like a viaticum. The water. The land shaved down to the bone, to its schistose skel-

130. This entry and the brief one that follows it do not appear in the handwritten notebook.

131. On December 2, 1952, Camus left Paris for Marseille, then traveled from Marseille to Algiers the next day. He visited his mother and brother, stopped in Tipasa, then arrived in Laghouat on December 14. He continued on through southern Algeria, before returning to Algiers on December 18.

132. Chebka refers to the arid land around Ghardaïa (more broadly, the M'zab) in the northern part of the Sahara. The descriptions in this entry bear resemblance to descriptions in Camus's short story "The Adulterous Woman."

eton. Ghardaïa and the holy cities buckled in a belt of ocher hills, themselves bedecked in red ramparts.

———

Like those desert stones that, suddenly piled one atop the other, hardly different from the other piles, teach those educated by poverty the mysterious routes that lead to water or dry grass.

———

Drought in the South—which leads to famine—eighty thousand sheep die. The whole population scrapes the earth in search of roots. Buchenwald beneath the sun.

———

In Vienna, doves perch on the gallows.

———

In every trade in France, the proportion of foreign workers is predetermined. So then, the deeper you descend into the mines, the higher the proportion. Land of asylum, but one where they ask for slaves first.

———

A.B. Oran's depressed Lucifer.

———

Don't forget—In Laghouat, a singular impression of power and invulnerability. Reconciled with death, therefore invulnerable.

———

Modern horrors explained by fear. Atom, Soviet trials, etc. The intellectual left's betrayal.

———

Actuelles[133]—Ten French doctors, half of them Jewish, sign, with no information beyond a communiqué issued by the Moscow government, a declaration applauding the arrest of their Soviet colleagues, nine-tenths of them Jewish. The scientific mind triumphs. A little later, the same government decreed the innocence of these still-imprisoned doctors.

———

133. During his lifetime, Camus published three volumes of essays and news articles under the title *Actuelles* (*Current Affairs*), and, at the time of his death, he was preparing a fourth volume. The third of these volumes, *Algerian Chronicles*, is the only one to have so far appeared in a complete English translation.

The reference here is to the 1951–1953 "Doctors' Plot." A version of this entry would be published in the October 15, 1953, issue of the Belgian magazine *Démenti*.

The desert and the hourglass.

———

Actuelles. Members of the National Assembly refused to give for housing the billions they granted alcohol manufacturers. Double whammy: at the same time, the slums increase the manufacture of alcohol. Six hundred Jacobins, giants of freedom, kneeling before the bars.[134]

———

Humanism. I don't like humanity in general. Mainly, I feel a sense of solidarity with it, which is not the same thing. And then there are some men, living or dead, who I like so much, with such admiration, that I'm always jealous or anxious to preserve or protect in all the others what, by chance, or on a day I can't foresee, has made or will make them like the former.

———

The folly of Fabre, administrator of the Française.[135] He believed only the world of mirrors was true. The rest was reflection.

———

Benjamin Constant—Diary.[136] "The precision of material descriptions of life has some attraction for the one to whom everything has become of equal indifference."

On Goethe's Faust, damning judgment p. 59.

". . . all people (like the Ancients) who have possessed that which gives value to life, fame and freedom, have at the same time felt it necessary to know how to despise life and renounce it. Those who preach to us the evils of suicide, precisely the men whose opinions render life despicable, are liars, partisans of slavery and vileness . . ."

"And I don't know anyone other than myself who knows how to feel more for others than for oneself because pity pursues me . . ."

Cf. p. 81. "Men who pass as tough . . ."

"Literature and fame disrupt life by obligating one to manifest and defend opinions."

---

134. In an October 31, 1952, letter to his own schoolteacher Louis Germain, Camus writes that his children "will be going to secondary school next year, if, that is, they're willing to devote to the classroom the billions they give to the alcohol manufacturers."

135. Émile Fabre (1869–1955), French playwright and administrator of the Comédie-Française from 1915 to 1936.

136. When this entry was written, the uncensored edition of the diary had just appeared in France, published by Gallimard. All page references are to that edition.

"Stroll with Simonde. He reproached me for not taking much interest in him or anyone else. It's because nobody knows . . . that I'm not in a normal situation, that my ties to Biondetta remove all thoughts and feelings of freely disposing of my life . . ."

Cf. 133–134.

"Ambition is much less interested than we think, because to live in peace requires almost as much laborious effort as to govern the world."

"My life trickles away like water."

"And alongside that I have a feeling so contrary to the brevity of life that I cannot stress strongly enough the importance of making a firm resolution, no matter what it is."

P. 201. On the futility of discussion with French men of letters: "We'd have to begin by explaining each point before discussing a question; without doing so, we'd only encounter people reproaching us for things we didn't say, and we'd tire ourselves out for nothing . . . We have to write, not argue."

"There's something vulgar and worn-out in irreligion that I find repulsive."

When a man is generous without affectation even those who are enriched by his generosity feel him only to be doing his duty.

Cf. p. 226. No matter how well-concealed his contempt, it's always sensed and not forgiven.

245—Death of Madam Talma.[137]

— . . . And all these people who say they are sensitive are worth nothing to me as a companion in adversity, misfortune, death.

. . . When, despite ourselves, we put up with a situation we despise, the slightest increase in inconvenience throws us into a rage.

Cf. 348. My misfortune is in not loving anything, and that makes even the simplest things hard.

My soul lives alone. I can only love in the absence of gratitude or pity. Do no evil, yes, but let's remember that I can't live from the bottom of my heart with anyone.

———

137. In the handwritten notebook, this line through the end of the entry appears following the earlier "Don't forget" entry (see p. 500). On the typescript, Camus noted that the lines should be moved to their current location.

When it comes to the cause of the people today, the Church gives the impression it yields not to pity but to force.

Novel. She didn't believe in love, and so in loving her, he felt ridiculous expressing love.

Cada vez que considero
Que me tengo de morir
Tiendo la capa en el suelo
Y no harto de dormir.[138]

Play about the Albigenses.[139]

Someone wrote to me: "In the twilight of our life, we will be judged on love." Then condemnation is certain.

She wore chaste dresses and yet her body was on fire.[140]

Socialism, according to Zochtchenko,[141] will be when violets grow on asphalt.

Jewish people, alive as a culture for four thousand years. The only ones.

Tolstoy writes: "Of Life and Death." He gets to work on it and decides death doesn't exist. That's how his essay came to be called "Of Life." See Tatiana Tolstoy's journal[142] p. 131: Story of three committed volunteers executed.

---

138. Spanish *Copla*: "Whenever I consider / That I myself must die / I stretch my cape on the ground / And am no longer filled with sleep."

139. A heretical movement of twelfth- and thirteenth-century southern France largely associated with the Cathari. See p. 155n104.

140. In the handwritten notebook, the entry is preceded by the word "Novel."

141. Mikhail Zoshchenko (1895–1962), Soviet writer and humorist persecuted by Stalin.

142. Tolstoy's daughter's journal had just been published in French. It appeared in English two years earlier as *The Tolstoy Home: The Diaries of Tatiana Tolstoy*. All page references above are to the French edition.

Tolstoy acknowledged that the first thing you feel when a beggar approaches your house isn't pleasant.[143]

He leaves a performance of Siegfried uttering insults.

He hated arrogant, ignorant revolutionaries "who seek to transform the world without knowing where true happiness is found."

February 15, 1953

Dear P.B.[144]

Let me start with the apology I owe you for Friday. It wasn't because of a lecture on Holland but because I was enlisted at the last second to sign books to benefit refugees. That sort of thing, which I'd never done before, seemed like something I couldn't refuse, and I'd imagined you'd forgive me for the small change of plans. But that's not what this is about; it's about these relationships you call difficult. On this point, what I have to say can be put quite simply: if you knew a quarter of my life and the obligations it entails, you wouldn't have written a single line of your letter. But you can't know it, and I can't explain it to you, nor do I owe you an explanation. That "haughty solitude" you complain about, you and so many others who don't have the same qualities you do, would be, after all, if it existed, a blessing. But it's a mistake to attribute such a paradise to me. The truth is that every working hour I have available is a fight against time and other people, and more often than not, I accomplish nothing. I'm not one to complain. My life is what I've made of it, and the first person responsible for the scattered, discordant way it's spent is me. But when I receive a letter like yours, then yes, okay, I feel like complaining, or at the very least asking that I not be so easily condemned. To get everything done today, I'd need three lives and several hearts. I only have one, one that can be judged and that I often judge to be mediocre. There aren't enough hours in the day to do what I need to do, let alone the leisure to see friends I'd like to see (ask Char, whom I love like a brother, how many

143. In *The Fall*, Clamence says: "A friend of mine, a great Christian, acknowledged that the first thing a person feels on seeing a beggar approach his house isn't pleasant. Well, for me, it was worse: I rejoiced. But let's move on."

144. A short interview with Camus conducted by the critic Pierre Berger was published in the February 15, 1952, issue of *Gazette des lettres* and was later collected in the second volume of Camus's *Actuelles*. A year later, Berger published an article on Camus in *Arts*.

The above letter, which Camus had tucked into the notebook and which is written on *NRF* letterhead, appeared in the January 4, 1962, issue of the French weekly *Démocratie*. In it, the roots of Camus's short story "The Artist at Work" can be seen.

times *a month* we see each other). I don't have the time to write for journals, neither about Jaspers nor about Tunisia, not even to rectify an argument with Sartre. You can believe me or not, it's up to you, I have neither the time nor the leisure of being ill, and when I am, my life is turned upside down, and I spend weeks just trying to catch up. But the real issue is that I no longer have the time, or leisure, to write my books, and so it takes me four years to write what, with a bit of freedom, would cost me one or two. Indeed, for the past few years, my work hasn't freed me, it's enslaved me. And if I continue to do it, it's because I can't help it, because I prefer it to all else, even to freedom, even to wisdom or true productivity, and even, yes, even to friendship. It's true that I'm trying to keep myself organized, trying to double my strength and "presence" by using a planner to structure my days for maximum efficiency. I hope to be able to get everything done, one day. At the moment, I'm not able to do so: each letter brings three others, each person ten, each book a hundred letters and twenty correspondents, all while life goes on, while there's work, while there are people I love, while there are those who need me. Life goes on and I, some mornings, wearied by all the noise, dispirited by the endless work to be done, sick from the world's madness assailing you as soon as you pick up the morning paper, certain, in the end, that I'm not up to the task and that I'll disappoint everyone, some mornings all I want to do is sit in a corner and wait for evening to come. That's all I want, and sometimes I give in to it.

Can't you understand that, B? Of course you deserve respect, of course you deserve to be included in conversations. Of course your friends are as good as mine (who aren't quite the grammarians you believe them to be). Although I can hardly imagine (and I'm not just saying this to say it) that having my respect could really matter to someone, it's true that you have mine. But for that respect to turn into an active friendship, it's only natural that we'd need to be able to spend a bit of free time together. The luck of my life has been to meet many fine people—but it's not possible to have so many friends, and that's my misfortunate, one that dooms me to disappoint, I know. I understand this is intolerable to others, and it's intolerable to me, too. But that's the way it is and if a person can't love me the way it is, it's only natural that they leave me to a solitude that, you see, is not so haughty as you say.

In any case, my reply to your bitterness is without bitterness. Letters like yours, coming from someone like you, bring only the gift of sadness, and add to all the reasons I already have for wanting to flee this city and the life I lead here. For the moment, even though there's nothing in the world I'd like more, it's not possible. So then, I have to continue on with this strange existence, and I have to figure words like yours into the price, a little steep in my opinion, that I have to pay for letting myself get cornered into this existence.

Forgive me, in any case, for having disappointed you, and know that you have my warm and faithful thoughts.

On Theater

The "laws" of theater. Action. Life. Action and life in great works. Theater is characters, characteristics pushed to the limits. Situations are only as good as the characters that are in them. Errors in design, staging, and performance come from ignorance of this truth. Relationship between style and theatrical convention. Toward the Grand Théâtre.

Novel. A coward who believed he was brave. A single occasion is enough for him to see otherwise—and he has to change his life.[145]

Id. He decides to fight against moral temptation. He *willingly* gives in to his instincts, which are strong.

Nemesis.[146] Love sometimes kills, but with no justification beyond itself. There's even an extreme at which loving one person amounts to killing all the rest.[147] In a way, there is no love without absolute, personal culpability. But this is a solitary culpability. Deprived of reason's alibis, it's heavy to bear. The decision to love is one that must be made alone, and it's all alone that one confronts the incalculable consequences of true love. To this adventurous solitude, man prefers a tepid heart and moral principle. He is afraid of himself and for himself. He wants to spare himself, so he refuses his condition. His

---

145. The novel in question is *The Fall*.

146. In the handwritten notebook, the word *Nemesis* is all that appears here, after which the rest of the page is left blank. Between this page and the next, Camus has inserted a typed copy of what is now the body of this entry.

147. The first complete draft of *The Rebel*, now housed at Harvard's Houghton Library, begins with the following lines, which were crossed out by Camus: "At one extreme, loving a living person amounts to killing all the rest. But loving all people leads to killing each one. Love kills with no other justification than itself. There is no love without personal and absolute culpability. That's why man lives with a tepid heart and moral principle. He's afraid of himself, he wants to spare himself, he refuses his condition." Camus, it seems, was now considering using these lines for his next longform essay centered on the myth of Nemesis.

first concern is to find a justification that will lift some of the weight of his guilt. Given a person must be culpable, at least let him not be alone. Militant.[148]

In love, hold on to what is.

Novel. Energy as a theme.

Pasiphae wants the bull in chastity. What it represents is a pure pleasure, a lightning bolt of pleasure and not that series of repetitive, polished acts, those cries, that breathless panting, those pleasures pursued year after year in an attempt to accomplish an impossible fusion. The bull is swift and searing as a god.

Pasiphae (when he enters): "O purity!"

Martyrs must choose to be used or forgotten.

Add to *State of Emergency*. Department of Suicide. "Impossible this year. The quotas have been reached. Fill out a form for next year."

Sex, strange, stranger, solitary, constantly making its own decision to press forward, becoming irresistible so it must be followed blindly, and then all at once, after years of frenzy, before other years of sensual madness, withdraws and falls silent—it thrives on routine, is restless with novelty, and only gives up independence when someone consents to fully satisfy it. Who, the slightest demanding, could ever wholeheartedly consent to such tyranny? Chastity, O liberty!

Honor hangs by a thread. If it holds, it's often by chance.

Fear of my profession and vocation. Faithful, the abyss, faithless, nothingness.

---

148. This last word was added to the typescript by hand; it doesn't appear in the typed version attached to the handwritten notebook.

A courageous cravat.

Novel. The two sons turn away when their mother, who is ill, takes out her dentures before leaving for the operating room. They know she's always been ashamed to admit she wears false teeth.

The only justification for my life that I've found is this effort to create. At almost everything else, I've failed. If this doesn't justify me, my life won't deserve absolution.

We put up with each other thanks to the body—to beauty. But the body ages. When beauty fades, then only psychologies remain present—and without intermediaries, they clash.

There are people who suffer rigidly and others who suffer flexibly: acrobats, virtuosos of (living with) sorrow.

Two common errors: existence precedes essence or essence existence. The two go hand in hand.

Letter from Green. Every time someone tells me they admire the man in me, I get the feeling I've been lying my whole life.

Nemesis[149]

Paris, July 9, '53
Dear Sir,

It's taken me a little while to reply to your kind letter, as these last few weeks have passed like the wind. All the same, I was deeply touched by your words of sympathy and by the way you expressed them. I liked the veiled radiance of your poems, that quality of "lagoon and sun" they share. And I'm happy to feel that, beyond this, we're in agreement.

Love without limits, the only desirable kind in fact, is the defining characteristic of saints. As for societies, the only limitless thing they've ever exuded

149. In the handwritten notebook, the word "Nemesis" is all that is printed on the page itself; a typed copy of the letter that follows was later attached.

is hatred. That's why to them we must preach an uncompromising limit. Limitlessness, madness, the abyss, for some these are secrets, and risks, of which we must not speak or which, at most, we should barely imply.

That's why poetry is the eternal nutrient. We must entrust it with our secrets. As for those of us who write in layman's terms, we have to understand that there are two wisdoms, and pretend, sometimes, to be unaware of the one that is higher. Please accept my best wishes and warmest regards.

If I've always refused to lie (inept even when I tried my best), it's because I could never accept solitude. But now solitude must be accepted as well.

Like when someone you love dies after a long illness. Even though you had been doing nothing but waiting, it's as if you had been fighting long and hard the whole time and in a single blow were defeated.

For some men, facing a simple street fight takes more courage than standing in the line of fire. The hardest thing to do is lay your hand on a person and, even more so, to feel the physical hostility of another human being.

M. "Two values for me: affection and fame."

To bring divine grace down on a B.O.F.[150] or predatory businessman—that's some feat. On an ordinary criminal, it's easy.

Van Gogh admired Millet, Tolstoy, Sully Prudhomme.

As a young man, Tolstoy goes to Saint Petersburg "in search of happiness." Result: cards, gypsies, debts, etc. "I live like an animal." (Tolstoy on Tolstoy, correspondence—1879.)

Tolstoy's brother: "He lacked the defects necessary to be a great writer" (according to Turgenev).

Id. Corr. May 3, '59: "For whom do I do any good? Whom do I love? Nobody. I have neither tears nor sadness for myself, only a cold repentance . . ."

Id. Oct. 17, '60, after his brother died: "And I've learned from thirty-two years of experience that in truth our situation is dreadful . . . Arriving at the

---

150. *Beurre, Œufs, Fromages* (Butter, Eggs, Cheese) is a derogatory term applied to dairymen who made their money off the black market during the Occupation.

highest degree of development, man realizes very clearly that all is but lies and stupidity, and that the truth that he loves more than anything else in the world is awful . . ."

Id. '61. Tolstoy challenges Turgenev to a duel, and Turgenev apologizes.

Id. '62. Search ordered on the Tolstoy residence: A colonel reads his diary. T. writes to Countess Alexandra Tolstoy, who is acquainted with the imperial court: "Fortunately for me and for your friend, I wasn't there, because I would have killed him." Alexandra's response to calm him: "Have pity. At bottom, nothing is more pitiless than a man unjustly mistreated who feels strongly that he is innocent."

'62. Meeting Sophie Bers: "I love as I never knew one could love. I'll kill myself if it continues like this . . ."

'65. "I'm glad you love my wife. Even though I love her less than my novel, she is still my wife, you know."

Cf. p. 285. Conception of Andrei Bolkonsky in *War and Peace.*

'65. On a short story by Turgenev that he doesn't like: "The personal, subjective element is only good when it's filled with life and passion, whereas here it's filled with a lifeless suffering." (apply to Rilke, Kafka, etc.).

'65. His indifference to politics—continuous—and stubborn. "Knowing who oppresses the Poles doesn't make a difference."

At fifty years old, he reiterates that it's not necessary to read newspapers (p. 405).

"During the summer . . . I daydream about death more and more then and always with a new sort of pleasure."

'69. He discovers Schopenhauer with admiration.

'70. Insomniac.

'71. When one of his friends dies, he doesn't miss him, he "rather envies him."

'72. To Strakhov. "Abandon the depraved activity of journalists."

Cf. p. 320. On a curve in which Pushkin would be the apex, Tolstoy places himself on the downward slope.

'72. "Boredom visits me with great rarity, but I welcome it with joy. It always heralds the coming of a great burst of intellectual energy."

'73. To a friend: "Don't live in Moscow. Two dangers: journalism and conversation."

Cf. p. 366. On the desert and primitive life.

'76. It's painful to finish one's life without respect for it.

'77. "We can't live without religion and yet we can't believe."

'78. He prays every day that Providence will grant him "peace in work." Alas!

Cf. p. 396. Against progress.

What they prefer, what makes them tender and melancholy, what makes them sentimental, is hatred. So then measure the sum of hatred and love each work contains—and then you'll be appalled by the times.

Lope de Vega, widowed five or six times. People die less often today. The result being that we no longer need to preserve in ourselves the strength to fall in love again, but, on the contrary, we need to extinguish it, to arouse another strength, one of infinite adaptation.

If the concern for duty is diminishing, it's because we have fewer and fewer rights. Only those who are uncompromising about their rights maintain a strong sense of duty.

Nihilism. Contentious little leveling dunces.[151] They've thought of everything so they can deny everything, feeling nothing, and relying on others—parties or leaders—to feel for them.

All their effort goes to discouraging being. When it comes to literature, for example, preventing a writer from writing is their main concern.

Cf. D.M. A hatred of writers such as can be contracted from a publishing house.

Virtue is not hateful. But speeches about virtue are. Likely no mouth in the world, and mine least of all, can utter them. In this regard, every time

151. In a biography of his father, Alphonse Daudet, Léon Daudet writes: "There's a type of person you often meet who drove my father crazy. For lack of a label, I'll call them the 'levelers of opinions and events.' / Whereas some people aggrandize everything, seeing in five soldiers an army, in a small gathering a riot, others deliberately diminish, destroy, and rob people and things of their importance, size, and vigor. The Protestant temperament, for example, readily reduces everything to a sort of average, to a vague neutral ideal, to a perpetual 'not so much as that.' This is one form of the wise, upstanding citizen. In this category we find the man so disproportionately proud that anything that turn the focus away from his actions, even if it be an eclipse or an earthquake, exasperates him, seems to him of no importance."

someone feels the need to speak of my honesty (Roy's[152] statement) there's someone inside me who shivers.

———

Title: Hatred of Art.

———

The artist and his time. Read Tolstoy's wonderful page about the artist (What must we do? 378–379 and R.R.[153] p. 113) . . . "the artist . . . is the one who would be happy not to think and not to express what weighs on his heart and soul, but who can't keep from doing so . . ."

Faced with this, "our current society's feelings are reduced to three things: pride, sensuality, and world-weariness."

Admirable letters about his remorse (R.R. pp. 189–190).

———

Novel. "I have nothing more to give you. I didn't love you enough and you didn't love me enough to allow me to give you my final thoughts. I'll have to manage on my own and die alone. For years, I waited for you to forgive my faults and accept me as I was. You never did. So, my faults remained, I'm still guilty, and today I have to come to terms with these faults alone. Leave me.

And then forgive me the wrong I've done you. And if you can, forgive me from the bottom of your heart. That's what I need most; the deprivation has for years prevented me from living.[154] If your heart remembered nothing more than its love for me, that would be in death the salvation I couldn't have in life."[155]

———

Don Giovanni. The pinnacle of all art. After listening to it, you've traveled the world and seen its peoples.

———

152. Jules Roy (1907–2000), a pied-noir writer like Camus, was highly critical of colonialism and of the role France played in Algeria. Roy was dedicated to his religious faith, and, though he and Camus remained friends, they often disagreed on specific issues.

153. The reference is to Romain Rolland's 1911 biography of Tolstoy. See p. 480n78.

154. This entry appears in Pierre's *The First Man* file with an extra line here: "Yes, I need your forgiveness." In the file, where the current entry ends, the following appears: "I'm not strong enough for the incredible effort it takes to be normal, to have a family, a wife etc. The work requires a level of energy I no longer have. I'd like to regain a little independence—to heal—to find a reason to live—and, to be honest, so as not to kill myself."

155. Although the editors of the French edition place this note a little later in the manuscript, an examination of the handwritten notebook shows that it appears here, as the only entry on the page, written in the top-left corner.

Focused. Sharpened—I ask only one thing, and I ask it humbly, though I know it's an exorbitant request: to be read carefully.

———

Too much safety for the child's heart and his adult life will be spent demanding that safety from other people—even though other people are but a chance for risk and freedom.

———

Novel. Jealousy. "I was careful not to let my imagination get carried away. I kept it on a leash."

"The adulterer stands accused before the one he or she has betrayed. But there is no sentencing. Or, rather, the unbearable sentence is to be eternally accused."[156]

———

Faust. Endymion. The death of the king. Rite—Pandora and the end of the golden age.[157]

———

Ferrero. "To finally pluck that exquisite little fruit from the tree of life, a fruit now so scarce that over the course of many years it blooms only once: rest without remorse."[158]

———

In France, talent always asserts itself *against*.

———

156. In *The Fall*, Clamence says: "The judgement you pass on others eventually comes back to slap you in the face." This entry also appears in *The First Man* files, where the "I" and "my" are changed to "he" and "his."

157. Faust and Endymion are two examples of the myth of eternal youth. In the penultimate paragraph of "Summer in Algiers," Camus writes: "From Pandora's box, where the evils of humanity teemed, the Greeks left hope, the most terrible of all, for last. I know of no more poignant a metaphor. For hope, contrary to popular belief, is the equivalent of resignation. And to live is not to resign yourself."

158. Guglielmo Ferrero (1871–1942), Italian historian and novelist. The citations over the next several pages come from his 1913 book *Fra i due mondi*. The French translation Camus would have had available to him at the time, Georges Hérelle's *Entre les deux mondes*, shows both significant and small differences from the quotations as Camus recorded them here. This first quotation, for example, reads "*des années mûrit à peine une fois . . .*" rather than "*des années, ne fleurit qu'une fois . . .*" Camus's paraphrases of Ferrero, sometimes unattributed in the notebooks, are generally faithful to his underlying ideas, though Camus's version often abbreviates a longer thought.

Beginning with Columbus, horizontal civilization, the one of space and quantity, replaces vertical civilization, the one of quality. Columbus kills Mediterranean civilization.

———

Ferrero. Contradiction of the machine world: it creates abundance through speed of production, yet it needs scarcity to thrive.

———

First, the natural.

———

Ferrero. A civilization such as ours, which tends to continually increase the quantity of objects while continually decreasing their quality, must end in an enormous, brutal orgy. And it's true. The end of history our men of progress speak of is an orgy.

———

Hegel. Measure, a synthesis of quality and quantity.

———

Without tradition, the artist has the illusion of creating his own rules. In this, he is God.

———

Antaeus is interred at the foot of Cape Spartel on the Atlantic Coast of what is now Morocco.

———

Ferrero. In Port Hercules, the Atlantic is an infinite beauty flowing into the narrow human mind and taking temporary form there.

———

Ferrero. The eternal voice crying out to the artist: "Create works of art and not aesthetics; discover new truths and not theories of knowledge; act and don't waste time worrying if you're in accord with history or not."[159] *Id.* "Believe in the principles you profess and don't compromise. But if the principal crumbles, deal with it. It'll be only a moment of universal truth."

Cf. p. 354: the Society's strength has limits. It's only through intense concentration and discipline that it accomplished the Greek epic, tragedy, and sculpture, Plato and Aristotle's aesthetics and morals, Roman law, the art

159. The official French translation reads "*et n'abuse pas de la gnoséologie*" rather than "*et ne fais pas la théorie de la connaissance.*" The second quote Camus records here is a significantly abbreviated rendition of the official French version.

of the Italian Middle Ages and Romanesque art in general, Galileo, Pascal, Racine, Molière . . .

Then the discovery of America, the French Revolution, the machine, the age of production.

Ultimately, it had to be done to feed the immense, starving multitudes roaming and languishing on the planet (check the growth rate of the human race since the thirteenth century). Perhaps we must pay for this with sterility.

France, which had the audacity and genius to produce that most amazing French Revolution, is also the country that has, due to apprehension, least given in to the madness of production.

———

Ferrero. "One of these days the exercise of limited willingness is going to break out."

———

With some people, we have relationships based on truth. With others, relationships based on lies. The latter are not the least durable.

———

Tocqueville (from *Democracy in America*): "It seems the rulers of our day seek only to use men to make things great. I would like them to think a little more about making great men."[160]

"Russia is the cornerstone of despotism in the world" (*Correspondence*).[161]

From the Revolution, Napoleon births an illegitimate child: despotism. The natural check on despotism is, according to T., the aristocracy.

These minds "that seem to make the taste for servitude a sort of ingredient of virtue." Applies to Sartre and the progressives.

"What do they need to remain free? What? The very desire to be so."[162]

———

Id. Tocqueville. The Ancien Régime and The French Revolution. T.I.

The general idea: it was the royalty that created the instrument of the Revolution—centralism—by cutting down the aristocracy and provincial liberties.

———

160. The quote is from *Democracy in America*, vol. 2, book 4, chap. 7. In this series of notes about Tocqueville, Camus crossed out one line, which can't entirely be made out, but which seems to say something along the lines of: "Only freedom delivers citizens from isolation."

161. From Tocqueville's correspondence with Pierre-Paul Royer-Collard and with Jean-Jacques Ampère.

162. This quote comes at the end of chap. 15 of Tocqueville's *The Ancien Régime and the Revolution*.

"It will always be regrettable that instead of bending the nobility to the rule of law, we cut it down and uprooted it. By doing this, we have . . . inflicted on liberty a wound that will never heal."

"Democratic societies that are not free can be rich, refined, pleasant, magnificent even, powerful by the weight of their bourgeois mass; private virtues can be found there, good family men, honest merchants and rather respectable landowners . . . but what will never be seen in such societies, I dare say, are great citizens and, above all, a great people, and I am not afraid to assert that the common level of hearts and minds will never cease to be lowered in such places so long as equality and despotism are joined together there."

Id. for our Progressives. "We have seen men who believed they could redeem their servility to the lowest agent of political power through their insolence to God, and who, while leaving behind all that was most free, most noble, and most proud in the doctrines of The Revolution, still flattered themselves that they were remaining faithful to it by remaining indevout."

Id. "They seemed to love freedom; it turns out they only hated the master."

Cf. p. 233. Modern socialism's fundamental thought, that ownership of the land ultimately belongs to the State, was taught by Louis XIV in his edicts.

Cf. p. 244. In '89 the French were proud enough of themselves to believe they could live as equals in freedom. Then . . .

Cf. p. 245, portrait of France.

The *Journals* of the nobility in Paris and elsewhere called for the demolition of the Bastille.

Chopin (born in 1810). Excellent player. Refuses the Opera out of certainty of what he is. Congratulates Tallberg, who, in playing a nocturne, deforms it as usual: "But by whom was it then?" Prodigal and generous. But merciless in his dealings with his publishers.

In Valldemossa, gulls lost in the mist come crashing into all the monastery's windows.[163]

---

163. In the handwritten notebook, this entry appears as the only one on the verso (which it seems Camus initially left blank), with an arrow pointing to its current location on the recto.

The initial reference is to Chopin's aversion to playing live, despite being an excellent concert pianist. As a result, Chopin turned to publishing his compositions as a means of making money, and, in an attempt to extract as much as he could from each publication, he sometimes pitted publishers against each other, breaking contracts along the way. The latter reference is to the monastery in Valldemossa where Chopin and George Sand, lovers at the time, stayed in the winter of 1838–1839.

Tolstoy, in the throes of death, wrote in the air.

———

According to Montherlant, all true creators dream of a life without friends.

———

In the Broadmoor asylum, where the criminally insane are reeducated, bloody arguments over an empty tube of aspirin.

———

Idea for the theater (still at Broadmoor): when the villain enters, a sign: "Boo." When the hero: "Applaud."

———

"In the eyes of the Chinese, the union of three people linked by a pleasant conformity of inclinations, qualities, and temperaments forms the pinnacle of earthly bliss . . ." Abel Rémusat.[164]

Id. "The Island Complex." Two women are needed, because the man has three souls and the woman four. This triangle is unbalanced on this square. But on two squares it makes a complete and solid pyramid.

———

Winter ends at El Kantara, where eternal summer begins. Black and pink mountain. According to Fromentin.[165]

Also Fromentin: small minds prefer detail in art.

"The Sahara remains brightly lit until the last minute of the day. Here, night arrives like a person blacking out."

Read Daumas's *Le grand désert*.[166]

———

We can't live everything we write. But we try.

———

164. Jean-Pierre Abel-Rémusat (1788–1832), French translator, teacher, and Orientalist scholar. The quote is from the preface to his 1826 French translation of the anonymous Chinese novel *Iu-Kiao-Li*, sometimes referred to as *The Two Fair Cousins*. The first English translation of the novel was done from Abel-Rémusat's French rather than from the original.

The quote recorded by Camus shows one difference from the source text, which has "dualities" rather than "qualities," a one-letter difference in both French and English. The rest of the line reads: "a sort of ideal happiness Heaven reserves for its favorites, as a reward for talent and virtue."

165. Eugène Fromentin (1820–1876), French writer and painter who, though not from Algeria, often focused his work on the country and its inhabitants.

166. Eugène Daumas (1803–1871), a French general who took part in the military occupation of Algeria in the early 1800s. He learned Arabic and went on to serve in various posts in Oran and elsewhere, eventually being appointed as the director of Algerian Affairs back in Paris. The book referenced above is *The Great Desert, or, Itinerary of a Caravan in Sub-Saharan Africa* (1848).

Kalyayev is wintry love. Victoria solar love.[167]

St. John. "He who says he loves God and who doesn't love his brother is a liar, for how can he say he loves God, whom he doesn't see, if he doesn't love his brother, whom he does see?" Similar to The Confused Mind, which says: "If I don't love God, it's because I don't love men, and in truth, why love them?" *Id.* John. "If I hadn't come and spoken to them, they wouldn't have been guilty of sin, but now they have no excuse."[168]

Altruism is a temptation, like pleasure.

Tolstoy: "One can live only so long as one is drunk on life" Confession (79).

In this same period: "I'm crazy about life . . . It's summer, delicious summer . . ."

Guilloux. When the Occupation begins in Saint-Brieuc, the town is cold and rainy, the shops empty. In the morning, he walks through the drizzly, deserted streets. On the empty town square, a German passes by, covered in an oilskin glistening with rain. Then, beneath a low sky, in the awful sadness of the hour, G. enters the church and prays, he, the declared atheist (prays to Mary, I believe). And then he leaves. Since then, every time he's tried to write about that moment of surrender or cowardice (he doesn't know which, he says), he hasn't been able to do it, or hasn't dared.

Roger Martin Du Gard and his mother's death. They hid from her that she had cancer. They changed the labels on her medicine bottles, etc.[169] But after she dies, the thought of the dreadful agony haunts M. du G., who tells

---

167. In *The Just*, Dora, trying to remind Kalyayev of the love they once shared, says: "The summer, Yanek, do you remember it? No, never mind. Winter is eternal. We're not of this world. We're the just. There's a warmth that's not for us." In *State of Emergency*, Diego equates his lover, Victoria, with sun and nature and heat, delivering lines like, "Behold, O city of light, you've been delivered to me for life, from now until the hour the earth comes calling. Tomorrow we'll set out together, the two of us riding on the same saddle."

168. The first quote is from 1 John 4:20. In most English renditions, "doesn't love his brother" reads "hates his brother." The second quote is in reference to Camus's short story "The Renegade," which is subtitled "A Confused Mind." The final quote is from John 15:22.

169. Roger Martin du Gard (1881–1958), French novelist and Nobel Prize winner. He and Camus shared a warm friendship, as can be seen in their correspondence and in Camus's 1955 preface to Martin du Gard's *Œuvres complètes* (*Complete Works*). In the notebook Camus was keeping separately

himself he can't bear it. His only hope would be to kill himself. But will he have the courage to do it? He tries, goes through several "rehearsals" with a revolver, but at the last minute (finger on the trigger) he feels his courage leave him. So then, the anguish grows, he feels trapped, until he finds a "method." He takes a taxi, brings the revolver to his forehead. "When I reach the third lamppost, I'll pull the trigger." Third lamppost and he *feels* he could do it with this method. From then on, an immense feeling of freedom.

This same man tells me he's suffering from a lack of wanting to do anything anymore, even live (see his letter).[170] The anorexia Gide spoke about. In Nice, suddenly a hope. He sees "Bouillabaisse" written on a sidewalk sign outside a restaurant and *wants some*. It's his first *want* in months. He goes in, joyfully eats. Since then, nothing. He is, he writes to me, in the waiting room.

The most human, which is to say the most worthy of affection, of all the men I've met.

———

Stendhal. "What is the self? I know nothing of it. One day I am awakened on this Earth, I find myself bound to my body, to my character, to my circumstance. Should I vainly amuse myself trying to change these things, all the while forgetting to live? Deception! I submit myself to these flaws. I submit myself to my aristocratic inclinations after having, for ten years and in good faith, railed against all aristocracy."[171]

———

The Philosophers' Farce as commedia dell'arte.[172]

---

for *The First Man*, he writes: "He knows that he has cancer, but he doesn't say that he knows. The others think they're putting on a good show."

170. The reference in this entry is likely to Roger Martin du Gard's July 22, 1953, letter, in which he writes to Camus: "I'm upset with myself for having such difficulty resigning myself to aging. But willpower wears out like everything else and has hardly any control over this malaise of the soul, this gloomy detachment I've been suffering these last months. Nothing to be done about this persistent feeling of being out of the game, this incredibly deep (and almost tender) feeling that 'all of this no longer concerns me.' That feeling you sometimes get in the waiting room—ticket in hand, bags packed, waiting for the arrival of the train that's going to carry you away forever—when people from the place you're leaving come to talk to you about small personal matters. You respond, you smile, you take part in the conversation in a friendly manner, but 'that no longer concerns you.' / Don't laugh. Yesterday, I would have also been put-out by such old people's talk, especially coming from a man in relatively good health. To understand, you have to already be seated in the waiting room."

171. The quote, from Stendhal's *Rome, Naples, and Florence*, appears in the section on Rome.

172. *The Philosophers' Farce*, a short play by Camus, was neither published nor performed during the author's lifetime, likely because the main character, a philosophical charlatan named Monsieur Nothingness, is a clear sendup of Jean-Paul Sartre (the character occasionally uses phrases straight from Sartre's work). Another reason for withholding the play may have been its similarities to

---

A "modern" title: The Hatred of Art.[173]

Write naturally. Publish naturally, and pay the price for doing so, naturally.

The critic is to the creator what the merchant is to the manufacturer. The mercantile age saw an asphyxiating multiplication of commentators, intermediaries between the manufacturer and the public. So then, it's not that we lack creators today, it's that there are too many commentators drowning the exquisite, elusive fish in their muddy waters.

Novel. See Weissberg notes.[174] During the interrogation, the Chekists placed a gilded paper crown decorated with swastikas on his head, a large swastika on his chest, and then beat him.

Id. The old anarchist tailor explains his point of view clearly. The judge insults him. "You have offended me, your honor, and I will not answer any more of your questions." Record of the interrogation: *31 days and 31 nights.* Madhouse!

Novel.[175] Part 1. Search for a Father or The Unknown Father. Poverty has no past.[176] "The day in the provincial cemetery when . . . X. discovered his father had died at a younger age than he was then . . . that the person lying there had been 2 years younger than he was now, even though he'd been lying there for 35 years already . . . He realized he didn't know anything about this father of his and decided to go in search of him . . ."

Molière's plays *Tartuffe* and *Sganarelle, or The Imaginary Cuckold* (a similarity Camus himself notes later in these pages). The play was published in French for the first time in 2008.

173. Perhaps supporting his claim to increased forgetfulness, Camus made almost the same note a few pages earlier.

174. Alex Weissberg (1901–1964), physicist and businessman who went on to write *L'accusé* (The Accused), a memoir and analysis of Stalin and the Great Purge, printed in English as *Conspiracy of Silence* with an introduction by Arthur Koestler.

175. Camus added "The First Man" between these two words on the initial typescript of the notebooks and then placed the typed sheet in the Education folder that was part of the larger folder containing ideas for *The First Man*. This first plan for the novel was likely written on October 18, 1953, as it was on that day that he wrote the following to Maria Casarès: "Unable to sleep last night, I got up to work at 4 in the morning. Guess what I worked on? The outline for my future novel."

176. In the separate notebook he was keeping for *The First Man*, Camus writes: "There was a mystery about that man, a mystery he wanted to bring to light. / But in the end, it was a mystery born of a poverty that leaves people with neither a name nor a past." The rest of the description given in the entry also appears in these pages, at the beginning of notebook VII.

Born during the move.

Part 2. Childhood (or thread this through the first part) Who am I?

Part 3. A Man's Education. Unable to tear himself away from bodies. Ah! The innocence of first acts. But the years pass, people form bonds, and each act of the flesh binds, prostitutes, and commits one more and more.

He doesn't want to be judged (he rarely judges, to be honest), but you can't not be.

Two characters:

1) The indifferent one: raised without a family environment. Without a father. An unusual mother. Figures things out for himself. A little haughty, though polite. Always walks alone. Goes to boxing and soccer matches. Likes only the most intense moments. Forgets the rest. At the same time, demands from others the affection of which he is incapable. Lies easily but has terrible urges to tell the truth. A little monstrous. Secretive as can be, because he forgets large parts of his life, because few things interest him—An artist by these very faults.

2) The other one, sensitive and generous.

They meet at the end (and are the same) at the mother's side.

O father! I'd been madly searching for that father I didn't have and what I came to find then was what I'd always had: my mother and her silence.

The five movements of Mozart's String Quintet No. 4 in G Minor.[177]

Love and Paris. Algeria. "We didn't know how to love."

Id. Childhood poverty. Life without love (not without pleasures). The mother is not a source of love. As a result, the longest thing in the world to learn is how to love.

Two people get together through looks and glances alone (let's say a cashier and a customer). When the opportunity arises, they go right for it. What does he say? "Do you have time?" What does she say? How does she respond? "I'll say I had to go somewhere."

---

177. The claim Camus is making here, and that music critics have made for many years, is that the aria that begins the fourth movement can be imagined as a separate movement from the allegro that follows, thus giving the "quintet" five movements.

Progress is an optimal balance of two forces in equal tension. It takes limits into account and subjugates them to a greater good. And not in a vertical arrow, which would imply progress has no limits.[178]

———

Play. They wait for him. He returns from the camp. He tells the truth about love (because he got close: now he knows what it means to be a man).

Scene with his wife in front of Philinte[179] and G., Philinte's wife. "For example, I slept with G. . . . Besides, I'm not so sure you and Philinte—"

Philinte: "No. It's not that G. isn't quite the dish, and even though I'm no fan of the truth, I'm going to make an exception and tell it. When I saw that you and G.—"

"How?"

"Yes, I knew. From then on, anything between your wife and I became impossible, because, really, this back and forth, ugh! You agree with me, don't you? So then, come have dinner tomorrow. G. will make you her chaud-froid.[180] No one makes chaud-froid better than she does."

End of the act.

"But your feelings of affection?"

"Well, what about my feelings of affection? They existed as all things do, here and there."

"And the rest of the time?"

"I was lying, of course."

"I preferred your lie."

"Of course you did. You've always liked a little shuteye."

"But you're a monster."

"And you, my angel?"

Id. "For example, my son's a fool."

"Oh, here we go," the son says.

"You see? You protest. That's how a fool reacts. An intelligent man always admits the possibility, or I should say the probability, of in some way being a fool. So then, my son is a fool (he looks at him). Not a complete fool, though.

———

178. See the fourth paragraph of Camus's April 12, 1951, speech, "A Europe of Loyalty," which was delivered to the Association of Friends of the Spanish Republic.

179. Philinte is also the name of a character in Molière's *The Misanthrope*, a character who seems to have much in common with the one Camus sketches here.

180. Literally "hot-cold," *chaud-froid* is a dish consisting of meat or chicken that has been cooled and coated with a jelly sauce.

He plays the part. He's cunning. He understands that acting the fool has its advantages, that it's the hearth around which society warms itself."

Id. The son becomes social. "When social plans and private plans coincide—"

"You mother will get wise?"

"No, but . . . you no longer covet the wife of another?"

"Surely."

"Why, will yours be perfect?"

"No . . ."

"You. I see what you're up to. You want to use the social strength of others to sort out your own little private problems. Leave it be, my boy. Other people's misery, that's their own private problem. They'll sort out their little affairs one way or another, don't you worry. But don't get yourself mixed up in it. Oh, don't get yourself mixed up in it."

Id. But he falls in love with Dominique and begins to lie again.

———

The intellectual who asks forgiveness.

"The worst was the Gospel. Yes, I read the Gospel, at first because it was the only thing at hand, and then because in reading it I realized I had more in common with Jesus than I had in common with a policeman. And in today's world, three-quarters are policemen—or their admirers."

———

A man whose life is full turns down many offers. Then, because his life is full, he forgets what he's turned down. But the offers were made by people whose lives are not full and who, for that very reason, remember. When the man later finds he's made enemies, he's astonished. Like this, almost all artists imagine they're being persecuted. But no—people are responding to being turned down and what they're punishing is an excess of riches. There is no injustice.[181]

———

181. In *The Fall*, Clamence says: "It was especially with those who only knew me from afar that I encountered hostility, with those whom I didn't know personally. No doubt they suspected me of living completely and totally abandoned to happiness—and that cannot be forgiven. The look of success, when worn in a certain way, is enough to drive an ass wild. In reality, my life was bursting at the seams, and, for lack of time, I turned down many offers. Then, because my life was full, I forgot the offers I'd turned down. But those offers were made by people whose lives were not full, and who, for that very reason, remembered me turning them down."

The First Man[182]

Outline?

1) Search for a Father

2) Childhood

3) Years of Happiness (sick in 1938). Action as a happy overabundance. Powerful feeling of freedom when it's over.

4) War and Resistance (Bir Hakeim and the clandestine newspaper, alternate).

5) Women.

6) Mother.

The indifferent one. A complete man. A high-caliber mind, a dexterous body well-versed in pleasure. He refuses to be loved due to restlessness, and due to a precise understanding of how he is: sweet and kind in illegitimacy, cynical and terrible in virtue.

He can do anything because he's decided to kill himself. Cyanide. So then, he joins the Resistance and acts with incredible daring. But the day he's supposed to take the cyanide, *he abstains.*

The First Man.

Search for a Father.

The hospital. The mother (and the notice from town hall that's brought to the two illiterate women peeling potatoes on the landing, and then the deputy mayor has to be brought in and the notice given back to him so that he can read it to them), the press, Cheragas,[183] etc. A sketch of the father begins to take shape. Then disappears completely. Ultimately, nothing remains.

That's the way it's always been in this land where, 50 years ago, 70 years ago, men and women came, plowed, dug deeper and deeper furrows or their opposite, more and more tentative, where they procreated then died, the lightest of soils covering their tracks. And so it went with their sons. And

---

182. This entry as well as the one that follows do not appear in the handwritten notebook. On the initial typescript, where the entries first appear, the title *The First Man* was still not yet present; Camus added it later in black ink. The addition of these entries creates some chronological confusion, as the initial outline for the novel was most likely written in October 1953.

183. An Algerian village in the Sahel region.

From this point on, Camus added the rest of the entry to the typescript by hand, in black ink. In the French edition of the notebooks, the entry ends at "(this is the book's main subject)," but the handwritten additions in fact continue, first onto a line written along the margin of the page and then onto an additional sheet of typewriter paper. These additional lines and paragraphs have been included here.

the sons of their sons found themselves on this land, without past, without morals, naked and happy to be so, everyday a day to be remade from scratch.

They were only, yes, this alone was certain, the sons of women—

After that, the sons of their labors, having to build themselves up from scratch, in strength, power, influence, having to fashion their own morality, their own truth, so as to at last be born as men, and then, all of that said and done, to achieve a second birth, the hardest one, which is to be born to others (this is the book's main subject).

They're born willingly or unwillingly into French or Arab life.

Yes, what's always separated him from the country where he now lived, what's kept him apart, it wasn't just the rain and the mist, the ugliness and clammy squalor, it was the absence of a past he had lived, one that had made him another man.

Id. Soccer and communism, two sports.

The flesh (the balls and the dance)

End. With the mother "He wept over the disabled woman's paltry fate. What it had taken him so many years to know—that others existed and that justice had to be done for them while they were alive—she had known from her very first steps. And she had acted in accordance with what she knew, taking the shortest path, the only one she could find, by accepting injustice for herself . . . if he was crying, it was out of love and admiration, and also for himself, for all that he knew about himself and on account of which he suffered, and because in his thirty-five years of life he'd never been able to reveal himself to that silent mother, the only person to whom he could have ever spoken."

Approach—The two characters. I and He? One develops a sense of self and then must learn that others exist. The second is born unto others from the very start, and something will always be missing for him.

For all the darker parts, the blood, the sex, etc., daydreams collected as *The Siesta.*

———

In '40, Maillol[184] meets V.B., a Romanian-Jewish painter who took refuge in Collioure to escape the Germans. He meets him in the street, recognizes he is a painter, invites him to come show him his work. The next day, V.B. goes, is welcomed with open arms, explains his situation. "My house is your house," M. says. That's all. He has a cup of coffee brought over. He opens the crate, smiling at V.B., and finally has a look at the first drawing, clearly surrealist: a woman who tapers into a tree. Maillol bursts out: "No, no, not that, it's not possible. Get out of here!"

Nietzsche. "They all talk about me . . . But nobody *thinks* of me."

The Pillory.[185] "He has to be held responsible. He has to be held responsible for his nasty habit of seeming honest and not being so." In the first-person. Incapable of loving. He forces himself to do it, etc.

What the collaborationist left approves of, passes over in silence, or judges unavoidable, in no particular order:

1) The deportation of tens of thousands of Greek children.
2) The physical destruction of the Russian peasant class.
3) The millions in concentration camps.
4) The political abductions.
5) Practically daily political executions behind the Iron Curtain.
6) The antisemitism.
7) The stupidity.
8) The cruelty.

The list goes on. But that's enough for me.

Tolstoy's Journal. Three demons:

1) the game (possible struggle)
2) the sensuality (very difficult struggle)
3) the vanity (the most terrible of all)

"I reckon," he says in a letter to his aunt, "that without religion man can be neither happy nor good . . . But I don't believe."

---

184. Aristide Maillol (1861–1944), a French artist who, like Camus, was killed as a passenger in a car accident. The V.B. mentioned here is most likely the surrealist sculptor and painter Victor Brauner.

185. An early working title for *The Fall*. A more literal translation of the quoted portion: "He must be blamed. He must be blamed for his nasty habit of appearing honest and not being so."

Id. "The truth is horrible."[186]

OCTOBER '53. Noble profession where you have to let yourself be insulted by a lackey of letters or the party without so much as flinching! In days gone by, which were said to be demeaning, you at least had the right to challenge without being ridiculed, and to kill. Stupid, to be sure, but it made insulting someone a little less comfortable.[187]

There are people whose religion consists of always forgiving offenses, but who never forget them. For my part, I don't have what it takes to forgive an offense, but I always forget it.[188]

Those fertilized by both Dostoyevsky and Tolstoy, who understand them both equally well, with the same facility, those people there: an always formidable nature, with themselves and with others.

OCTOBER '53. Publication of Actuelles II. Finished taking stock—the commentary and polemic. From now on, creation.[189]

In the aftermath of great historical crises, you find yourself as sick and discontented as on the morning after a night of excess. But there is no aspirin for the historic hangover.

Those unspoken thoughts that place you above it all, in an air that's brisk and free.

They say that Nietzsche, after breaking with Lou, entered a final solitude, in which he would walk around the mountains overlooking the Gulf

186. The rest of the page after this entry was left blank in the original notebook.

187. See p. 320, where Camus quotes Rousseau on dueling.

188. In *The Fall*, Clamence says: "Let's be fair: sometimes my forgetfulness could be meritorious. You'll have noticed there are some people whose religion consists of forgiving all offenses, and they do indeed forgive them, but never forget them. I didn't have what it takes to forgive offenses, but I always ended up forgetting them. And anyone who believed they were hated by me, well, they couldn't believe it when I greeted them with a big smile. Depending on their nature, they either admired the grandeur of my soul or despised my yellowbelly, never realizing the reason was much simpler: I didn't even remember their name. The same infirmity that rendered me indifferent or ungrateful also made me magnanimous."

189. The second volume of Camus's *Actuelles*, published October 29, 1953, was read by some as a response to the polemic surrounding *The Rebel*, though, on the whole, the book went largely un-

of Genoa at night, light huge fires there, and watch them burn themselves out. I've frequently thought of those fires and their flickering has danced behind the whole of my intellectual life. If I've happened to be unjust to certain thoughts, to certain people I've met in this century of ours, it's because I've inadvertently placed them before those blazing flames and they were instantly reduced to ash.[190]

Melville discusses Moby Dick in a letter to Hawthorne: "This is the book's motto (the secret one)—Ego non baptiso te in nomine . . ."

Id. "I had some vague idea while writing it, that the whole book was susceptible of an allegoric construction, & also that *parts* of it were . . ."

Id. After having finished M.B. and having read Hawthorne's admiring letter: "It is a strange feeling—no hopefulness is in it, no despair. Content—that is it; and irresponsibility; but without licentious inclination."

And then "I shall leave the world, I feel, with more satisfaction for having come to know you."

Cf. the theme of the tale "The Happy Failure": praise God for this failure.

Nietzsche. Religious men could be classified among the top tier of artists.[191]

Nietzsche: *Dawn.* "Never keep silent, never conceal what one can think against your own thoughts. Swear it solemnly. It is the first act of loyalty that you owe to your thought."

Beyond . . . : "If one has character, one has in his life a characteristic experience that eternally recurs." Question then: find the event and give it its name.

Genealogy . . . : "Whoever has ever built a new heaven has found the necessary power for this endeavor *only at the bottom of his own hell.*"

The "polyphony" of certain natures.

Nietzsche. (*Human, All Too Human*): "A little while after I fell ill, more than ill, tired by the continual disillusion caused by all that enthused us modern men . . ."

---

noticed by both the public and press.

190. Camus would use this entry, with minor revisions, in his essay "Create Dangerously."

191. In the handwritten notebook, this entry appears as the only one on the verso page, written in tiny print in the top-left corner.

... "Here a man who speaks suffers and is deprived, but he expresses himself as if he did not suffer and did not deprive himself."

... "From now on solitary, I take the side against myself and everything that, in fact, opposed me and made me suffer."

Single, gigantic goal: knowledge of truth.

Eternal return: Exalt what is and adore that it recurs. (Without metaphysics, this is all that really remains.)

Note to Lou (1882). "In bed. Acute crisis. I despise life."

Need for an aristocracy. At present, we can only imagine two types: one of intelligence and one of work. But intelligence is not in itself an aristocracy. Neither is work (the examples, in both cases, are obvious). Aristocracy is not primarily the enjoyment of certain rights, but primarily the acceptance of certain duties, which alone legitimize the rights. Aristocracy simultaneously asserts and erases itself. To move beyond the self (definition of duty) intelligence can't go toward privileges. Some privileges are part of intelligence, others are the opposite of intelligence. And duty consists neither in asserting yourself nor suppressing yourself, but in putting what you assert to good use. So then, intelligence can only go toward work, which is its duty and its limit. Work, for its part, can't go, consciously or unconsciously, toward stupefaction (generalized abasement of intelligence), which is either its own thing or the opposite of work (see above). So then, work can only go toward intelligence. Ultimately, the aristocracies of work and intelligence are, at present, only possible if they recognize each other and begin to move toward each other in order to one day establish a single greater vision of man.[192]

The obligation to hide a part of his life gave him the appearance of virtue.

The people are the sole source of aristocracy. Between the two, there's nothing. This nothing, which is the bourgeoisie, has, for the past 150 years, been trying to shape the world and has achieved only a nothingness, a chaos that still survives thanks only to its ancient roots.[193]

---

192. See the second paragraph of Camus's April 12, 1951, speech, "A Europe of Loyalty."

193. In French, this last phrase, *anciennes racines*, may call to mind the similar sounding *Ancien Régime*.

Walpole.[194] "His common sense went as far as genius."

———

Adaptation of *The Possessed*

Cf. Berdyaev. "Shatov, Verkhovensky, and Kirilov are all so many fragments of Stavrogin's disaggregated personality, emanations of that extraordinary personality that spreads itself so thin it disintegrates. The enigma of Stavrogin, the secret of Stavrogin, that's The Possessed's singular theme."

Dostoyevsky's thesis: the same paths that lead the individual to crime lead society to revolution.

Verkhovensky: "Revolution's greatest, most important strength is in making a person ashamed to have their own opinion."

Cf. Guardini,[195] pp. 40–41 and 202.[196]

———

Use your vices, be wary of your virtues.

———

Brupbacher.[197] "No one should produce more philanthropy or morality than they naturally exude." He thought the militant philosopher's mission was to foster all the factors of freedom in all classes.

———

W. Whitman. "When liberty goes out of a place, it is not the first to go. It waits for all the rest to go—it is the last."[198]

———

Van Gogh, stuck with a woman of the working poor, Christine, abandons her while she's in the maternity ward. Gaugin, waking in the night, sees Van Gogh leaning over him, staring at him. At the asylum in Saint-Rémy, the Count of G. beats his chest with a piece of wood, repeating: "My mistress, my mistress!"

———

194. Horace Walpole (1717–1797), English writer, historian, politician, and author of what's considered the first Gothic novel, *The Castle of Otranto*. In a 1769 letter to Horace Mann, he wrote: "I have often said, and oftner think, that this world is a comedy to those that think, a tragedy to those that feel—a solution of why Democritus laughed and Heraclitus wept."

195. Romano Guardini (1885–1968), German Catholic priest and author of *The Religious Universe of Dostoyevsky*, published in French in 1947. Perhaps the inspiration for the entry that follows.

196. This entry appears a little later in the published French edition; in the handwritten notebook, it is on its own page in this location.

197. Fritz Brupacher (1874–1945), Swiss physician and writer, author of *Socialism and Liberty*.

198. Camus may have encountered the Whitman quote when it appeared under the title "To a Foiled Revolter or Revoltress." The version Camus records here is slightly shortened.

In the notes accompanying Salacrou's[199] Theatre, Volume VI, he tells the following story: "A little girl going on 10 years old declares, 'When I grow up, I'll register with the cruelest party.' Questioned, she explains, 'If my party is in power, I'll have nothing to fear, and if the other party is in power, I'll suffer less because the less cruel party will be the one persecuting me.'" I don't really believe this story about the little girl, but I'm quite familiar with its reasoning. It's the unspoken yet effective reasoning of French intellectuals in 1954.

Dostoyevsky's father had both the peasants who bowed to him as well as those who didn't whipped. In his mind, they were being audacious either way.[200] After his wife, whom he bullied, died, he'd get drunk at night and talk to her, taking in turn a woman's voice and then a man's. He's murdered. His head smashed in, genitals crushed between two stones. Two months later, D., who hated his father, sees a funeral, collapses, and lets out the death rattle.

Id. Spechniov (the Petrashevskist[201]—"The man of irony, liberty, and power") and "each is guilty of all, for all." Etym. root of Stavrogin: *stauros*: the cross.

Russian hatred for forms that limit. They pushed the revolution as far as it could go. Berdyaev notes somewhere that they've never had a Renaissance. Anxiety, always. *Id.* According to Berdyaev the absence of chivalry has had disastrous consequences for Russia's moral culture.

Are Carlyle, Nietzsche, and Dostoyevsky revolutionaries? Yet they're called counterrevolutionaries.[202]

---

199. Armand Salacrou (1899–1989), a French playwright who took part in the Resistance during World War II.

200. In *The Fall*, Clamence says: "I would also tell anyone who would listen how sorry I was that it was no longer possible to act like that Russian landowner whose character I admired—he had both the peasants who bowed to him as well as those who didn't simultaneously whipped so as to punish an audacity that, in either case, he considered insolent."

201. In 1847, at twenty-seven years old, Dostoyevsky joined a group of liberal intellectuals, the Petrashevsky Circle, who wanted to prepare the peasants for socialist revolution. Nikolai Speshnev, a member of the group and model for Stavrogin, embodied a more radical view. During the night of April 22–23, 1849, Dostoyevsky was arrested alongside thirty-three other members of the group. He was sentenced to death, spent four years in prison, and was eventually pardoned.

202. The rest of the page after this entry was left blank in the original notebook.

A priest who regrets having to leave his books when he dies? You mean to say the violent pleasure of eternal life doesn't infinitely surpass the gentle company of books?[203]

———

MAY 8. Fall of Dien Bien Phu. As in '40, a mixed feeling of shame and fury.

The evening of the massacre, the balance[204] is clear. Right-wing politicians placed the poor in an untenable situation, while at the same time those on the left shot them in the back.

———

According to Johnson (Boswell) perfect courtesy consists in not bearing the mark of any profession whatsoever, instead having a general fluency in all manners and circumstances.

Id. On remarrying: "The triumph of hope over experience."

Id. J.'s friend: "I have tried too in my time to be a philosopher; but, I don't know how, cheerfulness was always breaking in."

Id. "When we have sat together some time, you'll find my brother grows very entertaining."

"'Sir, (said Johnson,) I can wait.'"

———

Socrates learned to dance at an advanced age.

———

Johnson: "No man is hypocritical in his pleasures."[205]

Before dying, a "curious thought" comes to him: we don't receive letters in our grave.

———

203. This is the only entry on the page in the original notebook.

204. As a noun, the French word *bilan* can refer to a "balance sheet," in terms of assessment or record keeping, as well as in terms of a "death toll" or human cost, and is often translated as simply "the result."

The dates of events in the closing pages of notebook VII do not always follow: this entry, which refers to an event that took place on May 7, 1954, precedes the two entries below about Marcel Herrand's death, which took place on June 11, 1953. It also precedes the entry Camus made about his April 12, 1954, letter to René Coty. The last entry in the notebook for which Camus himself gave both a date and year is October 1953. Given the end date Camus wrote on the cover of notebook VII, December 1953, which is also the start date he wrote on the cover of notebook VIII, it's possible that Camus initially left the last few pages of notebook VII blank—possibly because he had forgotten it or left it behind when he headed to Oran in December—and then came back to use the pages at a later date (see the note at the start of notebook VII), though this alone does not seem to fully account for the back-and-forth chronology.

205. In *The Fall*, Clamence says: "No man is a hypocrite in his pleasures. Did I read that or did I think it, my dear compatriot?"

Don Juan Faust

1) To be right

2) Nothing is allowed

3) He goes along with the Franciscans' ploy. They kill him.[206]

Aix-en-Provence? Romanticism?

In The Philosophers' Farce, Sganarelle would be Monsieur Nothingness.[207] He's the one who announces "He will not come" (he reproves Doña Anna's father, who questions him about his vices. See Farce)

Don Juan is Faust without the pact—(expand on this)

Act III, in Brazil with the slaves. Act IV, Act V becomes man and solitary. *Solitary with everyone.*

D.J. Pact with the devil but without the devil. *Betting on the world,* on sensation and pleasure, is making a pact with the devil. *Betting on justice* is also making a pact.

———

At Massignon's[208] request, I wrote to the President of the Republic to ask that the people sentenced to death at Moknine be pardoned. A few days later, I found a response in the newspaper: three of the condemned had been shot. *Fifteen days after the execution,* the Chief of Staff informed me that my letter "caught the attention" of the president and was, as such, sent on to the Conseil Supérieur de la Magistrature. Bewildering bureaucracy.

———

2 million union members out of eleven million employees. In 1947 there were seven million union members.

———

Play. A happy man. And no one can stand him.

———

In the water, the turtle becomes a bird. The giant sea turtle hovers in the warm waters like a beautiful albatross.

———

206. See p. 138.

207. The reference is to Molière's *Sganarelle, or The Imaginary Cuckold.*

208. Louis Massignon (1883–1962), a French scholar and Catholic who did much to advance the understanding of Islam in the West.

On April 12, 1954, Camus wrote to the French president, René Coty, on behalf of seven Tunisians who'd been sentenced to death for having killed three police officers. The introductory phrase, "At Massignon's request," was added to the typescript and does not appear in the handwritten notebook. On the chronology of the entry, see the earlier note on Dien Bien Phu.

Atonal music, music for voices, for the feverish voice of modern man.

Letter to M. "Don't curse the West. For my part, I cursed it at the time of its splendor. But today, as it succumbs under the weight of its faults, the weight of a glory that's gone on too long, I won't pile on top . . . Don't envy those in the East who sacrifice intelligence and heart to the gods of history. History has no gods and an intelligence enlightened by the heart is the only god that, in a thousand forms, has ever been recognized in this world."

Chekhov: "The essential thing for a writer isn't fame and glory . . . it's the patience to endure." "To bear your cross and keep hope alive."[209]

The Critics' School: the "laws" of the theater.

"If I've understood you correctly, Monsieur, I must follow with exacting precision the laws that neither Aeschylus, nor Shakespeare, nor Calderon, nor Corneille, nor any of the other great dramatic geniuses ever prevented themselves from breaking."

"It would be more accurate to say that only Shakespeare, Aeschylus, and the others could afford to break those laws."

"Following your advice, I'll never be either of those great creators."

"Would you claim to be?"

"To be, no. But to become. Otherwise, why bother writing? Sure, I'll fail, that's almost certain. But to have given it a try would infuse my life with a zest you'd take away before I even get started. And after all, Shakespeare was born of a hundred desperate and pretentious fools who wanted to be Shakespeare themselves. As for Feydeau, he could've only come from Feydeau (I laugh, nota bene, but rarely beyond one act)."

Play. Today King Lear is a patrician dispossessed by the socialists.

Id. A Caligula who no longer blames the world but himself.

Death of Marcel Herrand.[210]

---

209. These lines are spoken by Nina at the end of Chekhov's play *The Seagull*. Direct Russian-to-English translations show several differences from the French Camus records here, most notably, the word "faith" instead of "hope" at the conclusion.

210. Marcel Herrand (1897–1953) died on June 11, 1953, only days before the opening of the Festival of Angers, which he was set to direct. Camus met with Herrand in Nice a few months before his

Virtuous men often make spineless citizens. At the root of true courage, a little disorder.[211]

According to our existentialists, we're all responsible for who we are. Which explains the complete disappearance of compassion from their universe of aggressive old men. Yet they claim to fight against social injustice. So then, there are some people who aren't responsible for who they are: the impoverished are innocent of their poverty. Well? The disabled, the ugly, the shy. A return to compassion, eventually?

Pericles standing before a young man's grave: "The year has lost its Spring."[212]

When they referred to me as a "director" (that is, someone who is good at giving direction), of course a part of me puffed up with idiotic vanity. But another part has, through all these years, never stopped dying of shame.

M.H. The frightfully sad look of the dying—and the stubborn, provincial look of those who attend the death throes. He was so worldly, and then all of a sudden, practically hunted down into that alcove, where alone . . .

There are times when indulging in sincerity amounts to an inexcusable laxity.

The First Man:[213] Jessica's stages—the sensual girl, the young lover enamored with the absolute, the true lover. Fulfillment beyond dubious beginnings.

---

passing and went on to direct the festival after his death (though Herrand was still billed as director). On the chronology of the entry, see the earlier note on Dien Bien Phu.

211. Without further context, the final clause could be read in multiple ways: "a little misbehavior," "an imbalance," "a disruption," etc.

212. Henry Bordeaux (1870–1963), a French lawyer, writer, and member of the Académie Française, wrote a study of World War I French fighter ace Georges Guynemer (translated into English as *Georges Guynemer: Knight of the Air*), with a preface by Theodore Roosevelt. Early in the study, Bordeaux writes: "In Antiquity, they found moving ways of lamenting the loss of young people mowed down at their peak. 'The city,' Pericles sighs, 'has lost its light, the year has lost its spring.'"

213. On the original typescript, Camus crossed out the word "Novel" and replaced it with "The First Man."

"When I loved her most, someone deep inside me hated her for what she'd done, seen, and endured. Endured especially. I hated her for not having waited for me, dead, until the early morning hours. And I hated her when faced with that other person inside me who laughed at such ridiculous pretension."

Jonas.[214] A housing crisis. The paintings accumulate, crowding him out. So then, to the attic.

The moment he's no longer doing anything: "He heard them running through the rooms . . . life, the sounds people make, how beautiful they were. The little girl laughed. Oh, how he loved them! How he loved them!"

Play. The liar.

1) He lies. Two women enter.

2) He tells the truth.

3) Facing disaster, he lies again. (She tears up the paper that would get her out of the lie.)

A play about the impossibility of solitude. *They are always there.*

Novel. Best wishes (to my son who will begin again).

The most difficult thing for man to bear is being judged. This is where the attachment to the mother or to the blind lover originates, as well as the love of animals.

Thermonuclear bomb: ultimately, widespread death coincides with the human condition in light of this. All we have to do is come to terms with it. We're back to the first and oldest of problems. Having reached the infinite, we begin again from scratch. 2nd shift of the problem: the universal scourge no longer has God as author but man. Man is finally God's equal, but only

---

214. The notes that follow see Camus expanding on *The Life of the Artist*, a mimodrama he'd published in a small Algerian journal in February 1953 (the first English translation appeared in *The New Yorker* in 2013), which he would enlarge into the short story "Jonas, or The Artist at Work," collected in *Exile and the Kingdom*.

in his cruelty. So then, we have to resume the rebellion of previous ages, but this time against humanity. We call on a new Lucifer to deny man's power.

———

Bizarre. "Dirty kike," the bigger one says. And the little guy hits him. He had to hit him, but he didn't want to do it. He didn't hate the head he hit . . . And the bigger one didn't want to do it either, didn't want to call the nice little guy a kike, didn't want to hit him. But a person has to respond, has to hit back.

———

Fantastic tales.[215]

———

Pan-Christ.

———

Aesthetics. Sometimes we begin with the emotion, and the cry bursts forth. Other times, we set out to find the emotion, still alive in our memory, through a long detour of words and sentences that eventually lead us to it, that, in fact, resurrect the emotion, no longer a cry then but a great wave whose magnitude . . .

Id. If I say, "He has a nose like a pumpkin," that doesn't mean much, but "like a peach" does. In this way, art is a calculated exaggeration.

———

The love shared between Char and the lioness at the Jardin des Plantes. He strokes her head through the bars. She rolls over. Spreads her short legs . . .

———

Millions of people have preceded us on all the world's roads and their traces are still visible. But on the oldest sea our silence is always the first.

———

Nobody deserves to be loved—nobody measures up to that immeasurable gift. Whoever should receive it then discovers injustice.

———

If I hadn't given in to my passions, maybe I would have had what it takes to play a part in the world, to change something. But I gave in to them, and that's why I'm an artist, and only an artist.

———

215. With regard to fiction, the French *fantastique*, like the English "fantastic," is a contested term, with various definitions attributed to it. Tales of the fantastique are neither fairy tales, which are based in a world of magic, nor science-fiction, in which non-supernatural explanations are possible. Tales of the fantastique usually take place in an otherwise realistic setting invaded by an instance of the uncanny and weird.

Somebody inside of me has always, with all his might, tried to be nobody.

———

At the far end of this long thought, off in the distance, burns a total Yes.

———

At the very moment when, after so much effort, I was setting limits, believing I was reconciling the irreconcilable, the limits leaped forward and I plunged into mute misery.

Notebook VIII

DECEMBER 1953–JULY 1958

A plain spiral notebook with "Cahier VIII" handwritten toward the top-left side of the cover and the dates "December 1953 to July '58" written under it. See the note at the start of notebook VII for an explanation of the discrepancy between the dates given here and those given in the French edition.

8/15/1954

Mahler's Symphony No. 4 in G major for sopranos and orchestra. Sometimes Mahler makes you appreciate Wagner, showing, in the contrast between them, the extent to which Wagner remained master of his fog. Other times, Mahler reaches greatness.

———

8/16/1954

M. says to me: "Why don't we accept the idea of eternal life? Because it's ultimately a beatitude stripped of consciousness—and what we want is to be, which is to say to know that we are. But then why reproach the world for giving us precisely what leads to consciousness, which is to say pain and suffering (this is indeed the contradiction of modern atheism). Me? I've always accepted suffering with a sort of joy—the joy of being." I tell her that therein lies genius. Genius? Yes, a genius way of life, which she alone, among all the people I've met, carries off with a healthy sort of pride.[1]

———

17. Berl.[2]

It's easier for intellectuals to say no than to say yes. At the end of his life, looking over the volumes of his work, Doctor Reclus, who'd sided with Dreyfus, realizes there were two years during which he'd produced nothing. Ah, that's right, Dreyfus: he'd dedicated those two years to *studying* the case files. Today people take sides after reading a single article one time.

Wasted afternoon.

———

18.

No way out.[3] Suicide. So then what are you waiting for, you who are already dead?

---

1. Camus and Mamaine Koestler still shared a frequent correspondence when, on June 4, 1954, she died suddenly. Arthur Koestler wrote an undated letter informing Camus. On August 10, Camus wrote a condolence letter to Celia Goodman, Mamaine's twin sister.

2. Emmanuel Berl (1892–1976), French essayist and journalist who was friends with many well-known writers, Camus among them.

3. The entry begins with the clipped *N'en sortirai pas*, here translated as "No way out." A more complete version of the sentence, *Je ne m'en sortirai pas*, might be translated as, "I'm not going to make it."

The ivy in the Cimetière d'Anet broke through one of the old stones.

For years I lived cloistered in her love. Today I must flee, never having stopped loving her, or at least caring about her, which is difficult.

19.

Terrible morning. Cézanne exhibit in afternoon: first mad and morbid paintings (sexual obsession in particular). A madness of that sort demanded the terrible discipline that was Cézanne's. The mad alone are traditional because they're that or nothing. C. pushed the demand as far as his disorder would take it and he chose still-lifes and landscapes because he could find an architecture in them, a geometry. Toward the end he returned to bodies and faces and once again found madness, the madness he'd disciplined. It's here cubism takes shape (foretold).[4]

Mail.

20.

Mail. Large-scale general strike.[5]

21.

Large-scale general strike. N.A. (Derain went mad after being hit by a car, after hemiplegia. His wife and former mistress are putting official seals on his paintings while he's delirious in a clinic.)

The Gate of Hell.[6] Japanese film, some American influence. But our art is barbarous in comparison to this.

The Cimetière d'Anet, mentioned in the second line of the entry, is in northern France, on the grounds of the Château d'Anet, which was built in the 1500s.

4. The handwriting in the original notebook is hard to make out here. The sentence given is conjectural.

5. The term Camus uses here, *Journée morte* (literally, Dead day) refers to a strike or protest of such magnitude that it impacts a country beyond any one sector, usually causing major disruptions to normal functioning.

6. *The Gate of Hell* (*Jigoku-Mon*), a film by Kinugasa, received the 1954 Grand Prix du Festival at Cannes.

22.

Sad and wise nature of the Île-de-France.

23–24.

Large-scale general strike. Lunch with Berl.

25.

Work except in the morning. Afternoon: Musée de l'Homme. I leave with a mouth full of ashes, the bony ashes of skeletons and mummies. Peruvian mummy: [. . .][7] of history. Who was it?

Action and Writing: They're not so sure they're right, and this uncertainty leaves them with a guilty conscience. So then, they'll write to get rid of their guilty conscience. To make it work, they'll look for new rationales, find them, and then push them even harder. Those on the other side will do the same. Like this, the positions will harden. So many repeated assertions will be the equivalent of actions. Will soon provoke them. Like this, when the day of victory arrives, the victorious party will have plenty of charges to level. As a result of running from their guilty conscience, the vanquished will have found true guilt and will answer for it, not having wanted it to be like this. Another day, the victors will in turn be the vanquished and will answer, not having wanted it to be like this. History is one long crime perpetrated by the innocent.

[. . .][8]

September 7.

The children return. Catherine can't fall asleep because she's afraid of dying (she has chest pain). That this anxiety can already torment these little ones, is this not truly the ultimate outrage?

---

7. A series of illegible words.

The startling Peruvian mummy, discovered in 1877 and first displayed in 1882, can still be seen at the Musée de l'Homme (Museum of Mankind) in Paris. It has inspired many artists, from Gauguin to Munch.

8. In the original notebook, there are several illegible words at the end of this entry.

September 8.

N.A. called: Derain just died. Hemiplegic, gone mad, persecuted by his wife, who had seals put on his paintings. N.A. is desperate. Nothing to be done. Poor Derain, whose surly intensity I loved. Too alive for his own life.

———

19.

For F. (and her family) love blends with suffering and anguish. To love is to suffer from or for. For me, it never split away from a certain state of joyful innocence. No sooner had I met them than I was plunged into guilt and I could no longer truly love.[9]

———

20.

It's not dying that frightens me but living dead.

Annihilation can't frighten a person whose lived a full life.

God isn't needed to create guilt or punishment. Human beings do that just fine.[10] It's innocence he could set up in a pinch.

———

21.

How could he preach justice, he who hasn't even managed to achieve it in his own life?

When night fell, before chopping his family up with an axe, the murderer stripped naked.

M: "You're reserved, kind, and (to make up for what's repulsive in kindness) you're passionate and occasionally unjust."

———

9. This entry appears in Marie's *The First Man* file with an *M* instead of *F*.

10. The first sentence of this paragraph appears in *The Fall* unchanged. It is followed by: "Our fellow humans do just fine, with a little help from us." The general idea appears several times in the novel.

October 5[11]

Scenery in Rotterdam at night, its illuminated facades rising above the canals.

———

The Hague.

All these people packed together in a small span of houses and water, silently stuck to each other, the rain falling throughout the city, on and on, without a pause to breathe, the ugly, pouting little children directing the placid flow of cars and the beautiful [. . .][12] gates of the royal museum wash the pediment's opulent decorations while the rain continues to fall and a pianist on a tricycle [. . .][13] plays Chopin's Tristesse accompanied by a [. . .][14] violinist and a distinguished beggar collecting kindly given coins, oboles that make a soft sound and that are meant for the grimacing gods of Indonesia that can be seen in all the shop windows and that wander invisibly through Holland's air, populating the nostalgia of these dispossessed colonists. O Java, far distant island whose sons here serve coffee as the rain continues to fall, and in that rain-soaked air hangs the marvelous memory of a young girl on the brink of bottomless springs, the light of the tubercular, and the silence of Rembrandt's older brother, whose desireless eyes look out at the eternal country.

———

October 6.

It rains for days on end and the cold wind [. . .][15] the rain. It was over there in a freshly nickeled Rotterdam, in an Amsterdam always sopping; and here in The Hague, perched on bicycles with high handlebars like funerary swans circling the cold Vigver, between the fish market's live eels and the ugly

---

11. In October 1954, Camus was invited to give a talk in The Hague ("The Artist and His Times"). To Maria Casarès, he wrote: "I'm getting ready to leave, without much enthusiasm, as you might imagine, but happy all the same to find a little solitude. When I get back at the end of the week, I'll try to pull it together." Once he'd arrived, he wrote again, this time to say that Amsterdam had "completely seduced" him and that he regretted having to leave.

The handwriting in the next two entries is often hard to decipher in the original notebook, though Camus would go on to use many of the descriptions from these entries in *The Fall*, section 1.

12. Three illegible words.

13. One illegible word.

14. One illegible word.

15. Two illegible words.

windows displaying marvelous jewels, the color of the dead leaves pasted all over the earth and the smoked herrings that have long navigated in old gold seas. O Cipango, there and here [. . .][16] Holland, gentle Holland, where you learn the patience to die.[17]

———

Conversion to the serious. Seriousness is an accepted lie and recognized infirmity. For everything else, quiet sincerity.

———

Don Juan.
She: I always knew you didn't love me.
But I did love you.
You spoke to me and looked at me, sometimes past me.
He: I don't seduce, I adapt.

———

October 26.

The opposite of reaction isn't revolution but creation. The world is in a constant state of reaction, thus in constant danger of revolution. What defines progress, if such a thing exists, is that creators of all stripes are continually finding forms that triumph over the spirit of reaction and inertia, without revolution being necessary. When these creators are no longer to be found, revolution is inevitable.

———

According to Koestler, old Turkish law considered mitigating factors for a crime committed by [. . .].[18]

———

For me, the scent of honeysuckle is tied to Algiers. It drifted through the streets that led up to the high gardens where the young women awaited us. Grape vines, youth . . .

———

The white morning rose smells like water and pepper.

———

16. One illegible word.
17. The sentence given is conjectural; the handwriting is hard to make out in the original.
18. Two illegible words.

Julia.[19]

Last Act: J. I'm ugly

d'al: Yes.

———

Everything that, in me and in others, drags me down.

———

November 1st.

I often read that I'm an atheist and I hear people talk of my atheism. Yet such words mean nothing to me, they make no sense to me. I don't believe in God *and* I'm not an atheist.

———

As a creator, I gave life to death itself. That's all I had to do before dying.

———

Pavese: "We're idiots. We allow the little freedom the government allows us to be guzzled up by women."[20]

———

Rembrandt: fame until 1642, when he was 36. From then on, the long walk to solitude and poverty. Rare experience, and more meaningful than the banal one of the undiscovered artist. About such an experience, nothing has yet been said.

———

B.C: "Nature doesn't give such spiritual power to man for his own enjoyment. Nature entrusts it to him for a use greater than himself."

Id: "An authentic creator is organically subject to the law of pleasure."

———

Spengler says Russia's soul lies in a rebellion against Antiquity. True enough. See also Berdyaev: Russia has never had a Renaissance.

———

Text about Hébertot.[21] The great white sperm whale rests in the middle of the grotto. Using its teeth as filters, it lets only the plankton of tasty authors reach it.

———

19. The exchange here, for the project on Julie de Lespinasse, is between Julie and d'Alembert.

20. Cesare Pavese (1908–1950), Italian writer, translator, and antifascist, committed suicide August 1950, in part due to a failed relationship.

21. Director of the theater that bore his name and staged *Caligula* in 1945 and *The Just* in 1949.

Realism. Everybody's realistic. Nobody's a realist. In the end, it's not aesthetics that matter but inner disposition.

———

Literature in totalitarian countries doesn't die so much because it's controlled as because it's cut off from other literatures. Setting out without access to the whole of reality is a handicap for any artist.

———

November 7, 1954.

41 years old.

———

The Bacchae.

In Sicily. Present day. Small village near Palermo. Everything else follows suit.

Great works in preparation. In any case, there's more to be done. Ex: Don Juan, Faust, everything fits together.

———

Correct Rebel p. 225, 6th line (workers in place of monks)[22] and p. 229, 1st line.

———

Duperray letter. "The revolutionary syndicalists continue to do what they do best: search for reasons to separate over common principles."[23]

———

New title: A Puritan for our Times.[24]

———

22. The line reads: "[Ernest Jünger] had a vision of a 'technological world empire,' of 'an anti-Christian, technological religion,' whose followers and soldiers would have been the workers themselves, because—and here Jünger joins back up with Marx—by virtue of his human structure, the worker is universal." The only English translation of *The Rebel*, rendered from proof pages, reads "would have been the priests themselves. . . ."

23. Jean Duperray, author of *Fried Herring with Blood*, militant trade-unionist, and friend of Simone Weil.

24. One of the many titles Camus considered for *The Fall*.

November 24. 10:00 A.M.

Arrived in Turin this morning.[25] For several days, delight at the thought of rediscovering Italy, which I haven't seen since 1938, the last time I was here. The war, the resistance, *Combat*, and all those years of repulsive seriousness. Other travels, yes, but instructive, the kind about which the heart has nothing to say. It seemed my youth was awaiting me in Italy, and renewed strength, and lost light. I also came to escape that world (back home) that has for the past year been breaking me down cell by cell, maybe to save myself once and for all. In fact, by the time the train got moving yesterday, my delight was no longer as strong. Tired from the outset, and then the meeting with Grenier, during which I'd have liked us to speak freely and we weren't able to do so,[26] and F. didn't help to get the trip off to a good start either. During the night, however, between brief bouts of sleep, happiness arrived, still off in the distance.

At 7 o'clock this morning, the realization that we're in Italy. I give myself a shake and open the blinds: a countryside filled with snow and fog. It's snowing over all of Northern Italy. Alone in my compartment, a fit of laughter overtakes me. It's not cold, yet when we arrive at the station, the charming I.A.,[27] who's there waiting for me, claims she's freezing to death. With her lovely, hesitant French, her gentle, graceful little gestures (she reminds me of Maman), her cheeks rosy and cold like a little snow flower, she brings something of Italy back to me. The Italians on the train had already warmed my heart, those at the hotel soon would. A people I've always loved, who make my exile from the perpetual bad mood of the French evident.

From my hotel room, I can see Turin, snow steadily falling over it. I again laugh at my disappointment. Courage returns to me.

Turin beneath the snow and fog. In the Egyptian Museum, the mummies pulled from the sand without wrappings are curled up from the cold. I like these wide, spacious paved streets. A city built as much of space as of walls. I'm going to see the house at 6 Piazza Carlo Alberto where Nietzsche

25. Camus traveled to Italy at the invitation of the Italian Cultural Association. He gave talks ("The Artist and His Times") in Turin, Genoa, and Rome and met with friends such as Nicola Chiaramonte, Ignazio Silone, Alberto Moravia, and Carlo Levi. Though the next sentence says he was last in Italy in 1938, it was, in reality, in 1937.

26. The disappointment in attempted conversations with Jean Grenier runs throughout the notebooks, dating back to the earliest entries, and is also something that can be felt just below the surface of their correspondence.

27. Irma Antonetto, writer and founder of the Italian Cultural Association.

worked and then sunk into madness. I've never been able to read the account of Overbeck's arrival without crying, his entrance into Nietzsche's room, Nietzsche raving mad, throwing himself into Overbeck's arms and crying. Standing before the house, I try to think of him, he who I've always loved with affection as well as admiration, but it's in vain. I get a better sense of him in the city, which he loved, and I understand, despite the sky hanging low overhead, why he loved it.

———

Short Story. The concentration-camp prisoners elect a pope, choosing him from among those who have suffered most. They renounce the other one, the Roman, who lives in the luxurious Vatican. They call theirs *Father* even though he's one of the youngest there, they obey him completely, will die for him until he himself should die defending his sons (or if he declines death and decides to save himself instead, it'll be because he has others he has to protect and defend—and that's how it starts).[28]

———

November 25.

Hazy, gray day. I wander around Turin. Over the hill crowned with skull and crossbones. In the city, in the center of wide-open horizons, bronze horses rear up through the fog. Turin is a city of horses frozen mid-gallop, the city where Nietzsche, who'd gone mad, stopped a driver from beating his horse and then madly kissed its muzzle. Dinner Villa Camerana.

———

November 26.

Long walk on the hills of Turin. Surrounded by the snowy Alps, which rise into the sky and disappear in the fog. The air is brisk and fresh, humid and perfumed with autumn. The city below is covered in mist. Far from everything, tired and strangely happy. In the evening, a talk.[29]

———

28. Camus would use pieces of this entry in the closing pages of *The Fall*, where Clamence says that when he was held captive in Libya, his fellow inmates elected him pope.

29. Camus gave "The Artist and His Times" talk for the Italian Cultural Association, likely at the Teatro Reggio. Many of the details he records about Italy in these pages also appear in his November 25–December 12 letters to Maria Casarès, where they are at times described in greater detail, at times less.

November 27.

Depart for Genoa in the morning with I.A: strange little person, sharp, full of heart and determination, with a sort of thought-out renunciation that's surprising in someone so young. She wants to "laugh and regret." As regards religion, she believes in "indifferent love." A lot of things in common, obviously, with Maman, whom I think about with sadness. I always carry that grave, inconceivable death in my heart . . .

Rain and mist everywhere in Piedmont and Liguria. We travel through the mountains bordering the Ligurian coast, snowfields surrounding us. Four tunnels later and the snow disappears as the rain doubles down on those slopes cascading to the sea. Two hours after arriving, the talk. Dinner at the Palazzo Doria. The old marquise withered in all but eyes and heart. On leaving, I at last find myself walking in that Genoa I remember, thoroughly washed with rain. The black-and-white marbles glistening, the lights dripping down through the streets, the great boulevards well-tread.

———

From the 6th century through the year 1800, Europe's population never managed to exceed 180 million.

From 1800 to 1914, it rose from 180 million to 460 million!

———

Ortega y Gasset.[30] Wants to know to whom he speaks—for writing—

Distinguishes the corporation and the association.

Freedom and pluralism are the two dominant modes in Europe.

Philosopher and professor of philosophy, see p. 26—on true aristocracy, passion.

———

Humboldt.[31] For human beings to enrich and perfect themselves, a "variety of positions" are necessary. Maintaining this variety is the central effort of true liberalism.

———

30. Jose Ortega y Gasset (1883–1955), a Spanish philosopher whose work has sometimes been considered a precursor to existentialism. In his most famous and controversial book, *The Revolt of the Masses*—which Camus was reading at the time—Ortega y Gasset defends liberalism and meritocracy from the backwardness and barbarism he sees in the masses and expresses a fear of the "tyranny of the majority," while noting that the majority can come from any class background. Ortega y Gasset is critical of both the masses and bourgeois capitalism in its current form, and he expresses support for social-democratic reform.

31. Wilhelm von Humboldt (1767–1835), Prussian linguist, diplomat, and founder of the University of Berlin. Correspondent of Goethe and Schiller.

Today's Russia sees the triumph of individualism in its cynical form.

———

Ortega y Gasset. History: the eternal struggle between paralytics and epileptics.

———

Every society is based on aristocracy, because aristocracy, true aristocracy, sets high expectations for itself, and without such expectations every society would perish.

———

Ortega y Gasset. "A creative life implies a regimen of healthy living, of great nobility, of constant stimuli that excite the consciousness, and further, a creative life is an energetic life."[32]

———

How the narrow vicos[33] swarm with shadows. Tired and content.

———

November 28.

Long walk in Genoa. Captivating city, quite similar to the one I remembered. Superb monuments erupt in a tight corset of small streets teeming with life. Here, beauty radiates in everyday life, on any corner. A singer on a street corner improvises the latest scandals: a singing newspaper.

Small cloister of San Matteo. The wind blows sheets of rain against the large leaves of medlar trees. Brief instant of happiness. Now you have to change your life.[34]

Evening: depart for Milan in the rain. Arrive in the rain. What Stendhal loved here died long ago.

———

32. The quote comes from the end of chap. 14, sec. 4, of *The Revolt of the Masses*. In the authorized, anonymous English translation, it reads: "A creative life implies a regime of strict mental health, of high conduct, of constant stimulus, which keep active the consciousness of man's dignity. A creative life is energetic life, and this is only possible in one or other of these two situations: either being the one who rules, or finding oneself placed in a world which is ruled by someone in whom we recognize full right to such a function: either I rule or I obey."

33. Camus may mean *vicolo*, Italian for "alley."

34. To Maria Casarès, Camus wrote: "I think that, with a little luck, I'll find the strength to change my life here. For I have to change it, one way or another, and there's that misery I no longer want. Until then, I'm carrying Rome and its fountains in my heart."

November 29.

Last Supper—da Vinci is certainly at the start of Italian decadence.[35] Cloister of San Ambrogio. A talk. In the evening, I take the train to Rome, exasperated by the stupid social niceties that follow these talks. Unable to deal with more than a half-hour of such monkeying around. Sleepless night.

———

30

In the morning, the sun finally shines over the Roman countryside, faint but determined. Stupidly, tears come to my eyes. Rome. Another one of these hotels as luxurious and foolish as the people who keep them in business. I'll move tomorrow.[36] I see the Birth of Venus with N. Walk along the Villa Borghese and Pincio: everything is painted on the sky with a brush of few bristles. I sleep. Last talk. Free at last. Dinner with N., Silone, and Carlo Levi. Tomorrow will be good.

———

December 1st to the 3rd.

There are cities like Florence, some small Tuscan and Spanish cities, that carry a traveler along, supporting his every step and making each one lighter. Others, like New York, instantly weigh down on your shoulders, crushing you so that you have to learn, bit by bit, how to stand back up and see again.

That's how Rome weighs on you, but with a sensitive, light weight. You carry it on your heart like a corpus of fountains, gardens, and cupolas. You can breathe beneath them, a little oppressed, but strangely happy. This relatively small city that, seen from above, occasionally breaks out at the turning of a street, this sensitive, well-defined space breathes with the traveler and lives with him.

Moved from the hotel to a pension on the Villa Borghese. I have a balcony that extends out over the gardens, and the view, it pierces my heart every time I see it. After so many years in a city without light, of waking in the fog, between walls, I'm endlessly nourished by this line of trees and sky extend-

---

35. Leonardo da Vinci's *The Last Supper* is located in the dining hall at Santa Maria delle Grazie in Milan, Italy.

36. Likely the Grand Hotel Plaza on Via del Corso. N. refers to Nicola Chiaromonte.

ing from the Porta Pinciana to Trinità dei Monti, behind which Rome rolls out its cupolas and disorder.

Each morning when I step out onto that balcony, still a little drunk with sleep, the birdsong surprises me, reaches me in the depths of sleep, and touches a precise spot that in one fell swoop frees a sort of mysterious joy. The weather's been nice for two days now, the beautiful December light accentuating the rolled-up cypresses and pines in front of me.

Here I regret the black and stupid years I've lived in Paris. There's a conviction that I no longer want because it serves no one and brings me a hair's breadth from my own downfall.

The day before yesterday, in the truly ruined part of the Forum (near the Colosseum), not in that extravagant flea market of pretentious columns found beneath the Campidoglio, and then on the admirable Hill of Palatine, where nothing overwhelms the silence, the peace, the forever nascent and perfect world, there I began to find myself once more. That's what the great images of the past can do, when nature knows how to welcome them and extinguish the noise that sleeps inside them, they can rally hearts and energies, enabling them to better serve both present and future. You can feel it on the Via Appia, where, even though I'd arrived late in the afternoon, my heart was so full as I walked around that life could have left me then. But I knew that it would go on, that there's a strength in me that's moving forward, and that this pause would be useful for getting me there. (A year I haven't worked, haven't been able to work despite having ten different topics at hand, topics I know are worth exploring, but which I haven't been able to tackle—about a year now, and I haven't gone mad.) One could live well in this cloister, in this room where Tasso died.[37]

Squares in Rome. Piazza Navona. Sant'Ignazio and the others. They're yellow. The basin beneath the fountains has a pink tinge from the baroque spouting of water and stones. Once you've seen everything, or in any case seen everything you can see, ambling around with no particular *goal* in mind is a perfect happiness.

37. Torquato Tasso (1544–1595), Italian poet who seemed to suffer a form of schizophrenia in his later years.

In front of San Pietro in Montorio last night, at the foot of the silent riverbank where we were, there beneath its lights, Rome was like a harbor where the noise and movement went out.

———

Knowing that monumental beauty always involves servitude, that it is nevertheless beauty, and that you can't help but desire beauty and can't help but not desire servitude, is a strange, unbearable conviction; yet servitude remains no less unacceptable. Perhaps that's why I place the beauty of a landscape above all else: it's not paid for with any injustice and my heart is free in such a place.

———

December 3.

Superb morning in the Villa Borghese. The light of Algerian mornings flowing between thin pine needles and carving them out one by one. And the Berninis in the Gallery[38] brimming with blond light amuse me, delightful and disconcerting when grace triumphs, as it does in the highly surrealist Apollo and Daphne (as a form of art, Surrealism was initially a counteroffensive to the Baroque), hideous when grace disappears, as it does in the appalling Truth Unveiled by Time. A painter, too, and vivid (Portraits).

Correggio's Danae, and especially Venus Blindfolding Cupid, by Titian, painted at 90 years old and of timeless youth.

The Caravaggios, not the ones in St. Louis of the French,[39] seen in the afternoon, certainly superb in the way they contrast violence and a muted depth of light. *Before Rembrandt.* Especially The Calling of St. Matthew: superb. C. points out the recurring theme of youth and old age. Moravia had already told me about the type of person Caravaggio was: he committed several crimes, was robbed fleeing Tuscany by boat, and was then thrown on a beach where he died, crazy (1573–1610). Moravia also told me the true story of Cenci,[40] about whom he wants to write a play. Beatrice is buried under the altar of St. Louis of the French. Riots in Rome, the French Revolution. A French sansculotte painter takes part in the sacking of St. Louis of the

---

38. The Borghese Gallery in Rome.

39. The national French church of Rome, located in the heart of the city. Caravaggio was commissioned to produce paintings for the church's interior.

40. Beatrice Cenci (1577–1599) was at the center of a scandalous murder trial in Italy. She was eventually beheaded alongside most of her family.

French. The tombs are opened. Beatrice's skeleton is there, her severed skull resting in the center of her body. The painter takes it and leaves, playing with it like a ball. This is the last image related to the terrible history of Beatrice Cenci.

At the end of the afternoon, I head back to Janiculum. San Pietro in Montorio. Yes, this hill is my favorite place in Rome. High in the gentle sky, bands of starlings light as smoke flit about in all directions, cross, scatter, and then gather together and dive toward the pines, which they skim atop before returning to the sky. When we head back down with N., the felled starlings are there in the trees, the plane trees of Trastevere's Viale del Re, so incredibly many of them the trees buzz and crackle, covered with more birds than leaves. As evening falls, a deafening chirping blankets the sounds of this working-class neighborhood, merges with the crackling trams, and causes all the laughing heads to turn up toward those enormous swarms of feathers and leaves.

The tall, brown-haired Roman who looks after me at the pension has a gentle, noble face and carries himself with a proud ease. Short story. Love with painter. And all the nobility on his side.

Write BAROQUE text about Rome.

December 4

Morning. Barberini Palace. Caravaggio's Narcissus, and especially the Madonna attributed to P. della Francesca, seem like they belong more to the wispy manner of Signorelli. Admirable in any case.

Lunch with Moravia and N at Tivoli and a long afternoon in Hadrian's Villa, a perfect place. A superb day, it's true, with a rounded sky and not a cloud in sight, the light pouring out equally over the Villa's magnificent cypresses and tall pines. High sections of the wall, the ruins, receive this even light over their honeycomb surface and in turn drip honeyed light from their hives. Here, I'm better able to see the difference between the light in Rome and the light in other places, such as Florence, for example, where it's more diffuse, silvery, and, in short, spiritual. The light in Rome, on the other hand, is rounded, shining, and supple. It makes you think of bodies, the opulence of joyous flesh, of life well lived. Faraway places even more succulent. Birdsong among the ruins. Faced with this perfection, a curious, happy feeling that everything's been said.

Dinner Piovene.[41] After thirty or so conversations, I'm beginning to get an idea of what's really going on here. Not opinions but factions. Few liberals, poverty, making use of it, and the gradual creep of a certain inertia.

At forty years old, you no longer go around shouting about evils, you recognize them and struggle against them to the best of your ability. Then you can get busy creating without having forgotten anything.

In The Last Judgment's movement of ascension, to the right of the altar, Michelangelo had to make the bodies heavy with muscles so as to give the impression of overwhelming lightness. All the lighter because of the heaviness. This is the crux of art.

In the Borgia apartments Pinturicchio's Rhetoric carries a sword.

The heart aches a little at the thought that Julius II had some of Piero della Francesca's (and others) frescoes destroyed so that Raphael could paint his *bedrooms*; what price have we paid for the superb Liberation of St. Peter?

Caravaggio's Deposition from the Cross. We don't see the Cross; certainly a great painter.

———

December 6.

Gray day. Fever. I stayed in the room. Saw Moravia in the evening.

———

Novel.

The First Man retraces his background to discover his secret: he isn't the first. Every man is the first man, no one is. That's why he throws himself at his mother's feet.[42]

———

41. Guido Piovene (1907–1974), antifascist journalist and novelist and author of *The Cold Stars*.

42. This entry, which Camus initially wrote on the following notebook page and then circled and drew an arrow pointing back to its current placement, is the first time the title *The First Man* appears in any of the original, handwritten notebooks. All previous occurrences of the title were added at a later date.

December 7.

Depart with Nicola and Francesco. Roman countryside. F. is so beautiful and so far removed from everything without ceasing to be present and human. The village of Circe.[43] Arrive in Naples. Lunch in Pozzuoli at a restaurant that's Padovani's twin. In Naples, a diluvian rain that raises my fever. In the evening, the sky clears.

December 8.

Wake up with a serious fever. Last night I couldn't finish these notes. Still, I took a long walk in the "Barrios" behind Rue Santa Lucia. They're the slums behind the Champs-Élysées. Through an open door you see three children in a single bed, with their father, too, sometimes, not at all embarrassed to be so exposed. So much snapping linen gives Naples a feeling of perpetual festivity, which comes, after all, from the lack of linen, from the need to wash it every day. These are the standards of poverty.[44] In the evening, N.F. We head out in a damp carrozzella[45] that smells of leather and dung. Men's friendships always combine the perfect ingredients. N. takes us to the Porta Capuana neighborhood. The main street climbs upward. Lamps with lampshades are set out on all the balconies, giving the terrible poverty an air of extraordinary festivity. There's some sort of procession in front of the church. Standards wave above a tightly packed crowd trampling through a thick mud of cabbage debris left behind by the morning market. Firecrackers everywhere. In all the saints' backsides. The Virgin announces herself with a couple of real firecrackers. In one of the windows, a madman with an empty stare mechanically lights dozens of firecrackers, one off the other, throwing them out into the crowd, where the children below do a Sioux dance around them until they explode. The hospitality industry of the poor. They think big. The Escorial of poverty . . .

December 8.

All day in bed with a fever that won't break. In the end, I won't be able to go to Paestum. Return to Rome at the first sign of improvement, then to

43. Homer, Virgil, Strabo, and Pliny mention Mount Circeo, in the south of Lake Sabaudia, by the name Circe Island. The village at the base is also called Circeo.

44. "Standards" is used here in the sense of heraldic flags.

45. The word, in Italian in the original notebook, refers here to a cab or horse-drawn carriage.

Paris. That's all there is to it. There's something between the Greek temples and me. Something always intervenes at the last minute to keep me from going to them.[46]

No real mystery this time, though. This exhausting year has brought me to my knees. The hope of recovering my strength and getting back to work was purely sentimental. Instead of running toward a light I can barely see, I'd be better off taking a year to rebuild my health and will. But to do that I'd have to free myself a little from all the things that overwhelm me.

These are the thoughts of bed and fever and a cloistered traveler with Naples surrounding him. But they're true thoughts. Fortunately, I have a view of the sea from my bed.

F.'s painter friend, extremely ignorant, having to illustrate the Passion of St. Matthew for a radio program, depicts a saint surrounded by pretty women and scornful angels.

December 9.

When I wake the fever is gone. But I'm stiff and groggy. Still, I decide to leave as planned (and as always, I draw strength from recognizing that things could be worse: prisoner, etc.). The sun is beautiful as we set out. Sorrento (and the delightful Cocumella garden), Amalfi, where we stop for lunch, is a little too ornate, and then I drive to relieve F., who is tired, and as we arrive in Paestum, after having driven through an industrial region then a curious landscape that makes us think of Limbo (tall reeds, skeletal trees plucked bare), the sun begins to set. Here the heart falls silent.

(Later.) I want to try to capture our late-afternoon arrival. We were welcomed at the inn near the ruins by a good old-fashioned room with three beds and huge, whitewashed walls, rustic but absolutely clean. A dog followed me around. As the sun set, we scaled the ramparts, the gates being closed, to reach the field of ruins. The light coming from the nearby sea was still blue, but the hills facing the sea were already black. When we reached the front of the Temple of Poseidon the crows, already asleep, rose up in an extraordinary tumult of wings and caws, flew around the temple, came back to rest on all four corners, then took off again, as if to salute the admirable apparition before our eyes, a being made of stone but alive and unforgettable.

46. Camus had planned to travel to Greece in the summer of 1939, but the war intervened. He was finally able to make the trip in April 1955.

The hour, the black flight of crows, the occasional bit of birdsong, the space between the sea and the hills, a person holds onto such true, warm wonders, all of which, amid my fatigue and heightened emotion, set me a hair's breadth from tears. Then endless rapture, when all falls silent.

Evening, silence, crows, like the birds in Lourmarin, and the cat, my tears, music.

Morning in Tipasa, dew on the ruins. The most youthful freshness in the world on that which is oldest. There lies my faith and, in my opinion, the principle of art and life.

———

December 10.

Walked out to the beach last night, between the reeds, ramparts, and buffaloes. The vast, muted sound of the sea gradually increasing. The beach, the lukewarm water there beneath night's gray and luminous sky. On the way back, it rained a little and the sound of the sea faded behind us. The buffaloes took gentle steps, then bowed their heads, motionless as the night. Contentment.

After having looked out my window at the temples in the night, I go to sleep. This room I like so much, with its thick, bare walls, is glacial. Cold all night. I open the windows. It's raining over the ruins. An hour later, as we get ready to leave, the sky is blue, the light fresh and magnificent.

Endless amazement before this temple, its enormous columns of pink sponge and golden cork, its airy and ethereal weight, its inexhaustible presence. Other birds have come and mixed with the crows, but the latter still cover the temple in a black veil of batting wings and raucous caws. The temple grounds are blanketed with the fresh scent of small heliotropes.

Sounds: the sound of water, of dogs, of a distant Vespa.

It's not the melancholy of ruined things that makes the heart ache but the hopeless love of what lasts eternally in eternal youth: love of the future.

Still in the ruins between the hills and the sea. Difficult to tear myself away from such places, the first since Tipasa where I've felt my entire being let go.

———

December 10.

Continuing. We do leave, however, and a couple of hours later, Pompeii. Interested, of course, but never touched. The Romans are sometimes refined, never civilized. Lawyers and soldiers who we confuse, God knows why, with the Greeks. They are the first, the true, destroyers of the Greek sensibility. Alas, defeated Greece didn't defeat them in turn, for though they borrowed the themes and forms of great art from Greece, they never achieved anything more than cold approximations, which it would have been better they didn't make, so that Greek innocence and splendor could reach us without intermediary. Compared to Hera's Temple in Paestum, all the antiquity strewn across Rome and Italy crumbles, and with it the facade of false grandeur. My heart has always instinctively known this, and has never been set aflutter by a single Latin poem (not even Virgil, admired, not loved) but has always ached for the flash of a tragic or lyric stanza from Greece.

On the way back from this precious Buchenwald that is Pompeii, a taste of ashes and growing exhaustion. We alternate driving with F. and at 9:00 P.M. I arrive in Rome completely worn out.

December 11.

All day, or almost, in bed. Steady state of fever that takes away my desire to do anything. Build my health back up at all costs. I need my strength. I don't ask that life be easy, only that I be able to face up to it if it's difficult. That I be able to govern if I want to go where I'm going. Will leave Tuesday.

December 12.

A newspaper falls in my lap. The Parisian farce I'd forgotten about. The joke that is the Goncourt. Given to The Mandarins this time.[47] It seems I'm the hero. In truth, the author took a situation (director of a newspaper born out of the Resistance) and made the rest up, thoughts, feelings, and actions. Better still: the dubious acts of Sartre's life are generously heaped on my back. Aside from that, garbage, but not intentionally, for it comes as natural as breathing.

Improved state. Gray day. Rain falls over Rome, its well-washed cupolas weakly gleaming. Lunch at F.G's. Evening, alone, fever past.

---

47. Simone de Beauvoir's novel *The Mandarins*, a transparent roman à clef about a group of French intellectuals coming to terms with life post–World War II, won France's prestigious Goncourt Prize on the second round of voting. In personal letters and conversations, Camus expressed his bitterness and anger about the book, but when asked by Czesław Miłosz why he didn't respond publicly, Camus said: "You don't discuss things with a sewer drain."

December 13.

Caravaggio again. Santa Maria del Popolo. Also, Rome's sadness, its streets too high, too tight. That's why the squares are so beautiful here: they deliver a release, and the Baroque triumphs over the Roman. Like those Roman couples frozen in stone who share nothing in common other than how straight they stand. The twilight slips into the palace and crumbles its proud facades. In the evening, M. tells me about Brancati and his death.[48] Dinner alone.

December 14. Departure.

Existentialism. When they accuse themselves, you can be sure it's always to condemn others. Judge-penitents.[49]

In Luke, true betrayal begins, a betrayal that buries the desperate cries of Jesus's agony.

M., to whom I say that certain roles require only virtuosity from the actor, that the actor can put their craft to the test in these roles, their mastery, tells me that none of that interests her, that the only characters she likes to play are those she can marry, can inhabit, and through which she can feel she's living another life. She concludes with: "I like acting because I'm a romantic."

Morals. Don't take what you don't want (difficult).[50]

I've always hoped to become better. I've always been determined to do what it takes. If I've done it, that's another question.

For me, wasn't marriage a more sophisticated sensual affair? It was that.

If I blossom, she wilts. She can only live if I'm wilting. In this way, we're two opposite poles of psychology.

---

48. Vitaliano Brancati (1907–1954), Italian antifascist writer whose novel *Don Juan in Sicily* was later adapted into a successful film, had recently died after surgery.

49. The first appearance in these pages of the term "judge-penitent," Clamence's self-proclaimed profession in *The Fall*. After the book was published, Camus recorded some of his reactions to its reception and placed them in a folder alongside other materials related to the book. Among these notes, one sheet in particular seems to have been written out with care. It begins: "Those who accuse themselves to be able to better accuse others. We're all guilty of this, of giving ourselves the means or illusions of dominance. That doesn't ring any bells? But we live among the judge-penitents. You have only to read the weekly papers or specialized journals to see it."

A version of the second paragraph of this entry also appears in *The Fall*.

50. In *The Fall*, Clamence says: "Soon the words come without you having to think about them, they become a reflex: then one day you find yourself in a situation where you can take without really desiring. Believe me, for some people, not taking what you don't desire is the most difficult thing in the world. For some, at least."

The opposite of the underground man:[51] the man without resentment. But the catastrophe is the same.

This world only writhes as it does because, like a cut worm, it has lost its head. It's looking for its aristocrats.

The La Martinière: the white boat that transported convicts to Cayenne—and which stopped in Algiers to load up on new cargo (my article, on a day of torrential rain—the barge brimming with shaved convicts—the interior, the two cages, etc.—The same trip I made but in a comfortable cabin)—A récit?[52]

The First Man. Ambition made him laugh. He didn't want to have, he didn't want to possess, he wanted to be. For that, only persistence.

The moment someone's personal life is thrown out in the open and explained to so many people, it becomes a public life and it's pointless to try to keep it as it was.

That (empty) life of cities and those unbearable days without love.

For the past ten years, it's what's interested me most in the world.

The First Man. "And thinking about all the things he'd done without really wanting to do them, things that others had wanted or that he'd done simply because others had done such things in similar circumstances, all of it nevertheless added up to make a life, one he shared with all those who end up dying for not having been able to live the way they really wanted to live."

The First Man. Theme: vigor. "I'll prevail, but without compromising. Compromise, hypocrisy, base desire for power, it's all too easy. But I'll truly prevail, without trying to possess or have."

The only law of being is to be and to give it everything you've got.

Jonas. The crazy concierge (her son died): "Oh, Monsieur Jonas, you understand, of course, don't you?" Then two seconds later: "Don't go see Monsieur Jones—he beats his wife and children."

The First Man. Theme: friendship.

---

51. The reference is to Dostoyevsky's novel *Notes from the Underground*.

52. For the "article" referenced, see p. 87n69. For the term *récit*, see p. 33n56.

M. not highly cultured but making a solid entry into great works. Incapable of lingering in mediocrity, even out of laziness, and instinctively discerning greatness.

The First Man. Theme: anxiety (cf. Connaissance de l'homme, Adler, p. 156). Characters' main motivation: the desire for power, psychologically speaking.[53]

Don Faust (or Doctor Tenorio):[54] "I've never asked anything for what I've given, I've never spoken of what I've done, I don't hold myself in very high esteem, as I've never quite given enough, and the first thing on my mind is everything I've never given. But today I need a little of what I've given, I need other people to come, those to whom I've never refused my hand or my help, let them speak now and bear witness on my behalf. *Silence all around*. Well then, I'll speak. This one . . ." (rebel text).

First Man. With Simone. He has to wait a year to have her. Then the escape. She cries and that sets everything in motion.

Everything comes from my congenital inability to be a bourgeois, a happy bourgeois. The slightest hint of stability in my life terrifies me.

Ultimately, my great advantage over frauds and cheats is that I'm not afraid to die. I'm horrified and repulsed by death. But I'm not afraid to die.

Leftist intellectuals' betrayal. If their true goal is to preserve the revolutionary principles of the U.S.S.R. while progressively correcting its perversions, what reason would the Russian government have to renounce its totalitarian methods if it knows from the outset that they'll always be excused. In truth, only outspoken opposition from Western leftists can make that government consider such things, supposing that it can or wants to do so. But in truth, even our intellectuals' betrayal can be explained by something other than foolishness.

---

53. Alfred Adler's *Understanding Human Nature* appeared in French in 1949. Camus's page references are to that edition, published by Payot.

54. Another iteration of Camus's long-planned play, this time combining the ideas of Christopher Marlowe's *Doctor Faustus* and José Zorrilla's *Don Juan Tenorio*. Themes explored in *The Fall* can also be seen emerging in this passage.

Why should weakness in the face of pleasure be cause for more guilt than weakness in the face of pain. The latter sometimes causes incomparable devastation.

———

Don Faust. Scene I or prologue. Faust asks to know everything and have everything. "Then I'll grant you the power of seduction," the Devil says. And Faust becomes Don Juan.

Last scene. Time to pay up. "Let's get to it." No, the Devil says, I have to take you against your will or you'll die a normal death. "A normal death it is then" (here a male Chorus welcomes the hero among them—Better late than never).

The island complex of Russia and the communists (cf. Adler, Connaissance de l'homme, p. 154).[55]

In N.R.F.: dialogue (questions, answers) or imaginary letter[56] about Actuelles.

———

Novel. "The night didn't go so well: at the concert, he'd applauded after the third movement thinking the symphony was over, only to learn from the forceful, reproachful shushing that there were four movements. The look on his neighbors' faces, heavy with recent rhapsody and sudden scorn, still haunted him."

One of the short stories in the French style (Jonas).

55. Adler's work seems to have had its greatest influence on *The Fall,* even though Camus initially makes note of *Understanding Human Nature* in connection with *The First Man.* Several of the stories Adler tells on and around the pages Camus cites above would go on to appear in very similar fashion in *The Fall.* Adler's "island complex," for example, relates the story of a young man whose friend falls into the water and begins to drown, but rather than jumping in to try to save him, the man just watches the friend go under.

56. On several occasions, Camus employed "imaginary letters" as a literary technique, first in "Letter to a Young Englishman on the State of Mind of the French Nation," printed in the December 23, 1939, edition of *Le soir républicain,* then he sketched a "Letter to a Man Without Hope" here in these pages, and, most well-known, his series *Letters to a German Friend,* which were written for an underground newspaper and published in English in the collection *Resistance, Rebellion, and Death.*

Flooding of the Seine. During the night, a never before heard noise from the river.

Don Juan. The atheistic moralist finds faith. As a result, *everything* is permitted because *someone* can absolve what can't be forgiven by man. From this, generous libertinism crowned with living faith.

The desire to create is so strong that those who are incapable of doing so choose communism, which provides them with a wholly collective creation.

[. . .][57]

Theater. Timon—Possessed—Julie—Farce—Press—Bacchae.

Dante allows for neutral angels in the quarrel between Satan and God. He slips them into the vestibule to his Hell. III 37.[58]

January 26, 1955, Paris.[59]

My Dear Ravard.

My current silence is a personal matter. It involves too much of my own life to be able to explain it. But you'll be happy to know that if I had spoken, I wouldn't have said what you were hoping for, I wouldn't have made anyone happy. In any case, the cause that concerns you doesn't lack for appointed lawyers (I admit, however, that they haven't been very thorough in the matter at hand). But your letter gives me the opportunity to say something that I've

---

57. In the handwritten notebook, there are three illegible words here. The list that follows reprises Camus's plans for the theater: the previously mentioned translation of Shakespeare's *Timon of Athens* (a play thematically linked to Camus's own *Life of the Artist* and "Jonas"); the adaptation of Dostoyevsky's *The Possessed*; the long-planned, never-written plays about Julie de Lespinasse and the Bacchantes; the composed but never performed *The Philosophers' Farce*; and the *Comedy About the Press / Critics' School* play sketched earlier in these pages.

58. In *The Fall*, Clamence says: "We have neither the energy that comes from evil, nor the energy that comes from good. Do you know Dante? Really? Hot damn. So then, you know Dante allows for neutral angels in the quarrel between God and Satan. And he places them in Limbo, a sort of vestibule to his Hell. We are in that vestibule, my dear friend."

The reference is to Dante's *Inferno*, canto 3: "'This wretched state of being is the fate of those sad souls who lived a life but lived it with no blame and with no praise. / They are mixed with that repulsive choir of angels neither faithful nor unfaithful to their God, who undecided stood but for themselves. / Heaven, to keep its beauty, cast them out, but even Hell itself would not receive them, for fear the damned might glory over them" (trans. Mark Musa).

59. This letter, ostensibly a response to questions sent to Camus by a Mr. Claude Ravard, was inserted into the notebook. It is written on *NRF* letterhead.

wanted to say to you for a long time. Namely, that in the great controversy cutting the twentieth century in two, you have already chosen.

You know, for example, that East Germany long ago rearmed and that a number of former Nazi generals are operating there, just as they are in the West. The USSR has repeatedly recognized Germany's right to have national forces. Of this, you say nothing. You're okay with rearmament so long as it's carried out under the supervision of the USSR; within a Western framework, you reject it. And so it goes with everything. If worst comes to worst (ask yourself) you'll accept the transformation of France into a people's democracy under the protection of the Red Army (and I'd remind you that I am the one who defended the communists against any "Atlantization" of domestic policy). Every time you spoke or wrote to me about these issues, your implicit opinion was obvious, your indignation sincere only in the case of Rosenberg-type crimes,[60] whereas a sort of doubt-filled silence took over you as soon as it came to the suppression, courtesy of the communist regime, of a workers' revolt in Germany (this last point is important and seems to me a sad yet clear and decisive test of the attitude of leftist intellectuals).

In my opinion, then, you've chosen. And since you've chosen, it's only natural that you would join the Communist Party. I won't fault you for doing so. I have no contempt for militant communists, though I believe them to be making a fatal mistake. I do have contempt, an abundance of contempt, for intellectuals who are intellectuals without actually being so, who act as secular priests murdering us with their pseudo-agony, while allowing themselves a clear conscience at the expense of militant workers.

So then, once and for all, do what you want to do and come to terms with who you are. Then you'll see. You're constantly comparing two things, one of which you know and judge, that is the society in which we live, and the other which you don't. The Communist Party won't help you understand a people's democracy—it's far from being one—but it will help you understand communism, of which you know very little. If you find peace in it, a rule to live by, all the better. If not, at least you'll have gained a true understanding of the question.

So that there can be no mistake about it, I'll say again what I believe. German rearmament must be condemned in both cases, otherwise the whole

60. In 1953, under questionable circumstances, Julius and Ethel Rosenberg were convicted and executed for espionage in the US, while a budding workers' revolt in East Berlin was crushed by Soviet tanks. Camus's response here recalls his much earlier exchange with Jean Grenier about Communism.

thing's a charade. If I continue to find sending aid to Franco, or the "fruit-bearing" policy in South America, or colonialism, inexcusable, I also reject the fruit-bearing policy grafted on France courtesy of Russia and its unconditional supporter, the French Communist Party. Generally speaking, I remain opposed, fundamentally so, to the initiatives and methods of what I've called Cesarean Socialism.

These are things you know, of course. My books have simply meant a lot less to you than you say. Your fondness for me was more genuine. But a person who enters into religion also loves his friends and mother, and yet he abandons them. And you better believe you're entering a church the second you choose an orthodoxy like that of the Communist Party. Have no doubt about it. Instead, recognize in your heart that the communist temptation is, for an intellectual, the same sort of thing as religious temptation. There's nothing shameful about it, so long as you faithfully submit to it with full knowledge of the facts. As for me, you still have, even from a distance, my friendship. I ask only that if you follow through with your project, when you hear that I am, objectively speaking, as they say, a dreadful fascist, don't try to deny it, which would never work, try only not to believe it. Good luck, from the bottom of my heart, and please believe in my best wishes.

Albert Camus

February 17

Arrival in Algiers.[61] From high up in a plane skirting the coast, the city is like a handful of glittering stones tossed along the sea. The garden at the Hotel St. Georges. O welcoming night to which I finally return and which welcomes me as in times gone by: faithfully.

---

61. On September 9, 1954, a 6.7 magnitude earthquake ravaged Orléansville in northern Algeria. Over a thousand people died, and at least three thousand more were injured. The US Geological Survey called it "one of the world's deadliest earthquakes." The cost of rebuilding ran into the millions, and the destruction was so extensive that when the city was rebuilt—and in recognition of the then-ongoing Algerian War—it was given a new name, El Asnam (now Chlef). Camus hadn't been planning a trip to Algeria so close to leaving for Greece, but he wanted to take part in a book signing alongside other North African writers to raise money for the rebuilding.

February 18

Beauty of Algiers in the morning. Jasmine in the garden of St. Georges. Breathing it in fills me with joy, with youth.

Descent on the city, fresh and spacious. The sea glittering in the distance. Happiness.

François' death, crippled. Sent home from the clinic with tongue cancer. Dying alone in his hovel, vomiting blood all over the wall while slamming his fist against that thick, soiled wall separating him from his neighbors.

———

19

Not a single armchair at home. A handful of basic chairs. Always like this. Never neglect or comfort.

Visit the merchants in Belcourt. Three dead. The Massons. Marthe. Alexandrine. Juliette. Zinzin (protruding ears, contortionist, singer at the Alcazar cinema).

———

First Man

What year was Papa born?

I don't know. I was four years older than him.

And what year were you born?

I don't know. Look in the family record book.

OK, well, his family abandoned him. How old was he then?

"I don't know. Oh, he was so young. His sister left him. How old was his sister? I don't know."

"And his brothers? He was the youngest—no, the second."

"But his brothers were too young to take care of him."

"Yes, that must be the reason."

"They had no other option."

Apprenticed at sixteen years old as an agricultural laborer at his sister's in-laws. They work him hard.

"He didn't want to see them anymore. He'd had enough."

Id. He fights for the Arab cause. He and his wife are caught in an anti-French riot. He kills her to spare her from being raped but he survives. He's tried and convicted.

Or: I fought twenty years for them and the day of their liberation they killed my mother.

Id. X's suicide. St Germain-des-Prés. Friends of Méphisto.[62] Marinella. Drunkenness. Jean-Pierre insults X: "You succeed at everything. You disgust me."

20.

Tipasa. Rain and sun. Absinthe plants soaked with water. Streams of morning light on the dew-covered ruins. The same emotion, always new.

How lucky to have been born into the world on the hills of Tipasa, and not in St Étienne or Roubaix. Recognize my luck and accept it with gratitude.

21.

Radiant day. In the distance, the sea and sky sparkle and meld. As every morning, the garden and the scent of jasmine, and today the birds rejoicing.

22.

Hazy.

23.

Awakened by sun flooding my bed. The day like a crystal cup overflowing with a bottomless blue and golden light.

24.

Orléansville.[63] In the morning, the mountains carve out a delicate cyclamen petal. In Orléansville proper, tents and reconstruction: the Wild West.

---

62. Cellar club in Saint-Germain-des-Prés run by a Frenchman originally from Algeria.

A more complete version of this entry appears in *The First Man* folders: "St-German-des-Prés. Suicide. Nights at Méphisto. Marinella. In his drunkenness, Jean-Pierre Vivet insults J: 'You succeed at everything. You disgust me.'" Jean-Pierre Vivet wrote film reviews, humor pieces, and trial reports for *Combat*; later, he would be the first to write a graduate thesis on Camus. J. most likely refers to *The First Man*'s protagonist, Jacques Cormery.

63. Jean de Maisonseul, an old friend of Camus's, was director of the Urban Planning Service in Algiers at the time, and he took Camus to see the aftermath of the earthquake. The building of a youth recreation center, later to be named the Albert Camus Youth Sports Center, took on a some-

The team of young architects avoid despondency because they can see the future city.

25.

R.U.A.[64] Happiness of that simple friendship I lived.

26.

When the old queen gives birth to the young queens, they kill her or drive her out. And on the edge of the hive, she starves to death.

This ridiculous dance of love and its abominable demands, thanks to which the weak and the vulgar help each other to thrive and be noticed.[65]

April 26.

Depart from Paris. Heartbroken and emptied of all joy by F. The Alps. And the islands slowly come out one by one to meet us on the sea: Corsica, Sardinia, and off in the distance, Elba and Calabria. Cephalonia and Ithaca are almost invisible in the twilight. Then the coast of Greece, though at night, the muscular hand of the Peloponnese becomes a dark, mysterious continent covered in snowdrop petals, its snowy peaks glittering here and there. A few stars in the still-lit sky and then a crescent moon. Athens.

---

what symbolic air, as it was around this time that Camus, along with architect Louis Miquel, Roland Simounet, and Jean de Maisonseul, founded a Committee for a Civil Truce in Algeria. During the planning stages for the new center, Camus and Miquel corresponded about layout ideas for an "Elizabethan theater." The center wasn't completed until April 1961, just over a year after Camus died, and its opening became a sort of homage to Camus. In 1963, after Algerian Independence had been won, the center was renamed in honor of Larbi Tebessi. In the May 14, 1955, edition of *L'Express*, Camus would write an article extolling the virtues of Orléansville. And in the unfinished pages of *The First Man*, Camus left himself a note to "bring Michel back during the earthquake in Orléansville."

64. The Racing University of Algiers—where, in his youth, Camus had been a soccer goalie—held a reception in his honor.

65. *La parade*, translated above as "dance," can also refer specifically to a "mating dance," as well as to a "charade," or making a show of something, and to the transparent translation "parade." At the end of the sentence, *à vivre et à paraître*, given above as "to thrive and be noticed," literally means to "live and appear." See Camus's earlier comments on "appearing" (p. 53n99).

27.

At daybreak, wind, clouds, and sun. A few errands. My charming 21-year-old translator, with her adorable freshness (I told you I was close to the hotel, but it wasn't true, and I ran the whole way so I wouldn't be late, and that's why I'm out of breath), wins me over, and I adopt her.

Acropolis. The wind's chased away all the clouds, and the whitest, most intense light falls from the sky. Throughout the morning, a strange feeling of having been here for years, of being at home even, not really bothered by the difference in language. The feeling redoubles on the way up to the Acropolis when I realize I'm going "as a neighbor," without any emotion.

At the top, it's another story. The 11:00 A.M. light falls full-strength on the temples and the stone flooring that the wind seems to have also stripped to the bone, bounces, and breaks into a thousand scorching, white swords. The light digs into your eyes, makes them well with tears, enters your body with a painful quickness, empties it, opening it in a sort of physical violation that simultaneously cleanses it.

As you get used to it, your eyes gradually open and the extravagant (yes, that's what strikes me here, the extraordinary daring of this classicism) beauty of the place is welcomed into a purified being, exposed to the creosote of light.

Then the poppies, a dark red I've never seen before, one of them growing directly from bare rock, all on its own, the [. . .],[66] the mauves, marked by perfect vantage points, space all the way out to the sea. On the Erechtheion, the second Kore statue's face, the third's bent leg . . . [67]

Here you have to fight off the idea that perfection was reached then and that the world's been in decline ever since. But the idea ends up weighing on your heart. You have to fight it off once more, and then again and again. We want to live, and to believe such an idea is to die.

Afternoon, Hymettus, a violet-mauve color. Penteli.

7:00 P.M. A talk.[68] Dinner in a tavern in the old quarter.

———

66. One illegible word.

67. The south porch of the Erechtheion, a sacred temple on the Acropolis, featured a roof held aloft by six maidens, now known as Caryatids, then called Korai.

68. Camus gave "The Artist and His Times" talk at Parnassus Hall.

28.

Morning. With M.L.[69] Daphni. Clearly Byzantine, for sure. . . . The place is charming. A lot of imagination is needed in Eleusis. But the countryside before and after Eleusis is quite beautiful. In the temple, two routes lead to the sanctuary, the second veering off so that everything would be hidden from the uninitiated's sight.

Vital importance of what I know about Eleusis. Expand on this.

Some admirable pieces at the museum.

Lunch at the embassy. Tiempo perdido.[70]

Afternoon. Agora. Theseion.[71] Areopagus. In the Agora's small museum, statues from Heraklion: Athena, Hercules. Hercules is gnarled and hard beneath the flowery honeysuckles that cover him. Then I climb up on the Hill of the Muses. The sun, low on the horizon, hasn't yet reached the point when its red color etches it perfectly in the clear sky. But it's no longer at full strength. It's wasting away, losing its form. A subtle honey escapes its wavering circumference, spills out over the sky, gilds the hills and the Acropolis, and covers the scattered city blocks that extend to the four corners of the horizon, to the sea, with a soft and unrivaled splendor.

I head back down just in time for my controversial lecture.[72] After two hours of answering a host of questions, I leave exhausted. Dinner in Piraeus with Marguerite Liberaki. A curious person, secretive and bleak, with sudden bursts of life and laughter.

29.

Morning. National Museum. It contains all the world's beauty. I knew I'd find the Korai touching, but the wonderment they've left me with is still going strong. They let me visit the basement where they'd put some of them during the war to protect them from the invasion and destruction. And there in the basement where history tossed them, they were still smiling beneath the dust and straw covering them, and that smile of theirs, more than twenty-five centuries on, still warms, informs, and encourages. The funerary steles, too,

69. Marguerite Liberaki (pen name of Margarita Lymperaki), Greek novelist and playwright. "Daphni" refers to the eleventh-century Daphni Monastery near Athens.

70. *Tiempo perdido* (lost time) is written in Spanish in the original manuscript.

71. Known today as the Temple of Hephaestus.

72. The Greek-French Cultural Union had invited Camus to give a talk on "The Future of European Civilization."

with their repressed sorrow. On a black-and-white lekythos, an inconsolable dead man can't resign himself to never seeing the sun and sea again. Such perfection leaves me a little drunk and unhappy as I exit.

Then I'm on my way to Sounion. The midday light is still a bit clouded, an invisible mist suspended in it, but I admire the wide-open spaces and the vastness of these landscapes, even so reduced. As we get closer to Sounion, the light becomes fresher, brighter. Then on the Cape, at the foot of the temple, there's nothing but wind. The temple itself leaves me cold. The marble, too white, looks like stucco. But the promontory, an indescribable place, rises out over the sea like a poop deck from which one commands the squadron of offshore islands while, back and to the left and right, the sea foams along the flanks of sand and rock. The furious wind whistles through the columns so forcefully you could believe the forests were alive. It swirls the blue air, sucks up the fresh sea breeze, violently mixes it with the perfume rising from a hill covered in fresh, tiny flowers, and furiously, relentlessly snaps blue sheets woven from air and light all around us. Sitting at the foot of the temple to shelter from the wind, the light instantly clears in a sort of motionless gushing. In the distance, the islands drift. Not a single bird. The sea softly foaming to the horizon. A perfect moment.

Perfect except for that island facing Makronisos, empty today, it's true, but once an island prison about which people have told me awful stories.[73]

We have lunch down at the bottom, on the little beach, a meal of fish and cheese in front of the big fishing boats in the small port. Toward mid-afternoon, the colors darken, the islands solidify, the sky expands. It's a moment of perfect light, of letting go, of *All is well*. But we have to go, because of my talk. It's difficult to pull myself from such places and I never really leave them completely.

Out on the promontory again, before getting on the road, we catch a glimpse of Makronisos. The whole way back, the most beautiful light I've had here, over the olive groves, over the fig trees with especially green leaves, over the sporadic cypress and eucalyptus trees.

---

73. During the Greek Civil War (1943–1949), Makronisos was used by the military as a prison camp. Among Camus's papers, there is a document, not written by him, about the role Makronisos played.

A talk.[74] At dinner I get information about the deportations. The figures seem to line up. The number of deportees has been reduced to 8 or 900. That's what I should be focusing on.

30.

National Museum. I go to see the tall, thin kouros statue again. Rehearsal of Hecuba. With one exception, these young Greek women lack grace and style. Lunch in Kifissia, under a gentle light, in a garden vibrating with nightingale song.

Afternoon. Work then the Hill of Muses. The sun is nearing its end this time. Once again, a sort of delirious joy standing before the Acropolis' extraordinary audacity, where the architects played not with harmonious measures but with the extraordinary extravagance of the capes, of islands tossed over an immense gulf, of a vast sky swirled like a conch shell. It's not the Parthenon they built, it's the space itself, the wildly rapturous views. Over that entire squadron of islands and peaks dominated by that poop deck made of rock, the peacefulness of night suddenly falls and [. . .][75] on a silent navigation.

In the evening, popular dances at "Crazy Johnny's." I try to find the dances interesting but the dancers, especially the women, are too ugly.

May 1st.

Early morning departure for Argolis. The coast of the Gulf of Corinth. A shimmering, ethereal, exultant light inundates the gulf and offshore islands. Stopped at the edge of the cliff for a moment, the whole immensity of the sea before us, presented inside a single curve, like a cup from which we drink the light and air in long gulps.

After an hour on the road, I'm literally drunk with light, my head filled with bright bursts and silent shouts, an enormous joy in my heart's hidden lair, an unending laugh of understanding, after which anything can happen and everything is accepted. The descent on Mycenae and Argos. The Mycenaean fortress is covered in thick bunches of poppies that tremble in the wind above the royal tombs. (At the moment, every part of Greece I've traveled

74. The talk, "On the Future of Tragedy," was given at the French Institute of Athens.
75. One illegible word.

through is covered in poppies and thousands of flowers.) From the top of the fortress, the plane stretches out to Argos and the sea. Agamemnon's kingdom is no bigger than ten kilometers, yet the proportions are such that never has a larger kingdom extended beneath the sun. Ruined Mycenae, between two high boulders, enclosed by enormous blocks, beneath a brightness that here becomes dreadful, is today the savage queen of this unforgettable land.

The ruins of Argos don't interest me all that much. The young archaeologist, Georges Roux, from Vaucluse, so alive, such passion for his beautiful craft, he interests me quite a bit. I envy him a little and bitterly reproach myself for the lost time of these last years and for my profound failure. We lunch at Asini, and before lunch I swim in the beautiful beach's cold, crystal-clear water.

In the afternoon, Epidaurus, where the May Day kermis has filled the streets with joyous Greeks, but where, from the top of the theater, in a thick, tepid light that spills out over the slopes of olive trees, eucalyptus trees, [. . .],[76] and acacias, all the sounds echo at a sort of vast and gentle remove. Only the sheep herds' faint bells rise above the other sounds, though still at the same remove. Time here is again perfect.

Evening. Nafplion before the sea at this hour the Greeks call the royalty of the sun, which is the hour when purples fill the sky, when mauves and blues settle atop the mountains and bays.

May 2.

Leave for Sparta in the morning, beneath a formidable sun. Wide valleys, each of which forms a kingdom of olive trees and noble cypresses, of arid mountains, of a village from time to time, here where Greece is deserted. Only herds of sheep painted in pinks, greens, and reds cross it. On the Evrotas plain, beneath the snowy Taygetus, Sparta unfurls its fields of orange trees, their thick fragrance staying with us the rest of the way. Over the ruins of Mystras, flights of turtledoves. A quiet convent with whitewashed walls opens onto the immense Laconia plain, its well-rounded, well-spaced olive trees quivering beneath an unremitting sun.

On our way back, we descend on Nafplion, its gulf, the islands and mountains in the distance. Pause in Argos with the young archaeologists carrying out the excavations. Same feeling as with the small group of architects who

76. One illegible word.

are rebuilding Orléansville and living there as a community. I've only ever been happy and at peace when taking part in a craft, in work accomplished alongside other people I can love. I don't have a craft, only a vocation. And my work is solitary. I have to accept it and try only to be worthy of it, which isn't the case at the moment. But I can't help but feel a little melancholy faced with these men who're happy with what they're doing.

We return to Mycenae; the sun's just set as we reach the highest terrace. Between the steep peaks overlooking it, a transparent moon softly sails. But in front of us, the darkened plain spreads out from the foot of Argos's blue mountains all the way to the still-bright sea to our right. The space is vast, the silence so complete that the foot repents for having caused a stone to roll. A train huffs in the distance, a donkey on the plain brays a lament that rises up to us, the herds' bells rush down the hill like flowing water. Over this scenery, tender and untamed, [. . .][77] is magnificent. Over the now-blooming poppies, a light wind passes at ground level. The most beautiful evening in the world gradually sets over the Mycenaean lions. The mountains gradually darken until the ten chains reflecting as far as the horizon become a single blue vapor. It was worth coming from so far to receive this great slice of eternity. After this, the rest is of little importance.

———

May 3.

Work in the morning. Leave for Delphi at 1:00 P.M. Always the same light, though this time on less lofty heights, stony and without a single tree. This is when Greece seems a space made primarily of curved or straight lines, but always shaped. The entirety of the earth draws the sky, giving it its form, but the sky, in turn, would be nothing without these hills and mountains whose harmonious closure delineates its own space. That's why even the shortest mile here separated great kingdoms: the surface of the earth is double that of the sky. Having arrived in a sort of cup-shaped basin, we watched a single cloud thicken for a couple of minutes and in only seconds burst open in a rage, solid hailstones rifling the car with a deafening noise. Five minutes later, leaving the basin, we find the sky once again clear and we merrily get on our way.

77. One illegible word.

Delphi. Initially, the most striking thing about the grandeur of the site is, at the bottom of the valley, that dark-green river whose muscular ridges [. . .][78] toward the sea. The olive trees are so tightly packed together that, seen from above, they're like a single quivering path to the horizon. As for the ruins, the storm, which also fell on Delphi, soaked them. They seem more vivacious amid the more vivid perennials and vert grasses. A black eagle circles high above for a few seconds and disappears. Then the day lightens and from up in the high cliffs a mildness begins to fall, announcing the evening to come. Back at the stadium from which I leave happy.

Evening. At a bouzoukia,[79] four Greeks kindly invite me to dance, but their steps are too difficult. If I had the time to learn them, I'd like to do so. From my room, the shadow-filled valley extends out to that little necklace of lights bordering the sea. A moon wrapped in light scarves casts a fine, powdery light over the mountains and shadowy hollows. The silence, vast as the space, is good.

———

May 4.

Leave in the morning for Volos. Rugged mountains, then the plain of Lamia. Gentler mountains again, greener beneath the rising sun, and then the immense Thessalian plain. The Vlach's primitive huts—and the immense expanse. The East isn't so far away. Volos. 80% of the houses destroyed or damaged.[80] The whole city is in tents. The sun weighs on the canvas, on the dusty city. Few or no toilets. I wonder how they will avoid an epidemic. French school in a tent. And the sea so close, smooth and fresh, on the edge of the ruined city. The mayor receives me in a courtyard near a ruined house. An intelligent and elegant character. An offhand remark I make leads to a barber being called to cut my hair right there in the courtyard, in front of everyone, with the most charming familiarity. Still in the city. Mass celebrated outside, hospital tent, etc. Car ride back to Larissa. Railcar. Larissa to Salonica. In the night, we ride along a shimmering, moonlit sea. Arrive at 11:00 P.M.

———

78. Two illegible words.

79. Like an American nightclub, a *bouzoukia* is a Greek venue for listening to live music, drinking, and dancing.

80. A series of catastrophic earthquakes struck Volos in April 1955. Camus would end his first article for *L'Express*, published in France on May 14, 1955, with an appeal for donations. The article, "Le métier d'homme," makes use of many of the journal entries recorded in Greece, sometimes verbatim.

May 5.

Work. Lunch with Turner and Colonel Bramble[81] (or someone who certainly looks like him). Byzantine churches. The small monastery with the peacocks. St. David, St. Georges, St. Dimitriu. The twelve apostles (St. Sophie uninteresting). Byzantine art doesn't really move me. Have to admit it. But interested in the evolution that runs from the 5th to the 12th century and that allows for the reestablishment of a link between the Hellenistic period and the Quattrocento. The mosaics and frescoes of the twelve apostles are, for example, far from the stiffness and hieraticism of that art's first centuries. You can see Duccio's[82] origins in it. A little later (in the evening), I question a specialist, who tells me Byzantine artists emigrated to Italy after the fall of Constantinople. In this manner, over time, Eastern influence would be eliminated.

Evening. Talk.[83] Am touched by young woman enrolled there.[84] Reception with academics. At night, I relax on the bedroom's balcony, looking out at the port, the caiques, the quay flush with the sea, and breathing in the beautiful scent of salt and night.

May 6, 7, 8.

Lunch with T. on a clifftop facing the sea. The hour is pleasant. T. plays his latest compositions for me. I have to leave. Plane. The Sporades drift on a glittering sea below us. Dinner Merlier.[85] At midnight, D. comes to pick me up and we dash off for Piraeus, where Monsieur Algadès waits for us in his pretty cutter. A jolly fat man, joyous and cordial. We leave for Piraeus beneath an ashen moon that illuminates the sea with a warm, surreal light. I'm happy to feel water slapping beneath the hull and to once again see a light foam dashing down both sides of the ship's bow. But then, shortly after, we watch the fog being born, literally lifting from the sea, layer upon layer, thickening and gradually blocking out the horizon. It's cold and damp. Algadès claims he's never seen anything like this in the archipelago. He has to reroute the cutter to avoid two small islands. I go down to bed. Can't fall asleep until 6:00 A.M. I wake two hours later and head back up on deck. The fog is still there. Algadès and his navigator have been keep-

---

81. The reference is to a character in André Maurois's novel *Colonel Bramble's Silence*.

82. Duccio di Buoninsegna (c. 1255–1319), Italian painter.

83. Camus gave "The Artist and His Times" talk at the Lycée français de Thessalonique.

84. The word appears to be "enrolled," but it's hard to make out in the original notebook.

85. Octave Merlier was then director of the Institut Français.

ing watch all night, afraid we might run aground. But the sun rises little by little, comes out, pale, pierces the fog, and finally dissipates it. Around 11:00 o'clock, we set off (without sails because there's no wind) on a still sea, in a glittering, delicate light. The air is so crystal clear it seems the slightest sound can be heard from the other end of the horizon. The sun warms the deck, the heat rising little by little. Then the first island appears. We pass, because of the detour we made, between Seriphos and Sifnos. Syros and the other islands appear on the horizon. They appear in the sky with the sharpness of a sketch. On the overturned hulls of the islands, the small villages clinging to the slopes look like shells, like whitish concretions left by the ebbing sea.

The small yellow islands like piles of wheat atop a blue sea.

We sail through the center of these distant islands on a sea flooded with light, gently rippling, sailing along Syros, and soon Mykonos appears and, as the day progresses, becomes more clearly etched in the distance, its serpent's head, which bends toward Delos, still out of sight behind Rinia. The sun sets as we near the center of a circle of islands, their colors beginning to change. The gold smoldering, the cyclamen mauve green, the colors deepening, and the mass of islands turning a dark blue on a still-glistening sea. It's a strange, vast peacefulness that falls over the water then. Happiness at last, happiness on the verge of tears. For I'd like to hold it tightly to me, this inexpressible joy that I know must pass. But it has faintly echoed through so many days, and now holds such a tight grip on my heart that it seems I must be able to faithfully return to it whenever I'd like.

Night has fallen when we descend on Mykonos. As many churches as houses. All white. We wander through the small streets where colorful shops open up. The scent of honeysuckle finds us in the completely dark streets. The moon shines faintly above the white terraces. We head back aboard and I go to bed so happy that I don't even feel how tired I am.

In the morning, a divine light falls over the whitewashed houses of Mykonos. We weigh anchor for Delos. The sea is beautiful, crystalline and pure, and we can already make out the bottom. Approaching Delos, we can make out huge bunches of poppies on the island's first slopes.

Delos. Island of lions and bulls, depictions of which cover this island of animals, for we have to add snakes, too [. . .][86] and large lizards with dark

86. One illegible word inside parenthesis.

bodies but light-green heads and tails, and the dolphins in the mosaics. The marble the lions are made of has been eroded and pitted by the process of erosion, so much so that they look as if they were made of rock salt, a little ghostly, as if the first rain will dissolve them. But this island of lions and bulls is also covered in the friable, brown bones that are the ruins, and beneath these bones, suddenly, new and wonderful discoveries (mosaics of Dionysus at rest).

Also an island of ruins and flowers (poppies, convolvulus, wallflowers, asters). An island of the mutilated gods of the museum (the little kore statues). At noon, climb to the top of Cynthe, the gulfs surrounding it, the light, the reds and whites; the whole circle of the Cyclades slowly revolves around Delos, on a sparkling sea, in a sort of motionless dance. This world of islands so narrow and vast appears to me to be the heart of the world. And at the center of this heart floats Delos and the peak on which I stand, from which I can look out through the purest, clearest light in the world at that perfect circle that sets the limits of my kingdom.

Back at the rowboat later, a ravishing Greek teenager, dressed simply on the quay. As the rowboat exits the quay, I wave to her, and she instantly responds with a beautiful smile. Back on the cutter, I undress and plunge into the crystalline green water. It's freezing and I climb out after a few strokes. Then we return to Mykonos. Feeling of infinite freedom to travel the sea in all directions like this, one island to the next. And this freedom is not at all limited by the fact that this island world has boundaries. On the contrary, this freedom rejoices in their circle. For me, freedom wouldn't be to burst out of this circle and sail full speed for Sumatra, but to advance from this bare island to that island of trees, from this rock to that island of flowers.

In Mykonos for a few purchases. I preferred the city at night. We get back to sea late. Seeing Delos and Cynthe gradually disappear behind Rinia, a strange sadness so similar to the sadness of love. For the first time, I watch a land I love disappear with the painful feeling I may never see it again before dying. Heartache. The colors over the water and islands again change. [. . .][87] the sails, gently snapped by a weak wind. Hardly have we had time to taste the peace rising from the sea to a sky gradually drained of its light when already the moon rises behind a rocky islet, quickly lifting into the sky and illuminating the water. I sit and watch it until midnight, listening to the sails,

87. Three illegible words.

internally accompanying the movement of the water against the sides of the ship. The free life of the sea and these days of happiness. Everything is forgotten here, everything is remade. These marvelous days spent flying on the water, between islands covered in corollas and columns, beneath a tireless light, I hold the taste for all of this in my mouth, in my heart, a second revelation, a second birth . . .

In the morning, the wind whips, the sails snap, the boat lists more and more, and we dash off for Piraeus amid a racket of water and canvas. A rain of light, the drops falling and bouncing on the morning sea. Resigned to having to leave this archipelago, but the resignation itself is good.

May 9.

Depart for Olympia. Through the Gulf of Corinth. Beaches and gulfs. Swim in Xylokastro. This time it's the strength of the trees, the water, the fresh fruits of the earth. Shortly before Olympia, the hills are covered in fragile cypresses. The softness, the tenderness of these places beneath a light that is for the first time a little gray. The tall pines and the remains of the temples to Zeus and Hera. The birds call, the day wanes, peace will soon rise from the sleeping vale. During the night, I think of Delos.

May 10.

For the first time, the morning is gray as I look out over the Alpheios Valley from my window. Still, a soft light falls over the stones, cypresses, and green meadows. Since Delos, I've been able to feel nothing other than the peace of these hills, these soft shadows, this silence nourished on faint birdsong. Museum.[88] Along with the Siphnian frescoes at Delphi, this is the height of classical sculpture. Compared with the Apollo or the three male figures from the East Pediment, or the different Athenas from the metopes, the Hermes of Praxiteles is a sweet success that stinks of decadence. Behind it, two superb, life-size terracottas, one depicting a warrior, the other Zeus abducting Ganymede, are witnesses to a superbly different art. Strange archaic bronze kore

88. Camus is comparing what he sees here at the Archaeological Museum of Olympia with the reconstruction of the Siphnian Treasury and other works that he saw at the Delphi Archaeological Museum.

statues, griffins, figurines that seem to come straight from the East. Walk. A light rain falls and the vale's delicate, washed-out colors are easy on the eye. Amazed by the diversity of landscapes. Everything Greece attempts with its landscapes is a success carried out to perfection.

With the villagers and their friendly familiarity. Free in appearance and movement, even though political freedom doesn't exist here.

Brief evening rain. I climb up the hill through patches of fragrant flowers. Small village of Thronia. Impoverished houses. Children in rags, although apparently healthy.

———

May 12.

Clear, bright morning. The shade beneath the trees surrounding the ruins is all the more precious. The light is divine. Swim and lunch in Xylokastro. The water is clear and not as cold, but it's the air, especially, that's become crystalline, and the mountains lining the other side of the Gulf of Corinth are all visible with a strange clarity. M. has a sumptuous smile here, in this landscape.[89] And it's like this the whole way, and soon we're at the Gulf of Athens, and we can distinguish every house and tree on the islands. Such pleasures overwhelm me now, and I've stopped recording them here. Chaste, sober pleasures strong as joy itself, as the air we breathe.

———

Thission.

In the bright, clear sky, the tip of the moon like a hawthorn petal.

Evening with R.D. Honeysuckles, the bay in the distance at night, the mysterious flavor of life.

———

May 13.

These twenty days racing through Greece, I contemplate them now from Athens, before departing, and they seem like a single, long source of light that I can hold at the center of my life. For me, Greece is but a single glittering day stretched out over a series of crossings, but an enormous island covered in red flowers and mutilated gods endlessly drifting on a sea of light, beneath

---

89. In a letter to Maria Casarès from this period, Camus writes: "Do you know that you smile like the young women at the Acropolis?"

a crystal sky. Hold onto this light, return to it, no longer give in to the night of days . . .

———

May 14.

Leave for Aegina. Calm sea. Warm, blue sky. Small port. Caiques. Ascend to Aphaia. The three temples suspend a blue triangle in space: the Parthenon, Sounion, and Aphaia. I sleep on the temple's stone slabs, in the shade of the columns. Long swim in a small, lukewarm cove in Agia Marina. In the evening, large lilies with a suffocating fragrance are sold on the port. Aegina is the island of lilies. Return. The sun descends, gets lost in the clouds, turns into a golden fan, then into a large wheel with blinding spokes of light. The islands again begin to drift, and I'll leave them for good this evening. Stupid desire to cry.

In the evening, Variguerez and the shadow puppets.

———

May 15.

Sunday. Byzantine Museum. With the D's in Kifissia then on the Athenian beaches. Stroll along the sea in a fine wind full of light. These are the hours in which I say goodbye to this country that's poured the same long joy over us for weeks on end.

———

May 16.

Leave for Paris, heart aching.

———

Novel. He looked at the glittering shrapnel covering the engine, blinding in the sunlight, and a mysterious joy once again seeped in, a fountain flowing blindly inside him. It was the joy from Delos, circular, red and white, a swirling circle. In the plane plunging helplessly toward the sea, above the looming squall, life began again, identical to that impending death.

———

"The Guest."[90] The prisoner chooses the path to prison, but Daru had purposely misled him, had pointed toward the path to freedom.

---

90. "The Guest," Camus's best-known short story, provides a bit of a predicament for the translator, in that the title, "L'Hôte," can mean both "The Guest" and "The Host." It was, however, Camus himself who chose the English title.

Novel. A proud character. Who doesn't cry out in pain. Who doesn't give an inch.

A privileged man who discovers working-class life as an adult and gradually gives himself over to it. But it's never enough. Even becoming a worker doesn't change that he wasn't born one. Ultimately, you have to die for it.

I've tried to be the model of a man, to bring it all together inside me. And then . . .

First Man. Francine family. Wolfromm family.

Regarding genius, the Romans only had it in the way we refer to it in our armies.

History is made by blood and courage. No way around it. When the slave takes up arms and gives his life, he then rules as master and oppresses. But when an oppressed person, for the first time in the history of the world, rules by justice, without then oppressing, it'll all be over and it'll all finally begin.

My study on Grenier.[91] Difficult. It's like pulling logs from a brilliant flame one by one. And then you find yourself facing the blackened embers.

In Ancient Greece, people who wanted to become magistrates weren't to have had any business dealings for at least ten years.

Julia.[92] She believes she can pursue both her loves. But when Guibert suggests that he, too, pursue both his loves, she can't allow him to do what she permitted herself. But she can't judge him. Hence her "social disease."

Still enough tenderness to support . . . That kind of devotion supposes, however, that conviction is useful. I have the opposite impression and that's what disarms me.

Great suffering and sun, every day. He's cured and adores, alone, the red god.

Measure and madness. Measure in her relations with others, madness with herself; to force herself, to bend. And in both cases, both at the same time.

Jesus had 300 million contemporaries. He would have 2 billion.

Nothing burns in Hell but the ego (St Catherine of Genoa[93]).

---

91. Camus had written a preface for the new edition of Jean Grenier's *Islands*, which would be published by Gallimard in 1959.

92. A note for the planned play about Julie de Lespinasse.

93. St. Catherine of Genoa (1447–1510), author of *Dialogues of the Soul and Body* and *Treatise on Purgatory*.

Malice is the only industry in France that doesn't suffer underemployment.

First Man. A pacifist for so long. Then one day he agrees to fight and risk his life. His joy.

In Italian *talento* means desire.

First Man. "Many years later, when, worn out by our various endeavors, we'd part in the evening with the slightly disappointing feeling of not having truly loved each other that day, the small victory sign she flashed from the front door as I sat in my car waiting for her to slip inside, it tied that seemingly lost day to the sturdy thread of our steadfast love and saved it from any feeling of bitterness."

Id. Jessica's incredible toughness in breakups. The loss of love is the loss of all rights when once you had them all.

Play. A man appoints himself king today.

Étienne.[94] Roars upon waking and when he's alone.

Ultimately (if a life is worth a life) the condemned himself approves the death sentence. (Cf. Melville ultimately yielding in Billy Budd.)[95]

I am one of those whom Pascal deeply moves but doesn't convert. Pascal, the greatest of all, yesterday as today.

---

94. Étienne Sintès, Camus's deaf-mute uncle, who would appear as a character in *The First Man*.

95. Toward the end of *Billy Budd* (chap. 25), Melville writes:

> At the penultimate moment, his words, his only ones, words wholly unobstructed in the utterance were these: "God bless Captain Vere!" Syllables so unanticipated coming from one with the ignominious hemp about his neck—a conventional felon's benediction directed aft towards the quarters of honor; syllables too delivered in the clear melody of a singing bird on the point of launching from the twig—had a phenomenal effect, not unenhanced by the rare personal beauty of the young sailor, spiritualized now through late experiences so poignantly profound.
>
> Without volition, as it were, as if indeed the ship's populace were but the vehicles of some vocal current electric, with one voice from alow and aloft came a resonant sympathetic echo: "God bless Captain Vere!" And yet at that instant Billy alone must have been in their hearts, even as in their eyes.

Echoes of these ambiguous lines can be heard at the end of Camus's *The Stranger*.

First Man. The friend, Saddok.[96]

1) Young militant—My comrade—crisis of '36.[97]

2) Friend—Returns to Muslim customs because the others betrayed him. Marries according to his father's wishes. Fears failing his unknown wife.

3) Terrorist.[98]

Later, a European friend's wife is raped and killed. The first man and this friend rush to their weapons, apprehend an accomplice, torture him, then chase down the culprit, surprise him, and kill him. His shame, afterward. History is blood.

Id. Section about the Resistance. He'd rather be an R.A.F. hero. Be killed at a distance. Not have to suffer the enemy's presence, his cruelty. Really, he dreams of gigantic battles in the blazing skies above the metropolis while he takes the Métro to dusty, muddy places, from Paris to St. Étienne.

Id. Scene in Faubourg Montmartre. As the sound of S.S. pistol-whipping nears the gates and frightened neighbors recriminate against members of the Resistance, *he sees himself*: face full of contempt. But why contempt? He gets rid of the printing plate. After the S.S. have searched him, he goes on his way, a little ashamed. He finds a document on him that's just as compromising.

First Man. Pierre, militant, Jean, dilettante. Pierre is married. They both meet Jessica. Jean and Jessica as the *previous mistress*. In one of the interludes, she's with Pierre, whom she hurts and leaves, and who makes his wife suffer for it. That's how he learns, far from meetings, what justice *really* is. Jean, on the other hand, learns to love Jessica, and in doing so gets closer to other people. Pierre dies beside Jean (war, Resistance), who hated him *out*

96. Not long after this entry, Camus would draft a letter asking that Ben Saddok, a young Algerian militant accused of assassinating former vice president of the Algerian Assembly Ali Chekkal, not be given the death penalty. "Even though I entirely disapprove of his actions," Camus wrote, "it would be both humane and pragmatic for capital punishment not to be applied. Humane, for his act, senseless and stupid as it is, can't be compared to those racist acts of terrorism that indiscriminately kill women and children in the middle of an innocent crowd. Even if you disapprove of or condemn his motives, they're of a different order."

97. The crisis mentioned here is likely the defeat of the Blum-Violette Plan, which would have given immediate and equal voting rights to Muslims in Algeria. Some historians see this as the point at which a movement for integration became a more widespread movement for independence.

98. In *The First Man*'s Education file, this line has a parenthetical attached: "(scene with he and *the mother*, who is there and remains silent. At any price but the price of my mother. Wounded shortly after)."

of jealousy. And he cares for him with all his heart. He's the one she loved at least a little bit.[99]

Id. Discovery of love. Fascination M.A.

———

Giorgione, painter of musicians.[100] His subjects and his fluid painting, which, without contours, elongates, which feminizes everything, especially men. Voluptuousness is never sharp.

Venice in August and the swarms of tourists flock to St. Mark's Square right alongside the pigeons, pecking at the experience, vacationing on the ugliness they create.

———

Parma. And over there, the same thing. Here, these little places I loved 20 years ago and which still exist, apart from me.

———

Novel. Don't forget Italy and *the discovery of art*—and of religion suddenly revealed in its relationship with art.

Each time, this peace in my heart. And yet this time, continuously despondent, incapable of freshness or emotion. And yet, in San Leo, the heart opens on a soothing silence.[101] Dear Italy, where I would have been cured of everything. On the way back, the old smell of dusty trails. White oxen with long Romagna horns drag squeaky carts. The scent of straw and sun.

San Leo—and my desire to retire there. Make a list of the places I thought I could live and *die*. Always small cities. Tipasa. Djemila. Cabris. Valdemosa. Cabrières d'Avignon. Etc., etc. Come back to San Leo.

———

Urbino. These small, tightly walled cities, austere, silent, sealed up in their perfection. At the center of the fortified walls, the indifferent characters of della Francesca's *Flagellation*[102] eternally wait, standing before the angels

99. In *The First Man*'s Education file, this entry appears with several variations. In addition to being militant, Pierre is described as "sensitive, generous," whereas Jean is described as a "monster." It's clarified that Pierre is married to Marie. And instead of the single-line paragraph that ends this entry, we find "He takes his brother's hand (now", and the rest of the sentence is left incomplete.

100. Giorgione (c. 1477–1510), Italian painter.

Camus and Maria Casarès departed from Avignon on July 29, 1955, traveling through Italy until August 29, 1955.

101. A municipality a little south of Bologna, at an altitude of 1,932 feet. Known for the Fortress of San Leo, where magician and occultist Count Cagliostro died.

102. Piero della Francesca's *Flagellation of Christ* is housed in the Galleria Nazionale della Marche, which itself is located inside the Ducal Palace in Urbino, Italy. The gallery contains an extensive collection of Renaissance art by masters such as Raphael, Signorelli, and Titian.

and the high-and-mighty Madonna. Sansepolcro. Christ is risen. And here he stands, risen from the grave, fiercely militant. Piero della Francesca's new frescoes. The Sansepolcro valley, a place you have to return to at the end of your life. Vast, unchanging, it holds its secret beneath a calm sky.

I return to the sea once again, warm and relaxing for the muscles.

The weight of St. Croix. Madonna del Parto.[103]

At the end of my life, I'd like to return to this path that goes down into the Sansepolcro valley, descend it slowly, walk in the valley between the frail olive trees and long cypresses, and find, in a house with thick walls and cool rooms, a bare room with a narrow window from which I can watch night descend on the valley. I'd like to return to the Prato garden in Arezzo one evening and retrace my steps on the patrol path atop the fortress so that I can see night settle on this incomparable land. I'd like . . . Everywhere and always this desire for solitude that I don't even understand and that's like a harbinger of some sort of death to come, with the taste for recollection that accompanies it.

Come back to the Piazza della Signoria in Gubbio and watch the rain fall for a while over the valley, see Assisi without tourists or vespas, and listen to the harmony of the stars from S. Francesco's upper square. See Perugia on a crisp morning without the houses that are being built up around it, and be able, then, to see the frail olive trees on the hills that mark the bounds of Porta del Sole.

But most of all, most of all, take a backpack and walk the route from Monte San Savino to Siena again, follow along that countryside of olives and grapes, their scent palpable, pass by those hills of bluish tuff that stretch to the horizon, see Siena and its minarets rise in the setting sun like a Constantinople of perfection, arrive there at night, alone and penniless, sleep by a fountain and be the first on the palm-shaped Campo, which is like a hand offering up the greatest creation of post-Greek man.

Yes, I'd like to see Arezzo's sloping square again, the seashell pattern of the Campo in Siena, and again eat watermelon hearts in the hot streets of Verona.

When I'm old, I'd like to have the chance to come back to this route through Siena, equaled by no other in the world, and die there in a ditch, surrounded only by the kindness of these unknown Italians I love.

———

103. Piero della Francesca's fresco *Madonna del Parto* was originally housed in a small church in Monterchi, but when an earthquake destroyed the church in the late 1700s, the fresco was detached and moved above the altar of the new cemetery chapel. The fresco depicts the pregnant Madonna flanked by angels parting a red curtain behind her.

August 22, 1955. San Francesco di Siena. 11:00 in the morning.

———

In the Siena Museum, one of the many last judgments (Giovanni di Paolo).[104] On the right, among the blessed, two friends lift their arms to express their joy at seeing each other again. On the left, in Hell, Sisyphus and Prometheus, their sentence extended.

———

Novel. Portrait of the scorpion. It hates lies and loves mystery. Destructive element. Because the necessary lie fortifies. And the taste for mystery leads to inconsistency.

———

Novel. Grasshoppers—Earthquake—Attack on the isolated farmhouse—Philippeville attack—School attack—Typhoon in Nemours.

———

Sensual, victorious, at the height of a life of pleasure and success, he gives it all up, becomes chaste, because he walked in on two fifteen-year-olds discovering love on each other's face.

———

He wanted to be ordinary, to go out, to dance, to have the conversations and tastes everyone else had. But he intimidated everyone else. Based solely on his manner, he was assumed to have thoughts and preoccupations he didn't have or had without knowing they were on full display.

———

First Man. The mother, forced to flee Algeria, spends the rest of her life in Provence, in the country home her son bought for her. But she suffers from the exile. Her words: "It's nice. But there are no Arabs." It's there she dies and he understands.[105]

Title: The Father and the Mother?

———

October 24, 1955.

Death threats. My curious reaction.

———

104. Giovanni di Paolo (1399–1482), Sienese painter. His *Last Judgement* is in the Pinacoteca Nazionale in the Palazzo Buonsignori.

105. Camus tried in vain to convince his mother, his uncle Étienne, and his brother Lucien to move to France to escape the upheaval taking place in Algiers.

They're united beyond time. But as the years pass, she no longer dares show herself to him in the naked light of Parisian mornings.

———

Algiers. January 18.[106]

The anguish I'd had about Algeria while in Paris has left me. Here, at least, we're in the struggle, a difficult one for those of us who have public opinion against us. But it's in the struggle that I've always ended up finding my own sort of peace. Intellectuals, by their very function, whatever it may be—and especially if they only add their two cents to public affairs in writing—live like cowards. They compensate for their impotence with inflammatory rhetoric. Only risk justifies thought. And then anything is better than this France of resignation and malice, this swamp in which I'm suffocating. Yes, I woke up happy, for the first time in months. I've found the star once again.[107]

———

With everything that France has incessantly done to shape who I am today, I've tried to retain what Spain left in my blood, which was the truth, as far as I'm concerned.

———

January 21.

Threats for tonight and tomorrow.

———

January 22.

Adoration. The world's mystery.

———

106. On January 22, 1956, during a meeting in Algiers, Camus alongside other left-leaning Europeans and Muslims launched a "Call for a Civilian Truce in Algeria." In the weeks leading up to the meeting, as Camus notes above, and in the weeks after, he received death threats from both the Left and Right. During the meeting itself, protesters gathered outside the auditorium, some reportedly chanting "Death to Camus."

107. Regarding the "star," see pp. 426n39 and 492.

January 27.

First Man. X. declares that *only* the C.P. has always done what's necessary for its comrades.[108] Generational difference. They have everything to learn, too.

Every artistic doctrine is an alibi through which the artist attempts to justify his own limits.

St. Augustine lived in a totalitarian world: the Later Roman Empire. Marrou[109] called it: "The art of living in times of catastrophe." Resistance to Christianity comes from the peasants and the aristocracy. Pride in belonging to the Church of Africa. Faithful 14 years to that unknown woman who gave him Adeodatus. St. Paul's epistle sends him to the Church.

"Not in rioting and drunkenness, not in chambering and wantonness, not in strife and envying; but put ye on the Lord Jesus Christ, and make not provision for the flesh, to fulfill the lusts thereof."[110]

Always struggling to defend his work from the invasion of external occupations. His image of the divine *Sun* that illuminates our spirit.

"In the multitude of words there wanteth not sin."[111]

Chaste fear and servile fear. "You will at all times enjoy everything but you will not see my Face. Choose." Nobody wants to at all times enjoy everything.

Those who accuse the age of being an age of misfortune: "What they want is not so much an era of tranquility as security in their vices."

17th century, Augustinian century.

Novel. Portrait of V.D. She has big strong hands and, at the bottom of a slender, elegant body, dancer's feet. When she dances, everything is action, an unbridled intensity in which she completely reveals herself.[112]

---

108. In *The First Man*'s Education file, this line ends: " necessary for the Arab cause."

109. Henri-Irénée Marrou (1904–1977), historian who studied late antiquity, with a particular focus on Saint Augustine.

110. This passage, Romans 13:13–14, appears in French in Camus's notebook but is given here in the King James Version. It is the section of Paul's Epistle to the Romans with which Saint Augustine opened his Bible.

111. The passage, Proverbs 10:19, appears in French in Camus's notebook but is given here in the King James Version.

112. This entry utilizes a good bit of slang and innuendo, some of it uncommon and with no clear translation. For example, *Elle s'est renversé une omelette sur la tête* could be taken literally as "She dumped an omelet on his head" but more likely relies on a less frequent usage of *faire une omelette* or *attention à l'omelette*, which means to knock something fragile over and break it or to make a mess of

She celebrates the anniversary of the day she got her car. Puts the dress she just bought at the foot of the bed every evening so that she can have the joy of seeing it when she wakes.

She expresses herself only in indefinite terms. She has to go get someone at someplace to go somewhere else where she has to do something . . . etc. Her life hidden two or three times over (cf. X. "I have a lunch"). "I have impure thoughts," she says. Or about someone who doesn't exactly inspire impure thoughts in her: "It's in the bag."

The men with whom she's had liaisons. They're completely foreign to her. "Like Zulus," she says. "How can you not feel compassion for an intelligent man? People agree with all that he knows and sees precisely because they don't know or see it." "Women who place all their happiness in a man." "Women who don't please are stingy with the only man they have. Only women who please are capable of generosity." "I don't like especially young men. They're fools. A man always thinks he's superior to the woman he . . . I can accept such a feeling from an intelligent man, not from a young imbecile." Her little car. "I can't do without it. I love it dearly for all the freedom it gives me." She keeps a pair of old, worn-out slippers in the car and slips them on while driving, setting aside her elegant Louis XV heels. In fact, she leaves her flats everywhere she goes, in cinemas, restaurants, etc. Pretty feet of the dancer she is. "In my neighborhood, there are only grannies and people with pellagra, so I get noticed."

She arrives at the hotel with her baskets full of makeup and toiletries, her long blond hair a mess [. . .].[113]

Id. "Let's be frank—fame is an aphrodisiac."

If she became a billionaire, if, more precisely, she married Onassis, she'd have a bathtub made of gold or platinum, which would go better with her hair, and she'd fill it with her favorite perfume and macerate in it.

"I like my car better than my mother." She *likes the age in which she lives.*

Her readiness to laugh. Her determination to grab everything, to succeed at everything, to taste all the day's *pleasures*: skiing, the sea, dancing, society life, commercial success. And pure in this insatiable desire—because of him. "I've got a case." Her words: "She scrambled his brain" (speaking about a blond woman). "She'd raise Hell in a flock of Jesuits." "When we're doing

---

something. With this meaning in mind, and the context available in the entry itself, it seems the intention here might be to say something like, "She scrambled his brains." This is only one possible interpretation, though, and it is worth noting that this entry has several such instances of interpretation.

113. Four illegible words.

our thing, we can do some handstands or skin the cat, and they applaud no matter what." I'd cut my finger and had a bandage on it: "It makes you look like a clumsy carpenter."

What I love about V., what makes her attractive: she sticks to her class, however unpalatable, which is to say that she's figured out what she can give without complications (expand on this). V. and marriage. She'll be faithful if she marries. She'll owe that much to the poor guy who . . . etc.

You can always see her fresh girlish petticoat as she sits down.

"I don't understand these married women who harp on their husband. They have money, a father for their children, security, their golden years all set, and they expect fidelity on top of all that. They're asking too much." And again: "In marriage, the man has everything to lose, the woman everything to gain," etc., etc.

———

Don Faust and Doctor Juan. Leporello. Nothingness.

Id. He becomes an actor, of the theater, on the theater.

Id. Faust and women's youth (cf. Dupuis).

Id. When in love with her, I was unfaithful, and I was in love with her if she was unfaithful.

"Is this your new servant?"

"Yes, he's a philosopher. I bought him in Paris."

Id. Nothingness. There's a regret in you that rubs me the wrong way. There's nothing, I tell you. You can invite this statue. You won't see it coming.

D.F. Are you sure? Invite it.

Leporello goes.

D.F. No (he hesitates). Yes.

Leporello clowns around with the statue.

D.F. chooses chastity, looks for and finds a chaste girl. I would have converted long ago, but I've always been held back by a fear of what my friends would say.

The old doctor from the prologue is an atomic scientist. He could blow up the world. But he doesn't want that; he wants fun and experience.

End. The Franciscans have him locked up in a monastery. He rejects their god and confesses to them. Adoration of being-in-the-world.[114]

———

114. The final term in this entry, though one letter off in the French, seems to be referencing the Heideggerian term given above.

If a true creator were to find himself solitary tomorrow, he would experience a depth of solitude no other age could have even imagined. He'd be alone in trying to shape and serve a civilization that can only be conceived if everyone takes part. He'd suspect that such a civilization is on its last leg and that he's one of the last to know it.

F.M.[115] He has an answer for everything, except decency.

———

Before the third cycle: short stories for "A Hero of our Times." Theme: *judgment and exile.*[116]

The third cycle is on love: The First Man, Don Faust, The Myth of Nemesis.

The method is sincerity.

———

History is easy to imagine but hard to see for anyone who endures it in the flesh.

An oppressed person has no real duties because he has no rights. It's only through rebellion that he regains rights. But as soon as he has rights, he immediately becomes responsible for duties. That's why rebellion, the source of rights, is equally the mother of duties. Such are the origins of the aristocracy. And its history. He who neglects his duty loses his rights and becomes an oppressor even if he speaks in the name of the oppressed. But what is this duty [?]

———

Novel. A deportee is forced to strip naked. While undressing, a cufflink rolls into a corner. He goes to pick it up.

———

Paris. A late and sudden Spring. All the chestnut trees covered in their wax candles.

———

M: "How could I be jealous of someone who I know is going to die and slip away from me forever? Real jealousy would be for me to want to die with him no matter what."

———

115. Likely François Mauriac.

116. An indication that Camus didn't see *The Fall* and the stories that would be collected in *Exile and the Kingdom* as belonging to any of the formally planned cycles. *The Fall* would go on to be published as a standalone novel on May 16, 1956, while *Exile and the Kingdom* would appear around a year later, March 15, 1957.

The Stone That Grows. The Cook: "That's not so bad. You have to kill your enemy: wasn't he killed?"

D'Arras: He was.

The Cook: "Here, we kill our enemies and afterward there's the Good Lord, Jesus."

Chez Solidor: a man, Barbara, does his drag routine (as a society woman) in front of his guests: his mother, his grandmother, and a young man who is his current lover's son. The household is delighted.[117]

July. Palermo.

Three days of mistral had brushed, had planed the sky to its finest layer of thread, a thin membrane, transparent and blue, swollen with the heavy weight of golden water . . . and we waited for it, too, to break open, for a wave of vin jaune[118] to drown the earth beneath an exultant flood.

July 12. Palermo.

About the mistral. On hot days, I waited for it to pick up. Then I climbed on that hill covered in aromatic herbs and myriad tiny snail fossils. It would swoop down from the north, scour the nearby mountains, brush the sky to its finest layer of thread, toss and cleanse the trees, scream through the countryside, consign animals and people to their homes, reigning at last . . . Etc. And lying on the hill, crushing the shells, bathing in the intense wind and sun . . . a celebration.

A.B. wrote to me about the true story of the Van Eyck. Shortly after the theft, a priest attached to the church was suspected. He confessed. He stole the panel because he couldn't bear seeing judges so close to the Adoration of the Mystic Lamb. He receives absolution, given his intentions, promising to reveal where the panel is hidden the day he dies. The day comes. Extreme

---

117. Chez Suzy Solidor was a cabaret located on Rue Balzac in Paris's eighth arrondissement; it operated from 1954 to 1960 as a successor to Suzy Solidor's first club, La Vie Parisienne, opened in 1932.

118. Literally "yellow wine," *vin jaune* is a white wine from the Jura region of France.

Unction. He wants to speak. But his voice breaks. He utters a few unintelligible words and dies.[119]

Over the years, what I've always found at the core of my being is a refusal to disappear from the world, from its joys, from its pleasures, from its suffering, and it's this refusal that's made an artist of me.

———

Jean asks for fishing equipment, which I buy for him. Looks in vain for worms. Then finds some. Goes fishing. Catches six minnows and bursts into tears on seeing them struggle. He doesn't want to fish anymore.

———

July 22.

The moon above the poplars is light and full. The Luberon practically white, naked in the distance. A light wind through the reeds. Maman and I gaze at this marvelous night with the same heavy heart.

She's going to leave, though, and I'm always afraid I'll never see her again.

———

Nemesis. History-based thinking is the kind of thinking that despises time the most, its effects, its edifices, and its civilizations. For such thinkers, history is that which destroys.

———

End of July.

Nights full of moon and wind. The great [. . .][120] of the Vaucluse.

———

It seems no party in this country can sustain the patriotic effort for too long. So, the right falls apart in 1940 and then the left sixteen years later.

———

Stormy night. In the morning, the air is light, the contours clear. On a hill inundated with early light, a carpet of pink morning glories. The scent of young pines. Don't deny anything anymore!

———

119. A.B. likely refers to André Breton, who was then working on what would become his last major publication, *L'art magique* (*Magic Art*). The *Adoration of the Mystic Lamb* (also known as the *Ghent Altarpiece*) plays a central role in Camus's *The Fall*. It's possible that Camus first took an interest in the work when *Combat* published a front-page article on it on September 13, 1944.

120. One illegible word.

If you know nothing more than this: I'd like to be better.

———

Music on the South Atlantic transatlantic liner. Only music captures the dimension of the sea. And certain passages of Shakespeare, Melville, of [. . .].[121]

———

Russian anecdote (fictitious, I suppose): Stalin ordered Krupskaya[122] to cease all criticisms or he'd appoint Lenin *another widow*·

———

Novel-end. Maman. What was her silence saying? What was that mute and smiling mouth crying out? We shall rise again.

Her patience at the airdrome, in that world of machines and offices that are beyond her, waiting without a word, as old women around the world have for millennia, waiting for the world to pass them by. And then, very small, a little bent over, she moves out onto the immense fields, toward the screaming monsters, holding her well-combed hair with one hand . . . [123]

———

If nothing will redeem our days and our actions, then aren't we obligated to hold them up in the greatest possible light?

———

Novel. Étienne. Highly sensitive. The smell of egg on the plates. As a result, micro-tragedies.[124]

———

Paris. Beauty is perfect justice.

Freedom is not hope for the future. It's the present. It's being true to people and the world in the present.

Revolution is good. But why? You have to have an idea of the civilization you wish to create. The abolition of property is not an end. It's a means.

———

121. One illegible word.

122. Naydejda Konstantinovna Krupskaya (1869–1939), Russian revolutionary, advocate of public libraries, and wife of Vladimir Lenin.

123. In French, *dépasse*, here translated as "beyond," and *passe*, here translated as "pass," make for a stronger pairing than in English.

In the Yellow Notebook, Camus writes: "Contrast the mother with the universe (the airplane, the most distant countries linked together)." And in *The First Man*'s Mother file, this line ends: "holding her well-combed hair, mussed up by the propellers, with one hand."

124. Information that would be incorporated into *The First Man*.

Tolstoy's paternal grandfather sent his dirty laundry from Russia to Holland by sled at the first sign of snow and the sleds returned with clean laundry shortly before Spring.

Tolstoy: "Political literature, reflecting the transitory interests of the society, is important and is perhaps necessary for the development of the people, yet there exists another literature that echoes the eternal concerns shared by all humanity, and which includes creations dear to the people's heart, a literature accessible to a person of any class, of any time, and without which no strong and sturdy populace has yet developed."

———

Tolstoy had an illegitimate child with Axinia (peasant).

Id. Turgenev read *Fathers and Sons* to Tolstoy, who fell asleep.

Id. Cf. the countess: "He disgusts me with his people" (she copied out *War and Peace* seven different times).

Id. Tolstoy: "The savage criticism depresses me."

Id. "Madness is selfishness."

Id. Shakespeare. "An abomination is a scam."

The Optina Hermitage, which attracted all the Russian writers, was founded in the 14th century by a penitent brigand.

See Alexandra Tolstoy: *Tolstoy: A Life of My Father*, p. 302 and especially for me p. 444.[125]

Tolstoy on the Russo-Japanese war: "In a war with a non-Christian people, the Christian people must be defeated." *Id.* in the journal: "A criminal wishes to die." And at the moment of death: "Don't lose heart, Alexandra, everything's fine."

———

Novel (end). She goes back to Algeria, where the fighting is going on (because that's where she wants to die). They don't allow the son in the waiting room. He stays and waits. They look at each other, twenty meters between them, through three layers of glass, and give little waves from time to time.[126]

———

125. The book had just appeared in French as *Léon Tolstoï, mon père*, in a translation by Edmond Cary, published by Amiot-Dumont. Camus's page references are to this edition.

126. A slightly different version of this entry appears in *The First Man*'s Mother file, right after the previous entry that begins "Novel-end."

On August 5, Camus's mother, who had been staying with her son in Isle-sur-la-Sorgue, headed back to Algiers.

The world is collapsing, the East is in flames, people are tearing each other apart around her, and M., on a deserted beach at the very tip of Europe, runs through a howling wind, along the shaded path created by the clouds. She is life, triumphant.

———

August 1956.

C.S.[127] I love this little face, worried and wounded, sometimes tragic, always beautiful, this little being whose bonds are too strong but whose face is illuminated by a dark and gentle flame, the flame of purity, of a soul. And when she's onstage and she turns her back, insulted by her partner, then that slight unhappiness goes away, and her shoulders appear fragile.

For the first time in a long time, without any desires or intentions, without games, my heart is touched by a woman, loving her for her, not without sadness.

———

Novel. After loving Jessica for fifteen years, he meets a young dancer, who, with a couple of differences, has the same gifts, the same flame as J., and something is born in Jean that resembles the love he had for J., as if it were still possible to start over again (and as M.H., on the same premises, had loved Jessica without saying so). But he is old, she is young, and he still loves Jessica and the love he had for her. He says nothing. Withdraws. Life does not start over again. No sooner had he discovered, or believed he'd discovered, that he loved her than, terrified, he decided never to touch her. When you fall in love with someone, you wish they could have known you as you were before meeting them, so that they can see what they've made of you.

———

I'm old or I soon will be. I've spent half my adult life protecting one person at the cost of sacrificing another, and maybe a part of myself, too. I can't throw away what I've spent twelve years trying to preserve, not for a few months or years of living. The things I've broken in one person, I can't turn around and break in another, like a spoiled child who disfigures all his toys one after the next.

---

127. Catherine Sellers (1926–2014) was a French actress of Tunisian-Jewish heritage whose father died in the concentration camps. She would star in Camus's production of *Requiem for a Nun* (see below), and she and Camus would share an intimate relationship lasting through the end of his life.

I've always thought that love, that any feeling, always ends up resembling what it was at the very second it came into being. And what I've felt with you is love without possession, the heart's gift. Possession gets added, and brings a certain significance, but it's not a sensual one . . .

Maybe we could find a sort of alliance in this, a marriage known only to us, a commitment, a pact.[128]

Time no longer existed for me; ten hours a day in that theater basement, beneath the simultaneously dim and harsh light of those rehearsal lamps, I followed, fascinated, on that little face illuminated on the inside by another light, by a day of suffering, all the emotions the pain of living can bring into being on the human face. There, I was faced with what is deepest, most wounded, solemn, and powerless in man. And when we left, the unexpected rain, the gentle September night, was welcomed as it was, an immutable order, the stage setting for what stirs and suffers in the hearts of men and women, the only thing over these long weeks that's kept me alive and fulfilled.[129]

C., novel character.[130] Young Jewish deportee, used by the S.S. in the camp (X's sister). *She makes it through.* She becomes an actress: 1) because she develops a spectacular command of derision; 2) because it takes her away from the world; 3) because she lives all the lives that will forever be preferable to what she's seen and done. On her face: Belsen and pity. That's what we're applauding.

Her *clumsiness*. Burns, stains, losses, etc.

"They were alone in the car after a long night's work, the nonstop rain resounding on the metal above them, Paris deserted. Rolling over that face, illuminated only by the glow from a streetlamp filtering in through the glass, were the shadows of raindrops streaming down the windshield. They huddled there in that shadow, in their sheet-metal house, while the street, the silent city, a continent, the world in flames surrounded them, and he never tired of looking at that face streaming with shadowy tears."

---

128. This "entry," written on a separate sheet of *NRF* letterhead and placed inside the notebook, has no addressee listed but nevertheless appears to be part of a letter. The French word *alliance* can also mean "wedding ring."

129. At the time of this entry, Camus was in the middle of rehearsals for his stage adaptation of William Faulkner's *Requiem for a Nun*, which would open at the Théâtre des Mathurins on September 20, 1956. Catherine Sellers would play the role of Temple Drake.

130. The description given in this entry, as well as in the following entries marked "C," shares much in common with Catherine Sellers's background.

"Our deserted vacation, sweet and secret." He shook the tree branches above the walls and the drops of water fell like rain over his friend's upturned face. One by one, he drank those drops that shone like feverish, tender eyes.

———

Sunday, September 2, 1956.

The slowly sinking ship and her drowned face.[131] Birth.

———

Monday.

The faithful rain.

———

Tuesday.

A pure gift. Asking nothing for herself.

———

Thursday, 6.

Insurmountable fatigue and finally the confession of love.

C. I'd like to be able to breathe—to be able to love by memory or fidelity. But my heart constantly aches. I love you so much I can hardly bear it. The hand-kissing is painful. The annoying habit of always leaving something behind.

C's father—Jewish doctor—Stayed in Paris during the Occupation. Deported to Birkenau, dies there. Typhus. Crematorium. "I still think he had gold fillings." Separated from his wife, intense, passionate, seductive. C. loved him. Her life begins at sixteen years old, upon disembarkation.

Paris, where the sun is a luxury, where dying costs an arm and a leg, where there are no trees without a bank account. Paris, which wishes to give the world lessons.

———

131. In the short story "The Artist at Work," collected in *Exile and the Kingdom*, when the titular artist is questioned by his wife about his infidelities, the artist remarks that she has "the look of a drowned woman, that look that comes from surprise and an excess of pain." The idea of a drowning woman also plays a central role in *The Fall*.

Theater breaks through city walls. And these narrow-minded gnats want gnatty theaters that do nothing but reflect the city itself.[132]

———

At fourteen years old, C. sneaks out of her house in El Biar at night, her bedsheets tied into a rope.

———

C. Heart starving for sorrow. Her rage *against* her body.

———

Tragic love and only that. Tragic happiness. And when it stops being tragic it becomes something else and the person once more throws themselves in search of the tragic.

———

November 6, '56.

Facing the constant threat of total destruction posed by war—and thus deprivation of a future—what sort of morals can allow us to live solely in the present? Honor and freedom.

———

Industrial civilization, in suppressing natural beauty, in covering long stretches of it in industrial waste, creates and arouses artificial needs. In such a civilization, we can no longer live in or tolerate poverty.

———

Faust rejuvenated as Don Juan. A wise old spirit in a young body. Explosive combination.

Id. Scene where Don Juan witnesses his burial. Don Faust or The Knight of the West.

———

Dawn. A fable. The Don Juan of knowledge: no philosopher, no poet has discovered him. He lacks the capacity to love the things he discovers, but he's witty and sensuous, and he enjoys the allures and intrigues of knowledge—which he pursues to the highest and most distant stars—until finally there's nothing of knowledge left for him to hunt down except that most absolutely *painful* part, like the drunkard who ends up drinking absinthe and aqua fortis. That's why he ends up desiring Hell. It's the last bit of knowledge that *seduces* him. Maybe it, too, will end up disappointing him, like everything else he's

132. On the translation of the term *miteux,* here given as "gnatty," see p. 494n117.

come to know. Then he'd be stuck for all eternity, nailed to disappointment, and he himself would become the stone guest, would desire an evening meal of knowledge, a meal that will never be shared with him, for the whole wide world of things will find not another bite to give that famished mouth.[133]

———

Progressive intellectuals. They're the tricoteuses[134] of dialectics. As each head falls, they restitch the threads of reasoning torn out by the facts.

———

For forty-four years, Joanna the Mad[135] lived in a small windowless room, lit day and night by a lamp, and never left except to go to the neighboring convent to gaze upon her husband's grave. Maybe that's what real life is about.

———

The businessman who's had enough and so becomes a clown. But without quitting his house or business. He just dresses as a clown.

———

Mi. After long kisses: "How ravishing!"[136]

———

Custine:[137] "The contradiction that exists between a fiery soul and the uniformity of existence makes life unbearable."

Id. "These days speech is but a negotiation between verity and vanity."

———

The two greatest minds the heavens gifted the Romans, Lucretius and Seneca, committed suicide.

———

133. This entry reproduces Nietzsche's *Dawn* (sometimes translated as *Daybreak*), book 4, no. 327 in its entirety.

134. The *tricoteuses*, literally "knitting women," were the driving force in the Women's March on Versailles during the early days of the French Revolution. The group, made up of everyday market women, began to demonstrate when the price of already-scarce bread started to rise out of control. They won concessions from Louis XVI and were initially celebrated as heroines by successive governments, but by the time the Reign of Terror began, they'd been officially sidelined by decree of the authorities. With no political power left, they sat in front of the guillotines in the Place de la Révolution and knitted.

135. Joanna of Castile (1479–1555), mother of Charles V and sister of Catherine of Aragon. It's widely believed that Joanna suffered some form of schizophrenia.

136. Mette Ivers, a painter and illustrator of Danish heritage, is referred to in these pages by her initials, "Mi." She and Camus met at the Café de Flore in February 1957. Later, when Camus admitted he'd been writing about her in these notebooks, he asked her: "Does that make you happy?" To which she responded, "That all depends on what you're writing."

137. Astolphe de Custine (1790–1857), French writer and author of *Souvenirs and Portraits*.

After Noces, Summer. Celebration[138] (1—Soccer; 2—Tipasa; 3—Rome—The Greek Islands—The Mistral—The Body—Dance—Eternal Morning).

He loses his daughter. I'm an old man now. To be young, you need a future.

Massacre of the innocent during the life of Christ. To be born guilty, you must die innocent.[139]

Reprinting of Fall, p. 73: "melancholic surrenders." P. 126 masculine corporation.

Dr. Schnitzler. Multiple concentration camps. Saved in the end because he was *likable*. Everybody helped him.

Professor M.L: "People have to love one another," "we have to . . ." "we have to . . ." The reality surrounding him: indescribable chaos.

I sometimes feel overwhelmed by an immense affection for the people around me, living in this same century.

The Canadian prostitute in that café near the Folies-Bergère: "My father saw the world, and so have I, trust me, I've been to Germany, Algeria, I've suffered too much, I've starved, I'm in a bad way now and my mother hasn't seen me for two weeks, my father was blown up by a landmine, my brother, too, but you know, I'll do it for you because you're a girlfriend, and well, I'm waiting for him, and it's bad enough that I'm eating through my family's money, still going out with that asshole, oh, it's not going well, I don't know anyone."

N: strength in moderation is superior strength.[140]

---

138. A plan for a fourth book of lyrical essays, which would have been titled *Celebration*.

139. In *The Fall*, Clamence says: "The children of Judea [who were] massacred while his parents took him to a safe place; why did they die if not because of him?"

As the next entry points out, Camus was now combing through the initial printing of *The Fall*, which had sold a surprising 126,500 copies in its first six months. Neither of the corrections he mentions here were made in subsequent printings.

140. Possibly a reference to Nietzsche's *Beyond Good and Evil*, chap. 3, no. 51.

M. says: "The race of Christ—and the other."

Play. A writer (or scholar or artist or actor) overworked by social demands is lapped *by life*. Beside him, a quite dignified professor seized by love acts like a child: he pretends to know how to drink, to drive cars, to make love, practice judo, etc.[141]

There is in this world, running parallel to the forces of death and subjugation, an enormous force of persuasion. It's called culture.

In the Old Testament, God says nothing: it's the living who serve as his word. It's in this sense that I've never stopped loving what's sacred in this world.

N. carried out. A multitude of experiences but controlled by and oriented toward the greatest being and the earliest times, by extreme freedom but according to discipline—and a life endlessly risked as an ongoing punishment—an accepted and *prodigal* solitude, bowed only, secretly, before being-in-the-world. Say no more but do and in doing give meaning to a higher word, speaking only in terms of . . . (For he who is losing his memory, the journal is an instrument of such asceticism.)

Custine: "Arab architecture is the art of an effeminate people" (paper cutouts that confectioners use to cover their boxes of dragées[142]). He (Custine) cites the words of Voltaire or Diderot: "The Russians rotted before ripening."

At 10 years old, Nietzsche founds a *Théâtre des Arts* with his friends, and they put on two ancient dramas that he wrote.

---

141. *Se faire doubler*, given above as "lapped," is more transparently linked in French to Camus's interest in "doubling" and can mean "to fall behind," "to be undercut," or "to be double-crossed."

142. In English-speaking countries, dragées are often referred to as Jordan almonds or sugared almonds. Julius Dragatus, a confectioner in Ancient Rome, is thought to be the originator of the treat.

The quotes come from Custine's *L'espage sous Ferdinand VII*, book 2, 224.

June 1957.

Festival d'Angers finished.[143] Happy exhaustion. Life, marvelous life, its injustice, its glory, its passion, its struggles, life begins again. The strength, again, to love all and create all.

———

July 15.

Depart from Paris. Sleep in Guéret. Such is the life of the family poisoner.[144]

———

July 17.

Cordes. Silence and beauty. Solitude of this great house, of this ghost town. Time flows through me, delicately, bringing my breath back. Around Cordes, over the perfect circle of hills, the sky extends, tender, wide open, cloudy and luminous all at once. At night, Venus, plump as a peach, sets insanely fast over the Western hill. It stops for a moment at the ridgeline, then abruptly disappears, swallowed like a token in a slot. The stars instantly swarm and the Milky Way churns to cream.

———

July 18.

It's raining. This morning, the wild Aveyron Valley. Work. I can't bear these ties any longer, so crazy for freedom that I push deeper and deeper into a solitude that may be dangerous. I can't stop thinking of F., my grief.

Evening. Discouraged by myself, by my desert-like nature.

———

143. Camus played a key role in the 1957 festival, adapting and directing Lope de Vega's *Le chevalier d'Olmedo* (*The Knight from Olmedo*) and directing a revised version of *Caligula*. Actor Louis Jourdan asked Camus if he'd be interested in directing the production of *Caligula* in New York, to which Camus responded that, for him, an important part of directing a play is "directing the actors, and in that regard my weak understanding of English would be a major obstacle. . . . I'd be completely unable to say if an English intonation rings true or false."

144. The word Camus uses here can also mean, informally, "pest," "pain in the neck," or "nuisance." Camus's relationship with his wife, long in a bad way, had at this point become even more strained.

July 20.

A letter from Georges Didier's[145] superior telling me he died in a car accident in Switzerland.

July 21.

Rain that doesn't let up for days. Sharp and profound sadness.

July 22.

Letter from Mi about her family and their "feasts of bitterness." Telephoning the one she loves, 700 km away, she's at a loss for words. "I was miserable and merry there."[146]

July 23.

The truth! The truth!

July 24.

Beautiful, deserted countryside where every house you encounter has fallen into ruin. In gutted barns overgrown with nettles, old, wheeled-harrows rust, a desert kingdom haunted by ancient, enormous spiders. Flight to the cities, the factories, to collective pleasures. Here, a civilization slowly dies around us, the old houses bearing witness. I said this to M., who said she didn't have the impression of death but of waiting. Waiting for what?

"The Messiah."

It's always raining; I'm as hungry for light as for bread and can no longer bear myself.

---

145. Georges Didier was a childhood friend of Camus's who went on to become a monk. He was killed in a car accident at Chaux-de-Fonds, in Switzerland, on July 9, 1957. Camus's response to this letter, addressed to an unknown reverend, can be found on p. 636.

146. Mette Ivers spent the summer at her parents' house in Saint-Jean-de-Luz in southwestern France. There was only one phone, and it was in the middle of the main room, leaving no place for private conversation.

July 24.

Depart Roussillon.[147] The sea. Leucate. Return the evening of the 25th.

———

July 26.

Stunning mornings. Swallows drunk.

Those who aren't curious: what they know turns them off from what they don't (C.).

———

Buddhism is atheism as a religion. Rebirth *based on* nihilism. A unique example, I believe. And one worth meditating on for those of us grappling with nihilism.

———

If you asked suffering to explain its reasons you'd be liable to sympathize with next to nothing.

———

Cordes. Every night I went to watch Venus get under the covers, to watch the stars rise into the warm night above her bed.[148]

———

An old English lady who committed suicide kept a diary in which she'd jotted the same thing every day, for months on end: "Today, nobody came."

———

At the end of The Adolescent (and in its three alternate versions) Dostoyevsky ironically puts Tolstoy on trial.[149]

———

Cordes, August 4.

Thoughts of death.

———

147. Roussillon, now the Eastern Pyrenees, is a department in the southeast of France, bordering Spain and the Mediterranean Sea. Leucate is a nearby commune (township).

148. *Se coucher*, translated here as "get under the covers," can mean both "to go to sleep," as for a person, and "to set," as for an astral body.

149. At the time Dostoyevsky was publishing *The Adolescent*, also translated as *An Accidental Family*, Tolstoy was publishing *Anna Karenina*. Tolstoy's novel focuses on the aristocratic family, whereas Dostoyevsky's focuses on the conflict between adoptive and biological family.

August 6.

Visit to Cayla:[150] a silent, solitary place around which the world comes to die. I understand better now what I read in Eugénie de Guérin's journal: "I would gladly agree to be confined to Cayla. Nowhere else in the world pleases me like my home." And yet: "Where will I be? Where will we be when these trees once again grow tall? Others will take a stroll beneath their shadows, will see the winds pass just as we do, the winds that will bring them down."

———

The Old Believers in Russia thought we carried a little devil on our left shoulder and a little angel on our right shoulder. There's an idea for the theater in that (for Don Faust?): the angel and demon grow according to how much we feed them. In general, one *or* the other is much bigger. My character will enter with two smaller characters *of equal size*. The dialogue between them, from the character to the two creatures, from the two to the character, etc., etc.

———

"The lightest silk thread is more unbearable to me than a lead ball is to others." (N.) To me, as well, alas.

———

Svidrigailov from Crime and Punishment: "A small, smoke-filled room with spiders in the corners, and that's the entirety of eternity."[151]

———

August 8, 1957. Cordes.

For the first time after reading Crime and Punishment, absolute doubt about my calling. I'm seriously considering giving up. I've always believed creation is a dialogue. But with whom? Our literary society whose driving principle is second-rate spite, where offense takes the place of a critical method? Society as a whole? A population that doesn't read us, a bourgeoisie that, in a given year, peruses the papers and two trendy books. In reality, a creator these days can only be a solitary prophet, inhabited by, consumed by a limitless creation. Am I such a creator? I thought so. More precisely, I thought I could be. Today, I have my doubts and am quite tempted to cast aside this endless

---

150. Cayla refers to the Cayla Castle, today a museum honoring Maurice de Guérin, a French poet and painter born in the region. His sister, Eugénie, who took on the project of collecting and publishing her brother's work after his death, had her own *Journals* and *Letters* posthumously published. One of Maurice's two major works was *The Bacchante*.

151. In *The Notebooks for Crime and Punishment*, Dostoyevsky writes that Svidrigailov "believes in the future life, with the spiders, etc."

effort that leaves me unhappy in happiness itself, this empty asceticism, this call that steels me against who knows what. I'd do theatrical work, I'd write plays here and there, without worrying about a thing, and then maybe I'd be free. What do I care about respected or honest art? Am I capable of doing what I dream of doing? If I'm not capable, what's the point of dreaming? To free myself from that too and consent to nothing! Others far greater than I have done it.[152]

August 12.

C.S. "The greatest compassion should be aroused not by pain but indignity. Feeling ashamed of yourself is the worst of all miseries. The only kind of suffering all of you seem to have experienced is beautiful suffering, distinguished suffering." It's true.

Emerson: "The secret of genius is to suffer no fiction to exist for us."[153]

August 13.

Leave Cordes.

---

152. In a letter dated August 10, 1957, Camus expressed similar sentiments to Catherine Sellers: "No progress. For the past two days (after rereading *Crime and Punishment*), for the first time in my life, I've felt like giving up on being a writer. I could work in the theater, do the occasional adaptation, and I'd be free on the inside, without this soul-killing effort to unburden myself. Yea, perhaps I should give up, just like that."

The initials in the next entry likely refer to Catherine Sellers.

153. The quote comes from Emerson's 1850 book of essays, *Representative Men*. It appears as part of the closing line of the closing essay "Goethe; or, The Writer." In context, it reads: "Genius hovers with his sunshine and music close by the darkest and deafest eras. No mortgage, no attainder, will hold on men or hours. The world is young: the former great men call to us affectionately. We too must write Bibles, to unite again the heavens and the earthly world. The secret of genius is to suffer no fiction to exist for us; to realize all that we know; in the high refinement of modern life, in arts, in sciences, in books, in men, to exact good faith, reality and a purpose; and first, last, midst and without end, to honor every truth by use."

Atonal music is still dramatic, despite presenting itself as a reaction against musical Romanticism. This is because nonsignification is always poignant and dramatic.[154] *Id.* for painting.

———

A word about The Fall, given they don't understand. It's put together the way it is to mock a modern mindset and that strange, indecent secular remorse about sin. Cf. Chesterton[155] "The 19th century (*id.* the 20th) is full of Christian ideas gone mad."

Lenin never had to deal with the masses. Cf. Sperber: the left and Truman's Fourth Point.[156]

Id. Freud felt no medical calling, no "penchant for humanity's suffering."

Nemesis. Profound complicity of Marxism and Christianism (expand on this). That's why I'm against both.

———

The blind lovers who, groping about, kill the blind husband.

———

Un Théâtre Ininterrompu.[157]

———

Religion's attraction for theater people. Real life and the life of dreams.

I liked those places (well-lit restaurants, dance halls, etc.) people invented to take shelter from life. This wounded thing inside me.

———

154. In *The Rebel*, Camus writes: "The very expression of a philosophy of nonsignification creates a contradiction. Putting it into words gives a minimum of coherence to incoherence. It introduces consequence into something that, if the position is to be believed, leads to no such thing. To speak is to fix. The only coherent approach based on nonsignification would be silence, if silence itself carried no significance. Perfect absurdity tries to be mute. If it speaks, it's out of indulgence or, as we shall see, because it considers itself a provisional step."

Here, the term "nonsignification" might also be translated as "nonsense" or "meaninglessness."

155. The quote comes from G. K. Chesterton's *Orthodoxy*, chap. 3, "The Suicide of Thought." In context, it reads: "The modern world is not evil; in some ways the modern world is far too good. It is full of wild and wasted virtues. When a religious scheme is shattered (as Christianity was shattered at the Reformation), it is not merely the vices that are let loose. The vices are, indeed, let loose, and they wander and do damage. But the virtues are let loose also; and the virtues wander more wildly, and the virtues do more terrible damage. The modern world is full of the old Christian virtues gone mad. The virtues have gone mad because they have been isolated from each other and are wandering alone. Thus some scientists care for truth; and their truth is pitiless. Thus some humanitarians only care for pity; and their pity (I am sorry to say) is often untruthful."

156. The Truman Doctrine, conceived in 1947, aimed at containing Soviet expansion and led to the Marshall Plan, a vast program of aid for nations opposing Communism.

157. Literally, "An Uninterrupted Theater."

Necessity and exaltation of opposites. Balance, where contradiction lives. Sun and shadows.

———

At fifteen years old, Nietzsche,[158] while his friends dismiss what Mucius Scaevola's did,[159] takes a red-hot coal from the stove without saying a word and holds it out for them to see. He bears the scar the rest of his life.

Story about the brothel[160] (H. p. 48). Cosima is to blame for having destroyed all of N.'s letters to W. "Tragic knowledge and Greek gaiety." The Basel Cathedral's terrace, where Nietzsche and Burckhardt conversed. "A modern anchorite—the impossibility of living in line with the State." *Id.* "Aristocracy of the mind must conquer the whole of its freedom vis-à-vis the State, which today holds a tight grip on science"—*Id.* The dreamer, lying on a tiger.

The burning of the Louvre during the Commune causes him to cry and destroys him for days: "Never, no matter how sharp my pain, would I have thrown a stone at such sacrileges, which are only, in my eyes, the carriers of all our sins. Sins about which there is much to contemplate." "Make sure I'm buried as a faithful pagan, without lies." Sad without light, elated when it returns.

Plan for "ten years of meditation and silence." Idea of the "mask."[161] Praise for Napoleon in The Gay Science.[162] Affair with Mme V.P. in '87, last note

---

158. The following notes were taken during Camus's reading of Daniel Halévy's *Nietzsche*.

159. Gaius Mucius Cordus Scaevola (sixth century BC) was a Roman hero, perhaps mythical, who was captured by the Etruscans while on a mission to assassinate their king. Rather than naming his coconspirators, Scaevola let his right hand be burned, which is the origin of his nickname, Scaevola (left-handed).

160. Looking for a hotel in Cologne, Nietzsche was instead directed to a brothel, where he sat at the piano in the living room, naked women around him, and shocked everyone by bursting into an improvisation.

The "H" citation refers to *Human All Too Human*. "N.'s letters to W." refers to Nietzsche's letters to Wagner.

161. In *Beyond Good and Evil*, Nietzsche writes: "Give me another mask, a second mask!"

162. A copy of Nietzsche's *The Gay Science* was found in Camus's mud-caked valise, which was recovered at the scene of the accident that killed him. The reference here is to book 5, "We Fearless Ones," no. 362.

to Rohde, staggering.[163] Rohde doesn't respond. "Why are you crying, Lisbeth?[164] Aren't we happy?"

I was very skeptical about rationalism. But my colleagues' passion [. . .].[165]

September 8.

Death of Robert Chatté. At the Villejuif Hospital, alone.[166]

Refusing to shine when you can shine, to please, etc. It takes a little artifice but then artifice eventually consumes everything. Ultimately, moping about (as long as necessary) is more useful than gossiping and going out for nothing.

What it would take: not just someone you can love without asking anything of them but also someone you love who can give you nothing.

Novel. Mi: she breathed like a swimmer while making love, smiling the whole time, swimming faster and faster, running aground on a wet, hot shore, mouth open, still smiling, as if in passing through grottos and deep waters, water had become her element and the earth the arid place where, as a dripping-wet fish, she happily suffocated.

The greatest man, the greatest spiritual strength: the most, the most focused [. . .].[167]

Nietzsche. Irreligious by religion. Pascal—in his way—After all, according to Thomas, faith is courage of the mind.

---

163. Erwin Rohde (1845–1898), a German scholar and friend of Nietzsche's since their school years. When Nietzsche published *Human All Too Human*, Rohde was highly critical of the book, writing to Franz Overbeck: "The actual philosophical parts in it—when touched upon—are as paltry and almost childish as the political ones, fatuous and ignorant of the world." Nietzsche ends his November 11, 1887, letter to Rohde: "I now have forty-three years behind me and I'm as alone as when I was a child."

164. Elizabeth Forester-Nietzsche, Nietzsche's sister.

165. Two illegible sentences.

166. In the Yellow Notebook, Camus writes: "Chatté dies in the hospital while his neighbor's radio spouts nonsense. / —Heart disease. Deadman walking. 'If I commit suicide, at least I'll have taken the initiative.'"

167. Two illegible words.

Id. for him, Christ: the immoralist Savior.

Custine. "One day the sleeping giant will awaken and violence will end the reign of words. Then lost equality will call, in vain, the old aristocracy to rescue freedom, and the weapon, taken up too late by hands too long inactive, will be powerless."[168]

Id. about the French: "they would sooner paint themselves as ugly than let themselves be forgotten."

Don Faust. When he's transformed into Don Juan, the scene will start with a hearty laugh from a man backstage, which will signal Don Juan's entrance.

Nietzsche. "A few thousand years further on the road of the last century and the greatest intelligence will be on display in all that man does—but as a result intelligence will have lost all its dignity. It will still undoubtedly be necessary to be intelligent, but it will also be so ordinary that a nobler mind will experience this necessity as a vulgarity. To be noble might then mean *to have madness in one's head*."[169]

The Bible was born among stones.

October 1st.

Visit from G.T.[170] Before leaving for Algeria, she comes to tell me what she did. It was a month ago in Algiers. She was contacted by emissaries of the F.L.N. who proposed a meeting with their leaders, who wanted to ask her some questions about her pamphlet (Algeria '57). She accepted. Rendezvous, then procedures. In short, received in a house in the casbah by two

168. The quote is from Custine's *Letters from Russia*.

169. From Nietzsche's *The Gay Science*, book 1, section 20. The French translation shows significant differences from Walter Kaufmann's standard English translation. The above has been translated directly from the French. Camus cut the penultimate line from the quotation.

170. Germaine Tillion (1907–2008), French ethnologist, joined the Resistance as part of the Groupe du musée de l'Homme, was betrayed by the collaborationist priest Robert Alesch, and sent to the Ravensbrück concentration camp. After the war, she returned to Algeria and wrote a book, *Algeria in 1957*, in which she denounced the French state's use of torture and the way in which French colonialism had reduced the native population to a state of destitution. Camus wrote a preface for the American edition, published as *Algeria: The Realities*.

The National Liberation Front (Front de libération nationale, FLN) was established in 1954 to fight for Algerian independence.

women. Then two armed men arrived. They discussed. G.T. explained her thesis to them: a population reduced to destitution,[171] the bulk of supplemental income coming from mainland France, etc. (her opinion: politically valid, economically uncultivated). At that moment, the one who appeared to be in charge: "You take us for murderers." Then G.T: "But you are murderers" (this was shortly after the attack on the Casino de la Corniche). Then the other man's pained reaction: eyes welling with tears. Then: "These bombs, I'd like to see them at the bottom of the sea." To which G.T. said, "That's entirely up to you." They talked about torture. I'm a plaintiff, she said (she took part in the commission investigating [the] system of concentration camps). They arrived at [an] agreement: suppression of civilian terrorism in exchange for suppression of executions. More or less the terms I'd proposed (but the result, alas . . .). The other man, with regard to talks being spiked: "France is responsible." To which G.T. said, "You can go and tell that to your grandmother. I was there. It was the F.L.N. and you know it." The one in charge signaled to the other not to respond. She learned not long after that it was Ali la Pointe.[172] As she was leaving, she took him by the tie and shook him: "And don't forget what I said." And he replied: "No, Ma'am."

2nd interview after the execution, she learned that the one in charge was Saadi Yacef. He was arrested two weeks later.[173]

Also shows me responses written by 30 Arab students between the ages of 11 to 12 whose Arab teacher gave them the prompt: "What would you do if you were invisible?": All would take up arms and kill the French, either the paratroopers or the heads of state. I despair for the future.

That the slave is enslaved because he chose life over death is historically false. Budapest.

---

171. The word used here, *clochardisation* (derived from *clochard, vagrant*), was employed by Germain Tillion in her book *Algeria: The Realities* to discuss not only the overt effects of colonialism on native populations but also the systemic, societal, cultural effects that may not be as obvious. To a different effect, Charles de Gaulle proclaimed in March 1960 that, for Algeria, "Clochardisation is independence." The translation used at the time, "pauperization," seems somewhat antiquated now and, as a result, loses the harshness of the original.

172. Ali La Pointe (1930–1957) was one of the National Liberation Front's most trusted and terrifying fighters.

173. Saadi Yacef (b. 1928), head of the National Liberation Front's Autonomous Zone during the Battle of Algiers, was captured by French forces on September 24, 1957. On October 8, 1957, Ali La Pointe's hiding place was located (and he was killed) based on information provided to French forces by an informant. Saadi Yacef, who had been sentenced to death after being captured and was later pardoned, has denied being the informant.

October 17.

Nobel. Strange feeling of overwhelming weight and melancholy. At 20 years old, poor and naked, I knew true glory. My mother.[174]

October 19.

Frightened by what's happening to me, what I didn't ask for. And to make it all the worse, attacks so low they break my heart. Rebatet has the gall to say that I long to command firing squads even though he was among those for whom I, and other Resistance writers, requested a pardon when he was sentenced to death.[175] He was pardoned, but he doesn't pardon me. Again the desire to leave this country. But to go where?

Creation itself, art itself, its details, every day and the rupture. . . . I don't have enough strength to despise. In any case, I have to overcome this sort of terror, of incomprehensible panic, into which this unexpected news has thrown me. For that. . . .

"They don't love me. Is that a reason not to bless them?" N.[176]

Saints are afraid of the miracles they perform. They can neither love them nor lose themselves in them.

Three coughing fits this month alone, aggravated by claustrophobic panic. Unstable.

---

174. On October 16, 1957, Camus was eating lunch at Chez Marius with Patricia Blake when a representative from Gallimard approached the table to inform him he'd won the Nobel Prize for Literature. His first message was a telegram to his mother: "I've never missed you so much, Maman." Not long after, he wrote to his schoolteacher Louis Germain to say: "When I heard the news, my first thought, after my mother, was of you. Without you, without that affectionate hand you reached out to the poor child I was, without your teaching, and your example, none of this would have ever happened." To friends such as Nicola Chiaromonte, Camus expressed greater apprehension, writing: "I received the news with a sort of panic. What's helped is hearing from those I hold dear. . . . At the moment, I just want you to know that this event, which had redoubled my fear of public life, has only brought me closer to those few friends with whom I share a heart and mind." On October 17, Gallimard threw a party in his honor.

175. Lucien Rebatet (1903–1972), collaborationist journalist who wrote for *Je suis partout* (I am everywhere) and *L'action française* and author of *Décombres* (*The Ruins*). In 1946, he was sentenced to death for having collaborated with the Germans, but the sentence was commuted the next year.

176. From Nietzsche's *Fragments posthumes*, published as part of Gallimard's *Œuvres philosophiques complètes*.

The last sentence of the entry is literally: "love them nor love themselves in them."

The relentless effort I've made to come together with others on the basis of shared values, to establish my own sense of balance, isn't entirely in vain. What I've said or found can be of use, must be of use, to others. But not to me, now delivered unto a sort of madness.

December 29.

3 P.M. Another panic attack. It's been exactly four years to the day since X. became unstable (no, it's the 29th, so a day away, then).[177] For a few minutes, a feeling of complete madness. Then exhaustion and trembling. Sedatives. I'm writing this an hour later.

Night of the 29th to the 30th: interminable anguish.

December 30.

Better for a while.

January 1st.

Anxiety redoubled.

January–March.

The major attacks have passed. Only a constant, gnawing anxiety now.

March 5.

Meeting with de Gaulle. As I'm talking about the risk of unrest if Algeria is lost and of the French Algerians' fury in Algeria itself: "French fury? I'm 67 years old and I've never seen a Frenchman kill another Frenchman. Except me."

Comparing France to everywhere else. "After all," he says, "no one's come up with anything better than France."

---

177. Toward the end of December 1953, Francine Camus slipped into a serious depression and was admitted to a clinic for treatment.

1905 revolutionaries' song: "Toward the sun, brothers, toward freedom."

Sperber. The Achilles Heel, p. 202: "The idea of substituting a radical break for suicide is not new. The will to definitively disavow one's own actions, to be forever rid of them, is often found in the dreams of those for whom only the body's logic still links them to life and for whom nothing connects them to other people: neither what they've received from them nor even what they've given to them. These dreams are born of a solitude capable of destroying even the affection such people feel for themselves."

Kierkegaard waved a terrible threat at Hegel: to send him a young man seeking his advice.

Dostoyevsky, after his admirable Speech on Pushkin:[178] "Just look at the practically unanimous treatment the press gave me for what I said in Moscow, as if I'd stolen from or swindled a couple of banks. Ukhantsev himself (a famous swindler) doesn't get as much crap as I do."

Id. after his early success: ". . . they created this dubious reputation for me, and I don't know how long this hell will last."

"The question I think about most often is what constitutes our communion of ideas, what are the points on which we can all come together, no matter how we may lean . . ."

"No one should ever waste their life for any goal" (expand).

Those who truly have something to say never speak of it.

Marseille.

Algiers.—Aboard the *Kairouan.*[179] The sea spray doubles. Foams form and sizzle atop a first wave that breaks against the ship—and then a violent wind takes hold of it, suddenly twisting it, wringing it out, and then a second spray, less weighted with water, with a lace of fine vapor, lifts into mist.

Seagulls with wings broken exactly in the middle /\/\/ in the shape of a roof.

---

178. The speech was given on June 8, 1880, at the meeting of the Society of Friends of Russian Literature. It was later published in *A Writer's Diary.*

179. On March 26, 1958, Camus sailed from Marseille to Algiers aboard the ocean liner *Kairouan.* He would stay in Algeria until mid-April, visiting his mother every day, as well as meeting with other friends, such as the Kabyle writer Mouloud Ferraoun, who would be assassinated by the OAS in 1962.

Soldiers on deck, leeward, hunkered in the rigging, heads wrapped in scarves, capotes shapeless. Moments like this when man abandons pageantry and hunkers down at the level of need. That's history.

Motionless seagulls descend on the upper deck and continue their patient flight right next to me. Stubborn seagulls with their globular eyes, their witches' beaks, their muscles that never tire. Seabirds have nowhere to land. Either the hollow center of an ever-changing swell or the swaying cross of the mainmast.

———

Condorcet: "Robespierre is a priest and will never be anything but that."[180]

Among the *primitive* reflexes, those that are innate in the nature of man and animal, Pavlov includes the "freedom reflex."

———

Power can't be separated from injustice. Power properly applied is the sound, careful administration of injustice.

———

Never talk about your work.

———

Actor.

———

Nietzsche. "In a superabundance of life-giving and restorative forces, even misfortunes have a solar radiance and beget their own consolation . . ."[181]

Id. "Supposing that we are always waiting for something to go wrong, for an unpleasant surprise, we will remain in a state of tension and animosity, we will be unbearable to others, and we will see our own health suffer; such temperaments lead to their own extinction."

Id. "Fear of death, the European sickness."

Id. "Happiness lies in the promptness of feeling and thinking; the rest of the world appears slow, gradual, and thick-headed. Anyone capable of feeling the flight of a ray of light would be filled with happiness on account of its celerity."

Id. "Portrait of man to come: eccentric, energetic, warm, indefatigable, artist, enemy of books."

180. Originally from Condorcet's November 8, 1792, column in *Chronique de Paris*.

181. Camus concluded a 1959 interview with Jean-Claude Brisville with this quote, which was published in the volume *Camus* for Gallimard's La Bibliothèque Idéale series.

Id. "Men of very high culture and a strong body are above all sovereigns."

About the biophages:[182] Montherlant's Journals, p. 82: everything is said with excellence and moderation.

For me: "I would have succumbed to each of my remaining feelings. I've always placed two feelings in opposition to each other."

Tipasa: The gentle, gray sky. At the center of the ruins, the slapping sea, a little rough, covers the birds' chirping. The Chenouas,[183] enormous and light. I will die and this place will continue to pour out fullness and beauty. Nothing bitter about the thought. On the contrary, a feeling of gratitude and reverence.

The heavy, vertical rains of Algiers. Incessant. In a cage.

Algerians. They live in the richness and warmth of friendship, of family. The body and its virtues are at center—and the profound sadness of the body as soon as it begins to break down—a life without horizons beyond the immediate, the carnal loop. Proud of their virility, of their capacity for eating and drinking, of their strength and their courage. Vulnerable.

The stabbed dove.

Return. *Kairouan*. Storm. Irresistible urge to throw myself in the water. The solitude and surrender of someone left alone in the raging waters of a ship's wake as the ship continues on its way.

[. . .][184]

Stages of healing.

---

182. In his *Notebooks*, Montherlant writes of "biophages": "Those who corrode, who devour our life, are initially the indifferent ones to whom business obliges us to give sprigs of our time."

183. A mountain range on the Algerian coast, near Tipasa, as well as the language of a people living on the mountain.

184. Camus sailed back to France in mid-April 1958.

Two additional pages (numbered 79 and 80 by Camus and not printed here) follow this paragraph in the handwritten notebook. After pages 79 and 80, Camus inserted a sheet of paper that had been ripped from another notebook, which he numbered 80 bis and 80 ter (80a and 80b). Then, at the top of page 81, he drew an arrow and wrote: "here: Stages of healing |.|" The entries that appear

Let the will rest. Enough with "you must."

Completely depoliticize the mind in order to humanize it.

Write the claustrophobic—and comedies.

Come to terms with death, which is to say accept it.

———

Accept making a spectacle of yourself. Such anxieties won't kill me. If they did, done. Otherwise, worst comes to worst, a little careless behavior. It's enough to accept others' judgments. Humility and acceptance, purely therapeutic remedies for anxiety.

———

The world is moving toward paganism. But it still rejects pagan values. We have to restore them, paganize belief, Graecize Christ, and equilibrium will return.

———

Could it be that I've suffered from the burden of my responsibilities?

———

As I'm in the desert, lifeless, I have to push aridity as far as it'll go in order to reach the threshold and, one way or another, cross it. Madness or greater mastery.

———

Method: as the anxiety comes on, breathing accelerates or slows down the moment the alarm is sounded. *Along with* the immediate suspension of *every action* and gesture. Second association: general relaxation.[185]

In the long run: accumulation and transfer of the energy contained in every want or desire by the momentary suspension of that want and desire.

---

on this inserted sheet of paper (80a and 80b) are printed here, beginning with "Stages of Healing" and running through the word "Journal." That they were not part of the original notebook accounts for the seemingly anachronistic entry dated May 3. The notebook proper recommences with "End of April '58," which appears at the top of page 81 in the handwritten original.

185. In the handwritten notebook, Camus drew a large bracket alongside this paragraph and the two that follow, with the note "De. *Ascèse*," which may refer to Nikos Kazantzakis's book *Ascesis: The Saviors of God*, the contents of which fit the immediate, as well as larger, context of Camus's thinking.

Recognize that I expect nothing from society. Any contribution then becomes a gift that doesn't expect anything in return. Praise or blame then become what they are: nothing. Suppression of the herd mentality at last.

Suppress the brooding morals of abstract justice. Keep close to the reality of people and things. Return to personal happiness as often as possible. Don't refuse to recognize what's true even when it goes against what's desirable. Ex: Recognize that power—it, too, it, especially—persuades.[186] The truth is worth all the torment. It's the only basis for the joy that must crown this effort.

———

Recover energy—at the core.

———

Recognize the need for enemies. Love that they are.[187]

———

Systematically break down automatic reflexes from the smallest to the largest: tobacco, food, sex, defensive emotional reactions (or the reaction to attack—they're the same thing), and *creation itself.* Asceticism not with regard to desire, which must be kept intact, but with regard to its satisfaction.

———

Recover the greatest strength, not to dominate but to give.

———

May 3.

Near-total recovery. Even stronger than before, I hope. Understand better now what I've always known: he who drags himself through life, who succumbs under its weight, can't help anyone, no matter what duties he takes on. He who has his life in hand can be truly generous and effortlessly give. Expect nothing and ask for nothing other than this strength to give and to work.[188]

186. After the previous sentence, Camus circled the number one and drew an arrow to the top of the page, where he wrote this sentence.

187. Camus's third volume of *Actuelles* (*Current Events*), which dealt exclusively with matters related to Algeria, would be published June 16, 1958. It sold poorly and was mostly ignored or criticized by the press. On July 28, 1958, Camus wrote to Francine: "If they put the squeeze on me, it wasn't for the sake of Algeria, only to put me in a bad spot. But maybe that's a good thing as it pushed me to clarify my thinking a little. That's the proper use of enemies: loved be they. Amen."

188. Although this entry was written on the outside sheet of paper Camus inserted in the notebook, which accounts for the fact that it is dated "May 3" and then followed by an entry in the notebook proper that is dated "End of April," the outside sheet bearing this entry may be contemporaneous with the notebook proper, given that Camus wrote similar sentiments to Louis Guilloux on April 24, 1958.

Journal.

———

End of April 1958. Cannes.[189]

At sea every day. In the evening, the buoys attached to the nets (a bottle with a lead clapper, the whole thing floating on cork) make a sound like bells calling in the sea's flocks. In the port at night, the boats cry and moan from mast to plank.

The light—the light—and the anxiety recedes, not yet gone, but dulled, as if drowsy with heat and sun.

APRIL 30. Martin du Gard. Nice. He has to drag himself around because of his rheumatoid arthritis. 77 years old. "In the face of death, nothing matters anymore, not even my work. There's nothing, nothing . . ." "Yes, it's nice not to feel alone" (and his eyes fill with tears). We make plans to meet again at *Tertre* in July.[190] "If I'm alive." But his heart remains the same, interested in everything.

———

May 29, 1958.

My job is to write my books and to fight whenever the freedom of my people and those close to me is threatened. That's all.[191]

———

The artist is like the god at Delphi: "He neither reveals nor conceals: he gives a sign."[192]

———

Chekhov: "I am neither a liberal nor a conservative. . . . My holy of holies is the human body, health, intelligence, talent, inspiration, love, and the most absolute freedom. Freedom from all brute force and from all lies in whatever form they're expressed:

---

189. On returning from Algeria, Camus went to stay with Michel Gallimard in Cannes, where the two enjoyed his twenty-five-foot speedboat, *Aya*.

190. *Tertre* was the name of Roger Martin du Gard's property in Bellême (Orne).

191. May 29, 1958, is the date on which General Charles de Gaulle, amid the May 1958 Crisis (also known as the Algiers Putsch), agreed to return to power as prime minister of France. This essentially marked the end of the Fourth Republic and the beginning of the Fifth, which saw a much greater concentration of power in the executive than in the past.

192. The quote, from Heraclitus, is in reference to Apollo's cryptic manner of speaking. It reads in full: "The Lord whose oracle is at Delphi neither reveals nor conceals, but gives a sign."

That's what my agenda would be if I were a great artist" (letter to Pleshcheyev.[193] 1888).

Musil:[194] a vast project that requires all the resources of art, which he doesn't have. Thus this work that's moving on account of its failures, not what it says. In the author's endless monologue, genius shines through in spots but never illuminates the art as a whole.[195]

Musil: "Each of us has a second nature where everything we do is innocent."

"Ordinary life is the average of all our possible crimes."[196]

—Maman. If we loved our loved ones enough, we'd keep them from dying.[197]

JUNE 9, 1958. Depart again for Greece.[198]

June 10.

Acropolis. Not the same level of feeling as the first time. I wasn't alone and was preoccupied with my company. And then met with O., who annoys me. The Acropolis isn't a place where you can lie. At 2:00, plane to Rhodes. The islands, rocks on the sea, drift off behind us. A spray of continents. In Rhodes, we land in the middle of some fields where a short, flowering wheat

193. Alexey Pleshcheyev (1825–1893), Russian poet who was condemned to death alongside Dostoyevsky, then pardoned at the same time.

194. Robert Musil (1880–1942), Austrian writer whose magnum opus *The Man Without Qualities* was translated into French in 1957. Interestingly, Catherine Sellers told Olivier Todd that while there weren't many contemporary authors Camus truly admired, he did "like some things and he'd read to me what he'd just read and liked. When Musil's book came out, he fell in love with Musil; he admired him enormously."

195. The rest of the page after this entry is blank in the original notebook.

196. This is the only entry on the page in the original notebook.

197. In the original notebook, this entry appears at the top of the page, and the entry that follows appears at the bottom of the page. They are the only two entries on the page.

198. Camus and Maria Casarès met up with Michel and Janine Gallimard, Anne Gallimard, Mario Prassinos—designer of the original hardcover editions of Camus's books—and his wife, Io, and their daughter, Catherine, for a boating trip around Greece.

is growing, the wind blowing it toward the blue sea in waves. A sumptuous, flowery island. Stroll amid the Frankish architecture at night. Met with Father Brückberger, who told me he intended to break with the Church without defrocking. My feelings of friendship for him are still alive. Boat with Michel G.'s family and the Prassinos.

———

June 11.

I leave the boat early in the morning, alone, and go for a swim on a beach in Rhodes, twenty minutes away, alone. The water is clear, fresh. The sun, just beginning to rise, warms without burning. Delicious moments that bring me back to those Madrague mornings twenty years ago when I'd climb out of the tent half-asleep, only meters from the sea, and dive into the somnolent morning water.[199] Alas, I no longer know how to swim. Or rather I can no longer breathe as I once could. Still, it's with regret that I leave that beach where I'd been happy.

At 10:00 we leave Rhodes to double back around the northern tip of the island and make our way to Lindos.

———

12:30. Lindos.

A natural port, small, almost completely enclosed. A perfect bay. We lose an anchor in the crystal-clear waters. In the foreground, the village's white houses overlook the bay, as does the Acropolis behind them, fortified by medieval ramparts with Doric columns rising among them.

We reach the beach in a dinghy. Swim. As the afternoon comes to a close, we climb toward the Acropolis. At the top, a wide, steep staircase leads to a large, open-air square, one side overlooking the port where we're anchored, and the other, plunging in a vertiginous void, overlooking another enclosed cove, the one Saint Paul entered. The swallows zigzag above the space, drunk on light, diving vertically into the void then giving shrill cries as they come back up again. The day draws to a close over the columns, the two bays, the capes that multiply out toward the horizon and the immense sea before us. Feeling powerless to meet, to express so much beauty. But at the same time,

199. For a week in July 1941, Camus lived in a tent on the beach dunes of Madrague, near Oran. See the preface to the 1958 edition of *L'envers et l'endroit*.

gratitude there before the world's perfect being. On the way back to the city, the little donkeys, the barque in the evening . . . During the night, the donkeys' loud braying.

———

June 12.

I go up on deck at 6:00 to see the bay I love one last time. Everyone on board is asleep except the captain. In the mild morning air, the scent of Lindos, scent of froth, of heat, of donkeys and grass, of smoke . . .

———

Rhodes at 8:30.

Stroll to see a gorge full of freshly hatched butterflies. They're carpeted over the grass, the trees, the grottos, and they scatter in silent, agitated clouds as our footsteps approach. Crushing heat. Return. Depart at three o'clock for Marmaris, a Turkish port. Arrive at 5:00 P.M. The bay in the middle of which we anchor is beautiful but dark. From a distance, the small village appears impoverished. And we can see all the residents gradually gathering on the pier. Turkish police and customs officers arrive onboard. Interminable haggling to settle routine formalities. Then we disembark and are surrounded and followed by a crowd of impoverished children. The poverty, the derelict houses and streets, are heartrending, so much so we return to the boat without further delay. After dinner, another visit from the officials. More haggling (they don't speak any Western language), interminable. They hold onto our passports, etc. We'll get them back at 6:00 in the morning. The captain protests . . . etc. The truth is we'll have to go pick them up the next morning.

———

June 13.

Depart at 7:00 A.M. At 11:00 A.M., Symi island. Admirable Greek cleanliness. The poorest houses are freshly whitewashed, decorated, etc. That the Turks were able to dominate these people for so long is unbelievable and revolting. Swim. But increasingly claustrophobic. For all the rest, beautiful form. At 3:00 P.M. we leave for Kos.

———

KOS. Small port where life is easy in the evening. Music. News of the events in Cyprus blare from radio loudspeakers in a tone I recognize all too well.[200] We dine beneath pink lights.

June 14.

Island. Small temple on a beach with clear water. Swim and lunch in Psameros. In the small cove, five whitewashed houses, white and blue. A couple of little girls in shirts get in the water and swim out to us.

Every day the sun is monstrous . . . not thick or veiled in fog, but clear and pure, tossing its flames like ferocious darts. . . .

Head for Kalymnos at 6:00 P.M. The sea is covered in short, cool waves . . . Dozens of children with round heads escort us. Katina. June 15, the next day, she runs to the pass and continues to wave for a long time. Noon swim in Leros. Then head for Patmos, where we enter an almost completely sheltered bay. Evening time.

June 16.

We climb up to Patmos and the Monastery of St. John of P. on the backs of mules and donkeys. The two isthmuses from above. The violent northern wind (the meltem) picks up. This Greek mistral has the same effects: it combs the sky, bringing out a purified light, crisp, tight, almost metallic. But it prevents us from going back out to sea, and we have to wait here until it calms.

June 17.

Depart at 6:00 in the morning for Gaidaros, the meltem still going strong, the sea furious. Shaken for three hours by plunging waves, everyone onboard sick or shaken, the boat rerouted to the Fourni Islands. Shelter in a cove where

---

200. The Cyprus Emergency, an armed conflict in which the Ethniki Organosis Kyprion Agoniston sought the end of British colonial rule of the island, began in 1955 and officially ended with the signing of the London-Zürich Agreements in 1959, followed by Cypriot independence in 1960. In June 1958, when this entry was recorded, the violence between Greek and Turkish Cypriots had reached its highest point.

the wind blows less, but still blows. Day of waiting. Toward evening, the wind dies down a little. But it's too late to set out.

———

June 18.

The wind picked up again during the night, blowing violently. We give up on departing. Then, nothing having changed, bread running out, water soon, we decide to set out around 6:00 P.M. regardless. Everyone is in the cockpit. Serious squalls, but we arrive in sight of the fires of Tigani (ancient Samos) around 8:30 P.M.

After violent seas, the small, quiet port is gentle at night.

———

June 19.

In the morning, I go for a swim alone. Take a car to visit one of the islands. Among the most beautiful due to the great abundance of olive trees and filiform cypresses lining the slopes of the hills and mountains that run out to the sea. We lunch in a small village on the southern coast after we've swum. The table is outside. A crowd of beautiful children play around us, then come to watch us. One of the little girls, Matina, has gold eyes, and touches my heart. As we leave, she comes up next to the car and I take her little hand. In the evening, the Heraion of Samos, a ravaged temple whose formidable debris is strewn before the sea, among the reeds and oats, the debris itself destroyed by the recent earthquakes. Our drivers buy us a drink at a nearby café and begin to dance together to a radio, for their pleasure and ours.

Polycrates, tyrant of Samos, "the great statesman and depraved tyrant." Frightened by his own insolent, ever-present luck, and by his imperturbable success and fabulous wealth, he took a priceless ring from one of his fingers and threw it into the sea to ward off fate. But a fish served at his table brought the ring back to him, having swallowed it. Completed the Heraion, convened a sumptuous court there where the arts held great importance. Perished on the cross, crucified by Oroetus, the strategist who'd lured him into a trap (522).

———

June 20.

Day at sea sailing for Chios. In the morning, a manatee appears under the bow, does a couple of rolls, swims forward, prances around as if mocking us, and then dives down into the depths. A little later, a few miles from the coast, the wind carries the scent of oleanders out to us. An afternoon of sun and swimming in a cove with waters so clear it's ethereal. We enter Chios on a beautiful, quiet evening.

———

June 21.

Chios. Turkish quarter. Crossing the island. Huge cinder-block houses. Red earth. Huge olive trees. Beneath blinding heat, peasants thresh wheat using their mules' hooves. Summer of massacres. In a narrow, eucalyptus-tree lined ravine that ends in an impasse made of rocks, a leprosarium. A series of long, dilapidated buildings, brown and dark green. As evening falls, they leave their rooms, with their large iron beds covered in coarse, brown blankets. 11 leprous women and 3 leprous men wander around beneath the verandas. Some have lost fingers. Others have large eyes with neither pupils nor irises, only a cloudy yellow like a huge drop of putrid water. Under their heavy grayish outfits of boundless poverty, they wear a naturally cheerful demeanor. One of them laments that people want to remove them from this miserable place only to consign them to some other. . . . An evening of dancing and laughter that lasts well into the night.

———

June 22.

Head for Mytilene. A wide inlet cut along bays and beaches. The olive trees practically running into the ocean. P. is sick. Doctor (Paritis). Ascent to Ayassos. Dip in the water. I swim a little. Depart along the island. As the afternoon comes to a close, hundreds of terns, skimming the surface of the still water, fly up alongside the boat. Arrive in Sigris.

(We arrive in the ports at sunset. For a little while, the sun masks the port from us, then it disappears behind a hill and the port appears in the twilight . . .)

———

SIGRIS. Return to Sigris. Its two enclosed bays. Its bare hills. Its smooth water and evening light. Here the world and life come to an end. And begin again.

From the boat at night, we see the village lit up by Saint-Jean's fires.[201]

---

201. Though not celebrated as often today, *les feux de la Saint-Jean* were large communal bonfires that took place on June 24, also known as Midsummer Day, Saint John's Day, and Summer Solstice.

Depart during the night. Michel and I take the midnight watch. After the crescent moon sets in the west, the night stretches out over the sea. The constellations run down to the horizon, where unexpected islands take shape in the shadows. In the morning, Skyros, tiered atop its crests.

Depart at 3:00 P.M. for Skopelos. In the afternoon, the Northern Sporades. One, two, five, ten, fourteen islands hatch on the sea. In the evening, Skopelos, the ridges of its roofs edged in lime. Jasmine, pomegranate, hibiscus. Peaceful night. In the morning, Skiathos. We take the Euripus Strait.

———

June 26.

In the evening, the wide, silent Bay of Marathon. The waters suddenly calm. Only a brief, heavy surf. And night falls over the immense circle of mountains, over a suddenly mysterious bay. Beauty sleeps on the water.

Khalkis. Grenier's preface: "each conscience wants the death of the other."[202] Not at all. Master and slave. Master and disciple. History is built as much on admiration as on hatred.

I wish for this book to find young readers similar to the one I was.

Like the quest from island to island that Melville illustrated in Mardi, this book also concludes with a meditation on the absolute and the divine.

June 27.

In the early morning, as the cicadas begin to screech in the surrounding hills, a swim in the still, cool water. Then at sea and, at 12:00, under a slightly veiled sky, Kea, the island of green rocks and muddy-brown oysters. During the night the southern wind picks up, and the next day, the *28th*, we're stuck in Kea. *29th*. Depart in the morning on rough seas. Sounion. Light. Hydra, Spetsai for the night. *30th*. Poros, Egine, and once again Ayia Marina, as four years ago. Marvelous island in the center of a whirl of light and space. Come back here.

———

202. Camus drew a line around the first three parts of this entry, which he would use in his preface for Jean Grenier's *Les îles* (*Islands*). There, for example, he writes: "Among the half-truths that enchant our intellectual society appears this one: that each conscience wants the death of the other. We are all simultaneously masters and slaves, dedicated to mutual destruction."

July 1st.

Athens. Heat. Dust. Ridiculous hotel. Tired. *2nd.* Delphi. Once again, an extraordinary surge of light. I follow my own footsteps. Scent of evening over the small stadium. *3rd.* Back to Corinth. Then Patras. Alone, a swim, the water . . . Patras is a large, dusty, ugly, and lively Oran. *4th.* Olympia. *5th.* Mycenae, Argos. Olympia's tall pines sizzle with cicadas. Greece bursts with a sonorous braying in the valleys' hollows, on the islands' slopes.

———

Pavese.[203] As if the only reason we always think of ourselves is because we have to live with ourselves longer than with others.—As if genius is fecundity. To be is to express, to express constantly.—As if idleness makes the hours slow and the years quick and action makes the hours short and the years slow.—As if all libertines are sentimentalists because for them relationships between men and women are a matter of emotion, not of obligation.

Id. "When a woman marries, she belongs to another, and when she belongs to another, there's nothing left to say to her."

Id. The old Mentina woman who managed to ignore history for seventy years—she's lived a "static and unchanging life." That makes Pavese shudder. And if the old Mentina woman had been his mother?

———

Mi[204]

———

Live in and for *truth*. First and foremost, the truth of who you are. Give up compromising with people. The truth of what is—don't try to outwit reality. Accept originality and powerlessness. Live according to this originality, *to the point of* that powerlessness. Put creation at the center, with the immense strength of the individual finally respected.

———

203. Cesare Pavese's diary *The Burning Brand* had just been published in French by Gallimard, in a translation by Michel Arnaud titled *Métier de vivre*. The passages Camus refers to above appear on pages 86, 193, and 303.

204. In the handwritten notebook, the Pavese entry appears at the top of the page, and the only other thing on the page, halfway down, flush right, is: "Mi." On July 1, Camus had written to Mette to say he'd be back in Paris on July 6 and that he hoped to see her as soon as possible. The next page begins with two illegible words, after which the below entry begins.

Return. Lunch with A.M. He tells me Massu and two or three of his collaborators submitted to *torture* so as to have the right to . . . (the difference: they chose it. There is no humiliation.)[205] Strange feeling.

———

Since returning from Greece ten days ago, strength and joy fill my body, rest my heart and soul. Deep down, the convent sleeps, that strong, bare house where silence is contemplation.

———

Like illusions, lies lull you to sleep, to dream. Truth is the only power, blithe, inexhaustible. If we were capable of living only on and for truth: a youthful, immortal energy within us. A man of truth never grows old. Push a little further and he won't die.[206]

---

205. Camus returned to Paris on July 6, 1958. On July 4, André Malraux had written to him requesting a lunch meeting, so they could discuss Malraux's plan to send France's three living Nobel laureates in literature to Algeria on behalf of General de Gaulle. All three—Camus, Martin du Gard, and Mauriac—declined.

General Jacques Émile Massu (1908–2002), who encouraged the use of torture during the Battle of Algiers, claimed to have submitted himself to torture to test the method, so as to have the right to torture others.

206. The last page of the handwritten notebook is unnumbered and has two words crossed out at the top.

Drafts and Notes Tucked in Notebook VIII

November 19
My Dear Amrouche,[207]

Time—and health—have kept me from responding. Doing so was going to take a while, and I've hardly been able to keep up with my ordinary mail. Not that I'm any more up to it today. Only I didn't want to put off thanking you for your second letter, which touched me. Still, I have to be honest about what I think. Personal matters can't drive us apart. What do they matter in light of what's being done and planned? Nevertheless, I was painfully shocked by the generalizations you made about French Algerians, which you repeated on multiple occasions (in *Le Monde* and in *Commune*). You have the right to side with the F.L.N. For my part, I believe them murderous in the present, blind and dangerous for the future. But even if you side with them, you still have to make the necessary distinctions, which you have not made. I've given up on trying to present a voice of reason in public; I hope, against all hope, to be able to do so one day. But in private, I have to let you know my reaction, and you must not set aside that *indiscriminately* shooting at, or justifying shooting at, French Algerians who are only caught up in things, is to shoot at my people, who have always been poor and without hatred, and who cannot be taken as part of an unjust revolt.[208] No cause, even if it remained innocent and just, will ever separate me from mother, who is the greatest cause I know in the world.

In these sincere words, I know you will find an echo of our past brotherhood. May they inspire you to work for peace and unity, rather than for fratricidal separation. Therein lies the deep, heartfelt wish of your brother of birth and sky.

Albert Camus

———

207. Jean El-Mouhoub Amrouche (1906–1962) was an Algerian poet and journalist and editor-in-chief of the magazine *L'Arche,* in which he published Camus's "The Minotaur, or, The Stop in Oran."

208. This sentence was added in the margins. It's followed by several indecipherable words.

In the next sentence, the French word *désolidariser* (separate) has a more apparent connection to *solidarité* (solidarity).

April 3.
Monsieur,

My poor health has delayed this response, and I apologize for that. Over a year ago, after having recognized what irreparably separates me from both the left and the right on the Algerian question, I decided to no longer associate myself with any public campaign on the subject. Collective signatures, those equivocal alliances between people who share no other views in common, lead to confusions that far outstrip, and consequently compromise, the objectives they mean to serve. Even when such objectives are valid, as in the case at hand, I've nevertheless decided to act only in a personal capacity, under the conditions and at the time I feel it useful to do so, regardless of whatever pressures are put on me.

As for the rest of the questions you've asked, I intend to address them in a forthcoming book, which will speak for me alone. In any case, I entrust this personal response to your loyalty, and ask you to please accept my very best wishes.

Albert Camus

June 9, 1954.
My Dear Guérin,[209]

Your article in *La Parisienne* was passed on to me (I don't read that revue and I'm not subscribed to *L'Argus*). No, it's not for "ingratitude" or "severity" that I would reproach you but for the place and the discourteous manner in which they've been expressed, on top of which I don't appreciate you talking about what you don't know, by which I mean my life. If you did know about it, you wouldn't have mentioned it. As for the content of your article, you have the right to say you don't like what I publish and to say it without sugar-coating.

---

209. Raymond Guérin (1905–1955), French writer whose first novel, *Zobain*, was hailed by Jean Grenier and Jean Paulhan. After reading his second, *Quand vient la fin*, Camus himself began a correspondence with Guérin, who, having greatly admired *The Stranger*, welcomed the friendship. Unlike Camus, though, Guérin had no problem putting his most bitter thoughts in print, such as in his June 1954 "Literary Chronicle" for *La parisienne*, which Camus refers to here, and in which, after savaging Camus's essay collection *Summer*, Guérin openly admits: "You who have never been anything but kind to me, who has always been faithful to me, here I am betraying you, looking for a fight." Guérin later had the *La parisienne* article reprinted in his own essay collection *Humeurs*.

What I do reproach you for is an inexcusable breach of the common courtesy of asking for the sender's permission before publishing a personal letter. I didn't write to you, back then, so that my confidential letters, written with a raw and open heart, would ten years later be waved around in public. You have the right to make your own confessions to that public and to speak openly about those who were your friends, but you do not have the right to force those friends to make their own confessions. In reading those words of affection and friendship in the place you printed them, words written to a friend in pain, an intolerable embarrassment and a sort of disgust came over me, a feeling I can't forgive you for having inflicted, and which you should have been able to foresee.

In any case, I couldn't let you go on not knowing how I feel about the matter.

Yours
Albert Camus

July 20, 1956.
Madame,

I'm very sorry to hear what you've told me. And all the more so as, I assure you, the whole thing is quite clearly a misunderstanding.

It's possible I've met the doctor whose name you mentioned, but the name doesn't ring a bell. So then, you see he's not a friend of mine. And in any case, not someone I know well enough for him to have felt comfortable revealing confidential information about a third party to me. Moreover, supposing this confidential information had been disclosed, to imagine I would have used it so carelessly is not to know me very well.

I can guarantee you, on my honor, that the details set out in *The Fall* come from me alone. Your friend isn't the only one who loves the Hautes Plaines. I love them and I've lived on them. Having been treated for tuberculosis, I now suffer a type of pulmonary sclerosis that makes me claustrophobic. Anyone who has spent time with me can confirm for you my horror before chasms, caves, and all such enclosed places, which is a result of this quite personal infirmity. They joke about my impatience with speleologists, about my sadness in deep alpine valleys, etc. A similarly irrefutable explanation could be given for each of the details that struck your friend. As for the anecdote at the center of the story, you'll understand, of course, that I don't intend to divulge personal matters. However, I will quote a sentence from a letter I received the other day from one of my friends: "Each one of us, without exception, has a young woman in our life we didn't rescue."

Such evidence clarifies things, and your friend must realize that. You told me that he's always read me with a particular interest and respect, which means he must be aware that I'm incapable of lying about such things.

So then, let me say again, and on my honor, that I guarantee him he has nothing, absolutely nothing, to do with my character. He hasn't been betrayed by anyone, and if he's the type of person I think he is, he'll take his friends back into that circle of heartfelt trust without which all of life would be a wearying misery.

The root of your friend's current suffering is the exhausting life we all lead, which is all the more so for those of us who add personal work on top of modern life's never-ending weight. How could I not understand that? My days sometimes end with clenched teeth, and I often have the feeling that the only thing keeping me going, walking and working, is sheer willpower alone. But in such cases, we have to go easy on ourselves and our nature. We have to return to a more animal-like life, to rest, to solitude.

I hope that your friend, seeing what I've laid out here, will again find rest and peace. Then I will be able to console myself for having unintentionally created turmoil in a noble heart. At the moment, I feel only sadness for having done harm with one of my books, given that I've always thought art was nothing if it didn't ultimately do some good, if it didn't help.

Monsieur Reverend[210]

I received your letter very late and the news you gave me about the sudden death of my friend shook me, despite it all already being over and done. Still, I wanted to give you my heartfelt thanks for having thought of me. Didier was part of my childhood and youth, and when I ran into him later as a man of religion, I had no difficulty again loving what he had never ceased to be. He'd remained the same child, become the same man, with the same faith, purer and deeper, and the same fidelity. The discretion and unwavering tact that he brought to our encounters, too infrequent due to our different lives, could only enrich and make our childhood friendship that much deeper. This end, so abrupt, so unexpected, is a great sorrow for me. For several hours now, the world has been poorer in my eyes. I'm aware that for him death was only

210. See p. 607n145.

a passage—he spoke confidently about a certain sort of hope—but for those who, like me, loved him without being able to share that hope, the grief is all-consuming. You're right: his memory and example remain. Please know that, with gratitude, I carry a part of our long friendship over to those who've loved him and who've had the happiness of living by his side, and have no doubt that my faithful feelings are now with you.

A.C.

At the hospital, X. discovered something I've always known (due to a similar experience [. . .][211] youth—as well as to other things) the solidarity of bodies, unity in the midst of mortal, suffering flesh. That's all we are and nothing else. We're that plus human genius in all its forms, from a child to an Einstein.

No, dear Dominique, it's not humiliating to be unhappy. Physical suffering sometimes is, but the suffering of being can't be. It's as much a part of life as that happiness Bernard writes about in his text with such conviction that it deeply moved me.

I hesitate to tell you this, but the only thing you have to do now is live like everyone else. You deserve, being the person you are, a happiness, a plenitude that few people ever know. Even now, this plenitude isn't dead, is a part of life, and, to its credit, reigns over you whether you want it to or not. But in the coming days you're going to have to live alone, with this hole, with that painful memory. With that deadness we all carry inside us—and by us, I mean to say those who haven't been able to maintain our happiness and who painfully remember another happiness that fades from memory.[212]

For fierce minds, sometimes the time wrenched aside for work, which is wrenched out of time, is the best. An unfortunate passion.

---

211. Three illegible words. This entry and the two that follow it are written on a looseleaf sheet of *NRF* letterhead.

212. The above translation is conjectural, as the final clause is unclear in the original manuscript, with several sentences preceding it crossed out.

Gal[213] and I during the demonstration:
You're going to do something stupid again
Excellent! You don't want to come?
I'm going to smack you, Albert.

———

That guy's like a brother, and in my family, if you touch my brother, you're dead.

———

Fame is a convent.

———

Mi. Initiation by her mother's gymnastics teacher. At her mother's request, he prepares a course of sexual initiation for her (at 15 years old). Then persuades her mother it'll go better if it's done by an expert . . . [214]

Mi. One of the people traveling with her, who is reading a serial novel, repeats a sentence from the book: "Live each hour as if it were the last and most beautiful," and he cries out: "That's it exactly." But, Mi says: he doesn't even leave his room to visit the city and he divides his time between fine meals and bed.

At heart, Mi says, we're like those Christians. We're pagans, all right, but only pay lip service to our paganism. Her, too. A woman traveling with her, talking about her [. . .],[215] an athlete: she can neither make love with him before a match, because he has to preserve his strength, nor after, because he has no strength left. For these same reasons, they never go out. In the morning, he wakes her with a knee to her lower back so she'll go make breakfast . . . The Woman: "I don't fuck, I don't go out, I'm like a maid, and this has been going on for 3 years already."

———

From the prison ink
On the slave's chains

---

213. Pierre Galindo, brother of Christiane Galindo and a longtime friend of Camus's from Oran. This note and the three that follow it were written on sheets torn from an agenda with the word "NOTES" preprinted at the top of each page.

214. Mette Ivers recalls that the gymnastics teacher acted on his own, without her mother's knowledge, and that she, Mette, threatened to tell her mother if the gymnastics teacher tried anything again.

215. One illegible word, likely something to the effect of "boyfriend." In the summer of 1958, Mette Ivers was on a modeling tour through the South of France.

To the gentle faces of those shot down
I write your name
Liberty[216]

Your downstrokes are bars
Your face is a deadbolt
A brother to those who bring death
On the orders of the box office
I write your name
Liberty

Liberty, liberty betrayed
Where are your defenders?
In the cellars' darkness
Your gentle ego pitter-patter
I write your name
Kalande[217] dies.

Easy is writing
Terrible is dying
I write, I write
I write your adulterous name
On those close to you who hope in vain

Oh! What have you done with my young
Kalande? We die naked
When our brothers slay us
I write your sonorous name
With an ink that dishonors

---

216. A derisive retort to Paul Éluard's well-known poem "Liberty." The final line here, "In capitals of pain," makes the connection explicit, *Capital of Pain* being the title of one of Éluard's surrealist collections.

217. The reference is likely to Záviš Kalandra (1902–1950), Czechoslovakian journalist and critic, who was kicked out of the Communist Party for having publicly criticized the Moscow Trials. He was later arrested by the Gestapo, sent to a concentration camp, and sentenced to death. Following the sentencing, André Breton, who, along with Paul Éluard, had met Kalandra in 1935, started a petition that was signed by Camus, Sartre, Beauvoir, and other French intellectuals—a petition Éluard refused to sign.

To bar the future
To mar the memory
I write your name
Liberty
In capitals of pain

Pierre Serment[218]

218. The handwritten version of the poem is heavily edited. The name "Jean" Serment was initially written, then Jean was crossed out and replaced with Pierre. In French, *serment* means "oath."

Notebook IX

JULY 1958–

A plain spiral notebook with “Cahier IX” written near the top-center of the cover and “from July 1958 – ” written beneath it.

July 15 '58[1]

You have to resign yourself to keeping a healthy distance from this century's society. Live and suffer the same history, with all its struggles, as I have been doing, but when it comes to anything involving reflection, in order to rediscover that freshness, that boldness, and the truth, as well, press ahead and walk alone.

———

Greek anxiety was sublimated into the mind, Christian anxiety into love—modern anxiety into frivolous, mechanical life.

———

N. "He who has felt the pain of speaking the truth, despite his friendships and admirations, will surely fear new friendships."

JULY 21. Alone all day to think. Dinner in the evening with B.M. In that place inside me where M. lives, an uncomfortable emptiness all day long. I write to her.[2]

22–24. Nothing. Recorded Fall on my tape recorder. Mi's letter ("pure and ferocious nights"). Roamed around St. Germain-des-Prés last night—waiting for what? Spoke with a drunk painter: "What do you do for a living?"

"I'm not in jail."

"That's a bad thing?"

"No, it's a good thing."

He devours five hard-boiled eggs drizzled with cognac.

---

1. Camus drew an inward-pointing arrow at the top of the first page of the notebook, and above the arrow he wrote "July 1958," likely indicating that he wanted this entry and the two that follow it, which were written on a separate sheet of *NRF* letterhead tucked into the front of the notebook, to be inserted at the start of an eventual typescript. The notebook proper begins with the entry dated July 21. At the end of this entry, Camus crossed out two sentences, which are now illegible.

2. The initials B.M. refer to Jean Bloch-Michel (1912–1987), a longtime friend of Camus's, the two having worked together at *Combat*. The initial M. refers to Maria Casarès.

In a letter to Maria sent the same day that the above entry was recorded, Camus writes: "Maybe it's my fault you felt far away, driven away—and maybe it's because you doubted my love. So, it's not such a bad thing for me to tell you that I feel alone and filled with grief without you. You're my sweetheart, my tender one, my charming lovely, my one and only. . . . Outside of you, the entire world is nothing but a colorless shadow. Aside from my children, the rest of the world could fade away and nothing would change for me. You are my only anchor, the only thing that fills my life."

In the separate notebook he was keeping for *The First Man*, Camus writes: "That afternoon, on the road from Grasse to Cannes, in a moment of incredible elation, he suddenly discovers, after years of being with her, that he loves Jessica, that he truly loves her, and that next to her the rest of the world had become but a shadow."

Feeling hopeless about my inability to work. Thankfully there's Zhivago and the fondness I feel for its author.[3] Have given up on traveling to the Midi.

25. Nothing. Recorded Fall. Sun with A.C.[4] Casting Possessed. NRF. Dinner with A.C.[5] Makes love with M., who is impotent with his wife, which he confided to her.

"It's going better," she says.

"Which means"

"Well, he's not a man yet but he's not an old fogey anymore either."

This gray area hanging over their life. Over all lives. After having walked her home, I head over to St. Germain-des-Prés. I wait, like an idiot. Ah! If only the strength to work would return to me, it would bring the light, at last. The little hoodlums outfitted like James Dean, their blue jeans too tight, their hands moving like spoons, arranging their genitals with their ring fingers. I think of the naked, brown bodies of years ago, in my lost country. They were pure.

26. Recorded Fall. Have barely begun the preface for Islands. Dinner with C. Lazy and cynical, focused solely on pleasure. He's self-employed. Also a second-rate writer. But he's his own man. He's going to play poker, which bores me to tears, so I leave early and go home. On the way, a rather rude girl being hit on by an Arab man rejects him, saying quite simply: "I'm racist."

27. Finished recording Fall. Sun. Don Giovanni. Gray sky all day. In the evening, film about the World Cup. The young Black Brazilians cry after winning and try to hide their faces from the camera. This still touches and move me, as it did before.

28. Dinner with B.M. A.C. joins us—A storm weighs on the city—but doesn't break.

---

3. In 1958, Boris Pasternak was awarded the Nobel Prize in Literature, the year after Camus, and Gallimard published a French translation of *Doctor Zhivago*. Camus and Pasternak shared a brief, mutually admirative correspondence.

4. This third sentence, clearly present in the original notebook, does not appear in the French edition.

5. The A.C. mentioned here, and over the next couple of pages, may be Anne Cornaly, a young actress with whom Camus shared a short correspondence during this period.

29. Haunted by thoughts of Algeria this morning. Too late, too late . . . My land lost, I'd be worthless.

JULY 30. Solitary day. Unstructured work. At Nabokov's in the evening, Narayan, who is said to be Gandhi's successor, explains India's village and agrarian socialist movements (Vinoba).[6] I admire, from a distance. On the way home, passing the Aiglon, I see A.M.'s name on the illuminated marquee. I go inside. I had some good times with her, eleven years ago. Married now to an Air France steward with whom she goes fishing. And she sings every night.

JULY 31. A.M. comes to see me for half an hour in the afternoon. In the light of day, I see the lines left by those eleven years. She was 22 then, so she's 33 now. But we have a lot of laughs together.

AUGUST 1. Lunch at Barrault's in Chambourcy. A black sky the whole time due to an endless storm. B. again offers to connect me with Danchenko-Stanislavski.[7] In the afternoon, Colin Wilson.[8] A baby; clear to see that Europe has now conquered England. "We must now share faith in" [. . .][9] I know it well. That faith is mine—it has never left me. But I've taken the path of the times, with its setbacks, so as not to cheat and, after having shared in suffering and negation, to affirm on my own terms. Now I must transform, and that's what frightens me about and binds me to this book I have to write. Perhaps the portrayal of a certain distress has drained everything from men of my age and now we'll never be able to profess our true faith. We'll simply have prepared the way for the boys who come after us. I say this to C.W. and

---

6. Jayaprakash Narayan (1902–1979), a radical politician, joined the Indian National Congress, where he worked with and learned from Mahatma Gandhi.

The parenthetical reference is to Lana del Vasto's *Gandhi to Vinoba: The New Pilgrimage*, published in France in 1954 and in English in 1956.

7. In 1898, Konstantin Stanislavski and Vladimir Nemirovich-Danchenko founded the influential Moscow Art Theatre. At the time this entry was written, Camus was looking for someplace to put on his adaptation of *The Possessed*. The play was long, originally running five hours and later cut down to three, and it involved costly, complex staging that led to it being turned down by the Théâtre Récamier, among many others. With few options left, Camus reluctantly turned to Jean-Louis Barrault to try to help secure financing.

8. Colin Wilson (1931–2013), English writer and philosopher, wrote over one hundred books, the first of which was titled *The Outsider*, the same title used for the British edition of Camus's *L'Étranger*.

9. Two illegible words.

"if I don't succeed, at best I'll have been an interesting witness. If I do succeed, I'll have been a creator."

In the evening, I dine with A.C. and Karin, then Karin and I walk alone to Montmartre. The gardens are bathed in moonlight, but dark still. K is 18 years old. Parents divorced. She left Sweden, I don't know why, and earned her living as a model for a second-rate designer who exploited her. Thirty-five thousand francs for seven hours of work a day. The courage of these mid-century girls always fills me with the same admiration. Beauty a little boyish, but simple, as if not there. Return. Her natural ease. She immediately leans her tender mouth forward, then sets off, precise and reserved.

A2. I force myself to write this journal but find doing so repellent. Now I know why I've never done it before: for me, life is secret. It's secret from others (and that's what hurt F. so much) but must also be seen as secret from myself; I must not reveal it in words. When it's muted and unformulated, that's when it's rich for me. If I'm forcing myself to keep it at the moment, it's out of panic in the face of my failing memory. But I'm not sure I'll be able to continue. Even now, already I forget to note so much. And I say nothing about what I think. Which explains my long reflection about K.

SATURDAY 2. In the evening, with M. at the train station until Sunday evening. Tired and distant. She comes back to life later on and I'm happy about that.

MONDAY 4. Lunch with M. In the afternoon, Doctor X. According to him, because I have to be careful with F's health,[10] I've been living "in a glass ball." His prescription: freedom and selfishness. Superb prescription, I say. And by far the easiest to swallow. In the evening, K.

TUESDAY 5. In the afternoon, M. Long conversation. Few have gone further than she has in the acceptance of life. The 6th. Night out with Michel, Anne, and M. Dancing. The 7th. Again the feeling of estrangement from M. The fieriest person I've ever known is in fact the most chaste. Dinner with Brice Parain, at his place, with the Russian nurse and his nine-year-old girl.[11]

---

10. Francine Camus remained in a serious and prolonged depression, which was treated with, among other approaches, electroshock therapy.

11. Brice Parain's wife, Nathalie, had died earlier that year. She had a young daughter, Tatiana.

Like all religious minds, B.P. tries to justify all woes through the necessity for atonement. I tell him that, taken to the extreme, we end up with what's worst in dialectics. He knows this. He's thinking about it.

FRIDAY 8. Solitary day like almost all those preceding it. I'm trying to organize my work. It's been raining for two days. Letter from Mi: "haltering, superficial conversations" (on the telephone).[12] Warm, free, truthful.

SATURDAY 9—Sick. Sunday the 10th. [. . .]. Monday the 11th. *The Noose*. [. . .].[13] I go to bed and fall asleep with an awful headache. Bad night. Earlier in the day, Mi called from Marseille; she flees from city to city, pursued by anxiety and panic. I advise her to go back to Paris.[14]

TUESDAY 12. In the morning, C. comes to see me. Wednesday the 13th. Lunch with Char. We laugh a lot. In the afternoon, Ivernel.[15] In the evening, dinner at the golf course with M.G., Anne, and R.G. The evening on the meadows. Thursday the 14th. Ivernel phones. He read my adaptation of

The Possessed last night and wasn't able to put it down. He agrees to play the part of Shatov. In the evening, dinner with R. Jaussaud. He's been the same, physically, for the past 20 years. But his spirit's been broken ever since his nervous breakdown. He's clearly just going through the motions now. We meet up with K. Her natural ease astounds me (straight for the hand, then come with me, no why, I have a rendezvous). She eats nonstop.

AUGUST 15, 16, 17. This whole period since the 2nd has in fact been empty. You can't write without recovering vitality and energy. Without a healthy heart, even if what you have to say is tragic. Especially so. Finished Zhivago with a sort of affection for the author. It's wrong to say the book takes up the artistic tradition of 19th century Russia. It's much more heavy-handed and, for that matter, modern in its approach, with its continual use of snapshots. But it does better: it resurrects the Russian heart, crushed beneath

---

12. The published French edition reads *les conversations huilées et informes*, a misreading of *heurtée et infirme*, which is what Mette Ivers wrote in her letter and what Camus copied into the above entry.

13. The two bracketed ellipses each indicate a sentence removed by earlier editors.

14. Mette Ivers had recently learned that her sister, who was in Brazil, was gravely ill. See below.

15. Daniel Ivernel (1920–1999), a French actor, played the lead role in Camus's adaptation of Dino Buzzati's *Un cas intéressant* (*An Interesting Case*). Despite his initial interest, Ivernel did not end up playing the part of Shatov in *The Possessed*. The initials in the following sentence refer to Michel and Raymond Gallimard. Anne likely refers to Anne Gallimard.

forty years of slogans and humanitarian cruelties. Zhivago is a book about love. About a love so intense it extends to everyone all at once. The doctor loves his wife, and Lara, and others, too, and Russia. If he dies, it's due to being separated from his wife, from Lara, from Russia, and all the rest.

People without name are near to me
Trees, children, and sedentaries
I am overcome by all of these
And that alone is my victory.[16]

Pasternak's bravery was in rediscovering this genuine source of creation and then calmly getting to work on making it gush up in the middle of the desert.

What else? The evenings of the 15th and the 16th, recorded Char's poetry with M. Night of the 15th, strolled along the Seine. Under the Pont Neuf, some young foreigners (Nordic) were gathered around two people from their group, a trumpet player and a banjo player, and were lying on the street, couples embracing, listening to the improvisation. A little farther down, an Arab man was stretched out on one of the benches on the Pont des Arts, a portable radio by his head, playing some Arab tunes. The Pont de la Cité there beneath an August Paris sky, warm and hazy.

For Julia. Guibert is the noble progressive. Mora the face of the old world.

AUGUST 18. Lunch with M. Together again.[17] Evening dinner R. Jaussaud. Depression not improved.

---

19. Letter from F., which saddens me all over again.[18]

21→23, evening. Mi. Fills these days with beauty, with sweetness. Far from taking me away from work, such a stretch of joy turns me toward it. Her

---

16. A snippet from Pasternak's *The Poems of Doctor Zhivago*.

17. "M" may refer to Maria Casarès, who joined Camus in Cabrières-d'Avignon in August, before Francine and the children came to stay in September. It may also refer to Mette Ivers.

18. This entry is written in very small print at the bottom of the page.

sister, 22 years old, is dying from liver cancer. Her father orders her to admire the sunsets: "Because you're an artist."[19]

AUGUST 23. Death of Roger Martin du Gard. I'd delayed my visit to Bellême and suddenly . . . I can still see that man I so tenderly loved talking to me about his solitude, and about death, in Nice last May. He was hunched over, dragging his large, heavy body from the table to the armchair. His beautiful eyes . . . You could love him, respect him. Grief.

25. Dinner Brisville (and Thérèse). B.M. (and Vivette). Go for a walk. By the chapel and on the outer boulevards. Sordid Paris.[20]

26→29. Giacometti's example. Ah! M. and her life: "Those who, like us, have been through extreme experiences at a very young age (including love and fame), and who reach maturity desiring nothing more than life itself."

29. C. returns.

SEPTEMBER 2 at Isle-sur-Sorgue. Best way to use this notebook would be to occasionally summarize (2 times a week?) the important events of the preceding days. Saturday, the 30th, I saw Jamois[21] and agreed with her that we weren't ready to put on The Possessed at the Montparnasse. Despite her dry, bitter manner, she's rather charming, with those tight sandals, her small, well-formed feet, her long torso, and that sad, beautiful look in her eyes. Phoned Barrault afterward to tell him I agreed [. . .].[22] To bed early. I couldn't sleep at all, drifted off around 3:00 A.M., woke up at 5:00 A.M., ate heartily, and got on the road in the rain. Drove for eleven hours straight, occasionally nibbled a bit of melba toast, the rain also driving all the way to Drôme, where it lightened enough in Nyons for the powerful scent of the lavender to reach me, wake me, and invigorate me. Nourished by the familiar landscape, I

---

19. Mette Ivers's mother had traveled to Brazil to be with Mette's sister, while Mette returned to the family home in Saint-Jean-de-Luz to be with her father.

20. Jean-Claude Brisville, a novelist and playwright, wrote the 1959 volume on Camus for Gallimard's La Bibliothèque Idéale series. The initials refer to Jean Bloch-Michel, and the parenthetical to novelist Vivette Perret, his wife.

21. Marguerite Jamois, director of the Théâtre Montparnasse.

22. The bracketed ellipses indicate two sentences removed by earlier editors.

arrived happy. In Isle, I felt suddenly sheltered and pacified in that bare room at the Hotel St. Martin.

Met up with René Char in Isle. Sad to see him driven from his home, from his park (where a hideous cluster of H.L.M. buildings[23] now rise) and stuck in that small room at the Hotel St. Martin. At the Mathieu's place in Camphoux,[24] Mme Mathieu, an aged Clytemnestra, now wears glasses. As for M. Mathieu, the asset operations manager has become an impotent old man who can't even control his own outbursts. I look after the rental house, a little sad but charming nevertheless, with its view overlooking the Luberon. It surely won't please F. But I try to make it more comfortable for her. The 3rd long walk with R.C. on the road that runs along the peaks of the Luberon. The fierce light, the infinite space, transports me. I think again how I'd like to live here, find a house that suits me, finally get a little more settled. At the same time, I think a lot about Mi and her life here. At dinner, Mme Mathieu said: "Even the swallows are getting dumber. Instead of gathering silt for their nests, they're going around gathering crop soil. For the first time in decades, twelve of the thirteen nests in Camphoux crumbled with their eggs in them." Char: "We might have hoped the birds would at least maintain their reputation."

By the fourth I'm still waiting for a telegram or telephone call from F. letting me know when she'll be arriving with the children. Mme Mathieu is the one who ends up telling me that she's only planning to stay for four days and that her family will be in Paris. Anger and estrangement rise in me, anger at her and at me, who never stops looking for signs of affection where there are none and cannot be any.

———

SEPTEMBER 30. A month spent looking for a house in the Vaucluse. Purchased the one in Lourmarin. Then left for St. Jean to meet up with Mi. For hundreds of kilometers, through the scent of the grape harvest, a state of elation. Then the great, foamy sea. A pleasure like those long, flowing waves that scour the earth. Depart in the morning for Paris and the pink briars in the pine forests. Another twelve hours behind the wheel, then Paris.

---

23. Habitation à Loyer Modéré (HLM) were rent-controlled, government-subsidized housing projects that often took the form of large apartment complexes.

24. Camus, who initially met the Mathieu family through René Char, would become very close with Marcelle Mathieu's daughter, Jeanne, and her husband, Urbain Polge, who had two children around the same age as Camus's twins. The two families would often vacation together.

Visit from the writer *turned* miserable intellectual (the slum of the St. Denis suburbs).

———

Pasternak . . . "that living, vibrant element of artistry that, in Pushkin's wake, we call the highest Mozartian standard, the Mozartian element."[25]

J. de Beer. "Adultery should be punished by death. Then we'd see who's truly in love." That's not even true. Weakness is often stronger than fear.

OCTOBER 17. Depart Vaucluse. I should summarize the past 18 days and I will do so.

OCT. 18. When I get off the night train in Isle-sur-Sorgue, the mistral is blowing cold and dry. All through the day, a great, welcome elation beneath the glittering light. I'm filled with the full force of my strength.

19. Endless light. In an empty house without a single piece of furniture, stand for a long time watching the dead, red woodbine leaves being blown through the rooms by a fierce wind. The Mistral.

27. Return to Paris. At night, the voices that announce the names of the stations are reassuring. Nation.

———

Don't complain. Don't defend what you are or what you do. If you give, consider that you've received.

———

NOV. 5. Letter from E.B.'s husband telling me his wife wants to commit suicide and asking me to intervene. I, who so easily and often so stupidly feels such responsibility to others, I don't feel any in this case. The feeling is rather of being ambushed. That said, I have to intervene.

———

NOVEMBER 7, 45 YEARS OLD. As I wanted, a day of solitude and reflection. Now is the time to begin the disengagement that should be fully realized by fifty. On that day, I'll be in control.

———

25. The quote is from Boris Pasternak's comment about Russian poet Sergei Alexandrovich Yesenin.

Democracy isn't the rule of the majority but the protection of the minority.[26]

N. 22. Lunch with Char and St. John Perse.[27] Islands.

Afternoon with Waldo Frank in a sad room.

DECEMBER—Possessed rehearsals.[28]

Cuny seems too old to play Stavrogin. He's my age.

M. We're switching roles, that's all.

L. Yes, but the women will elude us and we're going to die.

Mi. Her wonderful appetite.

MARCH 3. I struggle like a fish caught in a net.

MARCH 17. Death of Paul Œttly at 69 years old.[29] His elderly mother (93 years old) commits suicide the next day.

Catherine's illness. I cancel my trip to the Midi. Heartache.[30]

MARCH 20. Maman's operation.[31] The telegram from L. reached me Saturday morning. Airplane the following night, at 3:00 in the morning. In

26. This entry is written in very tiny print at the top of the page.

27. Saint-John Perse (1887–1975), French poet, won the Nobel Prize in Literature three years after Camus, in 1960. He began his career in the French diplomatic service, serving in China, Germany, and the United States, among other locations.

28. Camus's stage adaptation of *The Possessed* premiered on January 30, 1959, at the Théâtre Antoine. Alain Cuny did not play the role of Stavrogin, though he did record a performance of *The Misunderstanding* with Maria Casarès, a snippet of which can be heard on the album *Albert Camus vous parle*.

29. Paul Œttly was Camus's uncle through marriage (Œttly married Francine's aunt). He was an actor and director, and he and Camus often worked together. His mother ran a boardinghouse in Panelier, near Chambon-sur-Lignon, where Camus lived from August 1942 to November 1943.

30. To René Char, Camus wrote: "[Catherine] had an infection that led to an acute rheumatic fever, which was very effectively treated with cortisone and penicillin. The fever has passed now, and the dramatic part of the story is over. . . . It's true that I was quite worried—and that I hate to see suffer this child, who you know is particularly dear to me."

31. On March 20, Camus flew to Algeria for a brief stay as his mother underwent a hernia operation. To Maria Casarès, he wrote: "In some ways, this hospital room, on the heights of Algiers, with a wonderful view over the gulf, is a good cell for meditation. And I'm happy to be with my mother. The most important thing is that she gets better." This would be Camus's last trip to Algeria.

The telegram from L. likely refers to Camus's brother, Lucien.

Algiers at seven o'clock. Always the same impression over the grounds surrounding the Maison-Blanche: my land. Yet the sky is gray, the air soft and spongy. I settle in at the clinic on the Heights of Algiers.

———

In the immaculate room with bare white walls: *nothing*. A handkerchief and a small comb. On the sheets, her knotted hands. Outside, an admirable landscape extending to the gulf. But the light and space bother her. She wants us to keep the room shaded.

———

About Philippe, who just got engaged to Paule, she says: "His father, he's good, his mother, she's good, his sister, she's good. They're old souls. Him? He did his duty. He saw Paule at a gas station and (she gestures, bringing her two index fingers together). Good for them."

"When I get back home, the doctor will give me something to get better." She says, "Thank you, Monsieur Doctor." She's unable to do anything: neither read, she doesn't know how, nor sew or embroider, because of her fingers, nor listen to anything, because she's deaf. Time flows, slow and heavy . . .

Her lips have disappeared. But her nose is so fine, so straight—her large forehead full of nobility, her eyes black and shining beneath that smooth bridge of bone.

She suffers silently. She *obeys*. The family sits around her, heavy, mute, waiting . . . Her brother Joseph, a few years younger, is also waiting—but as if he were waiting his turn—resigned and sad.

———

MARCH 23. Bad night. In the morning, it's raining over the hills and gulf. Wisteria: it filled my youth with its scent, with its rich and mysterious ardor . . . And endlessly once again. It's been more alive, more present in my life than many people have . . . except the one who's here suffering beside me, the one whose silence hasn't stopped speaking to me for over half a lifetime.

———

She says Vichy[32] for all mineral water.

———

The Maison-Blanche is the main airport serving Algiers.

32. A popular brand of mineral water derived from the springs in Vichy, France.

The flesh, the poor, miserable, dirty, fallen, humiliated flesh—the sacred flesh.

Léopold Flam on Nietzsche: "The affirmation of life that the union of patience and rebellion leads to is the height of life's great noon."[33]

The strange habit of putting Widow before her name, which she's been her entire life, and which still appears on hospital papers today.

She's lived unaware of all things—except suffering and patience—and she continues to absorb physical suffering today, with the same gentleness . . .

People whom neither newspapers nor radio nor any other technology has touched. As they were a hundred years ago, hardly warped by the social environment.

It looks like I passed blood. No? Oh, good.

The smell of syringes. The hill covered in acanthus, in reeds, in cypresses, in pines, palm trees, orange trees, medlar trees, and wisteria.

MARCH 29. Return to Paris.

Sophocles danced and was a *good* ball player.

"Detras de la cruz esta el demonio."[34]

Destroy everything in my life that isn't this poverty. Go for broke.

---

33. Léopold Flam (1912–1995), Belgian philosopher and concentration camp survivor. The reference Camus gives here is to Flam's "Signification de Nietzsche pour notre époque," an essay published in the October 1958–February 1959 *Revue de l'Université de Bruxelles*. Without further context—which can be found in Flam's essay, in Nietzsche's *Thus Spake Zarathustra*, and in the final section of *The Rebel*—the cited quote is difficult to fully grasp, especially given the loss of connection that occurs in translating *la pensée de midi* (Mediterranean thought) and *grand midi de la vie* (life's great noon). In short, Camus was likely attracted by Flam's synthesis of Nietzschean thought and Mediterranean thought, as seen in the segment of Flam's essay preceding the cited quote: "The long patience (the camel) and our self-will (the lion) form a whole, as seen in Mediterranean thought, where the atrocious experience of nothingness leads the individual to pull himself together and decide to live."

34. The rest of the page is blank after this entry in the original notebook.

"Behind the cross is the devil." Likely a reference to *Don Quixote*, in which different forms of the "proverb" appear.

Pasternak on Scriabin: "Each of us has experienced a similar moment in our life. To each of us the revelation has been offered, the gift of personality promised, and, in its way, this promise to each of us has been kept."[35]

Id: "The greatest works in the whole world, while talking about the most diverse subjects, in fact relay to us their own birth."

Id: ". . . you can run day after day to meet with a fragment of built-up earth, as if it were a living being."

Nietzsche. "No suffering has been able, or will be able, to induce me to bear false witness against life, *such as I know it*."[36]

Id ——"Six solitudes were already known to him
But the sea itself wasn't solitary enough for him . . ."[37]

On the use of fame as a camouflage behind which "our true self can once again play with and laugh at itself without being seen."

"Conquer freedom and spiritual joy, so that you're able to create and not be tyrannized by outside ideals."

Historical sense is only a masked theology.

N., a man of the North, suddenly placed one evening before the Naples sky: "And to think you could have died without seeing this!"

The August 20, 1880, letter to Gast in which he laments Wagner's friendship ". . . what

good is it for me to have been proven right over him in so many respects."[38]

---

35. Though Pasternak devoted a chapter in *An Essay in Autobiography* to Scriabin, this particular quote comes from chapter 2 of Pasternak's *Self-Conduct*. The quoted passage, in its official French translation, appears quite different from what Camus records here, and also much closer to Beatrice Scott's English translation, which reads: "This has been experienced by everyone. Tradition has appeared to us all, it has promised us all a face, and it has fulfilled its promise to us all in different ways."

The second quote appears in chapter 7. In Scott's English translation, it reads: "the world's best creations, those which tell of the most diverse things, in reality describe their own birth."

The third quote appears at the start of chapter 15. In Scott's English, it reads: "I too was fortunate enough to find that one can go day after day to meet a piece of built-up space as one would go to meet a live personality."

36. The quote comes from a January 14, 1880, letter to Malvida von Meysenbug.

37. From *Thus Spake Zarathustra*, reproduced in *Dionysian-Dithyrambs*.

38. The odd line break here is as Camus recorded the entry in the original.

A man of deep feelings needs friends unless he has his God
Men who have "a far-reaching will."

It's through Notes from Underground that Nietzsche discovers Dostoyevsky in '87. (he compares it to discovering The Red and the Black)
In '88 he discovers Strindberg's *Getting Married.*[39]

APRIL 1. [. . .][40] Love, on the other hand, is impossible. No longer *seek* it? Welcome it. An excess of power in creation.

N. in '87 (43 years old): "My life is only now at full meridian: one door is closing, another is opening."[41]

APRIL 28. Arrive Lourmarin. Gray sky. In the garden, wonderous roses weighed down with water, luscious as fruit. The rosemary is in bloom. Stroll and in the evening the iris's violet color grows ever deeper. Broken up.

For years I've wanted to live according to everyone else's morals. I've forced myself to live like everyone else, to look like everyone else. I said what had to be said to be a part of the group, even when I felt apart from it. And the result of it all was disaster. Now I wander amid the wreckage, lawless, torn apart, alone and accepting being so, resigned to my peculiarities and infirmities. I must rebuild a truth—after having lived my whole life in a sort of lie.

---

39. These three lines about Dostoyevsky are written in tiny print along the notebook's right margin.

In a letter to Overbeck dated February 23, 1887, Nietzsche writes: "A few weeks ago, I was still unaware of the name Dostoyevsky—I, a poor illiterate who doesn't read any 'journals.' A fortuitous gesture in a bookstore brought my eyes to *L'Esprit souterrain*, which had just been translated into French (it was by similar chance that I found Schopenhauer in my twenty-first year, Stendhal in my thirty-fifth!). The call of blood (or how shall I call it?) became audible immediately; my joy was extraordinary."

40. The bracketed ellipses indicate three brief sentences removed by earlier editors. Above this entry, which appears at the top of the notebook page, are several illegible words.

41. The rest of the page after this entry is blank in the original notebook.

The quote is from Nietzsche's December 20, 1887, letter to Carl von Gersdorff. Nietzsche goes on to write that until then he'd only been settling accounts and that it's only at this point that his real work is to begin.

At least the theater helps me. A parody is better than a lie: the parody is closer to the truth it performs.

MAY. Working again. Have progressed with first part of *First Man*. Gratitude for this land, for its solitude, its beauty.

MAY 18. Travel to Arles. M.'s splendid youth. Pentecost, travel to Toulon.[42]

Television broadcast.[43] I can't "appear" without provoking reactions. Remind myself, repeat to myself, again and again, that I have to eliminate all unproductive polemics. Praise what should be praised. Silence the rest. If I don't hold myself to this rule, with the current state of things, I'll have to accept paying and being punished. See stages of healing.[44] Hold tight this precious tremor, this complete silence I've found here. The rest doesn't exist.

For nearly five years now, it's myself I've been criticizing, the things I believed, the way I lived. That's why those who share these same ideas believe they're being targeted and bear such a grudge against me; but really, I'm waging war with myself, and I'll either destroy myself or I'll be reborn, that's all there is to it.

The Marseille lovers. Beneath a beautiful sky, on a juicy sea, in the garish, many-colored city, their desire is endlessly reinvigorated, initially exhaust-

---

42. The "M" here refers to Mette Ivers, who was then earning a living as a fashion model touring France. She'd given Camus a copy of her itinerary, and he would join her at different stops along the way.

43. On May 12, 1959, the television program *Gros plan* aired an episode in which Camus talked about his love for the theater. On May 15, he wrote to Maria Casarès that a newspaper had published the text of his talk without permission to do so, and that another newspaper to which he'd refused publication was now "dragging me through the mud." Those who knew Camus best felt he was unrecognizable onscreen. Speaking of the show, Mette Ivers recalls: "It wasn't very good at all. In life, he was simplicity itself, but standing there before the camera that day, he felt he needed to be theatrical to get his ideas across. That wasn't really his style, which was always devoid of the least affectation." Similarly, Catherine Sellers felt that it "wasn't at all the way he spoke, wasn't at all the way he moved, wasn't his natural way of being. I watched the *Gros plan* broadcast again and found it terrifying. It's not him, it's not his voice—it wasn't even *his voice*."

44. See the entry titled "Stages of healing" (pp. 620–21), which was written on a separate sheet of paper and inserted into the notebook at a later date.

ing them, ultimately sending them into an intoxicated binge. . . . Only the calanques, the white stones and sea burning with light, are chaste.[45]

Grenier. "Ermitages Maronites" (*Un Été au Liban*).[46]

> "In the same cave you can see, almost effaced, which is a shame, a smaller, much older crucifixion in which Christ, his knees half bent, seems to be wearing bouffant pants like the inhabitants of this country wear, and it's accompanied by an inscription in strangelo (what is Strangelo)."

Written under the title—The Strangelo—a not-quite comprehensible tale.

MAY 21. It's the red season. Cherries and poppies.

At noon, the sound of a tractor in the Lourmarin valley . . . like the one the boat's motor made in the sun-crushed port of Chios while I waited in a cabin full of shadows; yes, like today, full of a love without object.

I like these little lizards, as slender as the stones over which they run. They're like me: skin and bone.

PARIS, JUNE 59. I've given up the moralistic point of view. Morality leads to abstraction and injustice. It's the mother of fanaticism and blindness. He who is virtuous must cut off heads. But what is there to say about the one who professes morals without being able to live up to them? Heads fall to the ground and he legislates, unfaithful. Morality cuts in two, separates, rips the flesh from the bones. We must run from it, accept being judged and judge no longer, say yes, create unity—and in the meantime, suffer agony. [. . .][47]

Joski's Danish woman.[48]

---

45. "Calanques" refers to a type of high-walled cove or inlet found along the Mediterranean coast. Camus had gone to join Mette Ivers, who recalls the two having shared "an intoxicating boat ride in the calanques."

46. "Maronites Retreat" is a chapter in Jean Grenier's *A Summer in Lebanon*, which was published alongside his *Letters from Egypt*.

47. The bracketed ellipses indicate that the entry following this one was removed by earlier editors to protect the identity of a living person.

48. Daniel Joski played a small role in the traveling production of *The Possessed*. See "D.J." entry below.

The city drunk with heat.

VENICE FROM JULY 6 TO 13. A heavy, deadening heat pressed down on the lagoon like an enormous sponge, settling atop the city, weighing on it, cutting off any possibility of retreat via the Ponte della Libertà, obstructing the outlets of the streets and canals, filling all the free space between the closely built houses.[49] No exit door, no escape, a heat trap you had to live through while going around in circles. Which is precisely how that army of hideous tourists went around, furious, crazed, sweaty, ferocious, grotesquely decked out like the horrible troupe of an enormous circus suddenly gone idle and terrified of being so. The entire city is drunk on heat. In the morning, we read in *Il Gazzettino* that some Venetians driven mad by the heat were taken to an insane asylum. Felled cats lay all over the place. Every so often, one of them gets up, ventures a few steps on the burning Campo, and is just as quickly felled by the wicked, wearying sun that lies waiting for them. Rats hoist themselves above the canals' stagnant waters and three seconds later fall back in en masse. That scorching, wearying heat seemed to gnaw away at a city growing ever more decrepit, at the chipped splendor of the palaces, at the burning campos, at the moldy foundations and piles of mooring, and Venice sank a little deeper into the lagoon.

As for us, we wandered around unable to eat, fueling ourselves on coffee and ice cream, unable to sleep, no longer knowing where the days and nights began and ended. The day would catch us by surprise out on the Lido beach, in the warm and viscous morning water, or in a gondola wandering lost in the canals as the sky turned pinkish-gray above the suddenly turquoise tiling. The city was empty then but the heat didn't let up, neither at that hour nor in the evening, always the same, always burning and humid, Venice always encircled as, losing hope of ever getting out of there, we looked only for the next breath, and then the one after that, we looked for a way to make it through that strange time lacking bearings or breaks, nerves shot by coffee and insomnia, torn from life. We were people outside of time, but people who desired nothing in the world other than the continuation of that crazed, motionless madness, there amid that frozen fire devouring Venice, hour after hour, so relentlessly that we awaited the moment when that city that had just been bursting with color and beauty would in a single stroke collapse into

---

49. When *The Possessed* played in Venice, at La Fenice, Camus went along to help get things running. He would repeat much of this entry in a July 14 letter to Maria Casarès.

a heap of ashes that not even the absent wind would carry away. We waited, clinging to each other, unable to leave each other, and we were burning, too, but with a sort of strange and endless joy, there on that pyre of beauty.

———

D.J. notices a young Danish woman, rather unattractive, for what it's worth, on a café terrace and then at the theater. He approaches her, sits down next to her, then a few minutes pass, then they get up together. My heart aches seeing the submissive way she follows him. The submissiveness they all have in that moment.[50]

———

That's when J. tells me she's pregnant with P.'s child. I advise her to tell him. He laughs and an hour later comes back to the hotel with X., even though J. is there. J. stays with X., who loves her and says nothing. [. . .][51]

———

Novel. A fiery love explodes between them, a passion of body and soul.[52] For days on end they tremble, they merge so completely that their bodies grow as tender and stirred as their souls. United everywhere, on the sailboat, their desire is endlessly reborn as emotion. For him, it's a struggle with death, with himself, with forgetting, with her and his weak nature, and he finally surrenders, placing himself in her hands. After her there will be no one else, he knows, promises in the only place he still finds something of the sacred: Saint Julien le Pauvre, there where Greece and Christ come together. He decides to stick to this promise no matter what, so that beyond this person he's holding tight, there's nothing but a void, and he holds it tighter and tighter, melting into it, so completely open to it as to be torn to pieces, so as to at last take refuge there, to shelter forever there, in love at last rediscovered, there where the senses themselves are ablaze with light, are purified on an inextinguishable pyre, or in a gushing of jubilant waters—are crowned with limitless

50. In the handwritten notebook, the entry about Venice fills the whole page, and this entry about "D.J." is written sideways along the right margin, while the entry that follows about "J." and "P." is written sideways along the left margin.

51. The bracketed ellipses indicate a page-and-a-half removed by earlier editors to protect the identity of a living person.

52. A literal translation of the line: "Love erupts between them as a passion of flesh and heart." The word *cœur*, usually meaning "heart," is translated above as "soul," though here it has a more spiritual than religious connotation.

Saint Julien the Poor, mentioned just below, is a Greek church in Paris. Construction began in the 1100s and finished in the 1200s. It's one of the oldest churches in the city.

Mette Ivers accompanied Camus on this visit to Saint Julien the Poor. For the comment about the "sailboat," see p. 657n45.

gratitude. That hour when the boundaries of bodies fall, when the singular being is finally born in the complete nakedness of profound benefaction.[53]

This left to which I belong, despite myself and despite it.[54]

AUGUST 13. Absence, painful frustration. But my heart is alive, my heart is alive at last. So then it wasn't true that indifference had won the day. Gratitude, a fierce gratefulness for Mi.

Yes, jealousy bears witness for the spirit. Jealousy is the suffering born of seeing the other reduced to an object and the desire that everyone and everything recognize the other as subject. One is not jealous of God.

Evening falls on the valley, the old walls, the battlements, the patient houses. The grass rustles under my feet.

SEPTEMBER. Y. In spring she wakes at eleven, stays in bed, has lunch around 1:00 or 2:00 p.m., and then remains in bed until late in the afternoon, surrounded by *France-Dimanche, Match, Noir et Blanc, Cinémonde,*[55] etc., etc., which she devours.

Mi, to whom I speak half-joking, half-serious about extreme old age, when the rising action's all over, the jubilation of the senses, etc., bursts into sobs, "I love love so much."[56]

Before writing a novel, I'll have to spend years in a state of obscurity.

---

53. The French edition of the *Carnets* notes that a sentence was removed here, but aside from a sentence that Camus himself crossed out—something he does throughout the notebooks without comment from the editors—there does not appear to be any gap in the published version versus the handwritten manuscript.

One possible source of the confusion is that the entry that follows this one in the handwritten notebook ("This left to which I belong") appears at the very top of the next notebook page but was originally placed later in the first published French edition. It has been restored to its proper place here.

54. This entry is written in small print along the top edge of the page.

55. A listing of pop-culture French news and film magazines.

56. In the final pages of *The First Man*, Camus writes: "when, laughing, he told her one day that youth slips away and the daylight grows dim, she burst into sobs, saying through her tears, 'Oh, no, oh, no, I love love so much.'"

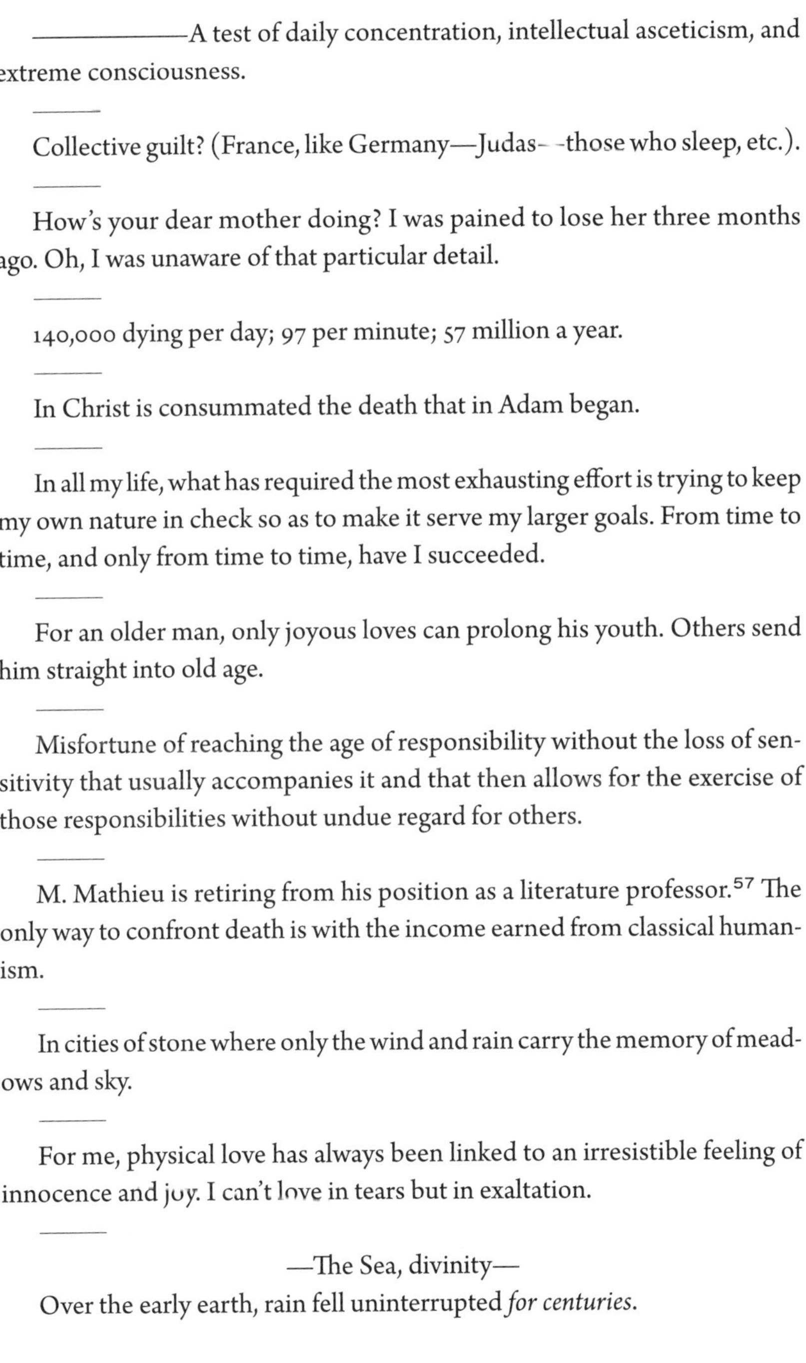

———————A test of daily concentration, intellectual asceticism, and extreme consciousness.

———

Collective guilt? (France, like Germany—Judas— —those who sleep, etc.).

———

How's your dear mother doing? I was pained to lose her three months ago. Oh, I was unaware of that particular detail.

———

140,000 dying per day; 97 per minute; 57 million a year.

———

In Christ is consummated the death that in Adam began.

———

In all my life, what has required the most exhausting effort is trying to keep my own nature in check so as to make it serve my larger goals. From time to time, and only from time to time, have I succeeded.

———

For an older man, only joyous loves can prolong his youth. Others send him straight into old age.

———

Misfortune of reaching the age of responsibility without the loss of sensitivity that usually accompanies it and that then allows for the exercise of those responsibilities without undue regard for others.

———

M. Mathieu is retiring from his position as a literature professor.[57] The only way to confront death is with the income earned from classical humanism.

———

In cities of stone where only the wind and rain carry the memory of meadows and sky.

———

For me, physical love has always been linked to an irresistible feeling of innocence and joy. I can't love in tears but in exaltation.

———

—The Sea, divinity—

Over the early earth, rain fell uninterrupted *for centuries.*

57. Monsieur Paul Mathieu was Camus's literature professor in 1932.

It's in the sea that life was born, and since time immemorial, from the first cell to complex marine creatures, the continent, having neither animal nor plant life, was but a land of stone, an enormous silence invaded only by the sound of wind and rain, crossed by no movement other than the swift shadows of large clouds and waters running over the ocean basins—

After billions of years the first living creature left the ocean and set foot on terra firma. It looked like a scorpion. That was 350 million years ago.

Flying fish make their nests in the deep to protect their eggs

In the Saragasso Sea, two million tons of algae.

The big red jellyfish, initially the size of a thimble, grows as wide as an umbrella in spring. It moves by pulsation, letting its long tentacles drag behind it, sheltering groups of codfish that move along with it under its parasol

The fish that swims up past its natural habitat cross an invisible border, bursts, and "falls back to the surface below."

Squid that live in the depths, unlike those on the surface that emit an ink, emit a luminous cloud. They hide in the light

Ultimately, terra firma is only a very thin plate on the sea. One day the ocean will reign supreme

There are waves that reach us from Cape Horn after a journey of 10,000 km

In 358, a tidal wave rose in the eastern Mediterranean, submerging the islands and lower coasts, leaving fishing boats perched on the forts in Alexandria

———

I'm a writer. It's not me but the pen that thinks, remembers, or discovers.

———

I can't live with other people for too long. I need a bit of solitude, a share of eternity.

———

A domestic horse escapes on the Greater Luberon and lives free and alone for years. Short story? A man hears about it goes looking for it. He's converted to a life of freedom.

———

For Nemesis (in Lourmarin December 59)[58]

Black horse, white horse, a single hand of man masters both furies. At breakneck speed, joyous is the race!

---

58. Among Catherine Sellers's papers, held at the Bibliothèque nationale de France, a copy of this entry, written out in her hand over several sheets of paper torn from a notebook, appears among her letters to Camus. Whereas Camus has written the lines as a single entry, Sellers has created sections separated by small sun-like drawings.

Truth lies, candor disguises. Hide yourself in the light

The world fills you and you are empty: plenitude

Soft sound of foam on a morning beach; it fills the world all the same as fame's roaring. Both come from silence

He who refuses chooses himself, he who covets prefers himself. Neither ask nor refuse. Accept to surrender

Flames of ice crown the days; sleep in the motionless fire

Equally hard, equally soft, the slope, the day's slope—but only one mountain at the top.

The night burns, the sun darkens. O self-sufficient earth

Freed from everything, enslaved to yourself. Enslaved to others: freed from nothing. Choose your servitude

Behind the cross, the devil.[59] Let them be together. Your empty altar is elsewhere.

The waters of pleasure and sea are equally salty. Even in the waves[60]

—The exile reigns, the king is on his knees. In the desert, solitude ends

—On the sea, unceasingly, from port to island, running in the light, over liquid abysses, joy, as long as a very long life

—You wear masks, here they are naked

—In the brief day given to you, warm and illuminate, without deviating from your course

Millions of other suns will come while you rest

Beneath joy's stone slab, the first sleep

Sown by the wind, reaped by the wind, and yet a creator still, such is man, through the centuries, proud to live a single instant

———

"Men's vanity erected these magnificent abodes, only to receive in them the unavoidable guest, Death, with all the ceremonies of superstitious fear" (Conrad, Suspense).[61]

———

59. The phrase, written earlier in these notebooks in Spanish, is here written in French. In the version of the entry written out by Catherine Sellers, the sentence is followed by "says the Spaniard."

60. In the version written out by Catherine Sellers, this section is followed by another section containing Nietzsche's "Six solitudes were already known to him, but the sea itself wasn't solitary enough for him," which Camus quotes earlier in these pages.

61. The quote is from Conrad's unfinished final novel, *Suspense*, which was published by Gallimard in 1944 under the French title *L'attente*. In the parenthetical above, Camus has given the title as "Angoisse."

Saint Ignatius (Spiritual Journal)[62] "indignant" at not receiving confirmation from heaven of his election by the Holy Trinity. But he wished "to die with Jesus rather than live with another."[63] He would be unhappier in hell due to the blaspheming of God's name done there than due to the suffering endured.

Id: he tells the devil tempting him: "Go back where you belong." Elsewhere: God is immutable, the devil fickle and immobile.

———

For Don Faust. There can be no D.J. in a time of free love. There are men who please more than others. But there is neither sin nor heroism.

There's Lope de Vega's Don Juan: *La Promesse accomplie* (translate it and also the Zorrilla). Philip IV's love affair with Sister Marguerite de la Croix (see Les Procès célèbres d'Espagne, see also (p. 189 and sq.) Don Juan and Gregorio Marañon's Don Juan)[64]

———

In *Parabole*[65] (p. 388) a man sentenced to death says he is innocent, then acknowledges that he isn't, and resigns himself to his fate. Then standing beneath the noose sees a bird fly to a branch, alight there, and begin to sing, and grabs the noose and screams that he is innocent[66]

———

62. In both French and English, the document is more commonly known as Spiritual Exercises. See p. 441n70.

63. In *The Rebel*, Camus quotes Meister Eckhart giving his assurance that he prefers Hell with Jesus rather than Heaven without Him. In *The Possessed*, Stavrogin tells Shatov that if it were mathematically proven that truth is separate from Christ, he would rather remain with Christ than with truth.

64. José Zorrilla (1817–1893), Spanish poet and dramatist. His *Don Juan Tenorio* is a Romantic play in which the doomed seducer is redeemed by the love of a woman. The play was written in 1844 and has been staged every November 1 since then in Spain.

Philip IV fell in love with an attractive nun from Madrid's San Placido convent. To be able to meet her, he dug a passage into the convent's cellar—but the Mother Superior, warned by the nun, had a fake scene setup. The king found his beloved stretched out on a bed, eyes closed, surrounded by candles, apparently dead. Seeing this, he fled, and although the incident was suppressed, the Inquisition was alerted, and there was quite a scandal.

Les procès célèbres d'Espagne is a 1931 book by Maurice Soulié.

Gregorio Marañòn (1887–1960) was a Spanish physician and critic who took a scientific approach to historical studies. His 1940 book on Don Juan was translated into French in 1958.

65. William Faulkner's *A Fable* was published in the US in 1954 and in French, as *Parabole*, in 1958. The translation was done by R. N. Raimbault.

66. The rest of the page after this entry was left blank in the original notebook. There is no period at the end of this sentence.

That's why I chose you and that's what will help me get back on track, will help me stop suffering the particulars of what I recognize as just and legitimate in principle . . .

What's also helped me: equity. That difficult acceptance of yourself and others is creation. But being in this crisis, in this sort of impotence, I now understand that despicable desire for possession that's always shocked me in others. You can conquer another person for lack of having conquered yourself. And it's true that at that very moment, I needed the sense of belonging you gave me. That's why I suffered as much from your lie as from your fleeing. But it'll pass. A little more pessimism and unhappiness will have its chance to shine through: I'll become myself again[67]

I've suffered as a result of what you revealed to me—that's a fact—but you mustn't be sad about my sadness. I'm in the wrong, I know, and even if I can't prevent my heart from being unjust, I can at least make it equitable. It won't be hard to overcome the injustice I do to you in my heart. I know I've done everything possible to drive you off. All my life, as soon as a person's gotten close to me, I've done everything possible to push them away. Of course, there's my inability to make commitments, my desire for other people, for multiplicity, and my own pessimism, too.[68] But maybe I haven't been as frivolous as I say. The first person I loved and was faithful to slipped away from me through drugs, through betrayal, and maybe a lot of things have come from that, from vanity, from fear of suffering again, and in any case, I've had my own share of suffering, too. Ever since then, I've managed to slip away from everyone, and in some way, I've wanted everyone to slip away from me, as well. Even M. I've done everything possible to discourage her. I don't believe she has slipped away from me, that she has given herself even fleetingly to another man. I can't be sure of it [. . .].[69] But if she didn't do it, it's because of a decision based on her inner heroism, not on an overabundance of the sort of love that gives without ever asking anything in return. So then, yes, I did everything possible to lead you away from me.

---

67. The rest of the page after this entry was left blank in the original notebook. There is no period at the end of this sentence.

68. In the margin of the original notebook, Camus wrote and circled: "The lie."

This final entry is fairly heavily edited, with many parts crossed out and many lines added.

69. One illegible word (the word may be "however"). These lines were added in along the margin.

And the more the infatuation of this past September grew, the more I wanted to break its enchanting spell. So that, in some sense, you did slip away from me. That's the sometimes-awful justice of this world. Betrayal responds to betrayal, the flight of love to the mask of love. And in this particular case, I, who have claimed and lived all freedoms, I know and recognize that it is just and good that you have also lived a freedom or two. The account is not even close to being balanced.

In any case, it's not just this cold equity of the heart that will help me through but the fondness, the affection, I feel for you. I sometimes accuse myself of being incapable of love. Perhaps it's true, but I've been able to *choose* a few people and to keep for them, faithfully, what is best in me, whatever they may do.[70]

---

70. In addition to the sheet of *NRF* letterhead that Camus had tucked in at the beginning of the notebook, three other looseleaf documents were also found in the notebook: a second sheet of *NRF* letterhead with a brief list of minor sentence-level corrections for *The Misunderstanding*, *Caligula*, and *State of Emergency*; a French newspaper clipping titled "A Mad Masquerade," which gives a sardonic account of a masked ball held at a psychiatric hospital ("an idea that would make Edgar Poe jealous"); and a handwritten list of responses to questions that Robert Donald Spector, an English literature professor at Long Island University, had sent Camus. After Camus's sudden death, an English translation of these responses, along with reproductions of the handwritten French originals, as well as the two letters Camus and Spector exchanged, would go on to be published as part of the Spring–Summer 1960 issue of *Venture* magazine, which featured a special dossier titled "Albert Camus: 1913–1960. A Final Interview." The list of responses found tucked into notebook IX is evidently a first draft, with some questions yet unanswered, and certain other differences from the final responses Camus sent to Spector on December 20, 1959.

Appendix I: The First Notebook

1933

Camus kept the following notes, a clear precursor to what would become the official journals, in a small school notebook he'd bought at the Ferraris Bookshop at 43 Rue Michelet in Algiers. He was nineteen years old at the time.

What you can gain from reading Stendhal: contempt for appearances.

I should learn to control my feelings, too quick to boil over.[1] I thought I'd mastered them by burying them beneath irony and coldness. I have to let go of such illusions. They are too intense, too excessive, unwelcome, untimely. They leave me too susceptible to the impressionistic, to the immediate, to the easy, to the "fatal." They lead me to wallow in senseless lethargy.

They should speak, not scream. They should, given that I want to write, be felt in my works, not in my life.

But is it really worth the trouble? I attach too much value to my contradictions. When faced with the occasional bit of energy, I spend too much time thinking about my naturally weak character, though it is quite real.

Finished my *Moorish House.*[2] Probably better than what I'd already shown G. I tried not to let any of my present sufferings show in it. But I did let a little of that suffering breakthrough in the final lines. That's just how it has to be. Not that I'm trying to hide from myself that the part where I tried to hide my need to cry is the best part.

Spent all day rereading Stendhal. Couldn't work. *The Abbess of Castro* and *Italian Chronicles*. They don't touch me; they satisfy me. What personal objectivity! An example for me to consider. G. is right.

At the moment, I'm surprised to be attributing more importance (I'm well aware) to my *Moorish House* than it deserves. Probably because of how much effort it took, despite how small it is. I forbid myself from rereading it before G. does.

Damned pride.

---

1. A literal translation of the line shows a greater connection to the first entry in the official notebooks: "I should learn to tame my sensibility, too quick to overflow."

The final clause of the entry is ambiguous in the French.

2. Camus's early essay "The Moorish House" was written in the same notebook and in the same time period as the rest of the notes given here, though it was kept separate from these entries.

The "G" likely refers to Jean Grenier.

Reread Aeschylus's *Prometheus*. Prometheus's romanticism. His complacence when faced with misfortune. Bitter satisfaction when faced with injustice. He's misunderstood, unsung, and it leads him to be proud.

The art of Byzantine portraiture: places emphasis on the eyes, overly enlarging them . . . as a constant reminder of the hereafter and the religious impulse. Interesting correspondence. Why the eyes? Fear the cliché.

When walking through the city with S.C., indulged in reciting verses and banalities as a way of hiding an all-too-natural excitement. The sun smelled nice on the quays.

The play of landscapes flitting past the car: those admirable sights that so sharply strike the senses only to disappear and end up a part of memory's misty magic.

The air is pure and clear. The sun soft and ethereal . . . Lying in the grass. Above my head, the oaks bear the brunt of the sun . . . I close my eyes, wounded by the light. An eyelid night. The slow feelings that build behind them, like in the cool shadows of closed-up rooms . . .

I can't imagine Gide loving an exclusive love. Maybe that's what he's after.

I can't imagine Gide on his deathbed.

Passivity of Gide's demeanor.

Reread my notes on Gide. Terribly banal. Infantile platitudes. I was infuriated by the mediocrity of my thinking in relation to the depth of my feelings for Gide.

I'm now convinced we can't talk about people we love so much.

Amazed by Lev Shestov.[3] The same feeling that seized me after reading Proust: so many things no longer need be said.

Dostoyevsky and Nietzsche, not Shestov: hopelessness set against ordinary life. The idea appeals to me, but I'm wary of its simplicity. It comes too naturally. Yet, digging a little deeper, Shestov seems to be making a new idea

3. Camus would go on to discuss Shestov in greater depth in the "Absurd Walls" section of *The Myth of Sisyphus*.

out of it. Anyway, maybe such an idea doesn't come naturally to Shestov, as a Russian.

You could argue that, at the same time as there's a need for unity, there's a need for death, because death give shapes to life, by way of contrast. Expand and clarify this.

Read Grenier's book. He is wholly present in it, and I feel the love and admiration he inspires in me growing. You can say about him that he embodies the greatest possible humanity, precisely in trying to distance himself from it. What ties his book together is the constant presence of death. This explains why the mere sight of G., while not changing anything about my way of being, makes me more serious, more deeply imbued with the gravity of life.

I don't know any other man who can make me feel this way. Spending two hours with him always enlarges me. Will I ever know how much I owe him?

Changed the end of my *Moorish House,* despite what I said before. It goes back to what I was saying earlier: my sensitivity must speak, not scream.

Is it not a mistake to record only my mental activity in these notes?[4]

Grenier: "All independence can ever be is a freely chosen dependence." Variant: "The freedom of slavery is given away to be free."[5]

The sun's eloquent volubility.

---

4. The French *spirituelle* could be translated as both "spiritual" and "intellectual," but given Camus's intentional effort to focus more on matters of the mind in his notebooks than on personal matters or what is commonly referred to as spiritual matters, the translation has been given here as "mental."

5. In an essay published over ten years later in the September 9, 1944, edition of *Les lettres françaises,* Jean-Paul Sartre would make a somewhat similar statement, writing: "We were never so free as under the German Occupation. We lost all our rights, first among them the right to speak. Every day we were insulted to our face, and we had to remain silent. We were deported en masse, as workers, as Jews, as political prisoners. Everywhere we looked—on the walls, in the newspapers, on our screens—we found that vile face our oppressors wished us to see as our own. That's why we were free: because of all that. Because, given that the Nazi venom burrowed all the way into our thoughts, every clear thought was a conquest; because, given that an all-powerful police force tried to force us into silence, every word spoken was as precious as a declaration of principles; because, given that we were hunted down, every action we took carried the weight of commitment. The often-atrocious circumstances of our daily battle had finally led us to live, unvarnished and unveiled, that unbearable, heartrending situation we call the human condition."

Art is born of constraints.[6] Let's generalize: life is born of constraints. The feeling that flourishes best must be the one that is constrained.

What they call Gide's need for justification is Gide's feeling that he needs to reconcile his lucid being and his passionate being. His lucid being demands justification from his passionate being.

If a need for justification there be, it's a justification to himself . . .

Counterfeiters: a writer grappling with Reality, which resists what he wants to make of it.[7]

So then maybe the real Gide is André Walter: "I am pure, I am pure, I am pure."[8] This feverish need for purity is found throughout his entire body of work.

It would be nice to be able to speak a few banalities about Gide one day, profoundly true banalities, as only banalities can be. Like this one: Gide is great only in banality.

Gide's work is a screen in front of his life: "Our books won't be the most truthful accounts of our miseries."[9]

When G. loves and speak passionately, there is always a Gide watching Gide. There is always a formidable duality in Gide between his need for childhood . . . and his ironic lucidity.

Gide is only himself when he sees that this conflict is one we all share and mythologizes it. He often sees this. That's why there are sobs in each one of his sentences.

---

6. Camus is referencing André Gide's comment "Art is born of constraints, lives on struggle, and dies of freedom."

7. *The Counterfeiters* (*Les faux-monnayeurs*), an experimental 1925 novel by André Gide, tackles questions of authenticity, as well as the spectrum of intimate relationships between men.

8. The reference is Gide's *The Notebooks of André Walter* (*Les cahiers et les poésies d'André Walter*).

9. The quote is from the opening of Gide's *An Attempt to Love, or The Treatise of Vain Desire* (*La tentative amoureuse, ou Le traité du vain désir*). As is the case throughout Camus's notebooks, the quote given here does not match the original, which reads: "Our books won't be the most truthful accounts of ourselves, but rather of our plaintive desires, our wish for other lives forever forbidden, for all those impossible acts."

Gide tries too hard to distance himself from Gide. That's the part of Gide I immediately understood. But isn't that because I'm trying to distance myself from me?

And Gide's tragedy, his suffering, is to find himself there in every step he takes. This can even be seen in his work. He tried in his most recent works to be objective: every landscape, every character is Gidian from whatever angle it's seen . . .

I no longer dare reread *The Fruits*,[10] so as to keep intact the memory of the intoxication and ecstasy they produced in me.

I've never been able to imagine Gide loving with committed love.[11] And yet that's what he's waiting for, what he has been waiting for·

I can't imagine Gide on his deathbed.

Fruits of the Earth: such an apologia for sensation . . . is never anything but an intellectualizing of the senses. Nothing is more intellectual than *The Fruits of the Earth*. The sole fact of having made a theory out of it annihilated and emasculated that Dionysian theory. Its truth can only be found in the very realization of that vicious circle. *Fruits of the Earth*: forbidden paradise . . .[12]

---

10. Gide's *The Fruits of the Earth*.

11. A more literal translation of the French might read "loving an exclusive love." That is, Camus can't imagine Gide being able to love someone, or sustain that love, while in a committed relationship.

12. The title of Gide's book, *Nourritures terrestres*, could also be translated as *Earthly Fruits*, which would correspond to the phrase *paradis terrestre* (earthly paradise). This invites several readings of Camus's final phrase, another version of which might be "heaven forbidden."

Appendix II: The Oran Notebook

MARCH 1938–AUGUST 1942

In July 1942, with Camus's health visibly deteriorating, Doctor Cviklinsky, a friend from Algiers, advised Camus that due to the condition of his lungs it would be in his best interest to spend some time in the mountains of France. Camus had been living in Oran at the time, and after a long, exhausting voyage that included a brief stop in Algiers, a boat to Marseille, a train to Lyon, another to Saint-Étienne, and another to Chambon-sur-Lignon, he and Francine would finally arrive in Le Panelier in mid-August 1942.

In the process of moving, the notebook that follows, a plain, dark-colored composition notebook similar in style to the others Camus had previously used, got left behind in Oran, and it wasn't until June 1988, long after Camus's death and the publication of the notebooks, that it was returned to the Camus family.

One of the things that sets this notebook apart from the others Camus was keeping at the time is its openly confessional nature, its unabashed use of "I," and its more personal, reflective content, all of which may have contributed to his decision to record these entries in a separate space, just as he'd recorded the more personal entries from his travels in South America in a separate journal.

Don Juan invited the Statue of the Commander [. . .][1]

He's been waiting at Doña Ana's since then. He's friendly but nervous. He falls into sudden silences. He seems tormented by an inexplicable longing. The arranged meeting time comes and goes. Dawn arrives and Don Juan falls into the most hopeless of silences. Doña Ana asks questions. Don Juan is speechless. Ana presses him and Don Juan bursts into sobs, sudden and sterile.

" "

A. laughs. "Naturally."

D.J. straightens up. Well said: "Naturally. But if it would have come, it would have meant that there's something greater than me. Greater than this life. Would have [. . .] a superior life [. . .] put mouths there where I've bitten. And now no. There's nothing. Nothing more. Statues don't move, miracles don't happen. [. . .] and its limits reign in the wake of its dead. I was right, Ana. I was right. That's why I'm crying. Have you ever known the awful feeling of being right when you've rejected everything and gambled on hopelessness.

You know very well that I don't love you and yet you pretend to believe otherwise. You gambled on me, the one who was gambling. And that gamble, that discernment: lies. There you have the whole truth [. . .] that I lived and will live and bear with my body until it fails me. The statue didn't come. There are no miracles. Everything is going to end in death."

March 17, 1938

No Tomorrows[2]

March 17, 1938

That day, every car was a temptation. I could see their wheels rolling over

---

1. This entry appears on a separate sheet of paper tucked in at the front of the notebook. A second entry, titled "Faith and Religion," which does not appear here, as much of it is difficult to make out, was tucked in at the back of the notebook.

Bracketed ellipses represent illegible words.

2. Following the inserted entry above, the first four pages of the notebook proper are blank, followed by the date and the phrase "No Tomorrows" on the fifth page, and then the first full entry on the sixth page. Camus has hand-numbered pages 6–14 as 1–9.

In notebooks I–IX, the phrase "No Tomorrow," in the singular, appears in several places during the same time period in which this notebook was being kept, and during which Camus was working on *The Happy Death*, *The Myth of Sisyphus*, and *The Stranger*.

me—and from within my otherwise motionless body, another being reached out to that soulless force that would have flattened me.[3] I searched the whole city for someone with whom I could do the things that people do: have a coffee, have a laugh with women, or go see a movie. But people tend to run from lepers, and if lepers can't find anyone, well, that's no coincidence.

As evening fell on the harbor, there before that soft light, with those mountains ringed behind it, the flaws that would've normally bound me to life began to dissolve into a peace that was seeping through me like a poison. I can hardly describe what my day had been like, the extreme hopelessness and madness into which I'd been thrown.[4] The essential thing for what follows is that on that evening, at that instant, without even thinking about it, I'd accepted the idea of dying and I was no longer thinking like a living person but like one who'd already been sentenced: it doesn't really matter how long it lasted. What matters is that in the night that followed I couldn't sleep and I paced back and forth. It doesn't really matter if I'm still capable of such extreme sorrow. What matters is that I didn't leave the house for three days, that I sat there staring at my hands for hours on end or running to the mirror to look for that icy, alien being who had just been born.[5] I wouldn't say that everything came from those three days—only the most essential thing. Until then, I'd had goals, concerns about the future and about justification (to whom or what is beside the point) that gave my life direction.[6] I used to evaluate the odds, to count on times to come. I used to act as if I could act on those odds and that future. That night, it all came crashing down.

It was then that I thought how illusory that freedom was, that idea that my days would continue to follow one after the next. That idea that "I was," the way I acted as if everything had a meaning (even if I occasionally felt that nothing did), it was all so vertiginously contradicted by the certainty of my death. Thinking about tomorrow, setting a goal, having preferences,

---

3. In French, *broyer,* which in its literal sense means "to grind" or "to crush," also carries the figurative meaning "to wreck" or "to destroy." It is also used in the phrase *broyer du noir,* which means to be depressed, to be down in the dumps, to brood.

4. Camus included an asterisk here with a note at the bottom of the page reading "Look at yourself."

5. The French *étrange,* here translated as "alien," also means "strange," as in the title of Camus's first published novel.

In French, *glace* (mirror) and *glacé* (icy) are only an accent apart, creating a stronger connection between object and condition.

6. An edited version of this sentence, as well as several others that appear in the following five paragraphs, would go on to be used in *The Myth of Sisyphus* in a depersonalized form.

all presuppose a belief in freedom—even if I sometimes told myself that I didn't believe—and that ultimate freedom, that freedom to be, which alone can serve as a basis for truth, it was then that I knew that it didn't exist—that death was the only reality, that after death all bets were off, and that, on account of this, I was no longer free to carry on but was a slave, and what's more, a slave without hope of revolution, without recourse to contempt. And who, without contempt, can remain a slave? What freedom can exist, in the fullest sense of the word, without the assurance of eternity.

So then, I wasn't free but a slave to death. I won't dwell on the overwhelming feeling that accompanied the discovery of that truth that I knew without truly knowing it, but in that moment I suddenly understood that up until then I'd been committed to that assumption of freedom, that I'd lived by it—that, in some ways, I'd been shackled by it—and that insofar as I saw my life as having a purpose, I actively pursued it, and in so doing became a slave to my freedom. I'd been holding onto that assumption of freedom without even realizing it, though, at the same time, it was also being reinforced by the beliefs of those around me, and, ultimately, by the prejudices of my environment. As removed as I may have been from such moral or social prejudices, I was still partly influenced by them, and I even modeled my life on the best of them (there are good and bad prejudices). So then, I wasn't really free. To be perfectly clear about it, insofar as I hoped for, as I worried about, a truth of my own, a way of being or creating, insofar as I made plans for my life, insofar as I unquestioningly accepted that my life had a meaning, I was erecting barriers between which I was narrowing the possibilities of my life, and, in taking man's freedom seriously, I can now see that I was doing the same thing that so many bureaucrats of the mind and heart do, those people who inspire in me nothing but disgust.

That sort of intellectual is something I ceased to be that night, for the certainty of my slavery carried away with it all concern for tomorrow. There could be no tomorrow.

Let me give two examples here. First, mystics find freedom in giving of themselves. By losing themselves in their god, by subjecting themselves to his rule, they remain inwardly free of their giving, and it's in freely consenting to slavery that they arrive at a profound independence. But are they really free? The truth is that they feel free. And most importantly, they feel free of themselves. And it's not so much free, in their eyes, as freed. Freed from everything. In the same way, turned entirely toward death, I felt released from everything that wasn't that horror crystallizing inside of me. I experienced an inexpressible freedom from basic norms and daily activities. And to give a sense of what that freedom was like, I'll set out my second example. In antiquity, slaves didn't have ownership of themselves—and there's a freedom in not feeling responsible for yourself. Death, too, has patrician hands that can crush as well as deliver.

Losing myself in that fathomless certainty, feeling that I was now enough of a stranger to my own life to stretch it out and explore it without the myopic eyes of a lover, in all of this I felt the birth of a certain kind of freedom, one that was finite,[7] but one that took the place of those illusions of freedom that all succumb to death. And the closer I felt freedom was to its end, the more aware I became of its exhilarating power. The divine freedom experienced by the individual sentenced to death as the prison doors open before him one fine and early dawn, that horrible disinterest in anything other than the pure flame of life, that's what I found to be the ultimate purpose of my groundless journey (free to act because forbidden to be, having lost all reason to hope and having gained the profound freedom of a life without direction). With a great, wrenching effort, I decided to apply my lucidity to playing all the parts of a game that I knew from the start I was going to lose. And my consolation (laughable even in my own eyes) was that it was precisely this freedom of mind that would give me the power to live, more than ever before, at a depth and with an intensity that would have driven anyone else mad.

This dreadful insight and that loathsome power to live had finally been given to me. Until then, I'd only had a vague sense of such an outcome. All those limited freedoms I'd experienced in my life, they made me realize that they weren't, that they lost all meaning in the face of those innumerable deaths that foreshadow the one solitary death: a deceased love and the ashy taste of every desire. Now I understood. Now I had glimpsed that burning, icy universe, that transparent, [. . .],[8] where nothing was possible but everything was given, beyond which all was collapse and nothingness. I decided that night to accept a life in such a universe and to draw from it my strength, my refusal to hope, to accept an overflowing life and a body of work without consolation, one that would bear lucid, determined witness, like a barren, magnificent desert.

In this regard, what need did I have of ethics or metaphysics? For a think-

7. The term in the manuscript is hard to decipher, and the translation given above, "finite," assumes that the original French reads *à terme*.

8. One illegible word.

ing man, the tragedy lies in having to reconcile his desire for unity with the irrationality surrounding him. For a man who is familiar with his death, it's a matter of finding unity in life, in the life of a single man, in his own individual, irreplaceable life: balancing body and mind, having both approaches and mastering them through an instinct that knows. This can only be resolved or represented in a body of work—like a clarifying mirror—the body of work was my ethic. But at the same time, this could only be justified by renouncing the "leap," whether it be that of religion or that of love. You had to know that love is not, was not, forever. You can love without it being so. To be the one who deliberately renounces love, who is content with a violent, mathematical universe—this doesn't mean living a sterile life or closing yourself off—It means quite the opposite, or you've understood nothing. If I only realize my unity and the unity of my life when facing my death, then that is when I fully grasp my life. Its diversity, its irreversibility, "its senseless sense" all end here, and its fountains of emotion[9] come together as hopelessness.

So then, to stretch your life, to seize every opportunity, to linger on every woman's face, is to give this mortal truth its full weight. For a truth is something that grows, that gets stronger. It's a work-in-progress. And it's this work that you have to pursue, both on paper and in life, and with all the resources lucidity has to offer.

ESSAYS	PLAYS	NOVELS
The Absurd or The Starting Point	Caligula or The Death Player[10]	A Free Man (The Indifferent One)
The Closed World An Essay on Tragedy	Budejovice	The Doric Plague The Player Punished
Greediness[11] (N)	Don Juan	The Lovers
The Gods of Death	The Anti-Faust	The Leper

9. The French word is hard to make out here, though it may read *d'émotion* (of emotion).

10. The first full version of the play, completed in September 1939, was titled *Caligula, or The Player*. The title given here in these pages could be interpreted in multiple ways, from the more literary *He Who Gambles with Death* to the more literal *Player to Death*, but given the title of the first completed manuscript, and for consistency, it has been given above as *The Death Player*.

11. The French word is hard to make out here, though it may read *L'avidité* (Greediness) or *L'aridité* (Aridity or Emptiness).

It was no longer a matter of explaining and solving but of experiencing and describing. Everything began with indifference.[12]

Not long after, I was able to make further progress on the path toward that freedom. Yet I was still bound to it by desire itself—the desire to exploit it, to depict it in that body of work I'd been contemplating—and everything that, due to me or to circumstance, got in the way of the daily fulfillment of that body of work, also got in the way of my own fulfillment, too. When I understood this obvious point, I stopped tormenting myself over who I was or what was happening to me. I came to accept that this body of work may itself never be, and in accepting this, I embraced the pointlessness of my own individual life. I accepted that I was who I was and that I sometimes disgusted myself. I accepted failing at things when it made no difference if I failed at them. And in accepting all of this, everything that then came my way truly came as an added bonus. I had to push my lucidity so far as to be aware of and accept those very things that might at times obscure or limit it. Then, I understood that nothing was an impediment. That a different profession, a different country, a different future, a different comportment, none of it changes anything—and that having created a work of genius puts you no further ahead than you were before it came to be. Such understanding should even make it easier for me to create this body of work, just as recognizing life's absurdity allowed me to fully immerse myself in it without reservation.[13]

I hardly had any difficulty in persuading myself that it didn't really matter whether I pursued this or that goal, whether I lived by a certain moral code or chose one experience over another. The essential thing was not to refuse anything. And not to do this by refusing to choose, because taking such a position would imply a qualitative value scale (and it would be better not to choose), but by indiscriminately welcoming all life's many faces, love and desire, desires and longing. For it made no difference if anything remained a part of me, given everything would inevitably go up in flames.

12. These two sentences would go on to appear in slightly different form in the fourth paragraph of the "Absurd Creation" section in *The Myth of Sisyphus*.

13. A literal translation of the end of the sentence might read "to dive into it with all its excesses." Up to this point, the handwriting in the notebook has been consistent, with both sides of the pages being used. In the next three paragraphs, the handwriting changes a little and only the recto pages are used, indicating that the paragraphs were recorded at a slightly later date.

I accepted life as it was. It became a matter of indifference as to whether I married or never did, whether I traveled or not, whether I became known or remained anonymous. But if I'm expressing myself clearly, then it will be clear to see with what magnificent ease I was then able to embrace marriage or travel or fame or anonymity, a life of seclusion or one of celibacy. And even to accept them all at once. I'd always had a penchant for secrecy, for a certain type of romantic outlook, that of the man who tries to find himself in silence, who tries to perfect himself outside the public eye. Then I came to see that such a penchant is both ridiculous and legitimate. And I felt that such a life was possible in principle but not in practice.

As all of this could have remained rather abstract, I decided to apply my thinking to the problem of love. A few lines back, I wrote that I'd accepted a life without love, and seeing as this is rather appalling from a human point of view, I should try to explain. In fact, I did try to specify that what was to be avoided was the "leap," which is to say the abdication of one's self to love or to religion, ideas that are irrational because we believe them eternal. But I was just as suspectable to love as anyone else. I only needed to know that it wasn't eternal, that it didn't last, and that nothing justified the way we've wrapped it all up in grandeur and wonder. Loving is one thing. But it's not the same thing as conceptualizing love. And not being able to live without loving, I could at least live lucidly without that idea of love.

It was a matter of accepting that love was a human concept and nothing more, just as I'd accepted that life goes no further than man himself. Accepting this allowed me to embrace love and to erect an ephemeral edifice of existence on the grounds of that most ephemeral of all feelings. This was logical. It was coherent. It satisfied both my passion and my rational thinking. It was in line with that awful truth at which I'd arrived, and accepting this particular point consummated my heartrending freedom, that most extravagant of solitudes.[14]

———

It took me three years to do the first part of that body of work in which I attempted to express the negative aspect of my thinking and that aspect

14. The seven paragraphs that follow this entry are in a distinctly different handwriting than the preceding paragraphs, indicating, along with the subject matter covered, that they were likely written after Camus had already completed a draft of *The Stranger* on May 1, 1940, and between the time he finished *The Myth of Sisyphus*, July 21, 1941, and mid-August 1942, at which point this notebook was lost to him.

While the entries are given here in the order in which they appear in the journal, a chronological reading would likely place the next entry last.

alone. I don't know why I felt the need to do so in three different forms: as a novel, *The Stranger*; as an essay, *The Myth of Sisyphus*; and as a play, *Caligula*. It may be that only the first two are worthwhile. I held onto *Caligula*, not yet sure if I would come back to it, and submitted the other two for publication.

Not long before publication, I was no longer so sure about what I had to say, no longer so sure about anything that had come before. Consequently, I was even less certain about what I still had to do. More specifically, these ideas, as soon as they were put in writing, they took on an air of atheism, which was not what I'd intended.

So then, I've managed to record my uncertainty in this notebook, to record the way in which I felt at odds with the essential idea that governed its writing. It seemed as if I should leave an account of things here, as doing so would allow me to pick the thread of my thinking up again.

So, I decided to start working on *Sunset of the Plague* and *Budejovice*, to think only of that body of work I'd been contemplating, none of which could be accomplished without a constant deepening of myself. A correction of my thought in relation to experience. A truth and simplification, ultimately. For example, it took me a long time to recognize that I was a man for whom intellectual matters were practically the only kind that counted, who knew deep down that it was unacceptable to conflate the man who creates and the man of action. I've always tried to be other things, *as well*. And naturally, I succeeded—it's not so difficult. But I was only playing games, having fun, and my aversion to the consequences was growing. I had to recognize that. It's always painful to categorize yourself, to limit yourself. But once you've taken that first step, you realize that everything can be accepted as a part of you.

In reality, these things weren't unrelated to the preceding pages. To the uncertainty that always preludes such essential simplifications. To the need to go further, to be a man who doesn't give personal observations. One who creates without engaging (do we ask sculptors for their observations?). A body of work without articles, without self-expression, without letters, without confessions, we can no longer imagine such a thing these days. You would have to turn your back on a certain number of facts and, what's more difficult, a certain number of problems. You would have to experience and embody the life of an artist, and that life alone. That's the essential meaning of making a choice. And that's where we find the apparent contradiction.

But the first part of *Sisyphus* gives the solution.

In any case, I can't help but find in these uncertainties precisely what I expected from life. It would have seemed contemptible to me to forever conform to some predefined image, whereas the opposite seemed quite normal (and once again, what I expected): that age would force me to correct that image. So then, my body of work would be shaped by my life and not the other way around. Which made that expectation seem easy.[15]

———

Naturally, I offer this manuscript for what it's worth. But on a first read, I was struck by the somewhat mathematical dryness of such a hopeless narrative. It casts a cold light on the problems that I, along with many other well-informed people, consider most pressing, and it does so with a categorical detachment more reminiscent of a lecture than a confession.

And yet (perhaps because I knew my friend well), I sensed a fierce determination beneath that implacable logic, a fiery love and rebellion known only to very young souls, a fervor Patrice Mersault sustained throughout the whole of an extraordinarily full and magnificent life. In a letter he wrote to me when he was already in his fifties, he said: "I can now die satisfied. Few of life's pleasures will go unknown to me; I've tasted all contradictions. I know my death will be something awful, something final, and I *know* (I truly know, or I should say that such is my faith) that there is nothing beyond this world and nothing beyond my desire."

Perhaps I'll come back to Patrice Mersault's death another day. It was terrible and magnificent. But it's reasonable to believe that the new manuscript, part of which I'm releasing to the public, will allow those who knew this remarkable man to better understand his behavior, his injustices, and his generosity.

15. In the handwritten notebook, the rest of this page is blank. The three paragraphs that follow this entry, which begin on the next page of the notebook, seem to be in the same handwriting as the earlier entry that appears on pages 9 and 10 (from "I had hardly had any difficulty" to "that most extravagant of solitudes"), indicating that Camus had originally left several blank pages after "extravagant solitudes" and later went back and filled them.

Index